LEVINAS, ADORNO, AND THE ETHICS OF THE MATERIAL OTHER

SUNY series in Contemporary French Thought
―――――――――
David Pettigrew and François Raffoul, editors

LEVINAS, ADORNO, AND THE ETHICS OF THE MATERIAL OTHER

Eric S. Nelson

Published by State University of New York Press, Albany

© 2020 State University of New York

All rights reserved

No part of this book may be used or reproduced in any manner whatsoever without written permission. No part of this book may be stored in a retrieval system or transmitted in any form or by any means including electronic, electrostatic, magnetic tape, mechanical, photocopying, recording, or otherwise without the prior permission in writing of the publisher.

For information, contact State University of New York Press, Albany, NY
www.sunypress.edu

Library of Congress Cataloging-in-Publication Data

Name: Nelson, Eric Sean, author.
Title: Levinas, Adorno, and the ethics of the material other / Eric S. Nelson.
Description: Albany, NY : State University of New York Press, 2020. |
  Series: SUNY series in contemporary French thought | Includes bibliographical references and index.
Identifiers: LCCN 2019055325 | ISBN 9781438480237 (hardcover) |
  ISBN 9781438480244 (pbk.) | ISBN 9781438480251 (ebook) Subjects: LCSH: Adorno, Theodor W., 1903–1969. | Lévinas, Emmanuel. Classification: LCC B3199.A34 N45 2020 | DDC 193—dc23
LC record available at https://lccn.loc.gov/2019055325

10 9 8 7 6 5 4 3 2 1

To Shengqing

Contents

Acknowledgments ix

Introduction: On the Way to an Ethics of Material Others 1

Part I
After Nature: Ethics, Natural History, and Environmental Crisis

1 Toward a Critical Ecological Model of Natural History 25

2 Natural History, Nonidentity, and Ecological Crisis 41

3 Communicative Interaction or Natural History?
   Aesthetics, Ethics, and Nature 65

4 The Trouble with Life: Life-Philosophy, Antinaturalism,
   and Transcendence in Levinas 91

5 An Ethics of Nature at the End of Nature 113

Part II
Unsettling Religion: Suffering, Prophecy, and the Good

6 Religion, Suffering, and Damaged Life: Nietzsche, Marx,
   and Adorno 149

7 The Disturbance of the Ethical: Kierkegaard, Levinas, and
   Abraham's Binding of Isaac   171

8 Ethics between Religiosity and Secularity: Kierkegaard
   and Levinas   197

9 Prophetic Time, Materiality, and Dignity: Bloch and Levinas   219

10 Ethical Imperfectionism and the Sovereignty of Good:
   Levinas, Løgstrup, and Murdoch   241

Part III
Demanding Justice: Asymmetrical Ethics and Critical Social Theory

11 Equality, Justice, and Asymmetrical Ethics   263

12 The Pathologies of Freedom and the Promise of Autonomy   285

13 The Limits of Liberalism: Cosmopolitanism, Tolerance,
   and Asymmetrical Ethics   311

14 Recognition, Nonidentity, and the Contradictions of
   Liberalism   333

Epilogue: Nourishing Life, Unrestricted Solidarity, and the Good 349

Notes   357

Bibliography   427

Index   459

Acknowledgments

A book is a social creation indebted to myriad voices and relations with others and the world. I have learned more from others than I can convey in words or expressions of gratitude. I would like to thank first Mark Cabural, Dennis Prooi, and Tung Tin Wong, as well as David Chai and Nahum Brown for their help with or comments on aspects of the argument and manuscript. I am also deeply thankful to my colleagues and students at the Hong Kong University of Science and Technology who helped provide a supportive and collegial setting for researching and writing this book. Particular thanks are also owed to my colleagues Charles Chan, Kim-chong Chong, Christian Daniels, Joshua Derman, Ilari Kaila, James Lee, Jianmei Liu, Billy So, Kellee Tsai, Simon Wong, and Kamming Yip, as well as to my previous colleagues Christa Hodapp, R. Eugene Mellican, Bassam Romaya, and P. Christopher Smith.

It is difficult to express how much I appreciate the many teachers, scholars, and friends who have helped shape my intellectual journey and the formation of the present book: Kelly Agra, Roger Ames, Emilia Angelova, Charles Bambach, Bettina Bergo, Robert Bernasconi, Jeffrey Bernstein, Peg Birmingham, Andrew Bowie, David Carr, Lulu Chai, Shirley Chan, Ching-yuen Cheung, Athena Colman, Deborah Cook, Christian Coseru, Bret Davis, John Deigh, John Drabinski, William Edelglass, Fiona Ellis, Thomas Flynn, Nicholas Fotion, Nancy Fraser, Matthias Fritsch, Linda Gossett, Namita Goswami, Saulius Geniusas, Margret Grebowicz, James Hatley, Jean-Yves Heurtebise, Joanna Hodge, Tzeki Hon, Patricia Huntington, Curtis Hutt, Leah Kalmanson, Antje Kapust, Halla Kim, Hyeyoung Kim, Kwok-ying Lau, Anita Leirfall, Claudia Leeb, David Michael Levin, Chenyang Li, Christian Lotz, Dan Lusthaus, Rudolf Makkreel, Bill Martin, Sarah Mattice, John McCumber,

Greg Moss, On-cho Ng, Stephen Palmquist, Michael Paradiso-Michau, Franklin Perkins, Diane Perpich, David Pettigrew, Ben Pryor, François Raffoul, James Risser, Tom Rockmore, Michael Rosen, Frank Schalow, Martin Schönfeld, Dennis Schmidt, Brian Schroeder, Daniel Selcer, Robert Stern, Kent Still, Kirill Thompson, Iain Thomson, Samuel Todes, Ranie Villaver, Bernhard Waldenfels, Mario Wenning, Cynthia Willett, Jason Wirth, and Dongming Zhao. I am also very grateful to Jenn Bennett-Genthner, Andrew Kenyon, and the entire editorial staff at State University of New York Press for their guidance and support. There are also many others to whom I apologize for not mentioning here.

My family has encouraged and supported my intellectual and academic endeavors throughout my life, for which I am grateful to Lydia, Rick, Jenny, and Dean Nelson, as well as Dianne, George, and Jim Filip. This book is fondly dedicated to Shengqing Wu.

This manuscript was completed with the support of the Hong Kong University of Science and Technology, the Hong Kong General Research Fund, and the Herzog August Bibliothek Wolfenbüttel.

The following chapters incorporate substantially revised and expanded parts of the following publications.

Chapter 2 draws on Eric S. Nelson, "Revisiting the Dialectic of Environment: Nature as Ideology and Ethics in Adorno and the Frankfurt School." *Telos*, no. 155 (2011): 105–126.

Chapter 5 draws on Eric S. Nelson, "Levinas and Adorno: Can there be an Ethics of Nature?" William Edelglass, James Hatley, and Christian Diehm, eds., *Facing Nature: Levinas and Environmental Thought* (Pittsburgh: Duquesne University Press, 2012), 109–133.

Chapter 7 draws on Eric S. Nelson, "Levinas and Kierkegaard: The Akedah, the Dao, and Aporetic Ethics." *Journal of Chinese Philosophy* 41, no. 1 (2013): 164–184.

Chapter 12 draws on Eric S. Nelson, "Against Liberty: Adorno, Levinas, and the Pathologies of Freedom." *Theoria: A Journal of Social and Political Theory*, 59, no. 131 (2012): 64–83.

Chapter Thirteen draws on Eric S. Nelson, "Cosmopolitan Tolerance and Asymmetrical Ethics: Adorno, Levinas, Derrida." Curtis Hutt, Halla Kim, Berel Dov Lerner, eds., *Jewish Religious and Philosophical Ethics* (New York: Routledge, 2017), 153–172.

Introduction

On the Way to an Ethics of Material Others

> The need to let suffering speak is a condition of all truth. For suffering is objectivity that weighs upon the subject.
>
> —Theodor Adorno, *Negative Dialectics*

> Has the material meaning of philosophical reflection been lost? And if there is no consideration of the materiality of human existence—no consideration of the negativity of starvation as a starting point (as Ernst Bloch makes it)—then it seems that the critical sense of historical reality (which was indeed this "material negativity" for the first school) has faded away. The "second generation," upon losing this material sense and thereby losing negative critique (not in relation to a discursive community, but rather a community of living humans), effectively fell into a moralistic formalism.
>
> —Enrique Dussel, "From Critical Theory to the Philosophy of Liberation"

Opening Reflections

Ethical Imperfection and the Priority of the Material Other

A common prejudice concerning ethics is that only the morally perfect should speak about it. The present work will trace possibilities of an ethics of "imperfection" in which ethical moments arise in the encounters and relations of bodily material others exposed through embodied desires and wants to need, suffering, injury, and death. This is an ethics that concerns what Theodor W. Adorno (1903–1969) diagnosed as damaged life in *Minima Moralia* and what Emmanuel Levinas (1906–1995) described in his 1935 work *On Escape* as the "insufficiency of the human condition" and later thought as incompletion, which cannot be understood as a limitation or negation of the "sufficiency of being."[1] Ethical incompletion and imperfection are heuristic expressions and inform critical diagnostic models deployed within and against existing material and social conditions, as in an ideology-critique of ethics, to contest disciplinary ideologies of the virtuous and morally privileged elites, and their judgments of who ranks as good, as well as the theories of moral perfectionism that dominate Western philosophical and practical discourses and that are integral to the social-historical perpetuation of damaged life against which that life resists and revolts: in its wounds lies hope.[2]

This volume consists of interwoven essays on critical natural history, mimesis and responsiveness, and the environmental crisis (part 1); religion, prophecy, and the good (part 2); and equality, liberty, and solidarity (part 3). These essays present in outline a critical model of an ethics of the material other addressing experiences, encounters, and discourses of the alterities, nonidentities, and the good that constitute, interrupt, and reorient ethical and social-political forms of life. The ethics of material others as "first philosophy" has a number of significant implications: (1) the self is constituted through material, mimetic, and communicative relations to others, as outside of and exterior to the subject, in "other-constitution" rather than individual or collective self-constitution; (2) encounters with the prophetic "other-power" or transcendence of the good in others, in the ordinary mundaneness and sufferings of immanent material life, disturb and place into question the economies of the individual ego relishing its own happiness and collective identities that codify themselves through the subjugation and refusal of nonhuman and human others; and (3) the infinite ethical and social-political demand of others calls for unrestricted solidarities that can reorient and transform ethical and social-political sensibilities and possibilities. Ethical and social demands are mediated by and contest existing material conditions and communicative processes of a given form of social reality such as the contemporary global capitalist order.

Given the persistent entanglements and mediations of the prophetic emancipatory potential of the present moment, with hegemonic power relations and ideological discourses that justify them, the imperfectionist ethics (in which the ordinary self, who can never be sufficiently ethical, is addressed by and responds to the material other) articulated in the current book must also be a politics and political economy of material others that would begin to transition beyond the confines of previous discourses.

The present inquiry into the material other is a heterodox response to the thought of the German philosopher, sociologist, and social theorist Adorno and the Lithuanian-born Jewish French philosopher Levinas, drawing on, interconnecting, and critically transforming their interpretive strategies with regard to the contemporary environmental and social-political situation. Their philosophies will be comparatively reconstructed in the chapters of this volume; some elements will be intensified and interrelated (such as nonidentity and alterity) while others are criticized (such as the Eurocentric hypostatization of modernity as an exclusively Western rather than an intercultural formation).[3]

The strategy of this project is to articulate a hermeneutics of alterity and nonidentity in regard to the relations of ethical life, or the lifeworld, and social totality (systems) as determined by the global exchange, circulation, and consumption of goods and labor. It deploys while critically revising examples, models, and strategies from Adorno, Levinas, and their interlocutors to address a series of interconnected ethical and social-political issues related to the relations between nature and nonhuman and human animals (part 1), religion's functions as ideology and as prophecy (part 2), and interhuman justice (part 3).

The Ethics of Alterity and the Negative Dialectics of Nonidentity

The logic of identity is, according to Adorno, a logic of exchange and equivalence. It requires universal fungibility, interchangeability, and a totality of relations that appropriates and commands the sacrifice of all things. In response to the hegemony of identity in the theoretical attitude and in practical life in which life has become the consumption of life, Adorno proposed a nonidentity that is not only conceptual but also material and indicates that which exceeds and interrupts identification and equivalence. While Levinas rejects dialectic as signifying mediation and closure (totality), dialectic in Adorno breaks totality by radicalizing the moments of the concept and of mediation that inevitably point beyond themselves. Both resist the totalizing movement of dialectic, but Adorno's negative dialectics is an aporetic and para-doxical (deconstructive of *doxa*) logic unfixing reified conceptualities and contesting practices of identification and identity formation.

Adorno heightened the negativity in the dialectic against the thinking of identity and totality that defined classical forms of dialectic logic. This intensification of negativity appears alien to while intersecting with Levinas's suspicions regarding negativity and dialectic altogether for an alterity and otherness that would be other than identity and totality. The strategies of Adorno and Levinas against negativity as derivative of positivity are distant and contradictory inasmuch as Adorno heightens the negativity that Levinas deconstructs. Their respective discourses are aligned in that they each develop a discourse of that which exceeds and disturbs forms of identity and totality that they both associate with the dominant paradigm of Western philosophy and social-political life.

The two paragraphs above used Adorno's language to clarify each discourse. It is already evident that the present work operates between the tensions and affinities of these respective philosophers, as well as others from Immanuel Kant and Georg Wilhelm Friedrich Hegel to Jacques Derrida and Enrique Dussel, thereby inevitably presenting its own third model that lacks the authority of these names and texts. Throughout this work, there will be transitions between these distinctive forms of communication as well as the emergence of creolized, mixed, or "hybrid" languages.

Whereas Adorno presents us with critical heuristic models of nonidentity and a radical negativity irreducible to logical negation, which need to be reconfigured in relation to the present situation, Levinas reveals the priority of "the other," who is primarily interpreted with respect to embodied human and nonhuman material others in the present work. This asymmetrical priority of the other is not reciprocal in the sense of a direct or indirect expectation of exchange: it is the "an-archic" (as intractable to an *archē* [ἀρχή] as origin or an ordering power), infinite (as irreducible to totality or an integrating system), and impossibly demanding (as unfeasible to perform and yet called for) condition of ethics as first philosophy: the responsiveness and substitution of one for the other without calculative exchange or an underlying principle of identity. Ethics transpires in its impossibility and tension with existing realities in which the encounter with the other is an indication of the good, and of its priority and sovereignty. All of ethics is in essence an ethics of the other, even as standard moral theories neglect the asymmetrical relations and responsibilities that the ethical encounter and situation entails. According to Levinas, "the Other" both is and is not the others who are materially and socially situated and address us in interpolation, need, and suffering. The interpretation articulated in the following chapters will stress the ethical demands of a multiplicity of human and nonhuman embodied material others without eliminating the prophetic and emancipatory dimensions (articulated in more directly political ways in Benjamin, Bloch, or Dussel) of Levinas's emphasis on transcendence, other-power, and the good.

A Materialist Interpretation of Nonidentity and the Other

What does "nonidentity" signify? To introduce a preliminary heuristic definition, which will be developed and modified in its elucidation, this expression refers to identity while endeavoring to say something other than and incommensurable with identification and the positing of identity. Nonidentity is an expression that does not make sense from the perspective of identity. In Adorno's strategy of negative dialectics, it is not merely a derivative negation or relative modification of identity (which would place it under Levinas's repudiation of negativity). It is something inevitably "more than" and excessive to experiential, affective, and cognitive-conceptual modalities of identification. Nonidentity is intimated in the object itself insofar as it evades and resists sublation in and reconciliation with the individual or collective subject and its theoretical and practical activities.

The very idea of nonidentity raises a number of problems. First, analogous to the Mādhyamika Buddhist discourse of emptiness (*Śūnyatā*) in Nāgārjuna, the concept of nonidentity faces its own reification that would turn it into another expression of identity thinking. A completely unconditional nonidentity is difficult to communicate in ordinary referential language given the identity-maintaining functions of language and concept formation. Given this problem, there appears to be no direct way to identify an absolutely nonidentical or a wholly other without reifying it in identification and reproducing the very identity it would evade.

Second, the intensification of Adorno's negativity and Levinas's alterity risks absolutizing nonidentity against any identity and the other as transcendent, infinite, "Wholly Other" (*Tout Autre*) against the multiplicity of concrete material nonidentities and others.[4] This potentially leads to moral perfectionist and mystical visions of nothingness, the supersensible, God, and the good while disregarding exploited and suffering existence. Levinas contests the idolization of God and the reification of the good, noting how—for instance—"God," as a distance indicating my own responsibility and as "transcendent to the point of absence," is a word arising in the ethical intrigue and divine comedy of responsibility.[5]

A reply to both of these problems is found in a pluralistic and materialist modification to nonidentity and alterity as interlinked with—to adopt the language of the early Marx's *Economic-Philosophical Manuscripts* and the *Theses on Feuerbach*—concrete bodily existence and sensuous material praxis.[6] "Sensuous" refers in this context to the mediation of life through the senses. In my reading, this modification is already at work in preliminary ways in Adorno and Levinas in their attention to sensuous temporal material life. The emphasis on embodied material alterities runs against interpretations of Levinas that wish to focus on religion and transcendence as exceeding materiality that is not sufficiently passive. But Levinas as well as Adorno recognized the ethical and social-political dimensions of the embodiment and sensory life of others in earthly joy and suffering. It is this regard for vulnerable life that this work proposes intensifying in a prophetic and ethical materialist direction. Drawing on Adorno and Levinas, this does not signify a materialism of naturalistic abstraction, individual contemplation, or the practical activity of a subject but rather the priority of ethical alterity, nonidentity, and responsiveness within the conditions of sensuous material life.[7]

Other-Constitution and Aporetic Thinking

Philosophies of radical alterity and nonidentity, of "other-constitution" through otherness and the nonidentical, appear nonsensical from the dominant perspective of identity thinking and the self-constitutive subject. Adorno's negative dialectics (negative in hesitating before the affirmative moment of synthesis and reconciliation, and in recollecting the violence done in the dialectic movement) and Levinas's ethics of the other who is beyond the self's grasping (that is, alterity in the sense of an otherness that cannot be subsumed or incorporated into the same or the one) share affinities with forms of skepticism in placing ideas of the system, totality, and ontology into question. Philosophers in Greco-Roman skepticism and South Asian Mādhyamika Buddhism, postmodernism and deconstruction, have questioned strategies of relying on identification that reproduce the predominance of identity, revealing the nonidentical at the heart of identity and the absence of unitary self-sameness at the core of the subject. Insofar as it contests identity thinking, skepticism relies on the empirical contingent nature of things as well as the aporetic conditions of language, thinking, and being.

A philosophy of nonidentity is an aporetic philosophy that risks perplexity in exposure to irresolvable aporia. The modern usage of *aporia*, as paradox and contradiction, stems from the classical Greek word ἄπορος signifying an impasse without exit or passage. As early as Socrates, as presented in the early dialogues of Plato, the aporetic lack of resolution itself operates as a means of dialogue and inquiry, and a way to begin inquiry anew in which the dialogue twists and turns in novel directions while keeping in mind its earlier attempts. The aporia revealed in dialogue has a double meaning of an impasse that cannot be crossed and a generative opening that cannot be closed. This enigmatic closure/opening conditions the structures of thinking and, dialectically speaking, the structure of what is to be thought. It is in this sense that modalities of aporetic ethics are considered in relation to the ethics of the material other.

What does "ethics" mean in this context? Ethical questioning and reflection should be distinguished from moralizing posturing, which Levinas as much as Adorno resisted, and moral theorizing. It is also not the listing of principles and rules. Ethics, according to Levinas, is a first philosophy that cannot be grounded in epistemology, ontology, philosophical anthropology, or other discourses of knowing, being, and the subject. It signifies the disorienting exteriority of the alterity and nonidentity (the affinities and differences of these two concepts are queried later) that places the self in its self-imprisonment and self-concern into question, a self who is shaped and threatened by natural and social forces.

Who is the self in this ethics? The question of how to articulate an ethics of nonidentity in the midst of relentless forces of identity, which require adopting and modifying interpretive strategies from Adorno, Levinas, and other authors, is bound together with the problem of the self. The self is simultaneously a subject (1) who is materially and socially conditioned, determined, and mediated by conditions and forces; (2) whose "selfhood" is defined by the impossible ethical demand of the other to be infinitely responsive and responsible; and (3) who is an embodied and temporally existing self who is called to nourish the material life of nonhuman and human others in asymmetrical yet unrestricted solidarity that would allow each to take its turn.[8]

The book before you is a consequence of an endeavor to pursue an inquiry into the good intimated in material life through the asymmetrical ethics of alterity and nonidentity with respect to nature, religion, and justice for the sake of articulating an ethics without a founding origin and governing power and as directed toward bodily material others in their height and priority. The asymmetrical difference between me and the other signifies in Levinas a kinship not based on being or nature, an ethical inequality that contests oppression and existing inequalities.[9] It offers an analysis of conceptions of the differences that aporetically unsettle fixations of identity. It pursues questions of whether radical difference can be constitutive of ethics and the ethical subject. The constitution at stake here is not transcendental self-constitution but what is better described as "other-constitution" in which the self is constituted "outside itself" in exteriority and otherness.

An Overview of the Work and Its Motivating Questions

Nature, Religion, and Justice

I consider in the following chapters the extent to which the "nonidentity thinking" of Adorno and the "ethics of the other" of Levinas point toward alternative ways of critically engaging three areas of concern: (1) the ethical status of "inhuman subjects" such as natural worlds, environments, and animals; (2) the bonds and tensions between ethics and religion and the formation of the self through the dynamic of violence and liberation expressed in religious and metaphysical discourses; and (3) the regressive uses as well as conceptual and practical limitations of classic, modern, and contemporary liberal and republican discourses of equality, liberty, tolerance, and their reified conceptions of the autonomous individual self and subject.[10]

Why do the three parts of this work address nature, religion, and justice? It could be objected that each concept has its own experts and theorists who do not need to converse with one another, and, more significantly, that each reality named has its own dynamics of oppression and emancipation. The argument traced in the following book indicates that what these three basic words name is deeply entangled and interconnected. Questions concerning a critical rather than reductive "natural history" (a concept rejected by Levinas in this sense) of the domination of nature and a brutal struggle for existence, religion as hope in suffering and the prophetic accusation against injustice, and interhuman justice and solidarity are interwoven in a form of life and its material conditions.[11]

Addressing these questions discloses different perspectives and examples for the ethics of material alterity that is at stake throughout this work. There are, as will be traced in the course of the following chapters, three overlapping concerns that orient this inquiry: nature (as entangled and crisis-ridden ecological-material life), religion (as the weak prophetic and messianic demand for a love and justice yet to come, and the good), and justice (as equality, liberty, and solidarity).

The five chapters of part 1 articulate a challenge and alternative to the anthropocentrism and intersubjective idealism of contemporary critical social theory maintained by philosophers such as Jürgen Habermas and Axel Honneth by pursuing questions of the materiality of human existence, nonhuman animals, ecosystems, and environments. These issues are of vital concern given the environmental and material crisis tendencies of contemporary—neoliberal and neomercantilist—capitalist societies. The stakes and strategies of part 1 are unfolded through reinterpretations of materiality and natural history in Adorno, and earthly embodied existence and the animal other in Levinas.

The five chapters of part 2 engage the multiple functions of religion as and contrary to political theology.[12] They address problems concerning the systematic complicity of religion with violence and subjugation while elucidating the an-archic and prophetic appeal to the good that is more than intimated in religious discourses and practices. Religion justifies and excuses systematic hierarchies and injustices. Yet the truth of religion and spirituality is, Levinas notes, prophecy that is a hearing without striving to hear.[13] As the "heart of a heartless world," it prophetically places exploitation and violence into question, intimating profounder forms of love and solidarity with the abject, exploited, and oppressed as well as between suffering vulnerable bodily beings.

Finally, part 3 turns toward topics such as equality, freedom, tolerance, cosmopolitanism, hospitality, and solidarity in order to interrogate their hegemonic theoretical and ideological forms. Its four chapters and the epilogue contest conventional liberal ethical and social-political philosophy—adopting and transforming (through the deployment of alterity, asymmetry, and nonidentity) radical republican (Rousseau through Levinas) and heterodox Marxist (Marx through Adorno to Dussel) political thought—for the sake of a radically nonidentitarian and unrestricted hospitality, solidarity, and welcoming. "Unrestricted" will be deployed in the double sense of decentering and undoing the fixed and fixating subject, of breaking down and relaxing the violence of essence, through the ethical priority of the other in Levinas's sense and formalization, experimentation, and responsiveness in freedom toward and felt contact with the object in Adorno's works. Ethical moments of the nonrestriction and nonindifference of the good occur in the midst of imperfect everyday life (in all of its affliction, damage, folly, ignorance, incompletion, and perplexity) in response to the earthly, embodied, and material other.

In the following chapters, I pursue a philosophical problematic and project through a historical study of philosophers associated with the critical social theory of the Frankfurt school (from precursors such as Kant, Hegel, and Marx to heirs such as Habermas, Honneth, and more recently Rahel Jaeggi) and the ethics of difference (from predecessors such as Nietzsche and Kierkegaard to Derrida and Dussel). However, the accent is placed on the writings of two twentieth-century European philosophers, Adorno and Levinas, since their works are to different degrees germane to articulating an asymmetrical and imperfectionist ethics from moments of otherness and transcendence within traumatized life.

Perfection and Imperfection

Ethical imperfection is a consequence of the concepts of damaged life and *minima moralia* in Adorno, and diachrony and incompletion (time as disquiet and unrest instead of continuity, flow, or a whole) in Levinas.[14] One objection to an imperfectionist elucidation of ethics is the claim that insofar as Adorno and Levinas have an ethics, it is either negative or morally perfectionist.[15] Levinas's reconstructions in *God, Death, and Time* of Plato's form of the good beyond being, Descartes's argument in the *Meditations* concerning the infinity of God, and Kant's articulation of hope and the supreme good can be interpreted as arguments for perfectionism insofar as the good places the imperfect into question, and ideas of infinity and perfection allow one to recognize one's own insufficiency and imperfection.[16] Such accounts (discussed in chapter 10) miss a key point: the good, the infinite, and the perfect are perfections beyond the dynamic of human perfection and imperfection that is at stake in the moral perfectionist perspective. Levinas persistently describes how the good and the infinite are other than and beyond the activity and capacity as well as even the receptivity and passivity of the subject. The infinitely affected and afflicted finite self can never respond to the infinity of the good, stirring inside its immanence, revealed in the other's demand. The anarchy of the good, a radicalization of the sovereignty of good outside the boundaries of moral perfectionism, is not known and mastered in the canons, customs, exemplars, and habits of moral elites cultivating and perfecting their virtues and arts of existing. It is not the idea of perfection in the good and infinite that constitutes what is objectionable in the moral perfectionist position. Perfectionist and virtue ethical models of morality are placed into question (as forms of domination) due to their assumptions of moral authority, expertise, mastery, and privilege that undermine both the singularity and the universality of ethics.

Where then is the good potentially revealed if not in the mastery of the self and others? Levinas clarifies in his reading of Plato's *Symposium* that the good is intimated not in knowledge but in affect and desire; that is, in desire and neediness in search of the other who is not merely a projection of that desire and need. Needy, wanting, imperfect life in its incompletion is not only necessary for the desire for the good, which, as disinterested and nonindifferent, surpasses being determined by hunger or need to the point of giving the other one's sole piece of bread, but is the locus of the alterity of ethical transcendence within worldly material immanence. Levinas emphasizes consequently that it is not knowledge or the idea but eros and desire—to the point of becoming a desire for the good in nonindifference without concupiscence and self-concern—that is operative in the Platonic good beyond being, the Cartesian notion of perfection that places my own freedom in question and welcomes the other, or Kantian hope as a hope beyond measure in and for the finite mortal life of subjectivity.[17]

Levinas does not portray the good as a mere normative ideal nor as a negation of imperfection. The transcendence of the ethical occurs within the immanence of transient material life, and the other-power of the good in the midst of incompletion and imperfection. The desire and hope for an undamaged life arises within—to modify Adorno's expression—the incompletion and imperfection of "damaged life" itself. In light of arguments unfolded in Levinas and Adorno, the good does not primarily address the morally perfected but rather those afflicted and subjugated by life's physical and moral evils in the midst of their ignorance and folly.

Why Levinas? Why Adorno?

Levinas might seem to be a dubious choice for such a project given his reliance on the religious language of transcendence and his suspicions concerning modern materialism and naturalism.[18] Naturalism, as the justification of what is and as a particular way of constructing and ordering nature, forgets what ought and should be, misses the enigmatic encounter with the transcendence of the other who is incompatible with ontology as the order of things. Levinas described in his 1947 work *Time and the Other* (*Le temps et l'autre*) how the personal is constituted in the event of the transcendent. The relation with the other (*l'autre*), whose absence is the relationship with the other person or someone else (*autrui*), and time, remains irreducible to power: "If one could possess, grasp, and know the other (*l'autre*), it would not be other. Possessing, grasping and knowing are synonyms of power."[19]

Levinas began his major work *Totality and Infinity*, described by Derrida as "an immense treatise on hospitality," with questions of war, betrayal, and the imprudence of the ethical.[20] He poses the basic problem of ethics in the following terms: how are we not duped and played for a fool by morality? Natural and ontological being presents itself as a state of competition and war that would make ethics impossible and the belief in ethics naïve. Levinas pursues the aporetic and paradoxical route of an ethics of alterity in response to its natural and ontological impossibility and its calculative and prudential foolishness. The height of ethics is the ultimate foolishness, which he calls holiness, of living outside of oneself for-the-other. The boldness of Levinas's project surpasses the limitations of his presentation of it and makes it difficult to ignore. Despite the genuine danger of reducing it to moralistic platitudes and narcissistic self-congratulation, its saying and unsaying continues to challenge ordinary reified conceptions of the self and identity.

Adorno also raised the prospect of the impossibility of ethics given its complicities with domination. He asked the question in *Minima Moralia*, echoing the suspicions posed at the beginning of Levinas's *Totality and Infinity*, can morality be anything more than ideological posturing? Is morality the smug expression of the comfortable bourgeoisie who can afford to moralize and assert their superiority over the poor and abject who struggle to survive? Morality serves to apologetically reconfirm and excuse the existing order in neoliberal and neomercantilist capitalism, just as in premodern societies, thus obscuring the inequalities and injustices perpetuated under the veil of abstract equality and justice.

Adorno's persistent suspicions concerning ethics and morality might imply a rejection of ethics as such, or his criticism might be informed by its own ethical perspective; that is, an ethics of nonidentity that challenges—with its "more than this" and "always not yet"—the ideology of identity and identification as forms of reification and fetishization. Thinking's genuine interest is the negation of the fixations of reification.[21] There are traces of resistance and hope within the negativity of manipulated damaged life that imagines possibilities of a genuine unforced reconciliation and a justice and equality that do not undertake violence toward the uniquely and concretely singular.

Despite their divergent philosophical orientations rooted, respectively, in critical social theory and the phenomenological movement, Levinas and Adorno addressed the questionable character of goodness and justice in the face of the totalizing power and hegemonic violence of modern societies and in the wake of the catastrophe of the Holocaust. The crises of modernity disclose the hypocrisy of conventional moral theories and normative prescriptions. Both thinkers eschewed normative ethical theorizing and prescriptive moralizing while pursuing their own forms of ethically concerned inquiry into living less wrongly a damaged life as a socially mediated and vulnerable material self. They challenged the unconditional monadic subject for the sake of a complicit and conditional individual subject who is betrayed and endangered by its naturalness and socialization, and its material and sensible embodiment, which threaten to overwhelm it.[22]

Three Queries about Ethics

The current ethical and social-political project faces a number of concerns, three of which can be outlined schematically here in a preliminary way and concretized in the subsequent chapters.

First, can alterity or the nonidentical be a necessary and sufficient condition for ethics? The answer to this is undoubtedly no. A different route is pursued in this work. The ethics of nonidentity is suggestive and formally indicative for ethical reflection and practice. It is a necessary and yet impossible condition, to speak with Derrida, remaining inevitably paradoxical and incomplete from the standpoint of the requirements of normative and prescriptive moral theories that themselves have been inadequate to address the ethical demand of material others.

Second, can an ethics of alterity be formulated formalistically only in outline? The answer to this must also be no. Such an ethics cannot be purely formal, as it is compelled toward concreteness because it is bound to sensible material subjects and their happiness and suffering. It must be bound to the multiplicity of material life in order to articulate the concrete differences that matter: specifically, the materially existing other. Asymmetrical or differential ethics requires encountering the differences and materialities without reducing them to identity. It must therefore emphasize recognizing and responding to the sensibility, sentience, and suffering of conditional material selves and fragile temporal subjects instead of eternal souls and self-constituting autonomous subjects. This entails encompassing more than human subjects, such as animals, organisms, ecosystems, and natural worlds. As Martin Buber noted in *I and Thou*, each one can be encountered as ethically addressing me.[23] The ethics of material others, as a result, to speak schematically here, are expansively naturalistic and materialistic while contesting reified and limited conceptions of nature and matter. The natural (the immanent) is already infected and recurrently interrupted by the ethical and the autonomous good (the transcendent) rather than in opposition to it.[24]

Third, if it is not to be an empty gesture and monotonous bourgeois moralizing, how can a materialist ethics of nonidentity—as distinct from an ethics of norms, prescriptions, and principles—be pertinent to contemporary sociopolitical issues such as the perpetuation of ecological devastation, identity violence, and social-political injustice characteristic of contemporary capitalist societies and the international order? The anomalous moment of the nonidentical reveals the nonharmonious dissonances and tense interconnectedness of conditional material subjects in relation to their environments and animals (the topic of part 1) and human animals (the topic of parts 2 and 3); that is, the nexus of complex and fragile formations of reciprocity and that which cannot be reciprocated or exchanged.[25]

Historical Contexts and Critical Departures

Marxism, Phenomenology, and New Critical Models

Karl Marx presciently depicted, initially in early works such as the *Economic and Philosophic Manuscripts* (1844), and later with more theoretical and empirical sophistication in the *Grundrisse* (the unfinished *Foundations of the Critique of Political Economy*) and *Capital*, how the paradigm of exchange dominates in capitalist societies, as values are reduced to exchange values and relations to exchange relations. Even as Marx's description and critique remain pertinent given the ecological and material crises of contemporary capitalist societies that damage life and endanger human survival, his ethical and social-political diagnosis and prescriptions do not offer an adequate response and require reinterpretation through an ethics of the alterity and nonidentity of embodied material others.

The disruptive logic of nonsymmetrical relationality and reciprocity (exemplified in hospitality, generosity, and gift giving) requires tracing existing and potential alternatives to the hegemonic logic of equivalence, exchange, and sacrifice determining conventional ethical and material life and moral-political discourses. This interpretive strategy allows difficult and complex questions concerning environments and animals, religious identity and difference, and the ethics and politics of justice to be reposed in the context of their asymmetries and materialities. Adorno and Levinas accordingly offer a significant alternative to orthodox forms of Marxism and anti-Marxism, phenomenology and antiphenomenology.

Marx remarked in *The German Ideology*, "Life is not determined by consciousness, but consciousness by life."[26] This claim is correct not so much in the sense of economic determination, which Marx had not developed at this point (if he ever did) to the degree later attributed to him, but in the sense that embodied conscious or self-reflective life is an ethos or praxis of living in and from the world and is called to respond to, address, and nourish its material others, contexts, and conditions. Ethics in the Levinasian sense signifies a stricter, more rigorous determination that interrupts the determinacy of being, including social-economic and anthropological-biological being. The unsettling and reorienting "an-archy" of the good is disruptively incarnate in the midst of material life rather than separate from it in an otherworldly or supersensible realm.

The thinking of Adorno and Levinas appears to intersect in a number of significant ways that other authors, such Hent de Vries, have examined. This impression is not incorrect insofar as there are striking affinities. Both discourses, as de Vries and others have described, engage in critiques of religious and secularized theodicies, the ordinary definition of which is the justification of God's justice in the world given the realities of suffering and evil, and its modern secularized incarnations.[27] Both confront modern Western society and philosophy, and in particular, in response to Martin Heidegger's ontology, through Auschwitz and the Shoah, which have thrown previous certainties concerning theodicy—or its secularization in progress, the invisible hand, and world spirit—into question.

Each of these philosophies has its own senses of "critique." Levinas speaks of philosophy as "justifying and critiquing the laws of being and of the city," deployed to assess ordinary conventional ethics, morality, and the social-political life that justifies and excuses the evils humans inflict upon one another.[28] These concerns encompass, more extensively in Adorno and less sufficiently in Levinas, animal life and the natural world. Although Levinas does not have as comprehensive a sense of nonhuman life as Adorno, he focuses on the significance of embodiment, sensibility, and the sensory that he links with the fragility and vulnerability of others, who are essentially concrete material others in their hunger and need for bread and daily sustenance, for habitation and care. This is a phenomenology of bodily others in Adorno and Levinas, which Adorno describes as the truth in materialism in contrast to its doctrinal and dogmatic forms.

Adorno and Levinas likewise retain a crucial phenomenological dimension in thinking that links thought to a care for concrete differences, to the primacy of the object in Adorno and the priority of the other in Levinas, even as they reject previous phenomenology for the priority it gave to conceptual cognition and subjectivity. One can perceive common emphases on irreducible differences, which Adorno analyzes through the notion of a nonidentity irreducible to and interruptive of the logic of identity and identity thinking, and Levinas depicts through the alterity of the other that is irreducible to and interruptive of the integrating sameness of the self-concerned self who is struggling in existence to preserve itself relative to the totality of social relations. The impersonal reality of totality, and its logic of exchange, sacrifice, and war, is that which Adorno and Levinas confront with moments of nonidentity and alterity, such that they might be thought to be allied sources for social critique—insofar as totality remains a problem at this stage of the capitalist social-economic organization of life.

At the same time, there are crucial differences between the two that should be kept in mind. They make it difficult and perhaps impossible to integrate the discourses associated with the proper names Adorno and Levinas. Accentuating the negative nonidentical moment in Hegel's dialectic Adorno's discourse is a dialectical one without—he stresses—the affirmative moment of identification: that is, the forced reconciliation and integrating synthesis that assimilate and preserve subsumed moments in an identity. Adorno's critical social theory concerns immanence, and the self-disruptive character of immanence to itself, in nonidentity. Its endeavor is to be a critical discourse of society that addresses and potentially participates in the transformation of the present. Levinas, in contrast, contests the very terms that are employed in Adorno's works: the language of dialectic, immanence, theory, and critique.

Levinas shares the phenomenological distrust of dialectic, which is also at work to varying degrees in the works of Husserl and Heidegger; dialectic is assimilative, and Levinas pursues the anarchic moments that surpass dialectic, such as the good beyond being in the dialogues of Plato. Levinas's mature works, which are already prefigured in the idea of escape from the immanence, positivity, and self-sufficiency of being in his *On Escape*, articulate a discourse of sweeping and excessive transcendence that is incompatible with and interrupts the order of immanence. Further, Levinas does not employ the language of negativity and critique, which would potentially reassert the dialectic in relation to what is critiqued, reestablishing totality. Negation and negativity are fundamentally inadequate to the encounter with alterity, an alterity that exceeds the attempt to identify or define it, including in terms of singularity, personhood, or ineffability. Critique as theoretical and practical self-reflection addressing the present situation is likewise insufficient. Levinas's thinking delineates what would exceed negativity and critique, allowing this work to rethink these very concepts beyond Levinas. Such excessiveness applies to Levinas's own discourse, which he describes in *Otherwise Than Being* as a passage and passing from an event of alterity to an alterity that cannot be conceptualized in or limited to the event of its encounter.

Cacophonies and Dissonances

In one sense to be elucidated in the present book, it appears as if Adorno and Levinas are speaking of overlapping questions and themes in the distinctive languages of nonidentity and alterity. Adorno's question "[H]ow is the right life possible in the midst of the false?" evokes Levinas's question, posed in the preface to *Totality and Infinity*, how is ethics not only possible but first philosophy given the omnipresence of the ego, its striving for existence (*conatus essendi*), competition, and war? Each not only articulates the vulnerability and perishability of bodily life in the context of racial oppression, national socialist extermination camps, and capitalist systems of exchange but also attempts to consider to what extent the promise of liberation and the otherwise than this lingers and speaks under these conditions.

In another sense, it appears that their respective strategies might well be incommensurable ways of endeavoring to articulate that which evades the identification of cognitive conceptual thinking, the sacrificial logic of social totalization, and confronts the pathologies of contemporary forms of life. Adorno embraces, often indirectly and through hesitation (except in occasional writings and more straightforward discussions in the lecture courses), the promise of freedom through the aesthetic moment, beginning with an interpretation of an experimental, formalized, and unrestricted mimesis. Mimesis in Adorno's reconceptualization is not mere identification, imitation, or realistic representation, and accordingly needs to be distinguished from its meanings in previous aesthetics.[29] It signifies in this context, to offer a preliminary description that is extended in chapter 3, a responsiveness to objects and others glimpsed in moments of childlike play, the tenderness of love, as well as in art. Adorno accentuates the emancipatory tendencies of the aesthetic dimension, to an extent that *Aesthetic Theory* is arguably his most revolutionary work, even as it is managed and manipulated under the auspices of consumeristic society and the culture industry. Levinas writes less frequently and more skeptically of the aesthetic, and much more of eros and love. His discourse relies heavily on ethical and religious vocabulary and interpretive strategies, only some of which find echoes or affinities in Adorno's works.

A number of Adorno-oriented commentators identify an ostensible theological moment in Levinas that is incommensurable with Adorno's more secularized thought and secularized use of the prophetic moment in Judaism that Adorno had encountered in the thought of Walter Benjamin. In contrast to Adorno's prophetic caution and modified Marxian social analysis, to speak summarily, Levinas inscribes Jewish prophetic and messianic inspirations, in conjunction with the idea of fraternity from the French republican tradition, in his most philosophical treatises as well as in his Jewish writings that emphasize its ethical moments.

There is also a rift between Adorno's and Levinas's use of the language and concepts of ethics and morality. Adorno avoids and contests the language of ethics and morality, particularly its moralizing perfectionist incarnations, famously naming a work of his most personal philosophical reflections *Minima Moralia*. Levinas appears to speak a language of *maxima moralia*. He can excessively exaggerate moral language and the ethical demand in a hyperbolic accusative manner that strikes a number of interpreters as the kind of moralizing that Adorno had challenged as bourgeois pretense. Whereas Adorno minimizes ethical and theological language, while still utilizing it for the purposes of social criticism (as a number of recent works on Adorno's aporetic and negative ethics have shown), Levinas amplifies and embellishes this language such that our desires and motivations are always in question. It might be inexactly said that Adorno intensifies negativity while minimizing ethics, and Levinas minimizes the use of negativity while intensifying ethics and its demands. At the same time, each rejects the moments of positivity (which justifies the world as it is) operating in the discourses of negativity of Hegel and Heidegger, even while Adorno extends Hegel's dialectic against identity and beyond this positivity.[30] It is the cacophony and dissonance of their disruptions of prevailing philosophical paradigms that indicate alternative critical models for contemporary thought.

If Levinas's works are read beyond the suspicion of their religious language, a suspicion that is turned around in a religion understood as the prophetic ethics for the other, it becomes problematic to read them as mere moralizing and theology, as they contest the economic and social-political pathologies of the present: the neglect and denial of the other, who, according to Levinas, is not God but the concrete material other who suffers from hunger and need, neglect and denial. The religious category of transcendence is transformed in being concretized in the material sensibility and vulnerability of this other who addresses and interrupts the "I," the my own, and the immanent sphere of the self-concerned ego.

Phenomenology and Antiphenomenology

Adorno and Levinas are each informed by and critically engage the phenomenologies of Husserl and Heidegger. Levinas's strategy in *Totality and Infinity* and *Otherwise Than Being* is not so much to moralize, or morally edify, as it is to enact a transformed phenomenology of the ethical in which the practice of phenomenology and the idea of ethics have been altered from their prior classical forms in Husserl and Heidegger's *Being and Time*. Levinas describes himself at points as a phenomenologist and a student of Husserl, and at other points as an antiphenomenologist who has broken the limits of phenomenology. Adorno recognizes an essential phenomenological moment of philosophy in the responsive encounter with the thing and the object in its primacy, while criticizing the reification that he diagnoses as being at work in the categories of consciousness and being thematized in Husserl and Heidegger.

Classical phenomenology, to briefly sketch it in a preliminary way, aims at a description of the phenomena as they show themselves to us and an analysis of the conditions of this appearing to us in intentional consciousness or ontologically in relation to being. Phenomenological descriptions of phenomena lead to the analysis of their conditions in notions of intentionality in Husserl and attunement and comportment in Heidegger, of consciousness in Husserl and the being-there of Dasein in Heidegger. Much more, of course, needs to be said than we have time to express here concerning how Adorno and Levinas have parallel concerns about the limits of classical phenomenology in terms of sensibility and the body, as well as a moment of difference that cannot be subsumed in the discourses of consciousness or being.

Levinas enacts a form of phenomenological description in his writings as he traces moments such as sensibility and insomnia, eros and the death of the other, totality and infinity, and being and that which is otherwise than being and not being. That is to say, Levinas's practice of phenomenological description leads to a distinctive analysis of its conditions: not activity but a passivity more passive than the activity of passive synthesis or the letting be of *Gelassenheit*; not the interiority of consciousness or the mineness (*Jemeinigkeit*) of Dasein but the exteriority, the exposure, and the nonmineness of the me and my own (its heteronomy); not the primacy of the ego, the self, or the subject but the priority of the other; not the phenomenon or that which appears but the inapparent, invisible, and impossible; and not the sphere of immanence but transcendence. This passing or passage, as Levinas calls this transition in *Otherwise Than Being*, is not a negation or reversal; it is noncoincidence, a transformation of a way of being by that which is otherwise than being.

Chapter 1 of *Otherwise Than Being* begins in a sense with the question of being as much as with Hegel's *Science of Logic* or Heidegger's *Being and Time*. Being is not construed as an abstract and empty category that passes over into its negation, nonbeing, and is then overcome in becoming (Hegel). Nor is being construed as fallen, or forgotten, and in need of authentic remembrance and retrieval (Heidegger). Being is interpreted instead as essence, interestedness, concerned with itself, and consequently as the striving for being, struggle for existence, and war. This condition of war is being without its other closed in upon and consuming itself.

In the midst of the closed immanence of being and its murmuring even in the deepest void, and the self-concerned care of being in the world, there are interruptive traces of transcendence, of the otherwise than being, that as anarchic is not nonbeing or the negation of being. This otherwise than being, according to Levinas, is not an otherworldly world behind the world or heavenly realm that would not signify the ethical but remain another form of being, "a celestial city gravitating in the skies of the earthly city."[31] The otherwise than being is thematized by Levinas as the interruption and reorientation of being, essence, interest toward the disinterestedness of the good and justice, which is how transcendence speaks in the realm of being.

Being and the otherwise than being have been interpreted as a dualistic or even gnostic interpretation of a reality structured by the diachrony of time, temporal noncoincidence and nonsimultaneity without synthesis. In such readings, Levinas's discourse is divided between being as the realm of egoism, the struggle to exist, and war and the otherwise than being as the anarchic good and ethical. Such interpretations are in need of complication: there is, to adopt Adorno's language, a third moment of nonidentity that is not a totalizing synthesis or a forced reconciliation in Levinas's description of the disruptive passing of the good into being and history. Levinas's analysis of the diachrony of time and the saying beyond being entail an intractability that is not merely a duality and consequently a far-reaching antireductionism to which even receptivity and responsiveness are inadequate.[32] Diachrony (as temporal nonidentity) in Levinas resonates with the prominence of dissonance over harmony in Adorno that he interprets temporally in his musical writings. While the former polemicized against totality and its form of temporality, the latter contested harmony both as a social as well as an aesthetic category. Levinas's strategy here brings to mind, to an extent, Adorno's articulation of nonidentity and its moment of materiality as moments that resist and undermine identification, synthesis, and totalization.

Conclusion

This volume addresses the historical contexts of Adorno and Levinas and their critical departures from their contexts. First, the disasters of twentieth-century history, in particular national socialism, from the initial emergence of Hitlerism to genocide and the Shoah, afflicted them in their reflections on ethical and social-political life and death. Second, the radical republican, socialist, and Marxist intellectual and practical tendencies that shaped twentieth-century life and thought form another significant historical context for this interpretation of Adorno and Levinas. Third, Adorno's and Levinas's adaptations, critiques, and transformations of Western philosophical traditions (in particular, the phenomenology of Husserl and Heidegger) also reveal their proximities and distances, sketched in the pages that follow.

The present inquiry is not primarily an intellectual history of two authors who did not discuss each other, nor a comparative reconstruction of their ideas. While considering the historical contexts of these two philosophers, it will think with and against them to address contemporary crisis tendencies that distort and endanger nourishing life in others and in oneself.

The succeeding chapters will illustrate how Adorno and Levinas offer two dissonant yet intersecting strategies for articulating an anarchic otherwise or nonidentity that cannot be pacified and that speaks in bodily sensibility and in the encounter with the other's suffering, need, and material life. Levinas's asymmetrical interpersonal ethics is arguably more phenomenologically developed than the portrayal of alterity and the dynamic of the other in Adorno's writings, despite provocative portrayals of the prejudicial and fascistic gaze. Adorno's depiction of nonidentity is provocatively linked with the problematic of the domination of nature and nonhuman life that shapes the contemporary failures of ecological politics and the ongoing ecological crisis, increasingly more devastating for human and other animal species, which require reimagining the conditions for ecological democracy and alternative ways of becoming-with and inhabiting-with (as the works of Donna J. Haraway disclose) other animals and the natural world.

This volume draws on and departs from Adorno and Levinas as sources for confronting the contemporary situation with a prophetic asymmetrical ethics and politics of material others that endeavors to respond to the harms and injustices being done to human and nonhuman life.

Part One

After Nature

Ethics, Natural History, and Environmental Crisis

Chapter One

Toward a Critical Ecological Model of Natural History

> Here, as everywhere, the identity of nature and humans appears in such a way that the restricted relation of humans to nature determines their restricted relation to one another, and their restricted relation to one another determines humans' restricted relation to nature.
>
> —Karl Marx, *The German Ideology*

Introduction to Part One

It is said that we live today in the epoch of the Anthropocene (which is very much determined as the Capitalocene) and after the "end of nature." But the denial that nature is a reality independent of human construction is a typical gesture of modern Western philosophy and its underlying rationalism (as identity thinking) and idealism (as the prioritization of the constitutive individual or a collective subject). Due to the complex and mediated tensions between human animals and their own nature as well as with animals and nonhuman nature, which are rooted in the material conditions of human life and the desire to master them, nature is reduced to a lesser stage or condition to be overcome by spirit, a concept to be posited and constructed by individual or collective human subjects, or—as in naturalistic and pragmatic models—an object to be controlled through instrumental techniques. Given these antagonisms, it might be the case that nature is not yet over but has not yet arrived.

"Nature," in Adorno's use of the word, does not name an essence, substance, or set of laws. It is mediated by, while remaining nonidentical and subaltern with, human thought and action, as "natural history," a concept that Adorno inherits and modifies from Karl Marx and Walter Benjamin. Marx revealed how, despite positivistic and social Darwinist elements in his thought, "[t]he objectivity of historic life is that of natural history" (*Naturgeschichte*) and "the development of society's economic formation of society [is] a process of natural history."[1] Marx's naturalistic interpretation of natural history, and the subsequent misappropriations that falsified Marxist natural law (see chapter 9), "does not rob Marx's talk of natural history of any part of its truth content, i.e., its critical content."[2] Marx's natural history discloses the historical-material interactions and entanglements of human subjects such that nature is also a social concept, and society a natural one: "The thesis that society is subject to natural laws is ideology if it is hypostatized as immutably given by nature."[3] Marx's notion of natural history, with its ethical dimensions inherited from the philosophy of natural law and radical republican politics, retains its critical potential in Adorno's *Negative Dialectics* and in the argument of the present work. Critical natural history challenges naturalism (which neglects natural historical subjects) and idealism (which feels itself to be the most immediate and certain vis-à-vis the object and the other that it posits derivative), and part 1 delineates a natural historical response to current ecological crisis tendencies as sedimented entanglements of nature and history.

Natural history is a primary critical model in the chapters of part 1, but not the only one: materiality, sensuous life, and alterity will also be addressed. Nature in its materiality, as well as in its "other-power" (*tariki* 他力) in contrast to "self-power" (*jiriki* 自力) to adopt a distinction deployed in Pure Land Buddhist and Kyōto school discourses that is related to the idea of "other-constitution" in the present work, for the most part is not experienced or conceptualized as an ethical reality in modern Western philosophy or moral theory.[4] Nature has become in globalized modernity primarily a disenchanted scientifically knowable order of efficient causes to be instrumentally managed by human subjects. Given the realities of current ecological crisis tendencies, which will be explored throughout part 1, one can pose the question of whether an appropriate culture and ethics of nature is possible, even if the existing environmental situation and disaster have established the need. What might a culture and an *ethos* of nature mean?

To offer preliminary heuristic definitions for the time being, which can be concretized only in the course of their exposition, it might be said that nature is the dynamic material transformation of things; culture a way of symbolically, linguistically, and intersubjectively relating to others, oneself, and one's world; and ethos a comportment or orientation in the midst of all this. "Ethics" is often defined as a normative discourse concerning norms and values about relations between human subjects, a definition that will be questioned in the following pages. Ethics is first and foremost concerned about someone else; that is, the (materially and sensuously embodied) others who are prior to (unconditionally prior in Levinas's language) and presupposed by imperatives, prescriptions, and values.

Alienated nature and reified culture are entangled phenomena such that a new culture, ethics, and political economy of nature and material relations are requisite.[5] The prospect of an ethics and culture of (nourishing or cultivating) nature might appear useless and senseless given that ethics is predominantly conceived as human-oriented and anthropocentric, and modern capitalist societies are primarily concerned with calculative means-oriented exchange and economic and bureaucratic forms of instrumental rationality. The very idea of an ethics of nature seems to hearken back to premodern sensibilities as well as to violate the "naturalistic fallacy" that posits a separation and abyss between the natural and the normative.[6] The current work contests the separation of the natural and normative, and the conflict between naturalism and normativism in ethics and social theory, since each is a one-sided expression of a more complexly entangled reality that is shot through with facticity and normativity. Nonhuman animals and ecosystems have had at best a secondary ethical status conceived through human affects and interests, and typically less than this in modern societies. However, the significant counterexamples of historically recent movements toward ecological, environmental, and animal rights illustrate how critical social theory and philosophy can take alternative routes.

The five chapters of part 1 will respond to this dire intellectual and existential-material situation by indicating alternative ways of encountering and interpreting nature and animals as an ethical reality and ethical demand. Part 1 will proceed through an interpretive analysis of the discourse of nature and animals in the works of Adorno (chapters 2 through 5) and Levinas (chapters 4 and 5) in relation to conflicting visions of ethical life (in particular Habermas). These discussions of nature suggest a solidarity of material life that will lead us to further question the encounter with life—in its damages, traumas, and sufferings—through the prism of hope and prophecy in part 2 and social-political justice in part 3.

Natural History and the Politics of Nature

Jürgen Habermas is a representative example of a contemporary critical social theorist who has neglected the ethical import of nature due to an interhuman characterization of ethics as communicative intersubjectivity. While Habermas insightfully recognizes advanced capitalism's antagonistic and destructive relationships with the environment in works such as *Legitimation Crisis*, and appreciates the important roles of environmental movements and green politics in the public sphere, he has at the same time limited the formation of critical models in regard to animals, ecosystems, and environments by emphasizing how issues concerning them are either derivative and secondary to interhuman communicative understanding or merely pragmatic decisions about nature as a realm of objects and resources governed by anthropocentrically defined human needs and the logic of instrumental means-ends rationality.[7] Habermas's articulation of postmetaphysical reason fails to overcome the neo-Kantian bifurcation of facticity and validity and the natural and the normative. It consequently anthropocentrically marginalizes the in- and nonhuman in eliminating possibilities of an ethics of nature as a metaphysical or romantic remnant.

This problematic is deeper than Habermas. Even thinkers suspicious of the philosophy of the constitutive subject and pure historicity have adopted constructivist positions that take nature and human anthropology to be socially and discursively determined. Benjamin claimed that "philosophical anthropology" is a bourgeois category and that the Marxist understanding of human beings demands recognizing their thoroughgoing historicity.[8] The interpretation of Marxism as socially constructivist, such that the bodily senses are radically revised in each new social configuration, misses the complex nexus of history and nature that is arguably addressed more consequently in Marx and Adorno. Benjamin himself introduced this mediation elsewhere through the dialectical concept of natural history irreducible to either nature or historicity. Such interpretations minimize the anthropological dimensions of Marx's historical materialism. Marx did not claim that human nature is historically relative, an idea he criticized in culturally oriented historicism, but rather that human nature, driven by its natural and socially modified drives and needs, historically and environmentally changes and adopts.

Problematic ideas concerning the ahistorical objectivity of natural processes underwrites the dichotomy between the natural and the ethical. Within more recent analytic Marxist theory, Jon Elster has claimed that the most fantastic element in Marx's philosophy is the idea of the domination of nature and the thesis of humans drastically transforming the natural world through labor, industry, and technology. Elster contends, "Marx's views [about the human relationship with nature] in this respect are either rambling and incoherent, or inherently trivial."[9] Benjamin rejected in his "Theses on the Philosophy of History" the vulgar Marxism that only perceives "progress in the mastery of nature, not the retrogression of society," as the mastery of nature is commentary to the exploitation of labor.[10] Nature is more than the heavens above, distant stars, and the vastness of the cosmos; nature encompasses the local places and spaces that have been rearranged and reconstructed through human activities. From small beginnings in agriculture and housing through industrialization and its effects, human activities have had massive effects on a planetary scale. Deniers of climate change contend that human activity cannot modify nature in any radical way. This prejudice has been repeatedly disproven by the disappearance of species, the destruction of ecosystems, drastic fluctuations in climate, and the increasingly chaotic weather patterns that are already underway.

Natural History and a Nature Still to Come

Nature is often presupposed to be an archaic past overcome by human activities, history, and spirit, resulting in the human-defined world and socially and economically determined ecologically destructive societies of the Anthropocene. There is a significant sense though in which nature is futural and yet to come. Chapters 2 and 3 of this volume clarify how Adorno's notion of natural history is not a fantastic metaphysical thesis by reconsidering the asymmetrical and dissonant mediations, without reconciliation or synthesis, of nature and history in the works of Adorno, who adopted this thesis from Marx and Benjamin. Given the current unrelenting and needful ecological crisis situation, in which human self-preservation is at stake, the hegemonic ideological separation between humans and nature is in need of reevaluation. Natural conditions and environments and humans are bound together in the changing configurations of natural history. Natural historical entanglements have led to our present environmental crisis-conditions. The "nature" that we encounter and experience is mediated by far-reaching social-historical transformations of environments and the human condition itself. Much has been undertaken in the last half century to attempt to change our thinking and modify destructive practices toward ecosystems, environments, and nonhuman and human animals. But this remains insufficient. Even the change in attitudes, discourses, and practices achieved appear to be too little and too late. Often the problems have been rearranged to soothe guilty consciences and shifted from the wealthy to the poor, and from the so-called developed to the developing world.

In part 1 of this work, I propose considering a noneliminative (i.e., nonreductionist or expansive) and dialectically inflected conception of nature. This conception is dialectical in the sense, inspired by Adorno, of the dynamic of nonidentity in which mediation is asymmetrical with itself, resisting closure into identity and totality. The strategy of natural history offers a revisable point of orientation and a "critical model" for confronting the ethics, politics, and political economy of animals and environments in contemporary global social-economic arrangements. The expression "critical model" is adopted from Adorno who speaks of a model immanently generated by the matter itself, and not merely external to it, such that its configurations, fault lines, and transformative potential are exposed. A critical model is a shifting range of internal perspectives and immanent heuristic and diagnostic strategies for reflection and praxis, yet it can also assume radically alternative perspectives such as contemplating things from "the standpoint of redemption" that in *Minima Moralia* is described as the only way to pursue philosophy in the face of despair and philosophy as mere technique.[11]

Adorno's reevaluation of the Marxist category of natural history challenges the idea of the "end of nature." The proposed elimination of nature undermines the nonidentity of nature and thereby the critique of the domination of nature that is intertwined with interhuman domination by obscuring their dynamic. Without their dialectical entanglement and nonidentity, environmental thought and practice are hampered by the lingering metaphysical duality of human subjects and nonhuman objects. Humans are not monadic ghostlike subjects hovering in the world but are materially and mimetically (in restricted forms of mimesis such as imitation and absorption) bound to their environments and to other organisms. Adorno described how ideologically informed discourses and social-historical constructions of nature reconfirm and perpetuate the existing state of affairs. Yet, contrary to the logic of constitutive idealism that in both its monadic and intersubjective forms cannot adequately recognize the material and the other-constitution of the subject, the ideological and social-historical construction of nature (which should be conceived in the plural) does not entail the conclusion that nature is purely or exclusively ideological. Nor does the critique of the ideological operations of discourses and "experiences" of nature preclude further reflection about the resistance and alterity of nature and the emancipatory potential in material relations that have been ideologically suppressed: namely, the truths of animal suffering, environmental degradation, and ecologically damaged life.[12]

The discourses of twentieth-century analytic and continental Western philosophy were dominated by forms of "linguistic idealism" (the privileging of language and the said over the others who are speaking) that are associated with proper names of philosophers, such as the later Wittgenstein (language games) and Heidegger (language as the house of being), and continues to shape contemporary social theory and philosophy, including the prioritization of intersubjective relations and communication (that is, a form of the constitutive collective subject) in the social theory of Habermas. The idealizing prioritization of language over sensuous material life and alterity was resisted by Adorno and Levinas, who still appreciated the significance of language in the formation of experience and subjectivity. This prioritization of language overly narrows ethics and critical social theory that should concern the suffering, exploitation, and domination of sensible subjects. The criticism of language, ideology, and consciousness is crucial to critique. But a critique of language and language games is insufficient to confront the social and material structures of society and their deformation and destruction of personal and natural life. The environmental-material and social-cultural reproduction of advanced capitalist economies continues to produce environmental havoc and damage across the globe, with the cumulative loss of species, the devastation of wilderness and forests, the production of endless pollution and waste, and drastic climate change. These environmental crisis tendencies are tied to the contemporary capitalist political economy and current forms of commodity fetishism and the culture industry.[13] They are internally entangled with, and not external to, the cycles of the material and social reproduction of global capitalist society. The contradictions of advanced neoliberal capitalist societies (which are modified but remain operative in the new forms of authoritarian populism and nationalism) have been sublimated and mediated as "problems" in the consciousness, discourse, and managerial style of contemporary societies. Unfixing and modifying our ways of speaking and playing our language games is indispensable. It is insufficient to confront present crisis conditions unless these games transition toward modifying society's damaged form of life and making its material relations less destructive.

The romantic aura, ideological deployment, and eco-consumerism of experiences of nature detached from ordinary human life are an aspect of the problem itself; symbolically evoking the environment as a consumable product partakes in the advertising and packaging of commodities. Environmental tropes and stereotypes have become a mainstay of the media and culture industry. Actions are deferred due to the promise that new technologies and polices will eventually limit the human impact on the environment. As the chapters of part 1 diagnose, environmentalism is itself interconnected with the ideology it confronts. Ideology, according to Adorno, is in essence identity thinking. The ideas of nature without history and humanity without nature reflect the maintenance of identity against the tensions and fractures that indicate their contested character and critical potential in relation to existing environmental and social-political conditions.

The Dialectic of Enlightenment, Damaged Life, and the Contemporary Ecological Crisis

Seventy-four years ago, in 1944, in their American exile from national socialist Germany, the philosophers and critical social theorists Max Horkheimer and Adorno analyzed the paradoxical developments of the Enlightenment, modernization, and technological progress in their coauthored work *Dialectic of Enlightenment* (*Dialektik der Aufklärung*) that was republished in a revised version in 1947. In this prescient work, Adorno and Horkheimer analyzed how technological development could outstrip human abilities to manage it, such that "the wholly enlightened earth is radiant with triumphant calamity [*Unheil*]."[14] They argued that the dialectic of enlightenment (typified by but not limited to the historical period called the Enlightenment), the way in which processes of enlightenment undermine and betray their own progressive aspirations and create conditions of disaster or, more literally, un-healing, driven by the compulsive mythologizing and sacrificial logic of the "domination of nature" that encompasses human nature and the natural world.[15]

Domination of one reinforces hegemony over the other in this critical model, such that life becomes—in the language of Adorno's most personal work—"damaged life." Although contemporary philosophers speak easily of the good life, of flourishing life, Adorno pointed to the necessity of addressing the systematically reproduced damages of contemporary forms of living and flourishing, not only in how I or we are damaged but also in how our own enjoyment and flourishing damages others and other forms of life. Without much exaggeration, we here today, not to speak of the coming generations with whom we are "taking turns" with the earth, are faced with the increasingly grim realities of climate chaos, overheated cities, plastic-filled oceans, pollution-filled air, perishing species, devastated ecosystems, and surviving in the increasingly seemingly unavoidable nightmarish reality of the "disaster triumphant" of an ecologically decimated earth.[16] If these phenomena are indeed rooted in the "domination of nature," what possibilities are there (if any remain) for a different way of living in and with animals, ecosystems, and the global environment?

Adorno's works confront the project of identity, the mastery of nature, and the instrumental rationalization that have produced ecologically damaged life. Given the "damaged life" prevalent in modern arts of existence, critical environmental reflection cannot simply appeal to the individual to be environmentally ethical. It should address the structurally—both materially and culturally—reproduced environmental crisis conditions. If this is the case, then discussion of "flourishing life" requires a confrontation with all that which materially and communicatively (to adopt a distinction from Habermas) reproduces life as "damaged" in which the ethical and the good transpires.

Aporetic Materialism and the Dialectic of Enlightenment

Chapter 2 is an inquiry into whether elements of an alternative ethical interpretation of nature are expressed in the first generation of the Frankfurt school. In the *Dialectic of Enlightenment*, Adorno and Horkheimer proposed that the domination of nature and interhuman domination are entangled in the same historical processes that have transformed the human species and resulted in the contemporary capitalist Anthropocene. As in later social ecology, with which it is in tension, each form of domination needs to be addressed in its relation to the other form for either to be addressed. Enlightenment and progressive rationalization have in this depiction of Western modernity (and—as Dussel demonstrates—the Eurocentric idea that modernity is exclusively Western rather than intercultural is itself a myth) become myth and ideology legitimating social irrationality and injustice.[17] In so doing, Adorno and Horkheimer conclude, natural and human relations are reduced to means through the ascendancy of instrumental rationality in its advanced capitalist form; fetishized in consumerist culture industries through the unconscious hegemony of symbolically reproduced values, styles, and practices; and reified and compulsively fixated in a consumeristic media-driven society.

Habermas criticizes Adorno and Horkheimer's portrayal of the project of the Enlightenment in his polemical work *The Philosophical Discourse of Modernity* (published in German in 1985) directed at regressive neoconservative and anarchistic postmodern critiques of the Enlightenment and modernity. *Dialectic of Enlightenment* signifies a withdrawal from interdisciplinary social scientific and normative inquiry and the emancipatory project of critical social theory as initially proposed by Horkheimer in the late 1920s in Frankfurt.[18] Habermas describes how Adorno's postwar critique of reason, as ensnared in identity and instrumentality, led him (inspired by Marx, Benjamin, and other sources) to locate sources of resistance in nature, materiality, and mimesis.[19] Habermas consistently opposes in this critical reading the categories of nature and history, and more broadly of facticity and normativity, and consequently underappreciates the extent to which Adorno conceived nature through the lenses of its historical entanglements in natural history.[20] Habermas construes Adorno's natural history in this context to be a warning against taking history as nature, which is only one of its features as shown in the subsequent chapters.[21]

As will be clarified in chapters 2 and 3, Habermas's assessment of Adorno's project appears overly idealistic in asserting the separation of facticity and normativity, whereas we see in Adorno the intractability of their historical entanglement and mediation in any given social nexus:

the good and the right are perceived (if at all) in the midst of the imperfections and damages of life. In Habermas's critique of the role of the mimetic in *The Philosophical Discourse of Modernity*, he misses how Adorno differentiates the restricted historical forms of mimesis linked with myth and power, and that is powerfully redeployed in authoritarian regimes and capitalist economies, and the potential of an unrestricted and responsive mimesis that is suggestively indicated in play and art. Its contents can inform multiple critical models of a life free of domination.[22] Adorno noted in his 1958/1959 lectures on aesthetics how the mimetic impulse, when formalized and emptied of fixations, becomes a responsive freedom toward the object (*Freiheit zum Objekt*).[23] Adorno attributes this expression to Hegel, who wrote only of *Freiheit zum Gegenstand* in the sense of freedom as an object of the will (for instance, in the *Philosophy of Right* § 10), and it appears to be more of a product of Adorno's reinterpretation of the priority of the object in negative dialectics that places constitutive subjectivity into question.[24] Adorno emphasizes in his readings of Hegel how his thought, despite his idealistic and totalizing tendencies, occurs "through discontinuity, alienation, and reflection" and remains entangled with the experientially concrete in ways that reveal the matter itself.[25] Hegel's dialectic reveals the limits of identity, as thinking without mimetic contact and referential exteriority loses itself in the obsessions of madness or ideology.[26]

Adorno described in the essay "Opinion Delusional Society" how this freedom toward the object potentially undoes the fixations of opinions and can "lose and transform itself in its encounter with the subject matter."[27] He also writes in *Minima Moralia* of gaining a sense of things entirely from "felt-contact" with them without arbitrariness or violence.[28] Adorno's freedom toward and priority of the object has a number of sources that come together in a new configuration in a critical model of contemporary society: (1) the objective material and social conditions confronting the subject (social objectivity in the Marxian sense); (2) the formalizing, experimenting, and playing with elements, forms, and models associated with aesthetic modernist avant-garde art and movements linked with the *Neue Sachlichkeit* (New Objectivity), such as postexpressionist painting, Bauhaus architecture and design, Brechtian theatre, and atonal music, which he himself practiced in music and advocated in his writings on music; (3) the transformation of moments of alterity, negativity, and nonidentity in Hegel's dialectic to prioritize the other, the object, and the thing and disrupt the totalizing movement of the subject and spirit;

(4) a secularization of prophetic and mystical sources, mediated through friends such as Benjamin, to give oneself over (*Hingabe*) to the thing, reconcile humanity with nature, and attend to suffering and subaltern life; and (5) the movement of mimesis from mere imitation, with its dangers of fixation, reification, and mythic violence, to responsiveness, as indicated in the transitions from eros to loving tenderness, intimate dialogue to unrestricted communication, and playfulness with others to solidarity.[29]

The articulation of mimetic contents is not only disclosed in experimental art, love, and play, but also in beginning to listen and respond to subaltern and silenced voices. Benjamin and Adorno show how the mimetic comportments can be responsive and emancipatory. It can but need not signify a return to archaic mythic and irrational powers, as Habermas and other critics fear. The repressed voices that come to be heard and the material contents released in an unrestricted mimesis can help reorient reflection and inform critical models that contest existing forms of domination. As such, the mimetic comportment (as intimated in love and play and as formalized and unrestricted) does not endanger but can help rearticulate and further the renewal of communication and rationality in materially and intersubjectively reproduced lifeworlds.[30]

Habermas proposed pursuing an alternative communicative model that is intended to correct the perceived failings of his teachers. However, his approach divorces communicative intersubjective rationality, oriented toward reaching intersubjective understanding (*Verständigung*), and calculative instrumental rationality, oriented toward maximizing means to successful outcomes. Such a model separates the problematic of interhuman domination (intersubjectivity) from the domination of nature that is left to instrumental rationality. For Habermas in an 1969 article that marks his departures from Adorno, the domination of nature is only a metaphor related to the secularized theology and empty idea of human reconciliation with nature instead of constituting a critical diagnostic model of the present.[31] Habermas's criticism of Adorno, and "Western Marxism" more broadly on the question of nature (he names Benjamin, Bloch, Horkheimer, and Marcuse), decouples the human and the natural worlds, sacrificing the latter, which offers an alterity and resistance that exceeds the transformative potential of the intersubjectivity of the lifeworld.[32] Habermas endeavors to dissolve the aporias—that is, the paradoxical entanglements and impasses that cannot be escaped and are constitutive of contemporary late modernity—of the

Dialectic of Enlightenment by removing the question of nature. He is on the way to *The Theory of Communicative Action* with its own categories of the (1) hermeneutic self-transparent lucidity of the lifeworld, and the intersubjective exchange of reasons in communicative action, and (2) its colonization by necessary yet excessive systems of power and exchange.[33]

It is argued throughout part 1, through a hermeneutical recovery and reconstruction of Adorno's philosophy of nature in contrast to recent thinkers identified with the Frankfurt school (particularly Habermas and, to a lesser extent, Honneth), that prioritizing human interaction through language and deemphasizing material and productive relations, which cannot be maintained in their classic Marxist form, are worse than the problem they are intended to resolve. Habermas's separation of labor and interaction, of instrumental and communicative rationalities, subordinates the "natural" and "material" to instrumentality, and subordinates the animality and materiality that humans themselves are. The bifurcation between the social and the natural in philosophy and in the lifeworld reproduces the anthropocentric forgetfulness that divides the human from the natural material world. The natural material world remains in turn unrecognized as something other than and in excess of human communication and rationality, and the hegemonic misuse and destruction of animals and environments is built into (with noticeable exceptions emerging in the nineteenth-century, such as Arthur Schopenhauer and Jeremy Bentham, who conceived ethics in relation to bodily suffering) the foundations of traditional forms of occidental ethical theory.

In part 1, a more appropriate natural historical conception of material life will be articulated in relation to Adorno's critical theory, which can be interpreted in relation to Levinas's notion of alterity to formulate an ethics of the material other that can orient critical social theory in an epoch of ecological crisis conditions. This strategy requires moving from Habermas to Adorno and Levinas to more appropriately confront contemporary material-environmental realities and crisis tendencies underemphasized in the communicative model.

Centered on a critical analysis of Adorno and Horkheimer's writings on nature and animals in light of the aporetic dialectic of nature and society examined in the *Dialectic of Enlightenment*—"dialectic" in the sense of both a way of thinking and the structure of the matter to be thought—I contend that environing material "outer nature" in its otherness and materiality, as much as subjective human "inner nature," can disturb systems of hegemonic domination and their ideological constructs through which they are predominantly (yet not fully) constructed and filtered. Adorno and Horkheimer's analysis of alienated human (inner) and reified nonhuman (outer) nature offers strategies for critically engaging contemporary environmental crisis tendencies: it does this by correcting the anthropocentric humanism and constructivist idealism of discourse ethics, dialogical ethics, and social contract theory. These prevailing ethical theories at best perceive the environment as a background for human activity and a secondary moral issue grounded on self-interest and anthropocentric analogical models.

The ensuing chapters are an attempt to illustrate how an "indirect" hermeneutically reflective ethics of the mimetic potential and responsiveness of sensuous existence, which operates as a critical orientation and model instead of a totalizing metaphysical doctrine, are unfolded throughout Adorno's mature works.[34] They present an argument for the critical interruptive significance of "nonidentity" (that is, alterity and otherness; the object or subject matter intractable to and potentially fracturing totalizing conceptualization)[35] and "nature" (or the animality, materiality, and worldliness of human praxis and reflection).[36]

Conclusion and Transition

> Today, however, where everything is included and the world constitutes a unity as far as one can see, the idea of "otherness" is one whose time has come. We might almost say that the dialectic, which always contains an element of freedom, has come to a full stop today because nothing remains outside it.
>
> —Theodor Adorno, *Towards a New Manifesto*

Adorno made this remark in his 1956 conversations with Horkheimer published in *Towards a New Manifesto*. Horkheimer stated in response that this otherness was ideological, and Adorno's hope a reversion to wishful utopianism. The dreams, hopes, and wishes that express the utopian dimension in Ernst Bloch's thinking are inadequate of themselves. Yet, they can be reimagined and reconstructed in critical models in relation to the present. In Adorno, as well in Levinas, otherness is not merely an ideological or utopian projection (a topic addressed in chapter 6) insofar as otherness places projection into question in and through the encounter. Otherness as revealed in encountering the object that eludes the subject's assimilating identification (Adorno) and the other who is someone else (Levinas) are diachronic moments of interruption and potential reorientation within the relentless reproduction and expansion of the forces of social totality.

The present approach articulates multiple critical models and shifting perspectives of a materialism of nonidentity (of mimesis, responsiveness, prophecy, and solidarity) and a critical or expansive (nonreductive) natural history and thus very different than the social Darwinist concept of natural history interrogated by Levinas as is discussed in chapters 4 and 5. Adorno's nature and Levinas's other bring attention to how otherness and alterity disturb the totality and unity characteristic of traditional philosophy and contemporary social organization, which are ruthlessly governed by equivalence and exchange.

The model of critical natural history (liberated from its reductive determinism and naturalism still operative in Marx) adopts elements from forms of materialism awoken to history as the history of species being and social history. The term "materialism" referred to in the present work is deployed in an antireductive direction, modifying its typical definition through the aporetic and ethical materiality operative in the discourses of Adorno and Levinas. In this context it signifies the thesis that material reality is the basis and point of departure for practice and reflection. Doctrinal and metaphysical materialism bracket the human practices and the dialectical and interpretive contexts that make a materialism of bodily existence and material others possible and necessary. Marx's dialectical or historical materialism integrated material reality and human praxis. In the writings of the early Frankfurt school in the 1930s, "materialism" signifies resistance to metaphysics rather than another metaphysical doctrine, including the eliminative and atomistic doctrinal accounts of materiality and sensation found in the Enlightenment and its positivistic heirs.[37]

Materialism, not as a metaphysical doctrine but as a critical perspective or diagnostic heuristic to confront existing social systems and their legitimating discourses that can involve ideological self-deception, requires the concrete analysis of the present social situation for early Horkheimer and his Frankfurt collaborators. The later recourse to materiality in Adorno's mature work retains a crucial materialist moment, as it indicates the corporeal, nonconceptual, and sensuous nature of existence. In the case of both early and later Adorno, natural historical materialism as a critical model does not imply a theoretical reduction to abstract nature or unmediated matter (as forms of identity). It is a futural orientation toward a promise of flourishing in the midst of the complexities and imperfections of damaged life rather than a reactive gesture of reviving or returning to a pure condition or origin. In Adorno's 1958–59 lectures on aesthetics, to be attentive and responsive to the object in interthingly playfulness and suffering requires the construction, formalization, and liberation of the disciplined and tabooed expressiveness and receptiveness of the mimetic comportment. Unfixing and unrestricting mimesis is not a return to a nonconceptual and unmediated nature. Freed mimesis occurs through provisional construction and experimentation, in responsiveness to its material and historical conditions that it can express, expose, and contest, as exhibited in radical modernist art.

In Adorno's context, materiality involves moments of constitution and mediation, power and violence (compellingly articulated by Levinas in *On Escape*), and also resistance and transformative possibilities. Accordingly, the emphasis on life in its materiality needs to be noneliminative, nonreductive, and experimental.[38] The current relevance of the early Frankfurt school's natural historical interpretation of material conditions consists in its transformative potential and advocacy of "aporetic" and ethical materialism—in contrast to a solely negative definition of Adorno's materialism—and its engagement through natural history with the constellation and mediated nexus of history and nature, rationality and power.[39]

Chapter Two

Natural History, Nonidentity, and Ecological Crisis

Introduction: Kant, Constitutive Idealism, and the Mythology of Reason

Idealism (as a reduction to the subject) and naturalism (as a reduction to the object as constructed by the subject) are both expressions of the philosophy of identity placed in question by nonidentity. Is this a fair conclusion? In a critical evaluation of Adorno and Horkheimer's depiction of Kantian rationality in the *Dialectic of Enlightenment*, Allen Wood proposes that Kant and the Enlightenment could not have reduced transformative reason to the means-oriented calculation of costs distinctive of instrumental rationality. Kant, after all, defended the precedence of practical reason that obligates us, as free rational agents, to recognize the noninstrumental and absolute moral value of human autonomy and dignity.[1] Wood's objection misses Adorno and Horkheimer's point that the noninstrumental status of human dignity is achieved in Kant by dividing practical from theoretical reason (i.e., the ethical from the natural world), which has the effect of promoting the instrumentalization of nature (i.e., the reduction of its meaning to means) and, consequently, of human beings *as* sensuous material and *as* animal beings. Pure and practical reason *both* promote the domination of nature. Nonhuman and human animals are instrumentalized as nature, even as humans are exempted as rational beings outside of the causal order of nature.[2]

The questionable status of Kantian reason is structural for Adorno. In a passage concerning Kant's lack of feeling for animals, worth quoting in full because of its vehemence, Adorno exaggerates the no doubt dubious categorization of nature and animals that informs Kant's practical philosophy:

> What I find so suspect in Kantian ethics is the "dignity" which they attribute to human beings in the name of autonomy. A capacity for moral self-determination is ascribed to humans as an absolute advantage—as a moral profit—while being covertly used to legitimize *dominance*—dominance over nature. This is the real aspect of the transcendental claim that humans can dictate the laws of nature. Ethical dignity in Kant is a demarcation of differences. It is directed against animals. Implicitly it excludes humans from nature, so that its humanity threatens incessantly to revert to the inhuman. It leaves no room for pity. Nothing is more abhorrent to the Kantian than a reminder of the resemblance of human beings to animals. This taboo is always at work when the idealist berates the materialist. Animals play for the idealist system virtually the same role as the Jews for fascism. To revile human animality—that is genuine idealism. To deny the possibility of salvation for animals absolutely and at any price is the inviolable boundary of its metaphysics.[3]

Further, even Kant's profoundest reflection on nature in the *Critique of the Power of Judgment*, in which nature is experienced as beautiful, sublime, and purposive without a final teleological purpose and which partially helps make up for the reductive account of nature in Kant's theoretical and practical philosophy, remains an anthropocentric and "bourgeois" gesture of spirit's dominion over abject nature that is inadequate to sensuous material existence and nonhuman animal suffering.[4]

A primary thesis of the *Dialectic of Enlightenment* is the mutuality of the human domination of nature and the domination of humans by one another. Tied together in the same integrative yet aporetic historical processes, Horkheimer and Adorno show that the highest ideals of modernity—of enlightenment, progress, and rationality—devalue themselves, becoming antienlightenment, through their historical realization. They are performatively undermined in their practice, institutionalization, and embodiment. Hegel argued in the *Phenomenology of Spirit* that the Enlightenment is fundamentally unenlightened about itself.[5] In contrast with Hegel's portrayal, the lack of self-insight of "radical rational insight" is not due to the Enlightenment's assertion of abstract and formal rationality against faith, tradition, and community. Instead, because of its one-sidedness, Enlightenment rationality undermines its own emancipatory promise by becoming increasingly complicit with domination. This collusion is reflected in its regression to pictorial thinking and the mythic—even if as a formal imaginary lacking the concrete images of traditional myth—that it once rejected as idolatry and superstition.

Modern rationalization requires adjusting to reality "as it is," reducing all actions and objects to their usefulness and exchange value, and without recognizing how this reality is itself materially and socially constituted and mediated.[6] Rationality in this critical model consequently loses its ethical and utopian dimensions. It becomes a new mythology in bureaucratic steering, in instrumental calculation, and in the manufactured spontaneity of consumerism as well as the affected freedom formed in the culture industry. The reversion to mythology, although now formalized and without a fixed particular content, is, for Adorno, "a second figurativeness, though without images or spontaneity."[7] This "mythology of reason" does not announce radical self-actualization and redemption through reason, as in the *Oldest System Program of German Idealism* that expressed the aspirations of the young Tübingen friends Hegel, Friedrich Hölderlin, and F. W. J. Schelling.[8] Rather, rationality is disenchanted and formalized and yet all the more mythic. It is complicit in the facticity of the domination that it once sought to unmask, and accepts and celebrates those powers as inevitable and good. It is not formalism that defies the decay of rationality if, as Adorno maintained, "Resistance to the decline of reason would mean for philosophical thinking . . . [to] immerse itself in the material contents in order to perceive in them, not beyond them, their truth content. Freedom of thinking is freedom in rather than from the object or subject matter."[9] Humanity's earthly dominion, or the transparency and controllability of nature for reified reason, is a defining tendency, according to Adorno and Horkheimer's argument, of the Enlightenment from its origins. Enlightenment betrays its own emancipatory impulses and legitimates interhuman domination because it has not questioned the human domination of nature.[10] If the thesis of the mutuality of natural history and human history can be upheld, then the two cannot be idealistically separated in the name of a deontological or communicative ethics that promotes human dignity by problematically isolating it from animality and materiality. Significant implications follow for diagnosing and responding to the intensifying environmental crises of our time.[11]

More recent generations of the Frankfurt school, from Habermas to Axel Honneth—a designation that disguises fundamental differences between those associated with the Institute for Social Research—have inadequately recognized the ethical and social-political significance of animals and environments. This is a serious lacuna; as social ecological, ecofeminist, and socialist environmental movements illustrate, the biopolitical contradictions of capitalism remain perilously unanswered. In contrast to social ecology, contemporary theorists associated with the Frankfurt school have failed to give the environment sufficient attention. The overlapping and closely aligned yet distinctive positions associated with Habermas (discourse ethics) and Honneth (the ethics of recognition) have made valuable contributions to egalitarian and democratic ethical and political theorizing.[12] Their work will operate as the primary ethical alternative to the "ethics of nonidentity" and material others elucidated throughout this volume.[13] This strategy is due to their (1) critical reception of the materialism of Marx and the early Frankfurt school, and (2) disagreements with the asymmetrical ethics of alterity on behalf of a different symmetrical model of interpersonal ethics. Their works are, furthermore, symptomatic of the overly anthropocentric and idealistic tendencies that deemphasize the material world and the multiplicity of material others. This neglect is a consequence of the preeminence conferred to human intersubjectivity and an impoverished analysis of the natural history of human-environmental interactions. In their reception of the *Dialectic of Enlightenment*, for instance, Habermas and Honneth maintain that the expression "domination of nature"—a key concept for Adorno and for the argument of this volume—is at best a metaphor extended to nature from the domination between humans in misshapen relations between socially constituted human agents.[14] Honneth remarks in *Reification* that the Hegelian Marxist concern with the reciprocal reification (the "thingifying" or "objectifying" in the reductive sense that should be distinguished from the freedom toward the thing and its priority in Adorno) of nature, society, and the self can be reconstructed through the prism of social reification and intersubjective relations of recognition and misrecognition.[15]

The symbolically reproduced lifeworld of human agents suffers from the inappropriate colonization and damaging reification by systems of bureaucratic power and market forces.[16] Reification consists of the socially reproduced control and marginalization of the nonidentical, the nonconceptual, and dynamic in Adorno. The critique of reification is unfortunately not applicable to nature for Honneth because the natural world cannot communicate even in a muted language or in its silent pain. Nature is fundamentally wordless, and the animal cry is meaningless to the anthropocentric gaze. Repeating the Kantian duality of the human and the natural that rationalizes intelligible value by irrationalizing brute facticity, the "domination of nature" is an analogy made from intersubjective domination and is therefore not domination at all.[17]

In response to this situation, it is worth reconsidering in our altered context the more empirical, materialist, and "naturalistic" (in an expansive sense) point of departure of the "interdisciplinary" and pluralistic materialism of the early Frankfurt school that continues to inform Adorno's later thought.[18] Horkheimer's initial program of an "interdisciplinary materialism" was an attempt to renew the obscured critical potential within Marxism. Marx's legacy had by the late 1920s already become primarily a rhetoric of legitimating new forms of domination in Eastern Europe and a conformist logic of adaptation in Western European social democratic parties. Habermas describes in this context how "[c]ritical theory was initially developed in Horkheimer's circle to think through political disappointments at the absence of revolution in the West, the development of Stalinism in Soviet Russia, and the victory of fascism in Germany. It was supposed to explain mistaken Marxist prognoses, but without breaking Marxist intentions."[19] The renewal was aimed at reformulating the theoretical foundations and social-critical intentions of historical materialism by integrating social-scientific, social-critical, and philosophical modes of inquiry. Traditional theory assumed a contemplative attitude toward reality; critical theory integrated the human sciences and philosophy with the practical aim of diagnosing the pathologies and transformative potential of the hegemonic social regime.

Adorno's heterodox metamorphosis of standard materialist interpretive strategies emerged from the early project of a critical theory of society formulated by Horkheimer and his colleagues at the University of Frankfurt in the late 1920s. This new theory, in its initial form, would consist of an "interdisciplinary materialism" integrating philosophy and empirically oriented social scientific research. Social theory, Adorno remarked in 1964, is philosophical insofar as it reflects upon itself.[20] As self-reflective concerning its own positionality in social reality in confrontation with society's ideological self-presentation, theory questions itself along with its objects of inquiry. This self-referential questioning served the twofold aim of explaining its own social-historical origins and accounting for its possible addressee.[21] In classical Marxist terms, a classicism that was questioned by this "school" from the beginning, the theory's origins rested in the economic and cultural conditions of advanced capitalism. Its addressee was that class that alone was capable of revolutionizing those conditions, the proletariat. This initial program already found itself in the ambiguity of asserting the universalizing tendencies of theory, and to a degree the legacy of classical Marxism, and of maintaining an awareness of the historical-contextual and reflexive self-referential character of knowledge. A more serious problem for its claim to practical import was that the early program of the Frankfurt school began in the affirmation of Marxism as a model for social theory and simultaneously in skepticism concerning its adequacy. It faced the inadequacy of that theory in two ways: (1) in how Marxism reductively related economic and cultural conditions, praxis and reflection, and (2) in skepticism about the historically determined revolutionary role of the proletariat and its self proclaimed directorial vanguard.

The later works of Adorno continued the project of an interdisciplinary and multidimensional materialism. Adorno dissolved the transcendental dichotomy between intelligible normativity and corporeality, an abyss that, once accepted, no amount of pragmatic application can overcome. Adorno dissolved the duality by thematizing the natural and human worlds as historically intertwined and mutually co-constituting. From this perspective, the antinaturalistic ethics of discourse and recognition of Habermas and Honneth limit the scope of the ethical to interhuman relations, while nature, the environment, and animals are abandoned to instrumentalization and reduced to what are at best indirect analogies with humans and extrinsic pragmatic calculations of their value for human purposes.[22]

Adorno cannot be appropriately portrayed as an ethicist if ethics is defined as a discourse of universal norms and prescriptions based on autonomy as in Kant, the calculation of overall utility as in Jeremy Bentham and John Stuart Mill, or the primacy of virtue and mastery as in Aristotle. Adorno mostly speaks negatively of ethics and morality as ideological instruments of power. However, his concerns remain ethical in a deeper sense that is also at work in Levinas: an infinite concern for the enigmatic Other that transcends any anthropological, biological, or natural reason or foundation for it. Adorno not only expresses care for the human other; care for nature shapes his critique of deontological ethics in ways that continue to be significant for their contemporary incarnations.

Adorno's argument against Kantian ethics in the quotation above remains applicable to contemporary deontological ethics: the devaluing of the natural in order to give absolute value to the human in effect devalues and instrumentalizes both. For Adorno, "Kantian ethics owes its semblance of objectivity exclusively to this formalism and hence to its utter subjectivism."[23] Its formalism neutralizes cultural and historical content, and thus neutralizes the rich bonds and fabric that inform and orient ethical judgment, allowing it to be used for regressive purposes.[24] Habermas intensifies this Kantian neutralization of cultural content. Habermas transformed the idealist self-constitution of the subject into an intersubjective constitution but did not arrive at the radicalness of the "other-constitution" of the subject indicated in the discourses of Adorno and Levinas. Habermas's discourse remains to this extent overly idealistic and subjectivist insofar as it does not offer adequate recognition of the asymmetrical material and intersubjective or ethical "other-constitution" of subjects that contests the dominant modern paradigm of the free self-constitution of subjectivity.[25]

Communicative Idealism or Natural History?

Adorno described the task of his philosophy as employing "the strength of the subject to break through the fallacy of constitutive subjectivity."[26] Habermas presents his "communicative turn" as a more adequate form of overcoming the philosophy of consciousness and the subject and as a correction to the ostensible failures of the first generation of the Frankfurt school, contending that critical theory can escape the "hopeless dead-end" of the *Dialectic of Enlightenment*, and the problem of reification through instrumental reason, by abandoning nature to objectification and technical manipulation while morally exempting intersubjective human relations. Habermas contends that human nature alone is to be redeemed from reification and disposability, rejecting Adorno's construal of the sensuous-material sources of rationality, and ignoring the task of a hermeneutics and ethics of natural history and environmental natural history.[27] The problem is resolved for Habermas by decoupling human nature from natural history and the natural world, and thus morally exempting human beings from inappropriate use and manipulation through biotechnologies and other means.[28] The domination of nature is not in itself objectionable, but only its illegitimate extension to human nature. Habermas's position (an idealism of a collective subject, the republic of spirits in the tradition of Leibniz and Kant) appears inadequate in downplaying the entanglement of communicative and natural worlds in natural history. In contrast with Adorno's insistence on the immanent interruptive moment of the nonidentical, no nonidentity or alterity in nature can challenge this departmentalization of the human and inhuman as moral and extramoral in Habermas.[29]

Habermas concludes in *The Future of Human Nature* that human nature ought to be normatively nondisposable for positive scientific and technological interventions, as distinguished from negative and curative ones, which serve to undermine the symmetry and equality of human relations, especially those between different generations.[30] Because nature does not involve the reciprocity of first- and second-person intersubjective relations, who address one another as "I" and "you," the natural world, the environment, and animals have no direct or immediate moral status. For intersubjectively defined moral philosophy, the nonhuman lacks intrinsic ethical worth. Ethical respect for the human other does not extend to animal others.[31] The nonhuman is left to disposability because it cannot even count *as* other, or as another ethically relevant "self." Insofar as humans are worldly bodily beings, with practical material lives, it is debatable whether the nondisposability of humans can be preserved in a world where everything else is disposable.[32] As Horkheimer remarked of the connection between human salvation and animal suffering, addressing the complicity of anthropocentric humanism with cruelty to animals in the *Eclipse of Reason*, "Only [the human] soul can be saved; animals have but the right to suffer."[33]

By not recognizing the animal in the human and the ethical in the animal, the partition of the human from the nonhuman devalues those forms of life that lack or resist this separation. In not listening and responding to animals, environments, and the materiality of the world, which correlates with being unable to address and be addressed by them, numerous human forms of life and suffering are silenced. The Kantian-Habermasian strategy of theoretically and practically domesticating and excluding the abject and the subaltern, that is, of that which and those who cannot come to "rational discourse," is as a consequence questionable. The young Marx spoke of the future reconciliation of humans and their natural world in his *Economic-Philosophic Manuscripts* (1844). György Lukács and Hegelian Marxism emphasized the difficulties of the reification of nature as part of human alienation under the capitalist regime of unrestricted exchange. The early Frankfurt school, with impulses from Marxism, focused on the domination of nature and animals in modernity.[34] Habermas rejects these ways of conceiving nature and the nonhuman. This rejection is made in the name of a—still all too metaphysical—"postmetaphysical" philosophy that is more metaphysical than past metaphysics in the way it transcendentally-pragmatically (that is, hierarchically) constructs the human in isolation from its suppressed worldly, material, and corporeal contexts.[35] As in the patriarchal dominion of Adam, who assigns names and significance to things, it is the constructors, givers, and masters of meaning who participate in and define the ethical.

Without returning to all the premises of classical Marxism, while being partially inspired by writings such as the *Theses on Feuerbach*, I propose that a nonreductive, aporetic, and ethical praxis-oriented—rather than a metaphysical or speculative—materialism is needed. An indirect approach to materiality is needed—that is, as in Adorno, one mediated through language and conceptualization. That is to say, it needs to be reconceived as an expansive materialism that is not restricted, as in vulgar scientism, to a restrictive model of matter and natural scientific inquiry or, as in statist forms of Marxism that justify the exploitation and domination that Marxism was intended to contest, to one paradigmatic deterministically interpreted form of human activity, such as labor or production. This indirect and expansive explication of materialism is more suited to reflectively engaging and potentially transforming both social and natural phenomena than the reduction of things and the world to discursive and ideologically constituted constructs.

Further, by confronting the perspective of the contemporary generations of the Frankfurt school with forgotten and repressed moments from its own past, in conjunction with Levinas's discourse of alterity, Habermas's communicative solution and cure is revealed—in overly neglecting animals, ecosystems/environments, and material others (as considered throughout this work)—to be worse than the ostensive aporetic disease diagnosed by Habermas in his polemical critique of the early Frankfurt school and antimodernism and postmodernism from

Friedrich Nietzsche to Foucault and Derrida.[36] As nature continues to be abandoned to instrumental rationalization, this communicative strategy is philosophically dubious and ecologically disastrous. The failures of twentieth-century positions that one-sidedly advocate linguistic and social construction without recognition of what is other than identity and its constructs, that is, the reductive thesis that things are basically reflections of concepts and words, demands a critical return to the role of the nonconceptual and nondiscursive corporeality and sensuousness of human existence, that is, as Adorno emphasized, a return to the nonidentity of the nonconstructed and nonconstructible. Adorno does emphasize linguistic critique as a form of ideology critique; yet a key constituent of the critique of language is the nonidentity between language and the contents and objects it seeks to signify.[37]

Three moments of identification can be differentiated in this context: (1) the identity of mimesis as imitative enslavement, fetishism, and idolatry, or adaptation and subordination to the object and the other understood in the Hegelian-Marxian context as the master who subjugates the servant and the laborer; (2) the nonidentification in mimesis as an unforced and noncoercive felt contact and "freedom toward the object" (*Freiheit zum Objekt*) and the other, which refers to the moment of anarchic nonidentity in life, nature, and the organic; and (3) the responsive and emancipatory potential of a formalized and unrestricted perceptual and imaginative mimesis, exhibited in avant-garde art and experimentalism, which cannot be separated from or preclude abstraction and conceptualization unfolded by way of Adorno's critique of the domination of nature as indifferent and unresponsive to the object (the question of mimesis will be further addressed in the next chapter).[38] Conceptual universalization, as partially constitutive of critique and nonidentity thinking, is needed if the nonconceptual singular is not to be betrayed. Adorno argued in his response to the student movement in the late 1960s that critical transformation is indicated not only in direct praxis or art; it also demands theory as the "open thinking that points beyond itself."[39]

The sensuous physicality of things does not consist in an extralinguistic unmediated substrate, as if language were not central to how the object is addressed, and merely external and secondary to it.[40] Even as communication and rationalization do not exhaust nature, humans do not intuit or access nature "in itself" or "as such," unmediated by their own historically situated activities and constructs. Since nothing seems more natural than attempts to master nature, this description applies to ideologies of nature consisting in what conceptually and practically counts as natural. Such ideological formations perpetuate human subordination and ecological devastation under the guise of creating the material means to promote human flourishing.

The continuing promise of Adorno and Horkheimer's strategy is found in their recognition of the dialectical entanglements and tensions of language and the materiality of life, social and natural history, and, through the aporetic moment of nonidentity, their potential disturbance of and irreducibility to either an ideological construct or an unchanging essence. Dialectical thinking is a hazardous game, given its mobility and transience, since it dangerously enables both apology and determinate critique.[41] Autonomous thought is inexorably bound to and cannot escape its heteronomous conditions. Given this dangerous state of affairs, in which dialectic is immanent yet not totalizing, Adorno's strategy self-critically disrupts itself.[42] This materially oriented and conceptually informed interruption enables the critical analysis of the one-sidedness of constructivism, naturalism, and environmentalisms that disregard human suffering and social injustice. In an age of deepening environmental crises, discourses that romanticize the natural, idolize the religious, and celebrate the supposed irrationality of life, that is, those that obstruct the disruptive movement of self-reflection and rationality, need to be confronted. If one mode of domination cannot be adequately addressed without other modes, there is no liberation of the natural that resists or transcends social life and intrahuman dynamics of communication and recognition.

Adorno's articulation of the paradoxical and aporetic mediations of nature and society suggests an alternative to (1) the contemporary ethics of discourse and recognition articulated by Habermas and Honneth; (2) the accounts of critical social theory and environmentalism, such as those offered by Steven Vogel and Andrew Biro, that construe discourses of nature and naturalness as inherently essentialist and ideological social constructs;[43] and (3) the potentially destructive dehumanization involved in submersing the human into the ideological construction of discourses of pure and untainted nature, in which biocentric ecotopias—or the eco-dystopias feared by critics of environmentalism—no longer address human suffering or attend to the human as the location where humans encounter or fail to encounter organic, biological, and animal life.

Nature as Ideology and Ethics

> [I]n keeping with bourgeois standards it is chalked up as a special merit that someone has feeling for nature—which is for the most part a moralistic-narcissistic posturing as if to say: What a fine person I must be to enjoy myself with such gratitude.
>
> —Theodor Adorno, *Aesthetic Theory*

Adorno and Horkheimer's *Dialectic of Enlightenment* has been described as a pessimistic work reflecting the failures of the democratic left, the rise and seemingly unlimited destructive fury of totalitarian domination in Hitler's Germany and Stalin's Soviet Union, the increasing pervasiveness of commodified and reified life, and the decomposition of the fragile individual subject under the hegemony of the culture industry and ideologically mass-manipulated society. Notwithstanding Adorno's insight that the critique of enlightenment's deformations through self-reflection and ideology-critique contributes to its continued transformation, and that an initial step of such self-reflection is to "stop slandering Enlightenment," Adorno and Horkheimer are blamed for the rise of a purportedly irrational left and even the destruction of Western civilization.[44]

Although Habermas interestingly relapses and partly adopts the language of the *Dialectic of Enlightenment* in his works on bioethics, he regards this work to be a retreat to a speculative philosophy of history and nature in negative form. In *The Philosophical Discourse of Modernity*, he considers it to be a flawed departure from (1) social scientific inquiry, (2) the normative and hermeneutical foundations of social theory,[45] and (3) the Frankfurt school's initial project of an emancipatory critical social theory conceived of as an "interdisciplinary materialism."[46]

Habermas contends that the excessively close linking of nature and history compelled the early Frankfurt school into a destructive aporia. Despite aporetic thinking's capacities to address mediated and contradictory conditions from Socrates to Derrida, as maintained in this work, Habermas promises to redeem the aims of critical social theory without reproducing these aporetic structures.[47] If this reconstruction is apposite, then Habermas has repressed rather than resolved the aporias and the questionability of the categories of nature and history in modernity. The attempt to repress the aporetic conditions of critical social theory entails the loss of critique and the impossibility of critical theory as understood by the early Frankfurt school.

Why is this strategy problematic? Habermas's communicative alternative decouples human domination from the domination of nature, as well as history from nature, by categorically and systematically separating instrumental rationalization from intersubjective communicative reason. Instrumental reason concerns the calculation of means for arbitrarily posited ends and the objectification of things from an explanatory third-person perspective, reflecting the irrationality of rational choice. Communicative action involves first- and second-person perspectives calling for the reciprocal respect of the other in the interpersonal exchange of impersonal reasons.

Informed by an ultimately anthropocentric and speciesist logic that severs interpersonal human relations from their natural and environmental contexts and conditions, a duality of instrumentalized nature and intersubjective spirit developed at length in *The Theory of Communicative Action*, Habermas argues in *The Future of Human Nature* for the nondisposability of human nature for humans and the disposability of nature for human calculation of its worth and value. Since animals do not partake in the relational symmetry of mutual respect, "they do not belong to the universe of members who address intersubjectively accepted rules and orders to one another."[48] Habermas pragmatically adjusts the unconditionality of his exclusion of creatures from ethics by adding, inconsistently, that "[a]nimals benefit for their own sake from the moral duties which we are held to respect in our dealings with sentient creatures."[49] Despite Habermas's uneasiness with his own position in this passage, his justification of morality through the recourse to intersubjective symmetry entails that human relations with animals and the environment are not directly or immediately ethical. Nature does not speak in a human tongue, and so cannot be heard. This silence is solidified to the degree that social history is divorced from the forces and relations of production, that is, interaction from labor, and its contexts or nexus in natural history. Habermas's reasoning is ethically doubtful and creates a paradox: either morality embraces human relations to the in- and nonhuman, such that it is not exclusively symmetrical and reciprocal by encompassing asymmetrical responsibilities and obligations, or else it is purely symmetrical and cannot concern animals intrinsically for their own sake.

Honneth's recognition theory is a significant modification of Habermas's model, which is based on communicative rationality as the ethically structured exchange of reasons, in reintroducing the affective and social-psychological dynamics of recognition and misrecognition.[50] He proposes a richer moral approach to animals and the environment, while concluding that such moral considerations are indirect extensions of human intersubjectivity. Honneth argues that Adorno's project fails to capture the ethical and critical character of practical life because of his commitment to the thesis of the domination of nature.[51] Because he finds Adorno and Horkheimer's intense meditation on the domination of nature to be an analogy, image, and metaphor constructed on interhuman domination, Honneth misinterprets the role that the domination and reification of nature plays throughout their works, including in their remarks on the direct moral significance of animal life and suffering.

Honneth problematically interprets and reductively excludes the idea of the domination of nature. Adorno's thesis should be interpreted instead in the context of Adorno's exploration of nonidentity as (1) a break with the absorption and mastery, and (2) the precondition of a genuinely pluralistic and unforced reconciliation.[52] Since Adorno did not restrict this moment of nonidentity to the human, as Honneth does in his critique of Adorno, "reconciliation with nature" remains an indefinite promise. Contrary to conventional expectations, such reconciliation is invisible in ideologically formed images of idyllic nature. It is rather indicated in the nightmares of the monstrous, the mutated, and the pseudoarchaic King Kong and the Loch Ness Monster—which express both human fear of nature and "the hope that animal creation might survive the wrong human beings have done it."[53] Discourses of nature require a more differentiated assessment than the arguments for the "end of nature" suggest. They are contested as ideological while also being deployed in critical natural history and environmental ethics to confront existing ecological crisis tendencies.

The alterity and nonidentity in nature depicted by Adorno are no longer meaningful in Honneth's critical social theory. Instead, the human other is the sole basic ethical concern. Honneth reproduces classical hermeneutical and neo-Kantian distinctions between interhuman understanding and objectifying natural explanation and a world of norms separated from a world of facts.[54] Fear of a return to romantic *Natur-* and *Lebensphilosophie*, with their ambiguous political entanglements, leads Honneth to deny teleological, metaphysical, and vitalistic conceptions of nature. By conflating different experiences of nature, Honneth rejects on this basis the possibility of an ethics and hermeneutics of nature that is suggested by Horkheimer in the *Eclipse of Reason*.[55]

The prevailing contemporary paradigm of critical social theory in Honneth and Habermas problematically approaches nature through the forced either/or of either enchanted romantic or reductive scientistic naturalism (which conflates nature and the human interpretation of the primacy of nature in reduced form) that are genealogically dismantled in the *Dialectic of Enlightenment*. Their dyadic strategy resolves the aporias of the *Dialectic of Enlightenment* in communicative rationality, or reciprocal interaction and recognition, by undialectically abandoning nature to the abjection of disenchantment and instrumentalization. It consequently disavows human dependence on the animality and materiality of life, a life that is presupposed by the theorist even as it is rejected. This solution reinforces the Baconian vision of the equation of knowledge and power that is achieved in mastery over nature and other humans.[56] This supposedly enlightened vision is oblivious to the natural environing world as something more than a projection of human rationality and symmetrical communication.

If the dignity of the human cannot be bought with the abjection of nature without undermining itself, then the communicative paradigm is inadequate to its own goals. This problem is indicated in Horkheimer's claim that the more nature is reduced to mastered material, the emptier the mastering subject becomes.[57] Adorno similarly describes how the Kantian "transcendental subject is nothing but the internalized and hypostatized form of human domination of nature. This always comes into being through the elimination of qualities, through the reduction of qualitative distinctions to quantitative forms."[58] It should be noted that Habermas in *The Future of Human Nature* does reject the bioengineering and reconstruction of human nature through eugenics while (if the arguments here are correct) insufficiently extending such concerns to nonhuman nature.[59]

We will continue to elucidate below two opposing alternatives for critical social ecology by addressing the conflicting conceptions of nature in Adorno and Habermas and the numerous reasons for the inadequacy of Habermas's discourse and communicative ethics as and for an ethics of nature and material others. Communicative ethics restores the mastery of a formalized "quasitranscendental" (although still too transcendental) subject in collective intersubjective form, emptied of qualitative content yet (as Nietzsche wrote of Kant's categorical imperative) still evocative of past and present violence, reproducing rather than questioning the radical deficits concerning animals, ecology, and the natural world of the contemporary world. These failures need to be addressed, first by rethinking and extending the ethical from the interhuman and the symmetrical from the asymmetrical, and second by articulating the differences, affinities, and inseparable interdependence of the natural and the human. This indirect and experimental materialist prospect indicated by Adorno reconnects with the organic basis of animal and human life, and reconnects as well in the bodily vulnerability, suffering, and happiness that bind them together.[60]

Historical Nature and Natural History

In *The Philosophical Discourse of Modernity*, Habermas portrays the *Dialectic of Enlightenment* as a totalizing and aporetic critique undermining rationality and the possibilities for emancipatory change.[61] Adorno and Horkheimer are engaged, Habermas claims, in an "ambiguous attempt at a dialectic of Enlightenment."[62] Adorno and Horkheimer "would still like to hold on to the basic figure of Enlightenment," but "it is no longer possible to place hope in the liberating force of Enlightenment."[63] What remains is a mournful hopeless hope. In contrast to this assessment offered by Habermas, and his abandonment of "nature" in the name of reciprocal and symmetrical intersubjectivity, the emancipatory hopes of critical theory—of an experimental hypothesis that aims beyond description and explanation at social transformation—cannot be based on neglecting the following factors: (1) the differences and affinities of nature and reason suppressed in the communicative turn; (2) the aporetic dialectical tension between nature and society characteristic of capitalist societies; and (3) ecological and environmental crisis-tendencies.

The "domination of nature" is in Horkheimer and Adorno an actual natural-historical process that asserts progressive human mastery and control over the natural world, and thus not merely a metaphor *pace* Habermas and Honneth. Despite the strangeness of this proposition to discourses that conceptualize the control of nature as material progress and human self-realization, Adorno and Horkheimer are closer to Marx and Marxist theorists such as Lukács in maintaining that nature can be an object of reification and fetishization (e.g., persons and relations becoming things and things becoming ideological and commodified)—concepts they modified from Marx and twentieth-century Hegelian Marxism in their own form of interdisciplinary materialism and ideology critique. Honneth's assertion is accurate that Adorno was distrustful of the romanticism and metaphysics of nature implicit in Lukács, rejecting the conflation of objectification with reification.[64] It does not follow from this disambiguation that nature is not reified or dominated in Adorno's sense.

Adorno's writings on nature show that "external nature," analogously to human "inner nature," is an object of domination, and that this process can be potentially displaced. Although the resistance and interruptive power of nature, what Horkheimer described as its "revolt,"[65] cannot be described as resistance in any sense that presupposes a choosing agent or subject, it does intimate a fuller and more appropriate critical model of nature than a strategy that abandons the natural world and denies any intrinsic value to it for the sake of morally reinforcing the intersubjective reciprocity of human relations.[66] Ways of life are formed by how humans encounter, engage, and respond to their world. Enmeshed in the facticity and material conditions of existence, ways of life presuppose and entail much more than the forms of communicative rationality, democratic deliberation, and intersubjective recognition emphasized by Habermas and Honneth. Yet ecodemocracy needs altered relations with nature.

Adorno and Horkheimer did not reject the hopes of ethical humanism and the traces of liberation at work in Enlightenment rationality, including critical and transformative projects of increasing freedom, solidarity, and social justice. For the sake of the betrayed hopes of the past, they skeptically examined how the realization of these hopes have remained incomplete and indeed become complicit with the regime of the calculative mastery of a subject that reduces others, nature, and itself to objects of technical management and propagandistic and media-driven steering. Given these circumstances, the promise of enlightenment and liberation can barely be articulated in the context of enlightenment's self-ruination: "Enlightenment, understood in the widest sense as the advance of thought, has always aimed at liberating human beings from fear and installing them as masters. Yet the wholly enlightened earth is radiant with triumphant calamity."[67]

In Hegel's *Phenomenology of Spirit*, the realization of freedom can be its destruction, and the rational moral law can become irrational terror.[68] Enlightenment produces the opposite of the aim of Enlightenment, returning to mythic violence in Hegel's assessment of the French

Revolution, when a state terrorizes a people with prophetic inspiration in the name of destroying superstition and achieving its freedom, and also in the early Frankfurt school's analysis of the material and political "progress" of advanced capitalism. Freedom from mythic nature itself becomes mythic, as the higher powers are less easy for Odysseus—for example, the prototype of the individual bourgeois agent—to trick and master. Individuality is increasingly lost unless it conforms to the ideological model of bourgeois individualism, as the mass-produced and officially sanctioned "pretense of individualism . . . necessarily increases in proportion to the liquidation of the individual."[69] Horkheimer describes elsewhere how social totality destroys individuality and forces the individual to accept inflicted damages as good.[70]

Maintaining the affinity of myth and Enlightenment, "myth is already Enlightenment: and Enlightenment reverts to mythology,"[71] Horkheimer and Adorno's account of the dialectic of myth and Enlightenment is comprehensible from the perspective of the question of how humans relate to nature through them: "Myth becomes Enlightenment and nature mere objectivity. Human beings purchase the increase in their power with estrangement from that over which it is exerted. Enlightenment stands in the same relationship to things as the dictator to human beings. He knows them to the extent that he can manipulate them."[72] At variance with the ideology of returning to the primitive and archaic, myth is already a form of Enlightenment attempting to distance itself from and control nature. Yet Enlightenment itself has mythical tendencies and, in conjunction with the unfolding material and cultural forces of modern societies, is forced to revert to myth: "Humans believe themselves free from fear when there is no longer anything unknown. This has determined the path of demythologization, of Enlightenment, which equates the living with the nonliving as myth equated the nonliving with the living. Enlightenment is mythical fear radicalized."[73] Myth and Enlightenment attempt to subdue the uncanniness and fear of existence, first compensated for in myth, and to drive the development of Enlightenment from myth to reason. Each step brings about a greater dominion over nature and the greater loss of the possibility of self-knowledge. Enlightenment is instrumentality tied to ends structured by violence and fear that results in domination.

As Adorno's assessment of Richard Wagner's contrived and romanticized naturalism demonstrates, which is further examined in chapter 3, the natural is an ambiguous and contested concept that both supports and potentially interferes with ideology. The ideological occultation of natural phenomena in society and the reification of socially constituted phenomena as if they were actually nature and human nature are processes rooted in exchange value and commodification.[74] Despite this, the phenomena designated as "nature" are not revealed purely in one manner such that nature or its idea can be overcome in the name of social progress. For Adorno, the reification and fetishism of nature is simultaneously human alienation—through processes of labor and consumption—from the natural world that subjects abject in exalting.[75] The dominion over nature is at the same time subjugation by nature and freedom from nature's liberation.[76] As a result of the logic of nonidentity, which destabilizes mediation and synthesis, and determinate (instead of totalizing) negation, which reveals truth in ideology, there can be neither a nostalgic return to nature as essence and origin nor an overcoming of nature by spirit—nor a linguistic-social construct to be effortlessly removed through good intentions. Adorno emphasizes in *Kierkegaard: Construction of the Aesthetic* how Kierkegaard's separation of spirit from nature and the body lead to their revenge on spirit that cannot separate itself from what it seeks to subjugate.[77]

If Adorno maintains that reflection must break with absorption in nature, and with nature's exaltation as an inhuman power and destiny unresponsive to human suffering, this happens because the break disturbs human mastery of nature, revealing possibilities for an unforced recognition of and reconciliation with nature.[78] Adorno identifies such a possibility with the promise of happiness; it is radically distorted in the fascist use of the beauty and sublimity of nature, when "[n]ature, in being presented by society's control mechanism as the healing antithesis of society, is itself absorbed into that incurable society and sold off."[79] Distorted nature is more than an epistemic mistake. It is, in Adorno's analysis of images of animals and nature in Wagner, a projection of domination, even as, at the same time, it "becomes the only gap in an all-encompassing prison."[80]

Materiality and a Critical Ethos of Nature

According to Adorno's "natural history" reconstructed in this chapter, nature is socially-historically configured and irreducible to any one conceptual or political economic system of that configuration. The human relation to nature is socially-historically mediated and configured. Material nature is irreducible to any given social system, insofar as nature is the material basis of human life and activity, and—as the nonconceptual and the object that has priority over the subject—inevitably more than what is posited in a conceptual model or reproduced in a social-economic configuration. Nature is accessed and mediated through language, history, and the sciences, while remaining irreducibly nonidentical with its appropriation, interpretation, and explanation through them. If nature were purely a social or ideological construct, it would disappear in its domination by "spirit," or the coercive integrating totality of the existing order and the calculations of instrumental rationality, such that ecological and environment crisis-tendencies would remain invisible. These crisis-tendencies, and the contradictions between the current socially organized configuration of human life and the natural world, have become more evident and heightened in their destructive and damaging effects. Heightening these environmental contradictions can potentially lead to the end of the human species, as climate crises are intensified. This intensification indicates the inappropriateness of the capitalist organization of society and previous and current antiecological Marxist models of human emancipation insofar as they fail to envision a solidarity of material others in the extended sense of an adequate culture of (cultivating) nature that responds to the mutual nourishing of life and nurturing the nonhuman as well as the human world.

"Nature" is, adopting Adorno's interpretive strategy, not given in immediate experience nor a univocal concept but is, rather, a socially and historically mediated configuration. The multiplicity of phenomena associated with the category of the natural, or with the animal, as Derrida has argued, does not appear in one homogeneous and invariable manner.[81] The natural reveals itself under various incommensurable guises, some terrifying and fateful, others liberating and redemptive for the ever-fragile historically and organically embodied subject joined through its biological life with the life of the world. Nature appears under the oppressive guise of fate and destiny, assigning bodies to abjection, destruction, and death via physical characteristics associated with race, gender, and class.

The experience and concept of "nature" are historical as they have been ideologically constituted and manipulated in legitimating injustice and inequality as "natural" phenomena. "Nature" has been continuously reconstructed in human natural history. Its invisible secrets have been grasped and made visible through scientific discourses and technologies.

Appeals to nature have functioned as an uncritical flight from an alienated and artificial civilization. Nonetheless, nature can also be articulated through traces of the nonidentical. Such traces are mediated even in their appearance of immediacy and spontaneity, yet they can still resist and confound or be hypostatized in the betrayal of the utopian and messianic in the idolatrous or violent instant of their adulation.

Domination appears to be primarily—perhaps even exclusively—a question of intersubjective recognition and undistorted communication for the contemporary critical social theory that claims the inheritance and legacy of the Frankfurt school (namely, Habermas and Honneth). This "intersubjective turn" signifies a diminishment to our critical reflection about human relations with animals, environments, and the encompassing natural world. Natural history was a crucial element in Marx's philosophy and in its reinterpretation in early Frankfurt school thinkers such as Adorno, Horkheimer, and Herbert Marcuse. Habermas describes the inability to distinguish labor (driven by need, fear, and instrumental calculation) and intersubjective interaction (a different form of praxis oriented toward mutual understanding) as the innermost failure of the orthodox Marxian paradigm.[82] He notes how this flawed paradigm failed to differentiate processes of intersubjective communication from the development of the forces and relations of production, and thus systematically misinterpreted the social. Marxism devalued the normative and interpretive dimensions of the lifeworld that are the prerequisites of ethical life, the human sciences, and social criticism.[83]

The justifiable rejection of naïve or direct forms of realism and reductive materialism, such as the economic determinism of orthodox Marxism that is inappropriate in a stage of capitalism in which socialcultural production and power takes precedence, need not entail the rejection of materialism or the idealistic subordination of facticity, materiality, and sensibility.[84] This is particularly the case if global rejection of materialism leads to a form of linguistic or communicative idealism of constitutive intersubjectivity that erroneously prioritizes validity claims and fatefully neglects the bodily entanglement of humans with animals and environments. Instead of being a residue of metaphysics, Adorno analyzes the loss of the distinction between cultural and empirical reality as part of processes of commodification and commercialization.[85]

Adorno and Horkheimer significantly transformed classical Marxism without abandoning the model of a critical and oblique materialism for which the interhuman domination cannot be solved exclusively in its own terms, that is, purely "humanistically" or "communicatively" through isolating human beings from natural and material relations. Questions of human justice and injustice cannot be removed from critical reflection on and engagement with both "external" and "internal" nature. The potential for a different relationship with nature and the environment informs the direction of the *Dialectic of Enlightenment*. Human domination presupposes nature and draws environments and animals further into its equation via the bodily and material bases of human "living from."

As materially conditioned, mediated, and reproduced natural historical lives, questions of the domination and mastery of nature—which Adorno identified as the core of identity and its dialectic rather than using it merely as a metaphor—are not only derivative of the dynamics of human intersubjectivity, as Honneth maintained in his work *Reification*.[86] The opposite is the case if the human misrelation with nature reinforces human domination of other humans as Adorno depicts.[87] Concerning the authoritarian irrationalism of contemporary culture, Adorno describes in his *Minima Moralia* (1951) how—after millennia of Enlightenment from mythic powers and superstitions—humanity's "control of nature as control of humans far exceeds in horror anything humans ever had to fear from nature."[88]

Habermas and Honneth have contended that the *Dialectic of Enlightenment* and Adorno's political-philosophical project constitute a pessimistic speculative effort, void of hope and critical potential. It is noteworthy in *Toward a New Manifesto* how Horkheimer maintains a pessimistic stance, joking that Adorno's belief that one can live differently is the hope of a country parson. Adorno's response is that everything appears bewitched and under a spell, yet the spell can be broken.[89] In Horkheimer's mind such hope is theological, but it is not so much theological as it is prophetic and ethical (see part 2). This chapter, and part 1 as a whole, has traced how Adorno's works indicate strategies for critically engaging the present and contemporary environmental crisis-tendencies underemphasized by Habermas and Honneth. But if the *Dialectic of Enlightenment* is interpreted according to a nonreductive materialist logic of nonidentity, as suggested in our reconstruction of Adorno's work, traces of the other of that domination can be heard, even as vigilance should be exercised against a cult of fetishizing the new and the other (as in consumeristic orientalism that Adorno notes in his comment on consumable Zen) in which, as the commodification of the modish and exotic, nothing other can disruptively disclose itself apart from the system of commodification and consumption.[90]

Conclusion

The critical model of ecological natural history sketched in this chapter indicates the need for a critical theory of the entanglements of nature and history and their potential transformations in response to ecological and social-political crisis tendencies. Natural history is emancipatory in the context of damaged life in contesting both the idealism that prioritizes the human world in ideologically fixated forms and the naturalism that reifies aspects of the natural world. What passes for "natural" and "naturalistic" is that which is furthest from nature: it is the socially produced and violence-distorted image of "nature."[91] Yet, in the midst of the seemingly unending suffering produced by regimes of domination and exploitation of human and animal life, something otherwise is still indicated.

The present interpretation will be outlined in subsequent chapters that extend and deepen the analysis of Adorno's critical conception of natural history and nature's nonidentity, showing how it offers alternative interpretive strategies with significant implications for a historical environmental philosophy, in contrast with the democratic yet overly anthropocentric approaches of Habermas and Honneth. Ecodemocracy requires (with Adorno) contesting and altering material and ideological misrelations with nature as well as—without the identity of a general will (as in Rousseau's *The Social Contract*) or collective subject (as in Lukács's *History and Class. Consciousness*)—intensifying and multiplying (with and beyond Habermas) public spheres and democratic communicative and deliberative practices.

The interpretive strategy proposed here will (1) reveal ways of rectifying the anthropocentrism and humanism of the ethics of discourse theory and social contract theory that at best observe the environment as a background for human activity and a secondary issue established on human self-interest, and (2) contest varieties of environmental thinking that interrogate the domination of nature without questioning human domination of humans through relations of status, role, and orientation (such as class, gender, and race), or that are complicit with views of nature that celebrate the reduction of life to "bare life" in the struggle for existence, the striving for the power of the self and for conformity within society, and the domination of animal and natural life.[92]

Chapter Three

Communicative Interaction or Natural History?

Aesthetics, Ethics, and Nature

Introduction: The Renunciation of Nature
in Habermas and Hegel

Axel Honneth noted in the essay "Communication and Reconciliation: Habermas' Critique of Adorno" the birth of a new vision of Frankfurt school critical social theory and the end of its previous project. He begins the essay with Habermas's declaration of the methodological poverty and end of Adorno's project with his death: "At the time of Adorno's death, Habermas pointed out a methodological bareness in Adorno's work. According to him, Adorno's theoretical veil no longer clothed the methodological skeleton. If one separates content from imagery, Habermas's comment signals a theoretical turn in critical theory from Adorno to Habermas."[1] This chapter continues to rediscover the significance of Adorno's thinking of nature and reverses the assessment of Habermas and Honneth by reflecting on the divergences between the two forms of critical social theory, associated with two intellectually divergent generations of the Frankfurt school, begun in chapter 1. In the current chapter, I propose a rejoinder to Habermas's negative assessment of the import of his teacher's work and its purported "aestheticism," which Habermas and Honneth (in his 1979 essay) consider a crucial debilitating fault.[2] Rather than leading to a theoretical impasse, *pace* Habermas and Honneth, Adorno's aesthetics discloses a less anthropocentric encounter with and responsiveness toward the natural world. His aesthetic writings will accordingly be examined in light of the issues of: (1) whether and to what extent there can be an "aesthetics of nature," and (2) the ethical and social-political significance of such an aesthetics.[3]

The disavowal of the aesthetic and ethical dimensions of nature and its restriction to the human is a key element of an idealist tradition articulated by Hegel, and reaffirmed in an intersubjective form by Habermas. Adorno depicted in *Negative Dialectics* how natural history remains canonical for history while being sublimated and repressed in history as the history of "world spirit."[4] Hegel does have a positive account of nature, to a limited extent, but its spirit is overwhelmingly "anthropocentric." Adorno elucidates in his 1958/1959 lectures on aesthetics how Hegel strives to reduce nature to the idea, minimizes the aesthetic category of "natural beauty," and links dignity (*Würde*) exclusively with humanity.[5] Nature is a dialectical part and entangled element in his philosophical system that will be redeemed in the ultimate reconciliation of nature and spirit (*Geist*) in the absolute.[6] Nonetheless, despite moments of recognition of nature, Hegel's nature is principally lesser than spirit, to be mediated and transformed by spirit's dialectic and human activity. Hegel's portrayal of nature (as separated from spirit) in his *Aesthetics: Lectures on Fine Art* as an empty external spiritless and unfree shell, lacking and requiring spirit's free and creative activity, remains representative of philosophical idealism: "For everything spiritual is better than any product of nature. Besides, no natural being is able, as art is, to present the divine Ideal."[7] Hegel contrasts nature with the human social activity that overcomes its lawful determinacy and gives it meaning, including aesthetic significance: "[T]he beauty of nature appears only as a reflection of the beauty that belongs to spirit."[8] For Hegel, aesthetics in modernity concerns human expressions and products (as a realm of spirit). It is humans alone who can appreciate beautiful sceneries, and therefore give neutral and indifferent nature its value and worth. For antinaturalistic anthropocentric philosophers from Hegel to Habermas, who lack appreciation of the category of the aesthetics of nature that was still of importance in Kant, there can be no aesthetics (or ethics) of nature except indirectly through human activities and projections. The present chapter will extend Adorno's arguments in his 1958/1959 lectures that the old aesthetics of natural beauty and the sublime cannot be resurrected, but the loss of the aesthetics of nature is interlinked with the intensifying domination of nature and the absence of nature distorts modern aesthetic theory.[9] While idealist aesthetics prioritizes the expression (*Ausdruck*) of subjectivity, materialist aesthetics attends to the object and the matter itself in its priority.[10] Accordingly, in the midst of nature's domination, a new aesthetics of nature is needed through the formalization and liberation of mimesis. Mimesis is often interpreted as imitation and realistic representation.[11] But the mimetic comportment gains a transformative and emancipatory positionality in Benjamin and Adorno when it is rethought with both (1) materiality, embodied sensibility, and eros, and (2) aesthetic experimentation, formalism, and construction.

Habermas is a critic of Adorno's appeal to mimesis, even as he recognizes how Adorno's interpretation of mimesis continues to resonate in his own conception of unrestricted communication. While the implicit experiential contexts of Habermas's thinking are entangled with mimesis and the materialism of the early Frankfurt school, the freedom of communicative participation becomes in Habermas a normative principle and regulative idea.[12] Habermas perpetuates the idealist subordination of nature in his aesthetic theory that construes art as expressive authenticity. He complements the aesthetic model of expression, placed in questioned by Adorno's aesthetics, with the neo-Kantian separation of facticity and validity, value-free nature from culturally formed value. Aesthetic judgments consist of intersubjectively redeemable validity claims about authenticity, genuineness, sincerity, and taste. There is at best an indirect aesthetic appreciation of natural phenomena, as these categories do not directly apply to the natural world. Hegel distinguishes natural beauty and the beauty of art (as an expression of spirit, as human) in his *Aesthetics*: "[T]he beauty of art is higher than nature. The beauty of art is beauty born of the spirit and born again, and the higher the spirit and its productions stand above nature and its phenomena, the higher too is the beauty of art above that of nature."[13]

Intersubjective Idealism in Habermas's Critique of Adorno

Adorno's analysis of the absence of and need for an aesthetics of nature can be extended to Habermas's lack of recognition of its significance. Further, this critique can be extended to questions of the ethics of nature. It could be argued in response that the radical separation of moral from aesthetic validity claims in Habermas's theory of communicative action entails that it constitutes a confusion of spheres, or a category mistake, to examine art and nature and aesthetics and ethics from their mutual entwinement in any given social-historical reality. In this context, Habermas has criticized the overreach of Adorno's "utopian aestheticism," that is, the interconnection between art, emancipation, and the promise of happiness in Adorno's works, as well as Adorno's use of unsystematically articulated experimental "speculative concepts," such as mimesis and nonidentity, which are constructive critical models with aesthetic and social-political functions in Adorno's discourse.[14]

Habermas pursues his communicative critique of Adorno in the name of rationalizing and redeeming the critical social theory of the earlier generation of the Frankfurt school. This revision of critical theory indexes the degree to which the critical significance and implications of the concepts of nonidentity, dissonance, mimesis, sensuous responsiveness, and imagination have been lost and constitutively excluded from playing a role in critical theory as reconstructed through Habermas's theory of communicative action. This loss signifies an impoverishment of the aesthetic and of critique, inasmuch as they both require a reference—however indirect and transient, as it is not an appeal to essence or substance—to sensuousness, nature, and materiality in their nonidentity and dissonance with human projects and constructions.

Adorno's aesthetics indicates a significant alternative to conceptualist and anthropocentric interpretations of aesthetics. First, even the most formal conceptual art and formalized avant-garde art, as a form of practice, is informed by the contingency and opaqueness of materiality and material conditions. Likewise, secondly, the aesthetic primacy of human expression cannot escape the nonhuman and natural. In contrast to the anthropocentric aesthetic tradition expressed in the aesthetics of Hegel and Habermas, there is an aesthetics of nature and materiality that has been articulated—albeit typically indirectly—as an alternative aesthetic tradition in modern philosophy from Kant's *Critique of Judgment* through Nietzsche to Adorno. All formalism, even the emptiest of abstractions, cannot escape the moment of empirical encounter with material nonidentity. Art can thus not overcome its character as art, as praxis, with conceptualization and theory. The theorization of art, including art as making validity claims about expression, results in aporias that reveal art's technical, material, and social-historical beholdenness, in particular when its formal and unconditional autonomy is asserted. The aesthetic moments have a broader context and significance than a discourse concerning validity claims about the authenticity and sincerity of states of mind and character to which Habermas has condensed it.[15] It goes beyond this to link with sensuousness, perception, materiality, empiricity, and consequently nonidentity with the conceptual and constructed.

Art can be an expression of sincerity and the human spirit, as Habermas defines it. Art is much more than this: it can confront and be confronted by its sensuous and material as well as its formal conditions and contexts. Aesthetic experience and reflection can encounter abstract forms and be unconcerned with or place in question authenticity of expression. It can also point toward the in- and nonhuman. Encounters with nature and animality can disorient and reorient ordinary human anthropomorphism even as they engage human capacities and organs. There are such moments, for example, in free natural beauty and the sublime, in Kant's *Critique of Judgment*. The Kantian sublime shakes the subject yet results in a heightened assertion of human dignity. Nature in Adorno is inevitably encountered in human social-historical terms that can challenge those terms themselves. To the extent that experiences have mimetic (a concept too often inadequately construed as solely "imitative" or "representational" as we have seen), sensuously embodied, and material dimensions that move toward the object as nonidentical to the subject, however conditionally this might occur, natural events and phenomena are potentially more than their intersubjective constitution and construction in which constitutive subjectivity is collectivized. The "wordlessness" of things without intersubjective processes of world constitution reflects the lingering idealism of the self-constitutive social subject—inherited from radical republicanism and Marxism, and which will be interrogated in later parts of this volume—in Habermas's conception of intersubjectivity. But is the object as passive, powerless, and mute as this philosophy of discourse concludes?[16]

Objects speak to those who listen, and they also speak in art. Aesthetic phenomena expose and open up nonhuman natural and animal worlds in Adorno's writings. This materialist element of the primacy of the object in the subject's receptiveness and responsiveness toward it is submerged in Habermas's reduction of the aesthetic to the expression of authenticity. This reductive strategy problematically assumes the precedence of the subject over the object. In *The Theory of Communicative Action*, the aesthetic is analyzed as an "authentic expression of an exemplary experience, in general as the embodiment of a claim to authenticity."[17] The aesthetic is not a purely human phenomenon for Adorno, by contrast, and the aesthetics of nature—reversing Kant's interpretation of the sublime as ultimately disclosing the primacy of the subject—exceed the power and subjectivity of the subject. Natural phenomena and animals are construed and conjured through human discourses and practices, such as normative ones of beauty and use, yet nevertheless resist them. Adorno illustrates such resistance and irreducibility in his works on music that reveal the domination of nature and a sense of nature's freedom.

Music expresses both the domination of nature and its—and thus our own—potential release from such domination.[18] Nature as represented in Wagner's music is analyzed primarily as ideology, that is, as a celebration of the magical aura and irrational power of nature that perpetuates the domination of nature and humans exemplified by authoritarianism and racism. Wagner would create a total work of art that does not allow the listener the freedom to escape for one second, offering a vision of redemption that belies its redemptive elements through compulsion in contrast to the unromantic and unsentimental freely felt nature of Georges Bizet's *Carmen*.[19] Nature as intimated in Mahler's *Song of the Earth* (derived from Tang dynasty poetry) evokes in Adorno a "promise of happiness" in the unforced reconciliation of humanity, animals, and environing worlds.[20] The domination of nature in music can be traced not only in Wagner's romanticism but also in the loss of free atonality in the development of Arnold Schönberg's systematizing of atonal music.[21]

Enlightenment and the Domination of Nature

The thesis that Adorno offers indications of an "aesthetics of nature"—one that is indirect to the extent that the reification and substantializing of its alterity can be countered—is itself controversial and contested, since Adorno is a thinker of the unending mediation of phenomena and is critical of appeals to the immediacy of nature or primordial experience. Accordingly, Adorno's suspicion against appeals to primordial experiences of nature and being, as in Heidegger's ontology, linked Heidegger's philosophy and politics for Adorno. Adorno found the ontological thinking of being to be complicit with the ideology of national socialism, an assessment that shapes and is articulated in the *Jargon of Authenticity* and *Negative Dialectics*.

Adorno remarked, "The more reified the world becomes, the thicker the veil cast upon nature, the more the thinking weaving that veil in its turn claims ideologically to be nature, primordial experience."[22] In response to the celebration of nature and life in German irrationalism and fascism, Adorno argued that the more nature is called upon, the more reified it is, and the more ideological its functions become. Discourses of nature are not innocent; they reflect the conditions and structures of social-historical life and domination. Such discourses are ideological in that the appeal to nature can be an expression of the "domination of nature." This expression is more than a metaphor for Adorno. To this extent nature is a socially constructed and sedimented object. What "nature" would signify is more than this, such that one can question anthropocentrism and anthropomorphism. Adorno's writings on nature reveal how the idea and practice of human sovereignty over nature is rooted in a deep-seated hostility toward nature. Animosity toward nature is self-hatred, given that humans are natural animal beings.[23]

Adorno's writing should be read in light of its nonidentical (as antiteleology and antitheodicy) materialist dimensions; nature is materially more than its construction by human individuals, groups, or the species. Giambattista Vico's thesis that the "true is the made" (*verum factum*) and the produced, a principle reformulated in Hegel's history of the development of spirit, is part of a humanistic cultural-social tradition in which nothing human is alien to us and nature is an alien realm. Contrary to this thesis, Adorno presents human and artistic making—creation from out of the damages and incompletion of existence rather than out of an external ideal or norm of perfection—with the enigmatic truth-content (*Wahrheitsgehalt*) of the unmade, and the determinate negativity of what is not. As emptiness shapes the vessel, the unmade, inhuman, and elemental shapes the crystallization of human works and products.[24]

Adorno's description of the domination of nature presupposes something about the dominated that is more than its domination. This "other than" points toward that which resists, escapes, and potentially interrupts domination. "Nature" is not only a construct of or fully mediated by existing social reality. It is aporetically an alterity to human constructs and practices:

> For our knowledge of nature is really so preformed by the demand that we *dominate* nature (something exemplified by the chief method of finding out about nature, namely the scientific experiment) that we end up understanding only

those aspects of nature that we can control. In addition there is also this underlying feeling that while we are putting out our nets and catching more and more things in them, there is a sense in which nature itself seems to keep receding from us; and the more we take possession of nature, the more its real essence becomes alien to us.[25]

As Horkheimer and Adorno argued in the *Dialectic of Enlightenment*, the domination of nature is a real process at work in the history of civilizations, from myth to rationality, and it is most fully realized in the project of modernity and the Enlightenment.

Owing to Horkheimer and Adorno's confrontation with the totalitarian, regressive, and destructive aspects of the Enlightenment and modern rationalization, and the Enlightenment's narratives of historical progress through increasing democracy and prosperity that can serve ideology critique and ideological self-deception, Habermas protests that Adorno and Horkheimer's analysis abandons possibilities for "hope," rational discourse, and progressive social action. However, the converse is true to the degree that furthering critical self-reflection and action requires critically diagnosing the regressive moments of the Enlightenment, of modernity, and of progress under capitalist and socialist regimes that have failed to pursue their promises of a free and equal society, rather than immunizing them as sacrosanct.[26] There are at least two problems with Habermas's critique of Adorno that can be mentioned here. First, there are legitimate reasons to doubt liberal and neoliberal ideas of progress, and to demand not only its further intensification and concentration but a more radical transformation as well. From the French Revolution to the present situation, appeals to norms such as justice, freedom, and democracy can in effect be their manipulation and self-destruction via external colonization, wars, and internal control and violence. Contemporary liberal societies have not only contingently failed to reconcile the antagonisms both within society and between society and nature that are threatening the destruction of species such as homo sapiens but are structurally incapable of doing so given their logic of exchange, equivalence, and identity. Secondly, Adorno's intimations, illustrated in mimetic relational bonds, of an unforced and noncoercive flourishing of life and a solidarity of material others, are perhaps too utopian, optimistic, and hopeful rather than hopeless and pessimistic, as portrayed by Habermas. They are not merely utopian, as they retain a critical orientation in response to the domination and mastery of nature that is insufficiently articulated in Habermas's revisioning of critical social theory.

Adorno's discussions of nature and animals, as illustrated in part 1 of this work, expresses a hopefulness without a fixed hope: it is purposive without a (teleological) purpose. Just as progress is simultaneously mythical and "inherently antimythological," embodying the magical spell of domination and the prospect of the enchantment being broken, it is, for Adorno, "[o]nly reason, the principle of social domination inverted into the subject, [which] would be capable of abolishing this domination."[27] Such nonidentical and an-archic inversion, which has its own prophetic "hopefulness" even without a predetermined "hope," can orient theory and praxis more flexibly and appropriately than a terminus such as the "modern Enlightenment project" that functions for Habermas as a normative and quasiteleological historical purpose.

The Asymmetrical Primacy and Intermateriality of the Object

By disallowing the possibility of being oriented by "the impossible," which Adorno introduces "for the sake of the possible," Habermas is in this respect insufficiently formalistic.[28] In subjecting the Enlightenment and its implicit modes of domination to critique, Adorno and Horkheimer are closer to Kant's striving for Enlightenment as a regulative and reflective project, that is, the idea that progress operates as an action-orienting if unrealizable reflective idea, and in particular Kant's notion of a "purposiveness without a purpose" (*Zweckmäßigkeit ohne Zweck*) in the *Critique of Judgment*. Kantian purposiveness without a purpose intimates for Adorno both the senseless brutality of purposeless work without end and the freedom of a playful and nonadministrated relating to the object in its asymmetrical priority over the subject. There are, as Adorno comments, moments such as tenderness that transcend purposiveness, even as such purposiveness without a purpose cannot completely rid itself of the question of purpose or "what for?"[29] In the negative dialectic of nonidentity thinking, the paradoxical structures of Kant's thought are radicalized rather than coercively resolved.[30]

In contrast to Kant's description of the Enlightenment as an orienting, but "not yet" demanding, self-criticism toward greater maturity, and also opposed to Marx's "ruthless criticism of all that exists" for the sake of a fairer more rational society, Habermas proposes that to criticize the Enlightenment is to reject the achievements of modern egalitarianism and democracy.[31] Habermas claims that "modernity, now aware of its contingencies, depends all the more on a procedural reason, that is, on a reason that places itself on trial. This critique of reason is its own work: this double meaning, first displayed by Kant, is due to the radically anti-Platonic insight that there is neither a higher nor a deeper reality to which we could appeal—we who find ourselves already situated in our linguistically structured forms of life."[32]

Adorno's self-referential critique of the Enlightenment and the problem of its potential complicity with domination are banished by Habermas as antimodernist. However, in contrast to the assessment of Habermas, one can affirm moral and political egalitarianism while rejecting the reasoning that restricts "postmetaphysical thinking" to the egalitarian and symmetrical interaction of human subjects and thus to a certain type of hegemonic identity thinking.

There are a number of reasons for undermining this restriction. First, Habermas's account of ethics conflates symmetry and equality. Acknowledging asymmetrical ethical relations with animals and environments can be compatible with maintaining, for instance, the equality of sentient beings in Buddhist ethics or the equal consideration of interests in Peter Singer's utilitarian animal ethics.[33]

Second, Habermas once stated that he did not have "any doubts about the primacy of natural history over the history of the human species."[34] Habermas claims to accept the Darwinian theory of evolution while developing a social theory that would switch perspectives and abandon biological third-person accounts of the lifeworld. This differentiating strategy is adopted from the hermeneutical and dialogical philosophical paradigms and arguably has its appropriateness. It is questionable to what degree Habermas's thinking about intersubjectivity idealistically perpetuates the division between the natural as material and the human as spiritual, an inheritance from Christianity and German idealism, while ignoring the potential and need for an aesthetics and ethics of nature that is intimated in the works of Adorno. The radical nonidentity and other-power of nature contests the reification of nature in ideological images and fetishes as well as the marginalization and exclusion of nature in a world constituted by social power and discourse.

Mimesis as Reification and Responsiveness

A critical materialist hermeneutics of nature is more adequately articulated in Adorno's nonidentity of nature. Adorno's aporetic natural history undermines the doctrinal and dogmatic naturalisms that dominate contemporary Anglophone philosophy, founded in identitythinking and ideological visions of nature; that is, the reified images and norms of nature found in romanticism and scientism, and in vitalism and positivism.[35] Such doctrines of nature preclude being responsive and answerable to the object in the priority of its own life, without either dictating to it or being absorbed in it as mimicry. That is to say, they preclude a spontaneous an-archic and intermaterial mimesis toward the natural that—through the acknowledgment of nonidentity—refuses an ideological "return to nature" or identification with the fetishized voice of "nature" that is its betrayal and domination.[36]

Popular cultures more directly express human damaged relations with the natural world and with other human and nonhuman animals. The fetishistic "ideologies of primitivism and return to nature" in music reproduce domination—and enforced childishness rather than spontaneous childlikeness and further resistance.[37] Adorno controversially extended this analysis to both elite and popular music, as in his flawed account of the dominance of capitalist exchange and the commodity form in the conformity of the "jazz business" through which he misconstrued the resistance and playful promise of freedom in jazz.[38] Jazz can be more experimental than avant-garde art, as it frees mimesis from mere imitation and the self from its bonds through a formalization. Due to Adorno's own limitations, he inadequately evaluated in his criticisms of jazz the dialectic of ideology and the promise of freedom and happiness that he reveals in the context of classical and modernistic experimental music and art. In his perspective, the archaic, original, and primordial are themselves products of fixation and reification: they are forms of "modern archaics" deploying the archaic and traditional for a specifically modern sensibility and purpose.[39] Even if one wishes to exclude varieties of popular culture such as jazz as forms of resistance, from the thoroughness of Adorno's social analysis, which depicts varieties of popular culture as ideological, the immediacy, intimacy, naturalness, and spontaneity that he criticizes in jazz is a central element of the commodity character, exchange value, and consumption of cultural goods.[40]

The aura and irrational powers of nature are socially produced and ideologically formed appearances, "the presence of that which is not present."[41] Against the aura of the ideological image, relentlessly reproduced through production, media, and consumption, Adorno's immanent critique fractures the prison of pure immanence in which all is perceptible and calculable to free the object. To free the object, whether human, animal, or material, is to engage its expressiveness and particularity while not being absorbed or enthralled by it, insofar as this is possible in current societies in which humans are "in thrall to the world of things."[42] Such receptivity oriented to the particularity, corporeality, and alterity of each thing is indispensable, since "[n]o theory, not even that which is true, is safe from perversion into delusion once it has renounced a spontaneous relation to the object."[43]

In Adorno's devotion to the particularity and suchness of objects, or the materialist commitment to the asymmetrical priority of the object that is not "the supposedly pure object, free of any added thought or intuition," he dialectically contests reductive doctrinal forms of materialism and naturalism with a phenomenological-hermeneutical moment of encounter and exposure to things.[44] Fashioned and damaged by structures of power and the demands of calculation and exchange, modern subjects are incapable of such encountering and experiencing of their world and things. Adorno disclosed the ideological character of appeals to natural and originary experience while calling for thought to remain in contact and in touch with immediate encounters and personal experiences.[45] His comprehensive appraisal of the early phenomenological movement, and what he considered to be Husserl and Heidegger's reification of receptivity and their ideology of the originary and the given, did not entail a rejection of the phenomenological elucidation of the experiential dimensions of perception and cognition.[46] Adorno's practice of immanent critique involves both a destructuring of ideology and reification and a phenomenological or perceptual dimension when he contends that "[s]uch criticism does not stop at a general recognition of the servitude of the objective mind, but seeks to transform this knowledge into a heightened perception of the thing itself."[47]

The intensification of a free identification moving toward the particular involves a mimesis that is liberated from magic and rituality. Adorno's nonreductive and anti-Platonic elucidation of mimesis cannot be reduced to the concept or the ideal. Since identification breaks with identity through the mimetic response to the freedom of the object, as will be considered further below, mutual freedom and a more responsive relational form of the concept are intimated in aesthetic experience, with significant implications for philosophy.[48] Art can encourage the explication of the affinities and differences of the human and the nonhuman. Adorno's descriptions of mimetic recognition are environmentally suggestive in that they entail the otherness of material nature without relying on one particular image or model of nature. Adorno and Horkheimer claimed, "Bourgeois society is ruled by equivalence. It makes dissimilar things comparable by reducing them to abstract quantities. For the Enlightenment, anything which cannot be resolved into numbers, and ultimately into one, is illusion."[49] Ecological mimesis intimates an alternative to this paradigm that reduces things, others, and creatures to symmetrical equivalence; that is, to an equality embedded in the division of labor, the formation of equivalence in exchange value, and money as the universal form of exchange and equivalence.

Mimesis is a mediated and hence ambivalent complicated concept in Adorno's writings. Mimesis can fetishize and reify objects; it can also indicate creativity, receptivity, and responsiveness to the object in its primacy. On the one hand, it can be mere imitation understood as copying, mechanical reproduction, and the repetition of a universal medium of sameness. Such mimesis reproduces the existing order of things; it is riveted in the connectedness and efficacy of myth, ritual, and magic or ideology; in media; and in consumption. On the other hand, mimesis and the pictorial character of thought speak to the entanglement of human life with its world, and of reason with nature. Artworks in particular are enigmas in their configuration of the mimetic and the rational.[50]

Mimesis is an expression and enactment of intermaterial or interthingly life. It binds to the singular in experience and material life; it is an indispensable moment of art and rationality.[51] Reason, despite itself, is a moment of nature that has separated itself from nature without being free of it.[52] Likewise, when image-oriented thinking is freed from its absorption in immanence without losing contact with it, and while not being eliminated in abstract conceptual thinking, it takes on an altered significance that is inherent in it from the start. Mimesis is in this sense the promise of a playful and receptive spontaneity of sensuous freedom that is not absorbed in the conformity and discipline of social integration. Adorno described the latter aspect of mimesis as the primal form of love.[53] Adorno's redemption of mimesis, against its degradation in Plato and the philosophical transmission, interprets it as receptivity and responsiveness to the asymmetrical priority of the object rather than as mere imitation, passivity, reproduction, or the copying of faded copies distanced from the reality of the ideal.

Andrea Oppo describes how for Adorno the "mimetic experience is precisely that of assimilating the self to other (object)."[54] Mimesis is a sensuous opening toward the material other. As such, mimesis is expression toward the other rather than the "self-expression" that Habermas identified with the aesthetic.[55] It is furthermore—here echoing a theme also articulated in Levinas—an eros, and a movement toward what is desired and loved.[56] Mimetic expression is more extensive than human intersubjective discourse and communicative action.[57] It is not only intersubjective but also intermaterial. Mimesis can operate as a compulsive and possessive repetition of identity, a coercive reconciliation with the object; yet it is more radically an emancipation of the material other. Mimesis need not be an enemy of the object in human activity and art—in abandoning reconciliation with nature—but can rather be reconciled with it.[58] There is another modality of mimesis than the one that stands in opposition to the false appearance of a harmony or reconciliation coercively forced upon the subject. In the form of a nonidentical transformative repetition, mimesis is a *metamorphosis* proceeding from the felt contact with and bodily nearness to its objects. This involves sensuous and material freedom, playfulness, and responsiveness toward objects or the things themselves that does not presuppose the self-identity of the subject.[59]

Adorno's an-archic mimetic, that is to say, the play that is free from purposiveness in contrast with "the repetition of prescribed models," discloses the possibility of transforming the compulsive and habitual repetition of identity and sameness into spontaneity and creative individuation.[60] Adorno notes, in a comment on Peter Altenberg, that "humanity" indicates individuation rather than being "a comprehensive generic concept," even if "the particularity of happiness" cannot be mistaken "for realized humanity."[61] Given the multiple modifications of mimesis, as a dynamic of servitude and freedom, its emancipatory potential is equivocal.[62] Rodolphe Gasché has argued that the indeterminacy of nature for Adorno indexes nature's interconnectedness with mythical violence and the promise of freedom from such violence.[63] Nature concurrently threatens violence and destruction while promising liberation from it in satisfaction, happiness, and flourishing.

Adorno's nonreductive and indirect thinking of the nonidentity of materiality, a thinking that recognizes the singularity of things rather than reduces them to an image or concept of what should count as nature, commits him to an animal-human continuum, which plays a revealing role in his posthumously published work *Aesthetic Theory*.[64] There is no reified division between the human and nonhuman, as reductive rationalism and spiritualism envision in their prohibition on mimesis and human animality, embodiment, and sexuality.[65] Through this taboo on mimesis, art becomes "the organ of mimesis" and a castrated "pleasure without pleasure."[66] The holy family reflects earthly families, and humans are much nearer to animals than constitutive idealism and its current incarnations imagine. Due to their diffuse mimetic capacities, which allow them to playfully create and ethically respond as well as reactively conform, humans are materially interconnected with environments and animals. Aristotle deployed mimesis to differentiate the animal and the human. Adorno's alternative is that mimesis brings nonhuman and human animals into nonhomogeneous asymmetrical relationships. In being nonidentically interconnected, or asymmetrically relational, humans can be potentially mimetically free toward the other, responsive, and ethically responsible in their distinction from and shared life with animals.[67]

Bodily and sensuous continuity (which does not signify identity or sameness) provides a more rigorous starting point for recognizing animal suffering and recognizing it as an ethical problem. Animal otherness counts ethically, since we are animals too and animals approximate us in their nonidentity. They perceive and use concepts—to the extent that concepts are already enmeshed in the mimetic and pictorial, as Hegel argued early in the *Phenomenology of Spirit*.[68] Adorno and Horkheimer depict in their 1944/1947 work how the human gaze regards itself as above that of the animal, unresponsively and irresponsibly lifting its eyes away from the suffering animal in the laboratory that is reduced to a mere exemplar of equivalence and universal fungibility.[69] In their presumed superiority and dignity, in the deformations of mimesis and ideology, humans do not consider how the human gaze is itself animal or the animal gaze already a human one.

Art and Nature between Suffering and Happiness

> For nature, although the opposite of human domination, is itself distorted as long as it is exposed to want and violence.
>
> —Adorno, *Mahler: A Musical Physiognomy*

Animals, as Peter Singer claims, are "treated like machines that convert fodder into flesh."[70] Their suffering is ignored and treated with indifference by the hegemonic ethical order. Horkheimer and Adorno's discussions of animal suffering and human cruelty to animals, although unsystematic, entail the possibility of a nonderivative animal ethics. The suffering of the animal demands ethical recognition in its asymmetry and beyond subjective feelings of anthropomorphizing empathy and identification. In this way, an asymmetrical and relational mimetic ethics offers a wider moral perspective than does the reduction of the ethical to the communicative symmetry of reason-giving human agents.

Nevertheless, to consider an objection to my thesis, there are additional statements in Horkheimer and Adorno's works that seem to limit the ethical status of animals and nature for which I am arguing. In what might seem an excursus, I consider how these apparently contrary arguments do not undermine the ethical character of human relations with animals and nature; they are aimed at their ideological misuse in perpetuating injustice toward other humans. Such criticisms, as shall be considered further later, occur particularly in the context of assessing discourses that advocate the prevention of animal cruelty and the preservation of nature within varieties of romantic, protofascist, and national socialist ideologies.

Adorno notes of the romantic and fascist reification of animals, "The prevention of cruelty to animals becomes sentimental as soon as compassion turns its back on humanity."[71] Adorno's attention to this sentimentality about animals and indifference toward other humans, which is still found today in some animal rights discourses, refers to the strange fact that national socialism condemned the Jewish people for their supposed cruelty to animals while attempting to reduce them to less than animals, and for their alleged rootless distance from nature even as they uprooted and destroyed their existence. This pretense with animal suffering and the "destruction" of German blood, soil, and natural environments masked the intensification of human suffering and annihilation while concurrently intensifying the technological domination of nature. Adorno's insight remains relevant to contemporary forms of racist environmentalist discourses that essentialize, racialize, and condemn whole peoples for their perceived crimes against animals and environments.

The national socialist aesthetic of "returning to nature" resulted in the utmost exploitation and destruction of humans, animals, and environments, and accordingly has been analyzed as the mythic and self-destructive fulfillment of instrumental rationality and Enlightenment mastery.[72] Because of a narrow interpretation of this historical context, some statements by Adorno, especially in the context of his responses to Heidegger and the emergent new age tendencies of the 1960s, and by leftist antienvironmentalists, seem to reductively condemn animal rights, environmentalism, and vegetarianism as eccentricities and modish fashions inherently connected with fascism, antihumanism, and irrationalism. This rhetoric suppresses the ethical claim of animal suffering, established via the affinities of human and animal beings, and excuses the exploitation of nature as a mere resource.

Instead of the mastery of nature being merely a metaphor or an incoherent thesis (which it is, if there is only intersubjectivity without material others), Adorno demonstrates—with reference to Arthur Schopenhauer's assessment of cruelty and human and nonhuman bodily suffering—both the destructive impulse as well as the interruptive force inherent in discourses about animals and nature.[73] This interpretation is strengthened by the connections Adorno drew between the dehumanization and animalization in racism, which subtracts ethical and legal status from its victims. In *Minima Moralia* Adorno relates racist dehumanization to the distancing abjection of nonhuman animals. Being completely othered, dehumanized humans and devalued animals do not ethically interrupt the sameness of the gaze. The sub- and nonhuman are categorically separated from the normatively human. Adorno describes how the prospect of pogroms and racial genocide is disclosed in the human gaze directed toward the wounded animal just as the powerful cannot value that which is different than themselves but only that which reflects and reproduces their own image. The sufferings of others cannot withstand this obsessive-compulsive gaze.[74] Vulnerability, injurability, and defenselessness are characteristic of organisms and not solely the human face. In its suffering, the animal is more than a passive object of use, misuse, and destruction who calls for a response to its suffering that intrudes on the indifference that would make it invisible. The pain of the animal inscribed into its body and expression indicates that it is more than a construct and product of human calculation, discourse, and power, that is, it is a subject and thus deserving of ethical consideration. The suffering of animals contests and challenges the anthropocentric prejudices and instrumental calculations of interests that would deny, obscure, and forget such suffering.

In a quotation from Adorno's 1960 work on Mahler, we see how the animal can unsettle and awaken the human: "Through animals, humanity becomes aware of itself as impeded nature and of its activity as deluded natural history; for this reason Mahler meditates on them. For him, as in Kafka's fables, the animal world is the human world as it would appear from the standpoint of redemption, which natural history itself precludes."[75] The awakening to animal life is not the romantic celebration of the violent forces of nature in the oppressive totalizing atmosphere of Wagner's music but instead the music of Mahler and the writings of Kafka that hint at an altered ethical relation between the human and the animal.

Music, Listening, and the Ethical

Music, as a domain of tonalities and gestures that humans share with animal life, is bound to the mimetic and cannot be reduced to the communicative space of reason.[76] Since Habermas prioritizes human speech and speaking over hearing, there is no appropriate role for music in his account. This is a social-political and ethical as much as an aesthetic deficit, as Adorno insightfully illustrates in his essay "The Fetish-Character in Music and the Regression of Listening" (1938). Human expressions in popular music and the idea of a communication that could occur without music are both features of the regression of senses in contemporary life. Under existing forms of communicative and cultural production, listening as mimetic and creative responsiveness (*zuhören*) increasingly becomes a mere hearing as registering and processing.[77] To deploy Habermas's more dualistic vocabulary, the habitualized reproduction of power in the lifeworld occurs in the senses themselves as a retrogression in hearing, as listening and hearkening are subjugated to the logic of exchange in increasingly commodified damaged life. Coercive hearing becomes a structure of the instrumentalized lifeworld itself, such that it is challenging to disentangle what has been imposed by power systems and what is internally formed in the lifeworld's intersubjective reproduction.

Adorno remarked in a letter to Horkheimer that artworks are preparations for happiness through the alienation of the alienation of damaged life.[78] The anticipation of happiness in the artwork does not preexist but is a response to the socially produced damages and imperfections of human existence. Music is an exemplary model of the intersection of art and reality, and the promise of happiness in response to suffering. It can express not only authenticity but also human existence in its damaged character and suffering, as well as its aspirations for happiness and a less systematically damaged life. Music indicates more than the suffering of the human world in extending beyond it and expressing—if only momentarily—the disavowal of a systematically damaged and suffering world. Artistic and aesthetic links with nature, joined to the sensuous and nonconceptual, are linked with this promise of happiness. This promise is at a minimum a negation of that world, intimating different ways of living; Adorno's negativity is not merely negative in once again being linked to possibilities of transformation.

The claim that ethics is confined to symmetrical rational relations blocks ethical reflection from recognizing the actual and existing asymmetries between humans and between human and nonhuman animals. The ethical reduction to the equality of rational beings brackets the ethical in activities that subordinate and destroy the asymmetrical and nonidentical.

Encountering asymmetry and a dissimilarity that is not merely an exchange of assorted reasons extends ethical reflection beyond what is categorized as human and therefore considered "intrinsically valuable."[79] The logic of equivalence involved in exchange relations, whether in speech or in the market, excludes and justifies the subjugation of those beings—however different from one another—who are not involved in the exchange.[80] Asymmetry challenges this dominant model.

Asymmetry is by itself insufficient for ethics insofar as (1) it potentially codifies inequalities, as in Confucian ethics, in which each human and animal has a hierarchically generated ethical status, or (2) it remains neglectful of or hostile to animals and the natural world by anthropocentrically giving humans unqualified priority over animals and environments. The ethical recognition of the asymmetrical and different should be distinguished from their asymmetrical nonrecognition in antiegalitarian political movements rooted in the domination of nature.

The recognition of the asymmetrical and nonidentical is related to mimesis through the category of aesthetics. Aesthetics is not merely aesthetic, as it is for Habermas, since it has an intrinsically ethical character via its connection with happiness. Habermas condemned Adorno for an "aestheticism" that conflates emancipation and aesthetic experience. The aesthetic intimates a promise of happiness connected to emancipation that resists being restricted to validity claims about taste. For Adorno, the aesthetic is in its richer significance not exhausted in the validity of communication. Thus, even the most abstract, formal, and experimental art involves relations to experience and perception, materiality and thingliness. The material moment in aesthetics is indicative of an alterity without which there is no art, even as the "inner historicity of artworks" is the "dialectic of nature and the domination of nature."[81] Art mirrors the existing order of society and the reification and commodification of things, persons, and cultural and spiritual products. A logic of exchangeability dominates the culture industry, even while consumers imagine they resist it through the aura of "uniqueness" and singularity of what have become fungible exchangeable objects.[82]

Remnants and moments of nonidentity, of sensuous freedom, and of the responsiveness of the mimetic, exist in art, such that art is not necessarily only the fetishism, idolatry, and myth mistrusted by moralists from Plato's *Republic* to Rousseau's admiration for Sparta to (according to critics) Levinas, who rejected the criticism that he fears idolatry in this sense, as argued in chapter 5.[83] Mimesis is more than an aesthetic phenomenon of imitation. It is the basis of identity and conformity, as well as the possibility of open and playful imitation, appropriation, and interaction, that is, of tenderness and, adopting a phrase that he attributes to Hegel, "freedom toward the object" in its asymmetrical priority.[84] Sensuous mimesis is the route to individuation: "The human is indissolubly linked with imitation: a human being only becomes human at all by imitating other human beings."[85] For Adorno, one must avoid the reduction of the mediated to the immediate, which serves ideological purposes, while remaining in contact with immediacy, as the relationship between subject and object is both mediated and asymmetrical in dissonance or in not being identical to itself, that is, empirical and material. In freeing oneself toward the object, and dereifying it by displacing its domination and exploitation, a transformative movement occurs in being addressed by the subject matter or the empirical material life of the object.[86]

Just as art and music are not pure responsiveness (to idealize Mahler) but simultaneously the domination of nature (to demonize Wagner), the experiment can be another instance of instrumental rationality and nature's domination. For Adorno, the preponderance of the object does not guarantee epistemic realism but designates the moment of non-identity and the potential for resistance that is either transformative or reabsorbed.[87] In the latter case, Adorno can speak of the experimental and the empirical as more than the compulsive repetition and preprogrammed calculation of the functional totality of the existing order.[88] In contrast with the empirical order of things, the experimental-empirical can indicate the capacity and willingness to encounter the object.[89] In the free mimesis toward the object, there is an encounter, intimacy, and felt contact.[90] In the encounter, rationality is related to the mimetic in being responsive to the object and, accordingly, to the new and the different that it might indicate.[91] In this context, the artwork and natural beauty are interconnected: "untrammeled nature provides an image of the non-identical" for art, and the "artwork's truth content can be viewed as a mimesis of the beautiful in nature."[92]

Such a perceptual shift occurring through the encounter reveals a dialectical materiality or empiricity that Adorno stresses in his reading of Hegel.[93] The dialectic between subject and object, or between perceiver and perceived, is not solely conceptual in remaining bound to the materiality and specificity of things. Just as Kant noted of the aesthetic in the *Critique of Judgment*, Adorno argues that the mimetic requires the conceptual and the discursive to come into word, even though it is not identical to the concept.[94] Art works through conceptualization without relying on or providing determinate concepts.

Deborah Cook has criticized the overemphasis on mimesis and the nonconceptual in recent interpretations of Adorno, preferring a more cognitivist approach to Adorno's thinking that does after all emphasize the deployment and dialectic of concepts.[95] Nonetheless, Adorno is neither a cognitivist nor an anticognitivist. The nonconceptual moments are stressed by Adorno himself throughout his works as part of the "negative dialectic" of nonidentity, and the nonidentity of the concept and the nonconceptual that motivates and conditions conceptualization. Concepts seek and fail to overcome and sublimate their other. All of the elements of the nonconceptual, given the asymmetrical primacy of the object, cannot be fully conceptualized, or mediated by other means, by the individual or collective subject. Accordingly, as there is no reason to posit either the complete idealist interpenetration or the complete realist separation of language and reality, conceptual meaning can refer to the nonconceptual. Indeed, if we are not to "fetishize the language or conceptual system that we use," then we must acknowledge that it is one part of reality rather than the whole itself.[96] While there is non-conceptual mediation invisible to the subject, there is the asymmetrical and dissonant "unreconciled matter" confronting processes of mediation.[97] Critique has an analogous operation: "[N]o critical theory can be practiced in particular detail without overestimating the particular; but without the particular it would be nothing."[98] Adorno illuminates how the thing, object, or matter (*die Sache*) is addressed in while remaining irreducible to communication. The specific is mediated by and yet resists identification and conceptualization.[99]

There is much that prevents the occurrence and practice of such mimesis interpreted as bodily and sensuous responsiveness.[100] Adorno analyzed the habitual and customary reproduction of power in our senses in the context of music as a regress in hearing as listeners are transformed into consumers.[101] The everyday transformation of hearing into consumption is even more coercive in that it is not merely superimposed by an external alien system upon the "innocent" native lifeworld, and hence easily correctable through a new consensus. Power relations are ingrained in the social-material fabric of the lifeworld itself.[102]

Mending Natural History

Nature and history, as disclosed in natural history, are bound together in one process such that ecology is as much about society as it is about nature. Environmental policies need to contest social pathologies to aid endangered creatures and ecosystems just as environmental damages most affect the abject, the poor, and the vulnerable in both the so-called developed and developing worlds.

Natural phenomena are relentlessly mediated by human activities and practices that partake in the material and natural conditions that they modify. Mediation—even in its extreme form of totalization—is as a consequence incomplete and uneven. Nature is disparate and not fully identical with modes of its social-historical mediation. The multiplicity of nature is indicated in experiences of the horrifying and terrible in nature, in the sublime that shatters and uplifts, and in natural beauty and its joys.[103] Such experiences are sources of the irrational in human life, of the supernatural and fatalistic, but also, as mimetic responsiveness, of the formation of meaning in aesthetics, ethics, and rationality.

Word and thing, experience and the experienced, are dialectically entangled yet mutually irreducible moments; in the tension of their conjuncture, neither moment can be grasped nor "intuited" in an immediate or originary way without one-sidedly missing the other.[104] In contrast to much of twentieth-century philosophy and its dogmatic semanticism, which still informs contemporary critical social theory and has been increasingly problematized in the contemporary revival of materialism, Adorno maintained the centrality of both language, as a medium in which words and concepts are inseparable, and physicality, as words cannot be separated from the nexus of things and the material relations that constitute them.[105]

The materiality of specific things—what Adorno depicted as the dynamic nonidentity that remains in tension with fixated words and concepts[106]—displaces the logic of integration. These moments of aporia, contradiction, and resistance are not limited to interhuman relations. They extend to all human comportments, even in regard to animals and environments. Aporetic concepts dynamically refer to their own conflicting tendencies. The dominant human discourse, according to Derrida, "imagines the animal in the most contradictory and incompatible generic terms."[107] Animals and environments are put to instrumental use, exploited as resources, eliminated and exterminated, and yet, conversely, there are nevertheless various ways—whether aesthetic or moral, emotional or conceptual—in which humans encounter and recognize them as other than this prevailing discourse.

A possible opening up of the medium of language in experimental openness and receptivity to the thing for its own sake occurs in "freedom toward the object." This assertion of the object's freedom indicates a different basis for considering the irreducible or "additional" (*das Hinzutretende*) significance of things that is necessary for a noninstrumental environmental and animal ethics that rejects the fixations of ahistorical essences and intrinsic natural values.[108]

The interwoven textures, the infinite multiplicities, and the transient contingencies of the material world resist being dwindled into a mere technical instrumental control over nature and the anthropocentric teleological purpose that excuses it. The natural historical material world resists not because of an inviolable essence, substance, or natural law but because of the prospect of the inexhaustible "more than" and "not yet" (*noch nicht*) that Adorno raises in his *Aesthetic Theory*. In the breakthrough of the "not yet" in mimesis, there is the trace of a memory and an anticipation of the future that lies beyond the division of self and other, subject and object.[109]

Animality, Happiness, and the Promises of Damaged Life

HORKHEIMER: Happiness would be an animal condition viewed from the perspective of whatever has ceased to be animal.

ADORNO: Animals could teach us what happiness is.

HORKHEIMER: To achieve the condition of an animal at the level of reflection—that is freedom. Freedom means not having to work.

—Theodor Adorno, *Towards a New Manifesto*

In the dialogues published in *Towards a New Manifesto*, Horkheimer and Adorno discuss the interconnections between happiness, animality, and reflection. Whereas Horkheimer emphasized a freedom that would be the reconciliation of animality and reflective consciousness, Adorno's comments take a different direction. Here and in the subsequent discussions, Adorno notes how happiness functions as ideology and also as a lesson to be learned from animal life. Adorno would repeatedly return to this thematic of how a damaged suffering animal could glimpse promises of happiness in animal and natural life.

Adorno spoke of the promise of happiness, of reconciled and undamaged life, immanently emerging within the alienation and reification of damaged life. Imperfection and suffering do not require an essence, substance, or ideal of perfection (in Stanley Cavell's sense) to be encountered, experienced, critiqued, and resisted. Imperfectionism is the reality that ethics occurs in the midst of ignorance and folly and calls for genuine forgiveness, mercy, and pardon in response to suffering whether it is caused by others or self-caused.[110] Ethics confronts the ordinary self-concerned self. It need not posit or construct a stratifying and fixating notion of the self who is striving toward an ideal or telos of self-perfection (see chapter 10 below).

The "yet not" and "still not" of nature, as implicit in animal and ecological life systems, and as more and other than human constructions of nature, is a materialist challenge to the intersubjective constitutive idealism and social constructivism of contemporary critical theory. The aporia of mimetic responsivity and constructive ordering, sensibility and rationality, cannot be resolved in either direction without the diminishment of human experience, since both are basic elements of the natural history of the human species.[111] Such nonidentity is the condition of critique and, as nonidentity that is dialectically nonidentical to itself, it challenges rather than presupposes an underlying essence or substance of nature—much less a mystical absorption or participation in it.[112]

While dissolving the natural material world into communicative rationality and intersubjective recognition is the overly idealistic aim of hegemonic forms of contemporary ethical and critical theory, as if humanity remained the moral republic of spirits articulated by Gottfried Wilhelm Leibniz and Kant, Adorno materialistically argued for a community of material others for whom the loss of nature is a diminution of the human and its possibilities. It is a denial of the hedonistic promise of happiness without which art and ethics lose their life and critical import. The loss of the material object is the impoverishment of the idealized subject, and the loss of natural beauty and sublimity is more than an aesthetic loss.[113] It is a damaged impoverishment of human sensibility, sensuous life, communication, and rationality itself.[114] Instead of constituting two distinct spheres of validity claims, *pace* Habermas's theory of communicative action, the aesthetic and ethical are interrelated in questions of the good life and the good in the midst of the imperfections of the damaged life that form their own ethical demand—to the point that one can stress the primacy of life over dialectic in Adorno, even as it is not the vital affirmation and celebration of the pure immediacy of life of vulgar life-philosophy, and life can only be lived less wrongly as damaged life in a society in which "[l]ife has become the ideology of its own absence."[115]

In the absence of life, one dreams of living and then questions how best to live. The desire to fulfill the promise of happiness, living otherwise, and undoing life's damages and suffering does not arise from an external norm or otherworldly realm. The intimation and promise of happiness in Adorno, and the prophetic good that is not the one in Levinas, transpire immanently within incomplete and damaged material and intersubjective life itself.

Chapter Four

The Trouble with Life

Life-Philosophy, Antinaturalism, and Transcendence in Levinas

> The phenomenological method wants to destroy the world falsified and impoverished by the naturalist tendencies of our times, which certainly have their rights but also their limits; it wants to reconstruct, to recover, the lost world of our concrete life.
>
> —Emmanuel Levinas, *Unforeseen History*

The Antinaturalism of Classical Phenomenology

The phenomenological movement has been ill at ease with nature, life, biology, and animality, due undoubtedly to the fundamental antinaturalistic heritage of the transcendental philosophies of Edmund Husserl and neo-Kantianism.[1] Categories related to biological life are suspected of reductively missing the intentional life of consciousness and the lived experiential human body, which classical phenomenology radically opposed to animality and the efficient causal order of nature, as phenomenology interprets consciousness and existence in transcendental or ontological senses distinguishable from their natural scientific explanation.

Levinas's philosophy likewise appears to be radically antinaturalistic and antibiological. The good prophetically contests being, and ethics radically places naturalness into question.[2] The category of "nature" is questionable in multiple ways: it can signify the "shameful materialism" of neutral naturalistic indifference toward the ethical and it can refer to a chaotic and contingent struggle of "bare life" for existential survival that endangers the ethical relation with the other.[3]

Levinas was deeply shaped by Husserl's antinaturalism and antihistoricism. He was a prominent figure in introducing the phenomenology of Husserl and Heidegger in France.[4] His later understandings of nature are related to his embrace of Husserl's antinaturalism in his earliest phenomenological writings. These quickly appeared after his initiation into phenomenology through his teacher and mentor, Jean Hering, at the University of Strasbourg and his studies in Freiburg in 1928–1929. They are associated with Levinas's tendency after 1932 to reject Heidegger's ontological phenomenology because of its presuppositions concerning being and nature (in their self-sufficiency) as violent and ethically indifferent in relation to human insufficiency.[5]

In contrast, other thinkers attempted to reconcile phenomenology and life-philosophy in ways that Levinas initially embraced and then relentlessly interrogated. Heidegger's philosophical trajectory, the most significant of these thinkers for Levinas, is partially epitomized by a succession of efforts to rethink "life"—in his early project of a hermeneutical self-articulation of factical life—and "nature"—as a primordial upsurgence and holding sway (*phusis* φύσις) in light of possibilities of poetic dwelling in his later thinking of being.[6] In Levinas's critique—and "critique" in Levinas should not be understood as operating through negation or dialectic unless reinterpreted in the context of Adorno's dialectic of nonidentity and the priority of the object—of Western ontology, life and nature continue to be overly anonymous and impersonal, tied to the self-assertion of the will and to a pagan participation and absorption in the mysterious powers of being that lets them be, rather than calling for interpersonal justice. Contesting the priority of biological life and being, which are interlinked in his reading of Heidegger, Levinas argues in *Existence and Existents* that the question of being is about not truth but rather the good.[7] In contrast to Heidegger's quest for origins, the ontology of nature and being is not to be rethought through more primordial sources, such as returning to the radical upsurge and sway of archaic Greek *phusis*, or by making it more dynamic and relational. Its power is unsettled by a transcendence that—like the Jewish understanding of God beyond being—is intractable to any form of immanence, such as being or nature conceived of as causal, constructed and sedimented, or as a primordial event.[8]

The displacements of nature, as a derivative construction and projection of spirit or as a separate phenomenal sphere left to scientific inquiry, is a principal thesis of transcendental philosophy that, as customarily portrayed, delineates the scope and limits of legitimate cognitive knowledge based on consciousness and the paradigm of modern scientific-mathematical inquiry—one of its primary achievements. In his *Logos* essay "Philosophy as Rigorous Science" (1910–1911), Husserl portrayed the crisis-conditions of the modern cultural situation—expressed in the naturalistic and historicist undermining of the sciences—and the potential resolution of this crisis in renewing philosophy as a rigorously scientific and transcendental enterprise and—as he subsequently argued in the Kaizō articles published in Japan in the first half of the 1920s and in *The Crisis of the European Sciences* (1936)—renewing Occidental culture itself in the face of its irrationalist deformations.[9] While neo-Kantian philosophers bifurcated nature and spirit into factuality and value, Husserl sought to rejuvenate and radicalize transcendental philosophy by providing it with an experientially richer and logically more sophisticated form associated with the phenomenological method.

It remains a contested question to what extent Levinas transcended or simply modified the transcendental paradigm of Husserl and their Kantian teachers in Freiburg and Strasbourg.[10] In the case of Levinas, like Heidegger, interpreters and critics dispute whether their respective practices of phenomenology embody a radical departure from Husserl or a subtler reorientation. Notwithstanding his appraisal of Husserl's ostensibly excessively intellectualistic and subjectivist conception of phenomenology, fundamental Husserlian concepts and strategies—such as phenomenological reduction, categorial intuition (*kategoriale Anschauung*), intentionality and temporality, and passive synthesis—inform and echo in Levinas's subsequent works.[11]

Intriguingly, given the respective questioning of the priority of consciousness and the transcendental subject through worldly "being-there" (Dasein) and the transcendence of the self through the other, Heidegger and Levinas's departures from Husserl's project do not lead them back to prephenomenological naturalistic or efficient causal explanations of the world. This is noteworthy given (1) Heidegger's deployment of his own unique language of the immanence of self-interpreting life and of nature and naturalness—from the violence of the upsurge and holding sway of *phusis* to the apparent nostalgic sentimentality for fields, forest groves, and riversides—and (2) Levinas's persistent identification and critique of this idiom of life and nature as the crucial element of Heidegger's thinking and its limitations.

Despite their transformations of phenomenology, Heidegger and Levinas remain beholden to its commitment to a realm of significance that is independent of the contingent causal nexus of the natural world and ontic empirical inquiry. The inheritance of transcendental philosophy, and its contestation of what Husserl called the "naturalistic worldview," joins them, even as the question of nature sets their thought into opposition—whether there is a more disclosive encounter with an "other nature" or an ethical revelation of an "other of nature" beyond calculation and instrumentalization. I consider in the following discussion to what extent Levinas's reorientation of phenomenology toward transcendence, excess, and escape suggest two divergent yet intersecting responses to the potential, risks, and problems of transcendental philosophy in light of the phenomenological critique of the nature of naturalism—as derivative of constitution and the sedimentation of lived experience—that orients and troubles their philosophical discourses.

Against Heidegger, Ontology, and Nature

Husserl's polemic against scientific naturalism coincided with his deep concern with the epistemological basis of and modes of inquiry in the natural sciences. Although present to an extent in their earliest writings, Heidegger and Levinas leave such concerns aside in intensifying Husserl's polemic against naturalism. Heidegger articulates the history of philosophy as the history of the forgetting of being. He rejected epistemology, a recent phase of this history of forgetting, as inadequate to genuine thinking, which concerns the question of the meaning of being prior to that of knowing. Levinas exposes ontology to be a history of the forgetting of the other. This undoing of ontology is pursued for the sake of an ethics prior to being. Although Levinas did not restore philosophy's epistemological dimension, as his postwar comments in essays such as "Heidegger, Gagarin and Us" make clear, he does not share elements linked with it in Heidegger's wariness of technology, science, and modernity in general. Yet Levinas maintains the phenomenological critique of scientific and poetic naturalisms in a desire for "a land foreign to every nature."[12] Levinas advocated this critique already in the 1930s, not in the name of a more fundamental encounter with being but for the sake of the concrete individual human person, who is irreducible to, while simultaneously riveted to, its biological and material facticity. Levinas's thinking in the 1930s of the person as both ethical and material is a precursor to an ethics of material others.

By the mid-1930s the questions of nature, life, and biology became entangled with Heidegger and national socialism. Levinas earlier—in the first chapter of his doctoral thesis *The Theory of Intuition in Husserl's Phenomenology* (1930)—focused on the reductive character of scientific naturalism.[13] Levinas commented in 1931 that the "world overflows nature," that is, the lived world exceeds and is irreducible to scientifically known nature, and, as quoted above, "the phenomenological method wants to destroy the world falsified and impoverished by the naturalistic tendencies of our times."[14]

Neither Heidegger nor Levinas questions in a sustained way Husserl's arguments that self and world cannot be adequately understood naturalistically or materialistically as a nexus of efficient causes. It is a significant question whether their strategies genuinely escape from transcendental idealism and continue to indirectly presuppose a transcendental constitutive subjectivity, even as it appears to be deferred through a transcendence that exceeds constitution, intentionality, and the self, and so consequently leads to aporia. Adorno, Heidegger, and Levinas endeavored to problematize constitutive transcendental subjectivity while arguably reemploying elements of the transcendental paradigm that was inherited from Kant, Husserl, and early twentieth-century neo-Kantianism.

Levinas remarked in *On Escape*, published originally in 1935 in Émile Bréhier's journal *Recherches philosophiques*, on the ethical social moment within materialism. In opposition to fascist asceticism, which intersects with what Adorno described as the coldness of the authoritarian and racially objectifying gaze, he articulates the significance of sensuous bodily existence and pleasure while also simultaneously rejecting any reification or fetishism of the body and biological or natural existence, however these are expressed. When Levinas mentions Hitler and Nietzsche, he deploys Heidegger's vocabulary, which entails that these figures belong together in a another nonpositivistic variety of naturalism linked with antimodernism.[15] Such a "fascist naturalism" borrows from the biological sciences but differs from the modern scientific worldview that Heidegger reactively rejects in Levinas's account. This nature is not objectively studied but rather romantically celebrated, heroically embraced, or tragically accepted. Levinas diagnoses this ideological configuration of nature, profoundly linking Heidegger with national socialism, as consisting of being, fatalism before nature, and the justification of barbarism: "Every civilization that accepts being—with the tragic despair it contains and the crimes it justifies—merits the name 'barbarian.'"[16] Heidegger is only indirectly mentioned in this passage by name through the reference to "ontologism" (which Levinas persistently links with his thinking).[17]

The underlying thread of Levinas's contestation of Heidegger's thinking from the 1930s to 1995 is of a naturalism in this second sense: being as nature—not as science or metaphysical essence but rather in the sense of accepting and advocating the brutality of the factuality, self-sufficiency, and "thereness" of being and accordingly of legitimating injustice and violence.[18] For Levinas, then, not unlike Adorno's assessment in *The Jargon of Authenticity*, no amount of poeticizing about the gift and generosity of being; the awe and sublimity of mountains, forests, and other natural phenomena; or the nostalgic simplicity of rural life can excuse it. The gift and generosity of being inadequately differentiates between the murderers who enjoy life and the murdered who are denied life and any of its happiness. Levinas accordingly in the essay "Everyday Language and Rhetoric without Eloquence" distinguishes the said of propositional and poeticizing language with the saying in everyday language with which one approaches and addresses the other person.[19]

Holy and Unholy Lands

Referring to Matthew 5:45, Kierkegaard posed the question under the pseudonym Johannes de Silentio whether the indifference of the external world, in which it shines or rains on the just and the unjust alike, is the rule of the spiritual world, concluding here that "it does not rain on the just and the unjust alike, here the sun does not shine on both good and evil."[20] Levinas asked the question in 1935 of the import of the indifferent neutrality of being for the individual person. Given what was to come under national socialism, the legitimacy of Levinas's questioning of Heidegger is undeniable. While Adorno criticized Heidegger for privileging the human in relation to nature, Levinas protested in the postwar period Heidegger's privileging of anonymous, indifferent, and neutral being in nature and mythic encompassing landscapes.[21] There are no individual persons to encounter in these environments: "In the *Feldwege*, there is a tree; you don't find humans there."[22]

Levinas praises in "Heidegger, Gagarin and Us" the monotheistic and modern technological destruction of pagan groves, sacred sites, and mystery-laden forest paths embraced in fascist ideology. The destruction of the logic of opposing self and other that Levinas designates paganism undermines the differentiation of native and stranger—and accordingly the distinction between the natural and artificial—and the violence that such distinctions have persistently justified. Nature is grasped in these passages as an antiethical nature-mythology governed by coercive force and violence. The bonds of native locality, place, and landscape are deconstructed as dividing humans into same and other, native and foreign. Levinas had previously presented an elucidation of phenomenology as humanizing things and "de-reifying the human being."[23] In this short text, written in the aftermath of the Holocaust, Levinas questions how Heidegger's letting responsiveness (*Gelassenheit*) toward beings appears to express cares for trees and nature while remaining indifferently silent about the national socialist mass annihilation of other humans.[24] It is and cannot be nature and its mysteries that makes humanity human, since the adoration of nature is compatible with the perpetuation of human suffering, as social ecology continues to describe. Humanity is then rather indicated in serving someone else, the others, by cultivating and reshaping the land to feed them.[25] As will be examined later, it is distance from nature that lets humans engage their earthly demand of not approaching "the widow, the orphan, the stranger and the beggar" with indifferent or neglectful "empty hands."[26]

The Holy Land is not Heidegger's sacred wilderness. What then does it signify in this context? The hunger of vulnerable bodily material others is holier than originary being and the abstract hypostatized grasping of God. This is revealed in the tamarisk, the desert evergreen planted by Abraham at Beersheba after digging a well there in Genesis 21:33. "Tamarisk" is an acronym: the three letters (aleph, shin, lamed) of the Hebrew word *eshel* (אשל) are initials for "food, drink and shelter, three things necessary to humans that humans offer to humans. The earth is for that."[27] Levinas endorsed in this regard a radical separation from nature in human responsibility as obedience to the earthly material needs of the other. This argument indicates an ethics of the material other operating in Levinas's discourse that should be further reevaluated in relation to a different interpretation of nature and animals, as developed in the works of Adorno and environmental philosophy. Accordingly, there is no separation from the sensuous material world; to echo Adorno's "promise of happiness," it is overcome in its fulfillment. Abraham materially welcomed the wayfarer and the stranger rather than meet them with empty hands. An intimation of a different sensibility about nature occurs when Levinas contends that humans inhabit "the earth more radically than the plant," and this earthly inhabiting is simultaneously material and ethical. Levinas's inhabiting is distinguished from Heidegger's care and dwelling by being turned toward welcoming and serving the other as Other rather than oneself (egoism) or neutral impersonal being (ontology).

Levinas, Heidegger, and Cryptonaturalism

Levinas portrayed Heidegger's ontology as a variety of naturalism that might be designated "cryptonaturalistic." It is not the naturalism of scientific causal explanation but shares its same impersonality in denigrating the interpersonal and consequently the ethical relation. This Heideggerian vision of being as a natural and ethically unquestionable holding sway or power must be heroically embraced in radical decision and resoluteness or patiently tolerated in resignation. Such naturalism is intrinsically inadequate to the ethical in that it accepts and thereby excuses the natural necessity of indifference and violence. Levinas portrays this dynamic self-unfolding striving power as central to Western ontology—encompassing philosophers through the conatus and will as diverse as Spinoza, Nietzsche, and Heidegger—through a line connecting the self-preservation and striving of the conatus, the struggle for and self-assertion of existence, the will to power, and Dasein's primary concern for itself in its individuation of its ownness and mineness.[28]

Heidegger consistently denigrated "biologism" (even in the period when he most actively engaged on behalf of the national socialist regime) in the first sense of naturalism discussed above; that is, as a reduction of human existence to its solely biological dynamics. He explicitly opposed notions of a biological or social Darwinist struggle for existence even during his national socialist period. Heidegger repeatedly rejected the notion of a "struggle for existence" (*Kampf ums Dasein*) occurring between natural entities from his early to later thinking.[29] Despite Heidegger's expression of suspicion against the Darwinian and Nietzschean language of survival, struggle, and will, Levinas identifies this as an essential moment in Heidegger's thought and of ontology as a whole. Beginning in his early writings on national socialism in the mid-1930s, Levinas links Heideggerian care for one's own being with the conatus and a Darwinian struggle for survival.[30] Adorno and Horkheimer also offer a diagnosis of the pathologies of self-preservation, interlinked with the domination of nature, in the *Dialectic of Enlightenment*. In a Levinasian manner on this point, Adorno describes Heidegger's Dasein as a sublimated form of idealist subjectivity and likewise connects the modern subject with self-preservation and self-assertion, noting, "The primacy of subjectivity is a spiritualized continuation of Darwin's struggle for existence."[31] Problems of subjectivity are not eliminated but sublimated in Heidegger's later thinking, as Adorno diagnoses Heidegger's ontology in *The Jargon of Authenticity* and *Negative Dialectics* as a form of rhetoric and a magic spell indirectly expressing actual conditions of alienation and servitude.

Levinas takes a step further in portraying the immanent totalizing tendencies of ontological thinking—in contrast with what he describes in this period as the transcendence of metaphysics—in this light in the preface to his *Totality and Infinity* (1961): being (*Sein*) *is* a condition of war, and ontology *is* violence.[32] To the degree that Heidegger himself opposed biologistic and anthropological accounts of human existence, Levinas's criticism appears misplaced to Heidegger scholars.[33] The biological and the natural are not only natural scientific categories applied to objective entities and their relations. Levinas does not consider Heidegger to be an acute naturalist, and Levinas is not so much concerned with biology put in terms of a natural scientific discipline as he is with a biological theory of evolution put in terms of natural selection in which Darwinism is taken to entail racial and social contest, hierarchy, and inequality. Levinas's "anti-Darwinism" is also not concerned with the evolutionary interconnectedness of species and life, which is considered to be the more radical point of the theory of evolution that angers religious creationists. His primary concern in these remarks is, rather, with social and ontological Darwinism and the ideological constructions of natural and racial "fitness" in national socialism and other forms of racism. Levinas identifies the affinities of Heidegger's language with this discourse. By celebrating individual egoism and self-interested concern as well as absorption and participation in collective organisms—and such narcissistic egoism and conformist collectivism are complementary in totalitarianism, as Adorno argued in corresponding ways—being and nature become justifications of the violence and injustice of humans against humans even when human individuals do not appear directly to be at stake. Yet, at the same time, as seen in the previous chapters, Adorno retained a sense of the redemptive moment in and of nature.

While Levinas was addressing the question of whether being and its fatalism that rivets the person to facticity can be escaped in 1935, he is not interpreting Heidegger merely externally by posing the question of violence.[34] Heidegger in the same year in his lecture course "Introduction to Metaphysics" was addressing the violent upsurge and holding sway of *phusis*, of the ontological and not merely ontic conflict of *polemos* and *Auseinandersetzung*, and spoke in his 1935 works *Introduction to Metaphysics* and "The Origin of the Work of Art" of the violent and creative upsurge and holding sway of founding and forming accomplished by great statesmen, artists, and thinkers. Heidegger's discourse of exemplary artists and originators differs from Levinas's oppressed who long for escape and Adorno's damaged lives. Heidegger increasingly—and this is not fortuitous—abandons this language of violence and creation that he embraced during the early national socialist period. It is in his late-war and postwar publications such as *Country Path Conversations* (*Feldweg-Gespräche*, 1944–1945) that he speaks of fields, forests, and rivers without the earlier violence of nature but in—as Levinas and Adorno repeatedly point out—nostalgic and sentimental ways. In both the case of his earlier and later thinking, as Adorno has argued, Heidegger is employing the language of nineteenth-century romantic naturalism with its categories of the sublime and the sentimental or pastoral idyllic, even if he rejected the Latin *natura* for the Greek—and thus for him more originary—*phusis* and Darwinian struggle for a more primordial *polemos*.

The different senses of naturalism considered so far—specifically, the efficient causal, the social-Darwinian, and the romantic-poetic—do not exhaust the question of nature, life, and biology in either Heidegger or Levinas. Levinas detects elements of vitalism in Heidegger. Levinas noted in 1935 that the discourse of creative life forces is tied to the self-assertion of life and thus to being, such that escaping or getting out of being cannot be renovation, creation, or return.[35] Yet Heidegger likewise disparaged intuitionist and vitalistic life-philosophies since they overlook the fact that perception and experience come to words through language and interpretation, and consequently that vitalism and *Lebensphilosophie* cannot provide a different and more appropriate sense of nature and naturalism for Heidegger or Levinas.

Levinas and the Other-Transcendence of Life

Levinas's endeavors remained tangled up with Heidegger's project through initially appropriating and then ruthlessly confronting it, at times polemically and unfairly. Levinas's commitment to Husserlian phenomenology was modified through his entanglement with Heidegger's thinking in the late 1920s. Heidegger's hermeneutics of factical life is one source for Levinas's work in the late 1920s and early 1930s, including the lectures Levinas attended in Freiburg, as he modified Husserl's transcendental project in a more existential, life-philosophical, and ontological direction. Despite his unfamiliarity with Heidegger's early lectures-courses, which were not published until the last few decades, he suggestively evokes the hermeneutical project of a self-interpreting life within a historical context, in contrast with its phenomenological neutralization as life and as historical in the conclusion to *The Theory of Intuition*.[36]

After a period of initial enthusiasm, marked in particular by his attendance at the Davos conference in March 1929, where Heidegger and Ernst Cassirer lectured and debated, Levinas was shocked by Heidegger's active endorsement of and engagement on behalf of national socialism. Through his increasingly critical stance toward Heidegger and growing interest in Jewish thought and culture in the circumstances of the rise to power of national socialism, Levinas can be described as moving from the phenomenology of the evident, the given, and the visible, of that which appears in intuition, to an excess or surplus incomprehensible to phenomenological description, hermeneutical interpretation, or systematic explanation, whether scientific or metaphysical.[37] Heidegger scholars might contend that Heidegger himself was moving in such a direction with his thinking of concealment/unconcealment, letting and withdrawal, and his later hermeneutics of responsiveness, openness, and the mystery of being. Nonetheless, Levinas indicates the inadequacy of the later Heidegger's philosophy of being as continuing to miss the fundamentally ethical demand revealed in other persons.

This "extra-" or "meta"phenomenology, which Levinas later calls ethics and religion, is of the inapparent, invisible, and transcendent.[38] Such transcendence is not the ineffable or mystical, nor an eternal absolute or determinate law known through intuition, revelation, or divine command. "Transcendence" indicates, instead, that which ethically resists reduction to the self and its world even as its traces are disruptively intimated in worldly encounters and experiences. The phenomenology and hermeneutics of experience, whether based in the intentionality of consciousness and the body or in the dynamics of self-reflexive interpretive life, are inadequate to this ethical suspension by the other of the self, society, and their ordering of the world. Levinas's interpretive strategy is in conflict with the hermeneutical maxim, adopted by the early Heidegger from Wilhelm Dilthey, of understanding and articulating life immanently in itself from out of itself. Levinas proposes instead a going behind and beyond the phenomenality and immanence of the world. Levinas interprets the self-disruption of immanence, that is, its multiplicity and difference, the blockages and breaks that place Dasein into question, as a relative nonabsolute difference that does not point toward the wholly Other.[39] But it should be noted that the empirical and ontic is not so much redeemed against the ontological by Levinas. The ontic is rather incorporated into an ontological state of self-interest and war that is interrupted through the transcendent ethical imperative indicated in the other.[40]

Levinas transitioned from a life-philosophical conception of "life," informed by phenomenology as well as the life-philosophy of Henri Bergson, into a conception of alterity as ethically irreducible to and interruptive of life in its immanence.[41] Despite Levinas's emerging assessment of "life" as brute factuality, immanent vitality, and self-absorbed virility, Levinas does not forget his earlier concern for the concrete life lost in naturalism. Life remains an ambiguous category in his works such that one must ask any call to embrace life the question, which life is it calling for? Life wants to live from the elemental and enjoy itself under the sun, yet is confronted by the ethical disturbance that does not occur as an existential shock or as the negation of the I. Instead it comes from afar and from someone else, addressing and contesting my life and enjoyment, my self-assertion and place in the sun for the sake of the other's life in its materiality and need. It is not an expression of spirit or God but the encounter with the fragility of the face, the embodied sensibility and lived materiality, who—as a material embodied and suffering other—calls for an ethical response. The other's face, as exemplary of the ethical encounter that is prior to and orients norms and values, is simultaneously ethical and sensuous, transcendental and empirical.[42] The face-to-face is not part of a causal sequence, even a multi- or nonlinear causality; yet it does have worldly effects.[43] This face is not only a human face, but appears in the abject and dehumanized.[44]

Levinas does not reject my hunger, satisfaction, or enjoyment for ascetic ideals or otherworldly spiritualism, nor does he instrumentally manage them for the sake of preserving a system of power.[45] Levinas stresses the disturbance of my own bodily life and satisfaction by "the Other" for the sake of the earthly and sensible needs of material others.

Levinas's most Husserlian work, *The Theory of Intuition in Husserl's Phenomenology* (1930), contains life- and existence-philosophical elements from Bergson and Heidegger, as when he defends Husserl against the Bergsonian charge that concepts inevitably distort experience. Levinas concludes then that one can still "reproach Husserl for his intellectualism," asking in light of Heidegger's care: "Is our main attitude toward reality that of theoretical contemplation?"[46]

In the conclusion to *The Theory of Intuition*, Levinas argues that the phenomenological reduction (retaining his gendered language here) "is an act by which a philosopher reflects upon himself and, so to speak, 'neutralizes' in himself the man living in the world, the man positing the world as existing, the man taking part in the world. The reduction consists at looking at one's life. But by virtue of the primacy of theory, Husserl does not wonder how this 'neutralization' of our life, which nevertheless is still an act of our life, has its foundation in life."[47] Levinas adopts the language of immanent historicity and "life," a term Heidegger had already abandoned in favor of "existence" in *Being and Time*, to criticize Husserl.[48] Following Heidegger at this time, Levinas portrayed Husserl as inadequately considering the historical character of that life: "The historical role of the reduction and the meaning of its appearance at a certain moment of existence are, for him, not even a problem."[49]

There is a significant variance between Levinas's assessment in *The Theory of Intuition* and the early Heidegger's departure from Husserl. It is admittedly deemphasized in *Being and Time* in comparison with the earlier lecture courses. Language is a primarily interpretive if habitually fallen practice of communication.[50] This absence is explicable as the lived nexus of life, history, and language as a hermeneutical issue in Heidegger stems from Dilthey.[51]

Nature, Life, and History

Before we continue, we should briefly consider the question of history: what is Levinas's understanding of the nexus of life and history that he faced through his engagement with Heidegger in the late 1920s?[52] Levinas espoused Husserl's rejection of historicism in *The Theory of Intuition in Husserl's Phenomenology*, which he interpreted in accordance with Husserl's criticism as the reduction of ideal validity to empirical historical contingencies. Still, Levinas recognized the necessity of tracing the "origins of reality," including the origins of consciousness, perception, and the sciences, in the context of the historical life situation: "Historicality and temporality form the very substantiality of human substance."[53]

While Levinas employed the hermeneutical language of returning to "historical life" as the context of intuition and theory in 1930, he did not deploy the existential life-philosophical strategy of escalating the feeling of life and its historicity in historical decision and resolve. Levinas's enthusiasm for Heidegger during this period did not remove his indebtedness to Husserl's phenomenology. Instead Levinas shortly criticized this strategy as the destruction of the freedom and personhood of the individual in his initial reflections on national socialism in *The Philosophy of Hitlerism* (1934).[54] In these critical considerations written during the early period of national socialism, fascism is linked with Heidegger's thinking of ontology and existence, and historical facticity and finitude are elucidated in relation to political brutality and violence. They are the brutal facts of being and the "being there" that assaults, traumatizes, and undoes individual freedom and the person's dignity.[55]

Facticity and finite historical life are an inappropriable oppressive presence that allows no refuge or escape. Levinas engages in *On Escape* the problematic of national socialism and Heideggerian ontology once again. Philosophy is not about finitude in experiences such as shame; it concerns the "I." In Levinas's later thinking, this theme is reinterpreted as separation that is radically opposed with any thinking committed to finitude.[56] The anonymous and impersonal "there is" impedes the temporality and individuation that occurs only through the diachronic and asymmetrical relation with the other.[57] Lost in its own historical and ontological immanence, finitude is the nonrecognition of the infinite. Heidegger's finitude, as an atheistic and cruel oblivion to the other, is "a regime of power more inhuman than mechanism."[58]

With the exception of his conclusion of *The Theory of Intuition*, in which the historicity of life is differentiated from reductive historicism, with intermittent comments on the interpersonal and potentially ethical character of history, Levinas is characteristically suspicious of the philosophical discourse of history and historicity and, particularly, their deployment in the philosophies of Hegel and Heidegger.[59] For Levinas, who is a critic of idealizing philosophies of history, history principally signifies totality and injustice that is interrupted through the prophetic and ethical. History is the order in which suffering is excused and justified, justice left unaccomplished, the other effaced, and the personal sacrificed for the sake of an impersonal order.[60] The philosophy of history, a secularized theodicy that is already injustice to humans and God, is contrasted with the ethics of otherness that disrupts the historical and its compulsive repetition in responding to others' needs and demanding justice. History contextualizes and relativizes suffering and murder; it is, as Hegel comments, a slaughter bench, which Levinas portrays as a realm of war. Yet despite the power of the totality of natural and historical conditions, the other person is irreducible to them. Speaking of history, Levinas argues, "History as a relationship between humans ignores a position of the I before the other in which the other remains transcendent with respect to me. Though of myself I am not exterior to history, I do find in the Other a point that is absolute with regard to history—not by amalgamating with the Other, but in speaking with the Other. History is worked over by the ruptures of history, in which a judgment is borne upon it. When the person truly approaches the Other they are uprooted from history."[61]

Nature and Justice

Existence was interpreted in Heidegger's early lecture courses, which provide the context for the emergence of *Being and Time*, through lived experience (*Erlebnis*), life (*Leben*), and historicity (*Geschichtlichkeit*). These contexts and conditions of historical life signify Heidegger's advance over Husserl for Levinas in his 1930 book. But they subsequently became—along with being toward death and ontology in general—more questionable for Levinas with the rise of national socialism and Heidegger's public embrace of it. The potential limitations of Levinas's later interpretations of Heidegger's thinking about being and its ethical import, insightfully analyzed by François Raffoul, do not undermine his overall assessment of Heidegger's ontology.[62] More adequate philosophical depictions of Heidegger's thinking do not resolve the ethical questions posed by Levinas.

In Levinas's later writings, which reflect on the pagan naturalism and vitalism of national socialism in the mid-1930s, Heidegger's language takes on a different tone for him: existence comes to signify a social Darwinian struggle for existence; life signifies the riveting of the individual to the biological and its arbitrary features; facticity signifies brutality without openness or possibility, and the anxiety of being-towards-death comes to mean the virile and "masculine" mastery of death in oblivion of the other's death.[63] "Ontology" signifies for Levinas the forgetting of ethical alterity, and "history" primarily signifies the murder, totality, and the systemization of oppression rather than the secularized theodicy of progress. The categories of being, life, and nature become prisons for human individuals. The inescapability of nature, life, and being in their brute and brutal facticity echoes a self-celebratory egoism that denies others whether through careless neglect or careful destruction.[64]

It is worthwhile to note that despite his hostility to naturalism in its various reductive forms, Levinas shows another face when he—admittedly infrequently—thematizes the otherness and radical exteriority of nature, and remarked that culture is the reduction of nature to presence and the same.[65] An ethically informed culture, oriented by the ethical uniqueness of the human other, might have a different relation to nature by not absorbing it in identity. Levinas's discussion up to a point indicates the prospect of an ethically attentive culture of nature, which one can think and imagine beyond Levinas, who concludes this promising discussion of the otherness of nature by once again linking the exteriority of nature with the brutality, cruelty, and self-interestedness of being.[66] There appears to be an absence of space, or a very circumscribed one, for ethical experiences and conceptions of nature in Levinas. The promise of an ethics of nature seems to be offered only to be withdrawn in moments when ethics and nature are set into opposition with one another.

The ethical occurs in disrelation to an alterity that necessarily and unconditionally disrupts the sacrificial orders of nature and history, calling the self to act for the other rather than out of self-interest or the self-assertion of the conatus in the "struggle for survival." "Conatus" is a commonly deployed in early modern philosophy. The "conatus essendi" is Baruch Spinoza's principle that "[e]ach thing, in so far as it is in itself, endeavors to persevere in its being" and has a fundamental "natural right to exist and act, without harm to himself and to others."[67] This principle prioritizes the self over others for Levinas even if Spinoza qualified this right with a harm principle that limited injuring oneself and others and developed arguments for republican government from it. As in natural law theory, rights are prior to any capacity or power of the self or the community; unlike natural law theory, they are also prior to any natural or religious origin that would be ascribed to them.[68]

Adorno and Horkheimer likewise identify Spinoza's conatus endeavoring to preserve itself as "the true maxim of all Western civilization."[69] The model of the *conatus essendi* shapes in Levinas and Adorno not only subsequent nineteenth-century discourses of the will (as in Schopenhauer and Nietzsche) and the struggle for existence (Darwinism) but the philosophy of life, existence, and being (Heidegger). Let's briefly consider the example of Schopenhauer before turning again to Heidegger. It is interesting that Levinas, unlike Adorno and Horkheimer, does not discuss Schopenhauer's thought at length given that in works such as *On the Basis of Morality* (1840) he identified nature and life with the conatus interpreted as will, and interpreted ethics as the abandonment of the will in compassion that operates as loving-kindness and justice in regard to the (human and nonhuman) other. The ethical comportment exhibited in saints and Bodhisattvas is likewise the exception to the rule given that life is dominated by direct and indirect forms of egoism and desire. *On the Basis of Morality* exposes moral reciprocity, and Kant's moral law and highest good, to be indirect passive forms of exchange and egoism, arguing that pure and active moral motives (e.g., placing the other before oneself without expectation of reward) must serve as the sole genuine basis of ethics.[70] This book contains a number of statements against the ego and for the other that, if taken out of context, could be attributed to Levinas, such as Schopenhauer's portrayal of ethical counterexamples to egoism in everyday acts of justice and kindness and the priority of others in encountering their suffering and pain. Nonetheless, this ethics founded in compassion is inadequate from a Levinasian analysis insofar as, to give only a brief sketch here, (1) the dynamic of the other's suffering and my compassion are only one aspect of the ethical relation, as Levinas remarks in one of his few discussions of Schopenhauer;[71] (2) the encounter with the other relies on a projection of the self into the other, who is then seen as having no boundaries with and as the same as oneself; (3) compassion, "suffering-with" (*mit-leiden*), is interpreted as the foundation of ethics rather than the other being prior to any attempt at or discourse of the justification or the refutation of ethics; and (4) Schopenhauer's philosophy, which is to simplify a secularized and naturalized form of the identification and participation of pantheism and mysticism, advocates abandoning a lower form of nature (the ego) for the sake of a higher form of nature (the egoless whole), reproducing arguably the problems of nature and the conatus at a cosmic level.

Levinas articulates analogous problems with Heidegger's philosophy, conceived in relation to Nietzsche rather than to Schopenhauer. Levinas controversially contends that not only Heidegger's early philosophy of life and Dasein but his later thinking of the primacy of being does not escape from this occidental history of the conatus. His question of being (*Seinsfrage*) is inexorably linked to a self-interested concern in the being that is always my own (*Jemeinigkeit*) and thus not the other who should be first and foremost: "Being is inseparable from the comprehension of Being; Being already invokes subjectivity."[72] There is accordingly an egoism at the heart of ontology, philosophies of existence, and natural history that reflects the "survival instinct," the self-interestedness that is the root of conflict and violence.[73] Heidegger's later thinking of being, in the at times polemical accounts of Levinas and Adorno, cannot escape the philosophy of the subject and constitutive subjectivity. Heidegger does not genuinely overcome this philosophy, but it is sublimated in the primacy of being and expressed in an indirect and passive form.[74]

Levinas's mature understanding of nature is informed by his earlier reflections in the 1930s that identify nature and the material world with the ontology of being and its indifferent coldness and violence. This fear does not fade in his later thought, in which Levinas would like to rediscover the person and dignity in the material world and the name in the midst of anonymity and impersonality.[75] According to Levinas, nature and matter are sites of the anonymous and depersonalizing forces of the "there is" (*il y a*), which has none of the generosity or giving qualities that Heidegger associates with the "there is" (*es gibt*) of being, against which human dignity must persistently struggle.[76] Natural and social determinisms inevitably hamper encountering others as irreducible to natural and social mechanisms.[77] These natural and social mechanisms operate as one in class exploitation and domination. In a discussion of Judaism, revolution, and workers' rights in 1969, Levinas defines "revolution," in an interpretation that goes back to the early humanistic writings of Marx, as liberation from economic determinism.[78] Adorno describes likewise the materialist overcoming of materialism as the moment of truth in idealism: "The realization of materialism would mean today the end of materialism, of the blind and degrading dependence of human beings upon material conditions."[79]

This line of prophetic argumentation for the sake of justice leads Levinas to condemn the ethical poverty of naturalism, while still thematizing the material bodily and earthly needs and joys, erotic sensual life and fecundity, and articulating the transition—provoked through the claim of transcendence and alterity—toward the exteriority of the good and, through the "third party" (*le tiers*), toward justice. Justice is already disorder and violence of the interpersonal ethical encounter. The word "justice"—which will be interpreted in the contexts of religion in part 2, and politics in part 3 of this volume—is not univocal in Levinas's works: it can describe the unique asymmetrical interpersonal relationship of self and other, the impersonal impartial attitude introduced by the third person, or a universal justice applied or misapplied by the state. Justice can be conceived as a ratio applied equally to all, or as love.[80] In this context, "justice" refers to emancipation from "natural" and social-political forms of oppression. This movement toward justice is not natural, biological, or immanent. It is primarily ethical. In the Jewish liberation from their oppression in Egypt, as described in Exodus, justice overturns the order of nature and empires. The biological as understood through categories of identity, genus, and race is opposed to the interpersonal constitution of meaning: "human community instituted by language."[81]

In a revealing conclusion to the essay "Notes on Meaning," Levinas describes how justice (in which the enthralled self is interrupted and reoriented by the other), of being for-the-other, and the constitution of meaning are, for Levinas, "against-nature, against the naturality of nature," as meaning cannot "turn toward any natural finality," and wherein life is not negated by meaning but "awakens to humanity."[82] Ethics is life freed of being (ontology) and nature (naturalism). It is life through the other rather than, as in the Hegelian model of recognition, the self who comes back to itself through the other. Levinas offers a radical transformation of classical phenomenology's privileging of the self. The self-constitution of meaning in Husserl's transcendental idealism is replaced in Levinas by the "other-constitution" of meaning (despite and outside the subject) through the face-to-face encounter that is material and sensuous life as ethical and as irreducible to fixed structures of materiality, naturalness, and sensibility. It is aporetically both immanent and transcendent. There can be no meaning without ethics, and nature is meaningful only through projection: "The significations of nature are but the result of a transfer of meaning from the anthropological to the natural. The human face is the face of the world itself."⁸³ A strong interpretation of Levinas's thesis entails the absence of alterity in nature, even as it might suggest a dubious way of moralizing nature through anthropomorphic transference, which would remain a form of identification.

Conclusion: Living beyond Idealism

Le matérialisme—c'est penser à l'avenir.

—Emmanuel Levinas, *Œuvres* 1

Materialism is a thinking to come, a thinking of the future, as Levinas once wrote in his notebooks in the 1940s. Materialism and naturalism are typically conceived of as ethically neutral and indifferent doctrines in which human meaning and subjectivity are lost in the coldness and vastness of the cosmos. Levinas is a critic of such forms of materialism and naturalism. However, Levinas does speak otherwise of materialism when it (as in ethical and utopian forms of Marxism) designates a condition for nonindifference and ethical subjectivity. It is in this sense that it can be a thinking of the future to come.⁸⁴

Levinas appears as if he adheres in reverse form (that is, through the other rather than the self) to the idealism (in Adorno's sense) of the phenomenological (Husserl and Heidegger) and dialogical personalist (Franz Rosenzweig and Martin Buber) paradigms that powerfully shaped his thought and he continues to maintain in the figure of the other the preponderance of spirit (*Geist*) over nature (*Natur*). The next chapter offers an opportunity to reconsider such as interpretation in further detail and examine whether a more adequate reflection on environments and animals can be reconstructed from the materialist dimensions of Levinas's analysis of materiality and sensibility.

The basic dissimilarity between Levinas's "ethics of the other" and Heidegger's "ontology of being" is more than a difference in climate and mood from which, for Levinas, we must escape.⁸⁵ Levinas's questioning of Heidegger's climate and mood announces a decision between "ethical responsiveness" and "ontological violence." His depiction of Heidegger is of a thinker of the receptivity of being, and hence of a variety of responsiveness that is inherently inadequate to the ethical transpiring despite and otherwise than being. Heidegger did not think of responsiveness—in its impossibility in the world, nature, and ontological being—to someone else, the others who are intractable to the presence of thereness and the "is." Levinas accordingly contested grounding ethics in being or human existence. This resistance included anthropological-psychological motivations and virtues such as pity, sympathy, and compassion, which Rousseau and Schopenhauer contended are the basis of altruistic behavior.

Levinas's Other is otherwise than being and its meaning no matter how profoundly the question of being is reposed. The transcendent absolute Other, if it is not to be an empty rhetoric, cannot be disembodied and separated from the fragility of the bodily life, needs, and suffering of others: that is, the embodied material other. This later thought distances Levinas from Husserl's constitutive monological subjectivity and Heidegger's solitary Dasein and brings Levinas into the vicinity of Adorno's critique of phenomenology if not directly into his nonidentitarian natural history and materialism. This is the matter to be thought that is at stake in the next chapter.

Chapter Five

An Ethics of Nature at the End of Nature

Introduction: Nature and History

A flaw in contemporary discussions of the environment, including environmental activism and philosophical approaches in environmental ethics such as environmental phenomenology, are their ahistorical character. Animals, ecosystems, environments, landscapes, that is, all that is associated with the ambiguous and difficult word "nature" are addressed as if they were either external to or permanently fixed throughout human history. Nature, whether interpreted as antagonistic or idyllic, is constructed and reified as the opposite of human culture, history, and social-political life.

Recent studies in environmental history and environmental literary criticism have explored the social, historical, and culturally mediated character of both conceptions and experiences of what counts as nature and naturalness.[1] As Levinas and Adorno pointed out, "nature" is bound up with human desires and practices, including those involving domination and exploitation. Contemporary environmental philosophy, both analytic and phenomenological, has not sufficiently attended to the consequences of the mutual interdependence of history and nature, even if this thesis is generally acknowledged. One reason for this is the concern that the universality of ethical claims (such as Peter Singer's argument that "all animals are equal" and have the claim to equal consideration) or the truth of phenomenological claims (such as encountering a stone, a tree, a river, or a woodchuck discloses a basic structure of existence) would be undermined by considering their human context and conditions.[2]

A second reason that environmental theories cannot be ahistorical lies in justifiable suspicions concerning the destructive effects of culture, history, and society in relation to the environment. These suspicions are a genuine response to the relentless environmental damages produced in modern societies. Traditional anthropocentric, idealist, and constructivist positions typically entail that (1) entities are social products or linguistic constructs, and (2) that the integrity and dignity of material and sensuous existence are secondary concerns, if considered at all. Constructivist theories, insofar as they are committed to both claims (1) and (2), do not appear to leave much room for the recognition of what should be recognized as autonomous in animals, ecosystems, and environments that was not conferred on them by a human or human-like agent, subject, or system of signification. In accordance with prevalent ecological arguments, it is difficult to have an ethics of nature *as* nature if nature is conceived as an instrumentalized resource for anthropocentric humanity or the invisible hand of the unregulated market.

There thus seem to be two interpretive choices. On the one hand, environmentalism appears to require an appeal to nature external to agency and representation, or naturalism, whether scientifically, phenomenologically, or romantically conceived. Nature is essence and identity. On the other hand, Judeo-Christian monotheism, philosophical idealism, and social-linguistic constructivism appear to exclude this recourse to nature on the grounds that it is pagan, intellectually naïve, or an ideological artifice. Against this either/or between the natural and native, on the one side, and the fabricated and foreign, on the other, I will consider two alternative approaches to the relation between the natural and the human.

It might be the case that there can be an ethics that is responsive to and responsible for animals, ecosystems, and environments without presupposing or requiring any concept or experience of nature—as it is formed in human discourse—at all. Instead of furthering environmental reflection, appeals to nature might impede and harm it. Environmental ethics might be better off "without nature." This possibility is articulated in the works of Levinas, who relentlessly criticized discourses of nature, naturalness, and naturalism in the name of the ethical. Levinas's interpretation of nature as derivative of ethics concerned, first, positivistic and reductive naturalism and materialism, which he analyzed as undermining the transcendence occurring through the ethical relation to the other.

Ethics requires the interruptive and reorienting force of transcendence, infinity, and the "otherwise than being" in relation ontological and natural or biological being.

Levinas's interpretation of nature as derivative of ethics concerned, second, the adventure of nature in its romantic, irrationalist, social Darwinist, and fascistic forms.[3] Adorno and Levinas were justifiably suspicious of both the nostalgia for the archaic and the "primitive," and of the "return to nature." This nostalgia construes nature, Adorno notes, through "the cultural desire that everything should remain unchanged," reflecting the failure and alienation of culture as a dialectical image of damaged life, instead of a genuine escape from it.[4] What appears as unchanging nature is doubly false, according to Adorno's analysis; nature is historically changing, and so are human experiences and interpretations of it. Adopting an argument from *The German Ideology*, Adorno stressed that such "naturalness" consists of the remnants and fragments of prior human activities.[5] Marx argued throughout his works that the visions of nature generated in social contract theory, German idealism, historicism, and Darwinism reflected their own social-historical context; as Rousseau pointed out against Hobbes in the preceding century, such visions project their own society's arrangement of social relations into the animal world. Nature is to this extent socially constructed.[6]

Nature functions as a social category of what appears to be nonsocial, and hence unalterable, as ideologies of nature and naturalness—reflecting the social and material nexus of human life—produce and enforce the cultural category of the natural. Rather than being the spontaneous and unmediated expressions of natural life that they are claimed to be, "natural activities" can be infantile and regressive when they hide their own social character and the fact that they are sophisticated products of a complex and mediated cultural and economic nexus.[7] For Levinas, the category of nature is a prison for human existence. The inexorableness of nature, life, and being in their brute and brutal facticity resonates in the self-regarding egoism that excludes others through careless neglect or carefully managed destruction.[8]

As discussed in chapter 4, Levinas infrequently mentions the otherness and radical exteriority of nature, and how culture can be its reduction to presence and the same.[9] An ethical culture, oriented by the ethical singularity of the other person, might have a different relationship with nature by not absorbing it in sameness. Levinas concludes, contrary to the earlier indication of the possibility of an ethical culture of nourishing the elemental and life that would be more responsive to nature, by reducing nature's radical exteriority to the identity and barbarism of ontological being.[10] The ethical occurs through a transcendence that necessarily and unconditionally upsets the sacrificial orders of nature and history, calling the self to act for the other rather than out of self-interest and self-assertion in a naturalistic "struggle for survival." If in fact there is no space for an adequately ethical nature or concept of nature in Levinas's own discourse, or if a space appears to be offered only to be taken away in the end, a radical ecological interpretation can resist this reduction for the sake of elemental life itself, and it need not follow Levinas to this conclusion.

As previously illustrated, Levinas primarily associated "nature" with the indifference and impersonality of the ontology of being that dominates Western philosophical traditions. For Levinas, nature and matter reflect the anonymous rustling of the "there is" (*il y a*).[11] Nature and matter accordingly designate the anonymous and impersonal forces against which human dignity struggles.[12] Levinas criticizes the ethical insufficiency of naturalism but addresses bodily and earthly needs and joys, carnal life and fecundity. He analyzes their movement—provoked through the claim of transcendence and alterity—toward the nonnatural and indefinable good and—through the figure of the third—toward justice. This transition is neither biological nor naturalistic. The biological adheres to the sameness of genus as opposed to "human community instituted by language" in which "the interlocutors remain absolutely separated."[13] Although Levinas spoke of ethics in relation to human others and perhaps God—as Derrida has contended, accusing Levinas of Cartesianism concerning the animal—I argue that there are traces of a broader ethics in his work that can be rethought and expanded.[14] There might not be only a "humanism of the other human" but also, as John Llewelyn proposes, a "humanism of the other animal" ("humanism" in this context meaning ethics and ethical humanism rather than necessarily anthropocentrism) and an alterity and transcendence to life and living beings insofar as they are ethically rather than biologically understood.[15]

We find traces of a nonnaturalistic animal and environmental ethics in Levinas through the moment of transcendence. Adorno's writings suggest a different alternative to the doubtful opposition between naturalism and constructivism. They do this by advocating what might be called a nonreductive and expansive ethically oriented "critical materialism."[16] Levinas takes the route of transcendence, as the disturbance of the logic of totality and "the Same" (*la Même*) through "the Other" (*l'Autre*), which leaves its traces in materiality and sensibility. Transcendence occurs within worldly immanence for Adorno, as immanence inevitably dislocates itself and its totalization. Adorno is as much a critic of totality as Levinas, identifying it as the undialectical element in Hegel and as the idealistic element in the communism of Marx and Engels.[17]

Peter Dews notes that although Adorno and Levinas both emphasize alterity in the face of totality, these terms do not have the same functions.[18] Alterity or absolute Otherness, as an unconditional and an-archic exteriority and transcendence in Levinas, in which the subject is outside of itself, is not found in the immanence of things or environments. For Adorno, however, nonidentity is immanent or internal to things themselves, their mutual yet heterogeneous relatedness, and their antagonistic mediations.[19] Adorno does not thereby exclude transcendence, even if it has no identity or positivity; transcendence is a paradox beyond which thought cannot reach and for which one cannot designate a name or engrave an image, as it reflects a life containing the "promise of something transcending life."[20]

Adorno engages the aporia of history and nature as constitutive and inescapable, such that critical reflection needs to proceed from "natural history." As with his nonanthropocentric humanism, which joins animals to humans through their common sensuous existence and suffering, Adorno's use of the category of "natural history" has its roots in Feuerbach, Marx, and Benjamin.[21] In contrast to the ordinary scientific and vulgar materialist conceptions, and particularly the reduction of history to nature, this critical notion of natural history entails naturalizing the historical by reconnecting it with its material conditions while historicizing the natural by revealing its socially mediated character. This creative aporia—the "without passage" that is dialectically a fertile opening to begin anew more than it is a desolate dead end—is seen in the tension between the ideological construction, on the one hand, and the implicit promise of organic and animal life, on the other. The sensuous, material, and bodily bonds between human and animal life, happiness, and suffering point toward the possibility of an unforced and noncoercive sensuous-mimetic and conceptual-rational responsiveness toward animals and the natural world.

Disturbing Nature:
Levinas and the Ethics of Other Animals

Whether environmental ethics is understood biocentrically or anthropocentrically, whether nature is construed as having its own intrinsic worth or as valuable only in relation to human self-interest, it is assumed that environmental ethics requires a notion of nature that gives it an independent or relative value. Given this thesis, and Levinas's hostility to discourses of nature, it seems questionable to consider environmental ethics in the context of Levinas.

The apparent impossibility of a Levinasian environmental ethics can be countered if nature is unnecessary for, or even an impediment to, environmental reflection and action. Some recent works in environmental thought have argued against naturalism and romanticism and for environmental aesthetics without nature, for denaturalizing ecological politics, or against nature as an ideological construct.[22] These writings proceed from the other side of the previously discussed opposition, that is, the social-historical context of understanding and experiencing nature. This strategy is inappropriate for approaching Levinas to the extent that history is as dubious a category as nature. Nature and history are objects of prophetic critique; neither one introduces the ethical or justice. For Levinas, nature and history are bound together in an apologetic logic of domination that sacrifices the other.[23]

Can there be an ethical responsiveness to and responsibility for animals and environments "without nature" or without the fetishized enchantment and idolatry of humans absorbed in natural forces and fixated things? Even if there can be, an affirmative response to this question faces the difficulty that Levinas does not explicitly leave adequate space for ethically encountering the in- or nonhuman except for his promising yet limited brief reflections on the faces of animals and the artwork that "gives a face to things."[24] Levinas's writings are devoted to the suffering, persecution, and hunger of the human other and, as has been noted, animals or environments are not discussed in ethical terms.[25] Indeed, some examples indicate the unethical anonymous, indifferent, and violent character of nature, in which humans are absorbed in participation, exiled, and prey to events.[26]

As delineated earlier, Adorno critiques the anthropocentric privileging of the human over the animal and the underlying intellectualism that ranks thinking over sensibility in Heidegger's thinking of the human and being. Levinas shared the latter concern about Heidegger, while rejecting Heidegger's "naturalism": the emphasis on anonymous and neutral being and nature over ethical persons.[27] Levinas noted how one encounters no persons in Heidegger's fields or forests.[28] In "Heidegger, Gagarin and Us," Levinas valorizes monotheistic and modern technological disenchantment and the destruction of sacred pagan groves and landscapes for the socialist purpose of redistributing wealth to feed the hungry and the poor.[29] This destruction is justifiable to challenge the differentiation between native and stranger and the violence that this artificial distinction authorizes. Levinas depicts nature here as an inhuman place governed by violent mythical powers. Absorbed participation and loss of humanity in native earth and landscape separates humans into native and foreign, friend and enemy. In this context, anthropomorphically and romantically humanizing nature is an enchanting reification (not as loss of essence but as fixation) complicit with cruelty toward other persons.[30]

Hunger is more sacred than being that is broken up through the material injurability and vulnerability of the other, whose face reveals precariousness and defenselessness. Serving others by transforming the earth through building and agriculture makes humanity distinctively human in an ethical sense.[31] For Levinas, science and technology facilitate the implementation of human rights and respect for others.[32] The early Confucian philosopher Xunzi (荀子) argued in favor of this same point, and against the Daoist Zhuangzi (莊子), by claiming that intervention in and control of nature is required for human flourishing and an ethical way of life: one cannot let the water of the river flow wherever it wills if this means the destruction of agriculture and lives.[33] Levinas proposes that the use of nature is necessary for ethical life and for the sake of the other, who cannot be left to starve and perish through indifferent natural forces. The moment of transcendence separates persons from nature and allows humans to engage in nature in an ethical way and not be empty-handed in reply to "the widow, the orphan, the stranger and the beggar."[34] The Holy Land of the Torah is not a land of idyllic or idealized nature. Abraham planted the tamarisk that symbolizes the necessity for human intervention in nature to produce and offer to others the bare needs of human life: "food, drink, and shelter."[35]

Levinas earlier interpreted phenomenology as "de-reifying the human being" and humanizing things.[36] Here Levinas is confronting the illusions of poetic and pagan nature that require an analysis of how discourses of nature can serve ideological functions. Even as Levinas promotes anthropocentrically separating the ethical and the natural in this line of thought, a hint of a different response to nature is intimated in his articulation of how humans inhabit the earth in a radically different way. Levinas differentiates between care and dwelling in Heidegger's sense and a radical inhabiting of the land guided by the promise of welcoming and serving others rather than prioritizing the self.[37]

Can this earthly inhabiting and use of the earth for the sake of the other welcome and serve animal others or ethically respond to ecosystems and environments? Can one respond to nature *as* nature?[38] This is not a possibility in the varieties of deontological ethics that dominate contemporary social thought. Habermas and other ethical universalists sacrifice the promise of happiness to demands for justice, and demand certain kinds of symmetry and equality as the condition of ethical responsibility.[39] Levinas's justice is rooted in the suffering of the other such that happiness must to a degree be part of ethics. Levinas held asymmetrical responsibility, as a response potentially without recuperation, to be the necessary condition of symmetry and equality.[40] Levinas maintains that the "I" is concretely and unconditionally responsible to and for each regardless of their equality, reciprocity, or symmetry with myself, since equality without asymmetrical responsibility is in the last analysis exchange and sacrifice.[41] I am even responsible and held hostage, in Levinas's more provocative formulation, to the other who bothers and troubles me and—in a ridiculous demand—the enemy who persecutes me.[42]

For Levinas, ethical inequality is "absolutely opposed to oppression," as it suggests a solidarity of alterity rather than the sameness of biological kinship or the genus.[43] The biological notion of the human—and thus the endeavor to biologically justify anthropocentrism—is ethically disturbed. In this context, inequality between humans and nonhumans for Levinas need not necessarily lead to the denial of the latter's moral status, and might indicate reasons for human responsibility to and for them.[44] Just as I am infinitely responsible for, without any expectation of reciprocity from, humans who require my help—the stranger, the widow, and the orphan—so there might be an analogous responsibility to nonhuman hunger, need, and persecution that is likewise seen in the faces, cries, and bodies of animals. Levinas has stated inconsistently that the animal has no face, in the sense of his account of the ethics of the face, and that it is a difficult issue. A third option is to consider the possibility of an epiphany of the animal's face. In its gaze and need, the face of the animal demands my response and care. Given the realities of ethical encounter, and mimesis freed of mythic identification and participation if we appeal to Adorno, the animal's face presents its own ethical demands without requiring positing a common identity or making an analogical inference between animals and humans. To the extent that human action is ethically defined by transcendence and responsiveness to alterity rather than nature or anthropology, as Levinas argued of biological categories applied to human existence, it is questionable to restrict the ethical to humans based on biological and anthropological reasons, such as the biological differentiation of species that the animal face transcends. Levinas himself notes in conversation with Philippe Nemo how the face-to-face encounter with the other person is an immediately ethical one that is also described by yet cannot be reduced to biological or perceptual features or processes:

> I do not know if one can speak of a "phenomenology" of the face, since phenomenology describes what appears. So, too, I wonder if one can speak of a look turned toward the face, for the look is knowledge, perception. I think rather that access to the face is straightaway ethical. You turn yourself toward the Other as toward an object when you see a nose, eyes, a forehead, a chin, and you can describe them. The best way of encountering the Other is not even to notice the eyes' color! When one observes the color of the eyes one is not in social relationship with the Other. The relation with the face can surely be dominated by perception, but what is specifically the face is what cannot be reduced to that.[45]

Another text reveals the difficulty of extending ethics to animals in the Levinasian context. The ethical respect for the human other does not easily translate into respect for animal others in their nonidentity and alterity from humans. In the short piece called "The Name of a Dog, or Natural Rights," Levinas described Bobby the dog as "the last Kantian in Nazi Germany."[46] Whereas the Germans offer not the slightest recognition to Levinas and his fellow prisoners of war—"stripped of our human skin [. . .] we were subhuman, a gang of apes" he remarked—a dog named Bobby recognizes them as more than an object of neglect, disgust, and negation: "[W]ith neither ethics nor logos, the dog will attest to the dignity of the person." Bobby the dog reveals what he depicts as a humanism, a Kantian respect for humanity lacking in the behavior of his fellow humans. Rather than other humans, it is the dog who attests to Rabbi Eliezer's insight in the *Pirkei Avot*, "The other's dignity (*kavod*) should be as precious to you as your own," which Levinas's linguistic strategy would intensify to "even more precious than your own."[47] The *Pirkei Avot* continues by stating that one must strive to be human in a place where there is no humanity.[48] In an abode without humanity, it is a dog who reveals the lingering possibility of humanity in the sense of an ethical comportment.

Levinas's apparent commitment to a humanistic interpretation of the animal in this passage poses the problem of whether there is a recognition or respect for animals in themselves in their alterity. Levinas has been interpreted as humanizing Bobby the dog rather than extend beyond the human sphere into the alterity of the animal, which arguably continues a long tradition of anthropomorphizing animals, and potentially undermines Levinas's rejection of reducing the other—if the animal can in fact be included as the other—to the Same (the human). Is Levinas inconsistent in his interpretation of Bobby the dog, or does the animal not belong to his conception of the other?

A number of readings, such as those of John Llewelyn and Christina Gerhardt, find an ethical alterity or animal otherness in these passages. Llewelyn even suggests that Levinas sets up an analogy between the Holocaust and the treatment of animals.[49] Jacques Derrida and David Wood, however, find an absence and lack of animal otherness.[50] The problem of anthropocentric humanism in Levinas persists for them insofar as Bobby is described as acting "more humanely" than humans in Levinas's account, and is not a genuinely nonhuman Other. That is, the dog is symbolically construed in this essay through humanity's lack of humanity and, to this extent, the dog enacts the ethical "without ethics or logos" and humanity while lacking actual moral agency of its own. This debate about Bobby raises an important issue: does Bobby's lack of ethical agency imply that the dog does not have an ethical status for Levinas and his fellow prisoners of war, who greeted and played with him? If ethics is exclusively defined by equality and symmetry, then this lack of agency and reflection would turn out to be the absence of the ethical. But if ethics is asymmetrical, that is, if ethics is an obligation prior to my reflection or the natural qualities of the other, then such asymmetries do not exclude the animal's ethical status. In this situation, the dog's asymmetry allows it to respond to humans in a way that other humans do not, whether they do so out of fear, hatred, or indifference.

What is needful, instead of the "inclusion of the other," is a radical undoing of the self and the same, and its powers of inclusion/exclusion, extending from the other to the self. The prospect of a more extensive ethics of nonhuman animals does not by itself necessarily entail a broader environmental ethics; ecosystems and environments cannot be as easily perceived or conceptualized as faces or others, and the needs of individual animals and species can come into conflict with ecosystems. Further, Levinas is critical of the pagan and nationalistic identification with landscape, locality, and place. In response to the rise of the fascist and national socialist ideologies of naturalness, Levinas distinguishes a Judaic diachronic separation between nature and spirit from the mythic and pagan participation in and celebration of anonymous monistic nature.[51] Levinas renounces "nature" (or a number of its interpretations), as he, perhaps overly polemically and almost gnostically, interrogates nature, life, and being as consisting of ontological conditions of war, and as complicit with egoistic self-assertion and indifference to the other.[52] In renouncing romantic and heroic conceptions of nature found in modern irrationalism and national socialism, Levinas loses track of the significance, and ethical import, of nature and the environment. Levinas moves in the wrong direction here, in my estimation; however, Levinas's ethics and suspicions concerning ideological constructions of nature and life, which operate as ideologies of mass-produced death, remain crucial sources for environmental thought and practice, as part 1 of this volume has endeavored to demonstrate.

Beginning in the early 1930s, in his initial responses to the rise of national socialism, such as *The Philosophy of Hitlerism* (1934), Levinas associated biology with fatality, spontaneous nature with cruel brutality, and the natural body with the enslavement of the human being to the mechanical and vitalistic forces of life and nature.[53] Socially marked through biological and naturalistic categories, humans are chained to natural bodies that are racialized through heredity and blood and are subjected to the extreme sacrificial logic of the "struggle for existence."[54] Levinas persistently associated this struggle for life with Spinoza and Heidegger as much as with Darwin and Nietzsche.[55] Subjected to nature, instead of individuating themselves in relation to it, humans are unable to escape the brutality of the facticity and thereness of being that Levinas later analyzes in relation to the indifferent "there is" of the *il y a*. He concludes *On Escape*, as quoted in the previous chapter, by noting how—in contrast to the insufficiency and incompletion of human life—societies that assent to being in its facticity and sufficiency are "barbarian" in that they lose themselves in despair and legitimate brutality and violence.[56]

In *Totality and Infinity*, as in other works, Levinas associated "nature" with ideas such as the striving of the self to exist (the *conatus essendi*), the identification and conflation of the divine and the natural, the reduction of human life to a bare life in a brutal struggle for existence, the Nietzschean self-assertion of the will, the nationalist socialist fetishizing of nature as native blood and soil, and the rusticity of Heideggerian being. In his analysis, the philosophy of nature, as assertion and struggle, is dominant in Western ontology from Heraclitus to Heidegger. It is in this situation that Levinas polemically assesses philosophies of immanence. They are absorbed within pagan participation in the sacredness of the world.[57] Levinas identified the philosophy of immanence with Heidegger in particular, yet also with Western ontology in general, as the absence of ethical alterity in absorption and participation in being.[58] An interest in being reflects the "survival instinct" for Levinas: self-interest and being are at the root of violence.[59]

Levinas distinguished life from nature in *Totality and Infinity* when he described life as "living from" or "living on" (*livre de*). Life—and here human life is meant—nourishes itself from the earth and the sun, bread and water.[60] This "living from" can be taken as a return to the elemental, as the naked will to exist and survive. The modern conception of the conatus and the life and death struggle for existence, with its Hobbesian state of nature as a war of each against the other, coincides with the awe and fear of the archaic and primordial that Adorno genealogically traces as the remnants of older, harder forms of repression.[61] Adorno and Levinas placed into question the privileging of self-assertion and the struggle for survival that they both associated with fascism and racism. Levinas contests such interpretations of life as power and will by showing how "living from" is not pure conatus or will, self-assertion in the struggle for existence: "Life is love of life, a relation with contents that are not my own being but more dear than my being: thinking, eating, sleeping, reading, working, warming oneself in the sun."[62] That is, already within the apparent unity of the biological, the I (*moi*) relates itself to a plurality of elements through nourishment and enjoyment prior and irreducible to even pragmatic relations to things: "[P]rior to being a system of tools, the world is an ensemble of nourishments."[63]

David Wood has criticized this thesis from the perspective of Heidegger's analysis of the pragmatic availability and usage of things as a referential context of practical signification that already informs nourishment and enjoyment.[64] Levinas's position opens up a different relationship to nature than Wood's portrayal. Instrumentality and possession presuppose rather than possess and instrumentally control the elemental that as "earth, sea, light, city" is nonpossessable and pragmatically determined.[65] In opposition to pragmatizing interpretations of reality that reduce reality to availability and usefulness, Levinas intimates an ecology of the elemental and nourishment with environments that are more and other than human pragmatic mastery of things.

Another response might be that Levinas's thesis can be elucidated as a form of the prioritization of praxis or sensuous practice, and its potential fulfillment in happiness and the suffering in "the pain of need and work," which is evident in Adorno.[66] By distinguishing bodily nourishment and joy from instrumentality, bodily experiences that contest the body's fatality and instrumentalization become visible in Levinas.[67] As an interpreter of Marx's historical materialism, Levinas indicates how the referential context of instrumental significance is historically variable rather than a fixed and inevitable structure of human existence. The prevailing regime of instrumentality is derivative even if inescapable in existing society to the extent that instrumental relations can potentially be reoriented toward the welfare of humans. Whereas Heidegger speaks of a formal "for the sake of which" governing pragmatic relations, Levinas addresses how they relate to potential happiness and suffering.[68] Levinas extends the argument in his later magnum opus from 1974. He contends in *Otherwise Than Being* that hunger and savoring are irreducible to pragmatic handiness or to appropriation and possession through their materiality and singularization in enjoyment and suffering. Only because life enjoys life in desire, eros, and pleasure can it leave the complacency of this enjoyment in response to the other.[69] Still, in the inadequacy and impossibility of this response, the self necessarily betrays the other and remains complicit with egoism and the logic of sameness. The ethics of the other that disrupts nonethical sameness is accordingly both constitutive of the ethical and aporetic and ungroundable. This ethics—which is not ethics in an ordinary or conventional sense—appears otherworldly and perhaps Manichean in its insistence on an infinity and transcendence that cannot be reduced to the order and structures of being, nature, and society.

Gnostic and otherworldly readings of Levinas set being and its beyond—or otherwise—into absolute opposition, reifying transcendence as "the Heavenly City" and "worlds behind the scenes."[70] Despite such interpretations, Levinas advocates a twofold exteriority consisting of both a worldly elemental and an ethical pluralism.[71] His thought proceeds, according to *Time and the Other* (1947), "toward a pluralism that does not merge into a unity," which emerges instead through the asymmetrical and uneven relationship with the other.[72] Such a radical multiplicity of singulars differs from a numerical multiplicity orderable by totality.[73] Contrary to the ascetic and Manichean self-denial attributed to him by critics, Levinas is a thinker who embraces ethics for the sake of eros, happiness, and sensuous existence.[74] Levinas can celebrate the enjoyment and happiness of the I that reveals that a life is more than nature or being, since through happiness it becomes personal. There is no life without affectivity and sentiment, and no person without the demand for satisfaction and happiness.[75] The I, individuated by its happiness in the particular contents of its life, is in this sense "beyond being" and the impersonal categories of the philosophies of life or race. In such impersonal life, life consumes itself, as all life is food for life, and all life is the same.[76] Levinas describes in a wonderful passage from *Existence and Existents* how in personal life, life is living for its own sake: "We breathe for the sake of breathing, eat and drink for the sake of eating and drinking, we take shelter for the sake of taking shelter, we study to satisfy our curiosity, we take a walk for the walk. All that's not for the sake of living, it is living. Life is a sincerity."[77] As an individuated affective life, the individual lives in egoism, but egoism is constantly being interrupted and potentially reoriented by the nonidentical other. It is in this regard that Levinas speaks of the other intruding on the sameness of the living being, and of tearing the bread away from one's own mouth and giving it to the other. Here too one should ask about the animal's hunger and satisfaction in its affective life of sensibility and nourishment, of eating, sleeping, and enjoying the warmth of the sun, or the coolness of the water. Levinas speaks of the "morality of 'earthly nourishments' [as] the first morality, the first abnegation. It is not the last, but one must pass through it."[78] This first earthly morality relates to justice and economy.[79] Given Levinas's critique of discourses of nature, naturalness, and naturalism, which are called into question by the other's face, and by the other's hunger and poverty, a Levinasian ethics of animals and environments cannot be adequately justified by appeals to nature or naturalism without reconceiving them as ethical.[80]

Appeals to "nature" have no primacy or justificatory power in Levinas. The ethical is perceived to be prior to, anachronistically older than, and more immediate than the natural, such that it cannot be derived or justified from it.[81] Levinas contests the naturalism and the reduction of the interpersonal to the biological characteristic of modern Western thought. Immediacy is not brute indifferent nature but rather the event of bodily sensibility and sentience, exposure and vulnerability. The exposed nonstructure of materiality and sensibility, the human body in its vulnerability and apprehensiveness, "are earlier than nature," as is evident in a maternity that is irreducible to the biological as perseverance in being.[82] The body in its "biological functioning"—in sexuality, pregnancy, and maternity—is ethical and accordingly prior to nature and biology.[83] Levinas describes how, in the drama of maternal natality, "I am bound to others before being tied to my body."[84] While natality in Levinas is primarily ethical, it is more immediately political and interconnected with rights themselves in Hannah Arendt's transformation of natural rights theory.[85]

Natality distinguishes the natural and the human orders in Levinas. The human is exemplified by the interpersonal; the nonhuman and natural is associated with the standpoint of third-person objectivity.[86] More radically anthropocentrically stated, human reality is the ethical reality for Levinas, because of the human face-to-face encounter, of "meeting and friendship" without any intermediary or communion. Levinas distinguishes the human from "all other reality," and thereby problematically limits the ethical to the human rather than expanding the ethical to other supposedly non-ethical forms of reality.[87] The concomitantly, Hebraically biblical, and prophetic materialist moment in Levinas's addressing of bodily and earthly needs and desires, sensual life and fecundity, interrupts the reduction of the nonhuman to objective relations by relating the human and nonhuman through embodiment and incarnation that is exterior to and exiled from itself. If such moments suggest an ethical obligation prior to and thus not isolated by intentionality and rationality, one can speak of a Levinasian, if not Levinas's own, animal ethics. This might be called, to use Llewelyn's phrase, a "humanism of the other animal"; yet this is still an overly anthropocentric expression in once again returning the animal to the human sphere and human values associated with humanism that in effect undermines what it intends: addressing animals in their own terms. The expression "humanism of the other animal" can be construed less anthropocentrically if one extends (1) Levinas's face beyond the human to the animal (an implausible option and misreading of the role of the face, as Diane Perpich has demonstrated), or (2) his concept of the ethically "human" beyond the factical biological species of the "human" (an option that does not recognize the problems of using the language of humanism).[88] A better alternative is to speak less anthropocentrically of an "ethics of the animal" in that the animal's "living from" is recognized as addressing me, demanding a reply that I answer or betray. If animal ethics is defined by empathy and identification with animals and their suffering, a strategy thrown into question by Levinas's ethics, then it will be inevitably inadequate and inappropriate to animal others to the extent that the heterogeneity of the human and nonhuman places such continuity and the solidarity of identification into question.

While Martin Buber's work *I and Thou* extends dialogical ethics to animals and vegetation, albeit not systematically, in disclosive encounters with the "bodying forth" (*leiben*) of the tree (encountered as a thou and other than an it) or the cat (its glance, the question posed to me in it, its communication), there is a scarcity of such moments in Levinas.[89] Even if there is a limited premonition of an animal ethics in Levinas that is in need of radical metamorphosis, as has been argued here, it remains questionable whether there can be an environmental ethics. Is the environment at best an issue of pragmatic concern insofar as pollution and global warming negatively affect human and animal life, or can environments and ecosystems place further obligations on human action and nonaction? Is it inevitably paganism to speak of an ethics of place and nature in the context of Levinas's writings, or can these be thought ethically—without nature or naturalism—through individuating encounter and confrontation that breaks with natural and social absorption and participation? Would not the claim that there is ethical transcendence in a melting glacier or in polluted wetlands be a perversion of Levinas's critique of personalizing the inhuman and depersonalizing the human? Glaciers and wetlands do not experience at all, much less experience need, want, and hunger.

Levinas's approach to nature is limited and inappropriate to the extent that the earth and its forests and mountains are places of exile over which the human individual and human sociality has unconditional priority.⁹⁰ Despite the suggestiveness of Levinas's "first" or "earthly morality" and his noninstrumental approach to the elemental, as well as his interlocking of sensibility and materiality, questions remain. First, as there is a limited role for the expression of natural integral wholes in Levinas, as exemplified by his rejection of the later Heidegger's quasienvironmental reflections, such a broader or more extended sense of environmental sensibilities or responsibilities appears dubious from a Levinasian perspective.⁹¹ Second, as there is no notion of the exploitation, domination, or reification of nature, but only of human and perhaps by extension animal life, it is difficult to make ecological claims ethical per se without fracturing Levinas's portrayal of the ethical itself given how closely it is entangled with the human. That is to say, it becomes possible by breaking with a number of assertions (the said) in Levinas's discourse by extending its potential to other creatures and modifying its orientation and direction to embrace animal beings and natural phenomena without reserve and restrictions.

Levinas suggests multiple beginnings for environmental reflection and engagement that can be extended and ecologically reimagined by his readers. He contests the limited materialism of the Enlightenment and Marxism while recognizing their ethical orientation and promise and the materiality of ethical existence that he returns to in *Existence and Existents* and *Totality and Infinity*.⁹² His "humanism of the other," an other who is not merely human understood as an anthropological category, incorporates elements such as sensuous fulfillment and happiness from humanistic materialism and socialism, which he praises to the extent that they rely on an ethical orientation toward the other as sensuous material other.⁹³ This meditation on ethical materiality, which insists that "matter is the very locus of the for-the-other" (which will be revisited below), is associated with the self being a sensuous creature.⁹⁴ Even though it is the human being rather than the animal that says "Here I am," the nonresponse of the other does not excuse my evading my responsibility for that other. This reflection should be extended to other animals to the extent that "our material nature is the very fulfillment of solidarity within being."⁹⁵ That is, insofar as asymmetry is the condition of responsibility, animals are encountered as material sensuous beings who enjoy and suffer, that is, who live from the elements and are invested with some form of sensibility and sense, and therefore cannot be excluded from human responsibility. As a consequence, the revelation of the "face"—to think with Levinas against Levinas—is ambiguously prior to a human face and can be a face without human biological or anthropological characteristics: that is, a nonhuman face.

Levinas's humanism remains, perhaps rightfully, structurally incompatible with ecological biocentrism and biological or other varieties of naturalism that affirm the priority of the natural or "nature as nature." Commenting on a second-century exegete, Levinas concludes, "[F]or if the earth had not been given to humans but simply taken by them, they would have possessed it only as an outlaw."[96] The earth is an issue of justice, not one immanent to nature. Accordingly, when asked about ecology in a late interview, Levinas considered it an issue of human economy and justice.[97] This answer might seem insufficient for antihumanist and deep green positions such as deep ecology, yet—as with Adorno's works—it presages the environmental justice movement.[98]

Natural Histories: Adorno on Animals and Environments

> Every single element in the web of delusion is nevertheless of relevance to the possible demise of that web. The good is what struggles free, finds a language, and opens its eyes. As something that struggles free, goodness is part of the texture of history which, without being unambiguously set on reconciliation, in the course of its movement illuminates the possibility of reconciliation in a momentary flash.
>
> —Theodor Adorno, *History and Freedom*

There is a potential if unrealized nonnaturalistic animal ethics via the moments of alterity and transcendence in Levinas, and a suggestive yet insufficient environmental ethics of urban and rural air, land, and water in their elemental import for humans. In the works of Adorno, another alternative is articulated through the oppositions between nature and history, and naturalism and constructivism, insofar as human beings are both natural beings and nonidentical with their immediate and natural existence.[99] Adorno advocates what might be described as an expansive nonreductive naturalness when he suggests that by becoming "conscious of their own naturalness," humans can "call a halt to their own domination of nature, a domination by means of which nature's own domination is perpetuated."[100]

Adorno and Levinas's argumentation and sensibility share overlapping features, while pursuing a different philosophical strategy with divergent premises and stakes. Despite their distance, to name one example, they share overlapping critiques of "totality," the comprehensible graspability of things in a system, which Adorno already critiqued in relation to what he considered to be Heidegger's residual idealism in his lecture "The Actuality of Philosophy" (1931).[101] The critique of totality as the "universal coercive mechanism" that unfolded in Adorno's mature thought occurs via the nonidentity that identity thinking denies and cannot overcome.[102] Adorno's tactics against totality have preconceptual and dialectically disruptive tendencies analogous to Levinas's nondialectical language of alterity. They both contested scientific and romantic naturalisms as reductive and reactionary, associating the latter with fascism. Although Adorno is closer to materialism than Levinas, they both stressed (with the 1844 Marx) the material moment of sensuous human activity and fulfillment.

Levinas addressed "living from" as nourishment, enjoyment, labor, and fatigue. "Pain cannot be redeemed," according to Levinas, and "retribution in the future does not wipe away the pains of the present"; without any just retribution, he continues, "[t]o hope then is to hope for the reparation of the irreparable; it is to hope for the present."[103] The utopian and messianic hope for the "redemption of the flesh," that is, of earthly existence and worldly needs and desires in the present, remains for Adorno a justification of materialism.[104] The implicit promise of society, however much betrayed, he writes, "would be to negate the physical suffering of even the least of its members, and to negate the internal reflexive forms of that suffering. By now, this negation in the interest of all can be realized only in a solidarity that is transparent to itself and all the living."[105] Life is not a factual biological claim for either thinker; it calls for addressing suffering and injustice. If letting suffering speak is the condition of truth, as Adorno notes, then truth is simultaneously material and ethical.[106] Truth is fundamentally an ethical imperative rather than an ontological event.

The Stendhalian "promise of happiness" remains unfilled. It cannot be fulfilled but remains utopian, while the historical materialism that would fulfill the call to more adequately recognize human rights and well-being has been debased and betrayed through its historical realization. Between utopianism and betrayal, the materialist and imperfectionist dialectic of suffering and happiness and of the damaged and the good life remains, for Adorno, crucial (if in negative form): "Art records negatively just that possibility of happiness that the only partially positive anticipation of happiness ruinously confronts today [. . .] the promise of happiness, once the definition of art, can no longer be found except where the mask has been torn from the countenance of false happiness."[107] This insight does not only apply to the aesthetic. Without the reference of reflection and rationality to concrete needs, interests, and their satisfaction, universal reason becomes irrational domination through the loss of the individual and its material nonidentical contexts.[108] This is the one-sidedness of Hegel's philosophy of history, and religious and secularized theodicies more generally, which ask the victims to acquiesce in their own mutilation in being consoled by the universal, as "the consciousness of non-identity that characterizes the particular is stripped of its own substantiality and survives only as suffering, as a consciousness of pain."[109]

Absorbed and spellbound in the appearance of immediacy, spontaneity is reduced to consumption, and happiness to pleasure.[110] Material and sensuous praxis and the promise of its fulfillment in happiness and the good life resists existing reality.[111] This promise continues to orient Adorno's critical social models and a negative dialectic that does not arrive at a final reconciliation or repose. Its infinite disintegrating movement seems, and not only at first glance or on a preliminary reading, to turn positive claims to naught in order to release their promise. The impression of a negativity without its emancipatory function of releasement informs many (mis)readings of Adorno. To take one example, in Robert Manning's reading of Levinas, he argues against Adorno's negativity in a similar vein to Habermas's separation of facticity and normativity but now in the name of a duality between immanence and transcendence attributed to Levinas, concluding that Adorno's thought "cannot excavate the meaning of its own ethical sense," since it "is an entirely negative strategy of reflection, an entirely critical theory."[112]

In "Marginalia to Theory and Practice" of *Critical Models*, Adorno does not reject the prereflective and pretheoretical spontaneity and positivity of praxis as such; he rejects rather the fixation on and reification of practice that devalues theory, reflection, and the labor of the concept to the detriment of practice itself.[113] Spontaneity needs reflectivity and the confrontation with material and social realities if it is not to be fully co-opted.[114] Sensuous enjoyment remains a reference point both in a moving constellation for critical thought as well as in its being compelled to obey the logic of the fetish character of the commodity. It is a suspect in that it is commodified and instrumentalized to the neglect of the individuation of the self and the injustice and suffering of others.[115] In his ostensible pessimistic late essay "Resignation," in which he challenges the student movement, Adorno articulates thinking as a practice of resistance that, however imperfect, damaged, and compromised, is still bound to its own and humanity's happiness.[116] Adorno is not a negative, reflective, or abstract theoretical thinker. The elucidation of suffering and happiness is at the core of his thought. This configuration involves both ethical and utopian moments that allow Adorno to articulate a powerful critique of suffering, which he extends to animals and nature itself.

Adorno, analogously with Levinas, criticized scientific and romantic naturalisms. Instead of destroying transcendence, according to Adorno, their portrayals of nature as objective factuality, struggle for existence and self-assertion, or idyllic paradise reflect ideology and consequently social domination. Ideology is relentless to the degree that it is most powerful in the construction of identities, where second nature takes on the appearance of an unchanging first nature, "at the very moment when people believe they are most themselves and belong to themselves."[117] Social domination, tied to human domination of nature, is revealed through immanent critique rather than being interrupted through a transcendence outside of natural history. The self-critique of immanence—which cannot result in an external or total critique, as it is mediated and tainted by what it criticizes—brings a different focus to the critique of nature. Adorno does not eliminate nature by reducing it to an ideological function. While interrogating its reductive, ideologically determined conceptualizations, social-ethical possibilities of nature in its nonidentity remain significant for damaged life. For Adorno, we are compelled to recognize the material and objective side of history "once we realize that we are its potential victims."[118] This same facticity is the possibility of critique and transformation.

As a result of Adorno's aporetic and ethical materialism—and "materialism" for Adorno means "the preponderance of the object" and the rejection of the reduction of objects to the organizing knowing subject—nature is not absorbed without residue or excess into subjectivity or an intersubjectively reproduced totality.[119] Normalizing discourses of the subject are themselves inadequate to the contradictory nonidentity of actual subjects in the conditionality and fragility of their material bodily being.[120] As John Drabinski aptly phrases it, in a depiction of Levinas's understanding of the self as a nonformal and sensuous contradictory configuration, which could well describe Adorno's thinking of the self: "Contradiction is the very life of the interrupted subject."[121] "Contradiction qua sensation," Levinas remarked, is "the ache of pain—woe."[122]

The forces of material nature and the contradictions between material and social forces not only haunt individuals and societies but also cause harm and suffering. Instead of taking Levinas's route of transcendence as the disturbance of totality and the same, it is worldly immanence itself that upsets itself, its social totalization, and fixation via the logic of equivalence through identity and exchange. The absolute Otherness of alterity is an an-archic exteriority and transcendence for Levinas, and negativity and nonidentity remain dialectical and insufficient in regard to the transcendent. Otherness and nonidentity are immanent or internal to things themselves and their relatedness for Adorno.[123] This is possible because Adorno does not identify immanence with essence, identity, or totality.[124] Accordingly, not only other humans—or their subjectivity—but things or objects themselves can be interruptive insofar as they resist assimilation or throw a systematic order into question. The social totality exercises power over each thing, and we are absorbed in and enthralled by those things.[125] Resistance is inevitably mediated by the categories and structures it defies: the "truth beyond coercive identity would not be its absolute Other, but would always pass through that coercive identity and be mediated by it."[126] In the face of a situation of unavoidable complicity with domination, even in resisting it, critical thought cannot evade its own weakness.[127]

Just as mediation is antagonistic and aporetic rather than completely integrated insofar as nonidentity constitutes the movement of identity, so too resistance still occurs.[128] It can come not only on the side of the object, in its irreducibility and transcendence, concerning which Adorno is more hopeful than Levinas. It can also occur in the moment of reflection and in the distance that thought can take in relation to its context.[129] In both cases, Adorno associates interruption with the interworldly instead of with otherworldly otherness. He considers that the ontic, material, and empirical character of worldly immanence acts to disturb and reorient thought and practice. Adorno's discourse achieves this without overly relying on a religious language of God and a transcendence and infinity that are beyond and otherwise than being, a topic addressed in detail in part 2. Such indirect attention to the empirical and to the object, the irreducible "additional factor" (*das Hinzutretende*), must remain risky and tentative given the ideological manipulation and loss of empirical reality.[130]

The critique of empirical and pragmatic perspectives as reproducing the status quo played a key part in Horkheimer and Adorno's dispute with pragmatic instrumentalists such as "Dewey's Bulldog" Sydney Hook in the 1940s and the "positivist dispute in German sociology" of the 1960s concerning whether the empirical corrects ideology or is already ideologically shaped such that it reconfirms pragmatically justified existing relations of domination and exploitation.[131] Nevertheless, while challenging its ideological uses, Adorno does not abandon the empirical moment. The Frankfurt school's early project of interdisciplinary materialism has not vanished: Adorno continued to pursue and theorize theoretically informed empirical inquiry and suggested that there is a dialectical tension in the empirical such that it is more than an ideological mediation.

Adorno and Levinas were the most relentless critics of ontological thinking in Heidegger, and not only due to its connections with national socialism. But their assessments move in different directions from one another. For Levinas, natural and material things have a relative otherness incomparable with the unconditional and interruptive alterity of the wholly Other. Levinas criticized Heidegger's being in the name of the human other that transcends it. Adorno criticized ontological being for the sake of beings, which dislocate it from within in their multiplicity, heterogeneity, and nonidentity. Adorno hence associates the nonidentity of nature with its multiplicity and diffuseness.[132] Such nonidentity already marks an ethical relation.

While challenging conventional understandings of nature and naturalism, for reasons similar to those of Levinas, the relation between history and nature is a central issue from Adorno's early to later works. In the early 1930s Adorno engaged the aporia of history and nature—or their intractable paradox—as constitutive and inescapable. He called for thinking both from the notion of "natural history" that removes the typical antithesis of nature and from the notion of history by naturalizing the historical while historicizing the natural.[133] Nature is history in the sense of what has already become. What is called human nature is a product of what humans have been so far.[134] History is nature in the sense of activating and forming nature, and the possibilities of the new that such transformation implies. That is to say, history and nature are both occurrences of second nature, of what is reified as fixed and unchanging.

Humans are natural beings, and nature is the inorganic body of human life for Marx. Along with the utopian ideal of an unforced human reconciliation between humans and nature, Marx had a second differential way of perceiving humans as a particular realization and universalization of nature. Despite the image of inverting Hegel, not by standing him on his head, as inversions usually go, but by putting him back on his feet, Marx retained the Hegelian overcoming of nature in depicting the realization of human freedom as the end of natural history and the beginning of genuine history as rationally shaped through human agency. For the young Marx, "nature as nature" is a fiction and the elimination of nature is the emergence of free individuality.[135] Adorno repeatedly employed the idea of "natural history" in both senses: one focused on entanglement and reconciliation, and the other indicating the lingering tension between nature and spirit in a being that is both naturally and socially conditioned and able to modify its conditions.

Adorno distinguished the vulgar naturalistic from the critical reflective use of the category of "natural history," addressing it as a productive paradox.[136] This aporia is seen in the tension between the ideological construction and the implicit promise of organic and animal life; between the material and bodily bonds at the juncture of human and animal life, happiness, and suffering; and the possibility of an unforced and noncoercive sensuous responsiveness and ethical appropriateness to animals and natural phenomena.

If we trace this material moment to art, we find an aesthetics of nature in Adorno that is lacking in Levinas, for whom the aesthetic and the cultural are derivative of the ethical.[137] Here too there is a moment of nonidentity and nonequivalence, of sensuous freedom and the responsiveness of the mimetic. Plato had argued, to speak summarily, that art is a copy of the real that in turn is a copy of the ideal, a copy of a copy, such that there is a double mimesis. Adorno elucidates the significance of the aesthetic moment against its idealistic and rationalist critics. As noted previously, Adorno's art indicates its disruptive and redemptive moments. Art is not inexorably myth and idolatry condemned by Plato, who exiled deceitful poets from his republic. Levinas expressed suspicions concerning the aesthetic and playfulness of obscuring egoism and violence in the essay "Reality and its Shadow" (1948), but this reflection should be situated in the context of his more affirmative depiction of aesthetics and its import for ethics in another essay from the same period "The Other in Proust" (1947).[138] Levinas noted in the latter essay the proximity of art to desire, eros, and sensibility. His later reflections on art, such as the interview in *On Obliteration* (1988), reveal its ethical character and how art interrupts and obliterates the enchantment of being and presence, thus calling to the sociality of being for others.[139]

Adorno does not only critique mimesis as enchantment and enslavement. He articulates the potential nonidentity of freedom and dependence in mimesis, and identifies a moment of Enlightenment in myth, rejecting the reactionary archaism that cannot find what it pursues—an origin uncontaminated by reflection. Adorno speaks of an art and a materialism without images, and critically employs the language of the Judaic prohibition of images and idols.[140] It is questionable whether Adorno enacts the emptying of form to the degree that Levinas does. Levinas traces how the image can be a nonidol teaching a disinterestedness the enchantment of what is.[141] The conditional embodied self mimetically models itself on its external world, whether in terms of its playfulness and ease or its hardness and coldness in Adorno.[142] Levinas analyzed the fixation of the spontaneity of the body in an analogous way: as it is "exposed to violence, spontaneity undergoes, turns into its contrary."[143] Absorbed and enchanted identification allows no distance, just as identity thinking endeavors to integrate and subjugate each alterity. Both are derivatives of mimesis that do not exhaust its other roles or possibilities.

Asher Horowitz argues that mimesis contains references both to the desire for the object and its irresolvable exteriority.[144] This is the ambivalent logic of desire for alterity that Levinas addressed in *Totality and Infinity* as metaphysical desire for the infinite.[145] Levinas described this mimetic moment as regressive, warning of how poetry can be magic and art idolatry insofar as it fails to obliterate presence.[146] The obliteration of being is not, however, a negation of desire, the material, and the sensuous, as he makes clear in his 1947 essay on Proust.[147] Art is intertwined with the sufferings and wounds of material existence in Levinas as well as in Adorno. Levinas cannot avoid presupposing and employing the mimetic to critique the mimetic, a possibility inherent in mimesis itself.[148] Mimesis, identification, and art can accordingly be either enslavement or emancipation, as it is for Adorno, who did not restrict it to the human, as Aristotle did. Thinking with and beyond Adorno and Levinas, such mimesis is erotic and sensuous in its spontaneity and receptivity across organic life hinting at the unrestricted solidarity of suffering material life. Such identification and recognition of alterity, that is, of a responsiveness irreducible to mechanical stimulus and reaction, is decisive for a more radical response to the question of the animal and its suffering.[149]

This revisionary nonreductive materialist strategy allows Adorno, similar to his colleague Horkheimer, to address animal as well as human suffering as part of the human domination of nature. Although Adorno does not appear to think much of animals' natural capacities, he does bring attention to their suffering. According to Adorno, obliviousness to suffering, whether animal or human, is based on the same coldness and insensibility that allows maltreatment of horses and Auschwitz to be possible.[150] In a significant passage from *Minima Moralia*, Adorno interconnects the racializing dehumanization to the distancing abjection of the animal.[151] Framed and constructed as other, dehumanized persons and degraded creatures are damaged life that cannot resist the totalizing gaze. The deep shudder and its absence in indifference and cruelty reveal fundamental characteristics about morality in human nature.[152] Adorno retains an anthropological element in his ethical reflections on living a damaged life in ways that contest the mechanisms of its damage. Levinas by contrast stresses the transcendent Otherness breaking in upon the immanence of human existence, revealing a passivity more passive—that is, responsibility—than can be found in the qualities of human anthropology and psychology.

Adorno links racism and speciesism as two consequences of the same dialectic of the domination of nature. Racism and speciesism both seek to animalize the other, as the inhuman that is categorically different from the standard of humanity. The inhuman is subject to human wrath, as the possibility of pogrom and genocide emerges in the power relation between human and inhuman subjects. "[It] is decided in the moment when the gaze of a fatally-wounded animal falls on a human being"; the powerful perceive "as human only their own reflected image, instead of reflecting back the human as precisely what is different." The stirring sufferings of the other in this case "can no longer refute the manic gaze."[153] Despite the animal's vulnerability and defenselessness, which are distinctive of organic life, and not the human face alone, its suffering reveals that it is more than a construct and product of human calculation, discourse, and power.

Human revulsion and fear of animality, employed to justify human degradation of animals, is part of humanity's own animality. The absolute difference between the body's animality and the humanity of the person, which Levinas himself upheld, is a thesis that Adorno condemned in Kant in a passage that Derrida employs to differentiate Levinas and Adorno regarding the animal.[154]

Animality links the mastery of both "inner" human and "outer" animal with environmental nature.[155] Adorno and Horkheimer analyzed the Baconian domination of nature, based historically in human lack and need and on the growing equation of knowledge and power, as part of the same historical process by which humans dominate one another.[156] This analysis, genealogically traced by Adorno and Horkheimer in the *Dialectic of Enlightenment,* allows Adorno in his later writing to diagnose environmentally destructive phenomena, without mystifying or sacralizing them. Romanticism concerning nature is part of its domination, as Adorno argues in his analyses of the natural in Wagner and Heidegger.[157] Different aspects of nature are tamed or marginalized, and celebrated or demonized.[158] The domination of nature is the social-historical subjugation of natural phenomena as alien, different, and other.[159] Such domination informs the exploitation and suppression of phenomena seen as natural, from the environment to the ideological naturalization of the human body in racism.[160] Adorno describes racism as a socially produced semblance of nature. Racism—which continues to fundamentally structure society under the guise of a liberal postracial polity—is the perverse revenge of mutilated natural life as dominated nature is put to work for its intensified domination.[161]

The thoroughly "planned, cultivated, and organized" designed formation of second nature, presented through natural reserves and the ideological construction of what is to be encountered as natural, appears as first nature.[162] Although the conventional and social are taken to be nature, "primary nature"—consisting of the objective and material context of human thought and practice—is irreducible to its social construction. That is, irreducible to the extent that the priority of the social in how humans interact with natural phenomena does not entail the reduction of nature to social ontology.[163] Idealism and its linguistic and social constructivist derivatives correctly historicize nature but misconstrue history as nature, reducing the nonidentical to the identity of mind, history, language, or society.[164] Such positions cannot take animals and environments to be ethical, that is—in the Levinasian sense of exteriority—any more than their construction and projection, which is, in effect, their domination. Although thought is interpretive, the reduction of reflection to interpretation undermines possibilities for critique and altered practice.[165] As an alternative strategy, Adorno argues that "natural history" itself indicates a model for interpretation, in which nature is read from history and history from nature.[166] Both are revealed in their antagonistic dynamism and ephemeral transience, in their nonidentity; immanent critique struggles to liberate immanence from itself, and its own fetishization, allowing what is other than itself to be encountered.[167]

Adorno's portrayal of the alterity of the natural, sensed through mimetic faculties, does not require that nature be defined via its reduction to the human or sacred, even if it is in relation to the human in their mutual natural history. As a consequence—and indications of this are found in Adorno's *Aesthetic Theory*—natural wholes, such as landscapes and environments, an acknowledgment of which is not completely absent in Levinas, can be recognized. They can be appreciated as having an immanent worth in their difference without necessarily appealing to what transcends them and only outwardly giving them meaning or value.

Adorno and the Culture of Nature

Adorno's works interlink history and nature and the various forms of communication and power, including the conformist and authoritarian character of how consensus reflects social mechanisms. This nexus is lost in Habermas and the later Frankfurt school.[168] Through this "critical model," one can attempt to respond to the heterogeneity of human and animal life without reducing that diverse and myriad life to either a hypostatized anthropocentric humanistic ideal, oblivious to the nonhuman in its presumed dominion over its world, or a predestined fatality of reified nature instrumentalized in the "struggle for existence" and biosocial mastery. The link between biologistic self-assertion and biosocial control is the domination of nature, an issue mentioned albeit inadequately addressed by Levinas, who does not sufficiently question the structures of modern Western civilization from the perspective of dominated nature.[169]

Freedom consists in the breaking of and resistance to such spells.[170] Freedom resists totalization and identity in Adorno, since it presupposes the category of the individual and the individual's reflection, just as a singular being in its ipseity resists its totalization through its separation in Levinas.[171] Resistance is possible at each conjuncture, since freedom is a social-historical category that is related to the natural bases of human life in impulse, spontaneity, and sensuous activity.[172] Although Levinas criticized the egoism, mastery, and virility of natural spontaneity, arguing that freedom is other- rather than self-constituted through responsibility and the ethical demand, he does not reject spontaneity or its ethical import entirely.[173]

The affective, bodily, and sensuous enactment of the ethical via responsiveness brings Levinas into an ambivalent proximity to a materialism of sensuous ethical existence without worldly enchantment and thingly idolatry, articulated by Adorno, which Levinas did not sufficiently foresee.[174] Levinas accordingly inconsistently points the way toward an ethical materialism of sensuous existence and material others. Levinas identifies materiality with the captivity and solitude of identity and matter, to be shattered by the time of the other, which becomes totalitarian through anonymity and the enchainment of the self to the body.[175] The body, as the experience of materiality—indeed of "a materiality more material than all matter"—is not a possession or instrument.[176] It is an affair or episode—which cannot be reduced to an ontological event—wherein humans encounter their existence, and "exposedness to wounds and outrage."[177] The self as body is affected and persecuted in spite of itself.[178] Materiality is ethical through the affectivity of embodied existence and bodily responsiveness to others in recognizing their distress, lack, and need. The ethics of the body is seen not only in response to bodily pain and need but also in moments of proximity and love, such as the receptive spontaneity of the caress in contrast to controlling, grasping touch.[179]

Adorno's receptive and spontaneous mimetic behavior is part of freedom itself, even if it cannot be reduced to reason; it is thus neither a merely negative freedom nor a rational freedom (autonomy), independent of the mediations of social and material life, in the classical Kantian conception.[180] The social and natural contexts of freedom do not inevitably entail its reductive elimination, since autonomy is bound to and only realizable in relation to the heterogeneity and materiality that constitute human life.[181] Resistance to injustice, Adorno states, is "the true primal phenomenon of moral behavior," and "[i]t occurs when the element of impulse joins forces with the element of consciousness to bring about a spontaneous act."[182]

Addressing ecological and environmental crises need not revert to metaphysical essentialism about inherent and eternal laws of nature. Nor must it romantically enchant us with fetishized images of nature that obscure the realities of human domination and suffering, nor be simply another anthropocentric calculation about how useful it might be to recognize the natural and the animal.

Even while Adorno and Levinas are—to varying degrees—complicit with what they criticize, as critique "lives from" its object, their interpretive strategies can be employed beyond the historical facticity and limits of their works to promote a critical environmental reflection that is necessary for environmental ethics and practical engagement.[183]

Ethical Responsiveness, Imperfectionism, and Minimalism

Adorno's articulation of a critical natural history in coordination with Levinas's articulation of a culture oriented toward the ethical offers a suggestive critical model for environmental reflection. Instead of appealing to nature in itself or as such, this model suggests an ethically informed society or culture that has the capacity to recognize, appreciate, and respond to animal others and the conditions of nourishment in the natural, the environmental, and the animal as more than a human construct or object of self-interested instrumental calculation. Such a culture of asymmetrically and mutually nourishing and cultivating nature would let beings and environments be encountered in their singular uniqueness as well as their nonhomogeneous organic continuity with our own life and well-being. Thomas Heyd has described such a prospect as "environmental culture," a society in which a practical and effective environmental conscience is possible.[184]

To echo Levinas's saying, the intensifying crises of the environment and the very existence of species in its "non-postponable urgency" calls for a response, that is, justice and solidarity in an ethical asymmetry and difference no longer restricted to the human.[185] An environmental society or culture of nourishing life presupposes individual as well as social transformation from—to adopt Levinas's language—an "allergic" to a "nonallergic" relation to the other that encompasses material others such as animals and environments. Levinas's use of these expressions keep the Greek sense in mind: *allos* (ἄλλος) signifies "other" and *ergon* (ἔργον) "work" (allergy as "other-effect").[186] Adorno and Levinas situate such hope in the context of the "critique of" (for Adorno) or "otherwise than" (for Levinas, who does not use the language of critique) totality and identity while recognizing the limitations and complicity of such critique. As Hegel's dialectic itself revealed, and to which Adorno in particular and Levinas to a lesser extent are indebted despite their criticisms of the Hegelian form of the dialectic, critique and "the otherwise" are inevitably to some degree beholden and indebted to the object that it seeks to betray.[187] Even if such concepts are to some extent exaggerated when applied to contemporary societies, they retain a critical import relevant to our current situation. Rather than demanding more overcoming and control, or a new union or fusion of nature and society, both authors advocate less. Such maximalism furthers more identity and consequently injustice to the nonidentical, and liberation from identity calls for "self-limitation."[188]

The project of a *minima moralia* allows for the resuscitation of spontaneity and responsiveness, which are frozen as clichés and compulsive consumptive behaviors in a form of capitalism that demands endlessly maximizing production and consumption and thus competition and conflict that is typically displaced to the edges and fracture points of the international order, as with the weakest points in the developing world. The minimalistic ethos and comportment of Adorno's *minima moralia* evokes a humility and self-limitation instead of self-assertion in relation to others in society and natural beings in the world. Such minimalism concerns nature and society, countering the logic of exchange, commodity fetishism, and consumerism diagnosed in varying degrees by both Levinas and the Frankfurt school. Their analysis of this logic has significant environmental implications in the face of the economic reductionism and commodification of nature that promotes both environmental devastation and social injustice.[189]

A responsive—rather than ascetic self-denying and disciplinary other-controlling—minimalism is appreciably rational in that it allows the critique of reified forms of rationality without rejecting the critical transformative nonidentical moment in reason. Responding to the object, such as animals and environments and their damages, calls for the nonabsorbed yet nonindifferent distance and reflection as well as the engagement of immediacy and affectivity. To succeed at being rational, reason need not be a form of totalizing identity thinking. Levinas contends that radical pluralism, and the responsibility it entails, is a condition of reason.[190] It is not rationality, the sciences, and technology that are irrational; the irrational lies in their overextension and instrumentalization. As reified, they can no longer be responsive to things or to their human agents.

The antinomies deforming and limiting modern rationality, distanced from its sensuous and mimetic sources, reflects processes of instrumental rationalization of nature and society from which it cannot be detached.

These antinomies are inescapable insofar as reason is caught up in domination and exploitation while simultaneously promising conciliation without force or coercion.[191] Adorno's conciliation, in the language of Levinas, would be the ethical peace of solidarity in relation to alterity, as opposed to the identity formed by the peace of absorption; and it would equate to what Levinas thematized as the eschatological moment.[192]

In accordance with its mediated dialectical formation, rationality precariously enables both apologetic ideology and its critique.[193] Levinas is distrustful of dialectic, in particular Hegel's dialectic, insofar as it is totalizing and ontological. Adorno's "negative dialectics" is antitotalizing, refusing the moment of synthesis and reconciliation, and antiontological.[194] Adorno describes in his *Lectures on Negative Dialectics* (1965–1966) how negative dialectics contests "the identity of being and thought" in articulating "the divergence of concept and thing, subject and object."[195] This aporetic and nonidentical dialectic—and dialectical thinking is aporetic after the collapse of metaphysics that would positively resolve aporias—breaches the ontology of being from within itself by exposing the falsity of forced alternatives. Forced alternatives one-sidedly hold on to their moment of truth (identity or difference, humanity or nature) as part of the reproduction of damaged life that immanently critiques its own damages according to the imperfectionist reconstruction of Adorno unfolded in this work (with its ruined figures and exhausted faces hoping for what is otherwise) instead of life as a dynamically open configuration.

Conclusion and Transition to Part Two

> Philosophy exists in order to redeem what you see in the look of an animal.
>
> —Theodor Adorno, *Towards a New Manifesto*

The look of the animal addresses me and makes a claim upon me. Philosophy is, according to Adorno, doing justice to the thing. The "thing" in Adorno is construed in its widest sense to address objects, minerals, plants, and nonhuman and human animals. The other, whether nonhuman or human, demands justice in the materially and intersubjectively reproduced world that conditions them and their circumstances. The material world is already the ethical world.

Part 1 has attempted to elucidate the natural historical entanglements; the material otherness of animals, environments, and nature; and the questionable consequences of the domination and mastery of nature for nonhuman and human animal life through an interpretative encounter with Adorno, Levinas, and the critical social theory of the Frankfurt school.

The transition from part 1 to part 2, from natural history to prophetic religion, consists of a shift between discursive-practical formations that institutionalize, reproduce, and ideologically promote visions of identity, sameness, and totality while nonetheless (in its prophetic and other-oriented moments) indicating what is otherwise through moments of radical alterity, materiality, and nonidentity. Discourses of nature and religion have ideological identity-forming and critical other-directed and constructive functions. As there can be no return to the immediacy of a pure nature free of social-historical and cultural mediations, and the labor of discourse and conceptualization, what is called for is the cultivation and formation of more appropriate cultures and political economies of nature (that is, after the end of nature, of nourishing life), in the context of natural historical analysis, beyond the opposition of the inhuman and the human, or biocentric nature and anthropocentric humanity.

Part Two

Unsettling Religion

Suffering, Prophecy, and the Good

Chapter Six

Religion, Suffering, and Damaged Life

Nietzsche, Marx, and Adorno

At bottom, the concept of life as a meaningful unity unfolding from within itself has ceased to possess any reality, much like the individual himself, and the ideological function of biographies consists in demonstrating to people with reference to various models that something like life still exists, with all the emphatic qualities of life.

—Theodor Adorno, letter to Leo Löwenthal, November 24, 1942

Introduction to Part Two

Adorno not only articulated a critical model or heuristic of damaged and mutilated life in his analysis of modern capitalist social intercourse and reproduction. He personally reflected on his own damaged life, in particular in response to the rise of national socialism, his exile, and the fact of Auschwitz. Adorno's discourse of negation (in which negation is not conceived as a reiteration of totality, as in Levinas) intimates an ethos of hope that is revealed in negativity itself as the denial of injustice and suffering. While Adorno does not as directly rely on prophetic language to the extent of Benjamin, Bloch, or Levinas, a prophetic response to reality emerges from within the damaged and destitute life that is the matter itself in question.

Questions of life and—to use Adorno's expression—damaged life are interconnected with the domination and mastery of nature, as nonhuman and human animals and ecosystems are damaged for the sake of profit according to the logic of exchange that is a form of self-domination for the sake of dominating what is otherwise, as has been diagnosed in part 1 of this volume. The question of mimetic and damaged life is bound up with nature and a primary topic of part 2: "religion" and its mythopoetic and prophetic relations with suffering and violence. As religion refers to diverse complexly and concretely mediated phenomena, it encompasses moments of repression (e.g., sacred violence, systematic domination, and arbitrary terror) as well as moments of emancipation (e.g., hope, prophecy, and witnessing for the abject and the oppressed).

Religions operate as ideological disguises and hegemonic regimes of this-worldly power that demand ascetic and sacrificial practices and exact heavy costs in lives and suffering according to their own logic of exchange. Nonetheless, at the same time, as will be examined in part 2, it calls for love and compassion for all beings and prophetically promises to break the spell of power, sacrifice, and suffering. Religion is, among many other things, in addition to the current attention to its pathology and promise, ideological and oppressive as well as expressive of prophetically inspired hope for forgiveness, happiness, and justice. Benjamin remarked in his "Theses on the Philosophy of History" that "our image of happiness is indissolubly bound up with the image of redemption."[1] Adorno describes in *Minima Moralia* how redemption is the perspective of philosophy that opposes despair by perceiving things in another guise than their domination.[2] Like the idea of communism itself, at least as the prophetic idea of an unrestricted solidarity intimated by Marx in the *Economic-Philosophic Manuscripts* (1844), religions legitimate and serve oppressive regimes and institutions as well as inspire reorienting critiques and transformations of the existing material and ethical conditions of life. According to Marx in *A Contribution to the Critique of Hegel's Philosophy of Right* (1844), "Religious suffering is, at one and the same time, the expression of real suffering and a protest against genuine suffering. Religion is the sigh of the oppressed creature, the heart of a heartless world, and it is the spirit of spiritless conditions."[3] Marx follows this statement with his well-known image of religion being the "opium of the people," the halo of this veil of tears, which temporarily helps to cope with the pain but fails to confront the underlying pathology. In the diagnosis offered by Marx and Nietzsche, who are both concerned with genuine real needs that are the basis of revolutionary change or self-transformation, religion establishes a false therapeutics that cannot heal the wounds that called it into being.

Religious desire and expression, born of suffering life itself, appears to be more and other than—as Hegel argued in his account of the Enlightenment's critique of faith in the *Phenomenology of Spirit*—reactionary repression and the priestly manipulation of desires.[4] Even as religion is this, and even worse in its social coercion, persecutions, and holy wars, it is otherwise than this, not so much in Hegel's idea of religious community as in its prophetic and ethical calling. Levinas remarked that prophecy is the fundamental form of revelation, as answering for others and a responsibility prior to natural or divine law.[5] This prophetic truth of religion is revealed in critical materialist demystifications of religion that would emancipate prophetic justice from Spinoza through Marx to Benjamin and Adorno.[6]

Horkheimer described in a *Spiegel* interview, "What We Call 'Meaning' Will Disappear" (1970), how the thought of Adorno and himself expressed a deep unattainable (*unerfüllbaren*) "longing for the other" (*Sehnsucht nach dem Anderen*), using a phrase now associated with Levinas.[7] Horkheimer notes in this interview how the two of them, relying on a Jewish understanding of refusing to name God or to idolatrize, rejected identifying this longing with names such as "God" or "Heaven" (determinate forms of religious language and imagery) or a determinate form of justice or utopia (as in dogmatic Marxism). The interview warns against both the reification of the religious in names and idols, and the ways in which its destruction would undermine meaningfulness itself. Meaning disappears and politics becomes mere business without that which is expressed in what Horkheimer designates theology. Whereas Horkheimer falls into an increasingly conservative anti-Marxist political theology, prioritizing theology over the political, his friend and collaborator Adorno intensifies the political theological problematic thematized in Marx's early writings: religion operates as power and ideology and as the expression of truth—the truth of oppression, suffering, and impossible hope that informs the aspirations of prophetic critique and critical social theory.

There are correlations in Levinas's argumentation, in which the good and the just have a prophetic exteriority to the social totality that cannot be eliminated if they are not to be lost in the equivalence and exchange of the logic of sameness. In expressing deep longings for what is wholly and infinitely otherwise, religion has multiple functions in relation to material suffering in that religion expresses it and potentially excuses and legitimates it. Religion, as prophetic, is accordingly the second name (after nature in part 1 and before justice in part 3) to be considered in this volume. Each name is a heuristic or critical model for interrogating the violence of discourses of nature, religion, and justice, and for prophetically exposing and questioning their violence. The "determinate negation"—to use this phrase in Adorno's sense—of priestly power (and their secularized incarnations in the economy, bureaucracy, and the intelligentsia) over the oppressed is not a liberal secularization complicit with the damage and suffering produced by the existing social-political order. It is "first philosophy"—reading Levinas apropos Enrique Dussel—in the sense of unruly prophecy of and for the abject and the oppressed: "Philosophical intelligence is never so truthful, pure, and precise as when it starts from oppression and does not have any privileges to defend, because it has none at all."[8] Privileged intellectuals can take the realities of injustice and suffering as the point of departure for critical diagnostic reflection instead of assuming justice is both the norm and the reality. The religious sense of hope for the hopeless, which can potentially issue in transformative prophetic critique of the hegemonic order as well as prophetic ethics (as indicated in Dussel's works), is expressed in 2 Corinthians 4:8–9 with reference to the persecuted: "We are troubled on every side, yet not crushed; we are perplexed, but not in despair; persecuted, but not forsaken; cast down, but not destroyed."[9]

To address schematically the transition from part 1 to part 2 of this volume, oriented by the discussions of material ethical life (for example, its material others and environmental situations and conditions) in part 1 of this volume, the topic of religion in part 2 intimates and prepares—through the religious topics of forgiveness and pardon, hope and prophecy, love and compassion, as well as the promise of happiness and redemption in encountering the inflicted damages and insufficiency, incompletion, and imperfection of existence (traditionally identified in occidental ontotheology with evil, sin, and fallenness from the sufficiency and positivity of being or God)—the way for questioning capitalist modernity with respect to the topics of equality, freedom, tolerance, and standard narratives of liberal justice in part 3.

Religion as and against Power

Levinas posed the question, how is one not duped by ethics? He designates the answer to this question "religion"—living for more than oneself in living for-the-other or someone else. But is religion not duping us through enchantment? Does religion not mandate conformity to a play of priestly illusion and power that numbs individuals and the masses into accepting their alterable conditions of life? Is religion, including Levinas's vision of religion as ethics and prophecy examined in chapters 7 and 8, another ideological narcotic, a variety of priestly power demanding the ultimate discipline of self-sacrifice for others and God?

Nietzsche's *Genealogy of Morality* constructs the image of priestly forms of power as a test stone for social-political suspicions about religion. This image continues to be a relevant critical model for examining ideological elites, particularly in light of the analysis of religion as ideology in Adorno's modeling of critical social theory. Comparable to an extent with Dostoevsky's exemplar of the Grand Inquisitor, Nietzsche's priestly figure is an exemplary portrayal of belief and fear employed to legitimate and orchestrate violence and domination, including violence against the self. Nietzsche's analysis entails more than this, since it radically interrogates its psychosocial dynamics. This destructuring strategy brings his discourse into proximity with those linked with the proper names Karl Marx and Sigmund Freud, which Paul Ricœur branded the hermeneutics of suspicion and yet which is not only suspicion.

This chapter examines the roles that pain, trauma, and damaged life—in Adorno's sense and in contrast to perfectionist and virtue ethical ideas of one idealized form of cultivation and the good life—play in the constitution and reproduction of power, with which religious and ethical discourses are inevitably entangled and can reproduce rather than cure, and the transformational aspirations that contest power relations. Nietzsche explored through the figure of the priest how the traumatic results of violence are concealed and deepened through a repetition that cannot realize its goal of healing the original wound. The pain is left unhealed and its suffering worsens in being left unencountered. Nietzsche's ascetic priests and their secular political heirs deal with pain and violence by not responding to their constitutive character. The reified self begins as a response to trauma, yet it is a response that repeats, reinscribes, and intensifies the trauma in denying this world and this life for the sake of a beyond or future devoid of conflict and alterity. Since it poisons the wound, and precludes genuine recovery, the therapy is more damaging than the illness. Pain is taken out on others; it is cultivated as revenge, resentment, and hostility toward what is other than oneself, and the other is identified as the source of pain and suffering.

The intrigue of trauma and violence, of love and revenge, are embodied for Nietzsche in the "gruesome paradox of a 'god on the cross,' that mystery of an inconceivable, final, extreme cruelty and self-crucifixion."[10] Theodicies, cures, and consolations that do not encounter suffering as suffering but justify and "redeem" suffering remain captured in the violence and trauma of their own origins. Accordingly, the passion, its reenactment, and anti-Semitism are symbiotic in legitimating pogroms and persecutions.

In his *Genealogy* Nietzsche unfolds a genealogy of the traumatic origins of the damaged life, aiming at the present by tracing the transformations of suffering and the damaged sublimations affecting human practices and institutions. Trauma is sublimated such that it is repeated and heightened; genealogy is a destructuring repetition that challenges compulsive repetition. The exemplar of priestly power remains—adopting Adorno's expression that indicates an interpretive strategy for defying the reification of concepts—a "critical model" given the skirmish of rival fundamentalisms, the violence involved in the "return to the sacred" and the arbitrary authority of the divine command, and the manipulation of ethnic, ideological, and religious sentiments. The social-political uses of religion are not accidental applications; they are its essence in the skeptical hermeneutics of suspicion, as Nietzsche, Marx, and Freud illustrate in their critiques of the systematic damages done to life and consciousness through religious forces and compulsions.

More radically, the damages revealed by the hermeneutics of suspicion are part of a hermeneutics of emancipation as a response to abjection and suffering. The damages done produce the aspiration and the critique that aspire to unfixate and undo them. Following the analysis of Adorno developed in part 1, as disclosed in his interpretations of the works of Wagner or Heidegger, dereification is not a return to an original natural or ontological condition. It requires challenging rather than presupposing and projecting a "first" unalienated natural condition that is a function of the system's reproduction of damaged life.

Suffering and the Truth and Untruth of Religion

Job asked, why do the righteous suffer? Arthur Schopenhauer posed the question, why is there suffering at all? The question of pain, of how pain permeates human existence, and of how to respond to it in its facticity, is a basic question inherited in part from Schopenhauer, whose philosophy of suffering related to his own experiences (such as his father's suicide) and which Nietzsche opposes as a nihilistic denial of life. This guiding question of the significance of suffering is recurrently reposed throughout Nietzsche's corpus and in his *Genealogy of Morality*. It is a focal point of the current chapter because of how it thematizes the dynamic relations between suffering and power: to live or not live, or to promote and intensify, or to limit and inhibit life. In this question, the possibility of an irreparable suffering emerges, of a wound that can be called traumatic in that it is without closure or healing. This problem does not represent a concern with the pain of the delicate and sensitive, the ostensible civilized Europeans who wither at the minutest exposure and that Nietzsche contrasts with the supposedly virtually infinite toleration of pain of the beast and the primitive, so much as a concern with pain as suffering.[11] Traumatic pain not only lingers after its initial appearance; it transforms how one animal relates to and experiences its world in health and sickness.

Elaine Scarry analyzed the transfiguring forces of trauma as "making and unmaking the world" in *The Body in Pain*.[12] Traumatic suffering is no less primordially world-disclosing or world-constituting than the Greek temple or Van Gogh's painting of peasant shoes analyzed by Heidegger in the "The Origin of the Work of Art," even as it constitutes and reveals a different world and sense of being.[13] Nietzsche's analysis of suffering entails that it is more than world-disclosing. In his thinking during the period of the *Genealogy*, radical suffering cannot be eliminated, and it is a dangerous symptom of religious and political utopians to suggest that it can be.[14] How individuals, classes, peoples, and races reply to suffering differentiates and individuates them, and forms the basis of aristocratic or slavish, noble or priestly ways of life. The noble is skeptical and unafraid in the face of suffering, and "wants it to be, if anything, worse and greater than before"; the priestly fears suffering even as it uses and manipulates it, and is consequently transfixed by and beholden to it.[15]

In the second of his *Untimely Meditations* Nietzsche portrayed forgetting as the power to heal wounds and enable individuals and nations to continue to act and achieve happiness.[16] *Thus Spoke Zarathustra* contains a number of passages that follow this initial model of forgetting as healing: the noble, the innocent, and the creators do not and should not take suffering seriously. Other passages disclose a second model of suffering in the 1880s that increasingly displaces the first one. In this second model, there is a shift from forgetting to nobility, freedom, and ease in the face of the worst suffering. Instead of an innocent and childlike disregard, suffering is to be affirmed not in the name of its future compensation by God or in the name of the state but as potentially transformative and creative, that is, as constitutive of the processes of life itself. Life is self-overcoming, according to Nietzsche's Zarathustra; it relentlessly wounds itself to procreatively transfigure itself into something beyond itself.[17]

Nietzsche's second model prescribes embracing rather than displacing one's suffering, such that the greatest tragedies lead the courageous to honor life all the more.[18] This model is articulated in Nietzsche's polemics against theology, theodicy, and metaphysics, the anaesthetizing and otherworldly justification and excuse of suffering that promises its redemptive end and compensation in a transcendent beyond (Jenseits).

Theodicy, which derives from the Greek words Θεός and δίκη, meaning "God's justice" or "God's justification," is the project of justifying God through the explanation of moral evil and physical suffering as part of God's design. Theodicy has a corresponding structure demanding tranquility of mind in acquiescence to social reality as a condition of felicity in its classical proponents such as Leibniz.[19] Nietzsche's secularizing disenchanting argumentation, insofar as it continues to speak of Stendhal's "promise of happiness" and of embracing one's suffering by affirming it and its world, risks becoming its own theodicy in the guise of a countertheodicy. That is to say, life is to be willed and reaffirmed again and again in all of its sufferings and joys, now for the sake of life itself rather than God, acts as a justification of and apology for the ways of the world, and for its violence and affliction. This is Adorno's assessment in Minima Moralia: whether in its Marxist or Nietzschean forms, the radical critique of culture, ideology, morality, and religion itself becomes ideological.[20] Liberal and radical modernist critiques of tradition have themselves become regressive traditions that preserve and sanctify existing power relations. Past violence against the self is structurally reproduced, retaining its grip on present virility, gratification, and self-affirmation; former pain masochistically becomes stereotyped pleasure.[21]

Adorno traces how Nietzsche's most decisive diagnosis of Christianity concerns its logic of sacrifice, "the sacrifice of the innocent for the sins of the guilty," of the earth and the body for phantoms, and that amor fati inevitably repeats rather than dismantles this logic of sacrifice and its violence.[22] Amor fati, embracing life even in its cruelties and suffering, does not arrive at the promised redemption of the child, of embracing immanence and innocence, of the body and the earth, demanded by Nietzsche, in the face of the damages of systematically degraded life.[23]

Nietzsche vigorously rejected the claim that pain is justifiable in the sense of its being deserved due to sin or guilt.[24] Nietzsche denied the foundations for theodicy, providence, and karma insofar as they are deployed to excuse and justify suffering.[25] Suffering is not holy or moral; it is often senseless. Nonetheless, in Adorno's reading of Nietzsche, pain is to a degree justified and to be accepted as part of life. Socially produced inequality and injustice are consequently naturalized as life itself.

Adorno and Horkheimer's sense of Nietzsche's problematic political implications moderates their appreciation for "the dark writers of the bourgeoisie."[26] Equality and justice remain key elements of critical social theory instead of being constituted by tarantula-like revenge and resentment. Nietzsche is echoed in Adorno's appreciation of the relation of individual suffering and social violence, of pain and its role in reproducing and deepening the mechanisms of power, the effects of which he designates as "damaged life." It is this life itself in its suffering that demands from its own imperfection that which would be otherwise. Adorno's genealogical strategies can be traced in his reflections on anti-Semitism and the Shoah, as well as in his ideology-critical explorations of suffering and authoritarian power in occultists and other broken personalities, such as newspaper astrologers and radio Christian evangelists.[27] Such popular forms of religiosity reveal as much about the social reality of religion as its higher, more reflexive forms, which can share the same underlying ideological dynamics. Adorno challenged the theodicy motif (which will be considered later with respect to Levinas)—irredeemable after Auschwitz and the Holocaust—in both its elite and popular cultural forms as being complicit with violence and suffering, while risking reverting to theodicy in another guise in regard to Stendhal's "promise of happiness," which for both of these authors is implicit in art and aesthetic-sensuous life.[28]

Notwithstanding the reference to potential sensuous and personal happiness—which is the guiding thread for social criticism, as I argued in part 1 of this volume—Adorno continues, "Art is the ever-broken promise of happiness."[29] Neither author can find satisfaction in the pursuit of pleasure in a hedonism that avoids responding to the question of suffering, which itself remains paradoxically implicated in ascetic and disciplinary ideals and practices. In *Thus Spoke Zarathustra*, Nietzsche presciently ridicules the contrived, banal, and agreeable pleasures of the last humans, for whom "[e]veryone wants the same thing, everyone is the same."[30] Adorno evoked his own variety of the last human in *Minima Moralia* in the form of a consumeristic individualism that leaves room for neither happiness nor individuals, in which the ideology of the individual corresponds to her actual subordination and elimination *as an individual*.[31] Autonomy is eliminated in the name of a freedom that is power over others, democracy is limited and undermined in its undemocratic and authoritarian maintenance, and individuality is eliminated in the consumption of the "unique" and mass-produced individualism. These themes will be examined in further detail in chapter 12. Planned, instrumentalized, and calculated, individuals are governed by the logic of equivalence and the same.

Nietzsche depicted in the *Genealogy of Morality* the subordination, inversion, and reinterpretation of instincts and desires in socialization, processes involving inordinate cruelty, mutilation, and suffering over enormous expanses of time.[32] These processes made humans "interesting" for the first time. Nietzsche recognizes his own and Zarathustra's proximity to the priestly character; yet the priestly character's "sickness" is increasingly dangerous as it deepens the wound and hastens life's decline.[33] Such suffering and traumatic violence against the individual remain integral to socialization. Adorno analyzes the traumas and their modifications in the damaged life of mass-consumerist societies. These traumas remain recognizable in the obsessive repetition and compulsive behavior of collectively mesmerized individuals.[34] Under such conditions of life, suffering is not liberated in happiness and unending pleasure, as promised in the past by religion and in the present by popular cultural images produced by advertising. Instead of addressing damaged life, suffering and happiness function as manipulated purposes under the aegis of the culture industry and media as mechanisms of social reproduction and social conformity.

In Adorno's later analysis of the culture industry, as well as in the cowritten work *Dialectic of Enlightenment*, the mutuality of pleasure and discipline, spontaneity and domination, characteristic of modern societies, is revealed most clearly not through its conservative and liberal apologists but through authors such as Marquis de Sade and Nietzsche. They both pursued the consequences and shadows of Enlightenment, modernization, and their dynamics of sadism and masochism, mastery and slavery.[35]

Between Marx and Nietzsche: Religion and Damaged Life

In the end the soul is itself the longing of the soulless for salvation.

—Theodor Adorno, *Minima Moralia*

The contemporary political situation, including the strength of religious fundamentalisms after the end of previous models of social-political alternatives to the capitalist mode of production, offers support for the early Marx's assertion that religion is not only a religious question but must be a social-political one. Exemplifying a strategy that has been criticized as a "hermeneutics of suspicion," in that it challenges the interpretive priority of the self-understanding of believers, Marx claimed in the fourth of his *Theses on Feuerbach* that Feuerbach "starts out from the fact of religious self-alienation (*Selbstentfremdung*), the duplication of the world into a religious, imaginary world, and a secular one. [Feuerbach's] work consists in resolving the religious world into its secular basis. He overlooks the fact that after completing this work, the chief thing still remains to be done."[36]

It is inadequate to reject religion as a purely untrue delusion that can be dispelled by rational argumentation. The self-estrangement of consciousness and a purely theoretical attitude, if it is implicated in the reproduction of the dynamics of the "concrete universal" of existing society, includes its estrangement and injustices: "Religion is the sigh of the oppressed creature, the heart of a heartless world."[37] As such, religion feeds off of alienation. Religion answers an alienated condition by reproducing estrangement, and the self fails to recognize itself in its own activities in relation to things, others, and its own self.

Religion is concurrently an expression of power and powerlessness. It calls on people to accept their socially produced suffering as fated and ordained while concurrently giving a possible voice to that suffering by potentially expressing a protest against that damaged life. Marx and Nietzsche expose how religion is both oppressive and more than an oppression; it is an expression of oppressed life that seeks to respond to its oppression. To speak schematically, while Nietzsche argues that powerlessness makes religion objectionable, Marx argues that religion's structure of power makes it objectionable. Nietzsche trenchantly articulates in the *Genealogy of Morality* the double movement of religion as both an expression of and opposition to oppression. The nexus of religion as an instrument of suffering and oppression, the expression of suffering, and the defiance against existing injustice, are the main dynamics taken up in the prophetic ethical dimension discernible in Adorno and Levinas.

Nietzsche's confrontation with religion's earthly truth occurs most forcefully in the genealogical exposure of the lowly origins of religious discourses in phenomena such as exchange relations and in ascetic, disciplinary, and priestly practices. According to Nietzsche, religion does not subjugate the masses by being externally imposed on them, even if the priestly employ it in this fashion. This system of symbolic, ideological, and in many cases physical power is generated within and by the lifeworld itself. Despite the potential misuses of genealogy in appropriations of Nietzsche's expressions and strategies, the transformative potential of genealogy contrasts with the implicitly conservative understanding of the lifeworld developed by Habermas. Habermas does not adequately address—from a perspective informed by Nietzsche's or Marx's analyses of social conditions—the sedimentation and stratification of power in the formation of the lifeworld itself such that the distinction between systems and lifeworld proves inadequately complex to address the complexity and ambiguity of the interpenetration of power and communication. The problem of intersubjective or communicative idealism is not adequately resolved in Habermas's later work on the lifeworld, which incorporates precommunicative and prerational elements within the "embodied space of reasons" that—given his conception of reason—is not sufficiently embodied or material.[38]

Nietzsche's analysis circumvents Marx's objection to Feuerbach, given that it does not humanistically contest religious ideals while avoiding recognizing their practical social structures. It does more than this by revealing the dependency and conformity of religious life to be self-created by a disfigured and monstrous self who is unable to confront and embrace itself and its world. The relationship between priestly power and the masses consequently serves as an exemplar of the heteronomy of social life, including secular priests leading complicit masses on the basis of their damaged affective lives in mass political movements.

To use the schema from the second *Untimely Meditation*, the *Genealogy of Morality* is a variety of "critical history," albeit enacted in the name of present life, rather than against it. As Nietzsche's *Genealogy* offers a variety of critical histories, the question arises of his relation to the priestly character. The question arises also, as posed by Adorno, of whether Nietzsche's discourse on agonistic life is intrinsically apologetic in its demand for a life of amor fati, and of whether each "it was" should become an "I will." Does the *Genealogy* offer an inverted worldly theodicy vindicating the ways of the world, nature, and life to humans, and thereby encouraging them to accept their role and fate, or is it a variety of immanent self-cleansing critique? Does genealogical history uncritically conceal the present and its immanent promise of and hope for happiness, or is it a relevant critical model for examining the intersection of power and suffering, or—in more social theoretical language—for examining ideological elites and mechanisms of the reproduction and perpetuation of power? To respond to these questions, a closer look at the strategy and structure of the portrayal of priestly power and sickly life in Nietzsche's *Genealogy of Morality* is called for.[39]

One might be tempted to juxtapose Nietzsche's priestly figure with other portrayals of priestly power, such as Dostoevsky's Grand Inquisitor, who employs devotion, faith, and fear to legitimate and perpetuate violence and domination. However, Nietzsche did not reveal in his description that such a contrast between the priest and an exemplar of true religiosity is warranted. Nietzsche's genealogical interpretation does not offer a standard liberal or neoliberal narrative regarding the risks of overly enthusiastic religiosity. Confronting and questioning its psycho-social-political dynamics, Nietzsche's genealogical suspicion uncovers the historical constitution and formation of the religious soul itself, which, as Nietzsche remarked of Blaise Pascal in *Beyond Good and Evil*, is a deep, wounded, and monstrous soul, one shaped by a "multitude of dangerous, painful experiences."[40] Even if one should avoid reducing Nietzsche's thought to another instance of "virtue ethics," this and related passages nevertheless illustrate how his critique of morality and religion evokes the "good life" in a biological language of health and sickness, ascending and descending life.

Priestly Powers, Damaged Lives, and Imperfectionist Promises of Happiness

> I know that everything is false as long as the world is as it is.
>
> —Theodor Adorno, *Towards a New Manifesto*

Key aspects of Nietzsche's discourse of suffering arise in the context of his early adaptation and later rejection of Schopenhauer's philosophy and his interpretation of will, creative spontaneity, life, and suffering.[41] Nietzsche's later thinking of suffering appears to be articulated in response to the fourth book of Schopenhauer's *The World as Will and Representation*, where—to briefly summarize—the basic argument is that beyond aesthetic contemplation (as described in book 3), the relief from the suffering of the world (as he argued in books 1 and 2) comes from the willless contemplation of the ascetic.[42] The ascetic practices of letting go of strife and pain by forgetting the self and subjectivity, with its opposition to the world as object, results in the subject's ceasing to perceive determinate being and instead dissolving into nothingness. In Schopenhauer, the ascetic can redeem suffering by letting go of earthly matters and identifying with the cosmic processes of nature. Schopenhauer's philosophy is accordingly a point of reference for Nietzsche, who turns from an early embrace and critique of Schopenhauer in *The Birth of Tragedy* to a more comprehensive rejection in his later writings.

The perspective of what might be designated as the Nietzschean "good life" is at work in Nietzsche's rejection of Schopenhauer's self-denial of the will and the Buddhist self-negation of attachment as forms of passive nihilism. Nietzsche would overturn these teachings with the promise of the self-affirmation of life, if not achieving happiness in an ordinary sense, and this ethos enables Nietzsche's evaluation and ranking of various forms of life.[43] Nietzsche's vision of a "good life" is not a life without damages and suffering; it is a life that does not understand itself according to the fatality and "it is" of these damages. It affirms precisely that life. This Nietzschean strategy is modified in Adorno's imperfectionist argumentation that the promise of happiness emerges from within and in response to damaged life itself rather than appealing to a teleological historical goal or fixed moral ideal of perfection.

Religion functions both as a promise of the otherwise within life and as a power that subjugates life. Moral and religious discourses and practices operate as reproductive mechanisms of ways of life that damage individuals at the same time as individuals are compelled, as Horkheimer noted, to accept the damages they suffer as justified and indeed good.[44] Through the disciplinary ascetic ideal, as epitomized by the formation of the priestly character in Nietzsche's genealogical model, suffering is interpreted in ways that reinforce and result in greater amounts and new forms of suffering.[45] Pain and suffering are not merely part of the contingent fabric of becoming but are rather part of what come to be perceived as "deserved" and justified debts that are part of the reproduction of the logic of sacrifice and exchange governing religious cultures and political economic systems. Pain and suffering, discipline and punishment, become ideologically warranted due to the construction of life as guilt and sin that continue to resonate beyond the problematics of existential philosophy.[46] As the *Dialectic of Enlightenment* describes in its discussion of Nietzsche, Marquis de Sade, and sadomasochism, an interrogation that links with the study of the authoritarian personality, pain itself thereby becomes both a need and a pleasure. It is potentially the final remaining one under the regime of priestly power and its secularized incarnations that sacrificially promise heaven or an infinitely deferred happiness.[47]

Nietzsche's characterization of priestly power exposes violence against the instincts and the self, the trauma of a socialization that traumatizes life to make it malleable, and how these traumatic results of violence are concealed and deepened through a repetition that does not realize its purpose of healing the initial wound. The pain not only remains unhealed but deteriorates into a condition of suffering by lingering pathologically without being either overcome through forgetting or liberated through being encountered and illuminated. Nietzsche's ascetic priests and their secular ideological heirs accordingly deal with pain and violence by not responding to their constitutive character for the vulnerable conditional material life that is both repressed and presupposed. The truth of religion, returned to in the prophetic concern for worldly suffering, is accordingly material earthly life in its suffering and happiness—or the promise thereof in the entwinement of happiness and redemption articulated by Benjamin.[48]

The fixated and reified self, a product of sacrifice and exchange, is a damaged individuality formed through two aspects of the same dynamic process that result in individuation and socialization. This self begins as a response to suffering; asceticism accordingly promises to be a means to end suffering. But, with Schopenhauer in mind, Nietzsche contends that asceticism cannot redeem the suffering that it itself enacts and heal the wound that it poisons. Ascetic practices are an answer that consequently repeat, reinscribe, and intensify suffering in denying the immanence of this world and this life—even as it attempts to assert absolute control over it—for the sake of a beyond or future that would be devoid of resistance and alterity. Accordingly, Nietzsche writes, the priestly cure is worse than the disease itself.[49] As noted above, life-denying disciplinary practices do not heal the wound but poison it.[50]

Nietzsche explicates how pain is patiently cultivated through suffering into a condition of ressentiment. The wounded self is educated into a spirit of revenge and hostility toward what is other than oneself, including the good life itself.⁵¹ All selves suffer and are wounded, but not all selves become embodiments of ressentiment and revenge. This intrigue and complicity of peace and violence, of love as the deepest revenge, is embodied most emphatically in Nietzsche's depiction of Christ, already quoted above, as the "gruesome paradox of a 'god on the cross,'" which Kierkegaard identifies as *the* redemptive paradox, and the "inconceivable, final, extreme cruelty" of "self-crucifixion."⁵² The passion of Christ and the violence of Christianity are interdependent phenomena for Nietzsche. Hence there are deep connections that are not merely accidental between Christianity's reenactment of the passion and anti-Semitism.

Religious cures, consolations, and theodicies—as in Adorno's vision of advertising—do not allow the encounter with suffering *as* the suffering that it is. Instead they work at transforming, justifying, and redeeming suffering as necessary and even good. They establish suffering, including self-inflected suffering in the name of redemption, as meaningful, just, and holy sacrificial demands through an underlying logic based on nonmoral motives and relations of exchange and debt.

Nietzsche traces in the *Genealogy* how Christianity functions as a form of capitalist loan sharking, in which all debts are allegedly freely paid off through the redemptive suffering of Christ only to increase one's debt. Nietzsche describes how the debts are to be paid back to the same being that created them by establishing individual actions as faults and sins that must be paid off. These debts cannot be paid even in principle. Hence, the debtor's indebtedness not only persists but is deepened in being unconditionally indebted to the ultimate redeemer of debts. The debtor is not allowed to pay off her own debt through her own actions and, at the same time, is intrinsically in need of forgiveness while never receiving the genuine forgiveness that releases her from the redeemer of the debt and his earthly representatives. The sinful person is thus in constant need of the grace and mercy of the debt collector, who assumes all debt in order to impose an infinite obedience and guilt onto the debtor that cannot be repaid. In being "freely" redeemed by Christ, Nietzsche concludes that the human agent is reduced to an absolute debtor by taking on an infinite obligation to the redeemer. The debtor is then expected to love and be joyfully thankful for this state of an eternal unconditional indebtedness and infinitely deferred forgiveness. Nietzsche's analysis in the *Genealogy of Morality* concludes that the Christian notion of forgiveness is not forgiving enough. This argument applies to more than pathological forms of Christianity. It casts suspicion on religious and social-political discourses that promise liberation through eschatological redemption yet bring with them real servitude.

Beyond the heteronomy of an everlasting debt constituted in a forgiveness that is in fact the unforgiveness of a never-ending forgiving, the ascetic and priestly ideal remains captured in the sacrificial logic of the violence and trauma of its own origins even when it promises forgiveness and mercy for earthly beings in their imperfection and incompletion. It cannot rescind suffering or heal the wound as it promises, since suffering is its primary basis and need. It reproduces suffering to propagate itself. If this suspicion is the case, even if this structure would incarnate the language of the oppressed rather than the oppressor, it cannot overcome the logic of exchange and sacrifice. The logic of religion diagnosed by Nietzsche inevitably precludes the "weak messianic power," which is for Benjamin "a power to which the past has a claim," and the prophetic dimensions that Benjamin—and Adorno, Bloch, and Levinas in their own ways—perceive in the prophetic moment and its emancipatory temporality.[53] At the same time as each moment is an entrance for this redemptive promise to enter, the hope for justice characteristic of weak messianic power is dialectically entangled with and in danger of being replaced by the sacrificial logic of an infinitely deferred messianic forgiveness and debt. Prophecy without ethics risks unleashing the terror of prophetic justice, "breathing wrath to come," applied via this infinitely demanding and relentless logic of religious sacrifice and exchange.[54]

Nietzsche's suspicions continue to be pertinent with the contemporary return to and revival of the religious after the disenchantment and secularism of modernity, in spheres as diverse as politics and philosophy. Religious forms of life assert themselves in the shadow of sacred discipline and violence, in which the nonreligious and the otherly religious symbolize an evil to be eliminated. The desire to negate religious and nonreligious others is motivated by the disquiet of religious belief, the fear of alterity, and the longing for power over the other, even if it would proceed in the name of others and ethics, as the religious exercise sacred power and violence in the guise of rejecting ordinary imperfect earthly powers.

Nietzsche presciently surveyed not only the dogmatic but also the skeptical and relativistic legitimization of religiosity in the *Genealogy*. Since there is no knowing and only questioning, one worships the question mark, and the question mark is in the end the same old God.[55]

Nietzsche described this in *Human, All Too Human* as the more subtle obscurantism of Kantian critical philosophy and modern skepticism: it does not obscure thinking as much as it does existence itself.[56]

Nietzsche analyzed the wounds and trauma within power and how it operates in constructing social-political authority in customary morality and religion. Cynthia Halpern commented, "We remember trauma. We are made as selves out of trauma. Nietzsche is saying that memory itself [. . .] is created by trauma."[57] Katrin Froese construes Nietzsche's Zarathustra as "a testament to the powerful hold such trauma has on his psyche."[58] Nietzsche's *Genealogy* could be read as articulating a genealogy of the traumatic origins of the damaged life, directed at the present condition by tracing the metamorphoses of suffering as well as the damaged sublimations that shape human practices and institutions. Trauma permeates the image of priestly rule as it is sublimated in religious experiences and practices that heighten its power through repetition. Genealogy contests such pathological compulsive repetition through a destructuring repetition. Priestly power in Nietzsche's analysis is, as mentioned previously, a critical or diagnostic model of the present. It remains a critical heuristic given the ongoing conflicts between faith and reason, the competition between conflicting fundamentalisms, the discourses of returning to a lost mythical and sacred age that legitimates social-political power and violence, the capriciousness of divine commands that undermine rather than motivate responsiveness to the other's ethical demand, and the ideological management by elites of ethnic, ideological, and religious sensibilities for the sake of constructing images of the other and the enemy.

Religion, Oppression, and Prophecy

What is the truth in religious ideological untruth that makes it necessary for thinkers such as Nietzsche, Marx, and Freud to deconstruct it? Nietzsche's atheism, as could be said of Marx's, has a prophetic and religious atmosphere. Nietzsche did not reject all that can be characterized as religious, as he celebrated the Dionysian elements of religion that rejoice in sensuous life in festivals, dance, and music. Nietzsche's imagining of Dionysian release is ambiguous as—in Adorno's language that indicates an alternative to Nietzsche and Marx—it retains dimensions of the restricted mimesis of mythic and sacred powers as well as of an anarchic and freed mimesis. While in Marx the religious dimension operates through the prophetic concern for justice, Nietzsche expresses appreciation of the expressiveness of religion and its intensification of the dreams, drunkenness, and imagination of individuals and peoples. Nietzsche's recognition of the earthly life and virtue of the religious in its Dionysian, noble, and tragic forms is not limited to the *Birth of Tragedy* and his early writing. These images of Dionysius and Christ with their affinities and differences are redeployed throughout his later works and reinscribed onto his own life and fate in *Ecce Homo*.

Nietzsche's polemic against religion offers a powerful analysis and critical model of the persistent pathologies of the religious as a traumatized and oppressed form of life that repeats its trauma and intensifies its oppressiveness by denying itself as life; not as the idea of pure natural or biological life that Adorno and Levinas questioned, but as "a" singular life. As seen in chapter 10, "a life" is interpreted as a temporal material ethical reality that makes an ethical demand that it be nourished as *a* life. A life calls forth prophecy that transpires on its behalf rather than being the negation and denial of life that Nietzsche diagnosed as pathological.

This chapter has examined the roles that pain, suffering, trauma, and the damaged plays, in contrast to Adorno's sense of the good life, in the constitution and reproduction of power and the self. The contemporary relevance of Nietzsche and Adorno lies in their alternatives to the simplifying categories of naturalism and antinaturalism, their linking of history and nature—natural history—and historical processes of rationalization, power, and self-formation to one another.[59] There is the question how to respond to the heterogeneity of the human without reducing the human to either a reified anthropocentric humanistic ideal, unaware of the nonhuman in its power over its world, or a predestined fatality of instrumentalized nature that is reified as the struggle for existence and biosocial mastery of human and nonhuman others.

Autonomy is bound to heterogeneity in Adorno as much as it is for Levinas, as will be examined in further detail in chapter 12 on the pathologies of freedom.[60] Dialectical thinking facilitates both critique and apology and requires the recognition of the apologetic moments in critique as well as the critical potential in apology.[61] Insofar as the aporetic and nonidentical dialectic expose the falseness of forced alternatives that one-sidedly hold on to their moment of truth until they are capable of no more than reproducing the damaged life, Adorno comments that "freedom would be not to choose between black and white but to abjure such prescribed choices."[62]

Religious justifications and ontotheological theodicies of supernatural justice and secularized theodicies of teleological progress in freedom are questionable given the realities of mass suffering and the destruction of peoples in war and genocide. Adorno and Levinas articulate antitheodicies, as a number of authors, such as Hent de Vries, have shown.[63] The realities of suffering speak against the notion that nature and life can be understood as generosity and a gift for Levinas, as the *es gibt* occurs as anonymous terror (see chapter 10 below). Life is a nightmare and worse for its victims. They are hostages to others' irresponsiveness and irresponsibility. Their hearts beat in and contest a heartless world. They hope and prophesize for the sake of incomplete life in a hopeless condition. Their suffering sensibility and material life constitutes an ethical and social-political demand on the selfish and the virtuous, the imperfect and perfect, who would ignore them. Levinas's ethics is in this sense an ethical imperfectionism of incompletion, which is not merely a negation or derivative of completion, a concept that will be further delineated in chapter 10.

Dussel explains Levinas's responsibility in the language of an ethically responsive rather than neutral materialism, which is a source for the strategies of the present work, as an appeal to sensibility from the other's vulnerable corporeality that is "shaped by the needs inherent in suffering. The other's demand upon me emerges out of that desperate condition of suffering."[64]

Levinas points us toward those to whom flourishing life has been denied in works such as *Totality and Infinity* and in his critique of theodicy unfolded in the essay "Useless Suffering." Theodicy, the hope that there is a divine meaning in the meaninglessness of senseless suffering, can neither save God's innocence nor help ethics and ethical theory. The supposed rationality of suffering in theodicy appears to be at best an avoidance and escape, and at worst an apologetic excuse for violence. Theodicies function as ideological forms of repression, naturalizing human injustices as if they were natural facts: "the arbitrariness and strange failure of justice amidst wars, crimes and the oppression of the weak by the strong, rejoin, in a sort of fatality, the useless suffering that springs from natural plagues, as if they were the effects of an ontological perversion."[65]

Conclusion and Transition

Questions can be formulated at this point that will lead into the next two chapters (7 and 8) focusing on the tension between ethics and religion in Kierkegaard and Levinas.

The first set of issues concerns the interconnections between religion, promise, and violence: Is the religious primarily a projection of power or a consequence of violence and trauma? Can the prophetic moment of promised happiness and justice have a transformative rather than apologetic function? Further, what of the biblical story of Abraham and Isaac that has been significant for Western debates concerning the appropriate relation of religion and ethics? Does it illustrate the deep complicity of religion with mutilation, oppression, and sacrifice?

The second set of issues concerns Levinas's specific understanding of ethics and religion in Levinas: Is Levinasian ethics another incarnation of ascetic and disciplinary "priestly" power turned against the self in the name of altruism that should be regarded with suspicion? Does Levinas's use of religious language in the service of articulating his philosophy and ethics deserve the same ideology critique as exhibited in Adorno's social analysis of astrologers and evangelist preachers? Does the ethical critique of the logic of sacrifice in the call for unrestricted solidarity necessitate (adopting the suspicions of Marx, Nietzsche, or Freud) the abolition of prophecy as violence and religion as a mythological and ideological form of ascetic, disciplinary, and sacrificial logic?

These questions are more than rhetorical issues. The problematic of the religious in Levinas, in relation to Kierkegaard and other thinkers and traditions, will be the focus of the following two chapters.

Chapter Seven

The Disturbance of the Ethical

Kierkegaard, Levinas, and Abraham's Binding of Isaac

Introduction

Levinas presents an alternative interpretive strategy to Kierkegaard's retelling of Abraham's binding of Isaac, as will be examined in the current and next chapters, and accordingly the relationship between ethics and religion. In this chapter, I bring a cross- or intercultural perspective—drawing on Jewish, Christian, and Chinese sources—to bear on Kierkegaard's depiction of the suspension of the ethical through his reading of the narrative of Abraham's binding of Isaac in *Fear and Trembling* in relation to Levinas's articulation of the disturbance and provocation of the primacy of ethics.[1] Kierkegaard's and Levinas's respective analyses of the *Akedah* narrative—which is the older transliteration of *Aqedah* עקדה used by the authors under discussion—of Abraham's binding and near sacrifice of Isaac is indicative of the distance and nearness in their thinking that each pivots on the relationship between the ethical and the religious in the encounter with alterity, infinity, and transcendence.

In Kierkegaard and Levinas, the encounter with God occurs as a traumatic interval and aporetic encounter with a transcendence that cannot be defined, categorized, or sublimated under a concept. While in Kierkegaard the self is forced back upon itself, exposed to the otherness of its singular unfathomable source, in Levinas, in contrast, a traumatic exposure and delivery over to the unconditional transcendent Other—who is inseparable from if irreducible to the empirical other person—occurs to the self. In this incalculable exposure, I am inescapably "accused"—to use the language of Levinas—called, chosen, and elected to an inescapable and irreducible ethical responsibility even before those who do not recognize me (a maxim articulated by Confucius, or Kongzi 孔子, among others) or persecute me (a maxim advocated in other-oriented altruistic and saintly ethics such as the Buddhist philosopher Śāntideva).² This is more originary than practice and theory, and prior to faith, knowledge, and morality.

The paradox and aporia of Abraham's sacrifice might seem to break and transcend the ethical, leaving us with a voluntarism and terror of arbitrary divine commands or with a nihilistic loss of ethical orientation and sensibility. However, the troubling narrative of Abraham and Isaac in the land of Moriah also suggests something other than either a nihilistic or voluntaristic destruction of ethics. It provides a different modality of experiencing and reflecting on the ethical, indicating the aporetic and deconstructive performative character of the ethical that resonates in part, as will be considered below as intercultural examples are explored in this chapter, with early Chinese "Daoist" (*daojia* 道家) sources such as the *Daodejing* (道德經) and the *Zhuangzi* (莊子), which offer an alternative perspective on the problematic of ethics and religion as well as critical models of unrestricted mimesis and responsiveness, as I have argued in my book *Daoism and Environmental Philosophy: Nourishing Life*.³ These various sources and examples from divergent linguistic and cultural contexts provide no unified understanding of ethics, nor do they form the basis of a system of ethics. They do each suggest the impossibility of such a system and different variations on how alterity "other-constitutes" the good and the ethical.

"Here I Am" in an Intercultural Context

In Bereshit 22:1–2 (Genesis), Abraham responded to God's call with the words "Here I am":

וַיְהִי, אַחַר הַדְּבָרִים הָאֵלֶּה, וְהָאֱלֹהִים, נִסָּה אֶת-אַבְרָהָם; וַיֹּאמֶר אֵלָיו, אַבְרָהָם וַיֹּאמֶר הִנֵּנִי.

> And it came to pass after these things that God did prove Abraham, and said unto him: "Abraham"; and he said: "Here am I."

The Disturbance of the Ethical

אֲשֶׁר-אָהַבְתָּ, אֶת-יִצְחָק, וְלֶךְ-לְךָ, אֶל-אֶרֶץ הַמֹּרִיָּה; וְהַעֲלֵהוּ שָׁם, לְעֹלָה, עַל
וַיֹּאמֶר קַח-נָא אֶת-בִּנְךָ אֶת-יְחִידְךָ אַחַד הֶהָרִים, אֲשֶׁר אֹמַר אֵלֶיךָ.

> And He said: "Take now thy son, thine only son, whom thou lovest, even Isaac, and get thee into the land of Moriah; and offer him there for a burnt-offering upon one of the mountains which I will tell thee of."[4]

It is noticeable in this passage that the verb "to take" in "take now thy son" is in the imperative form *qakh*. Abraham is being commanded to act. It is a commandment (*mitzvah* מִצְוָה). This word for "commandment" would be recognized outside of the Abrahamic religions by, for example, the orthopraxic Hindu Mīmāṃsā school, with its prioritizing of Vedic commandments and their self-justifying character. In Levinas's reading of the Torah, a name that is derived from the Hebrew word for "guiding" or "teaching" rather than "law," God's guidance or instruction occurs prior to its communication, and prior to a list of commandments. Exposure to God comes by way of a summoning. This exposure is enacted through an appellation and questioning prior to reflection and communication, which Levinas identifies with the constitution of responsibility through the asymmetrical and aporetic relationship with the irreducible and nonrelational Other who must somehow but cannot be addressed.

Derrida's reading of the *Akedah* narrative suggests that the asymmetry comes from the secret of God's command that is revoked before it is enacted.[5] There is a different strategy found in Levinas. In a communication without restriction or symmetry, God's interpolation is answered—in a sense anachronistically, before it is articulated—with the performative utterance or speech act *hineni*. This is the "Here I am" of Abraham, Jacob, Moses, Samuel, and Isaiah, in which the stress is on the "here" rather than the "I" that modifies it. This place of the "here" singularizes the "I" in its response to the divine address.[6] Or it is evaded. In evasion, Cain denied his responsibility for his brother Abel.[7] Jonah fled from himself in trying to evade his responsibility, fleeing his prophetic vocation without being able to escape God even inside the belly of a whale.[8] God's question "Where are you?" (*ayekah*), Adam cannot hide, as he is exposed in his nakedness in communication and is consequently summoned to respond.[9] With God's personal call of "Abraham" and "here am I" as his confirmation of obedience, Abraham is himself bound in being bound to God's command in the sacrificial binding (*akedah*) of his beloved son Isaac.[10]

Abraham's "Here I am" has a deep resonance in the Jewish tradition. Adam's hearing the voice of God is an an-archic shattering of the self-enclosed garden of the egoistic self by the glory of the infinite that leads the ego, which is subordinated to the other's height but not eliminated, to sincerity before and responsibility to the other.¹¹ God's initial question, "Where are you?" calls for the "Here I am" that Adam refuses to speak. Levinas notes that it is here that God becomes involved in words to bring humans to words.¹² This entering into language—as an interpersonal performative vocative and responsive saying (*le dire*) that is more fundamental than the solidified and propositionally stated and said (*le dit*)—is an awakening to responsibility.¹³

Adam's utterance "Here I am," to introduce a cross-cultural example to help clarify its distinctiveness, differs from the "Here I am" uttered in a creation narrative from the Bṛhadāraṇyaka Upaniṣad. There was in the beginning in this South Asian creation narrative one single mass in a shape resembling a human. The first being (*puruṣa*), the primordial self (*ātman*), utters "Here I am" (*aham ayam*)—that is, a self-reflexive "It is I"—out of its solitude, thus bringing the "I" into being from itself.¹⁴ Motivated by the desire, fear, loneliness, and solitude of this self-reflexive I, the plurality of the world unfolds from out of its own immanence.¹⁵ The ultimate reality of things in this Upaniṣadic narrative is the self coming to know the entirety of the world by awakening to itself. This "I," or "self," likewise differs from the impoverished, foolish "I" and the "I alone" (*wo du* 我獨) of chapter 20 of the early Daoist work called the *Daodejing*. This "I" parts from the ordinary customary life of people and things and responsively nurtures them by being nurtured, as in the image of the nourishing mother (*shi mu* 食母), that is, the generativity of the *dao* 道, in this chapter's concluding statement (*wo du yi yu ren, er gui shi mu* 我獨異於人，而貴食母).¹⁶ This deployment of feminine and maternal imagery of the mutual nourishing of life here could be compared to nourishment, maternity, and fecundity in Levinas delineated previously in chapters 4 and 5.¹⁷ This expression of being singled out in the *dao*, the overturning of everyday attitudes and the reorientation existentially indicated in the "I alone," occurs in three chapters of the *Zhuangzi*.¹⁸ The an-archic and transformative immanence of the *dao* can be explained from the terms of the solitude of the "I alone" of Laozi 老子.

Levinas distinguishes between the immanence of things and the transcendence of others.¹⁹ This distinction does not hold, and needs modification, when things are encountered as others and others as things in Marx's analysis of reification and fetishism or in Adorno's prioritization of the object in its alterity. Levinas stresses the disorderly moment of unconditional exposure and an-archic transcendence to which the Hebraic "Here I am" answers. This is not the self-assertion of the I asserting its place in the sun and maintaining its virility and mastery in the world. This saying of the I cannot be described as a speech act, much less a propositional thesis in its passivity. This saying is an accusation, accusing and signifying "me" in my nakedness before God. The accusative "me" is at the service of others who gaze at me and speak to me, "without having anything to identify myself with, but the sound of my voice or the figure of my gesture—the saying itself."[20] Such a response to God's provocation—the saying is an unsaying in its nudity and sincerity prior to the reification of the propositional and ontological said that needs to be in a sense rectified—is to bear witness, offer testimony, and enter into prophecy for God and others. "Here I am" is a response to an accusation and command that occurs before calculative prudence and rational deliberation about self-interest and rule following take hold. The self is brought neither into being nor into the truth of itself through a self-reflexive feeling such as anxiety or a self-reflective awareness. Responsibility in response to the "in-finite" is the condition of becoming a self and the ethical condition of individuation for Levinas: "The word ['I'] means ['Here I am'], answering for everything and everyone."[21]

Levinas does not beg the question in regard to Kierkegaard's challenge of the universal, that is, that it is lower than the singular, by arriving at a universal altruistic benevolence, which, as with its contrary egoistic self-interest, already presupposes the interruptive ethical episode exposing the self to the other.[22] More radical than a generalizable and universal altruism is the message Levinas finds in Isaiah's "Here I am! Send me."[23] Here "the ego," Levinas claims, is "stripped by the trauma of the persecution of its scornful and imperialist subjectivity" and is reduced to "a transparency without opaqueness."[24] The obligation enacted in the "me, Here I am for the others," of the accused I "in its non-interchangeable uniqueness of one chosen," is without reciprocity.[25] This is the condition of uniqueness, individuality, and election. That is, it is a being chosen prior to and without my voluntary choice, a responsibility that I either confirm—for example, "Send me!" (*shelakh-ni*)—or I attempt to evade as did Jonah. This unique chosenness is at the same time substitution of the self for the other, to the point of dying for the other and being responsible for and to each person, even—in passages that evoke Judeo-Christian images of saintliness and the Buddhist portrayals of the Bodhisattva offering her own body to the antagonist—my oppressor and tormentor.[26]

Substitution—which Levinas describes as "being a hostage"—is the most intensified and interruptive form of otherness in the self, commanding it as an ethical demand without excuse or evasion. Substitution, and accordingly the ethical displacement of the ego, is intrinsically asymmetrical for Levinas. The asymmetrical priority demanding recognition of the other person over one's own self is maintained in numerous passages of the *Analects* (*Lunyu* 論語): whether *I recognize* others is more important for me ethically than *whether others recognize me*.[27] The asymmetry of radical otherness operates differently from the asymmetry of gradated benevolence or humaneness (*ren* 仁) articulated in Confucian conceptions of the interpersonal relational priority of others in asymmetrical reciprocity in "establishing others" (*liren* 立人) and "promoting others" (*daren* 達人).[28]

Since the thesis attributed to Confucius of an asymmetrical priority of the other person is not based on instrumental calculation and exchange but rather transcends it, Confucius's philosophy can be said to be genuinely ethical. Still, can it be genuinely ethical without the moment of radical or absolute transcendence? Interpreters such as David L. Hall and Roger T. Ames find this sentiment, as it has been articulated by Kierkegaard and Levinas, to be foreign to classical Confucian thought.[29] Early Confucian discussions of asymmetry do not displace or bracket the reference to self-concern found in the demand to broaden, cultivate, and improve oneself. This is not the self-negation and self-sacrifice of radically altruistic moralities. Nor is the human respect for heaven (*tian* 天) and its mandate (*tianming* 天命) in the thought of early *rujia* 儒家 (the school of the erudites, called Confucianism in the West) equivalent to the asymmetrical disrelation between the transcendent monotheistic God and the individual self that is at work in Kierkegaard and Levinas. In the case of Confucian ethics, which does not rely on the monotheistic language of transcendence, and consequently serves as a counterexample to the idea that asymmetrical ethics requires an absolute other, the asymmetrical priority of the other person occurs as an immanent relational demand compelling me to respond to the other in the context of ethical self-cultivation and communal ethical life, rather than as an absolutely transcendent divine command.[30] To this extent, in contrast to Levinas's radical hyperbolic strategies, Confucian ethical discourses offer a significantly more immanent and relational ethical alternative to

Levinas's argumentation that the asymmetrical ethical relation requires the most extreme conception of the transcendence of otherness.[31] This strategy includes moments of exposure and encountering transcendence as well as ethical prophecy and critique.

Substitution is for Levinas an-archic and anachronistic even as the command is obeyed before it can be made or heard.[32] This can be understood in the context of the Jewish tenet that obligation precedes understanding and interpretation, or, as Levinas would say, that ethics is prior to hermeneutics. This primacy is articulated in Exodus 24:7 in which the people say first "We will do" and then add "and we will listen" (na'aseh ve-nishma').[33]

Levinas insists that I am asymmetrically responsible to the point of substitution for the other, even as I cannot expect the other to substitute herself for me, since such an expectation "would be to preach human sacrifice."[34] An expectation of substitution, in which the substitution is perceived as reciprocal, would form a symmetrical rather than asymmetrical relation, and it would be another form of equivalence and exchange. This nontransferable, irreversible, and gratuitous responsibility is the traumatic passivity of my obligation for and to the other in its priority over my claims to obligate the other.[35] Such substitution is intensified to the point of persecution. I become hostage to the other, even when the other troubles and—in a preposterous demand—persecutes me.[36] The I is addressed and singled out as responsible through the other's unavoidable face and irrevocable height.

In *Otherwise than Being*, Levinas does not establish a moral theory or guidelines to moral action but instead interrogates the conditions of the ethical.[37] Nevertheless, the *hineni* ("Here I am") of the *Akedah* presents his thought with a peculiar challenge, insofar as Levinas is committed to interpreting the experience and category of the religious in an immanent way through the asymmetrical ethical encounter and relation; there can be accordingly no separation of the obligation to God, the Other, and the other even as he stresses their nonidentity.[38] In fact, Levinas's argumentation compels us to avoid reifying the distinction between the unconditional constitutive Other and the conditional relative other in ways that undermine responsibility for the latter empirical ontic others.

Levinas's understanding of the religious motivates his criticisms of visions of participation in the divine and enthusiastic, fideistic, and voluntaristic portrayals of God. Analogous to the portrayal of Confucius in the *Analects*, speculation concerning the otherworldly and supernatural is deemphasized and bracketed without religious language being eliminated, such that the ethical, and one's own ethical disposition and comportment, becomes a crucial concern.[39]

In neither Levinas nor early Confucian thought is there a "secularization" of the religious, since religious practices are interpreted through the ethical without being thereby eliminated. Yet the aporetic paradox of absolute sacrifice revealed in Kierkegaard and Levinas appears to be distant from classical Chinese philosophy, which has no drama comparable with the *Akedah*. The Confucian interpretation of ritual sacrifice to spirits (*shen* 神) prioritizes their ethical significance in maintaining a sense of tradition for the sake of sincerity (*cheng* 誠) and ritual propriety (*li* 禮) as normative conditions of social life and self-cultivation. Confucianism gives the impression of being a variety of this-worldly thinking, as seen in the charges articulated by Mozi 墨子 against its disenchantment of heaven's will (*tianzhi* 天志) and of ghosts and spirits (*guishen* 鬼神). Even the judgmental heaven and spirits of Mozi enforce a worldly moral order that they do not contravene. An intriguing affinity between Confucian ethics and Levinas's vision of Judaism is that the ethical, preoccupied with the practical dimension of "behavior, actions and rites,"[40] orients the religious as the ethical is enacted in everyday practices of rituals of politeness.

Despite the centrality of Abraham's "Here I am" in his writings, Levinas elucidates this utterance through Isaiah's inspirational call to prophecy, in which the reply precedes the appeal: "Before they call, I will answer."[41] Abraham is an indication of Jewish ethical humanism in interceding humbly for mercy for Sodom and Gomorrah. Isaiah's prophetic mission is more radical in responding not only to God's interpolation but to the contrite and the humble as well, as he calls for sharing bread with the famished and welcoming the most wretched into one's home.[42] Isaiah is in fact the one who expresses God's consecration of "the stranger, the widow, and the orphan."[43] Focusing on the ethical significance of the "Here I am" in the Hebrew Bible, Levinas's most explicit and detailed discussions of the difficulties of the *Akedah* appear in his criticisms of Kierkegaard's retelling of the narrative of Abraham's binding of Isaac.

Confronting Abraham

Abraham did not only reply to God with the words "Here I am." He used these words in response to his son, Isaac, whom God commanded him to sacrifice:

וַיֹּאמֶר יִצְחָק אֶל-אַבְרָהָם אָבִיו, וַיֹּאמֶר אָבִי, וַיֹּאמֶר, הִנֶּנִּי בְנִי; וַיֹּאמֶר, הִנֵּה הָאֵשׁ וְהָעֵצִים, וְאַיֵּה הַשֶּׂה, לְעֹלָה.

And Isaac spoke unto Abraham his father, and said: "My father." And he said: "Here I am, my son." And he said: "Behold the fire and the wood; but where is the lamb for a burnt-offering?"[44]

The priority of ethics has led to using moral norms as the measure of religious truth and validity for thinkers such as Kant. Since morality sets the measure by which the validity and worth of religious claims should be evaluated, claims contradicting that measure ought to be rejected—despite the appearance of being a genuine religious command, miracle, or revelation. In Kant's deontological understanding of the ethical, morality necessitates the universality of practical reason and the recognition of each person's autonomy as an inviolable end-in-itself, which challenges the particularity and partiality of positive religions.[45] The Enlightenment's reduction of religion to its rational ethical core was contested by Friedrich Schleiermacher in *On Religion: Speeches to Its Cultured Despisers*. His argument offers one interpretive strategy of accounting for religion within modernity. In this work, the incomprehensible is disclosed as a condition of comprehension, the incommunicable reveals possibilities of communication (*Mitteilung*), and the other necessary to becoming a self.[46] Schleiermacher did not articulate the relation of the ethical and the religious as an aporia or paradoxical deadlock; he argued for the uniqueness of the religious experience that had its own social and ethical character in contrast with the morality of abstract universal reason.

Another strategy highlighting the ethical truth of religion was proposed by Leibniz, who did not reject the *Akedah* narrative, but relativized its sacrificial dimension by differentiating the obligation and the act: "It is true that God may command something and yet not will that it be done, as when he commanded Abraham to sacrifice his son: he willed the obedience, and he did not will the action."[47] In Leibniz's *Theodicy*, in which voluntaristic and legal positivist conceptions of God's will are rejected as arbitrary, despotic, and irrational, God's command to bind Isaac and his later command, through the angel, not to sacrifice him are—through the distinction between command and will—both ostensibly consistent with one another and the goodness distinctive of God.

The traditional Jewish reading prioritizes the ethical moment of God's mercy, which does not permit Isaac's sacrifice and "represents the abandonment of pagan sacrifice" that hitherto characterized proto-Judaism itself.[48] This is the reason why, as Hermann Cohen notes, it is called binding (*akedah*) rather than sacrifice and "manifests the reciprocal effect of Abraham's love for God and God's love for him and his descendants."[49] Religious responsibility calls for and culminates in ethical responsibility to the extent that the actual drama—that of living within the interval of the ethical indicated in the face of the other—commences for Levinas after it has concluded for Kierkegaard.[50]

Detractors depict the *Akedah* as reflecting the primordial paradigm of patriarchal monotheistic violence that they claim continues to inform the reality and practices of followers of Judaism, Christianity, and Islam, especially in terms of the exclusion of women from decision making and public roles.[51] The sacrifice of the one beloved son prefigures the central Christological event, in which God's mercy does not intervene for the sake of this one singular concrete human being, who is sacrificed for the sake of redeeming the many. Even if this story were not the negation of the ethical, it remains a difficulty for interpretation and—given its questionability and horror—it should not be too easily reconciled with the ethical as Kierkegaard emphasizes. But it is not only Kierkegaard: there are authors in the Jewish tradition who emphasize the horror, questionability, and uncertainty of Abraham's trial and the extraordinary and exceptional character of the *Akedah* that can and should not be explained away.[52] Philo in particular insisted that Abraham's conduct is "wholly novel" and cannot be derived from custom or tradition.[53] Abraham's unique significance cannot be underestimated; indeed, it serves to distinguish the Judaic from the pagan: "It is of more importance than all the actions of piety and religion put together."[54] No one is similar or equivalent to Abraham, as the pseudonymous figure Johannes de Silentio (the authorial name Kierkegaard uses in this work) maintains.

Portrayals of the *Akedah*, such as that of Kierkegaard, present a challenge to Levinas's interpretation of the religious. One can well ask whether Silentio's paradoxical trial of faith, in which the ethical is the temptation, in which murder becomes "a holy and God-pleasing act," and in which responsibility is beholden to no one except God, is inherently incompatible with Levinasian ethical responsibility for human others.[55] In emphasizing the conclusion of the *Akedah* and God's benevolent mercy, instead of emphasizing Abraham's traumatic exposure to the order to sacrifice his one beloved son as a burnt offering, does Levinas underestimate the significance of its drama, as stressed by Silentio? Does Levinas miss the shudder and paradox of a God whose primordial command is

"Thou shall not kill" as shown—prior to the announcement of the Ten Commandments in Exodus 20—by the narrative of the advent of murder in Cain's killing of his brother Abel, and the command to kill Isaac on Mount Moriah? Does he misunderstand the faith that overcomes despair and the obedience that overcomes one's questionability, which makes Abraham a new and unique hero for Philo and Kierkegaard?[56]

These suspicions can be pushed further: does Levinas's assessment of Kierkegaard's reading as a variety of fideistic enthusiasm, and his avoidance of a Christian—or modern Protestant—understanding of faith, lead Levinas away from the *Akedah*'s questionability and horror? Should one conclude that Levinas, as previously with Kant, did not allow the religious to exceed and challenge the ethical that is ultimately its measure? Is this another reduction of the religious to a modernist ethics that undermines its meaning? In response to such questions and suspicions, and readings that promote them, I suggest that Levinas's explication of the *Akedah* is more multifaceted, just as the Jewish tradition itself is.[57] The *Akedah* cannot be read purely ethically for the sake of the human other, nor as a story of moral edification; nor is it the transethical suspension of the ethical suggested in *Fear and Trembling* by Silentio.

In Levinas's analysis, the binding of Isaac cannot represent either the negation or the affirmation of the ethical. It cannot be contained by Kierkegaard's either/or as a choice between the ethical and the religious, because it constitutively presupposes violence, betrayal, and the aporia of the ethical; that is, it presupposes mercy for the other appearing within the midst of and interrupting this scene of patriarchal religious violence. Levinas concludes that the founding moment of Israel, and of Abrahamic religiosity, is not then Abraham's willingness to ritually perform the sacrifice of his beloved son commanded by God, but the intervening interruptive mercy that intrudes upon it. That is, the ethical is the suspension of the merely religious rather than, according to *Fear and Trembling*, the religious constituting the suspension of the ethical. The ethical event is not found in God's command to sacrifice but, on the contrary, in the interruption of this command by the ethical demand not to kill.

The Suspension or the Provocation of the Ethical?

Abraham responded to the call of God's intervening angel with the words "Here am I":

וַיִּקְרָא אֵלָיו מַלְאַךְ יְהוָה, מִן-הַשָּׁמַיִם, וַיֹּאמֶר, אַבְרָהָם אַבְרָהָם; וַיֹּאמֶר, הִנֵּנִי

And the angel of the Lord called unto him out of heaven, and said: 'Abraham, Abraham.' And he said: "Here am I."[58]

On being asked in an interview whether one should evaluate biblical characters such as Samuel according to ethical criteria, Levinas responded, "I don't believe one can kill like this face to face as easily as Samuel does. There are definitely certain things in the Bible that shock us, and I think that one shouldn't start with these. But even in these texts, you need to listen to what they are saying."[59]

It is undeniable that Levinas prioritizes the ethical moment of the *Akedah*, arguing for the primacy of the third *hineni*, when Abraham listens to "the voice that brought him back to the ethical order."[60] Levinas notes that it is remarkable that Abraham listened to and obeyed the first voice, God commanding his son's binding, but "that he had sufficient distance with respect to that obedience to hear the second [divine] voice—that is the essential."[61] Listening and responding to the second voice from God, the command not to sacrifice Isaac spoken through the interceding angel, does not negate his obedience to the first voice of God; yet it does transform its significance by placing God's first traumatizing address, and Abraham's two prior utterances of "Here I am" to God and to Isaac, in their ethical context. To this extent, Levinas recognizes the enigma and violence of the transcendent that "traumatizes and compels."[62] Given this trauma and violence in the midst of which the ethical appears, Levinas cannot be said to sublimate or overcome the religious for the ethical, as might be said of Kant's rational religion, even as the ethical is the necessary and genuine, albeit impossible and hence aporetic, demand of the religious.

Levinas accordingly insists that the intervening moment that intrudes on human sacrifice and reveals God's mercy for Abraham and Isaac should be interpreted in the context of Abraham's failed intercession with, and plea for mercy from, God for the sake of Sodom and Gomorrah.[63] That is, for Levinas, Abraham is not Johannes de Silentio's "father of faith"; Abraham's story in its fragility is a more elevated revelation of mercy.

Kierkegaard did not forget how Abraham prays for others, and not selfishly for himself, as evidenced by his prayers to God to spare Sodom and Gomorrah.[64] Instead of being a Kierkegaardian hero of faith or new model for faith, with the activity, subjectivity, and return of the self to the self that this suggests for Kierkegaard, Levinas comments on how "Abraham is fully aware of his nothingness, mortality, and fragility: 'I am but dust and ashes.'"[65] The humility of "me, dust and ashes" is a "destitution which reveals glory."[66] It is such humility for the sake of others in dialogue with the transcendent that marks Abraham's elevation and election as the father of ethical humanism.[67] For Levinas, it is Abraham's humility rather than a masculine pride and virile self-assertion that, as Catherine Chalier notes, leads him to the urgency and promptness of the "Here I am" "without taking time to inquire about his reasons."[68]

The divine law, therefore, is not the voluntaristic or positivistic command of a great yet arbitrary and despotic will, "an oppressive grip exerted upon the freedom of the faithful. It signifies, even in its constraining weight, all that the order of the unique God already provides for participation in his reign, for divine proximity and election, and for accession to the rank of the authentically human."[69] Not dissimilar to Leibniz's antilegalistic conception of God on this point, yet without his concern for systematic reconciliation of Abraham's initial and final *hineni* in the *Akedah*, Levinas insists that God is best interpreted through universal goodness rather than the primacy of will, power, or subjective faith. However, Levinas is not the sole thinker who prioritizes goodness over the will. The primacy of the good over the sovereign will serves, for Leibniz as well, as an interpretive guide to those difficult biblical passages that present God as despotic and as the contradiction of divine goodness. By not taking these exceptional passages as the norm but, instead, by listening more carefully, another form of hermeneutics is possible. Given such an interpretive approach, the *Akedah* discloses neither the primacy of subjective faith nor the voluntaristic conception of God suggested by divine command theory; it is an indication of the priority of the ethical demand of the good that is shown in divine mercy and grace.[70]

The humanism of the other, as it is revealed in Abraham and the prophets, exhibits the ethical truth of monotheism more fundamentally than do faith and its subjectivity. The different responses to alterity distinguish Judaism and Christianity for Levinas. Though it should be noted that faith is for the sake of "this life" and is "a task for a whole lifetime" that culminates in the moment in Johannes de Silentio's account,[71] prior to faith and its subjective "I believe" is the embodied and performative "Here I am," in which one is singled out before God and in service to others, and "in which God comes to be involved in words."[72]

Despite Kierkegaard's decentering of the conventional self, and his emphasis on how faith makes one an alien in the world, Levinas regards Kierkegaard's Abraham as still having too much expectancy and hope, too much activity and agency. Levinas, differently and to a greater degree—if it indeed requires such radical transcendence—than the immanent passivity of *wuwei* 無爲 articulated in the *Daodejing*, the *Zhuangzi*, and later Daoist influenced works, stresses passivity and responsiveness through which exteriority disruptively enters and overcomes the narrowness of the ego and its interiority.[73] In spite of Kierkegaard's provocative elucidation of the paradoxes of interiority and subjectivity, Levinas suggests that Kierkegaardian subjectivity remains too close to the self-concerned and self-involved egoism of the same, an irresponsible faith and thus essentially "atheistic" egoism.[74] Levinas rejects the thesis that religion concerns faith as a form of belief, a subjective truth, or what he argues is an egotistical and self-interested search for consolation, redemption, and salvation. Faith is not even primarily about God for Levinas in his claim, echoing the *Works of Love*, that "[f]aith is not a question of the existence or non-existence of God. It is believing that love without reward is valuable."[75]

Focusing on the Kierkegaard of *Fear and Trembling*, Levinas contends that in Kierkegaard faith belongs to the egoism of salvation and thus indirectly to the violence of the self-concerned conatus and its preservation in being, instead of being turned around and moved by the other.[76] Faith, even in this radical Kierkegaardian form, continues to speak "the language of being," which in Levinas's analysis is inevitably egotistical and narcissistic in its self-concern.[77]

Levinas persistently distinguishes between the indifference of the ontological "there is" (*es gibt*) and the nonindifference of the personal "Here I am" (*me voici*). Abraham's relation with God reveals a more fundamental passivity, the passivity of inspiration that is a waking and sobering up, rather than the enthusiasm of participation and intoxication.[78] It is a passivity that would be more passive than even the abjection in faith and suffering truth imagined by Kierkegaard: "Life receives meaning from an infinite responsibility, a fundamental diacony that constitutes the subjectivity of the subject."[79] Levinas interprets "diacony," which is a Christian conception of care for the poor and serving those in need, as the condition of becoming a self. The ego cannot posit or produce itself; it comes into being through the other such that ethics (alterity) precedes ontology (identity). Levinas's reading resists reducing the biblical narrative of Abraham to this conclusion, or to mercy alone, since they would suppress the suffering and trauma vital to the dynamic of the ethical self. The story of Abraham is a teaching of mercy and grace without excluding the problematic of justice, as God commands both the binding and unbinding of Isaac, and destroys Sodom and Gomorrah despite Abraham's pleas for mercy and forgiveness.

Levinas interprets *hineni* as a fundamentally ethical saying that interrupts the self for the sake of the other. Yet the first instance of *hineni* in the *Akedah* appears to be not for the sake of the human other (Isaac) but in response to the pure command of the divine Other.[80] And Abraham's second *hineni* appears to be a lie and an evasion of Isaac's question—which as inadvertent prophecy might become the truth as events unfold—or is it, as Levinas's comments on the author Shmuel Yosef Agnon reveal, a question without answer or response?[81] Does it indicate the impossibility of responding, the impossibility of ethics without the unethical, without betrayal, complicity, or sacrifice?[82]

In Levinas's depiction, it is the third *hineni* in response to the angel (the second divine voice of interceding mercy in Levinas's account) that is crucial. This third *hineni* reveals God's mercy in a call that turns Abraham toward the ethical. Does this reading underestimate the trial, temptation, and suffering, emphasized by Kierkegaard, that leads up to the ethical turn? Levinas does underemphasize the moment of faith and its suffering, which would turn the exception into the norm, because in his interpretation the narrative does not concern God's capacity to supersede the ethical (as in fideistic interpretations of Kierkegaard) or to arbitrarily decree any possible command through the divine will (as in voluntaristic divine command theories). This need not imply a return to the ethical after its religious suspension, as a particular reading of Kierkegaard might suggest, but indicates instead an intensified affirmation of the primacy of the ethical beyond sacrificial exchange of the firstborn for a god's disfavor or favor.

Levinas's interpretation of the ethical is defined by singular mercy rather than universal justice or brutal compulsion. It places in question the strict and limited conception of justice governed by an identitarian logic of equivalence, exchange, and sacrifice. The angelic intervention upsetting human sacrifice binds God and the other more tightly together for Abraham; God's command becomes incomprehensible without service to others. Despite appearances, then, and in keeping with one traditional Jewish reading, the *Akedah* teaches a lesson about the interruptive possibility of mercy in opposition to the despotic power and obedience that disregard mercy and compassion. Cruel justice demands its retribution, revealing how unethical the fixated equivalence and identity demanded by this form of justice can be.

Is the Ethical or the Religious Primary?

Silentio delineated the ethical as the universal that annuls the singular.[83] Levinas interprets the singular that breaks with the ethical as violence. Suspicious of the violence in the language of Kierkegaard's reading, Levinas explicitly challenges his point of departure, and thereby his distinction between the ethical as the universal and the religious as the singular. There is no irresolvable aporia between the ethical and religious in Levinas. An interruptive aporia does not take place between the spheres or levels of the same existence, as it does in Kierkegaard's writings. It occurs "between" the self and other. Yet it is not this "between" that binds them together and separates and individuates the "I" and the "you," insofar as the "between" is a space of immanence, but only the transcendence and height of the other, the formless and the invisible that shines forth in the epiphany of the other's face. Accordingly, both the ethical and the religious are interpreted as proceeding to my singular and asymmetrical responsibility from the other who transcends my existence.[84]

Although Abraham bound and nearly sacrificed his beloved Isaac to follow God's initial command, Levinas does not follow Leibniz's or Kierkegaard's attempts to resolve the disparate elements of the narrative into either God's goodness or the power and truth of faith. Despite the sacrificial command and near killing of Isaac, the narrative's meaning becomes apparent when God's mercy is revealed. Levinas insists that Abraham's asymmetrical responsibility is for the singular human other and not for the divine other. This is so even as it has a moment of universality, to the extent that ethics concerns the fate of all, including those who are deemed unworthy of life. The disturbing *Akedah* narrative culminates in the mercy that saves Isaac as this singular concrete human being. This is a form of mercy that breaks through the violence of the ontological realm of being and its logic of sacrifice: and it is here exactly where the ethical is discovered. In this sense, ethics cannot be subordinated to theology or religion, as "creation, omnipotence, rewards, and promises" are secondary to responsibility of one-for-the-other and to love, "the trace of the coming of God to mind."[85] Nonetheless, one might ask from the perspective of Kierkegaard: does Levinas adequately account for, or does he evade, Abraham's lack of initial resistance to God's order to sacrifice his child Isaac?

Levinas describes how ethics cannot be derived from theoretical or cognitive knowledge of the ontic facts of the world and their ontological conditions, including theological ones, even as my prereflective responsibility inherently elicits reflection. Reflection, and its tendency toward rationality and universality, is not omitted from the ethical or the religious, as maintained by anticognitivist interpretations of Kierkegaard and Levinas. Instead, they are related to practice, and derivative of being singled out as responsible for others in chosenness and election, in being uniquely and singularly responsible for the other without expectations about the other.[86] Such chosenness, as an irreducible responsibility of the one for the other, rather than as superiority, is indicated in the Jewish conception of "covenant" (*berit* בְּרִית). Ethics is accordingly inherently religious, in the sense of being irreducible to and intruding on the logic of exchange, the economy of being, prudential calculation, and the human sacrifice these require and excuse.[87]

The multifaceted threads interweaving Levinas's interpretation of the *Akedah* with traditional Jewish readings consist in the intervention of mercy that disorients and reorients the self toward the ethical order, and the renunciation of human sacrifice. The disorienting aporetic narrative of Abraham's binding of Isaac consists of God's command that binds Abraham to sacrifice Isaac, and God's merciful unbinding of Abraham's sacrificial action. His drama does not so much transcend or suspend the ethical in devotional faith (Kierkegaard). It indicates the "an-archic" (orderless) and immemorial (originless) sources of the ethical in generosity and the gift. That is to say, ethical moments such as mercy, grace, and love disrupt the logic of the sacrificial demand.

Levinas portrays how there is a "Torah before Sinai." That is, reconceiving the Jewish idea of law, a law prior to the law and an ethics prior to its discursive justification and argumentation, which, from Adam and Eve to Cain and Abel, to Abraham and Isaac, already involves the drama and complication of the ethical.[88] Ethics does not begin in the self and totality (i.e., in the order of the same) that precludes recognition of the other and refuses even its own brother and neighbor, as will be considered further in the chapters of part 3. The ethical is anachronistic; it can be neither pure nor "original," since it arrives with fall and betrayal. Neither law nor faith can be separated from the betrayal, the complicity, and the fragility that is constitutive of the human condition. Ethics means to be complicit—to be simultaneously and unavoidably both betrayer and betrayed—and yet to be without excuse for one's complicity with betrayal. It arrives from afar and in the night in the intensity of the prophetic moment. It breaks through in the other in whom the self hears God's word.[89]

The holy word is irreducible to the rules of conventional morality and the instrumental calculations of politics. Yet, Levinas insists its prophetic resonances can disorient and reorient routine expectations and instrumental calculations. The holy word as the prophetic saying of a justice to come is unsettling. Prophecy arising from the other is more exceptional than any form of faith occurring from the self. Prophecy is a unique noncalculative temporality that—depicted as being struck and overcome by the "other-power" (an idea interconnected with compassion and forgiveness in Japanese Shin Buddhist thought) of the transcendent good beyond being—exceeds, escapes, and resists both the naturalistic objectivity of beings and the subjective interiority of the individual self (its self-power), which are opposed in Kierkegaard's discourse.[90]

Interlude: Levinas, Moore, and the Priority of the Good

"The Good is before being."

—Emmanuel Levinas, *Otherwise Than Being or Beyond Essence*

It is thought-provoking to compare the good in Levinas with the priority of the good in philosophers such as G. E. Moore here as well as Knud Løgstrup and Iris Murdoch in chapter 10 below. Moore upheld in the *Principia Ethica* (1903) the Platonic priority of the good.[91] The good cannot be defined by other properties in his account, since it defines every other ethical property. It is "first" in not being definable through other properties and is thus incapable of proof according to standard Western interpretations of argumentation. Furthermore, the good is nonnatural, as it cannot be explained by the natural sciences or deduced from the order of nature, which would be to commit the naturalistic fallacy of illegitimately closing the "open question" of whether what is natural is good.⁹² Ethics proceeds through self-evident moral intuitions incapable of proof or disproof.

Levinas rejected arguments for the direct intuition, experience, or disclosure of the good. The good is exteriority, radically striking the self from the outside, from alterity rather than being a product derived from one's own intentions and will (deontological ethics) or one's own cultivation of virtue and perfection (virtue and perfectionist ethics), as examined in chapter 10. Levinas describes the good as occurring beyond the order of being and knowing while continuing to evoke the good's intuitive qualities found in the Platonic tradition, from Plato's vision of the form of the good, which Levinas addresses as the good beyond being, to G. E. Moore's simple, indefinable, nonnatural good and Iris Murdoch's sovereignty of good.

The "an-archy" and "in-finity" of the good expressed by Levinas appears analogous to Moore's conception insofar as it is nonnaturalistic and ungroundable. First, the good cannot be known through other properties or explained through the order of nature. The ultimate orientation of ethics is "first" and incapable of direct proof or disproof according to the standards of traditional Western logic. Is this then moral intuition after all? The good is not positively revealed, as it is for Moore, through self-certain intuitions that result in a list of incommensurable goods and an impartial consequentialism. Levinas might appear to this extent to be a "negative" moral intuitionist who reverses standard moral intuitionism found in Moore. Although it does appear to have a quasi–a priori character for Levinas, as it does in Moore, the good is not disclosed in intuition. It is revealed against experience and intuition through the disturbance of the Other who is foreign and alien in the realm of the visible, a nonpresence in the regime of presence. The good appears—insofar as its traces appear and can be traced at all (and one might here compare Derrida's thinking of the trace in this context)—as paradoxical from the perspective of and as irreducible to the common space of identity; that is, as diachronic, asymmetrical, and aporetic. One should question whether "apophatic" or "negative" "ethics (as an ethics that unsays in saying and is defined through what it is not) shares the same plight as negative theology, and whether one can appeal to something like Platonic qualities of the good, characterized as they are through ineffability and an infinite deferral of meaning, without presupposing intuitionism or even the Platonic intellectual vision of the good.

Is Levinas in the end a cryptointuitionist in the lineage of Plato? The good is not, however, only and purely transcendence, as it can appear for Levinas as the human good in the midst of daily life. The human genuinely occurs "between two," in not denying, as Cain did, that one is one's "brother's keeper." Such constitutive cohumanity, and the priority of the ethical, is indicated in a different manner in the ethical-anthropological understanding of the human (ren 人)—which can commonly refer to the other person—as "cohuman," or as constituted between two humans (ren 仁) in the *Mengzi* (孟子).

The self seeks and desires and yet is unable to control, equalize, or neutralize the other that seeks to evade and escape it. This would be a struggle for recognition if not for the radical disruptive appearance of the good in the midst of contest and struggle. The paradigm of agonistic and antagonistic contest in Hegel, Nietzsche, and Heidegger is one that Levinas problematizes. Levinas's concern, as will be considered further in part 3, can be extended to Honneth's modification and reconstruction of the paradigm of the struggle for recognition. The primacy of the ethical as first philosophy signifies for Levinas that the self or ego already presupposes an other exterior to itself that escapes its confines and presuppositions and that is prior to all struggle and contest as well as exchange and equivalence.

Ethical relations, based on alterity and nonidentity, are shot through with paradox, impossibility, and aporia, and so demand the constant vigilance and renewal of the ethical in response to the other; there is at the same time nothing prior to or more ancient than the ethical that did not "begin" with the written laws handed down at Sinai. The ethical moment is aporetic as it is "im-possible": the possibility of the impossible, the otherwise, disturbing the usual, the probable, and the calculable. What is impossible here is not only the inability to recognize, grasp, and control the other, which remains an ontological concern, but the ethical movement itself that has to do a with relation that is significantly divorced from ontology, sameness, and the reduction of the other to identity. Ethics can be manifested in interruptions and failures to grasp and mediate the other, yet the ethical is much more than and irreducible to the frustrations of the ego and the self in such breakdowns and failures.

Whereas Moore perceives the good to be indefinable yet knowable through intuition, Derrida articulates the aporetic necessity of ethical action through its very impossibility. Ethics is paradoxically an impossible yet unavoidable obligation: "To do the impossible cannot be an ethics and yet it is the condition of ethics."[93] The aporetic and interruptive is not the destruction but the condition of the ethical. As such, ethics is an-archically irreducible to either a given form of historical ethical life (Sittlichkeit) or a realm of abstract moral principles and deontological understanding of duties (Moralität). The ethical is a promise, if an impossible one, as Derrida proposes.[94]

Aporetic Ethics in Early Daoism, Kierkegaard, and Levinas

Kierkegaard and Zhuangzi have been interpreted as religious thinkers who share a spirit of antirationalist skepticism about the claims of reason and logical argumentation, all as part of an ultimately soteriological strategy.[95] Nothing might appear more foreign to Levinas—with his defense of the ethical, the humanistic and personal, and the rational—than the standard interpretation of early Daoist discourses as problematizing and overcoming ethics, humanism, and rationality through a naturalistic, impersonal, and "amoral" sageliness.[96]

The Daodejing and the Zhuangzi place conventional, rule-based, and moralizing sensibilities profoundly into doubt as the decay and loss of the dao. Nonetheless, the problematizing of limited conceptions of morality need not entail the rejection of the ethical. The Daodejing and Zhuangzi, as with Levinas's ethics, problematize—in their own contexts and ways—the notion that fixed moral codes and laws are the source of ethics and recognize how the objectification and institutionalization of morals and laws signifies the loss of the originary ethical as nourishing and nurturing life (yangsheng 養生) that cannot be limited to the self-satisfaction of the ego or the instrumental use of things (recall chapters 4 and 5). In Ethics and Infinity, among other works, Levinas considers how "thou shalt not kill" is prior to any ethical codes a society might write down and try to live by. The encounter of the face is the demand "thou shalt not kill," which appears prior to the structure of a fixed law, since a fixed law carries with it the possibility of transgression. But from the encounter of the face there is no possibility of transgression. It stands as prior even to the universality of a law. The infinite overflowing systematic totality is a characteristic of the ethical as an interruptive and transformational transcendence. The unruly and reorienting moment of impossibility that Levinas and Derrida describe—in joining their names here we must also keep their dissimilarities in mind—is the ethical as it is articulated in its own way in the "uneven" and aporetic ethical sensibilities evoked repeatedly in the *Daodejing* and the *Zhuangzi*. That is, the ethical is immanently hidden in the flow of the visible world (hiding the world in the world) rather than sustained through the appeal to the transcendent as in Levinas.[97] Early Daoism indicates paths to a different materialist interpretation and reinterpretation of Levinasian ethics.

Early Daoist sources such as the *Daodejing* and the *Zhuangzi* reveal the paradoxical call to cultivate what cannot be cultivated and to not harm, to care for, and to nurture all things by an-archically abandoning both conventional and philosophical models of ontology (that dictate how the world is) and morality (that dictate how one should behave). In contrast to the coercive imposition of one vision of totality contested by Levinas in *Totality and Infinity*, one cosmological model of the world, or one moral ideal of behavior onto oneself and others, Daoist philosophies offer an ethics of transformation. This ethical attitude is indicated in an immanent "shifting rightness" (*yishi* 移是) expressed in the *Gengsangchu* 庚桑楚 chapter of the *Zhuangzi*. In this later "miscellaneous chapter," which sheds light on themes throughout the *Zhuangzi*, one is said to freely comport oneself toward and thus nourish life—processes different from controlling, manipulating, and regulating the forces and conditions of life to their detriment and needless sacrifice.[98]

Basic words at play in the *Daodejing* and the *Zhuangzi*, such as *ziran* 自然 (as a natural or artless attitude of self-generating self-so-ness), *wu* 無 (nothingness), and *wuwei* (as a dispositional "nonacting action" or a noncalculative unforced responsive and nurturing being in the world) do not entail either amorality or immorality, much less nihilism.[99] They suggest instead an ethical disposition and way of comporting oneself through the aporias and paradoxes that constitute the nonindifference toward and the care for nourishing and nurturing life.[100]

The an-archic moments exposed by Zhuangzi in the reversals of the *dao* resist reified cognitive and linguistic categories by unfixing the fixity of the said. Such a saying of the ethical cannot be reduced to moral propositions, or to calculations, conventions, or rules that in fact betray and undermine the ethical itself. This impossible responsiveness of aporetic ethics, its uselessness in the face of the purportedly useful, is articulated though the ongoing transformation of immanence in the texts associated with early Daoist aporetic linguistic strategies and through the moment when transcendence breaks through the rigidity of immanence in Levinas. In these two ways of thinking, there is an ethically motivated suspicion of abstract transcendence and of reified unchanging immanence. Kierkegaard challenged these two ways of thinking through his existential psychologically oriented analyses, as it is found most intensely in *Fear and Trembling* (1843) and *The Sickness unto Death* (1849).

The texts identified with Laozi and Zhuangzi have been depicted as offering a more naturalistic way of being attuned within the natural world, in a way that is unencumbered by the restrictions of "Western" morality, monotheism, rationalism, and scientism. Daoism is consequently presented as an alternative to the flaws of "Western" reason and Middle Eastern religiosity. Early "classical" Daoism appears as a way of liberation in both religious readings, emphasizing soteriological mysticism and, in philosophical interpretations, accentuating an an-archic and poetic naturalism.[101] Both discourses coincide, despite their divergent strategies and stakes, concerning the need to liberate oneself from restrictive conventional moralities that reproduce alienation and violence; early Daoist sources can be interpreted in relation to Levinas as a radical inhabiting of the elemental and nurturing of the earth as traced in this book, and my other works on Daoism, in contrast to construing them as unfolding an antiethical, fatalistic, and unresponsive absorption in nature or a mystical cosmic order.[102]

Both the mystical and philosophical readings present early Daoist texts as a mythic exotic other of modern Western rationality and individual personalism. The impersonal interpretation of early Daoism as undermining the possibility of the ethical self and ethical agency is shared by its Chinese and Western critics, who perceive it as an inhuman and inhumane doctrine that depersonalizes individuals, sacrificing them as "straw dogs," and fatalistically letting them be as if they were floating leaves in the river of incontrovertible fate.

Conclusion: Contesting Conventional Morality

The misconceptions about early Daoism as expressed in the *Zhuangzi* text, Levinas, and Kierkegaard discussed above need to be further problematized. First, an unconventional yet nevertheless ethical dimension can be found in the works attributed to Laozi and Zhuangzi in the notion of nurturing and nourishing life (*yangsheng*) that encompasses nonhuman and human animals and inhuman things and nature.[103] Second, Levinas's thinking cannot be reduced to a thinking of transcendence alone. In addition to his rhetoric of radical transcendence, Levinas's writings articulate an immanent dimension in elucidating a this-worldly sensibility and sensuousness of both bodily and social affectivity. In these ethically oriented criticisms of morality, ethics is not rejected. It is broader and more radical than moralistic judgments or a customary or habitual morality based on conformity and instrumental calculation. In Levinas's face of the other and in the more encompassing Daoist working with, nurturing of, and responsiveness toward the "myriad things" (*wanwu* 萬物), as a mutual nourishing of life and solidarity between material beings, one can ascertain intimations in both discourses of an ethical event that transpires in the place of the encounter between self and the other/things that cannot be reduced to customs, norms, rules, or conventions and prejudices.[104] The *Akedah* and the *dao* are to an extent two distinctive instances of aporetic ethics that—despite one being personalist and the other expansively naturalistic—challenge conventional moralities for the sake of another ethical sensibility, and another way of relating to ourselves and the others around us.

If one turns one's attention toward the Kierkegaard of *Works of Love* (1847), it becomes clear that he cannot be interpreted solely as an antinomian or fideist antiethical thinker, despite the conclusions of several readings of *Fear and Trembling*.[105] The paradoxes of the ethical in Kierkegaard's latter work, in fact, lead to an ethics of love for the neighbor, in which the unique ethical significance of the ipseity of the singular person is revealed. This ethics of love of the other cannot be reduced to the morality that sacrifices the singular to the universal, as Kierkegaard articulated it in *Works of Love*. To this extent, it is dubious to overidentify Kierkegaard with Silentio's suspension of the ethical, which is one step in the realization of a different conception and experience of ethical life.

In summary, Levinas and Kierkegaard indicate divergent ways of confronting the Akedah narrative and rule-based morality for the sake of encountering and enacting the ethical in how one—the "I alone" as the singular unique one or as singled out in responsibility—dialogically lives in the midst of others.[106] These occurrences of aporetic ethics, albeit with the undeniable plurality and the irreducibility of their voices, strategies, contexts, and contents, might be said to converge in the endeavor of reorienting their readers toward the ethical through destructuring crises and paradoxical impassable aporias that express what resists being said and the gaps and fractures of totality, intimating possibilities of individual conversions of the heart and social transformations of peoples.

Levinas observes in his reading of the Akedah narrative how the ethical demand is a conversion from religious violence, sacrifice, and exchange. Ethics (as the other's demand) and politics (as dramas of institutionalization and betrayal, power and resistance) are formed in the negativities and contradictions of material life that is called to answer for its own conditions and promises. The prophetic demand is to end the brute command and its logic of sacrifice. The transformative positionality of the ethical—an-archic (that is, without one governing principle or temporal origin) and reorienting in life's alterity, materiality, and singularity—is disclosed in the imperfection and inconstancy of damaged life through the aporetic tensions in which the self is constituted and awakened by others. To speak with Adorno, ethical language can function as ideology and as protest. To echo Derrida's language from *Adieu to Emmanuel Levinas*, the impossibility of ethics (in and of itself) is a condition of its possibility in the lifeworld.[107]

Chapter Eight

Ethics between Religiosity and Secularity

Kierkegaard and Levinas

Introduction

It is a contested question whether the religious has any sense outside of the ethical in Levinas's works. He recurrently and emphatically used religious language and evoked a monotheistic sensibility in his philosophical and Jewish writings of the "God who comes to mind." However, he also praises secular ethics and can quote Vasily Grossman's words that "there is neither God nor the Good, but there is goodness," remarking that this "is also my thesis."[1] It is a legitimate question to pursue if the God evoked by Levinas is the same God of ordinary religious and theological discourses. Such tendencies in his writings have led interpreters such as Samuel Moyn to argue that Levinas secularizes the vocabulary of religious transcendence by prioritizing its ethical moment.[2] Yet, even if one were to assume that he has such a secularizing intention—and that secularization typically signifies the desacralization of God as well as the disenchantment of the world—Levinas's commitment to religious language and forms of life, such as his use of the word "God" and interpretation of Judaism, might appear perplexing to secularizing interpreters. It is indeed questionable given the interpretation of the secularization of God as signifying the destruction of transcendence. Levinas is inevitably ontological despite himself in construing God in reference to being as completely otherwise than beings and being.[3]

Speaking schematically at this point, key interpretations of the priority of the ethical in Levinas diverge into two general positions: (1) an ethical-political reading emphasizing the primacy of the human other and the rhetorical or deconstructive character of his religious language, and (2) an ethical-religious reading focusing on the inherent mutuality of the human and divine Other in which the religious is not to be secularized as a linguistic strategy but is necessary in being pretheoretically constitutive of ethical life. For the former interpretation, Levinas's discourse of God is an expression of what Benjamin described as the "weak messianic power" discussed in chapter 6.[4] The prophetic and messianic appears as an interruptive breakthrough of the good and the just into the injustices and horrors of historical life, a promise and break that, as "weak," does not require a present God or Messiah and might well be violated by them. For the latter approach, the religious signifies more of an ethical way of life than faith, given Levinas's rejection of the language of subjective faith, and insofar as the good is exhibited in the performance of the ethical demand in the activities and rituals of the daily life of a community. Addressing the other with "pardon," "God bless you," and "after you" are ethical examples that are much more than formal or ritual politeness. Both interpretive strategies, which have their sources in Levinas's own work and are at their most divergent in interpreting the political implications of his thought, agree that the religious—whether it is understood as an ethical idiom or a transcendent trace from beyond ethically intervening in worldly immanence—occurs in altruistic and responsive behavior toward others. In other words, the religious occurs in charity from kindness (*chesed* חסד) and proximity to the neighbor and in responsibility for "the stranger, the widow, and the orphan" as well as the exiled, the destitute, and the proletarian.[5]

Questioning Levinas Questioning Kierkegaard

Levinas's portrayal of the interpersonal as "originative religion" and religion as unconditionally and solely ethical in opposition to religion as faith and theology diverges from standard interpretations of Kierkegaard's religious thinking. Levinas repeatedly denies that religion concerns faith as a variety of belief, subjective truth, or what he argues is an egotistical and self-interested search for consolation, redemption, and salvation. For Levinas, "[W]hile remaining outside of reason, or while wanting to be there, faith and opinion speak the language of being. Nothing is less opposed to ontology than the opinion of faith."[6] Even in Kierkegaard, faith operates as a modality of being shaped by the desire and violence of the *conatus essendi* and the struggle for existence rather than being a movement toward ethical alterity.[7]

Levinas's strategy articulates a "religion for adults," an expression that evokes overcoming authoritarian tutelage in achieving moral maturity in Kant's essay "What Is Enlightenment?" Levinas perceives the ethical moment in monotheism in the example of Abraham's coming to adulthood through his break with idolatry and his disenchantment of the violence of participation in the ecstatic and the numinous for the sake of saintliness.[8] If, as Levinas maintains, "religion is to coincide with spiritual life" then "it must be essentially ethical."[9] All genuine spirituality is according to this argument interruptive as prophetic while being oriented toward the good in the midst of this life.[10] As a movement without teleology, an insatiable "metaphysical" desire for the good beyond being that outstrips all decisions, intentions, and projects that can be activated in the realm of being, Levinas's use of the word "religion" results in "no theology, no mysticism."[11]

Levinas portrays freedom in *From Existence to the Existent* (1947), a work begun in wartime captivity, as consisting of responsibility rather than grace, and messianic prophetic hope as hope in and for the present.[12] One can glimpse a comparable yet distinctive form of hope, as it proceeds through the grace of the absurd, in *Fear and Trembling* that emphasizes the fulfillment of faith in this life in the present instant.[13] Levinas, Dussel notes, "was a victim of the Jewish holocaust in the heart of Modernity."[14] Levinas thus speaks otherwise of religion in the flames and shadows of the systematically mass-produced violence and annihilation and of the Shoah.[15] Religion is for Levinas understood as lacking any consolation, guarantee, or promise; it is a "faith without theodicy."[16] It is furthermore "an awaiting without an awaited, an insatiable aspiration," which is due not to the limits or finitude of human existence but to the "in-adequation" (*in-adéquation*) and noncoincidence of infinity itself.[17] Religion is interpreted through its prophetic and ethical dimensions. But here prophecy is without expectancy, without future, even if these are understood as impossible promises on the paradoxical basis of and in the face of the absurd. Religion takes place beyond both Heideggerian possibility and Kierkegaardian impossibility. Although Kierkegaard's absurd exceeds one's own intentionality and activity, as reliant on the other-power of God as the transcendent that individuates and singularizes, it cannot adequately break with the dramas of participation in the divine and the egotistical self-concern for salvation according to Levinas.

Despite the abyss that appears to open between Kierkegaard and Levinas concerning the import of faith in his comments, Levinas further remarks, with regard to a religion without nostalgia about the past and expectation about the future, that all one can require ethically is to assume responsibility for oneself without demanding it of others. Levinas described the solitude of universal responsibility in his prison notebooks.[18] It is "only me" singled out and alone who is responsible to the extent of substitution for the other, and at the same time there can be no expectation that the other substitutes herself for me. Such a relentless demand would teach "human sacrifice."[19] Responsibility is accordingly a traumatic passivity for me through the obligation for and to the other. My being obliged does not symmetrically entail that the other is obligated toward me.[20] This disturbing interruptive substitution is an ascetic negation not of the I but of the self who is coming into its responsibility. Its scope does not even exclude my persecutors: I am hostage to the other who disturbs, wounds, and persecutes me.[21]

In a Prophetic Voice

It is only me—and no other—who is called and singled out as responsible via the prophetic demand toward others rather than a legal command or order. The face and height of the other not only orders but disorders and reorients. Contemporary normative moral theory from Habermas to John Rawls typically grounds ethics in the mutual and symmetrical relations between equal agents. Levinasian responsibility is asymmetrical in that it is not grounded in but precedes the symmetry of reciprocal recognition and communication. It unequally holds me in suspension as it demands more of me than it does of anyone else and, as such, it is a singular obligation addressing "each" rather than a universal duty addressing all. For Levinas, this inequality and asymmetry is the prophetic and ethical basis of equality itself: "The equality of all is borne by my inequality, the surplus of my duties over my rights. The forgetting of self moves justice."[22]

How can Levinas link the ethical with the prophetic? Divination and prophecy have been contested notions in Western religion and philosophy. Kant praised morally informed divination as a form of genius that can contribute to progress and enlightenment while denouncing prophecy as useless superstition.[23] Heidegger linked Jewish prophecy with the calculative-predictive mastery of things characteristic of modern temporality in his *Black Notebooks*.[24] Levinas has a fundamentally different understanding of prophecy—the temporality of expectancy and waiting for the other—as the Other within the Same.[25] Prophecy designates an appeal to goodness and justice that dislocates the paradigm of calculative exchange and instrumental rationality governing an impersonal and indifferent social totality.

Heidegger is mistaken to claim that Jewish prophecy concerns only calculating the future. Prophecy in the Tanakh is first and foremost concerned with a moral and social critique and transformation of the present. The visions of the future of the Hebrew prophets (*navi* נָבִיא) address present injustices. They are predictions not of what will happen but of what would occur if the advice of the ethical-political critique were not followed. Based on the classic Judaic understanding of the evils of divination and the glory of prophetic saying, interpreted as saying/unsaying, Levinas distinguished the "subjective and arbitrary divination of the future" from "the extraordinary phenomenon of prophetic eschatology" that concerns the ethical priority of the other person.[26] Levinas accordingly maintains the unique ethical temporality of prophecy missed by Heidegger: "Prophecy as the very duration of time, which is not identical to the vision of the visionaries and the diviners; prophecy that must be understand as the very *a-Dieu* of time, as its inspiration, with all the ethical conjunctures."[27]

Pluralism, Religion, and Faith

Levinas's conception of other-regarding asymmetrical responsibility, depicted as prophetic holiness beyond the expectations and promises of reciprocal exchange, brings to mind the notion of responsibility communicated in Kierkegaard. However, Levinasian asymmetrical responsibility is not identical with Johannes de Silentio's vision of Abraham in *Fear and Trembling*. Levinas himself differentiates these two perspectives. Kierkegaard's interpretation emphasizes Abraham's asymmetrical responsibility to God and separation from the human. Levinas criticizes this for the sake of ethical responsibility to the human other, in this case, to his son Isaac, and to God via this human other. Religious responsibility in Kierkegaard's sense, as alone singled out before God in one's responsibility, seems incompatible with ethical responsibility to God exclusively through responding to the human other.[28]

The question of the relation of the religious and the ethical cuts both ways, however; it might be asked whether Kierkegaardian faith is possible given Levinas's interpretation of religion, in which the objectivity of the book and the demand matters more than phenomena such as subjectivity, interiority, and conscience. Although Levinas's elimination of the modern Protestant religious categories at work in Kierkegaard's discourse might well be unproblematic, more troublesome is Levinas's contention that Kierkegaard's wound, passion, and turning in of the self upon itself is not sufficiently monotheistic but essentially "pagan."[29] This is a damning claim, because Levinas identifies, even if only rhetorically, modern paganism with evil and the return to the primitive, identifying its darkness as the absence of God's light.[30] In discussions of Heidegger's politics, Levinas ascribes paganism and atheism to national socialism, as if they were necessarily identical.[31] Nature itself, as seen in chapters 4 and 5, falls under a pagan "logic of indifference" as brutal, inhuman, and without God: that is, without the ethical.[32]

While there can be apparently no ethical pagans or atheists for Levinas, at least on conservative religious readings that have sources in Levinas's own texts, Kierkegaard is in multiple ways less reductive and more pluralistic. Kierkegaard contests fallen Christendom as self-deceptively Christian and actually pagan; the genuinely pagan (in contrast to what Kierkegaard designated the "Christian pagan" obsessed with worldly power and wealth) can achieve a more fulfilled religious consciousness than indifferent monotheists through passion and awe for the incommensurable, the eternal, and the divine. In a similar way, in Kierkegaard (or at least some of his personalities), the pagan, the atheist, and nonmonotheist can attain the virtues of ethical life, if not the faith that constitutes the fullness of the religious as distinct from the ethical that cannot overcome sin.[33]

By separating the ethical and religious spheres, and describing the abysses and breaks requiring leaps between them, Kierkegaard more adequately differentiates religious and secular ethical life without assimilating one to the other. In *The Moment* and other late polemical pieces, he fiercely radicalizes such separation for religious reasons to focus Christianity on individual freedom and responsibility and away from

Christendom's coercion and constant calculations concerning power, status, and wealth.[34] Levinas criticizes the "violence" of Kierkegaard's language, but it is noteworthy that Kierkegaard interprets Christianity as the renunciation of authority and power, whether of the self and other. Kierkegaard contests concrete instances of church control over secular life traditionally thought to be within the power of the church, maintaining that war and regulating marriage are secular and political rather than Christian practices.[35]

Based on Levinas's portrayal of the ethical as fundamentally monotheistic, even if this appears as a rhetorical strategy, as liberal and deconstructive readings contend, it is a genuine question whether Levinas allows ethical significance to nonmonotheistic ways of life and whether the atheist, the pagan, or the nonconforming pan-entheist Spinoza can be genuinely ethical. Levinas rejects mystical and monistic interpretations of God, as they—as in Spinoza's unity of nature and God or Hegel's absolute spirit—fundamentally lack alterity and transcendence, which are better indicated in the good beyond being in Plato's *Republic* and Descartes's argument in the *Meditations* for God's existence from infinity.[36] This issue of Levinas's apparent orthopraxy does not appear resolvable by arguing against religious appropriations of Levinas, and "secularizing" his way of speaking and taking it as a merely rhetorical linguistic strategy, if it remains privileged as a rhetorical and argumentative strategy. Why does Levinas assert at times that ethics is intrinsically atheistic and secular and at other times that ethics is essentially interconnected with monotheism and atheism signifies the absence of the ethical?[37] Over the course of his works, Levinas uses multiple diverging and conflicting senses of terms such as "atheism" and "paganism," such that, as we have seen, atheism can be identified with evil in one context and with ethical maturity in another. Atheism and disenchantment can be praised by Levinas as purifying religion of idolatry as well as the supernatural and superstitious that would undermine the ethical truth in religious discourses and practices.[38]

There are a number of interpretations of Levinas that risk reducing ethics to the religious and religion to the ethical, thereby doing injustice to the asymmetry between both, an injustice that Kierkegaard, the mere religious writer and theologian—as Heidegger categorized him—would have contested. At the same time as Levinas suggests that the tragic pagan is unethical, the Kierkegaardian perspective exposes Levinasian ethics as a lot closer to this position than Levinas himself would have accepted. If the tragic ethical hero acts for the universal by altruistically and therefore asymmetrically sacrificing what is most precious—child, life, or the self—for the sake of others, that is, by assuming a more extensive responsibility without the paradoxical absurdity of faith that distinguishes the hero of faith, then Levinas's idea of responsibility without hope or promise is closer to the altruistic resignation of Kierkegaard's tragic hero than to his hero of faith.

If it is the case that Levinasian ethics is neither secular nor religious in undermining both by confusing their terms, then his ethics must be interpreted either, on one hand, as a theological ethics for the religious or for a religious form of life, without pretending to be an ethics for each human, or, on the other hand, as a secular ethics that has abandoned its religious pretenses for each irreplaceable person and hence applicable to each regardless of religious affiliation, belief, or practice. This group consists of atheists, pagans, and pantheists who, as the supposedly hypertheological and "fideist" Kierkegaard recognized, do not and need not partake in monotheistic language—whether as truth or as rhetorical linguistic strategy—to have a form of ethical life. This applies even if Kierkegaard ultimately deemed it inadequate in comparison with the religious that overcomes sin. The inadequacy of paganism for Kierkegaard consists in the fact that it is tragic because it lacks the possibility of salvation, not because it is intrinsically evil and dark, since: (1) ethics is ultimately futile without the category of sin (which is to be transcended together with it);[39] and (2) the demonic is one form of the tragic illustrating how ethics and society can intervene yet not save.[40]

In the editor's preface to *The Book on Adler*, Kierkegaard repeats his critique of the dangers of secularization as part of the confusion of modernity that he illiberally analyzes as an inability to obey. Kierkegaard is opposed to cultural and political liberalism, yet he continues by presciently warning that the greatest danger is not the self-willfulness of secularization but rather the self-willfulness that in the name of God illegitimately assumes authority from God by attempting to collapse the religious into each aspect of life, even that which is nonreligious, such as the political sphere. The crisis of modernity rests in the confusion and totalization of the divergent and plural spheres of existence; for example, the destruction of the religious by overzealous religious enthusiasts who force everything nonreligious to be religious, thereby making the religious nonreligious.[41] As Kierkegaard contends in his critique of the fallen Christianity of Christendom, the drama of faith and redemption are lost in the machinations of earthly interests and power.

A number of approaches to Kierkegaard, Levinas, and the philosophy of religion have staked their claims based on the ambiguity that Kierkegaard diagnoses through the inability to distinguish between the secular and the religious. As a critic of the Enlightenment who places in question the overextension of the secular in modernity rather than its difference from the religious, Kierkegaard is closer to its aspirations in rejecting the conflation of the religious and the secular characteristic of "Christendom." Instead of making the decision for Christianity, which is a disturbance of and differentiation from the secular world, the decision has already been made by society, consequently taking it away from the individual.

Kierkegaard's analysis of placidity evokes Nietzsche's argument in the *Genealogy of Morality*, where the worshiping of uncertainty, the question mark, the inability to know, and the identification of this uncertainty with God is described as the intensification of the priestly ascetic ideal under the conditions of modernity.[42] Instead of concluding with the undecidability and consequent conflation of the religious and the secular, Kierkegaard sharpens the discrepancy by criticizing the confusion of the secular and the religious, or *dulia et latria*, as what is ethically owed to other humans as distinct from what is owed to God. He does this to contest religious confusion about the religious as a symptom of the modern crisis of religion. Such tendencies promote totality antidialectically rather than dialectically in the name of rejecting it, insofar as they subordinate the plurality of ways and spheres of existing to one inflationary or conflated term. No term is magically protected from the uprooting process of dialectical reversal. Not only are terms such as "ontological" and "aesthetic" vulnerable but "ethical" and "religious" are as well. In the name of messianic justice, Benjamin's weak messianic power is at risk of being converted back into worldly power; yet there is injustice not only in separating the secular and the messianic but also in sacrificing secular life for religious dominion. This is perhaps why philosophical and theological discourses denouncing pagan idolatry and atheistic evil resonate with contemporary religious fundamentalists, and their ideological and social-political uses.

Whatever proximity Levinas and Kierkegaard share concerning the interruptive character of being called to self-responsibility in being called by the transcendent, and concerning the abjection and suffering of witnessing,[43] their accounts of ethics and religion, and their relation through shared and overlapping concepts such as asymmetrical responsibility, appear disjointed and potentially irreconcilable as explored in the previous chapter and in this one.

Abraham, Isaac, and the Ends of the Ethical

How then do asymmetry, responsibility, and the nonuniversal concrete singular allow us to interpret the story of Abraham and Isaac examined in the previous chapter? On the one hand, Levinas argues against Kierkegaard's definition of the ethical as the universal and the religious as the singular. Both can be construed as proceeding from "my own" singular and asymmetrical responsibility in which I am singled out and individuated through "other-constitution."[44] Levinas contrasts this interpretive strategy with Heidegger's depiction of the mineness (*Jemeinigkeit*) and individuation of Dasein in *Being and Time*, which Levinas interprets as self-interested and solipsistic.[45]

On the other hand, the significance of the narrative of Abraham and Isaac is in Levinas's reading the moment in which Abraham hears "the voice that brought him back to the ethical order," adding that we should think of Abraham in this moment as the one who pleads with God to spare Sodom and Gomorrah before their destruction.[46] Abraham's asymmetrical responsibility, as argued in chapter 7, is for the concrete human other rather than the divine Other, even as it has a moment of universality to the extent that ethics concerns the fate of all, even those deemed unworthy of life. In Levinas, ethics cannot be derived from theoretical or cognitive knowledge even as my prereflective responsibility inherently elicits reflection. Reflection and its universality are not excluded from the ethical but derivative of my chosenness and election in being uniquely and singularly responsible for the other without expectations about the other.[47]

Universal responsibility for the other is at the same time the individuation of my singularity.[48] It is neither a universal property nor the uncanniness of Heidegger's being-towards-death that individuates; it is rather the "other [who] individuates me in the responsibility I have for him."[49] The moment of this each-time singular and unique universality in my responsibility contrasts strongly with the general and abstract universal normativity and symmetrical reciprocity as conceived from Kant to Habermas and Honneth that will be further analyzed in part 3.[50] According to Kant in *Religion within the Boundaries of Mere Reason*, "[I]f something is represented as committed by God in a direct manifestation of him yet is directly in conflict with morality, it cannot be a divine miracle despite the appearance of being one (e.g., if a father were ordered to kill his own son who, as far as he knows, is totally innocent)";[51] and "even if [a revelation] were to appear to him to have come from God himself like the command issued to Abraham to slaughter [*tevah* טבח] his own son as if he were a sheep, yet it is at least possible that on this point error has prevailed."[52] Since morality determines the criteria by which the validity and worth of religious claims ought to be evaluated, claims contradicting that standard should be rejected notwithstanding the semblance of being an authentic religious command, miracle, or revelation.

In Kant's ethics, as evident in the justification and formulations of the categorical imperative, morality demands universality and the recognition of each person's autonomy as an inviolable end in itself.[53] Kierkegaard's *Fear and Trembling* takes such an understanding of the ethical, as universal and applying equally to all, as its point of departure for what Abraham must contend with and potentially overcome. If ethics is indeed universal normativity, then Abraham is lost, as Kant himself recognized. Despite Kierkegaard's way of speaking about faith as embodied in the figure of Abraham, as entailing a suspension of the ethical, a number of recent interpreters contend that this is not so much a departure from the ethical per se as it is the recognition of ethics of the singular.

T. P. S. Angier proposes that the works of Kierkegaard cannot be appropriately read as advocating a choice that is antinomian and unethical, inherently arbitrary and irrational, or hyperexistentialist—a choice he links with Nietzschean nihilism—but instead promotes a different nonuniversal and personal ethics of humility, self-giving, and self-sacrifice.[54] The ethical as universal duty is suspended for the sake of the more genuine ethics of charity, friendship, and the neighbor unfolded in *Works of Love*. Unlike Kierkegaard's edifying discourses and sermons, ethics has a different function in *Fear and Trembling*. Johannes de Silentio asked "whether this story contains any higher expression for the ethical that can ethically explain his behavior, can ethically justify his suspending the ethical obligation to his son, but without moving beyond the teleology of the ethical."[55] He answered that it is the tragic hero who has his "*telos* in a higher expression of the ethical."[56] However, "Abraham's situation is different. By his act he transgressed the ethical altogether, and had a higher *telos* outside it."[57] Instead of being another variety or understanding of the ethical, it is the ethical itself that tests and tempts Abraham. Abraham's situation entails a "unique responsibility" rather than an aesthetic irresponsibility.[58] To conclude that Kierkegaard is defining the ethical in accordance with Abraham's paradoxical situation, much less a divine command theory, would undermine the significance of Kierkegaard's reading of the text: that the singular interrupts and exceeds all (including ethical and theological) justification. Such a normalization of the exceptional, given his respect for the ethical even in the *Akedah* narrative of Abraham, would have horrified Kierkegaard as not ethical at all if it does not rise through the level of the universal and does not arrive at the singular but falls back into the particular.

The figure of Abraham is an exception to the moral order, yet not on the basis of another morality considered as a discourse that could justify and explain him to the public and the world. Kierkegaard does not articulate another normative or prescriptive ethical theory or a religious alternative to Kantian ethics. *Fear and Trembling* indicates the tensions and limits of the ethical as such. Kierkegaard's exploration of boundaries in *Fear and Trembling* should not be mistaken for an ethics, even a religious or asymmetrical one, since Kierkegaard's portrayal of an ethics of the concrete existential other is articulated more fully in writings such as, in particular, *Works of Love*, which prioritizes the ethical concretion of love of and for the neighbor in relation to God's command.[59] Of diverse provenance, because of the use of various and conflicting pseudonyms, the ethical is not simply a Kantian and universalistic category to be eliminated in the name of faith. Kierkegaard repeatedly asserted that there can be no character, culture, or propriety without passion, highlighting the role of the affects and emotions in ethics even if—as Adorno argues—in pathological forms.[60]

Adorno, Kierkegaard, Levinas

According to Adorno in his 1939 essay "On Kierkegaard's Doctrine of Love," Kierkegaard's *Works of Love* "supplements his negative theology with a positive one."[61] As in his Kierkegaard book, Adorno identifies the primary role of subjectivity and an objectless interiority in Kierkegaard's discourse in ways that echo Levinas's criticism of egoism. The *Works of Love* reduces love to an object-less and other-less "endless monologue" of pure interiority in which the other cannot disappoint love, since it is not love for the concrete other that is at stake but love is only "practiced for the sake of God's command to Love," reproducing the cold calculative eros of Kierkegaard's seducer in *Either/Or* within love itself.[62]

Yet Adorno also recognizes that there are elements of social protest and critique in Kierkegaard's suspicion of the ideological functions of bourgeois ideas of equality and welfare, his ironic rejection of "seriousness," and his ethos of hope as a sense of possibilities.[63] This seriousness is the bodily actuality of redemption.[64] Adorno specifically links its critical potential against the logic of exchange with the tenacity of hope in his discourse: "Kierkegaard's doctrine of hope protests against the seriousness of a mere reproduction of life which mutilates humans. It protests against a world which is determined by barter and gives nothing without an equivalent."[65] Kierkegaard expresses through multiple fragmented and wounded voices, using pseudonyms or his own name, diverse indirect discourses from Socratic "ethical-ironic" to Christian love. He indicated the minutest steps from mourning to happiness, the "power of powerlessness," and thus critical images and models of the present.[66]

Kierkegaard maintained the moral rather than the aesthetic-romantic character of Christianity; even if he undermined it—as Adorno argued in his 1933 book *Kierkegaard: Construction of the Aesthetic*—in obeying a fundamentally aesthetic dialectic concerned with a poetic interiority that flees objective conditions and material contents.[67] In *Either/Or* and *Works of Love*, despite Adorno's trenchant criticisms, ethical life is unfolded—in contradistinction to both romantic aestheticism and deontological normative moral theory with which his thought is ensnared in Adorno's analysis—as being much richer and more complex than a vacant universal applying equally to all without consideration of particularity. Yet neither the earnestness of Judge William's life of Kantian-Hegelian social duty (which Kierkegaard ironically teases as misunderstanding the aesthetic from the perspective of the ethical but does not therefore dismiss) nor the rich texture of religious-ethical love, as it is revealed in *Works of Love* and in his upbuilding confessional writings, can make Abraham explainable to the understanding or ordinary life, which is how it should be, given what is about to take place on the mountain. For Kierkegaard's purposes, nonetheless, Abraham is an exemplar of and model for faith and its unique responsibility before God. Moreover, it is in its paradoxical form an example of what cannot be modeled and used as a model by others, as it tells of what stands in disorderly incommensurability with human normativity, judgment, and activity.

The discourses of Kierkegaard and Levinas diverge on religious responsibility that resists the ethical as universal in Kierkegaard but which calls for and culminates in an ethical responsibility as singular demand that eclipses command and faith theories of ethics in Levinas. The real drama of the narrative of Abraham and Isaac begins for Levinas after it has already concluded in Kierkegaard's account that centers on the dynamic of Abraham's faith and interiority.[68] If this reading of the two authors is appropriate, then Kierkegaard's paradox of faith and its responsibility is inherently incompatible with Levinasian responsibility, in its prediscursive passivity and dependence on the wholly Other, as a discourse concerning ethical justification and practice.

Demystifying Levinas: Must One Be Religious to Be Ethical?

Although one can interpret Levinas as a religious author and edifying moralist, the religious is by no means a simple, univocal, or unambiguous category in his works. In this section, I problematize the religious reading of Levinas unfolded above while avoiding excising the religious from his thought. This is possible insofar as the ethical and the religious are intertwined and cannot constitute an either/or for Levinas: the religious is the height of the ethical. At times Levinas emphasized the need for some sense of monotheism and God in constituting the ethical; at other times, he can speak more radically of a Comtean secularized "religion of humanity" that does not utter the word "God."[69] For Levinas, one cannot avoid the confusion of terms of referring to God and the human other, of employing an earthly horizontal and heavenly vertical religious language. Such ambiguous tension is inescapable due to the transcendence that exceeds intentionality.[70] God and the human other cannot be adequately identified or separated: "[T]he distinction between transcendence toward the other person and transcendence toward God should not be made too quickly."[71] There is a hesitation in distinguishing them while at the same time their irreducibility prevents the assimilation of the divine and human other.[72]

Fear and Trembling does not offer an ethics, much less an ethical theory; instead, it explores the limits of the ethical in religious experience. The main philosophical works of Levinas offer not a religious or theological ethics but a philosophical exploration of the conditions of the ethical that addresses all as a responsible singular each. Ethics is not so much a belonging to any order or institution of being, including religious belonging. Ethics is primarily the transcendence and utopia of "small goodness," to use Vasily Grossmann's expression, in everyday life.[73] It relies on the commonplace rituals of kindness and politeness that Levinas highlights in a number of contexts.[74]

Levinas's thinking of the ethical in *Totality and Infinity* begins precisely with disturbing yet unavoidable questions about the normalcy of the condition of war, violence, and complicity, and the states of emergencies that excuse the deferral of the ethical to better days.[75] Rather than naively asserting the ethical, Levinas's preface presents the reader with questions that seem to suggest its impossibility. Given the facticity and power of the Hobbesian state of war of all against all (*bellum omnium contra omnes*)—described in the preface to *Totality and Infinity*—and the allergic, almost spontaneous reaction against the other, how can ethics be possible? Supposing the ordinary self-interested egoism of self-enjoyment and possession, absorbed participation in the daily world, and disregard for the suffering of others, how can the ethical response to the other even begin? Can there genuinely be an ethics that extends beyond the friend and the neighbor to the stranger and even the enemy who persecutes me, or is this merely an overly demanding and outrageous hyperbolic rhetoric?

Notwithstanding religious and theological interpretations and appropriations of Levinas, the significance of religion for Levinas is ambiguous. It is neither the conquest nor reward of heaven but the invisible height that elevates in deference, wonder, and worship, and that cannot be located in consumption, caress, or liturgy.[76] In its alterity, infinity, and incommensurability, transcendence indicates the distinction and separation of the human and the divine, in such a way that the ecstatic and mystical, the violent and orgiastic (and its symbolic substitutes) assimilation of participation, and direct union and communion are not characteristic of the religious as ethical rather than mythical.[77] For Levinas, who praises the Pharisees' nonparticipation in divine drunkenness,[78] the divine is not absorption and subsumption into sameness and undifferentiated totality;

it is the interval in which identity is placed into question. Its meaning is not revealed in the ecstasy and enthusiasm of story, myth, liturgy, the supernatural, the miraculous, or faith.

Levinas's elucidation of the word "religion" in *Totality and Infinity* disrupts standard definitions of the religious for the sake of the nonidolatrous transcendence in ethical invocation and interpolation. The religious emerges as "the bond that is established between the same and other without constituting a totality."[79] It is a responsibility and obligation to the other as a beyond and excess that transcends the sameness of the ego and the reproductive identity of conceptual thinking and social totalities. This includes the sacred and holy violence of religions. Levinas claims that the religious is enacted in moral responsiveness to the other—that is, in the concrete reality of the transcendent Other appresented in the empirical other—as exemplified in the vulnerability and height of the face. This dimension of height is associated not with heaven but with invisibility.[80] Levinas's religiously inflected language of revelation, testimony, and witnessing refers to the heterogeneity of the other by whom I am already addressed and to whom I am called to respond.[81] I am pressed to reply to others prior to ideology and theology, indeed prior even to the self-conscious recognition of being a self, and their forgetting of the other as more than and external to myself. For Levinas, "[T]o wish to escape dissolution into the Neuter, to posit knowing as a welcoming of the Other, is not a pious attempt to maintain the spiritualism of a personal God, but is the condition of language."[82]

It was the Carthaginian convert to Christianity and polemical fideist Quintus Septimus Florens Tertullianus who formulated the radical opposition between Athens and Jerusalem in its classical form in his *Prescription against Heretics* (*De praescriptione haereticorum*): "What has Athens to do with Jerusalem?" This question was asked as part of a trinity of questions separating Christianity from Greece: "What indeed has Athens to do with Jerusalem? What concord is there between the Academy and the Church? What between heretics and Christians?" Tertullian answered by citing Acts 3:11: "Our instruction comes from 'the porch of Solomon,' who had himself taught that 'the Lord should be sought in simplicity of heart.'"[83] The philosophers are "patriarchs of the heretics." The faithful should, he asserts, be on their guard against the "vain deceit" of philosophy, since no bridge exists between Socratic reason and the simplicity of heart and faith in Christ.[84] Tertullian, of course, never stated the assertion falsely attributed to him, "Credo quia absurdum [est]" (I believe because it is absurd); he did assert concerning the resurrection, "Certum est, quia impossibile" (It is certain because it is impossible).[85]

Levinas's prioritization of Jerusalem over Athens is not an either/or between faith and reason. It does not designate the primacy of faith over reason as depicted in the Christian fideistic tradition from Tertullian to Kierkegaard. Jerusalem does not signify in this context fideistic faith but the prophetic priority of the good and justice over discourses of knowing and truth that presuppose the interpersonal encounters and intersubjective relations of self and other.

Levinas reveals the ethical core of knowledge through the "religious." He exposes the ethical core of the religious by "atheistically" confronting and destructuring the sacred violence of Dionysian participation and irrational faith. Levinas rejects atheism as the loss of the ethical demand. It is critiqued in the sense that it constitutes the denial and absence of the transcendent, while he praises atheism in another sense as the break with mythic absorption and monistic participation. Atheism in this second sense echoes Nietzsche's category of the Apollonian, except that it is primarily ethical rather than aesthetic. This ethical form of atheism is, for Levinas, also a revelation of God's glory in denying the allure of mythic powers and by allowing genuine ethical individuation in response to the other to transpire. Levinas depicts the atheistic break with enchantment and myth as a condition of monotheism in that it separates the alterity of the transcendent from immanent participation and the religious as ethical responsibility from mythic irresponsibility.[86] He comments, "The idea of infinity, the metaphysical relation, is the dawn of a humanity without myths. But faith purged of myths, the monotheist faith, itself implies metaphysical atheism." Unfortunately, in the previous sentence, Levinas mentions that "the believers of positive religions, ill disengaged from the bonds of participation, [. . .] accept being immersed in myth unbeknownst to themselves."[87]

The religious as ethical is announced in the disturbance of sacred violence and holy war, which is the true meaning of the pagan for Levinas. The invisible and unknowable God challenges idolatry by evading identification through speculative argumentation and enthusiastic participation, since God is not a presence but the absence of signifiers—an infinity and "relation without relation" that cannot constitute a totality.[88] Given this account, which overlaps at points with Kierkegaard's polemic against pagan success and power-oriented Christianity that culminates in *The Moment*, Levinas fears that monotheism does not necessarily overcome but can remain trapped in the idolatry and paganism of which it accuses others.

Infinite and beyond, without mediation or incarnation, God is accessible in and through the human relation and in justice.[89] That is, the transcendent as infinite occurs in its ethical enactment in the rituals and practices of everyday human relations and encounters, in acts of responsibility. The ethical relation therefore has precedence over theological and religious considerations. Not only can the ethical not be reduced to supernatural rewards and punishments, it disturbs the logic of sacrifice, the theodicy that excuses the facticity of actual suffering and horror, and what Levinas described elsewhere as "the egotism of grace" and salvation.[90] He accordingly claims,

> When I maintain an ethical relation I refuse to recognize the role I would play in a drama of which I would not be the author or whose outcome another would know before me; I refuse to figure in a drama of salvation or of damnation that would be enacted in spite of me and that would make game of me. This is not equivalent to diabolical pride, for it does not exclude obedience. But obedience precisely is to be distinguished from an involuntary participation in mysterious designs in which one figures or prefigures. Everything that cannot be reduced to an interhuman relation represents not the superior but the forever primitive form of religion.[91]

In addition to this unconvincing, overly generalized concept of paganism, a Levinasian insight familiar from communitarian virtue ethics is disclosed in this passage to the extent that everyday "small goodness" and the ethical are embodied and cultivated in practices and rituals, such as those of solidarity and, as evident in his Talmudic writings, of the Jewish community. Although both emphasize the nontheoretical and experiential character of the ethical, this comparison is deceptive. A significant dissimilarity between Levinas and Aristotelian or neo-Aristotelian communitarian virtue ethics is that Aristotle described ethics as following an end (telos) of life that guides practical appropriate judgment (*phronesis*). Levinas portrays the ethical as an-archic and as exceeding all intentional and teleological order. In a rejection of prudence as inherently calculative that recalls Kant's distinction between morality and prudence, Levinas polemicizes against habituation and prudence as the comfortable and calculative betrayal of the ethical.[92] Levinas's concern can be extended from prudential to universalistic ethics; even the expectations of equal dialogical reciprocity and deliberative participation developed in discourse ethics are too calculative and confining from the perspective of the priority of the other, the good, and an unrestricted sense of justice that confronts existing associations and systems.

Between Religiosity and Antireligiosity

What is religion for Levinas when one poses the question whether ethics requires religion? Religion consists of the communal and individual practices of the ethical, of solidarity between distinct persons who need to be recognized as such rather than assimilated to the logic of "the Same" that is placed in question in the appresentation of "the Other" that exceeds psychic and intentional structures. Levinas endeavors to rethink the meaning of the religious in distinction from all myth and mysticism, that is, as ethics, without reducing the ethical to the particularity of one faith or religious form of life. "Religion" is a relation to the wholly Other, the transcendent, the infinite "that is not structured like knowing" and does not concern "an abstract eternity and dead God."[93]

Religion is not a doctrine or theory about God as an entity or person that can be used to convert the nonbeliever or produce a theological discourse or religious-political ideology about God. Yet it is not the negation of God implied by the secularization thesis, which allows Samuel Moyn to conclude that Levinas failed in secularizing God radically enough.[94] A caveat should be added to this thesis such that its nonfulfillment is not simply a failure by Levinas to carry out his own project and intentions. If Levinas was truly interested in "secularizing ethics"—and, to an extent, he was and must be—then why did he retain and rely on highly charged religious language? Can "God" and the language surrounding God ever be truly "secularized"? Given the importance of the religious and the word "God" for Levinas, and the pertinent detail that he explained the religious through the ethical but did not reductively eliminate religion in ethics, religious language must be more than rhetorical while not dogmatic theological truth.

If the religious in Levinas is not so much a failure at secularizing ethics as it is a vehicle of its enactment, then the dogmatic content of theology from the philosophy or phenomenology of the religious should be cautiously distinguished. After all, Levinas does not so much want to secularize God as secularize pseudoreligious idolatry, and it is this atheism and secularization that join the God of Israel with Western philosophy and science.[95]

Levinas praises atheism as disenchantment while at the same time rejecting atheism as the absence of transcendence. The former "ethical atheism" preserves rather than destroys the invisible. It confronts the anonymous indifference of participation in the sacred, which institutes religious violence against others, and challenges the idolatry that endeavors to reduce the transcendent to the immanent by making visible the inherently invisible. Levinas has his own distinctive interpretation of invisibility: the Other and the monotheistic God are invisible as "beyond being" and "unthematizable."[96] It does not demystify God to the extent that, following the logic of the *Bilderverbot* (ban on images) linked with prophetic justice and the messianic in Benjamin, it is not the invisible but the visible that is at the root of mystification, idolatry, and fetishism.[97] Levinas's secularization questioned the theological not by dismissing or excluding all that is suggested by the religious but by performatively addressing, saying, and unsaying what it indicates.

One can therefore question claims that ethics needs to be secular, immanent, and autonomous rather than involving passivity and obedience to something outside of oneself—the heteronomy to the transcendent that Levinas described as the "impossibility of escaping God, the adventure of Jonas"[98]—if excluding all dependence would not simply exclude relations of power and domination but also charity, compassion, and loving-kindness (*chesed* חסד), which is the ultimate form of the ethical and holiness for Levinas. The fecundity and singularity of ethical life, as opposed to the subordination of the individual to common life, requires distinguishing rather than conflating ethical responsiveness—that is, heteronomy as the other in the self that is the prerequisite of acting for the other as a defining instance of the ethical—along with the elimination of responsiveness in religious forms of power: disciplinary regimes of ascetic self-denial, exchanges with and sacrifices to higher powers that are mystified earthly powers, and authoritarian and hierarchical subordination that would erase the other's face.

Conclusion: Double Strategies in Levinas and Kierkegaard

According to the argument articulated in this chapter, Levinas pursues a twofold strategy that undoes identity thinking of the secular and the religious by sanctifying the secular and secularizing the religious via the ethical moment of the transcendence of "the Other" (*l'Autrui*) disturbing the immanence of "the Same" (*la Même*). This double strategy, which Levinas does not continuously sustain and further complicates, is depicted as a transversal of the ethical rather than—refusing Hegel's dialectical language—a double negation, resulting in a positive, or reversal culminating in synthesis. Levinas is not familiar with the possibility of a "negative dialectics," articulated by Adorno as discussed in earlier chapters, which explicitly rejects—contrary to what Adorno portrays as the undialectical element in Hegel's dialectic—construing the negation of the negation as culminating in an affirmation, a reconciliation, or a synthesis (which Adorno describes as a positive dialectics).[99]

Given Levinas's dual and aporetic strategy, Levinas should not be construed as a secularizing atheist, a deceptive obscurantist mobilizing religious language for ulterior motives, nor a theological, literal, or dogmatic theist. The other is not, of course, God, and God is not the other; and transcendence is neither exclusively atheist nor theist. It is tied to these two terms that indicate different aspects (horizontal and vertical) of that which escapes the self and in doing so disturbs and addresses the self as an ethical claim within the dominion of everyday and immanent life. Ethical claims can be glimpsed in the revolutionary temporality of prophetic justice (chapter 9) and in ordinary acts of kindness and goodness (the topic of chapter 10).

Kierkegaard's and Levinas's approaches to the secular, the religious, and the ethical can inform and complement one another in the tension of their interactive divergence. Levinas is skeptical of Kierkegaard's strategies while still praising his works for proceeding from transcendence: "His point of departure is no longer experience, but transcendence. He is the first philosopher who thinks God without thinking Him in terms of the world."[100] Both to name and to keep silent about God are betrayals—not of a potentially angry being but of transcendence itself, which cannot be spoken and yet (in its otherness) elicits its saying.

The suspension of the ethical, interpreted as universality and symmetry, in *Fear and Trembling* and other works does not and should not by itself constitute an ethics, yet it can contribute to a broader alternative ethics that embraces considerations of the asymmetrical relations between singular subjects. Although intersubjective universality, reciprocity, and equality are in a sense suspended, they are not bracketed for the sake of the unethical, violence, or domination but for a different way of enacting the ethical itself in its nonuniversal and nonreciprocal singularity. The ethical encompasses virtues such as humility, generosity, and gentleness in order to attend to what the other needs and wants instead of projecting one's own needs and desires upon the other as if she were another "me."

Adorno recognized the critical impulses in Kierkegaard's "misanthropic" discourses. They appear in his calls for "sobriety" with respect to ideological forms of happiness and his suspicions concerning modern ideas of civic equality and engineered welfare as a wretched form of happiness.[101] This radical potential is evident in the *Two Ages*. Kierkegaard reverses there potential egalitarian criticisms of his work by arguing not only for the individuating power of passion—even the passion for equality and democracy of the revolutionary age, as opposed to their calculative and manipulative established forms of the present age—but, further, that religious asymmetry leads to an elevating equality between individuals qua individuals before God, and in contrast to the leveling equality of symmetrical public life of modern mass societies.[102]

Kierkegaard's interpretation of the asymmetrical responsibility, silence, and self-relation of the "knight of faith," and its accompanying notion of an essentially objectless and otherless self-absorbed subjective interiority critiqued by Adorno and Levinas, differs from Levinas's articulation of the religious as an asymmetrical ethics involving disrelations of height, distance, and alterity. Levinas interrogates the failures of modern universalism to live up to its own aspirations. He confronts the subjective interiority of Kierkegaard and the dialogical symmetry (no doubt exaggerated) in Buber (for whom dialogical participation is not absorption or appropriation) in the name of the priority of the unqualified Other who is irreducible to the interchangeable relative-reciprocal other.[103] Asymmetry entails that I do not expect or demand reciprocity, as returning reciprocity is the affair and concern of the other person.[104] But, as examined further in part 3, Levinas does not deny the importance of symmetry and equality in questions of politics, justice, and the citizen, relations involving the third party or person to be further explored in the subsequent chapters of this volume.

Chapter Nine

Prophetic Time, Materiality, and Dignity

Bloch and Levinas

> That the assumption of natural laws is not to be taken *à la lettre*—that least of all is it to be ontologized in the sense of a design, whatever its kind, of so-called "humanity"—this is confirmed by the strongest motive behind all Marxist theory: that those laws can be abolished. The realm of freedom would no sooner begin than they would cease to apply.
>
> —Theodor Adorno, *Negative Dialectics*

Introduction: Marxism and Dignity

Marxist discourses, beginning with Marx and Engels, have had an ambivalent historical relationship and record with dignity. On the one hand, communism for Marx would signify the realization of dignity for the abject, and its universal achievement has been perceived to be the goal of social-historical struggles and revolts for unrestricted democratic participation and social-political equality. On the other hand, following Marx's prophetic diagnosis of the ideological functions of bourgeois ideas, dignity has been dismantled as a reactionary residue of metaphysical and theological thinking that is inherently interconnected with human inequality, privilege, and rank. Michael Rosen describes in *Dignity: Its History and Meaning* how Marx accordingly condemned human dignity as an "empty phrase" that "[takes] refuge from history in morality."[1] In addition, deconstructive and poststructuralist philosophizing has more recently exposed how the discourse and institutionalization of human dignity operate to justify regimes of indignity that subjugate human and nonhuman animal life. The equivocal meanings and multiple functions of concepts expressed in such philosophizing, with both egalitarian and hierarchical connotations, might give reason for trepidation. Should the notion of dignity be abandoned altogether, as advocated in many forms of Marxism and posthumanism, or can the emancipatory connotation of dignity be disentangled—either in a heuristic "critical model" or as a "fundamental right"—from its ideological and repressive functions?[2]

Notwithstanding dignity's ideological functions, the elimination of the "bourgeois" idea of dignity has been a risky and dangerous pursuit due to the close interconnections between dignity and fundamental rights, as the history of communist regimes that have sacrificed dignity for the sake of utopian planning and future historical progress have persistently demonstrated. In this chapter, two heterodox philosophies of dignity (namely, those of Bloch and Levinas) will be retrieved to address this problematic. Both Bloch and Levinas offer alternatives to the reification of dignity in the conventional natural law (*ius naturae*) tradition as well as the social utopian marginalization of dignity for the sake of constructing and managing general happiness. The alternative to conventional natural law that their works suggests is that dignity should be rethought through its embeddedness and enactment in the temporality and materiality of life itself.[3] The thesis developed here should be—following the arguments of part 1 of this volume—extensively transformed in relation to animal life.

Two distinct strategies for linking the ethical-political demand for achieving dignity and human rights for all persons with the temporal embodied character of human existence are articulated in Bloch's underappreciated classic work *Natural Law and Human Dignity*, first published in German in 1961, four years after his relocation from East to West Germany, and in light of Levinas's sympathetic critique of Bloch.[4] Levinas examined Bloch's thinking of death presented in the third volume of *The Principle of Hope* in *God, Death, and Time* (*Dieu, la mort et le temps*). This work was based on two lecture courses ("Death and Time" and "God and Onto-theo-logy") given during his last year at the Sorbonne in 1975–1976 and was published in French in 1982.

Bloch and Levinas could appear to be an odd pairing. Their intellectual contexts and perspectives diverge in significant ways. Bloch adopts the critical materialist transmission from Aristotelian materialism through Spinoza and his heirs traced by Idit Dobbs-Weinstein, who in *Spinoza's Critique of Religion and Its Heirs* analyzes how this transmission is concerned with two senses of time and history: (1) a future-oriented "onto-theological" one, and (2) a past-oriented political one concerned with remembrance, past aspirations, and the dead.[5] These two dimensions intersect in prophetic ethics as a model of social-political critique.

Bloch's critique of the present draws on the traces of hope revealed in the past as well as in present counter-tendencies. Prophetic temporality is not only futural as Bloch articulates the prophetic in the form of a historically immanent and transformative concrete utopia of hope in the "tendency-latency" toward well-being and dignity.[6] This concrete utopia is set in opposition to the present and to the planning of happiness in abstract social utopian/dystopian administrations or in the culture industry's manipulation of utopian desires and images diagnosed by Adorno. In contrast, modifying transcendental phenomenology and prioritizing ethical transcendence over this-worldly immanence, as previously noted in chapter 4, Levinas speaks through an intensified sense of an infinite responsibility to the other that presupposes the other's vulnerable bodily existence and suffering.

Bloch and Levinas each seek to address suffering existence, from which their thinking of sociality and utopia arises.[7] They share, at least in part, the task of articulating the "breakthrough of transcendence," the redemption of the sensuous, and an ethically-politically oriented sense of the interruptive and reorienting temporality of the prophetic in response to suffering and abjection.[8] In both cases, temporal material life does not entail the elimination of dignity, as standard natural law theories assume. It rather proves to be dignity's very condition calling for its prophetic fulfillment in ethical and social-political life. In the dialogue between the works of Bloch and Levinas, a new critical model of the dignity of temporal material life emerges that opposes the reification and destruction of the other's dignity.

Marxism between Dignity and Happiness

Bloch is often seen as a utopian thinker, which he no doubt is, without recognizing how profoundly he engaged in a critique of utopian thinking. Bloch's groundbreaking work *Natural Law and Human Dignity* is a plea for dignity in response to its loss under the communism that he earlier embraced. This work, initially to be titled "Natural Law and Socialism," traces the tensions between two competing paradigms in the formation of Western social-political discourse: (1) the "natural law" paradigm that is principally concerned with human dignity and rights; and (2) the abstract "social utopian" paradigm that predominantly aims at the achievement of eudaemonic general happiness and well-being.[9] While natural law traditions tend to essentialize ahistorical laws and eternal rights stemming from God rather than from intersubjective relations, social utopian constructions are primarily eudaemonic and consequentialist. Marxism shares a number of features with utilitarianism in addition to the suspicion that dignity and rights are rhetorical devices, and it is typically construed to be dedicated to the social utopian formation of a just social order that will realize equal conditions of prosperity.

The social utopian view of Marxism is correct with regard to historically existent communist societies such as East Germany and the Soviet Union that suppressed dignity and justified sacrificing individuals for the sake of the progress of a collective whole. This understanding of Marxism is problematized in Bloch's reconsideration of the revolutionary impulses in Marx and Marxism. It is misleading to conclude that Marx was exclusively concerned with partiality for the economically exploited and oppressed, since the struggle for the dignity—in the spirit of natural law—of the humiliated and degraded, irrespective of authority, was constitutive of Marx's socially transformative project.[10]

Why does Bloch disconnect Marx's thought from social utopianism and relate it to natural law? Marx explicitly critiqued the abstract social constructions of the utopian tradition, refusing to design the communist society to come. He adopted—albeit in an overly circumscribed way that would be exploited by its totalitarian appropriations—natural law from the critical form of natural law theory that Bloch ascribes to the names Epicurus and Rousseau, as well as the latter's radical republicanism.[11] Radical natural law in these discourses does not plan happiness. It posits human freedom in solidarity, contesting the injustices allowed by and perpetuated under established positive laws.[12] Adorno, like Bloch, recognized the capacity of natural law to be employed in the critique of natural law: "Every positive, substantially elaborated doctrine of natural law leads to antinomies, and yet it is the idea of natural law which critically maintains the untruth of positive law."[13]

The natural law heritage of radical republican and socialist politics demanded liberty, equality, and solidarity, and confronted the injustices of existing positive laws and social-political structures. It dismissed dreaming of idyllic islands with ideally constructed society.[14] Although Bloch expresses mistrust toward Sir Thomas More's image of social utopia, the utopian managerial construction and planning of happiness by elites, the fantastic revelations of utopian visionaries, he refuses at the same time to abandon the essentially ethical demand expressed in utopianism. He therefore seeks to distinguish the social utopian planning mocked by Marx from the imagining and dreaming forward of concrete utopian aspirations that would establish dignity as well as economic well-being that by itself is insufficient for genuine flourishing.

Bloch recognizes the "dreaming ahead" from and against the present of concrete utopia in Marx's writings as in his September 1843 letter to Arnold Ruge where Marx describes how "the world has possessed the dream of a matter" (*den Traum von einer Sache besitzt*) and the world can "wake up from the dream about itself" (*aus dem Traum über sich selbst aufweckt*). This self-awakening to the matter in the dream not only denotes a "secularization of religious transcendence"; it also indicates the actualization of the aspirations of the past in a praxis that would intensify rather than minimize religion's interruptive and reorienting force (compare chapter 6).[15] Bloch shows how the revolutionary emancipatory impulses in Marxism and socialism are informed by prophetic and radical republican inspirations rather than by the architectonic construction of an ideal social utopian society on an enclosed island. These impulses are inherited from the aim of natural law to establish general human dignity with the fundamental right to a life that is not governed by regimes of alienation and reification or domination and exploitation.

The conservatism of standard natural law theories and their institutionalization masks natural law's more radical and transformative tendencies in Bloch's reconstruction.[16] Bloch describes the radical potential of the inviolability of dignity in natural law in how it aims at human dignity by raising abject bodies to an upright stance that cannot be deduced from the existing relations in which their dignity is systematically distorted and undermined. Bloch's image of the ethical "orthopedics of upright posture" (*Orthopädie des aufrechten Gangs*) could be better described as a bodily composure of dignity. It is not inspired by being, existence, or presence—Bloch's critique of being is not foreign to the discourse of Levinas, where it has a more radical form—but rather in an aspirational interruptive hope and not-yet (*noch nicht*) that cannot be detached from justice and solidarity. In Bloch, time is hope itself.[17]

What is this hope such that it is not an empty or manipulative utopian gesture? Bloch does not reject the term "ontology" unlike Levinas. Bloch's "humanism" is more expansive as he describes how it is impossible to distinguish whether ethics and ontology is more fundamental in carrying the other and to separate interhuman solidarity from solidarity with the world.[18] Bloch's "humanism" entails not a restricted but rather an unrestricted understanding of solidarity that can help us to reimagine Levinas's more anthropocentric tendencies.[19] Levinas's portrait of Bloch marks labor and material life as dignity, time as hope and solidarity, in contrast to time as isolation in being and death in Heidegger. Bloch transforms time in relation to the other (and not merely human other) by articulating an ontology of hope, the not-yet, the new, and transcendence as the world existing otherwise through which existing being is interrupted and reoriented. Hope is implicit in sensuous material existence not as an otherworldly presence but as time itself.

What are the implications of Levinas's reconstruction of Bloch in which time is hope? To return to Bloch's *Natural Law and Human Dignity*, temporalized natural law is concretely enacted not in the soul but in the body's capacities to maintain its dignity in resistance against oppression.[20] Temporalizing hope is an anticipatory prefiguration of a new conception of what it signifies to be human: the liberation of the systematic distortions of productive forces and a different way of existing in love and solidarity.

Luxemburg, Bloch, and Democratic Socialism

> Freedom only for the supporters of the government, only for the members of one party—however numerous they may be—is no freedom at all. Freedom is always and exclusively freedom for the one who thinks differently. Not because of any fanatical concept of "justice" but because all that is instructive, wholesome and purifying in political freedom depends on this essential characteristic, and its effectiveness vanishes when "freedom" becomes a special privilege.
>
> —Rosa Luxemburg, *The Russian Revolution, and Leninism or Marxism?*

In the previous discussion, Bloch is committed to Marxist theses concerning productive forces and solidarity. He is concerned in the political situation after the Second World War, during his life in and exile from the German Democratic Republic (where he had enthusiastically moved in 1948 and departed in 1961), with a problem of principle in existing communism that betrayed Marxism's fundamental aspirations for a just society. He perceived that the problems of existing communism were not merely ones of the inadequate application of Marxist theory or corrupted leadership. The brutality and violence of communist regimes revealed deeper questions of the very principle and theory not only of its Soviet and Eastern European institutionalization but of Marxism itself.

Bloch's response to this situation was to identify the nonconsequentialist dimensions of dignity operative in Marx's writings that are in tension with and contest the instrumental managerial calculus and unrestricted use of power in which life and dignity are sacrificed for the goal of realizing a general social happiness to come. The planned future of social utopia fails to meet, as expressed by Levinas, the demand of time as hope. *Natural Law and Human Dignity* reveals how this temporalizing hope is dignity in response to existing conditions.

This problematic is not limited to Bloch's analysis. The tensions between the goals of dignity and happiness within socialist discourses were also visible in the debates during the concluding years of the Chinese Civil War, from 1946 to 1948. I have described elsewhere the political thought of Zhang Junmai 张君劢, a Confucian social democratic advocate of constitutionally established rights. Zhang articulated in his writings concerning a new Chinese democratic constitution the necessity of a constitution that would guarantee a full range of social, political, and economic rights as fundamental rights in order to appropriately realize socialist planning while restricting its destructive implementation and consequences.[21]

The conflict between rights and collective planning is noticeable in the political works of Rosa Luxemburg, which are overly neglected as a point of departure for twentieth-century "Western Marxism" and the early Frankfurt school, as evident in their prioritization of democratic practices, institutions, and flourishing public spheres that are lacking in Soviet communism. The trajectory of Bloch's rethinking of Marxism, particularly after his experiences in East Germany, was informed by Luxemburg and the 1919 Spartacist revolution that had initially inspired his commitment to socialism. Bloch referred to the continuing importance of Luxemburg's philosophy in his last years, such as in his dedication of *Experimentum Mundi* (1975) to her memory due to her emphasis on an experimental and open Marxism that rejected old dogmas and formed new insights. *Experimentum Mundi* is another example of how Bloch is offering a new conception of time. This work temporalized epistemology by dereifying the doctrine of categories as historically productive formations of "bringing forth." He also contrasted the lessons and continuing potential of Luxemburg's political positions with Lenin's in the 1974 interview "Rosa Luxemburg, Lenin, and Their Lessons or Marxism as Morality."[22]

Why was Luxemburg's construal of socialism compelling to Bloch, the resonances of which can be glimpsed in Levinas's interpretation of Bloch's "humanistic Marxism"? Luxemburg had argued for radical socialism, unlike the German social democrats who had compromised with war and capitalism, in conjunction with a comprehensive commitment to participatory democracy. In her 1918 critique of the establishment of dictatorship in the newly forming Soviet Union, Luxemburg described how "[w]ithout general elections, without unrestricted freedom of press and assembly, without a free struggle of opinion, life dies out in every public institution, becomes a mere semblance of life, in which only the bureaucracy remains as the active element."[23] She described how the Soviet destruction of democratic rights and institutions "is worse than the disease it is supposed to cure."[24]

Bloch not only thought of time as dignity in the face of suffering and death, he also confirmed the interconnectedness of democracy and dignity. Democratic constitutions and institutions preserve dignity in encompassing guaranteed rights and freedoms that limit sacrificial violence in the name of general economic development as administered by fanatical or self-serving managerial elites. Socialism, as Bloch insisted, citing Luxemburg in *On Karl Marx*, cannot persevere without democratic enfranchisement: "The realization of this inheritance, of a no longer bourgeois but socialist emancipation, will be the decisive factor in the future with regard to the countenance of freedom within communism. The orthopedics of the upright posture is one of its most pressing obligations, and none other than humanistic socialism features it as the supreme human right."[25]

Bloch's argumentation in *Natural Law and Human Dignity* contested the actually existing Marxism that Bloch argued had betrayed its own fundamental principle of achieving human dignity. In Bloch's analysis, the social utopian demand to attain equality as general economic happiness had undermined equal regard for the dignity of subjects, with disastrous results in human life and suffering. The Soviet-dominated sphere failed to actively maintain its relationship with the anticipation of a just and right form of life—in natural law philosophy and in Marx's works—in which the economic and political conditions of dignity (which could today encompass bioenvironmental, expressive, healthcare, and labor rights) would be structurally guaranteed.

While the assessment of Marxist failures in conservative and liberal discourses leads to demands to restrict solidarity and excuse social-economic forces and systems that reproduce domination and exploitation, Bloch shows in this work how immanently confronting liberal modernity with its own unrealized principles and dreams leads to further unrestricting ethical demands for solidarity and dignity with respect—as Levinas noted in Bloch's aligning of ethics and ontology—to the world as well as to humanity.

The History and Paradox of Dignity

Bloch's works reveal how it is not only Marxism that faces problems of principle. His deconstruction of Soviet forms of communism are interconnected with his confrontation with Western forms of capitalism. Actually existing liberalism, whether in its contemporary neoliberal or nativist incarnations, is justifiably suspected of avowing dignity in general while systematically perpetuating the social forces that violate dignity in racial, gender, and class relations. In such systems, the migrant worker and encaged refugee are not perceived as bearers of dignity deserving respect. In his own interpretive situation, Bloch did not forget the deployment of dignity in subjugation, as he works through its repressive functions and emancipatory potential in his 1961 work. How is it that dignity has both ideological functions as well as emancipatory potential? This is a question repeatedly faced in this volume with regard to discourses of nature in part 1, and discourses of cosmopolitanism, freedom, justice, solidarity, and tolerance in part 3.

Dignity's ambiguous functions and possibilities reflect its history. As Bloch depicted in *Natural Law and Human Dignity*, the classic Roman conception of *dignitas* did not require the equal ethical or political worth of human individuals. Indeed, the assertion of dignity, much like the concept of "humanity," presupposed deep-seated inequalities. *Dignitas* concerned the ranking, relative merit, and comparative worthiness of persons within a hierarchical community and political order. It was the assertion of a height and privilege that should not be disturbed by the claims of lessors who were intrinsically unequal and should by no means receive equal consideration. This sense of dignity dominated the history of the word "dignity" until recently, as can be seen in the usage of the word. "Dignity" continues to be linked in ordinary English-language expressions with a superior worth associated with a hierarchical status, an office ("the dignity of the president"), or personal character ("she maintained her dignity despite the insults"). In such cases, dignity is not a right that must be upheld for each and all; it is a privilege hierarchically limited to specific social classes, ranks, and roles.

Dignity and humanity have lowly origins in relations of power, while undergoing processes of "ethicalization" and universalization. It was Hellenistic and Roman philosophy, particularly in Stoicism, that coupled the concepts of *dignitas* and *humanitas* in a moral stance that is cultivated by the sage and the wise in the midst of the anxiety and turbulence of everyday existence.[26] The Stoic cosmopolitan conception of human equality and dignity belonging to all from birth is a significant source for the modern egalitarian interpretation of dignity.[27] Such dignity is detached from the social rank and status of the person, becoming a universal feature of human beings, and as such, however it might be defined, calling for love and solidarity.[28]

From this brief reflection on Bloch's genealogy of dignity, a first tension in the historical concept of dignity can be recognized. This first tension consists in the difference between dignity as hierarchical rank and dignity as equal for all. There is also a second tension between the religious and ethical moments in natural law traditions that have emphasized a dignity that modern liberal secularization has failed to resolve or reconcile. Bloch depicts in his work how natural law is an ethical secularization of religion.[29] The second tension rests accordingly in the political theological conditions of the formation of the concept of intrinsic dignity, as interconnected with divinely given inalienable individual rights and the idea of an individual soul, and the secularization and globalization of what is described either as an initially or inherently Western paradigm. The formulation that identifies natural law as preeminently Judeo-Christian is typical of conservative natural law discourses that underemphasize its Greco-Roman heritage as well as its later radical republican incarnations.

This historical outline indicates how these historical and conceptual tensions are potentially explosive for coherent interpretations and social-political enactments of discourses of human dignity and concomitant human rights.

Natural Law and Prophetic Critique

The Harvard University historian Eric M. Nelson (unrelated to myself) has delineated in *The Hebrew Republic: Jewish Sources and the Transformation of European Political Thought* the Jewish and Christian sources of the modern liberal and republican political paradigms.[30] Neonatural law theorists have argued for an intrinsic systematic conceptual link between theology and dignity that liberal secularization and republican and socialist actualization can only undermine. Although the political theological idea of dignity is often seen as conservative, and even reactionary, it has a noteworthy role in "prophetic" ethical and political diagnosis that provides a clue for its reinterpretation. The prophetic temporal moments in Marx and Marxism have been articulated in heterodox Marxist philosophers such as Bloch and Walter Benjamin, non-Marxist ones such as Levinas and Derrida, as well as contemporary decolonial critical theorists such as Dussel.

What, then, is the meaning and import of "prophetic critique"? To define it in a preliminary heuristic way, it is to witness the oppressed, exploited, and abject. This sense is palpable in the book attributed to the prophet (the *nevi'im*, or spokesperson) Isaiah (Yeshayahu), with its vision of a righteous kingdom and radical condemnations of the injustices of the existing social-political order for the sake of defending widows, orphans, strangers, and helping the subjugated and the wretched. The prophets could appeal to an earlier sense of justice stated in, for instance, Deuteronomy 24:17, which demands that one not undermine the justice due to the stranger, the orphan, and the widow. This is not a task left to God, as in theodicies, which justify God's justice by projecting it into the future or afterlife. It is an ethical and social-political demand of the nonpresent on the present moment for confronting injustice and cruelty.

As social-political liberation has been interconnected with violence and terror in revolutionary politics, the prophets do not speak only on behalf of the deprived and oppressed. They also communicate God's wrathful punishment and destructive power, as evident in the depiction of the "wrath of the Lord" in Isaiah 9:18. Some if not all of the authors of the book of Isaiah, however, envision God's wrath as motivated not merely by upholding the convent and proper rule following but rather by a primary concern for justice. The prophetic voice consequently communicates catastrophe as well as hope. It intimates in Bloch's interpretation of prophecy a community of egalitarian communistic solidarity in the destruction of domination and hierarchical social stratification.

According to Bloch in *Atheism in Christianity*, a work that articulates the radical potential of prophecy in Judaism and Christianity, the prophetic denunciation of exploiters, despots, and masters, particularly the socially subversive announcements of Amos and Isaiah, prepared the way for the communist communities of love from which primordial Christianity emerged.[31] The concrete utopian moment in prophetic critique is for the moment, the temporalizing here and now, and anarchically opposed to social utopian architectonics. It is neither the projection of a distant island or otherworldly realm, nor is it administrative and managerial. Rather, according to Bloch, utopia is disclosed in the nonsimultaneous temporalities of the oppressed in relation to the "historical time" that it exceeds and reorients.[32] The prophetic time of dignity, the time of the other, interrupts the present.

What sense can be made of this idea of "prophetic critique" being reassembled here from the works of Bloch and Levinas? It is not "otherworldly" in the sense of escaping or retreating into another world to avoid the suffering and evils of this world; it is not the negation of life but a critique of oppressed life, as it does precisely the opposite of flight in witnessing and responding to material suffering life. Witnessing is not a neutral observation of states of affairs; it is an ethical reply. It perceives states of affairs through the lenses of a radically other version of life and way of living that lies within while also contesting the existing order, as in Marx's image of awakening to the dream within the dream. It can arguably be traced at points in Marx's writings, in forms of heterodox Marxism (Benjamin and Bloch), the quasi- or postphenomenological ethics of Levinas and Derrida, and Latin American liberation theology, as well as Dussel's prophetically oriented decolonizing liberation ethics that developed in part in dialogue with Marxism, the Frankfurt school, and Levinas while contesting their Eurocentric elements as when he repeatedly writes of "Asiatic masses" lacking "sacred history."[33] The implications of prophecy for justice will be examined in part 3. What then of time?

Prophetic Temporalities

> Everywhere one looks, the Messianic is the last handhold of life and the ultimate resultant of the light of Utopian truth. To the clever that is folly, to the pious it is a pre-fabricated house, but to the wise the sense of Utopia is the most real and pressing problem of an unsolved world. It follows that life itself has sense inasmuch—precisely inasmuch—as it forms itself in dissatisfaction, in work, in rejection of the inadequate and in prophetic premonition of the adequate. Humans do not lose themselves in these heights; they surpass themselves.
>
> —Ernst Bloch, *Atheism in Christianity*

Bloch depicts how the messianic and prophetic tendency-latency (the presence of the ethical in the ontological, to adopt Levinas's interpretation of Bloch) occurs in forms of distress, labor, and negativity—in the natural histories of damaged lives to speak with Adorno—in his writings on the utopian promise in religion. Religion, insofar as it can be distinguished from ideology (see chapter 6), points toward transcendence as life self-surpassing itself. While both are articulate forms of earthly self-affirmation, Bloch's socialistic self-surpassing is an alternative to Nietzsche's individualistic prophetic ethos of self-overcoming. Prophecy in this sense does not fall under Nietzsche's critique as life negation, as it negates unjust life in order to nourish earthly life. It does not arise from an otherworldly or supersensible realm. It is rather an expression of temporal material life itself calling for justice and solidarity without poisoning itself as an otherworldly negation of existence. Prophecy, as future-oriented and aspirational without reducing history to the expectancy of theodicy or teleology (recall chapter 8, section 2), is a question of the time that is hope itself and the basis for transformative aspirations.[34] Is time sufficient for dignity?

The dominant paradigm perceives dignity as the negation of time and history that devours material life but not the soul. Conservative and orthodox political theologically oriented natural law theories appeal to a standard sense of the divine and the eternal as super- or nontemporal properties underwriting inalienable dignity and fundamental rights. Any other model, including any sense of dignity within historicity and temporality, undermines it. Prophetic ethics and critique signify a challenge to this paradigm in expressing a distinctive understanding of the importance of prophetic and messianic temporality to justice itself. Evocative examples of prophetic temporality can be glimpsed in Benjamin, Bloch, and Levinas, in addition to later thinkers of prophetic time such as Derrida and Dussel, who should be kept in mind.

To sketch one model of prophetic time, Benjamin elucidates in "On the Concept of History" (1940) how the "weak messianic power" disrupts the linear, homogeneous, empty time of the historical present in the immediacy of the "now-time" (*Jetztzeit*). This time would give justice to the living and the dead by redeeming their aspirations. Weak messianic time, messianism without a messiah, is revolutionary time. Like his friend Benjamin, Bloch heretically conjoins Marxist materialism and religious mysticism, already in the early works *The Spirit of Utopia* (1918) and *Thomas Müntzer as Theologian of the Revolution* (1921), written in the wake of the Bolshevik and repressed German Spartacist revolutions, to interpret radically interruptive temporalities that reorient toward the new as radically other rather than merely transform the already existent.[35] This focus on prophetic and utopian temporality is articulated in a variety of ways through Bloch's works. For instance, Bloch articulates in his later works different modalities of time that challenge the present, such as the temporality of hope, being as the not-yet of being (*Sein als Noch-Nicht von Sein*), nonsimultaneous temporalities, the radically different new (*Novum*), and that which is painfully missing.

Moments of existential and prophetic interruptive temporalities are also unfolded in Levinas's works. For example, he thematizes in *Existence and Existents* (1947) the time of the "instant" revealed in the night, insomnia, and the mere thereness of being (the *il y a*). In *Time and the Other* (1948), Levinas contests the identification of time with the "identity" of substance and the subjectivity and the self in classical Western thought. Time is not a property of the self and self-presence. It is rather intrinsically from the other who is temporally and ethically "prior to" the self. Temporality is examined further as exposure, exteriority, diachrony, and transcendence in Levinas's works. However, time is described not only in existential terms but also in prophetic language. The time of the future (*avenir*) is interpreted as the "what is to come" (*à-venir*) that haunts the present existing order of things. The interruptive temporalities of Benjamin's "now-time," Bloch's "not-yet," and Levinas's "to come" resonate with the rethinking of time and the prophetic in

Derrida and Dussel. In distinctive ways, Dussel more directly politically, these trace the radical reorientation of prophetic temporality.

While Bloch directly thematizes the revolutionary core in natural law theory, Levinas communicates through a negative natural law theory without identifying it as or with natural law, which shares a number of its basic properties: namely, being prior to authority, tradition, or positive rights and laws, and operating as an excessive demand and measure that can never be enacted. The demanding and impossible justice of Levinas and Derrida (discussed later in this volume in part 3) operates like natural law theory in a negative form. It is without the foundationalist metaphysics of nature, reason, or God that grounds traditional natural law theories. However, Levinas's demand for justice is more radical than natural law theory in that justice is more fundamental than and prior to any divine, natural, or human property that would ground it.

The arguments of Bloch and Levinas considered in this chapter indicate how prophetic ethics is distinctive from conventional natural law traditions in at least two ways: (1) it is temporal rather than nontemporal, and its temporality is unstable and nonlinear, interrupting natural historical time and problematizing the existing order of things rather than justifying a stable normative order; and (2) it is "materialist" in being primarily concerned with suffering, material life, and human sensibility. Materialism is consequently (and we see this understanding at work in Adorno, Bloch, and Horkheimer as well as Levinas) necessary for the ethics of temporal material life.

Politics and the Dialectic of Dignity

There are a number of questions to pose at this point: (1) Does a prophetic ethics indicate a genuine alternative, a supplement in desperate times, or a mere historical curiosity with regard to dignity and human rights?; (2) Are the temporality and materiality of human existence compatible with a full or adequate conception of human dignity, or do they undermine it?; and (3) Does any form of Marxism, even in the heterodox versions of Benjamin or Bloch, or the interpretations of their thinking of temporality unfolded in Derrida or Levinas, prove to be incompatible with human dignity?

Let us consider these issues in reverse order. Levinas's most hostile detractors reject his thought as that of a conservative believing Jew, overly religious, a "Zionist ideologue" who ignores Palestinian alterity and suffering despite their primacy in his own discourse.[36] Slavoj Žižek and Alain Badiou are typical examples of such reductive simplifying interpretations, given Levinas's differentiation of ethical ideals and political realities, as they polemicize against prophetic ethics in Levinas and Derrida as empty messianic posturing. Howard Caygill, Simon Critchley, and others criticize (as will be considered in further detail in part 3) Levinas's political thinking as a form of republicanism with all of its perceived limitations. However, the discourse of republicanism is more complex than Caygill and Critchley assume. Bloch offered a republican socialist critique of existing statist communism in *Natural Law and Human Dignity*, and Hannah Arendt and Jürgen Habermas have presented nuanced accounts of the varieties of republican thought (see part 3 below).

Bloch and Levinas share emancipatory interpretations of the radical republican tradition while interrogating their conservative communal forms. Levinas does not restrict republicanism, as do his Anglo-American critics, to a delimited ethnic or national community based on perpetuating and expanding its identity. As is evident in Bloch's Luxembourgian argument that socialist liberation requires a radical republican commitment to democratic participation, constitutional rights, and infinite and unrestricted solidarity that confronts every restricted solidarity based in affiliation and identity, the republicanism of the other (that is, of the nonnative and stranger) signifies in Levinas's discourse the contestation of the restrictions of ethnic and other forms of identity through the emancipatory hope in freedom, equality, and solidarity reconceived vis-à-vis the primacy of the other. This is the other who is both materially and communicatively constituted (immanence) and is irreducible to and who contests the conditions of present existence (prophetic transcendence) through the ethical and social-political demand.

As described later in part 3, Levinas's republicanism has both Jewish prophetic sources and a Rousseauian lineage—which Bloch has described as a critical natural law theory—in being informed by progressive French republican inspirations.[37] More radically, Levinas's interpretation of republicanism through the primacy of the other, a radical democracy of the other person, prioritizes the moments of other-determination and unrestricted solidarity, overturning the discourse of republicanism (also articulated in Rousseau) as the self-determination and will formation of a collective subject identified with the people.

Levinas's republican political commitments should be read in light of the differentiation made by Arendt and Seyla Benhabib between republicanism's cosmopolitan aspirations (which oppose the reduction of republican institutions and practices to the nation-state or national identity) and their nationalist abandonment (which embraces a restrictive view of the nation state and national identity).[38] The radical republican impulses toward liberty, equality, and solidarity are interpreted universally in contrast to pathological self-undermining nationalist forms. In nativist and nationalist ideology, restricted fraternity is ethnocentrically and patriarchically defined and pathologically limited in opposition to unrestricted solidarity. Levinas's discourse suffers no doubt from Eurocentrism in a number of ways, yet it is universalist in its intentions and aspirations, stimulating a confrontation with Levinas's own Eurocentric elements, as Dussel has argued.[39]

Levinas's thought in these and other writings is not Marxist, which degraded into an apologetic ideology for nationalistic and totalitarian political systems in postwar Europe. It does have a complex and at times affirmative relation with Marxist discourse. It encompasses Marxist moments and sympathetic readings of Marx, Bloch, and—deploying a type of argument also evident in Bloch's *Natural Law and Human Dignity* and Herbert Marcuse's 1958 *Soviet Marxism: A Critical Analysis*—the repressed yet latent humanistic dimensions of Soviet communism.

One complex instance of Levinas's position is developed in the essay "Dialectics and the Sino-Soviet Quarrel" (published in the liberal anticommunist periodical *Esprit* in 1960), in which he sides with Soviet internationalism, because of its reliance on universal human dignity and thus its potential reactivation, against what he construes as Chinese nationalism using the racialized language of the "yellow peril," which continues to dominate Western discourses regarding China, and which he claims to deploy in a "spiritual" nonracial sense.[40] One cannot simply bracket the many difficulties with this essay, including its problematic Eurocentrism concerning lifeworlds outside the West that Dussel has interrogated, and how dignity is reductively identified with Western humanity in opposition to its lack of recognition in non-Western contexts.[41] Levinas fails to recognize here the problem of the not merely accidental Eurocentric delimitation of dignity that denies it to most of humanity.[42]

In this short piece, Levinas documented the tension and paradox in Marxism between the realization and destruction of dignity. There is a Marxist notion of dignity linked with the critique of its flawed abstract bourgeois form. Marx's early existential-ethical and later social-systematic critiques of capitalist societies share an ethical thread: individual and social flourishing in the radical demand for the realization of human happiness and self-worth for the abject and oppressed.

The Marxist critique of dignity qua bourgeois ideology operates against the assertion of dignity as rank and ingenuine equality in contrast to the concrete realization of equality, against a religious understanding that denies in reality what it affirms as an ideal, and against an ideological structure that is complicit with the denial of actual flourishing. Marxist discourses accordingly have an ambivalent relationship and historical record with the concept of dignity. On the one hand, Marxism's universal achievement has been seen as the goal of social-historical development and revolutionary struggles for the oppressed. On the other hand, dignity has been critiqued as a reactionary bourgeois residue of metaphysical and theological thinking that is inherently tied to inequality, privilege, and rank. Marx's analysis of dignity signifies in Bloch the criticism of its inadequate realization rather than the elimination of individual dignity for the sake of collective development. More recently, Dussel has rethought dignity through labor's alterity and exteriority to capital.[43]

A Dusselian Interpretation of Bloch and Levinas

This chapter has traced in outline the works of thinkers who have disclosed the bonds between dignity and temporalizing material life, delineating how the works of Bloch and Levinas offer two strategies for relating the ethical-political demands for dignity and rights with the temporal sensuous embodiment of existence.

In *God, Death, and Time*, Levinas reflects on dignity in the context of human temporality and mortality. Bloch provides a more adequate way of conceiving this nexus than Heidegger, who—Levinas contended—prioritizes one's own death and one's mastery over it rather than the death of the other and the dignity of the other in material moments of suffering and death.[44]

Levinas's reading of Bloch can be situated in the larger circumstances of their thought as argued in this chapter. Bloch and Levinas unfold the social-politically oriented implications of the interruptive and reorienting temporality of the prophetic. Bloch undertakes this in terms of the anticipation of that which exceeds and disturbs the present, a historically immanent and revolutionary concrete utopia of hope—hinted at in dreams, imaginings, stories, and religious visions—in the realization of the flourishing of temporal, sensuous, material subjects with ethical poise and dignity.[45] Levinas proceeds in contrast through an infinite (which is not merely the negation of the finite) asymmetrical (in contrast to hierarchically superior) responsibility to the other's vulnerable sensible existence and suffering.

Finite temporal material life is thought by neonatural law theorists to entail the elimination of human dignity through the reduction of validity to facticity, and universal natural law to positive historical laws. But is this the case? Can natural law be "naturalized" in the sense of being linked to material sensuous existence?

Levinas's reading of Bloch concludes that love—the receiving of the other—is as "strong as death" and the anxiety of "my own death."[46] Bloch expresses not only the love of the other in response to the other's mortality and vulnerability, instead of the Heideggerian "my own," but also solidarity to others in their material life. Bloch's unrestricted solidarity offers a correction to Levinas. Levinas's Bloch offers an alternative interpretation of time based on the other rather than the self, which my argument in this chapter has extended from Heidegger's Dasein to the soul of the natural law tradition. The nothingness in the utopian confrontation with the present is not the nothingness of death, as Levinas noted, but it is also not the nothingness of a nontemporal eternity. Levinas's reading of Bloch reveals how temporal material configurations of labor and hope reveal dignity and glory in a time that is defined neither by death (Heidegger) nor deathlessness (as in natural law).

If the arguments of Bloch and Levinas are correct, the materiality of concrete sensuous life does not entail the elimination of dignity. The early Marx could contest the commodification of existence and labor by presupposing the distinction between price and dignity that capitalist economic processes dismantle. Dignity is not solely a concern of Marx's early works. In *Towards an Unknown Marx*, Dussel analyzes how the exteriority of labor constitutes a dignity in conflict with the subjugation and appropriation that produces the surplus value necessary for the reproduction of capital: "'Living labor,' as human labor, actualization of subjectivity, as person, and as manifestation of his dignity, is placed as such outside, beyond, transcending [. . .] the exteriority of capital."[47]

Prophetic ethics and the ethics of material others in Bloch, Dussel, and Levinas reveal how dignity does not, as in Kantian ethics, belong primarily to reason and spirit.[48] Transcendental reconstructions of dignity are inadequate to their own intentions if dignity requires precisely embracing a prophetic ethics of temporal sensuous life.[49] In Bloch's reassessment of Marx's early works, sensuous material existence proves to be dignity's very condition.[50] It is its condition by calling for prophetic critique of structures that undermine flourishing life and the fulfillment of claims to a dignified life without subjugation and exploitation. It is the face and material life of the other in which dignity is to be recognized.

A Concluding Note on Adorno

What about Adorno's positionality in this nexus of prophecy, sensuous materiality, and life's dignity? Adorno described Bloch's *The Spirit of Utopia* as a rebellion against renunciation in thinking, a motif to which his own work constantly returned.[51] Bloch and Levinas can be said to share an alignment—of prophetic ethics and radical republican political thought—which is less visible in Adorno's writings, which illuminate the role of receptivity and the imagination (see part 1) and offer a sociologically informed analysis of democratic social structures and their deformations in advanced capitalism.

Although Adorno's hermeneutical strategies rely less explicitly on the intensification of prophetic and radical republican discourse, in comparison to Bloch and Levinas, prophetic motifs appear throughout his works. Moments of hope and utopia appear negatively (in Adorno's complex understanding of this word), avoiding picturing positive utopias, within this "imperfect" and insufficient damaged life (see chapter 6). Paths of ethical and social-political resistance, critique, and transformation emerge from suffering damaged life itself, which is not intrinsically evil or corrupt. Damaged life is the site of the good, which appears in the concept's attention and doing justice to the thing, in Adorno's thinking rather than external perfectionist ideals and norms.[52] Ideas of flourishing, nourishing, and reconciled and redeemed life are not a presupposed essence, nature, or teleological purpose from which humans have departed, as described in philosophies of origins. They are immanently formed in natural history and in the very aspirations, dreams, and hopes (that is, the transcendence operating within immanence) of alienated and damaged forms of life. The facticity of damaged and distorted life is sufficient to motivate aspirations of a different way of life. In this context, Adorno can also speak of the prophetic good and modalities of possibility that are other than the plans and projections of social utopianism, revealing a correlation of his thought with Bloch and Levinas.[53] To return to a previously cited quotation in chapter 5, Adorno describes in his lecture course "History and Freedom" how the good is that which contests the present and "struggles free, finds a language, and opens its eyes." In struggle itself, the good is revealed as operative in damaged life and the textures of history and, we should add, natural history.[54]

Given Adorno's antimoral critiques of theodicy, teleology, and moral perfectionist and moralizing moralities, three tendencies that intersect with an antiperfectionist interpretation of Levinas, his ethics is and yet is more than a "negative ethics" that would solely speak of the ethical through negation or in immanently negating the suffering and unjust conditions of present existence. Because of the conditions and promises of the material bodily life of self and other, as illustrated in part 1, the promise of happiness is intimated in resistance and negativity. There is the nonidentical and otherwise in that life such that *minima moralia* is an ethos of "ethical imperfectionism," understood as a heuristic to deconstruct theories of moral perfectionism and associated ideologies of moralizing posturing disparaged by Adorno in *Minima Moralia*. This ethos will be elucidated in the next chapter in opposition to moralizing and perfectionist interpretations of Levinas. Adorno's social-political thought will be a focal point subsequently in part 3.

Chapter Ten

Ethical Imperfectionism and the Sovereignty of Good

Levinas, Løgstrup, and Murdoch

[A]lthough [philosophers] constantly talk of freedom they rarely talk of love.

—Iris Murdoch, *The Sovereignty of Good*

Everywhere bourgeois society insists on the exertion of will; only love is supposed to be involuntary, pure immediacy of feeling. In its longing for this, which means a dispensation from work, the bourgeois idea of love transcends bourgeois society. But in erecting truth directly amid the general untruth, it perverts the former into the latter.

—Theodor Adorno, *Minima Moralia*

Introduction

This chapter on love and the good, which are more elemental to life than the autonomy and perfections of the individual self, marks a transition between parts 2 and 3 of this volume, between—so to speak—the prophetic tendency in religion and social-political justice via a reflection on the good that is revealed in the ethical demand of the other. It describes how Levinas, Knud Ejler Løgstrup, and Iris Murdoch (1919–1999) developed divergent overlapping conceptions of the good, and the former two authors, alternative models for asymmetrical ethics of the ethical demand—a demand that cannot be conflated with an authoritarian command.

Standard theories of social-political equality depend on a notion of ethical reciprocity that abstracts from the concrete alterity of the other. Levinas and Løgstrup argue by contrast for egalitarianism on a different ethical basis: namely, the asymmetrical responsibility of the self for the concrete singular other as the unconditional demand on me from the life and suffering of the other. Despite a number of palpable affinities, the respective formulation and justification of the ethical demand diverge in a fundamental way. Levinas interprets the other as wholly interruptive and disrelational to the self. Ethics is anarchically irreducible to worldly immanence and order. This strategy is linked to a distrust of discourses of life in Levinas.

Løgstrup, in distinction from Levinas, interprets the unconditional radicalness of the demand in terms of the "sovereign expressions" of the life of the other. Ethics is moral anthropology, as he proposes articulating the very radicality of the demand "in a purely human manner."[1] Ethics must disrupt as transcendent the order of life, its egoism and self-assertion, for Levinas, while it is immanently rooted in life as its primary expression for Løgstrup. We will consider the consequences of this difference over the question of life and what Murdoch designates "the sovereignty of good" for asymmetrical ethics.

What does asymmetry mean for these two authors? There are many examples of asymmetry in Levinas. The Levinasian understanding of asymmetry can be perceived in claims such as the following: (1) it operates as the nonidentity of self and other when Levinas asserts "the radical impossibility of seeing oneself from the outside and of speaking in the same sense of oneself and of the others";[2] and (2) it operates as a purely altruistic responsibility without reciprocation prior to the derivative and conditional responsibility that operates according to reciprocal relations, impersonal laws, and negotiated contracts.[3]

In Levinas's thinking, there is an asymmetry of the claims of others upon the self. The other's face, suffering, and vulnerability constitute a demand to respond. Not responding, due to the excuse and "justification of the neighbor's pain," is according to Levinas "the source of all immorality."[4] In this articulation, the stress is placed on the other in all of its radicality, transcendence, and interruptive power in the immanent realm of the sameness of the self and its life. Yet, at the same time, otherness is not pure transcendence in the sense that it does not take place in the immanent empirical encounter, as the stress is also placed on the suffering and pain that transpires in encountering a sensuous material human or (to reimagine Levinas's discourse of the animal as in part one) nonhuman other.

Løgstrup similarly albeit not identically emphasizes in his underappreciated 1956 work *The Ethical Demand* (*Den Etiske Fordring*) and later works such as the 1972 *Norm and Spontaneity* (*Norm og Spontaneitet*) the asymmetrical one-sidedness of the ethical demand: the ethical demand is "silent, radical, one-sided, and unfulfillable."[5] Løgstrup describes the ethical demand as radically one-sided in its responsibility for the other. The ethical demand is furthermore radical (unconditional), silent (unarticulated and incapable of systematization and institutionalization), and anonymous (not belonging to me, my ego, or my power).

Responding to Philosophies of Life, Existence, and Being

It should be noted how the ways of thinking of Løgstrup and Levinas were shaped by their education in and interpretive responses to phenomenological, neo-Kantian, life-philosophical, and Kierkegaardian personalist sources in the 1920s and 1930s, as well as their own respective concerns with Lutheran and Jewish religious and ethical themes. Løgstrup is deeply influenced by Kierkegaard while critiquing the self-orientation of his vision of salvation, his overweighing of the importance of choice and decision, and his reliance on a model of command rather than the ethical demand. Their thought, as well as Adorno, can be interpreted through their critical transformative reception of Kierkegaard and Heidegger.

These intersecting historical constellations are not only visible through comparing their conceptions of ethics. There are concrete overlapping connections in their life histories as well, as they both studied with Jean Hering in Strasbourg during the same period (it is unknown if their paths crossed then) and attended lecture courses by Heidegger at different times: Levinas in the spring semester of 1929, and Løgstrup in 1933–1934. This experience inspired Løgstrup to publish a critique of Heidegger and national socialism, "Nazismens Filosof" (The Nazi's philosopher), published in 1936 in *Dagens Nyheder* (Daily news), which shares concerns with Levinas's 1934 essay *The Philosophy of Hitlerism*.[6] Løgstrup's postwar assessment of Heidegger's philosophy, which brackets his political involvement, appears in the 1950 German work *Kierkegaard's and Heidegger's Analysis of Existence and Its Relation to Proclamation*.[7]

Neither thinker can be described as belonging to the movement of "life-philosophy" even as its motifs linger in their thinking. It is evident that they are using two divergent and conflicting notions of life. In Løgstrup, life is an anonymous gift, generosity, and goodness. Life is spontaneous and sovereign in being shared, in common, in not being limited to the decisions of the subject. Løgstrup's argument is ethical anthropological as it thematizes the radicalness of transcendence as transpiring immanently within the relational processes and structures of human life: if life is acknowledged as a gift, then one cannot deny the ethical demand.[8] To not listen and respond "to the demand is to be indifferent to the question whether life is to be promoted or ruined."[9] In contrast, Levinas argues that the egoism of life is ruined by the ethical encounter, and indicates that the demand occurs even in the midst of the giftlessness of being and life, when the starving victim in the death camp gifts his last piece of bread to the other.

In Levinas, life is the life of the self, the subject, and ego. Life is competition, conflict, and the "struggle for existence" that Levinas identified as the core feature of Western ontology from Heraclitus to Heidegger.[10] Levinas repeatedly critiqued the notion of the gift and generosity of being poetically thought by the later Heidegger. Levinas's criticisms center on the lack of ethical significance of Heidegger's discourse of being, even when it is spoken of in its generosity, as well as its immersion in pagan nature and reductive worldly immanence.

A number of questions arise from Levinas's and Løgstrup's distinctive approaches to the discourse of life. What if, following Løgstrup, the immanence of life's gift is conceived in light of the monotheistic idea of creation (ethically interpreted), rather than pagan participation and absorbed immersion, and as expressing the ethical demand instead of hiding it? This strategy would be adequate if the radicalness of Levinas's language is downplayed. The more seriously it is maintained, the more the suspicion arises that the ethical idea of creation remains complicit and caught up with absorption and participation, and is thereby inadequately ethical. It is a serious question whether the ethical requires the sweeping amplification of alterity, separation, and transcendence demanded by Levinas or whether it is loving the neighbor and the stranger and responding to others that matters in ethics. We turn to this problematic, which obsesses Levinas's detractors, next.

The Problem of Moral Perfectionism

Is the ethics of Levinas a hyperbolic moralizing perfectionism and ascetic disciplinary puritanism? Simon Critchley has argued that there is a shared moral perfectionism underlying both conceptions of asymmetry.[11] Moral perfection establishes the measure and criteria to interpret the self's responsiveness and responsibility (or lack thereof) to the other even as it places the other in a privileged nonreciprocal relationship to the self. That is, paradoxically perhaps, the asymmetrical priority of the other is inevitably a concern for a self and the sense that this self has of itself. To sketch the implications of this argument, the focus on alterity itself can be complicit with and reproduce a problematic sense of identity formation and ethical privilege that leaves no space for the compassion, forgiveness, and pardon that are necessary for an ethics of mortal earthly beings.

This variety of moral perfectionism collapses into the traditional variety focused on the self's striving toward a more "realized" ethical condition. The "Emersonian perfectionism" articulated in Stanley Cavell, Hilary Putnam, and Critchley is inadequate to the ethical demand of alterity on the virtuous and unvirtuous.[12] The perfectionist model is flawed in simultaneously stressing the self's moral striving (instead of the priority of the encounter with the other) and one objective form of the good life to be cultivated (instead of the anarchy of the good itself in its intrinsic separation from the self and in its other-power). Goodness is prior to freedom and self-realization, choosing me before I can choose it: "Goodness in the subject is anarchy itself."[13] Only the good itself is genuinely an-archic in its nonindifference that preserves difference, which every anarchist subject fails to achieve.[14] The ethical imperfectionist model developed in the present work has been reconstructed from the analyses of damaged life in Adorno and insufficiency and incompletion in Levinas. In this context, the self's assertion of its own self-power and self-constituted perfectibility appears to be a form of self-absorption and moral narcissism in light of this critical ethical model of encountering the other and the other-power of the good in which the self can be radically reoriented. That is, one must change one's life through encountering the reality of the other rather than through one's own project of perfection through self-cultivation. Critchley's perfectionist assessment is too quick given that the paradigm of moral perfectionism is inadequate to describe, assess, and modify these two discourses of the ethical demand that is irreducible to the self or a moralistic hierarchy of social status that does not merely neglect the dispossessed and the marginalized.

Moral perfectionism is based in conceptions of a realized good life, human flourishing, or authenticity such as through (1) the cultivation of virtues and character (as in portrayals of Aristotelian or Confucian ethics);[15] (2) the educational perfectibility and ethical progress of the person toward a moral ideal (as in the early modern moral theories of Rousseau or Leibniz); or (3) the radicality of a decision and the ethical consequences that follow from the self's following through on that decision (as in depictions of existential ethics). It is questionable whether the self who responds to the other, insofar as that happens, achieves a higher, more perfected or authentic ethical condition in the writings of either Levinas or Løgstrup, who radically diverge from the perfectionist models attributed to Aristotle, Ralph Waldo Emerson, or Cavell.

Levinas and Løgstrup cannot be moral perfectionists in senses 1 through 3. Indeed, both challenge and place not merely the unattained ideal but the very motivation and goal of the moral perfection/perfectibility of the self, which explicitly and implicitly shapes much of Western moral thinking, into question. Levinas and Løgstrup are antiperfectionist in fundamentally different ways, as evident in their conceptions of (1) "interruptive" ethical transcendence of the good (Levinas), and (2) the immanence of the good in ethical life (Løgstrup).

Ethical Decision or Ethical Demand?

There is a priority of the ethical encounter in both Levinas and Løgstrup. It would be contentious to claim that they offer ethical theories, or the systematic and normative basis for an ethical theory, as they resist ethical theorizing in their own way for the sake of a phenomenology (broadly construed, given their criticisms of its classical forms in Husserl and Heidegger, and the "antiphenomenology" of the inapparent in Levinas) of the ethical encounter. For each, the ethical encounter is not a matter of ethical decision, judgment, or the will. The encounter is an exposure "prior to" the activities of the subject, its will, and its intellect. As Murdoch remarks, it is not the will but the good that is transcendent, an invisible center of attention.[16]

Decision ethics submerges the priority of the object, the other, and the good in processes occurring within the power of the human subject.

Such an ethics is based on forms of judgment by a subject that can be portrayed in multiple registers: existential, emotive, rational-cognitive, or instrumental-calculative. Cognitive accounts of decision emphasize getting the understanding and the application of theory and rules "correct," and the judgments leading to good decisions (whether theorized in deontological or consequentialist language games). Noncognitive accounts stress getting community, situation, emotions, or authenticity "right" to lead to better decisions. Examples of such forms of ethics, which are inadequate for an ethics of the other, range from Aristotelian *phronesis* through Hegelian *Sittlichkeit* to the idea of authenticity in existential ethics in Kierkegaard and Heidegger.

Ethics is not primarily about the self and its self-interests and care for itself. In the egoism of prevailing Western models of morality, ethics is obsessed with the perfecting and mastery of the self, the self's self-relation, and its care for itself that typically becomes a disciplinary mastery of self and others. This is the civility and propriety of the "good person," mentioned by Adorno, who is a model of morality, ruling over oneself in the same way as one rules over one's property.[17] The self-interested "moral" care of the self is the dominant Western moral paradigm rather than the ethical demand of the other. That is, decision ethics is not an ethics. This conclusion leads away from the primacy of the subject, and its perfections and rules, to the radical exteriority of the ethical demand placed on it. This is the good that is invisible and indefinable yet appears within reality without being reducible to the natural or metaphysical structures and processes employed to explain reality.

The Ethics of Demand

The ethical "relation" between self and other is before or prior to the agency of the subject, its decisions and judgments: whether these are existentially or rationally construed, they arrive too late. Levinas and Løgstrup rejected construing this "before" as transcendental. Though the "beforeness" of the ethical demand echoes Husserl's "always already," it cannot be passively or actively constituted by an individual or collective subject.

There is a sharp contrast between the thrust and rhetoric of the two thinkers that needs to be made at this point. Løgstrup interprets the relation between self and other as asymmetrical, transecting with Levinas, and as a relation of what can be described as the "ethical immanence of life." This-worldly ethical immanence is developed in Løgstrup's portrayal of the "sovereign expressions of life" (*suveræne livsytringer*) in his 1968 book *Opgør med Kierkegaard* (Settling accounts with Kierkegaard) and further articulated in 1972 in *Norm and Spontaneity*.

The sovereign expressions of life (characteristically in Løgstrup's portrayal) encompass other-oriented phenomena such as trust, openness, sincerity, mercy, or forgiveness; he also mentions (less typically in his works) personally oriented phenomena such as integrity. The sovereign life-expressions encircle "thoughts and emotions"; they are latent presuppositions of communication and action, they cannot be systematized or institutionalized, even as they ethically orient and guide. They turn into their opposites when they are compromised, corrupted as belonging to self rather than to life beyond the self: "Or else we corrupt the sovereign expression of life by, for instance, crediting ourselves with what the sovereign expression of life achieves and thus, flattering our will, we deprive the former of its sovereignty."[18]

The ethical expressions of the good in the midst of life and the thick of things are presupposed in their distortion, as trust is the basis of distrust. Løgstrup gives as an example that everyday social life, including distrust, presupposes trust and reliance on others, recognition of dependency. Dependency is a form of power, and in power there is a demand to be responsible toward those one has power over. "Sovereignty" here does not signify the ascendency of the self, the ego, or the vitalistic life that are questioned by Levinas. It refers to the independent functioning of the good and forms of common ethical life over the individual subject's decisions and self-concern.

The Immanence and Transcendence of the Good: Murdoch, Løgstrup, and Levinas

Religion is primarily ethical for a number of other thinkers besides Levinas. An intriguing approach to religion as an awareness of the good is proposed by Murdoch, who demarcated religion as "a mode of belief in the unique sovereign place of goodness or virtue in human life."[19] Religion consists in this context in recognizing the functioning of the forms of the good not merely as ideals but also as constituent aspects of life and the world. The recognition of the autonomy of the good and its "creative force" developed in Murdoch's ethics could be further distanced from perfectionist ideas of virtue that relativize the autonomy and other-power of the good to social and individual habits and cultivation practices.[20]

Murdoch described love as the tension between imperfection and perfection, pointing to Plato's claim in the *Symposium* that love is impoverished and needful. Arising in poverty and need, the relation to the other in humility is the ethical moment in love.[21] Humility, a healthier virtue than freedom or courage, recognizes the transience and nothingness of existence, and thus can see reality as it is. Love of the good joins one to the world. Murdoch's insightful analysis of the limitations and imperfections of every human virtue in relation to "the endless extent of [the virtue's] demand" might be amended to "the endless extent of the other's demand" that both virtues of the self and ideal perfections and principles are unable to satisfy.[22]

To adjust Adorno's strategy of disclosing the promise of happiness within damaged life itself, and the tenderness of love in a society structured by instrumental purposiveness, the good is revealed in the evils and sufferings afflicting others as the demand to respond. It does not demand ethical or social theorizing, nor congratulatory moralizing claims about who is morally superior, but responsiveness from the (supposedly) "inferior" and "superior" alike. This imperfectionist rectification of the moral elitism and vanguardism characteristic of virtue ethics and moral perfectionist ethical theory signified that those relegated to abject, marginal, and subaltern positions can do more than speak. That is, the good can occur through both uncultivated and cultivated human attitudes and practices of goodness, such as the small everyday acts that all three philosophers elucidate to different degrees.[23] Løgstrup's sovereign life-expressions indicate the ultimate "sovereignty of good"—to deploy Murdoch's apt expression—immanently in the midst of life in human terms. This reflection finds resonances in Levinas and Murdoch to the extent that they thematize everyday acts of goodness and kindness—such as saying "Hello," "Thank you," "After you," and "Adieu"—in ordinary life.[24] Ordinary acts of goodness can occur in the most mundane and horrifying conditions, as all three philosophers recognized, and also expose the Luciferian secret of moralistic vanity.

The good's transcendence occurs within this-worldly immanence in love and solidarity. Murdoch describes how the good operates with the authority of a "beyond," a transcendent background checking our selfishness and self-interestedness.[25] The good is not defined by freedom, decision, or the will, but rather these aim at the good, which appears as vanity and good for nothing (invisible and nonrepresentable) in resisting the reductive perspective of usefulness and purposiveness that it places into question.[26] According to Murdoch, the good is in itself invisible and imageless while leaving images for our focus and attention: "The image of the Good as a transcendent magnetic center seems to me the least corruptible and most realistic picture for us to use in our reflections on the moral life."[27] The good's "other-power" (an expression adopted from Hōnen, Pure Land Buddhism, and the Kyōto school) is revealed in Murdoch's account in how it confronts the limiting prioritization of self-interest, the will, and power in moments of love and unselfing.[28]

Murdoch calls her ethics "perfectionist," given the notable roles she gives to cultivating virtue and disposition. Yet, I would add, it is imperfectionist in the sense that her ethics prioritizes the good over the striving and perfectionist telos of the individual and collective subject. In her redirection of Platonic eros and the good into the world, love is the overcoming of the self in encountering reality: "Love is the extremely difficult realization that something other than oneself is real. Love, and so art and morals, is the discovery of reality."[29] Murdoch's elucidation of love in *The Sovereignty of Good* is a significant point of departure for this work's notion of an unrestricted solidarity immanent within the nexus of damaged and incomplete life that embraces and nourishes—to speak once more of the material dimension disclosed by Levinas—sensuous and transient material life living in and from the elemental.[30]

The reconstructed conversation between Murdoch, Løgstrup, and Levinas presented here points toward the following theses: (1) the good's sovereignty (its irreducibility to any other natural or nonnatural qualities or motivations); (2) its other-power in relation to decision, the will, and the self; (3) its conceptual and theoretical indefinability as an inexhaustible or infinite aspect of reality; (4) its an-archy (its nonidentity with being, God, nature, or the supersensible); and (5) ethical imperfectionism (it is an interruptive and reorienting demand on finite, destitute, and damaged lives regardless of their perfection or virtue).

This imperfectionist heuristic or critical model has sources, as observed earlier, in Adorno's ethics of damaged life, which encompasses its own promise of happiness, and in Levinas's ethics of the other's abjection, destitution, and suffering that calls for our response in the context of our incompletion. As described in the introduction, imperfectionism results from damaged life and *minima moralia* as well as the diachrony, disquiet, and incompletion of time described by Levinas.[31]

The good's "other-power," interrupting the self in its immanence, is given a more radically intensified and hyperbolic expression in Levinas in comparison to Murdoch and Løgstrup. The good confronts not only the evil but the just and the virtuous. It unsettles and reorients damaged life and human imperfections in both the virtuous (the perfected) and the unvirtuous (the imperfect). Ethical imperfectionism is therefore an implication of Levinas's qualifications against the self-righteous moralism of the virtuous, the pure, and the perfected for the sake of the awakening of vigilance (in contrast to moralistic self-satisfaction) in encountering and responding to others: "[E]thics is no longer a simple moralism of rules decreed by the virtuous. It is the original awakening of an 'I' responsible for others, the accession of my person to the uniqueness of the 'I' called and elected to responsibility for others."[32] It is the task of responding to the good in the midst of a constitutive (not merely contingent) ignorance and folly.

Levinas commented, again in relation to Vasily Grossman, that "in the decay of human relations, in that sociological misery, goodness persists."[33] In the relation of one person to another person, goodness is possible. In Levinas's extensive reflections on the most extreme horror and terror in concentration and death camps, the autonomous sovereign good appears to function as the exception—intimated in the gaze of the dog Bobby or the handing over of a piece of bread—rather than the rule, even as (according to Løgstrup) it is presupposed in its brokenness and ruination. In contrast to the sovereign self-interested individual of modern capitalist societies or a community's self-assertion of a collective identity, it is the good that is sovereign as "first philosophy" irreducible to instrumental calculations and other purposes. Nonetheless, whereas the autonomy of the good is the immanent significance of life itself as a moral reality in Løgstrup's ethics, and "naturalistic" in Murdoch's sense of being "a real constituent of the world," it is the transcendence striking against reality understood as suffocating presence in *Of Escape*, as war and violence in *Totality and Infinity*, and life's egoism, and the self-interestedness of perseverance in being.[34]

To speak heuristically in a Kantian language at this point, a reader might wish to interpret the sovereign life-expressions as being closer to an indeterminate reflective judgment in search of a rule rather than a determinate judgment that follows a rule. This strategy would be inadequate insofar as sovereign life-expressions are neither reflective nor prereflective indeterminate judgments. They are determinate and presupposed in a preexisting common ethical life or an ethically orienting lifeworld. To a degree, Løgstrup's depiction of sovereign life-expressions is proximate to Husserl's notion of lifeworld (without the theory of passive sedimentation) and Habermas's portrayal of the ethical preconditions of communicative action and his distinction between lifeworld (as normative source) and systems (of power, wealth, and status that cannot reduce or exhaust the normativity and critical capacity of the lifeworld).

Murdoch, Løgstrup, and Levinas each configure the relations between immanence and transcendence differently while endeavoring to address how the transcendence or otherness of the good occurs within the immanence of reality and life. Løgstrup prioritizes immanence in his approach to the asymmetrical ethics of the other, stressing the immediacy and spontaneity of the ethical encounter with the other in the sovereign expressions of life. These expressions of the good signify that life expresses itself as the trust and openness that is always presupposed by distrust and the lack of or denial of openness. The ethical demand in this case presupposes an account of life in terms of the sovereign life-expressions and understanding of life as fundamentally being a gift. This creational gift (*donum*) of life demands that we share in the life and suffering of others.

Naturalism, Antinaturalism, and Life's Sovereign Expressions

To return to the topic of section two above at this point, Løgstrup develops a phenomenological anthropology of the pre- or protoethical moral capacities that is informed by the work of Hans Lipps and that was developed in different forms in the philosophical anthropology of Lipps's contemporaries, such as Max Scheler, Helmuth Plessner, and Georg Misch.[35] The human capacity to respond to others and act for them is possible because of the immanence of the good in life and the naturally and anthropologically rooted capacities to respond to ethical demands. There is in this case no dichotomy between the ethical care of the self and care for the other.

Levinas rejected notions of immanent community, ethical life, and the lifeworld for the transcendence that disrupts them. Would he respond to the sense of immanence in Løgstrup's sovereign expressions of life in an analogous way? As in Heidegger's description of inauthentic everydayness in *Being and Time*, immanence (including the immanence of human life) is already fallen. It is ethically malformed in egoism and war, requiring a radical transformative break. In Levinas's response to Heidegger, absorption and participation in immanence and relationality by themselves are inadequate to the ethical that is radically transcendent, interruptive, and "disrelational" to identity and sameness.

Levinas's thinking is shaped by the phenomenological distrust (evident in Husserl and Heidegger) of philosophical anthropology. The good in its alterity is irreducibly transcendent and interruptive to the self-absorbed self. The ethical demand cannot be situated much less rooted in any capacity or characteristic of the self, however passive it might be. Recognition of marks or features of the alterity of the other already presupposes the responsibility of the self for the other in the ethical encounter, even as moral reflection and theorizing presuppose and elucidate rather than create the ethical relation. The good occurs as the self's distress, trauma, persecution, and its being confronted by the face, life, and suffering of the other. Ethics thus has the characteristics of compulsion and heteronomy that Levinas employs against the ethics of autonomy understood as the primacy of one's own autonomy instead of the autonomy of the other.

Insofar as one can speak of the same "ethical demand" in Levinas and Løgstrup, as Critchley and others have done, despite their different accounts of how such a demand occurs and grasps the self, one can claim in both cases that ethics does not primarily concern the perfectionist care and cultivation of the self. It is the exposure to the other, and calling forth responses to the other, that matter more than one's own moral status or virtue. Appropriately responding to the other is the primary ethical issue. This approach involves perplexities from the perspective of classical moral theory. Getting theory, judgment, and decision "right" does not guarantee the response in contrast with the ethics of decision. More radically, they are "after the fact," distance the self from the other, and deform the response. There are no explicit "rules" for deciding or evaluating whether the response is appropriate or not, yet we can clearly assess or criticize departures from the ethical. How then can there be ethically oriented judgment and criticism on the basis of the ethical demand?

As noted in chapter 4 on naturalism and antinaturalism in Levinas's works, nature and science are significant because of a metalevel of concrete interhuman relations that make them meaningful.[36] Levinas can consequently be portrayed as engaging in a hermeneutics of suspicion against the ethical failures of naturalism and philosophies of self-enclosed or totalistic immanence. In such philosophies of presence, being, nature, life, and no doubt the lifeworld are critiqued as realms of egoism, self-interest, the struggle for existence, competition, and war. Levinas's critique of immanence and presence is not accidental. It is a defining aspect of his works from *Of Escape* in the 1930s through *Totality and Infinity* to *Otherwise Than Being*.

Whereas Levinas argued for the radically nonnaturalistic conception of the good as indefinable, invisible, and transcendent, which is beyond being itself, Løgstrup is aware that his strategy of approaching the invisible, one-sided, silent, radical—and nonetheless immanent—demand is in jeopardy of committing a form of the naturalistic fallacy through his identification of creation, createdness, and the good. This is an odd form of naturalism, if it is one at all, given the brokenness of the human relationship with external or internal nature.[37] "The good" is not prescriptive for Løgstrup, as in natural law theory, nor did he identify this good with pleasure, drives, or other any other aspect of human nature. Yet the ethical demand must have a weight for the person it addresses, orienting and becoming part of human personality and character.[38] Although Løgstrup's moral anthropology and psychology do not underwrite or undermine the unconditionality of the ethical demand, the demand and the good are immanent in life.

The ethical demand, according to Løgstrup's argumentation, is underwritten by life's immanent goodness. Løgstrup's language seems to suggest that there is an eternal invisible and silent—though indirectly seen and heard—law orienting practical life through its historically shifting social norms and their relative and finite institutionalization and practice. The sovereign life-expression of trust, for example, is irrevocable for communication itself. Communication cannot persist without the dimension of openness and trust: "So robust a phenomenon as mistrust arises from disappointed trust."[39] This means that the systematic distortive powers of distrust and suspicion presuppose trust as the source and point of departure they betray and misuse. Due to its fundamental constitutive character, trust can be institutionalized and practiced only in partial and imperfect ways, through which it continues to operate even in distorted and misused forms.

The Good of Ethical Life and the Good beyond Being

Løgstrup's argument focuses on the immediate individual encounter of the self with the other, as the happening of the ethical relation. However, the nexus and weight of ethical tradition, the totality of the relations of ethical life, or the lifeworld plays a significant role for Løgstrup—to the extent that it determines relations in ways that agents cannot radically change or alter its content, as seen in his description of love relations. This approach would appear to be opposed to Levinas's sense of the ethical defined as an inherent transcendence to natural and social life: a break and interruption of unethical ethical life or objective spirit understood as a system of self-interested egoism or systematic totality.

Løgstrup's social enactment and mediation of the ethical demand intensify it as well as potentially hide it. In Løgstrup's discussions of mistrust and the misuse of trust, as in the manipulation of trust and openness by the secret police in a police state, trust cannot disappear in the social totality or in the political. It is not infinity and the transcendent that is exterior to totality, as in Levinas's *Totality and Infinity*. It is perceived as the immanence of the good itself in life, and which is expressed in life, that is irreducible to its social form and totalization.

To return to a question previously raised in chapter 7, is Levinas committed to another variation on moral intuitionism or a variety of "Platonism" (analogous to Murdoch's realistic interpretation of it)? Løgstrup's affirmative assessment of Moore's simple perception of the good in *Principia Ethica*, noted by Brenda Almond, is revealing in relation to Murdoch's naturalizing reinterpretation of Moore's intuition as a natural or worldly moral perception.[40] Løgstrup rejected the intuitive knowing of the good presupposed in Moore's formulation of the naturalistic fallacy; that is, the naturalistic fallacy fails as an abstraction that allows the separation of the good from descriptive content and the significance of the situation in which the demand can be enacted. Does this concern apply to Levinas's diachronic separation of the good from being and the self? He certainly does not argue for the ethical intuition of the good as a form or supersensible reality; neither do we intuit "the good" (Moore), the intelligible, nor "obligation." As Hilary Putnam remarks, there appears to be an affinity between Levinas and intuitionism, and if anything is intuited in Levinas it would be "the presence of the other person."[41]

The good is a "nonnatural quality" for Levinas, as it is for Moore. However, they have radically different interpretations of what counts as nature and nonnature. In Levinas, the good revealed through the other is radically exterior to nature and self-nature, striking the self from the outside. It does not strike from the supersensible but rather from the alterity in the sensuous material face and life of the other, which should be interpreted through natural history, as claimed previously in part 1. In Levinas's discussions of Plato's vision of the form of the good as the good beyond being, his description of the good echoes and evokes its intuitive qualities found in the Platonic tradition. In this way there is both proximity and distance between Levinas and G. E. Moore's simple, indefinable, nonnatural good or Iris Murdoch's moral realist—and immanent and naturalized Platonist—conception of the autonomous yet worldly sovereignty of good.[42]

Levinas, as well as Adorno, have been identified in some interpretations with "negative ethics."[43] As was asked in the previous discussion of Platonism, Levinas, and G. E. Moore, one could well ask again if negative ethics (defined through that which it is not) has the same predicament as negative theology (as inconsistently presupposing what it denies asserting) and question whether Levinas assumes an intuitive Platonic understanding of the good, characterized through the ineffable and a meaning that is infinitely deferred, while simultaneously striving to distance itself from the Platonic metaphysical vision of a supersensible form of the good. If negative ethics and its ineffability are undermined by their hidden presuppositions, then Murdoch's naturalization of Plato's sovereignty of good, which makes it a constituent part of the sensible world, offers an alternative route.[44] Another interpretive route is the positivity of responsibility in material existence. Levinas's discourse of ethical embodiment, sensibility, and the materiality and suffering of the other, as particularly explicated in the interpretation of Dussel, indicates how this ethics is not merely a "negative ethics" depending on a hidden intuition of the supersensible but rather depending on an ethics of the material sensible other.[45]

The radicalness of Levinas's language, of responsibility and sacrifice even to one's persecutors, has struck his critics as unnecessary exaggerated rhetorical hyperbole, an accusation also used against Løgstrup despite the comparative mildness of his language. Levinas's and Løgstrup's different linguistic strategies are not only stylistic; they are part of a larger pattern of differences concerning substantive philosophical concerns about the ethical. This point can be unfolded with regard to the difference between Løgstrup's "gift of life" and Levinas's transcendent good in light of Murdoch's ethics of the good. Levinas's antinaturalistic conception of a good irreducible to immanence or nature intersects with Murdoch's expansive naturalistic reformulation of Plato's discourse of the good in a number of ways. In their readings of the good in Plato's *Republic*, the good can only be beyond and otherwise than being. However, rejecting the reification (or reifying interpretation) of Platonism, the good does not persist in another ontological realm as a supersensible form. Levinas's transcendent good, again reminding one of Murdoch's naturalized realism, transpires immanently—or as a transcendent exterior operating disruptively within the system according to Dussel—in life, interrupting the very egoism of life and its enjoyment in and through the other.[46]

Such an ethics is not "negative ethics," if negative is construed as negation, but is negative in the sense that the interruption and other-power of the good is a constituent part of life and the lifeworld. They are ethical realities in which not only power but kindness and generosity take place. This attention to the responsibility in our power over others and the good in everyday interactions is expressed in Løgstrup's statement affirming the importance of how small ethical acts affect the other and human flourishing:

> A person never has something to do with another person without having some degree of control over him or her. It may be a very small matter, involving only a passing mood, a dampening or quickening of spirit, a deepening or removal of some dislike. But it may also be a matter of tremendous scope, such as can determine if the life of the other flourishes or not.[47]

Suffering, Useless Suffering, and Theodicy

The reality of suffering speaks against the notion that life should be understood as a gift. As we know too well, life can be a nightmare and worse. Levinas points us toward all those to whom such a life has been denied in works such as *Totality and Infinity* and his critique of theodicy in his essay "Useless Suffering" (1982).[48] Theodicy can neither save God's innocence nor help ethics. The supposed rationality of suffering in discourses of theodicy and punishment give the impression of being an excusing suffering by erasing it in a happy conclusion. Discourses that excuse and justify suffering appear "suspiciously like repression." Levinas claims that "the arbitrariness and strange failure of justice amidst wars, crimes and the oppression of the weak by the strong" in such discourses perpetuate the fatalism of "the useless suffering that springs from natural plagues," and operate as "the effects of an ontological perversion."[49]

Løgstrup likewise rejects appeals to religious and secular theodicies and the justification of suffering that they presuppose. One could ask whether the gift of life is an implicit immanent "theodicy" or shares its structural problems. The problem of "theodicy": if life is inherently good, then how can it be filled with such suffering and horror? Løgstrup does not offer a justification, explanation, or excuse for this situation, as there cannot be one. There is no escape from the aporia of suffering. He describes how life as gift is the measure of the denial and loss of the gift; that is, we recall and mourn the dead and respond to suffering precisely because life is a gift and we perceive this sharing in life's gift to be lacking or annihilated. The ethical demand accordingly addresses us through the shared life and the lack of life, the shared good and the lack thereof. It does not guarantee that life is a gift in each case; yet it is the source from which we recognize the injustice and evil that occur.[50]

Levinas, Løgstrup, and Murdoch offer alternative strategies of interacting with the good and for addressing ethical asymmetries in responsibility and love. Relational ethics could potentially be egalitarian or hierarchical, symmetrical or asymmetrical. Levinas and Løgstrup are both generally—albeit not sufficiently politically radical—egalitarian thinkers on the basis of an asymmetrical responsibility of the self for the concrete singular other; that is, the unconditional demand of damaged and destitute life and the other's suffering that cannot be justified.[51]

Conclusion and Transition to Part Three

Part 2 of this volume has explored how the category of the religious can express—through its prophetic and redemptive moments and in its dreams, hopes, and visions formed and expressed in abject, damaged, and wounded life—the good itself and the ethical aspirations and demands of the other that calls for a society that would not only preserve but heighten the radical republican and social democratic alignment in the direction of equality (fairness), liberty (autonomy), and solidarity (love).

As the analysis of Nietzsche and Marx illustrated at the beginning of part 2, the religious is employed to justify and sanctify violence, terror, and power, and repress life and its aspirations of equality, freedom, and happiness, which it promises and encloses in a distant supersensible realm. Nevertheless, their critiques of religion—often despite themselves—reveal how the religious dreams the truth of the matter that can contest and disrupt—through that redemptive promise and the demand for unconditional love and compassion not delimited by instrumental purposiveness—domination and the all too profane tendencies of politicized religious ideologies and institutions, as analyzed in Marx, Nietzsche, and Adorno in chapter 6.

In part 3 of this work, questions of equality, freedom, and solidarity will be pursued in the context of an asymmetrical ethics of material others. Asymmetrical ethics, or the claim that individuals are unequal in their moral obligations in a way that disturbs the realities of inequality, is supposed by its detractors to be incompatible with political equality. In Habermas and Honneth, whose critical social theories were interrogated in part 1 in regard to nature and natural history and will be encountered again throughout part 3 in relation to justice, ethics is justifiable based on norms grounded in intersubjective relations of communication and recognition between symmetrical agents. The denial of moral symmetry necessarily undermines political equality in their closely aligned conceptions of ethical life. In addition, the phenomenological and deconstructive emphasis on receptivity, passive synthesis, passivity, openness, and letting be—a language that operates at times in Adorno and that Levinas radicalizes by speaking of dependence, heteronomy, and a passivity beyond all passivity—is interpreted as being a "postmodern" philosophical elitism complicit with political subordination and oppression, and involving a submissive and potentially reactionary political sensibility.

The responsibility of ethical responsiveness, constituted in "ethical imperfection" and in the impossibility of ever adequately responding to the other qua other, challenges political dominion, as shown in Levinas's reflections on twentieth-century politics, with its numerous failures and horrors. Rather than establishing a static and hierarchical ethics of subordination, as feared by Habermas, Honneth, and other theorists of moral egalitarianism, the variety of ethics identified with Adorno and Levinas, and more recently Derrida and Dussel, offers a basis for and correction to standard liberal and socialist accounts of social-political equality by attending to questions of alterity, heterogeneity, materiality, and singularity. Discourses of prophetic ethics and politics offer vital critical alternatives to the contemporary paradigm of ethical and critical social theory insofar as practical inquiry is nontrivially extended beyond the equal yet abstract symmetry and prudential negotiations of mutual recognition and consensus formation.

At this juncture, this work turns from the natural (part 1) and the religious (part 2) to explicitly social-political concerns (part 3). The third part of this work concerns the drama of the demands of justice. Justice promises equality and fairness and is at the same time part of the formation and maintenance of regimes of institutionalized domination and exploitation. This work now turns to justice as a third name for the drama of oppression and liberation, and considers examples of how this dynamic operates in contemporary globalized yet hierarchically organized—in spite of its egalitarian and universalist claims—contemporary capitalist societies in their complexly interconnected cosmopolitan neoliberal and neomercantile nativist and nationalistic ideological variations. While neoliberalism affirms in discourse the primacy of the free global circulation of capital and unrestricted exchange, neomercantile discourses (reflecting the crisis conditions of capitalist societies) assert in the guise of populism the primacy of racialized and nationalized capital in the service of elites. Both varieties need to be confronted with an ethics, politics, and political economy of the other.

Part Three

Demanding Justice

Asymmetrical Ethics and Critical Social Theory

Chapter Eleven

Equality, Justice, and Asymmetrical Ethics

Introduction to Part Three

The present part of the volume operates in the intersections and margins between ethics and politics and how these discourses function as ideologically mystified untruth and as prophetic truth. Every ideological phenomenon (including the highest democratic norms of equality, freedom, justice, and solidarity) is simultaneously untruth and truth. According to the double operation of the dialectic in relation to the present described by Marx, and modified by Adorno, who rejected its inevitability, dialectic "includes in its comprehension an affirmative recognition of the existing state of things, at the same time also, the recognition of the negation of that state, of its inevitable breaking up."[1] Oppressed and damaged forms of life already indicate their negation and therefore their potential transformation. Levinas rejected the discourses of negativity, dialectic, and critique (in particular in its Hegelian form) while also revealing the otherwise (as other than positivity and negativity) in the midst of identity, the same, and the totality. Part 3 of this volume traces how Adorno's and Levinas's distinctive strategies entail an asymmetrical ethics of material differences that can be deployed against standard liberal ideas and practices of contemporary capitalist forms of life.

Detractors of the asymmetrical ethics of alterity prioritize social-ethical symmetry in a just social arrangement. The argumentation of Habermas and Honneth is examined throughout this volume (previously in part 1, and further in the following chapters) as a significant counterposition. They maintain that prioritizing the alterity and asymmetry between subjects undermines social-political equality and justice. This claim presupposes the reciprocal recognition of autonomous subjects as posited in classical and contemporary liberal political philosophy. Habermas and Honneth have linked recent French postmodernism with "Nietzschean elitism," systematically misinterpreting the works of both Nietzsche and these authors.[2] Furthermore, both have criticized the affinities that they identify between Adorno and deconstructive philosophy, such as the critique of Enlightenment, modern rationality, and secularized apologetic theodicies that overlook the victims.

However inadequate their specific readings of authors and works (including Adorno and Levinas, as already argued in part 1, as well as others, such as Derrida) might be, particularly Habermas's in his adversarial *The Philosophical Discourse of Modernity*, it is worthwhile to address it to articulate an alternative.[3] Habermas and Honneth raise real challenges and pose genuine questions to asymmetrical ethics. A fundamental question is, to what extent, if at all, is an ethics stressing the asymmetry and alterity between self and other compatible with the demands of social-political equality and justice? This question is justified insofar as Adorno, Levinas, Derrida, and other thinkers associated with alterity, nonidentity, and the ethical priority of a nonrelative difference express commitments to and articulate options for egalitarian political philosophy and politics by advocating alternative transformative approaches to such a politics oriented by the alterity and singularity of the other and multiplicity of material others.

The five chapters of part 3, including the epilogue, will consider the ethical-political significance of the works of Adorno and Levinas on the basis of the notions of mimetic intermateriality, the solidarity of material others, damaged and nourished life, and prophetic critique introduced in the first two parts above. It will challenge the argumentative, interpretive, and rhetorical strategies of these two philosophers with the alternate conception of egalitarianism and liberalism, developed in contemporary critical theorists such as Habermas and Honneth, for the sake of articulating an asymmetrical ethics and politics of material others in the sense of the unrestricted solidarity articulated in the three parts of this volume in relation to nature, religion, and justice.

Asymmetry and Equality

The current chapter focuses on selected works of Levinas in contrast to the ethical-political discourse of the recent generations associated with the Frankfurt school (e.g., Habermas and Honneth), and consider whether the social-political equality that he himself supported is consistent with the ethics of the radically transcendent Other. I argue in this context for the more far-reaching thesis that asymmetry and equality are not only not incompatible; more significantly, egalitarian politics can be adequately analyzed and articulated only in relation to the real existing asymmetries between self and other, their ecological and political economic material conditions, and their ethical import, which demands responsibility and calls me to respond. That is, the actually existing asymmetries between individuals and groups, their passions and sufferings, call forth an ethical and political response that would begin to address and redress them.

Conceptions of equality that negate the heterogeneity between self and other risk falling into the invalidation of the factual life of actual individuals in identity thinking and the assumption of totality that has produced the violence, terror, and totalitarianism of movements that offered promise while undermining the equality of individuals. This betrayal occurred in the inversion of the defense of the person into the brutality of Stalinist communism.[4] The history of the establishment and institutionalization of communist regimes in the twentieth-century saw the betrayal and destruction of the ethical orientation toward human liberation. Even as Levinas distinguished his asymmetrical ethics from symmetrical egalitarianism, he defended Marxism from the accusation that it is only a form of domination. He stated in an interview, "[I]n Marxism, there is not just conquest; there is recognition of the other. True enough, it consists in saying: We can save the other if he himself demands his due. Marxism invites humanity to demand what it is my duty to give it."[5] Levinas observes of the heterodox Marxist thinker Bloch in *God, Death, and Time* (1973–1974), "What incites this revolutionary movement is the meaning of human misery. What led those to socialism who had no need for it? Perhaps the soul, perhaps the conscience that throbs in the silence of those who are sated."[6] There is an ethical core orienting political activities on behalf of justice, which are betrayed if practiced and institutionalized without the sensibility that is ethically addressed in and responds to injustice.[7]

Levinas recognizes the prophetic and messianic moments in socialism and Marxism, along with their historical betrayal.[8] The Marxist paradigm was flawed because of its ontological misinterpretation of materialism and reduction of ethics to an ideology secondary to the movement of historical necessity (that is, the reductive sense of natural history). It did not adequately perceive the ethical moment in materiality or the material moment in ethics. In his writings on the prospects of socialism and Marxism, which resonate with heterodox Marxists such as Bloch and Marcuse on Soviet communism's stifled emancipatory elements, Levinas is both sympathetic to the ethical and egalitarian claims of communism and intensely critical of the infidelity to and betrayal of these claims. Levinas is a thinker who reflects on the political that adopts and transforms elements of republicanism (at least in its modern egalitarian form) and socialism in the changed conditions of the twentieth-century. The historical context of the disappointments and aporias of modern Western reason and democracy encompass a variety of phenomena for him, including "two world wars, oppression, genocides, the Holocaust, terrorism, unemployment, the never ending poverty of the Third World, [and] the ruthless doctrines of Fascism and National Socialism."[9] Levinas reframed questions of liberty, equality, and solidarity from within this historical situation of continuing suffering and consequently injustice, as the excuse before and "justification of the neighbor's pain is certainly the source of immorality."[10] These issues are not pursued from the primacy of the individual autonomy of the self-interested subject, happily pursuing its own goods and rights in oblivion to its responsibility to the other; they are instead questioned and rethought in relation to the interruptive encounters between inherently asymmetrical subjects and the priority of the other over myself. Levinas articulated this situation of encounter through exemplary ethical occurrences such as the face and height of, and sacrifice and substitution for, the other.

The ethical encounter is unsolicited and disquieting in that it simultaneously demands too much responsibility of me while providing too little guidance to me in its an-archy that disrupts ontological and ontic determinacy. The ethically insufficient and imperfect self is paradoxically obligated without end even in the lack of economy and empirical impossibility of ethics. An asymmetrical and an-archic (or non-rule-based) ethics and humanism proceeding from the other person enables the confrontation with contemporary moral and social issues involving unequal situations, opportunities, and resources between pluralities of nonidentical concrete individuals and groups. Such an ethics calls, awakens, and sobers me to my unwelcome yet inescapable responsibility to the other—prior to and regardless of any relation of sympathy or antipathy, mutual exchange or recognition, compromise or negotiation, which underestimate and undermine the ethical by excusing suffering and neglecting the enormity of a responsibility uniquely my own.

Equality and Freedom

Equality and freedom have ideological and ethical functions that are constantly entangled to block their transformative realization. Equality has multiple contested meanings, such that one is forced to reflect on whose and which equality.[11] To consider one example, in two essays in the *Frankfurter Allgemeine Zeitung* published in 2009, Peter Sloterdijk has declared the issue of inequality to be an anachronistic concern enslaving our thinking to conformity and our institutions to the administration of funds.[12] In a rejoinder, Honneth argues for the continuing ethical and political relevance of equality in the face of irresponsible and elitist fantasies of individual freedom.[13] In this discussion, the primary options appear to be between a libertarianism (fearful of losing its freedom to the fairness of others) and egalitarianism (afraid of the reactionary potential of asymmetry and nonidentity). Neither author notices that these two distinctions between equality and liberty and asymmetry and symmetry are not identical, and that they can match up in ways that neither envisions.

The limited debate between Honneth and Sloterdijk is representative of the dominant ways of conceptualizing the political, and raises questions concerning the assumptions made about the relation between the ethical and the political and how human relationships are structured and how they ought to be. This debate brings access to the following questions: Are human relations inherently motivated by and oriented toward mutual reciprocity and symmetry? Or can the ethical be more broadly understood as openness, responsiveness, and responsibility toward one who is different and other and not equivalent to myself?

First, on one side of this dispute, is the concern that difference necessarily entails superiority and subordination or a distance and separation that indicate a refusal to share or speak in common. To deny the moral symmetry of persons is to undermine a major, if not *the* major, device necessary to contest and correct the social and political inequalities and injustices that still afflict much of humanity. Indeed, to deny this principle is seen as leaving us defenseless and open to justifying relationships that are fundamentally repressive and unjust, insofar as asymmetry is identical to—as it is in Honneth—hierarchical privilege.[14]

Second, on the other side, there is the suspicion that the universal, even when it appears as the benevolently structured thought of inclusion, justice, fairness, and equality, fails to appropriately address and appreciate the ipseity and singular life of the other, in the concrete and contingent specificities of a life, insofar as the other is not merely a standardized particular subsumable under and typified by a universal category. Even the dynamics of mutual consensus and recognition proposed by Habermas and Honneth, in which "all humans are to reciprocally respect each other as free and equal persons," falls under this domain.[15] Despite the fact that Habermas abandoned the consensus theory of truth, upheld by Karl-Otto Apel more consistently and comprehensively over the long term, consensus remains a basic ideal of his social-political and ethical reflections. Levinas's critique of the absorption of participation extends from irrational organic wholes to the most rational systematic totality. It throws into doubt the constitutive idealism in the prioritization of intersubjective consensus and recognition. Such universality presupposes an abstract totality reducing individuals to a formal relative alterity and conformity, leaving them vulnerable to manipulation and elimination in the name of the collective and universal. As Adorno described enlightened liberal perspectives concerning race in *Minima Moralia*, tolerance can rebound like a boomerang against stigmatized difference that appears to it to be a form of ungratefulness.[16]

Habermas, Honneth, and the Problematic of Asymmetry

Habermas has been a persistent critic of the ostensible antimodernism and antihumanism of recent French philosophy, both through his concern for an ethics of difference and through his analysis of asymmetrical power relations, arguing that social-political equality can be justified and achieved through a dialogical ethics of rational discourse that is uncoerced—or maximally free from power—and in which each one is symmetrical with each other.[17] There are two different but interconnected forms of the asymmetrical in question in this context: (1) asymmetrical power relations, which are the concern of Foucault's analysis of power/knowledge complexes; and (2) asymmetrical ethical responsibilities and demands, such as those of benevolence, charity and goodwill, generosity, guest-friendship, and hospitality, which will be considered in chapter 13. Both forms of difference (hierarchical power and asymmetrical responsibility) concern the variances between self and the other, and the latter concerns the ethical demand on the self to be more responsive and responsible to the other beyond the equal reciprocal exchange of goods and recognition of rights that are relative to their exchange.

Feminist critics of Habermas have illustrated hierarchical power relations inadequately addressed by his social theory. Claudia Moscovici concludes that there are a "number of asymmetrical power relations which Habermas does not even mention," since his account of ethical and social-political equality fails to recognize real gendered inequalities in the workplace, the home, and the public sphere.[18] Marie Fleming likewise analyzes communicative rationality as missing "the asymmetrical representation of women and men in public" and concludes that "Habermas does not address these issues."[19] Insofar as such criticisms share the same presupposition that asymmetry is inherently repressive, Habermas's discourse ethics would be in need of only correction and supplementation concerning gender rather than radical transformation. But such a radical if not conditional critique *is* necessary only if asymmetry is inherent in human relations and is not exclusively oppressive, that is, if asymmetry is not merely the exercise of power but the basis of interpersonal relations. The political philosopher Iris Marion Young accordingly argued along these lines for an "asymmetrical instead of symmetrical responsibility."[20]

In response to such challenges, a number of authors (including Habermas) have attempted to show that discourse ethics—the project of Apel and Habermas to revise Kantian deontological ethics by grounding moral norms in communicative action—can be more inclusive of the other, including others who cannot speak or who lack access to the means of communication.[21] As a result, Habermas has added the principle of affectively oriented solidarity (a modification of the Rousseauian republican legacy) alongside normative justice, although both are conceived as symmetrical reciprocating relations between the self and other.[22] Beyond the reciprocal solidarity between equals, some authors maintain that Habermas can extend a humanistic sense of equality between rational agents to those who are considered asymmetrical: nonhuman animals, as well as the silenced, the poor, and the oppressed.[23] This is based on an argument by Habermas that introduces a principle of asymmetrical respect into his account, thereby signifying that the equal respect fostered within communicative action and ethics can be extended outward to embrace asymmetrical others who are marginalized in and disbarred from participating in that communication.[24] This is problematic insofar as the asymmetrical other remains derivative of symmetrical reciprocity rather than primary as other.

Honneth has justifiably sought to remedy the deficits of discourse ethics. He argues that this problem can be resolved through a more flexible model of reciprocal yet dynamic recognition on the basis of Hegel's dialectic of recognition and recent interpersonal psychology.[25] Honneth incorporates the affective basis of interpersonal relations and moral life to strengthen moral egalitarianism. Yet, as will be further clarified, it is difficult to be as optimistic as Honneth about reconciling the ethics of difference and the ethics of recognition.[26] Honneth's reconciliation of the two is forced in his insistence that, in the end, it is necessarily and exclusively symmetry, and not asymmetry, that can stand in as a universal moral principle.[27] He concludes in his single essay concerning Levinas that asymmetry is a genetic rather than a logical aspect of ethics and that it is ultimately incompatible with "the moral point of view" of reciprocal autonomous subjects.[28] Manuel P. Arriaga describes this essay with the conclusion, "The most that Honneth can grant in this regard is to view the asymmetrical as the genetic foundation of the symmetrical."[29] Yet it is not so much a foundation as it is an imperfect stage to be developmentally left behind. Asymmetry is a stage of misrecognition to be dialectically overcome rather than valorized.[30] Asymmetry—like "particularity" and "singularity"—is an antithesis to be dialectically sublimated. In this strategy of synthesis that levels out alterity and asymmetry, Honneth, who promoted a Hegelian correction to Habermas's Kantianism, is committed to a positive dialectic of identity rather than a negative dialectic of nonidentity. Asymmetry fails to legitimate or further the aims of egalitarian ethics and politics, being the primitive precondition and irregular exception and not the genuine foundational normative ideal.

Deconstructive and postmodern intellectuals have claimed that "Habermas cannot deal with the demand of the asymmetrical other."[31] He incoherently presupposes the asymmetrical that he attempts to suppress through a nearly classical metaphysical systematizing and equalizing.[32] Honneth recognizes this problem more fully yet still inadequately. He acknowledges the genuine ethical impulses in the ethics of alterity to the extent that he considers the asymmetrical responsibility between persons to be the most difficult ethical challenge to universal equality.[33] Honneth's answer to this challenge is to embrace asymmetrical "care" (*Fürsorge*) along with equal "justice" (*Gerechtigkeit*) as constitutive of ethical life, while subordinating it to a universalist ethics with Hegelian premises. This requires progressively overcoming care with equal treatment and equal opportunities and correcting asymmetries and inequalities as imperfect and corrupt forms of recognition.[34] Honneth's spheres of recognition, an account developed in *The Struggle for Recognition*, encompass relations of (1) parental and familial affection, (2) legal rights, and (3) social solidarity.[35]

Despite the potential pertinence of the criticisms of Habermas and Honneth, deconstructive and postmodern authors—such as Hent de Vries and Mark Devenney—have yet to adequately make the case for an ethics of difference, since basic issues remain unclarified, such as whether asymmetry and equality are compatible, and how one can proceed from an asymmetrical ethics to social-political equality given the absence of natural and universal equality.[36] For Levinas, there is no natural or foundational equality, as in traditional or contemporary contract theory and liberalism: "To emphasize a notion of asymmetrical obligation, Levinas rejects the notion of natural equality as the first principle of ethics."[37]

The question that could be posed here is, how and why—if at all—can any ethical relation be derived from the asymmetrical and disrelational? It seems difficult to articulate the relational in the ethical given the radical questioning and lack of relationality. For the Kantian and Hegelian ethical paradigms, and in most interpretations of ethics for that matter, "an asymmetrical, one-sided relation is no relation at all."[38] The abandonment of exchange and reciprocity in ethics appears to undermine the negotiation and compromise characteristic of everyday ethical life and consensus formation: "That is, we need an account that abandons the purity of asymmetry [and the] utter repudiation by Levinas of the whole space of negotiation."[39]

Two further objections in line with Honneth's objections follow from this. The first is that the phenomenological emphasis on receptivity—on passive synthesis, openness, and letting be—is complicit with political subordination and oppression, involving a submissive, or in the case of Heidegger, reactionary political sensibility. Levinas further radicalized this phenomenological language of responsiveness by emphasizing the dependence, heteronomy, and passivity (beyond the passive synthesis that is still too intentional and active) of ethical obedience of the self to the other.[40]

Second, the ethics of an absolute but impossible hospitality, the thought of an infinite generosity under the conditions described by ethical insufficiency and imperfection, and an unsettling and impossible "justice to come" in Levinas and Derrida has been decried by social theorists such as Slavoj Žižek as a hyperbolic yet ultimately empty responsibility and an exaggerated but politically ineffective messianic utopianism.[41] Criticisms of the language of absolute Otherness are correct to the extent that it is construed to aim at overcoming the Same in attaining the other. But, as discussed previously, alterity and nonidentity aporetically express their relationship to sameness and identity while indicating what is otherwise and irreducible to them. Asymmetry, whether in aesthetics or ethics, is "comprehended in its relation to symmetry."[42] The ethics of alterity is possible only in its impossibility (from the hegemonic perspective of identity and completion), that is, as an aporetic (see chapter 7) and imperfectionist (see chapter 10) ethics of damaged life. These two elements entail the radicalism of ethics in the dynamic conjuncture of moments of alterity and nonidentity and the structures of abjection and injustice that they place into question and contest.

The Good, the Just, and the Material Other

> Goodness, a childish virtue; but already charity and mercy and responsibility for the other, and already the possibility of sacrifice in which the humanity of [humans] bursts forth, disrupting the general economy of the real.
>
> —Emmanuel Levinas, *Entre nous: On Thinking-of-the-Other*

Habermas and Honneth's assessment rests on the proposition that there is no moral point of view without universality, and no justice without symmetrical equal relations in both ethics and politics. Levinas's ethical thought challenges the basic assumption of this paradigm, since the ethical is unethical without the unequal first-person perspective of an irrevocable responsibility to and answerability for the other person. Levinas transforms the standard portrayal of the first-person point of view, since the "first person" is second in being dependent on and a hostage to the "second person." In this interpersonal perspective, instead of maintaining the priority of the I or the equal mirroring of self and other, I am confronted by and exposed to the singular other who does not parallel myself in the reciprocal commerce of goods or exchange of reasons.[43] Habermas and Honneth move astray from Levinas's actual account, as their critique does not describe the asymmetries of ethical life to reify the facticity of social stratification or of power relations.

Løgstrup, discussed previously in chapter 10, noted in *The Ethical Demand* the interconnection, invisible to egoistic self-interest, between these two kinds of asymmetry: power and responsibility. If I have power in relation to the other, then I am responsible and must serve that other: "Because power is involved in every human relationship, we are always in advance compelled to decide whether to use our power over the other for serving him or for serving ourselves."[44] Asymmetrical power is confronted with asymmetrical responsibility in Løgstrup and Levinas, both critics of the ethics of decision on behalf of the ethics of the demand, and existential and material need and suffering demands a response.[45] If we recall Adorno at this juncture, actual suffering and injustice are the point of departure for justice and equality in which individual existence—and the life projects, goods, and joys they involve if Adorno's negative ethical formulations are transversed—still matter and matter unconditionally.

Ethical asymmetry contests the interchangeability of the logic of exchange and commerce that sacrifices individuals for things. Ethical asymmetry contests the formalism of justice that allows injustices to continue, since all are already ideally equal without regard for the specific conditions and circumstances of a particular life.[46] Levinas's challenge does not arise from faith or the mysticism that calls for participation in a mysterious inhuman beyond. The ethical challenge is announced in the abrupt epiphany of the face, in the sudden striking immediacy and urgency of the face-to-face encounter in its an-archic anteriority (ungroundable primacy) that is exemplary of the ethical.[47] Levinas's quasiphenomenology of the face is articulated as an ethical and figurative expression that would defy its own reification.[48] The ethical interval in the an-archic materiality and empirical life of the good takes place in encountering the other's face and bodily life in its vulnerability and need. The ethical encounter is both material and transcendent: it signifies the "radical turn around" of my mundane self-regarding egoism (in which the "I" means "I have") and an awakening or conversion in which I experience my responsibility to the other as inescapable and nontransferable.[49]

The ethical encounter occurs *before* my intentionality and freedom, and cannot be created by choice or deliberation. It is preconceptual in being *prior* to the justification and application of normative concepts and theories. Nonetheless, despite the radical and un-Greek separation between ethics and knowledge, and between the responsibility in which I risk myself and the mastery and security of calculative prudence, the ethical reorientation of the "one-for-the-other" does not exclude but is the possibility of ethical judgment, reasoning, and theory, which articulate this preintentional constitutive episode as an ontic or empirical event in however diminished or unfaithful a form.[50] Existing normative and prescriptive ethics have been inadequate to the "other-constitution" of the ethical through alterity and nonidentity.

My moral feeling for and normative reflection about others—Honneth respectively discusses these through care and justice—are not constitutive of ethics, as prevalent affective-expressive and cognitive moral theories maintain, since they are elements of my response to the ethical event of the other's excessive proximity. My decision is *not* freely made insofar as it takes place as an answer to an encounter that is already occurring, and a denial of or beginning to live up to my responsibility to the other. Ethical representation and conceptualization, in contrast with the engagement in the ethical encounter in which I must respond in one way or another, is after the fact, *nachträglich*. It is exposed to the diachronic temporality that cannot be harmonized.[51]

Without the asymmetrical ethical encounter, without charity, generosity, and the naïveté of loving-kindness "responding without reasons or reservations," there can then be no formalization of the ethical into the symmetry and reciprocity of justice.[52] This is not an accidental genetic moment of the ethical, as Honneth argues; if the asymmetrical interpersonal relation is effaced, only the interchangeability of commerce remains in effect.[53] Reciprocity grounds and thus conditions and limits responsibility, according to the logic of the economy of being, whether it is understood as Habermas's procedure of the equal communicative exchange of reasons or as Honneth's agonistic struggle for recognition (*Kampf um Anerkennung*).

The ethics of the struggle for recognition is not yet genuinely ethical in light of Levinas's understanding of ethics as first philosophy in contrast to what he considers its secondary and derivative—and therefore defaced—status in the Western ontological tradition culminating in Heidegger.[54] As Levinas rejects the ontology of fundamental conflict (*Kampf*) that pervades Western thought, including its Hegelian dialectical form that aims at reconciliation, Honneth's vision of a fundamental struggle for recognition would still be too close to the idea of a struggle for life or existence (*Kampf ums Dasein*; *Kampf um Existenz*), the state of war, and the peace that is a mere continuation of war, disturbed and problematized through the height of the other that cannot be equalized. This disruption does not happen as shock and negation but as a call to gentleness and generosity.[55] Levinas considered in his notes whether giving is the highest exemplar of the interpersonal relation and materiality, the reverse of having and possession, as the condition of giving and the self.[56] The self is constituted through the materiality and alterity that it cannot possess, instead of through an idealist process of self-constitution. Neither the self nor the expectation of mutual reciprocity grounds ethics; forms of reciprocity and recognition are possible from a prior responsibility that responds to the other in the risk of the "here am I" addressed in chapter 7.[57]

Levinas concluded his essay "Uniqueness" with a claim that Honneth calls *überraschend*: "justice is always a revision of justice and the expectation of a better justice."[58] Levinas's claim is surprising because this moment cannot be mediated or overcome to achieve a reconciled and stable universal moral point of view. Justice without an other justice risks becoming exchange and calculative prudence, and risks becoming injustice to those who cannot fairly partake in this exchange or (to recall Adorno) are systematically disadvantaged by it and its logic.

Insofar as symmetrical ethics persistently expects the reciprocal exchange of goods, duties, or rights, it is all too ready to assimilate or exclude the other who does not partake or cannot respond in kind in this exchange—as in justifications of opening countries by force in the name of cosmopolitan free trade—and hence inadequate to the excess and an-archy of the good that disturbs and transcends the determinations of being and its ontological and ontic conditions. This unrestrictable good, if the good is not to be a betrayal of the good, is irreducible to determinacy and contests self-interested egoism that feels good about itself in evading the other's pain and suffering.

One decisive problem for universalizing ethics is that power operates not only through physical force but also ideologically through the tacit yet mutually agreed upon exploitation and misuse of others who are left voiceless.[59] Exploited workers from the developing world have no chance if efforts to achieve comprehensive equality concern only formal and elite participation. Levinas's point entails the more radical conclusion that symmetry is in effect mutual indifference. The autonomy of each permits one not to perceive the other's face—who must be, as previously established, a bodily material other—in their heteronomy. It allows one to attempt to excuse oneself and not encounter or engage the passive and epidermal fragility, vulnerability, and suffering of the other, subject to wounds and outrages, whose face is precarious and defenseless and yet unassailable in its alterity. If the logic of symmetry and consensus is inherently indifference, what is nonindifference? The ethical encounter, "otherwise than being," is "the shattering of indifference."[60] Nonindifference "with regard to the difference or the otherness of the other" is the irreversible asymmetry that compels me to do what is right by the other person, without the self-righteous posturing that denies what it would assert, to do "justice to the difference of the other person."[61]

In *Totality and Infinity*, Levinas defines "asymmetry" in imperfectionist terms as the fundamental impossibility of externally grasping oneself and of conceiving oneself and the other as identical or the same.[62] Asymmetry is the break and gap, the nonidentity and inequality, between the self and the other, rather than, as some definitions of asymmetry might imply, the codification of hierarchies and privileges between different types of persons—often according to class, ethnicity, and gender—in traditional moralities. Habermas and Honneth, for instance, conflate asymmetry and privilege in a nearly libertarian manner that privileges liberty over responsibility and conflicts with asymmetrically favoring those who are oppressed and exploited. Honneth's 2011 book, *Freedom's Right: The Social Foundations of Democratic Life*, identifies autonomy as the most fundamental value of modernity, which prevails over all others, whether love and solidarity, humility, or generosity and hospitality. Honneth articulates the primacy of autonomy as the center of modernity: "As if by magical attraction, all modern ethical ideals have been placed under the spell of freedom; sometimes they infuse this idea with greater depth or add new accents, but they never manage to posit an independent stand-alone alternative."[63]

Other fundamental orienting values, namely, equality and solidarity, are to be derived from the notion of autonomy insofar as it is a social conception in which autonomy must answer for itself to others. A crucial difference concerning freedom's unright is at work in Levinas. It is not a return to premodern ethics for the sake of a modern antiindividualism, visible in recent Western appropriations of Aristotelian and Confucian ethics. Traditional hierarchical moralities presuppose an identity of self and other in which the other is intended as known, subordinated, and mastered; no "recognition" occurs in such moralities of the impossible and interruptive other—the other who is inexcusably my responsibility—of whom Levinas speaks. I am not to oppress the poor, hungry, and dispossessed, but they rightfully and justly oppress my freedom by calling for a nonindifferent response.[64]

Contrary to Honneth's positing of the fundamental value of autonomy, welcoming and hospitality are more basic to the self in its other-constitution than freedom for Levinas: "To welcome the Other is to put in question my freedom."[65] Freedom and unfreedom are not the measure of ethics.[66] Freedom is derivative and dependent on something more fundamental, the ethical encounter with the other that questions my "freedom" and "right" to dispose of the other as I will. Otherwise, indifference is legitimate and murder justifiable: "To approach the Other is to put into question my freedom, my spontaneity as a living being, my emprise over the things, this freedom of a 'moving force,' this impetuosity of the current to which everything is permitted, even murder."[67] If this is the case, then ethics is incompatible with much of Western ontology, from the metaphysics of independent and self-sufficient substances, through the self-willing *conatus essendi* and self-interested ego, to the affectivity and rationality of the free or autonomous subject. This ontology still underlies the contemporary moral universalism of Habermas and Honneth, as "postmetaphysical" thinking does not question its basic assumptions.

Are Equality and Asymmetry Incompatible?

Levinas's ethics of alterity does not so much undermine as reorient egalitarian politics by (1) problematizing the assumption of a freedom unlimited by responsibility to the other, and (2) indicating the priority of the other that is the prerequisite of such a politics. The priority of the other is a prerequisite insofar as goods should correspond to needs through human kindness and the institutionalization of goodness in justice. The state, institutions, and laws are inadequate and incomplete in relation to such a goodness. Accordingly, they must be persistently questioned in regard to and prophetically reminded of justice mediated through the third and the asymmetrical interhuman goodness and gratuitous kindness between self and other.

Asymmetrical ethics promotes political and social equality through its connection with welcoming the other even in the other's need and desperation. Levinas notes, "Equality is produced where the other commands the same and reveals himself to the same in responsibility;

otherwise it is but an abstract idea and a word. It cannot be detached from the welcoming of the face, of which it is a moment."[68] Instead of the absolute insistence on liberty and egoism in the struggle for existence that continues to haunt the modern liberal political paradigm, especially whenever confronted with the other's suffering in poverty and neglect, Levinas rethinks the relation between liberty and equality through the demand of the other in exposure to the face. Instead of calculating and deliberating about whether there have been equal chances and rights, and thus whether the suffering is somehow "deserved," one can respond by avoiding the gaze, by defying it, or by offering generosity.

In addition to overturning conventional republican and liberal notions of liberty and equality, Levinas challenges the third Rousseauian and French republican expression "fraternity" through the other who is not a "brother" or "like me" but is a nonfraternal stranger.[69] In contrast to Rousseau's claim that humans were born free and found everywhere to be in chains, Levinas interrogates the movement from egotistical freedom, asserting its place in the world to the heteronomy of the self for the other, to systems of domination.

Rousseau, in the *Social Contract*, maintained that a republic, a society governed by laws and civil associations (civil society in distinction from the state apparatus), is the only form of legitimate government insofar as the people make the laws to which they are subject: the participants determine the conditions of participation. Rousseau and radical French republicanism—in contrast to its earlier hierarchical and later nationalistic forms—speak of liberty, equality, and fraternity as coming from the claims of the self and its self-realization. Levinas did not directly discuss Rousseau while frequently evoking republican ideas. He places into question and transforms the republican revolutionary trinity of demands by articulating it as an an-archic (perhaps this would be called "irregular duties" in Kantian ethics) demand that accuses me. As clarified in chapter 10, the ethical demand places "me" directly into question in the other person. Accordingly, despite its questionable gendered character, which Levinas fails to consistently resist, "fraternity" is not to be based on a resemblance that excludes those who do not participate in it; on the contrary, it is solidarity in noncoincidence without identity.[70] The ethical demand surpasses and interrupts the society limited to the equality and symmetry of the brother, the friend, and the neighbor. In the interpretive context of the Tanakh, particularly prophetic passages such as Isaiah 58, Micah 6:8, and Zechariah 7:10, the ethical demand signifies breaking every yoke and caring with justice and mercy for the concrete, bodily, and material other, the orphan and the widow, of welcoming the other, and of hospitality and guest-friendship toward the stranger and the foreigner.[71]

According to this reading, while challenging the failed theoretical and fractured practical realities of modern republican and liberal discourses, it can be argued that Levinas reorients according to the singular—while not abandoning and without eliminating—the universalistic categories of modern ethics, politics, and human rights.[72] For Levinas, liberty, equality, and solidarity are limited and self-undermining in proceeding from the self who withdraws from these claims in the name of an originary freedom indifferent to others, that is, from a subject who cares for others only insofar as they are reflected in this subject's self concern. Although autonomy dreams of itself as a will free of all exteriority, exposure, and dependence, Levinas questions whether individual freedom can excuse or provide an alibi for what I do or do not do to others. If the self-assertion of the self—the *conatus essendi* in its self-satisfied freedom and mastery of things—defines the modern ethico-political project of autonomy, then its crisis is not easily resolved through heightening and refining this universalism.

If there is no genuine dialogue without concrete material others, universal reason, and its discourse of formal or logical alterity in which each can be exchanged with any other, remains in effect a monological "egological interiority" (related to the constitutive subjectivity dismantled by Adorno) that is lacking an adequate conception of ecological and material alterity (as argued previously in chapters 1 through 3).[73] Since liberty, equality, and solidarity become genuinely possible in the other person from whom they originate for me, Habermas and Honneth's endeavor to redeem the emancipatory core of modernity (which they conceptualize according to Eurocentric presuppositions even in their most recent works) in response to its many pathologies is self-undermining without the reorientation from the same to difference, and the self to the other: that is, to the humanism and cosmopolitanism of the other person, of the stranger, rather than of the identity of the same. For Honneth, discourses of alterity are ultimately about the self; what is valid in the "postmodern" ethics of difference and poststructuralist elucidations of power is an implicit value of autonomy as self-determination.[74]

Liberty and equality are not problematized in Levinas to eliminate them for the sake of the unethical, violence, or domination; nor is the ethical reduced to a heteronomy of mere obedience and sacrifice. Instead, an alternate way of enacting and reflecting on the ethical is revealed. Ethics primarily refers first to the responsibility to one's Other, and second to the autonomy and self-determination of the self. This entails a negatively defined notion of the ethical: to not exclude, marginalize, or inevitably sacrifice the nonuniversal and nonreciprocal ipseity and singularity; to risk oneself for others in being vigilant against excusing and legitimating the pain of the neighbor that is "the source of immorality."[75] Through the pain and suffering that are necessarily material and sensible realities, Levinas articulates a universally and globally oriented ethical singularity materially constituted through relations of the ethical encounter and responsibility for others.

Levinas rhetorically exaggerates the ethical with the hyperbolic excessive and accusative demands of justice. Does Levinas forsake with his extreme rhetoric the key device to challenging exploitation and dominion in critiquing the reduction to identity that operates in the name of reason? To answer this question in the affirmative is to misread the import of Levinas's endeavors, as one key result of such extreme rhetoric is that he does not abandon rationality. He is rearticulating it beyond mathematical ratio to preserve it against the irrational powers and forces of life. Rationality is derivative of the ethical rather than vice-versa. The rationality of difference and the difference of reason evident in Levinas (and Adorno) entails that sociality precedes and is irreducible to identity thinking. Levinas's preoccupation with alterity and nonidentity brings into play the nonconceptual ethical and bodily-material aspects of human existence as well as the critical reflection and reasoning that constitute a breach with absorption in everyday life.[76] This is the prospect of ethical awakening, sobering up, watchfulness, and vigilance.

Ethical responsiveness occurs in the ethical encounter prior to calculations and deliberations concerning profit, right, and virtue. This responsiveness appears as a form of moral spontaneity or through a preinstrumental awakening and vigilance to the other. Despite the impossibility of satisfactorily responding to the other qua wholly Other, such ethical spontaneity and prophecy contest injustices by reminding us of a more human order.[77] They challenge political dominion, as shown in Levinas's critical reflections on twentieth-century politics, with its all too abundant devastation.

Does an ethics of alterity necessarily establish a static, hierarchical, and elitist ethics of subordination, as Habermas and moral egalitarians contend is necessarily the case with asymmetrical ethics? Such a criticism is inappropriate to the extent that this form of asymmetrical ethics signifies a way of correcting standard liberal and socialist categorizations of social-political equality: it does this by attending to questions of the other person and the other's alterity, heterogeneity, and singularity as being more than derivative accidents and threatening hindrances to social-political life. This indicates a noteworthy way of revising the contemporary discourses of ethical and critical social theory insofar as practical inquiry is nontrivially extended beyond the ideal consensual symmetry and pragmatic negotiations of mutual recognition, consensus, and belonging. Issues of local and global equalities and inequalities cannot be adequately posed—despite monistic demands for constant identity—without considering the concrete particularities and asymmetries of an intrinsically diverse and pluralistic world.

It might be that the degree of peace and justice that Levinas proposes is impossible to institute and institutionalize in the world, and is at risk of being betrayed in this world. If these did not speak to and in it, they could not be either interruptive or prophetic, and the ethical would not only be an impossible demand but a deception that—as Žižek accuses of Levinas—hides the everyday socially sanctioned injustices of the world under an unconditional and completely impracticable justice.[78]

To summarize and restate the argument to this point: Levinas's articulation of asymmetrical ethics, involving disrelations of substitution, height, distance, and alterity, is not so much a rejection as it is a critical transformation of the categories of modern universalism. Levinas does not deny the importance of social, political, and even economic symmetry and equality for questions of politics, justice, and citizenship that involve relations between self, other, and the third (discussed previously above and again below). Levinas intensifies and reorients equality and justice by indicating the sources of justice and economic equality and fairness in asymmetrical responsibility, that is, in the dys-symmetrical interruptive encounters between inherently asymmetrical selves in the ethical revelation of the other's face in its height and transcendence.[79] Levinas argues this to the extent that there is no self without passivity, no subjectivity without sacrifice and substitution, and that the self is responsible even for the enemy and the persecutor.[80]

Given the an-archic exposure to the good in the existential facticity of my unrequested responsibility for-the-other, no proportionality, symmetry, equality, or mutual exchange exists that could serve as an appropriate measure or principle, legitimation or excuse, for me.[81] Levinas cites in this regard Dostoevsky's statement, made by the character Father Zossima in the *Brothers Karamazov*: "We are responsible for all and before all, and I more than all the others."[82] Levinas contests the dialectic of recognition, which is still tied to exchange, with a prior responsibility.[83] To be responsible is described as obsession and persecution, it signifies to be without justification before the other and therefore infinitely responsible or not responsible at all.[84]

Ethics beyond the Dialectic of Recognition and Misrecognition

Who is the other for Levinas? Is the other someone "like me," "equivalent" to me, or, as Levinas insists, someone else, "the widow, the orphan, the stranger and the beggar"? What does it mean to begin with the asymmetrical, with the other who is not me or the same as me, and the abject who suffer, rather than with the normative principle of symmetry and sameness? The other who appears strong, powerful, and rich is in a sense as destitute and in need as someone who is weak or impoverished. Yet it is in encountering the weak and the poor that my freedom is more forcefully called out as my responsibility for the other.

My freedom is, furthermore, inaugurated and constituted through the other for Levinas; it is not a property of the "self" that can deny others their lives and freedom as in the ideological and oppressive deployments of freedom considered in chapter 12. In the depth, height, and ipseity of the other, and in the other's fragility, nakedness, and misery in face and body, the "I" is singled out and individuated as distressingly responsible: "Responsibility is an individuation, a principle of individuation."[85] Since reciprocal exchange (no matter how generalized and rationalized through an impersonal exchange of reasons) is structured by expectations of equivalence, it is not genuinely ethical. Ethics calls on me to be responsible to the other "despite myself" and regardless of what the other expects or exchanges in return; it is a "service without promises."[86]

This ethical responsibility of me for the other is the primary way to draw near a genuinely ethical economic and political equality between citizens. Equality requires the movement from charity to equity, that is, from the interpersonal face-to-face encounter to the generalized reciprocal contractual and legal relations between citizens, via the intervention of the third. Therefore, equality cannot be limited to symmetrical rational agents exchanging reasons or rights. Such an abstract ideal misses the reality of exchange as an economic commerce structured by desires and interests, relations of power, status and wealth, and the social-economic reproduction of society. Social-political equality is conceivable only in a reality shaped by competition, conflict, and war as well as the peaceful violence of exploitation through the breakthrough of the ethical in the other into the self and of my unavoidable obligation to the other.

Any recognition of a determinate mark or characteristic of the other presupposes this responsibility in the transcendence in immanence of the asymmetrical face-to-face encounter, just as all moral reflection and theorizing presupposes rather than justifies the ethical relation. By making ethics dependent on communicative rationality and the struggle for recognition, Habermas and Honneth endanger it to the extent that no dialogue, reasoning, or recognition of another person and her/his priority occurs without the ethical encounter. Because recognition and other universalistic categories such as consensus operate at the level of the ego, and thus of the logic of belonging to and participating in the same, the ego replicates rather than resists the logic of totality and identity that exploits, excludes, and dominates others in classifying them as others. This point is made by Levinas as well as by Jacques Lacan. Both question the ego's recognition and knowledge of the other as belated and anachronistic in relation to the encounter with the other, the other's singularity, and the fundamental materiality and interruptive resistance of the good where the ethical already occurs.[87]

The ethical encounter has its own "formalism" in that it does not depend on recognition or any act of feeling, intellect, or will. These presuppose and are elements of such an encounter and ethical event. Instead, our responses and nonresponses, our indifference and making a difference, occur in relation to this encounter. There is neither charity nor justice without singularity, since the relation to the unique other is what generates them. The point of departure for justice and equality is not abstract; it is the individual's earthly and bodily life in its needs and suffering that stubbornly require our attention whether we recognize, feel, or conceptualize them or not.

The discourse of recognition, whether recognition is conceived as the agonistic struggle to be acknowledged by the other or as a more sedate dialogical mutual understanding, is haunted by the seemingly intractable facticity and deeply rooted systemic character of misrecognition and its social-political as well as ethical damages.[88] The self that ought to recognize the other might well be constitutively or systematically implicated in power, defined by self-interest, or conditioned by finitude, such that dialectical reversals of power and dialogical communication do not conclude with free and uncoerced reconciliation for each but collude with another constellation of inclusion and exclusion.

Given the misrecognition and ethical damage involved in all recognition, the carelessness in all care to which Honneth attempts to reduce the ethics of Levinas and Derrida, such affectively or emotionally rooted principles cannot save moral universalism unless they involve a more basic event of responsibility that is immemorially prior to and infinitely more demanding than affective care and cognitive justice.[89] The responsibility of ethical responsiveness—which is constituted in the impossibility of ever adequately recognizing and responding to the other qua Other—as a result challenges domination, exploitation, and injustice.

Conclusion

Habermas and Honneth contrast the concept of the asymmetrical as intrinsically hierarchical with the concept of the symmetrical as egalitarian. Critical social theory and ethics accordingly must rely on symmetry as its fundamental norm. Levinas offers reasons to doubt this strategy, which informs most liberal ethical and political thought. He places into question the hierarchical, symmetrical, and universal through the anarchic, asymmetrical, and singular Other who, as upheld in this volume, is primarily a material, embodied, and thus ethical alterity.

Rather than limiting ethics to a shared space of reasons, the interstitial positionality of embodied asymmetrical persons constitutes and orients ethical practice and reasoning. Levinas's variety of asymmetrical ethics offers a source for and alteration to the normative liberal, republican, and socialist accounts of equality by attending to the ethical-political event of alterity, heterogeneity, and singularity that have been ignored or dismissed as threats to identity formation. This is, I have argued, a significant modification to existing discourses of ethical and critical social theory because practical inquiry is nontrivially extended further than the equal yet abstract symmetry and calculative prudential negotiations of mutual consensus and recognition.

Chapter Twelve

The Pathologies of Freedom and the Promise of Autonomy

The human subject is bewitched by the idea of its own freedom as if by a magic spell.

—Theodor Adorno, *History and Freedom*

Introduction: The Problem of Freedom

Freedom is characteristically taken in modern Western philosophy as well as in the popular Western imagination, even if only as a rhetoric and ideology that simultaneously negates the freedom and life of others, to be the original source (as freedom of the will to formulate, choose, and determine its actions) and ultimate value (as the liberty to pursue one's own will and interests as one sees fit) for action.

Freedom should not be, contrary to Axel Honneth's assertion questioned in part 3, the primary value or norm of modernity that awakens to and problematizes the neglect of material others. Too often appeals to one's own freedom function to justify power over others and deny the freedom of others to live without coercion and violence. Freedom characteristically functions in the Western social-political world (whether in its contemporary neoliberal or nativist understanding) as the power to do what one desires and likes while others are left in exploitation, servitude, and suffering. The question of freedom should not then be how to maximize freedom as power to the exclusion of the other but how to maximize freedom in accordance with the freedom and nonexploitation and nonoppression of others. The freedom of the ego and the self is not always necessarily born of the desire to conquer and kill the other, since it can also be due to a self-involved indifference toward others. Even so, this freedom is in need of being exposed to the freedom of the other.

How did the idea of freedom as the negation of the other emerge, and how does it function in advanced capitalist societies? This will be the primary issue of the current chapter. Negative liberty, as elucidated by thinkers such as Isaiah Berlin, typically signifies freedom from constraint.[1] It is commonly defined as independence from an arbitrary external will and authority, if not necessarily the condition of law established through consensus. As such, it can be seen as the defining feature of classical liberalism as well as contemporary neoliberalism and libertarianism. The recent forms of populist nativist movements are part of the neoliberal paradigm insofar as they appeal to a liberty and justice that belong to specific ethnicities and that are construed as being under threat by others constructed as enemies to justify brutal reactions of exclusion and internment.

What is "neoliberalism"? It refers in the context of this work to the contemporary globalized stage of capitalist social organization, which prioritizes speculative finance and the idea of unrestricted markets, according to which all institutions and practices, from the university to the government, must conform to the logic of exchange value and to the arguments of the ideological defenders of classical liberal capitalism. Neoliberalism is linked with growing inequalities within the developed world and between developed and developing countries. It appeals to an abstract ideology of individual freedom and free market exchange while undermining genuine forms of individuation and community. Some if not most culturally oriented gender, race, and recognition theorists have rejected the concept of neoliberalism, but it is a useful category to adopt in confronting the structurally mandated inequalities of the current forms of the capitalist mode of production. Race and gender cannot be abstractly detached from economic inequality and material need for the sake of a politics exclusively concerned with issues of identity and recognition—just as the standard orthodox Marxist notion of social class is inadequate to critique forms of power governing gender and race relations insofar as the proletariat and the poor in the contemporary "Western" world are primarily female and of non-European descent.[2]

Liberal and Neoliberal Freedom

Already in the "classical liberalism" associated with John Locke, a figure who can justify individual freedom in conjunction with coercive colonial expropriation and racial enslavement, liberty as free consent is theoretically opposed to while concretely being entangled with brutality and coercion against the bodies of Africans and the theft of Native American lands. Locke's conception of liberty is tied to the validation of practices of war, slavery, colonialism, and the appropriation of others' collective common property in order to "freely" (defined according to the interests of English elites) force property to be usefully and individually one's own.[3] Locke's political writings systematically reveal how the theodicy and political theology of the liberal Englishman's individual freedom legitimates the exploitation of those incapable of realizing such liberty.

In a similar manner, in Adam Smith and in orthodox interpretations of bourgeois capitalist freedom, the larger amount of wealth produced by capitalist inequality justifies its unequal distribution according to the agent's individual initiative. Nineteenth-century North American individualists, including Ralph Waldo Emerson and Henry David Thoreau, celebrated the self-initiated responsibility and generosity of the individual, and presented solitude as a condition of a deeper sociability and solidarity. Nonetheless, the popular authoritarian libertarianism of contemporary politics does not recognize this free generosity of noble souls, nor does it acknowledge community as an intended consequence of liberty. Instead, it locates the primary virtues of liberty in the fear and distrust of others and the politics of mass resentment. This chapter supports the conclusion of deeper connections existing between self-assertion and negation of the other. One should bear in the mind that there are differences between elite theoretically oriented libertarianism and its popular "vulgar" incarnations; there is a distinction between libertarian theory, "which is racism-free by construction," and "racism camouflaged behind libertarian rhetoric."[4]

Social-political forms of life indicate how "freedom"—despite its utopian promise and critical potential for individuals and communities—can be problematic in validating what should otherwise not be justified. Freedom has become, as David Harvey described, "a freedom to dominate and exploit others."[5] Insofar as capitalist freedom justifies "a politics of unequal rewards," and sanctions not only vast inequalities of wealth but more active forms of exploitation and marginalization, it is questionable whether freedom and liberty are the unconditional goods they are construed to be when they are deployed in an ideological and mythical manner that is pathological and destructive to the flourishing of individual and common life. In Adorno, or in Honneth, the pathologies of the authoritarian personality, fetishized individuality, and so on, can be immanently critiqued through critical models without essentializing an unchanging state or natural condition from which every deviation is deemed pathological.[6] The contemporary pathology of freedom, with its dialectic of self-assertion (against those who are different, weaker, poor, foreign; against "the enemy" who is not with us) and authoritarian submission (to those whose image is "like us"; to "the friend" who is with us) is an all too apparent tendency in media, politics, and social life, even while acknowledging that there are tendencies that attempt to challenge it.

This chapter offers an analysis of the philosophical issue of the value of freedom, with an eye toward this contemporary situation. Modern Western philosophy tends to demand and reify the absolute freedom of the ego and glorify the possessive individual through individual spontaneity and striving for self-preservation. A series of thinkers in the twentieth century have questioned this priority of the self, and the identity demanded by its logic, for the sake of the other person and what remains nonidentical.[7] Frantz Fanon described how "some want to impose their presence on the world, fill it up with their presence," a "some" that applies to groups as well as individuals. The ideology of individuality absorbs and excludes others according to its own conditional standard of freedom. This is the freedom of the self that sets itself against others in order to assert and stabilize its own sense of self.

Fanon remarked that "one German philosopher described the process as the pathology of freedom."[8] The German philosopher that Fanon is referring to is Günther Anders, who, in a neglected yet trenchant and prescient essay, detailed the corrosive and pathological characteristics of self-assertive freedom. The nihilistic freedom that neglects and negates the other is a condition of national socialist totalitarianism. Anders demonstrates how an ideology of freedom—the notion of a unique "German freedom" in this case—is complicit with practices of domination. Instead of being the contrary of freedom, as libertarian theory maintains, Anders's conception of "German freedom" is intertwined and complicit with domination as the will to fill the world with oneself and force it to conform to one's own liberty and identity.[9] Negative liberty (as freedom from social and governmental interference) is the defining characteristic of liberalism from John Locke through Adam Smith and James Mill to contemporary neoliberalism and libertarianism. Negative freedom is an important norm with which to check abusive power, as John Stuart Mill contends in *On Liberty*. Yet, as Mill perceived by introducing the "harm principle" to limit unconditional freedom that damages others in *On Liberty*, it can function not only as a rationalization for indifference and irresponsibility toward others but also as a validation for active injustice. As a social ideology, if not necessary as philosophical theorizing, it opens the space for the realization of one's freedom over others who do not deserve to share in it, because of God, fate, or the market that invisibly and ineluctably determines all merit and value.

To critically evaluate contemporary capitalist societies, an inflationary understanding of "liberalism" needs to be challenged. "Liberalism" should not be understood in so broad a sense that one cannot distinguish classical liberalism and republicanism, capitalist-oriented libertarianism and varieties of contemporary liberalism compatible with more robust forms of social responsibility. This chapter, in light of ethical and social-political argumentation unfolded in the works of Levinas and Adorno, is concerned with the variety of liberalism defined by negative liberty, possessive individualism, and the limitless circulation and nourishment of capital.

The Ideological Functions of Freedom

> The idea that freedom consists in self-determination is really rather pathetic, if all it means is that the work my master formerly ordered me to do is the same as the work I now seek to carry out of my own free will; the master did not determine his own actions.
>
> —Max Horkheimer, *Towards a New Manifesto*

In the ideological assertion of freedom, with its anti-intellectualist ressentiment, freedom appears as the opposite of social critique and as the negation of the need to answer to the other. Critique is initiated in the materiality of others rather than in the ideality and ideology of the autonomous subject. This critique is not autonomously self-initiated and underwritten by itself in the Kantian fashion. It is formed in freedom's irresponsibility and injustice to the other person. Identifying the habitual and unthought with nature, critique is accordingly suspected of being the destruction of natural liberty via its problematization of routine unreflective action and belief by potentially placing it into question and calling the self to offer an account of itself. Adorno and Levinas are both acutely aware in their own ways of how rational freedom betrays itself. The ostensible critical freedom of self-reflection and the give and take of reasons in communication, praised by socially oriented and progressive thinkers of autonomy from Kant and Mill to Dewey and Habermas, can become an impediment to rather than the fulfillment of freedom, as consent becomes the coercion to assent.

The issue of self-negating freedom, already described by Hegel and Marx, was intensified in the Frankfurt school's project of critical social theory as interdisciplinary materialism, which did not consist of the idealizing normative theorizing characteristic of Habermas's "communicative turn."[10] Normativity is everywhere for antinormative thinkers such as Hegel and Adorno.[11] Yet, through the negativity within and in relation to exiting norms, Adorno more adequately addressed the double role of norms as ideological and as potentially transformative than either the Kantian or Hegelian ethical traditions. Adorno and Max Horkheimer traced the aporias and collusions of autonomy, heteronomy, spontaneity, and instrumentality in "Western modernity," diagnosing society's constructed image of freedom as the ideological destruction of the autonomy promised by the Enlightenment. The ideology of individualism, in which individuals are mass-produced copies of what the individual is projected to be, corresponded with the concrete individual being undermined and absorbed by the pseudoindividualistic conformity of the culture industry and mass consumerism: "The total effect of the culture industry is one of anti-enlightenment, in which, as Horkheimer and I [i.e., Adorno] have noted, Enlightenment, that is the progressive domination of nature, becomes mass deception and is turned into a means for fettering consciousness. It impedes the development of autonomous, independent individuals who judge and decide consciously for themselves. These, however, would be the precondition of a democratic society which needs adults who have come to age in order to sustain itself and develop."[12] Kantian autonomy and the Enlightenment's promise of rational independence is reductively narrowed to "free self-interested choices" between predetermined brands and prefabricated activities. Mature individuation and responsive or relational autonomy are blocked and frustrated, and free spontaneous activity is reduced to a repressive entertainment and relaxation, a reactive realm of escape and irresponsibility rather than the flourishing and fulfillment of life.[13]

Adorno has shown how a purportedly democratic and popular culture, in which each new technological and cultural fad is advertised as liberation, can be dialectically a vehicle for its opposite. For Adorno, "the ideology of freedom and autonomy" camouflages an "actual state of unfreedom and dependence."[14] The culture industry, "the most inflexible style of all," is the "most effective form of ideology today," since it is no longer dependent on any particular ideology or perspective but appropriates and transverses them.[15]

Adorno's analysis of how popular culture and its appearance of freedom were structured by the culture industry, commodity fetishism, and consumerism has been criticized as undemocratic elitism. Yet questioning mass-produced culture and its illusion of freedom is an interrogation of self-negating democracy and self-undermining freedom.[16] The logic of the culture industry and deformation of the public sphere undermines the conditions for a democratic society and the authentic individuation needed for such a society to exist. Adorno's analysis does not entail a denial of the emancipatory potential of the Enlightenment and modernity, as Habermas and other critics of Adorno dread. It entails, instead, the diagnosis of its ideological uses and deformations.[17]

It might be argued that even if Adorno's criticism of consumerist individualism is accurate, it does not follow that liberal and neoliberal capitalist accounts of free market liberty are wrong; these accounts expose that such liberty has not yet been effectively achieved. This argument reflects the dialectical ambiguity of freedom as future promise and negated present. The critique of liberal freedom need not necessarily be the denial of freedom, as the libertarian objection suggests. Critics of existing conditions of unfreedom in advanced capitalist societies can distinguish between freedom's role in the structural inequalities of society; its ideological falsification, which excuses these inequalities of class, gender, and race; and its interruptive and transformative promise in relation to the present.

Adorno's analysis adopted Marx's thesis of the heteronomy of the individual in the face of the commodification of nature and society and the autonomy of the commodity in the enchantment of commodity fetishism.[18] In the first volume of Marx's *Capital*, a work Adorno described as a phenomenology of antispirit (*Wiedergeistes*), the fetishism of the commodity signifies the illusion that humanly produced objects appear and operate independently of human labor.[19] In the age of the primacy of social reproduction over material reproduction of a society, which is the inversion of Marx's thesis that is characteristic of the early generation of Frankfurt school thinkers, freedom and individuality have become commodified and autonomy is the manifestation of heteronomy.

Still, one cannot be reduced to the other to the extent that the promise of freedom and the tenacious facticity of hegemonic domination are asymmetrically dialectically mediated.[20] The logic of war and totality posits the forced either/or of one or the other, being for and against, and the friend and the enemy.[21] Adorno has articulated the incompleteness of ideological mediation, in identity and social totality, and the prospect of its interruption, and Levinas has also articulated this in a nondialectical vocative and accusative saying and unsaying that undoes the solidified and neutralized said.[22]

Questionable Liberty

According to Peter Dews, the question of "why human beings prefer an inadequate, self-destructive freedom to genuine freedom" raises difficult issues of human motivation and the prospect of evil.[23] The conformist and destructive tendencies of individualistic and democratic freedom have been at issue, from Plato's diagnosis of the feverish conditions of the Athenian polis in the *Republic* to Hegel's dialectic of the self-destruction of the French Revolution to Alexis de Tocqueville's portrayal of the tyranny of the majority and conformity that characterize the political life of the United States.[24]

We must consider how liberty can be betrayed in the name of liberty, and authentic freedom can be ideologically distorted and masked by inauthentic and pathological freedom.[25] Indeed, perhaps freedom is much more questionable than the distinctions between authentic and inauthentic, negative and positive, freedoms suggests. Perhaps prioritizing freedom is not as innocent and natural as it appears; perhaps it is intrinsically questionable as a betrayal of the other person. In Levinas's works in particular, one finds a thorough questioning of the freedom of the "I" in its naïve and irresponsible spontaneity, insofar as this is oblivion to the other.[26] This concern is already evident in the notebooks Levinas composed in Germany captivity; there is no liberty without service and the subordination of one's liberty to another's liberty.[27] Levinas conceives of liberty, in a republican manner, as conditioned by sociality, through the relationship of appeal and address in which I am called to act for the other's freedom. The tragedy of difficult finite liberty is its decay into the arbitrary freedom and injustice of the subject.[28] Genuine freedom means answering for it to others.[29] But freedom is frequently conflated with power, with which it is ideologically mystified to justify harming others. When it is recognized in the sense of heightening power and increasing enjoyment without concern or obligation toward others, asserting its place in the sun unconcerned with any other (except to evade the other's shadow), freedom is arbitrary and tyrannical.[30] To this extent, contrary to Honneth's assessment discussed earlier, freedom cannot be the ultimate ethical horizon, norm, or value.[31] Responsibility is the condition of freedom and provides a strategy for pursuing a morally adequate understanding of freedom.

In *Otherwise Than Being*, Levinas deploys "unlimited responsibility" to contest freedom as the measure of ethics and undermine the idea of the primacy and originality of freedom: "The responsibility for another, an unlimited responsibility which the strict book-keeping of the free and non-free does not measure, requires subjectivity as an irreplaceable hostage. . . . This finite freedom is not primary, is not initial; but it lies in an infinite responsibility where the other is not other because he strikes up against and limits my freedom, but where he can accuse me to the point of persecution, because the other, absolutely other, is another one."[32] Levinas describes how freedom as the feeling of self and its power, threatened by the other, is interconnected with the conatus and its self-assertion in the struggle for existence. Similarly to Adorno's analysis of the sociopathological sublimation of self-preservation, Levinas identifies this experience of freedom as central to modern philosophy's preoccupation with the self, its compulsive care and self-concern, and its perseverance in being in contest with others.[33] At the same time, insofar as this historically formed egoism is tied up with a calculative self-interest that is defined by social conventions, this form of self and subjectivity is a product of the ritualized logic of sacrifice. Despite its numerous suspicions of morality, justice, and altruism, this sacrificially constituted self is conformist, moralistic, and vindictive to those who do not follow the rules of the game with its sacrifices and privileges. Adorno and Horkheimer uncover in the *Dialectic of Enlightenment*, and in the studies of the authoritarian personality, how strategies of adaptive self-preserving reason become maladaptive, irrational, and authoritarian through their redeployment in unequal systems of exchange structured by power. In this configuration of exchange and sacrifice, the individual's pursuit of the good life and the "natural goods" prized by classical capitalist liberalism—the culture of total mobilization for the sake of life, liberty, and the pursuit of happiness—systematically reproduce damaged life rather than the "good life" that is thought to be the goal of classical ethics.

While the freedom of the subject is typically prioritized and valorized in modern Western philosophy, Levinas concludes that responsibility necessarily precedes and is the condition of any freedom: "To be obliged to responsibility overflowing freedom, that is, responsibility for the others [. . .]. The pure passivity that precedes freedom is responsibility."[34] This passivity is not the docile weakness of egos administered by the culture industry, as depicted by Adorno, locked into their private, infantile patterns of consumption and lacking the relational and responsive autonomy (in contrast to its "cold" Kantian form) of integrity, intimacy, and maturity that can resist subordination to social totality.[35] Adorno remarked that bourgeois coldness made Auschwitz possible, and described how genuine maturity retains a kind of childlike sense of playfulness capable of gentleness and tenderness.[36]

Chapters 4 and 5 portrayed Levinas's analysis of how need, enjoyment, and seemingly natural desires are bound to and complicit with structures of power and consumption. Levinas's radical passivity is not a departure and safe haven from social mediation; it is entanglement in the life, needs, and suffering of others. Passivity signifies the one-for-the-other of responsibility that is the necessary condition—if not a sufficient one given the demands of the third—for social-political equality in Levinas. My dependence on the other—to the point of being a substitute for and prisoner to the other—is the facticity of freedom; the fact that freedom is without excuse and must answer for itself before others. It "must justify itself" in response to the other person.[37]

Ethical freedom—that is, social other-oriented freedom—is impossible without the ongoing critique to which it must respond. Anticognitivist interpretations of Levinas deny that he engages in argumentation or criticism, as these concern discursive truth and validity claims. Levinas questioned the concept of critique, in its Kantian and general sense, and so critique is supposedly absent in Levinas.[38] Nonetheless, Levinas engages in practices of critical reading and reflection: the interrogation of institutions, practices, and reasons.[39] He not only engages in reading as "cloture"; his reading is vocative and interrogative, as he disputes, reverses, and transverses the claims of the philosophers.[40] Levinas engages in questioning and critique in the sense of responding otherwise. One concept that does not mean what it is usually assumed to mean is freedom.

Without the social-theoretical strategies of critical social theory developed by Frankfurt school thinkers, Levinas exposed in his own way the ideological function of freedom understood as egoistic indifference toward others or as a playful spontaneity in undermining responsibility. Levinas criticizes Eugen Fink and Jeanne Delhomme, who "demand an unconditional freedom without responsibility, a freedom of play."[41] Despite the popularity of radically anti- and nonconceptual readings of ethics in Levinas, there are discursive, cognitive, and normative dimensions to Levinas's ethics, as Diane Perpich has convincingly demonstrated.[42] In contrast to readings that interpret Levinas in a religious-theological vein or as offering a deconstructive ethics with no relation to normative questions, Perpich establishes in *The Ethics of Emmanuel Levinas* how Levinas offers an account of normative force, without principles and prescriptions, which does not issue in specific norms or prescriptions. Her portrayal is one in which ethics is not the name for a set of principles that guarantee right action. It is the enactment and performance of a relation to the other that is constitutive of the space in which ethical demands come to be heard.[43] Levinas's ethics is strikingly different here from noncognitive accounts of ethics that suggest that getting community, situation, emotions, or authenticity "right" in a sense leads to an authentic self or a more appropriate social community in noncognitivist accounts of existential ethics, situation ethics, or Aristotelian *phronesis*. Levinas's inclusion of and orientation toward noncognitive ethics reorients the cognitive: it is not an exclusion of discourse, argumentation, and reasoning from the ethical, insofar as he himself engages in them, even as reflection and conceptualization necessarily remain derivative to the encounter with and exposure to the other. All knowing, all discourse, already presupposes the encounter of self and other even if it is suppressed, distorted, and bracketed. This encounter does not end communication and reflection; it is their transient point of departure.

Levinas's reassessment of freedom places freedom in risk while not being able to abandon or eliminate it either: "One is not against freedom if one seeks for it a justification."[44] But, as he points out against Heidegger and Jean-Paul Sartre's portrayal of freedom as the spontaneity of the self, "freedom is not justified by freedom."[45] Responsibility is an-archic in that it goes beyond the mastery of the self, beyond intentions and calculations. It involves a displacement in the encounter between self and other, such that one can speak of a "difficult freedom" confronted by the legitimate and inescapable claims of the other rather than resistance, negation, and limitation. Consequently, an unlimited or unconditional freedom that does not acknowledge or respond to the other's interpolation, suffering, and illness—as in the denial of healthcare—is not freedom; it is sanctioned systematic neglect in the self-reproduction of power.

Rudi Visker has deemphasized the radicality of Levinas's argumentation by claiming, "Instead of limiting my freedom—as is the case in pathology—Levinas's trauma constitutes it, or 'invests' it; yet this investment is the limitation of the freedom of play without responsibility."[46] Attempts to force Levinas to sound less challenging to standard notions of freedom—for example, that he is only limiting its playfulness, not limiting my freedom per se or questioning the priority of freedom—deradicalize his strong claim to the weaker version of his thesis, which is that freedom has sources outside of itself but that these external origins should not change how one conceives of freedom. This weakening strategy is explicitly denied by Levinas: "It is for the free self to fix the limits of this responsibility [. . . but] it can do so only in the name of that original responsibility."[47] Freedom is not self-initiating and then either morally or pathologically limited; freedom is already configured through the tension of an ethical response to others and complicity with their betrayal. Levinas's freedom is for that reason not only an initial trauma that is integrated and superseded; it is characterized by its restlessness, wakefulness, and vigilance.[48]

Such readings do not adequately articulate the pathological freedom that is a crucial concern for Levinas and for those who interpret contemporary political appeals to freedom as involving an ethical promise while being acutely ideological and pathologically absorbed in domination, exploitation, neglect, and violence. Levinas does not abandon the word "freedom"; he questions whether its self-presentation as freedom can operate as the justification for avoidance, exclusion, and violence. Levinas asks how free persons "can be subject to reason without losing their freedom" and how one can "give meaning to this notion of finite freedom without striking a blow against freedom in its finitude [. . .] how can freedom be, while also being limited?"[49] This prospect of a responsible freedom proceeding from and in response to the other suggests an alternative to the aporetic dynamic of moralizing and irresponsibility that characterizes ideological discourses of individual liberty.

Asymmetrical Freedom

Another question worthy of an interpretative strategy comes from the assertion that Levinas is too willing to abandon freedom and its privileges. In his account of Levinas based on his interpretation of the Frankfurt school, C. Fred Alford misses an important dimension of Levinas's thesis about freedom in claiming, "Against freedom of the will in all its guises, Levinas posits freedom of the abandonment of the will, an openness to the world."[50] Levinas overtly and repeatedly rejects Heidegger's openness, letting be, and releasement (*Gelassenheit*). Levinas does not argue for an altruistic and receptive openness without will; he argues for a dependence and passivity that is at the same time active responsibility—arising in extreme vulnerability—to the other and to the other's freedom.[51] Although Adorno rejects overusing the language of passivity and receptivity as the abandonment of critical thought, associating this language with Heidegger's poetic acquiescence, it should be noted that, for Levinas, this language is the point of departure for discourse. The concept might arrive "after the fact," yet it does arrive to mediate the relations between self and other. Consequently, the immediacy of the ethical is incessantly mediated and caught up in the betrayals and complicities of the political.

Levinas accusatively and exaggeratedly demands beholdenness and service to the other. For Levinas this service is not servitude. He does not advocate the abandonment of the will in a tranquil condition of letting be nor as a complete giving over (*Hingabe*) of oneself and subservience of the self to the other, whether human or divine, with its potentially reactionary political consequences, feared by critics who reductively associate forms of passivity at work in Husserl, Heidegger, and Levinas. Levinas does not abandon willing; he shows how the will is already informed by responsibility from the beginning and without evasion: "To reflection, this responsibility is astonishing in every way, extending all the way to the obligation to answer for the freedom of the other, all the way to being a responsibility for his responsibility."[52] Freedom as responsibility for the freedom of the other confounds the philosophy of the primacy of the self and the uninterrupted subject; it entails that my freedom is implicated in the fate and freedom of others, and I cannot deny them on behalf of my freedom.

It is a false dichotomy to maintain that either Levinas negates freedom by responsibility to the other or that he must leave the priority of the freedom of the subject intact and unaltered. The configuration of freedom is rethought through asymmetry and the asymmetrical freedom between self and other.[53] I do not choose my or the other's freedom; instead I am other-constituted. The self does not choose its own responsibilities. There is a gap and asymmetry between freedom and responsibility, other and self, which contests the Kantian model of reciprocal autonomy and the mutual deduction of autonomy and responsibility in the "fact of reason."[54] More than this, I am more responsible and less free than the other due to the passivity constitutive of the ethical: "Pure passivity preceding freedom is responsibility. But the responsibility that owes nothing to my freedom is my responsibility for the freedom of others."[55]

Passivity means that I am not free to pick and choose in relation to the other; I respond and must respond infinitely to the chagrin and discomfort of self-interested calculation and egoism: passivity "implies responsibility—which should surprise, nothing being more opposed to freedom than the non-freedom of responsibility. The coinciding of freedom with responsibility constitutes the I, doubled with itself, encumbered with itself."[56] Does such a strategy reductively eliminate freedom by making it superfluous to ethical responsibility?[57] Does this movement from the other subordinate the individual too completely to the ethical or the religious? Hent de Vries remarks, "What is at stake here, however, is an asymmetrical freedom in which God in the very donation of His presence retains the initiative at every single moment."[58] To return for a moment to the topic of Levinas's deployment of the language of "God" more fully discussed in part 2, Levinas speaks of God in the context of the priority of the ethical, as in the claim "It is a responsibility that precedes freedom, which would mean precisely belonging to God, a unique belonging which, anterior to freedom, does not destroy."[59] This is a sense of religion determined by the ethical. It is the other that places the ethical demand upon me: "Suffering the weight of the other person, the 'me' [*moi*] is called to uniqueness by responsibility."[60]

While there are critics who find asymmetrical ethics to be too burdensome and demanding, because it calls us to our nonindifference and responsibility for others, other detractors assert that asymmetrical freedom is inherently conservative and elitist in negatively privileging myself over others, as if injustice were solely my responsibility.[61] Žižek, to take one example, asks whether this "self-questioning" is not—through the dynamic reversal of the position interrogated by Hegel and Nietzsche in their depiction of the dialectic between master and slave—in fact "self-privileging": "does this asymmetry not effectively end up in privileging one particular group that assumes responsibility for all others [and] embodies in a privileged way this responsibility[?]"[62] Are not such fears of asymmetry warranted insofar as neoconservative ideologues: (1) demand an aggressively interventionist international politics based precisely on the asymmetrical responsibility and exceptionalism of the United States, and (2) criticize ethical symmetry and its associated liberal freedoms for the sake of an authoritarian paternalistic tradition that they intend to undermine?[63]

Questions concerning the social-political consequences of asymmetry are intensified in the case of Levinas because his ethical-political skepticism has been interpreted as part of postmodern and communitarian critiques of liberal Western modernity. Levinas is at times interpreted as rejecting liberalism and modern Western political thought in these readings rather than rethinking its sources.[64] However, Levinas's assessment of liberalism is based in premodern traditional Jewish and Greek sources. Furthermore, it should be understood in the modern context of his overt reliance on and appeals to the French republican inheritance as he deploys in his political argumentation the progressive universalizing yet masculine republican language of the "rights of man," and liberty, equality, "fraternity."[65] It is a genuine issue, raised by Simon Critchley, whether the classical modern republican discourse of the "rights of man" and "fraternity" is inherently masculine or whether it can be universalized as "human rights" and "solidarity."[66]

Levinas is an ambiguous inheritor of the radical republicanism of Rousseau and the French Revolution insofar as solidarity, which is the asymmetrical ethical condition of the liberty of each individual, has priority over the liberty that neglects and denies the other's suffering. This ethical claim bears on the political through the intervention of the third party. Through the third-person perspective, abstracted from the asymmetries of the self-other encounter, it calls for the institutionalization of justice, equality, and liberties that threaten their own ethical sources. Processes of institutionalization are a necessary infidelity to the primacy of the ethical that would keep institutions and their impersonal logic in check. Adorno warned of the liquidation of the individual for the sake of the impersonally administered socialist or capitalist collective. But Adorno is closer to the Marxist and sociological understanding of the priority of the social ethics of justice over personal ethics that is largely ineffective in challenging and changing systemic social institutions and processes.[67] Levinas agrees and disagrees with the Marxist prioritization of the collective social and political sources for obtaining individual liberties for all.[68] These structures must be equally for the sake of all (as political) and asymmetrically for the other individual (as ethical). For Levinas, the asymmetrical and ethical is more essential and orienting than the political. The political wavers between real forms of domination and the normative demand to institutionalize equal justice.

Levinas's deployments of the republican and democratic socialist political traditions are simultaneously their critique insofar as these political registers—whether liberal, republican, or socialist—can become the means to subordinate rather than recognize the other. The "ideology of freedom and equality" in its modern technological and consumeristic context is the foundational ideology for liberalism and conservatism, capitalism and socialism.[69] The underlying philosophical ideology of freedom remains questionable.[70] The ideology of self-assertive and self-centered freedom, with its political consequences of indifference and oblivion toward others, needs to be confronted, and freedom itself needs to be rethought to the extent that autonomy functions to isolate the subject and deny its fundamental mutuality and relatedness.[71] In the context of the problematic consequences of autonomy and freedom, a profoundly altered conception of the subject and its emancipation is required.[72]

Though the affirmation of relatedness in variance and responsibility in alterity entails the risk of acting in place of the other rather than only for her or him, it is the asymmetrical difference of responsibility itself that does not allow the self to replace the other. My responsibility is conditioned by being toward the other. This involves an externalization and expropriation of the self that upsets responsibility taken as privileged mastery over others and challenges absorbing and controlling the other in the name of being responsible for the other. Asymmetry entails an irrevocable interval between self and other that paternalistic responsibility wants to remove for the sake of an identity that hierarchically identifies and ranks individuals, groups, and peoples. A distinction between an-archic difference-preserving and hierarchical difference-integrating asymmetries can be upheld such that they cannot be assumed to be the same.

Levinas's interpretation of asymmetrical responsibility both exaggerates and limits responsibility; it problematizes ossified asymmetrical hierarchies, reductive symmetrical conformism, and the avant-gardist esoteric assumption of power that purports to act in the best interests of equality. The denial of asymmetry and otherness risks becoming totalitarian indifference and depersonalization, where there are those who enjoy power and privilege while others are pressed to conform or are eliminated under the guise of equality. This betrayal occurred, for instance, in what Levinas described as "the supreme paradox in which the defense of the person is inverted into Stalinism."[73] This remark illustrates Levinas's appreciation and criticism of the history of socialism insofar as its political instrumentalization and institutionalization undermined its ethical and prophetic motivations.

Levinas critiqued (a critique that is more than negation and self-reflective positionality) existing communism and socialism, as discussed previously and indicated in a revealing passage in his notebooks, due to its deformation into a calculative instrumental doctrine enforcing the compulsion of work.[74] He considers in these passages an alternative experience of property as intimacy instead of possession and ownership by the individual or the collective; this intimacy with things is the condition of enjoyment and happiness.[75] Levinas reflects on the hither side of socialism in more radical messianic and prophetic sources, in which things are shared like air—in not possessing things and thus not being possessed by them—and being becomes the present.[76]

Just as pathological forms of equality have occurred in Stalinist terror, there are pathologies of freedom in the indifference and irresponsibility toward the other of libertarian freedom; a condition where some enjoy the leisure of their freedom while others—who are "not my concern," as I am not my brother's keeper, as Cain said of Abel—are condemned to the regime of toil, fatigue, and suffering. In reply to such denials of answerability, Levinas comments, "It is as if, behind being, one could hear the sarcastic laughter of irresponsibility, for which the freedom within being is not free enough; but beyond being there would extend the goodness of unbounded responsibility, for which that freedom is not generous enough."[77] Responsibility, as irrevocably asymmetrically heavier for me than for anyone else, is inevitably a heteronomy and subordination to the other for the leisurely freedom for which responsibility is persistently excessive: "One thus reproaches one's freedom for losing itself in the burden of responsibility for oneself and others; and concern for others can, of course, appear as a form of subjection, as an infinite subjection."[78] This subordination is justice, and no ethical subject exists without such subjection. Ethical individuation occurs through substitution rather than through self-creation. There is not heteronomous subordination but the determination of the self through the anarchy of the good; a good that is irreducible to calculation, exchange, principles, and norms. This good is prior to and "other-constitutes" the freedom of the self for Levinas.[79]

The Idolatry of Liberty and the Pathology of Freedom

Nietzsche's Zarathustra warned of the new idol of the state, requiring idolatry and human sacrifice from good and bad alike, such that the human individual begins where the state ends.[80] Nietzsche, as de Tocqueville before him and Adorno afterward, describes the conformity of ordinary social relations beyond the state. Precisely in the valorization of the individual, the individual is lost through the media and instruments that are supposed to preserve and support it. Adorno repeatedly diagnosed in his analysis of the North American culture industry how a cultish idolatry of individualism exists that is the management of individuals. It can be more dangerous than that demanded by the state, because it is more effective through accepted background conformity.

The fixed typology of what it means to be an individual reifies individual life and does not permit individuality to be different from mass-produced individuals. These forms are not only externally imposed, and thus more easily remedied, but structure the prereflective and nonconceptual dimensions of individual life where the ethical takes place for Levinas.[81] Although Adorno likewise brings into play the noncognitive, mimetic, and sensuous to challenge identity thinking, anti-cognitivism based on the prereflective without critique or argumentation reproduces damaged life without any prospect of challenging it. The natural and the transcendent are not unambiguous; they have been already stylized and restylized through society, history, and culture, even if their heterogeneity remains irreducible to human activity.

Freedom, whether it is thought of as a natural capacity or as grounded in a transcendent referent such as God, is already ideologically preformed. As ideological, freedom can function to compel and integrate without interruptive or transformative promise or prospect. Günther Anders consequently diagnosed how autonomy and authenticity can be the compulsion of power demanding surrender before those interests that put individuals in their place, negating their freedom in the name and fantasy of their freedom.[82]

Adorno notes how in antiquity and modernity, negative liberty, as the separation of freedom from freedom in society, undermines the freedom to actively participate in social life: "The situation in which the individual was vanishing was at the same time one of unbridled individualism, where 'all was possible.'"[83] Freedom from society robs the individual of the strength for freedom. Asocial freedom limited to an absolutized private self, and divorced from the sociality of the other, is not the "natural" negative freedom envisioned in libertarianism. It is rather a denial of the freedom that participates in and helps shape society.[84] Unlike the responsibility of nonidentical sociality, the absolutization of the separated and unconditional self and its "theodicy of the individual" impose conformity by excluding nonidentity.[85] The privatized and reified freedom of the self is correlated with its unfreedom in the social totality. In Levinas's language, the freedom of the self is the imperialism of the same.[86] Far from being unconditional, such freedom is suspect as socially mediated illusion and as ethical irresponsibility. It denotes not only avoidance but also "the determination of the other by the same," instead of the openness of the same to the other, and is in need of a reversal where it learns its responsibility to the other.[87]

The abstract and ideologically configured individual of fetishized and mass-produced "individualism" betrays and negates actual concrete individuals, as negative liberty becomes lack of autonomy in society and the self becomes reduced to conformity and consumption: "[T]he official culture's pretense of individualism . . . necessarily increases in proportion to the liquidation of the individual."[88] On this basis, Adorno concludes—not unlike de Tocqueville a century earlier—that North American individualism and libertarianism are deeply conformist in their simultaneous demand for "pragmatic" adjustment and accommodation to the existing order that provides the standard for what should be considered popular, successful, and useful.[89]

The libertarian ideology of absolute freedom masks power and violence. It cynically assumes that persons have equal opportunities but do not make the same effort to realize their aspirations. It actively restricts actual difficult liberties—which are conditional, fragile, and plural—to the extent that its freedom is the freedom to accept social compulsion.[90] The utopian and narcissistic liberty of the self becomes the inverted totalitarianism of the harshest legalism applied to others, as genuine variance is restricted by the identity of unrestricted exchange "freely" operating in the name of the abstract autonomous individual and corporate profits.[91]

The modern bourgeois individual is constructed from its socially trained instincts to dream of realizing itself, its feeling of power, and uniqueness in economic exchange; and yet it is used, exhausted, and replaced by an identical product in a larger indifferent systematic process. As intimated in Adam Smith's invisible hand and Hegel's cunning of reason, the idea of asocial freedom motivates social individuals who reproduce a fateful whole. The "individual" is the mass-produced instantiation of a category, concealed in an aura of false uniqueness that has been cheaply designed to appeal to each person's desire to feel special. Yet this individual is pathologically conformist; afraid of people, ideas, and cultures that are perceived as other; and easily manipulated by the advertising and "spin" that create and regulate its desires. The heroic virile individual, a product of the culture industry and the system of exchange that it expresses, proves to be impotent in regard to the forces that constitute it and dictate what type of individual it should be. As freedom dialectically undermines itself by creating the conditions of its opposite, and as my own idea of freedom claims to defend the freedom of others while actually betraying it, extreme vigilance is needed to confront our equivocal freedom—freedom that is both an ideological fabrication, designed to compensate individuals for their actual lack of freedom, and an immanent emancipatory promise.[92]

Levinas, intersecting with Anders and Adorno at this point, is concerned with the aporia and self-betrayal of freedom as well as its prophetic promise.[93] Even as freedom can be a denial of responsibility and justice, freedom presupposes the society that threatens to destroy it.[94] It is not merely that responsibility is intimate and personal and that mass society undermines such responsibility.[95] While recognizing the material conditions, desires, and needs that constitute a vulnerable, injurable, and fragile subject, such that materialism is a necessary condition of the ethical as much as transcendence, it is through responsibility and ethical love that freedom is invested, elected, and individuated as unique.[96] As Adorno recognized, autonomy without intimacy is pathological.[97] The asymmetrical mutuality and nonindifference of love is more fundamental than the virility, solitude, and cold indifference (toward the other) of individual freedom. Levinas's rhetorical strategies of overemphasizing a hyperbolic sense of responsibility risks dangers such as its thoughtless reproduction by hypocritical epigones, where it becomes a narcissistic virtue-signaling incapable of a genuine response to real concrete material others, and the self-undermining of asymmetrical responsibility in an empty or puritanical piety and wretched moralistic posturing in the name of humanity of which Adorno warns in *Minima Moralia* and other works.

Is Levinas's understanding of responsibility too extreme and ultimately, despite the discursive assertion of the absolute priority of the other, still—in demanding that "I" act as the sole one who is singularly singled out and responsible—all too heroically individualistic? Levinas's responsibility is not that of an isolated subject valiantly or guiltily assuming every burden of the world, since this conditional self is inevitably social and oriented toward others in the community of neighbors as well as responsive to the face of the stranger. The ethical orientation of the political should not lead to the moralistic reduction of the political to the ethical—whether it is represented by the heroic individual saving the world through power and violence or a self-reliant resilient community that helps its own members without regard for nonmembers. For Levinas, however, the appearance of the stranger is not outside the ethical. This encounter is a primary exemplar of the enactment of the ethical, as the stranger calls for an ethical response from me.

Another set of concerns involve issues regarding whether interpersonal ethics prioritizes friendship, family, and social connections in a way that would be unfair to others lacking those relations, and whether Levinas's ethics of the other is too demanding in sacrificing the personal for another. There is a parallel debate in consequentialist ethical theories as to whether and to what degree one can prioritize intimate relations and bonds over the happiness and suffering of strangers, which can reach the seemingly strange conclusion that consequentialists often hold: we might have to sacrifice those we care for if this is for the good of the many or the whole.

A different example of the need for justice through the third is how fairness and equality might be missing in a system of communitarian situational and relational morality such as—according to some overly simplified interpretations—*guanxi* 關係 in Chinese culture, wherein hierarchically organized interpersonal face-to-face relationships predominate (*renqing* 人情) and the "face" (*mianzi* 面子) is identified with status and prestige. The emphasis on the alterity and transcendence of the face differentiates Levinas's approach from communitarian moralities and nationalist identity-oriented forms of republican fraternity that promote helping one's own community or ethnicity and overlook the stranger. Levinas's ethos, oriented by his reading of the Jewish tradition of Israel among the nations and modern republican political thought, resists—despite failures on his part—limiting the ethical to one community and the enclosed boundaries of a nation.

Levinas's vision of responsible freedom is interlinked with his understanding of classical republicanism.[98] Freedom is one element of the classical French republican triad, which Levinas reinterprets rather than abandons. It is bound up with equality and solidarity, the heteronomous conditions of ethical autonomy: "One's duty regarding the other who makes appeal to one's responsibility is an investing of one's own freedom. In responsibility, which is, as such, irrecusable and non-transferable, I am instituted as non-interchangeable."[99]

Responsibility, as elected and invested freedom, is more than Kantian autonomy or the free limitation of freedom that comes and goes and picks and choses as it wishes.[100] Kant's analysis already begins too late after the fact of the ethical encounter prior to freedom, spontaneity, and the self. Describing the transition of the Jewish people—the liberation from servitude associated with the name of Abraham in the *Pentateuch*—from slavery to a condition of receiving the moral law, Levinas reverses the standard interpretation of the Nietzschean narrative of slave-morality: "The negative freedom of those set free is about to transform itself into the freedom of the Law, engraved in stone, into a freedom of responsibilities. Is one already responsible when one chooses responsibility?"[101] Does Levinas mean that there is not a real choice, and that there only appears to be a choice through the folds of subjectivity's emergence in its responsibility? Are we effectively bound to be responsible in the sense that responsibility involves already finding oneself to be responsible? Here Levinas reflects on the biblical and Kantian thematic of the interconnectedness of freedom and law. In contrast with such a difficult responsible freedom that does not deny the poor and the weak but responds to their distress, Levinas describes how in the freedom to exploit others, economically and otherwise, the law—originating in freedom—comes to repress the freedom it ought to uphold and secure. There is no freedom without the moral law even as the institutionalization of law can institutionalize freedom in ways that produce injustice and suffering. However, in the unlimited freedom of desire that knows no laws or boundaries in relation to others, and in distinction from the an-archic desire for the other in transcendence, love (which suffers from its own pathologies) without law becomes pleasure without love.[102] Others become for the freedom and pleasure of the ego—in its authoritarian imperialism and pragmatic instrumentalism—impediments to be removed and objects of calculation to be controlled. Within this interwoven nexus of instrumental power relations, there rests the possibility of encounter and, in the contingent exposure and risky exteriority of the encounter, the aporetic reversal of the self that is the opening toward the other.

Fraternal Republicanism and the An-archic Republic

In *The Government of Poland,* Rousseau cautioned against appeals to liberty that in reality reaffirm servitude, noting the importance of citizens mutually digesting and cultivating freedom in contrast with its rhetorical abuses. Rousseau concluded, "Liberty is a food that is good to taste but hard to digest: it sets well only on a good strong stomach."[103] Liberty requires digestion, the hardship and "difficult freedom" of living and working in sincerity not only for oneself but for others and their bodily and material life.

Levinas and Adorno are "against liberty" in its ideological forms that systematically deny justice and the freedom of others. Their thinking is informed by, respectively, progressive Rousseauian republican and Marxist social democratic sources that they critically rethought, as well as appeals to the an-archic promise of freedom that unsettles the indifferent functioning and autopoietic reproduction of the present social totality. Totality is neither interrupted by the egotistical self who strives endlessly for more in the name of its freedom, nor by what Adorno and Horkheimer describe as "the wretched moralistic attempts to propagate humanity as the most rational of means."[104] While the latter leaves the systematic sources of injustice uncontested and intact, the former is an expression of the relentless reproduction of the structural processes of exchange and making equivalent. This acquisitive selfish ego, despite its intentions and wishes to simply enjoy itself and "simply be itself," is intertwined with the mechanisms of commodification, consumption, and consumerism. This "natural" self reflects and intensifies the social totality that Adorno and Levinas recognize as structured by the identity of equivalence and exchange. The promise of freedom cannot originate from me, or the sovereignty of the subject; it must disturb my freedom and its illusory power from beyond it. It approaches from the abject and the other to whom it is systematically denied, unsettling the ego-oriented subject and alarming those who ideologically identify their present advantages with natural liberty.

Despite their own complicities with instrumental reason and identity thinking, Levinas and Adorno's writings suggest critical models and indicate strategies for diagnosing and confronting the structurally formed pathologies associated with reified visions and the manipulative misuses of liberty. The problem with pathological freedom is that it is a structure of privilege. Despite its undeniable accomplishments and promise and potential for letting individuals pursue their own course, the modern reified conception of liberty is conjoined with the actual lack of liberty in its enactment, institutionalization, and practice. This is due to its being preempted by conformity, irresponsibility, and indifference to others' well-being, and the rejection of what is different in the ideologically constructed resentment against the alien, the foreign, and the enemy.

Possessive individualism, libertarianism, and liberalism in their classical Lockean and capitalist senses are not the neutral theoretical positions in accord with "nature" or "natural law" that their proponents interpret them to be. They are socially formed positions, even as the occupants of these roles deny their own sociality and entanglement with the others whom they ignore and disavow. This is by no means a novel claim. Still, its importance calls for its repetition: the doctrine of natural liberty serves to mask and justify socially contrived injustice. As they are lived and not merely thought, these ideological positions can be the symptom and mask, if not the toxin itself, of a social condition appropriately described as the pathology of freedom and idolatry of liberty. This is appropriate to the degree that there is willingness if not eagerness to engage in the sacrifice of actual concrete individuals and their ability to participate in society and have a degree of well-being and flourishing without the incessant and excessive anxiety of socioeconomic and personal ruin.

Conclusion: The Priority of the Freedom of the Other

The radical republican, Marxist, and anarchist political traditions offer—to varying degrees—in their an-archic prophetic moments indications of another form of politics if interpreted from the altered perspective of ethical asymmetry and nonidentity articulated by Adorno and Levinas. Rereading Levinas beyond Levinas, the prospect of a pluralistic and an-archic "republicanism" of the other emerges that would not be based on or restricted to political theological, nationalistic, fraternal, and ethnic identities.

The ideas of republicanism and socialism, unrestrained by the identity thinking (such as the *volonté générale* in Rousseau or the collective subject in Lukács) that has deformed (as Arendt exposed) their emancipatory dimensions, indicate an unrestricted and not merely negatively (i.e., liberally) defined solidarity, equality, and liberty. That is to say, they indicate in outline, to speak in a summary fashion: (1) an infinite or unrestricted solidarity—manifest in welcoming, hospitality, and generosity—that is not restricted to personal connections, communal roles, and national identities; (2) an asymmetrically oriented equality that reaches toward the singular, the suffering, and the vulnerable and is not limited to calculative exchange; and (3) a liberty that does not deny or neglect its unconditional responsibility to the other. Whereas classical liberal and contemporary neoliberal liberty justifies the institutions and practices of appropriation and enslavement in the name of one's own pursuit of happiness and the good life, its transformative negation and critique reveals that the freedom of the other (from injury and harm) has priority over my own (as the pursuit of desires regardless of others).

In the next two chapters and in the epilogue, the potential of an an-archic (in a modified Levinasian sense) and nonidentitarian (in a modified Adornian sense) solidarity necessary for democracy and equality will be pursued further as an alternative to (1) communal and nationalistic understandings of fraternal identity, and (2) liberal cosmopolitan ideas of neutrality and negatively defined tolerance that function as means of adaptive (Foucault) or integrating (Adorno) construction and repressive control (Marcuse). Levinas's works move between liberal rights-oriented and radical republican and socialist political philosophies in which liberty, equality, and fraternity are prophetically reconceived through the other. This prophetic orientation indicates (in light of critical social theory) a critical model of mimetic and communicative forms of praxis that are not constrained by and a solidarity that contests coercive regimes of exchange and identity.

Chapter Thirteen

The Limits of Liberalism

Cosmopolitanism, Tolerance, and Asymmetrical Ethics

Introduction: Colonialism and the
Aporias of Cosmopolitan Tolerance

Tolerance is taken to be an elementary virtue of modern liberal societies and to be constitutive of a universal (within the limits of anthropocentrism) cosmopolitan moral or legal order. April Carter notes, "Although there are a range of possible reasons for advocating toleration as a policy, an attitude of tolerance is essential to cosmopolitanism, which values the mingling of different peoples and the ability to live harmoniously together."[1] The modern liberal idea of society (*Gesellschaft*) is distinguished from "traditional" communities (*Gemeinschaft*) that presuppose and require a basic common identity that by definition excludes and subordinates others on the basis of race, religion, sexuality, or other specific characteristics.

Recent liberal cosmopolitan political theorists—a group that embraces significant moral philosophers such as Jürgen Habermas, John Rawls, and Martha Nussbaum—construe tolerance to be a fundamental element of a conception of justice that endorses a plurality of forms of life on condition that they are compatible with justice toward others.[2] Such an envisioning of cosmopolitan tolerance and pluralism is opposed to the communitarian and conservative republican demands for a dominant integrating framework of the good and the good life. Rainer Forst has historically traced and systematically articulated this vision of liberal tolerance in his work *Tolerance in Conflict*.[3]

Despite the prevalent supposition that tolerance is intrinsically a force for justice, a number of thinkers have critiqued the potential intolerance and ideological function of classical liberal capitalist conceptions of tolerance.

First, using cross-cultural examples to develop this point, there is the suspicion that, in the words of Martin Buber's description of the multiethnic tolerance of the Austro-Hungarian Empire of his youth, "mutual tolerance" can exist "without mutual understanding."[4] The imperial function of universalism is expressed by the Chinese anticolonial and nationalist leader Sun Yat-Sen 孫中山. He maintained in his lecture "Nationalism and Cosmopolitanism" (1924), published in *Sanmin zhuyi* 三民主義 (The Three Principles of the People), that the cosmopolitan vision can further the interests of the stronger party (e.g., the colonizing West) against the weaker party (e.g., the colonized peoples) who require an appeal to their own particular self-interests and particularity to resist their oppression. The Western powers and Westernizing Chinese claimed that cosmopolitanism was progressive and modern, even as the "opening" of Asia meant in reality its domination and exploitation, and as imperial powers pursued their own nationalist self-interests in the "civilizing" cosmopolitan façade that is a characteristic integrating ideology of multicultural empires and neoliberal exchange.

Sun Yat-Sen noted how earlier Chinese Confucian thought was both cosmopolitan and imperial. The cosmopolitan imperial version of Confucianism allowed traditional China to rule over other non-Han nationalities and to be governed by them in the Yuan and Qing dynasties. Cosmopolitanism is accordingly an advantage of empires and a flaw for weak vulnerable nations. Furthermore, traditional Confucian cosmopolitanism prepared the way for China's modern status as an exploited "hypo-" or "semi-" colony that required a progressive anticosmopolitan and nationalist response.[5] Without national identity, the Chinese and other oppressed peoples of the earth were like heaps of "lose sand" (*yipan sansha* 一盤散沙) unable to resist their exploitation by their cosmopolitan oppressors. Asymmetries of power require the weaker powers to affirm themselves in patriotism and nationalism to resist their oppression. This argumentation maintains that identification can play radical roles in forms of resistance such as anticolonialism and antiracism in contrast to a neutral universalism that ignores the realities of discrimination and power dynamics. Identity orients the dominated against their oppression.

Notwithstanding the separation of the cosmopolitan ethical ideal from worldly international politics in liberal theorists such as Nussbaum, the universality of cosmopolitan tolerance in its appeals to a collective world interest or common universalizing perspective might be distinctive of specific forms of power. Among these are multiethnic empires or a multinational capitalist order that exercises hegemony over each particular rather than bringing about genuine fairness and equality between them.[6]

Second, given the history of Western colonialism and its appeal to exercising power in the name of progress and modernization, there is a historically justified concern that cosmopolitan universality and tolerance might undermine instead of enable the critique that rests in the particularity of the oppressed and exploited. It might be the specific conditions and experiences of the victims that allow them to speak and resist their oppression in a way that is unrecognized from a privileged neutral point of view or consciously or unconsciously opposed by those who benefit from and perpetuate oppression. Herbert Marcuse described this situation in the 1960s as the passive "repressive tolerance" of advanced capitalist societies that gives everyone a voice so long as the voice does not intrude on privilege. "Liberal" tolerance contrasts with the "liberating critique" of confrontational "active tolerance" that promotes social change and genuine democracy.[7] The earlier generation of the Frankfurt school, especially Adorno and Marcuse, critiqued the repressive side of tolerance in relation to those who are different as part of the logic of conformity operative in existing societies. Wendy Brown's *Regulating Aversion* has suggestively illuminated how tolerance functions as a means to assimilate and ostracize in North American society.[8]

Third, thinkers associated with what could be described as the asymmetrical ethics of difference, particularly Levinas and Derrida, in their own ways have examined the aporias, false universalism, and limits of tolerance, liberalism, and cosmopolitanism. They have interrogated the category of tolerance as a variety of indifference that places the other at a distance and at a disadvantage; this is in contrast with the nonindifferent and asymmetrically charged ethical encounter of self and other in generosity, hospitality, and welcome. Such welcoming consummates infinity and defines subjectivity for Levinas.[9] Levinas interrogates an indifferent tolerance for the sake of a dissimilarity that is ethical in its nonindifference. In Derrida's later ethical-political reflections, cosmopolitan tolerance is similarly a failure to welcome the other. In the context of hospitality, it is inevitably not "hospitable enough." But is this ethics of the priority of the other a banal inversion of the ethics of identity? When it is applied to issues of cosmopolitanism and internationalism, is it itself a "lukewarm tolerance" wherein particular cultures and forms of life are, as Bonner (one of its critics) asserts, "turned into a set of competing cultural ghettos"?[10]

The three issues analyzed in this chapter (cosmopolitanism, tolerance, and asymmetrical ethics) present us with a number of questions: Are cosmopolitanism and tolerance minimal yet nevertheless necessary elements of just societies? Or do cosmopolitanism and tolerance instead perpetuate indifference toward others and potentially disguise the concrete and particular forms of domination and exploitation of others? I explore the complications and aporias of liberal conceptions of tolerance with an eye toward potential critical alternatives to consider whether they can be reformulated—or more adequately thought—in the context of the critique of ideology and power articulated in the critical social theory of the early Frankfurt school (Adorno and Marcuse) and asymmetrical ethics (Levinas and Derrida) that accentuates the alterity and priority of the other.

The Complicity of Cosmopolitan Tolerance with Domination

Discussions of cosmopolitanism typically contrast the "liberalism" and "internationalism" of Kant, on the one hand, with the "communitarianism" and "nationalism" of Hegel, on the other hand.[11] This distinction is questionable if the categories of personal freedom, civil society, and tolerance are considered more attentively. Hegel did not oppose the cosmopolitan tolerance advocated by the Enlightenment with a communitarian sense of identity or sameness that lacked tolerance. In reality he argued, on the contrary, that a strong sense of identity—or the universal realized in the concrete—is the condition of the tolerance and individual freedom characteristic of modern societies. Hegel did not reject "modernity" for the sake of an imagined community to be found in the past that could be preserved against historical transformation.[12] Hegel justified modernity as a unique achievement of Western history and identified it with the stability, legality, and power of the state that can guarantee tolerance and the free exchange of goods and ideas between individuals in civil society.

Kant's cosmopolitan law holds between nations and peoples in war (just war), commerce, and travel by guaranteeing freedom of movement and "universal hospitality." Kant's cosmopolitanism was both too pragmatically weak and too rigidly moralistic in its universality. In contrast to the standard assessment of Hegel as a thinker of totality, Hegel argued that cosmopolitanism must fail to be genuinely tolerant, as it is a political vision of integration and totalization that cannot effectively manage social diversity. Hegel remarked, in defending the virtues of robust individual nation-states, that it is such states that can effectively ignore, manage, and "tolerate anomalies" such as the "particular" commitments of religious and ethnic minorities.[13] Hegel linked attitudes of tolerance with the pragmatic qualities of maturity and mildness of judgment and with the power of the state while questioning the liberal cosmopolitan vision of a tolerance without borders.[14] Tolerance is embedded in a concrete social configuration and actual way of life that to this extent requires the borders and laws of the nation-state and the resilient and dynamic spirit of a community to flourish. The practice and institutionalization of tolerance cannot be effectively based—in accordance with Hegel's argument for the concrete universal of ethical life—in the disinterest, indifference, and neutrality of an abstract and disembodied universal ethical principle.

Hegel separated the reflective critical thought associated with modernity from the project of the Enlightenment. He maintained instead that reflective consciousness problematically undermined itself when it embraced cosmopolitan abstractness "in opposition to the concrete life of the citizen" and the tangible contextual mediations of ethical life, civil society, and the state.[15]

Adorno traces in his lecture course "History and Freedom" (1964–1965) how for globalized capitalism and its vanguard of Americanization, and contrary to Hegel's defense of concrete ethical life (*Sittlichkeit*), "it is no longer the case that so-called cosmopolitanism is the more abstract thing in contrast to the individual nations; cosmopolitanism now possesses the greater reality."[16] Hegel's anticosmopolitan vision of the existing contextual community has consequently been shattered, according to Adorno, by the relentless developments of the logic of advanced capitalism and ideologies of neoliberal capitalist internationalism. By implication, universal cosmopolitan tolerance is a "positive freedom for" that has been managerially steered and disfigured in being restricted to processes of commodification and consumption.

Adorno's concerns intersect with those of Marcuse in his analysis of the repressive functions of liberal tolerance. Nonetheless, Adorno did not attempt to resolve the aporia of tolerance into a choice between the passive repressive tolerance of the established neoliberal order, including its nativist and racist variations, and the active emancipatory tolerance of the oppressed and exploited that necessitated employing intolerance to challenge limited tolerance. Adorno is more wary than Marcuse of the potential for immediate social transformation, and repeatedly warned of the dangers of new forms of oppression emerging under the guise of emancipation in the charged political atmosphere of the 1960s.[17]

The cosmopolitan vision of a humanity transcending all local bonds as well as the particularities of race has its sinister dimensions in Adorno's reflections on the failures of the project of the Enlightenment. Adorno analyzed the close historical connections between the humanism and cosmopolitanism of the Enlightenment with anti-Semitism, colonialism, and racism—which are not only past issues. Adorno noted in a number of his works how anti-Semitism "can be found even in the works championing tolerance and humanism."[18]

Adorno contests the totalitarian tendencies inherent in nationalism and patriotism and in the cosmopolitanism and internationalism that reject those who obstinately stick to their own particularity. This is a characteristic of multiethnic domains from the Roman Empire to contemporary international mechanisms that reproduce and further capitalist markets and the neoliberal and neoconservative ideologies justifying them.

Adorno concluded of enlightened cosmopolitan attitudes about race in *Minima Moralia* that tolerance is a boomerang insofar as all are equal and any mark of dissimilarity is perceived to be an ingratitude and a stigma.[19] An analogous issue is seen in the *Mencius* (Mengzi 孟子) in the early Confucian critique of Mohist (*mojia* 墨家) conceptions of universal, impartial, and equal love (*jian'ai* 兼愛); universal impartial love forgets those nearest to oneself in the name of an abstract and impossible universal love of all that can entail neglecting one's actual responsibilities for the sake of responsibilities to distant others one does not fulfill. The dialectical movement from universal tolerance toward particular intolerance is evident in the cosmopolitan attitude of the civilized European against the "stubborn particularity" of the colonized and those who refuse to assimilate to the established order of things.

Echoing Marcuse's thesis about the repressive social role of tolerance, Adorno claimed that cosmopolitan tolerance is itself the ideology of the bourgeoisie who love people as they are—in their atomistic separation and lack of solidarity—and despise how people otherwise can be.[20] Cosmopolitanism does and can occur at the same time as a form of violence against persons as they actually exist in the name of universal ethical ideas.

Cosmopolitan tolerance functions in the neoliberal international order, as Wendy Brown has more recently argued, as a form of acceptable and excusable dislike, disapproval, sanctioning, and regulation.[21] The ideology of a tolerant cosmopolitan world-civilization can itself justify and excuse violence against those who are perceived as recalcitrant, that is, those who are branded as intolerant, primitive, deviant, barbaric, and backward.

Given the historical difficulty and ideological complicity of normative ethical and political theory, such concerns about the ideological uses of cosmopolitanism and tolerance cannot be too easily dismissed. The actual deployment of cosmopolitan ideas should not be displaced by invoking a cosmopolitan ethical model that is disconnected from and uncontaminated by the historical facticity of the cosmopolitan project, from the multiethnic imperial cosmopolitanism of traditional empires, such as Stoic Rome and Confucian China, to liberal and neoliberal capitalist internationalism that allows no borders to be closed to the power and interests of the ethically neutral and socially indifferent market.

Cosmopolitan Tolerance, Colonialism, and Racism

Levinas and Derrida reveal in their own ways different forms of inquiry regarding cosmopolitanism and tolerance. These resonate with Adorno's analysis of their complicity with anti-Semitism and racism while introducing additional considerations concerning alterity or otherness and its ethical implications. As discussed further in detail previously and again below, these elements are neglected in the framework of critical social theory as it has been reformulated—in a broadly liberal style—by Habermas and Honneth.[22]

It is striking how small a role the word "tolerance" plays in recent French thought, given its importance in the French Enlightenment and French republican thought. This absence is not accidental, as Derrida once remarked: "The fact that I never use the word 'tolerance' is not fortuitous."[23] It is not accidental for a negative and a positive reason that are at work in a comparable manner in Adorno. First, Adorno and Derrida were both wary of the oppressive functions of tolerance that are at work in the anti-Semitism of Enlightenment thinkers such as Voltaire as well as the French republican tradition. Second, they each sought to articulate in different ways a more robust critical or ethical stance toward the moment of nonidentity (Adorno) or trace of alterity (Levinas and Derrida) that challenges the formulaic universalism of cosmopolitanism that ideologically masks and legitimates power.

Notwithstanding his identification with the image of the "urban, cosmopolitan intellectual," Derrida skeptically questioned the universal pretensions of the cosmopolitan project.[24] Derrida intensified his concern with issues of the ethical significance of difference, including the arrival and welcoming of the other, in his later works.

Marcuse noted how, "[u]nder the rule of the repressive whole, liberty can be made into a powerful instrument of domination."[25] The free movements and choices of the few are historically interlinked with the economic and social coercion of others. Earlier discourses of cosmopolitan freedom focused on the arrival of the European traveler across the globe. Early modern thinkers theorized and justified the demands that the European visitor placed upon others: "his" claims for free travel and the open exchange of goods and ideas that arguably prepared the way for colonization as colonies expanded from trading centers. China and Japan were forcibly opened for the sake of the "free market" and in the name of the freedom of the European. India, Indonesia, and others were colonized via European trading companies. Discourses of cosmopolitanism have in reality legitimated the subjugation of the provincial and the particular that were perceived as making no claims to cosmopolitan, that is, European universality. Such discourses, to give another example, include John Stuart Mill's use of universalistic arguments to justify British dominion over India as a civilizing and progressive force in contrast with the vulgar self-interested colonialism that he criticized.

More recent poststructuralist and postcolonial discourses, in comparison, have not only placed the universal scope of cosmopolitanism in doubt but also, as in the case of Levinas, the complicities of its own earlier thinkers and theorists with Eurocentrism as an ideological privileging of the Western world.[26] These discourses have in several cases turned to issues of the arrival and status of migrants from the former colonized territories in the heartlands of the former colonizing powers. European cosmopolitanism faced a dilemma with the influx of foreign others and, above all, the particularist other who does not partake in the same vision of cosmopolitanism and tolerance. In the context of hospitality, Derrida questioned the self-image of fairness, openness, and tolerance in republican France with its questionable longstanding treatment of its Jewish population and the current tensions with its newer migrants from Africa and the Middle East.[27]

The problems and aporias of cosmopolitanism articulated by Adorno and Derrida cannot be adequately explained as the inadequate application of an adequate theory or ideal. As Derrida demonstrates, they are structurally rooted in the nature of a cosmopolitan cause that "presupposes the categories of the state and the citizen, even if the citizen is a world citizen."[28] Cosmopolitanism is defined as world citizenship and assumes a specific nonuniversalizable conception of the world (*cosmos*) and the political (*polis*).[29] In Kant's account of cosmopolitan right, according to Derrida's analysis, what first appears as if it were unlimited "universal hospitality" is revealed as inexorably conditioned and restricted.[30]

The classical liberal conception of tolerance operates as a vehicle of intolerance, just as cosmopolitanism can function as the ideology of globalizing and universalizing empires and international regimes regulating nations and markets. These, as recent neoconservative international polices have demonstrated once again, sacrifice the particular to an abstract universal—and democratic participation and self-determination to an elitist cosmopolitan regime.

In confrontation with cultural "coloniality," Derrida consequently clarified the "conditions and auto-limits" of even the most "cosmopolitan" law, as envisioned in Kant's thinking of universal right and perpetual peace.[31] Derrida argues concerning this potential colonialism and monologism of universalism, "My language, the only one I hear myself speak and agree to speak, is the language of the other."[32] The center is unthinkable without its periphery and margins; the universal is unimaginable without the singularities it intends to transverse, integrate, and regulate as particulars subsumed under a universal order or principle.

To encounter and confront our contemporary situation, which is characterized by a limited inadequate form of tolerance reactive against others in their concreteness as much as by allergic intolerance, must we not break with the naïve dichotomy between universalist tolerance and particularist intolerance? Is there in the Levinasian motif of the "language of the other," introduced by Derrida in the last passage, the possibility of an alternative to both the false universality of liberal and neoliberal cosmopolitanism and the false concreteness of communitarianism and racialized particularism?

How might Levinas's thinking of the other indicate an alternative to this impasse? To begin to formulate a response, Levinas's conceptions of cosmopolitanism and tolerance ought to be reconsidered.[33] Derrida provides a sense of the import of this question in his remark in *Adieu to Emmanuel Levinas*: "Levinas always prefers, and I would want to say this without any play on words, peace now, and he prefers universality to cosmopolitanism. To my knowledge, Levinas never uses the word 'cosmopolitanism' or adopts it as his own. I can imagine at least two reasons for this: first, because this sort of political thought refers pure hospitality, and thus peace, to an indefinite progress; second, because of the ideological connotations with which modern anti-Semitism saddled the great tradition of a cosmopolitanism passed down from Stoicism or Pauline Christianity to the Enlightenment and to Kant."[34] The unmasking of the anti-Semitism of the cosmopolitan tradition from antiquity through modern European Enlightenment is similarly evident in the writings of Adorno and Derrida, as discussed previously.

The three modernistic (and still too Eurocentric) critics of modernity discussed in this chapter (that is, Adorno, Levinas, and Derrida) are skeptical concerning the modern conception of progress and its linear perception of time—not in the name of a past that is being lost through modernization, of course, but rather for the sake of the present. The liberal conception of progress toward the future realization of peace and fairness signifies a denial of peace and justice to the other in the present moment, as they are deferred infinitely into the future. In contrast to this anticipation of a future that cannot become present, the welcoming of the other, transpiring through interruption, cannot be reduced to the concept or principle of tolerance, nor can it be deferred to a progress to come.

Love and Justice beyond Communitarianism and Liberalism

Levinas uses the word "politics" in multiple inconsistent ways: it can mean a domain of war and conflict, prudential calculation, justice established via the figure of the third, or the achievement of democracy and fundamental human rights. The first two usages are characteristic of *Totality and Infinity* and earlier works; the latter predominate in Levinas's later writings.

Levinas's postwar political sensibilities were shaped by the catastrophe of the Holocaust, the terror of Stalinism and actual communist regimes, and the legacies of the French republican and Jewish prophetic traditions. Levinas's political thinking is in multiple ways, as argued previously in this work, an ethically informed and other-oriented transformation of French republican thought.[35] Levinas has been criticized for his reliance on French republican ideas by Critchley, who interprets the concept only through its conservative and nationalist deformations. Republicanism is, however, a multivocal concept with a revolutionary and radical democratic heritage that remains suggestive for contemporary models of democratic political and civic participation, and popular will formation.[36]

The republican political tradition has had communal and cosmopolitan, nationalistic and universalistic, regressive and revolutionary social-political tendencies. It has through complicated histories developed into nationalist and internationalist forms stressing various kinds of identity. One lesson of Arendt's *The Origins of Totalitarianism* is the possibility of rehabilitating republican traditions against their fascistic and communist incarnations in which the bureaucratic and colonial expansion of the modern state and limiting notions of the people eclipse the drama of democratic participation and self-determination.[37] The French theory and practice of republicanism has been a series of sites of struggle between the rightwing deformation of republicanism in anti-Semitic and racist French nationalisms, which limits solidarity to ethnicity, and the possibility of an inclusive republic that would welcome the stranger, the exile, and the stateless who have lost the very right to have rights.[38]

Levinas accentuates the latter tendencies toward an-archic republicanism of nonidentity in focusing on solidarity for the other and human rights (*droits de l'homme*) that can be turned against humans if they are not oriented by their interpersonal and prophetic sources that cannot be established and institutionalized.[39] Levinas introduced the term "anarchy" to describe his ethics. His ethical conception of an-archy can be extended to reconsider an anarchistic politics that would go beyond the idea found in Marx and the anarchist tradition of a free association of producers who self-organize themselves such that the free development of each is the condition of the free development of all.[40] Without alterity and nonidentity, this potentially emancipatory idea achieves the opposite in retaining the coercive aura of a restricted republican fraternity and popular will, even if the state apparatus appears to wither away.

Habermas proposes an alternative to classical republicanism that would not abandon its ethical motivations toward participation, solidarity, and popular sovereignty. He stresses the mutual correction needed between republican solidarity and popular sovereignty and liberal rights and liberties in deliberative democracy, while decentering and pluralizing the republican notion of corporate association and collective will in "Three Models of Normative Democracy."[41] Habermas argues for an alternative to liberal and republican models of democracy with the deliberative model that corrects the overemphasis on the collective or the individual. Habermas strives for more inclusiveness and pluralism in deliberation and the public sphere, but does not adequately attend to the role of alterity and nonidentity. An-archic and nonidentical elements in republicanism are indicated by Levinas. These tendencies in Levinas suggest, according to Derrida, "a political *res publica* that cannot be reduced to a version of 'tolerance,' unless this tolerance requires the affirmation of a 'love' without measure."[42]

Liberal accounts of passive and negative tolerance fail to reach the material other in her suffering and need. Levinas erases the distinction between perfect and imperfect duties—a conception of duty that cannot prevent murder when duty outweighs suffering, as Arendt and Levinas have argued against Kantian ethics—with the immediate immanent transcendence of the face of the other who demands and obliges infinite solidarity, love, and charity without restriction: that is, the *chesed* חסד that in rabbinic traditions is constitutive of healing the wounds of the world (*tikkun olam* תיקון עולם) that was discussed as a reconciliation with nature in part 1. Instead of being imperfect duties and "supererogatory" actions that go beyond what is required by duty, loving-kindness and charity constitute a more originary obligation emerging from the asymmetrical encounter with the other person.

One might argue here that, comparable to utilitarianism, Levinasian obligation is open to the objection that it is overly ethically demanding in requiring too much sacrifice by ethical agents and violates the moral idea that ought implies can. One significant difference in this comparison is that Levinas offers not a normative rule or prescription but a phenomenological description of the ethical and an indication of the injustice of the alternative when law, which constantly asserts its precedence, overlooks charity and mercy. Levinas is closer to Leibniz than to

Kant in recognizing the unconditional primacy of the good (even over God's will) and prioritizing charity, generosity, and mercy above duty, justice, and law.[43] The liberal priority of justice over care, charity, and republican and communistic solidarity functions as a veil of indifference for excusing injustice, given the structures of domination imbedded in the institutions and practices of social-political life.

The impersonal application of norms and calculative measure associated with liberal notions of tolerance as a negative and imperfect duty are confronted with the incalculability, immeasurability, and unconditionality of the encounter with and solidarity for the other person. The actual limitation and restrictedness of "universal" cosmopolitan justice is revealed in contrast with the "infinite" and unrestricted responsibility to the poor, the needy, and the abject.[44]

Why is this? As already delineated in earlier chapters, Levinas calls the revelation of the other in the encounter "ethics" and, as noted previously above, love, kindness, and charity. A love without concupiscence and an unconditional charity for-the-other without expecting reciprocity indicate possibilities of a relationship with the other not based on calculation, exchange, or fungible interchangeability. Asymmetry does not monadically preclude reciprocity; it is its condition.[45] Due to asymmetrical separation, I do not ask what the other would prefer if she were me or similar to me, but what she would prefer granted that she is other than, and cannot be compared with, me. This critique of the logic of equivalence and exchange at work in administrative and managerial justice, an unending debt without forgiveness and mercy (compare chapter 6), applies to the strict forms of exchange involved in the cruel retaliation of "an eye for an eye, a tooth for a tooth"—the principle of retribution (*ius talionis*) endorsed, for example, in Kant's retributivist defense of the death penalty in the *Doctrine of Right* in the *Metaphysics of Morals*—such as the use of capital punishment.[46]

Ethical-political life cannot be reduced to the immediacy of loving-kindness and care, a pure solidarity without institutions, given the problems of steering and management in large-scale societies and the need for justice beyond the scope of one's friends, neighbors, and community. Levinas is right to insist that justice requires and is warped without the charity that precedes it and that gives it a bad conscience by beckoning to it, even as charity likewise requires and is fulfilled in social justice.[47]

Levinas appears to be inconsistent about the primacy of love or justice. He asserts at various points the priority of love or justice, the spirit or the letter, as each presupposes and fulfills the other due to the asymmetrical triadic relationship of self, other, and the third. Levinas consequently switches between the first-person and third-person perspectives without being able to reduce one perspective to the other or to an ultimate neutral and impersonal view from nowhere of the brute "there is"—such as the murmuring of the *il y a* in the ceaseless night of insomnia.

Levinasian love is distinct from the bonds based on identity articulated in communitarian ethics and the care of the other expressed in the ethics of care in not being grounded in human moral psychology or anthropology. As described in chapter 4, Levinas is rightfully suspicious of naturalistic and biologically based models of the ethical, which I advocated replacing with natural historical models in part 1 and the prophetism of the good in part 2, while tracing the operation of the transcendent and infinite (that is, the ethical) in the affective and sensible conditions of human life. Since the words "hospitality" and "love" are open-ended and multivocal, and not grounded in abstract reason or in concrete human nature, Levinas's reflection on the ethical is not ethics in the familiar sense: it does not establish universal norms and formulas for action, nor does it establish models of virtue and care to cultivate or particular prescriptive maxims to guide situational behavior. Levinas's "ethics" operates as a "first philosophy" before and beyond ethics as it is ordinarily conceived in common life and in moral theory.[48] Ethics is first and foremost the responsibility of the "I." As discussed previously, ethics is distinguished from virtues, values, norms, prescriptions, and perfectionist moralizing. Ethics is not the "moralism of rules decreed by the virtuous," as it is a prior "awakening of an 'I' responsible for others, the accession of my person to the uniqueness of the 'I' called and elected to responsibility for others."[49] Instead of offering an ethical program of cultivating virtues or duties, or setting up procedural normative guidelines, Levinas speaks of the other as a who. This "who" cannot be defined by ethics in the sense of a normative theory or moral code. This other cannot be reduced to my interests without violence, no matter how universally those interests might be conceived. This is the paradox of a liberalism that strives for equality and fairness while undermining their realization through neglecting the tensions of nonidentity and asymmetry in ethics and politics.

The universalism of cosmopolitanism, liberalism, and tolerance can be inattentive to the asymmetries of power that they help reproduce and the asymmetries of responsibility that they evade; they presuppose a logic of exchange between self and other that—demanding equivalence—is reductive of the other *as* other no matter how equally, fairly, and symmetrically this exchange is conceived. The inherent limitations of symmetry are revealed in its underlying economic and calculative character. Liberalism fails insofar as it does not question its own hither side, the underlying logic and machinery governing the actual reproduction of societies and the international system. Its limits entail the need for an "asymmetrical ethics"—as well as a political economy of exteriority and difference in contemporary capitalism indicated in works such as Dussel's reconstruction of living labor as exterior to capital in *Towards an Unknown Marx*.[50]

Asymmetrical ethics is exemplified in welcoming and greeting the other, and in generosity and hospitality. Derrida describes how Levinasian hospitality opens the path to humanity from out of the context of hospitality in the Jewish tradition and its ethical personalism, observing how for Levinas "this duty of hospitality is not only essential to a 'Jewish thought' of the relationships between Israel and the nations. It opens the way to the humanity of the human in general. There is here, then, a daunting logic of election and exemplarity operating between the assignation of a singular responsibility and human universality—today one might even say humanitarian universality."[51] The references to Israel can lead one to believe that Levinas is articulating a variety of Jewish communitarian ethics: a vision restricted to an ethically defined Jewish community, or a form of political Zionism that is complicit with the Israeli treatment of the Palestinians. There are commentators and critics who advocate this interpretation, which represents genuine concerns about Levinas's thinking and its application to politics.[52] Such interpretations enact a hermeneutics of suspicion against Levinas's texts insofar as he repeatedly rejects communalist, ethnocentric, or racial interpretations of Israel and Judaism, contesting nationalist and a merely strategic political Zionism in writings such as "Means of Identification" (1963), a reflection on how Jewish identity is both lost and retained in questioning it.[53] Levinas's vision of Israel as an ethically and prophetically oriented community that is to judge the suffering, injustice, and cruelty of history, instead of naturalistically participating in them, can be conflated with the existing state of Israel to obscure and justify its injustices in a "Levinasian" inspired apologetics; yet the ethical idea of Israel can be used to assess unjust Israeli policies and practices, as is evident in Levinasian-inspired critiques of Israeli politics.

Yet can the state of Caesar and the state of David be so easily disentangled? In contrast to communitarian and conservative political and religious readings of Levinas that stress Jewish social cohesion and identity, Derrida rightly insists upon the role of an interruptive universality and humanity in the thought of Levinas even as he indicates—from his earliest writing on Levinas to his later works—the potential and latent violence within it: there is, he notes, a "price to pay for not injuring or wronging the absolute Other. Violence of sacrifice in the name of non-violence."[54] However, Levinas does not portray acting for the other as ascetic or self-sacrificial violence against oneself; it is rather gentleness and generosity that disturbs egoism (being as possessing) in moving us for the other.

Due to its aporetic structure, Levinas's thinking cannot be, despite potential communitarian limitations and ascetic self-sacrificial violence raised by Derrida and Critchley, confined to either a definitive sense of a limited community (e.g., communitarianism), such as a specially defined Jewish community or nation of Israel, nor to a universal liberal and accordingly ethically neutral society (e.g., cosmopolitanism). Hospitality is an exemplar of a different constellation of the ethical and political than is found in communitarianism and liberalism, which is the pair of alternatives that governs the moral theorizing of later generations of the Frankfurt school such as Habermas and Honneth.

Hospitality, Substitution, and Tolerance

In Levinas, the home is not constituted through itself but rather in a drama of interiority and exteriority through hospitality and welcoming. This home diverges from the experience of "home" (*Heimat*) that Levinas relentlessly criticizes in Heidegger for its exclusivity and allergy toward the alien and other. There is thus the positionality of an acquired home and soil in contrast to an originary one.[55] Interiority and subjectivity presuppose and are permeated by alterity, exteriority, and—we should also add, according to the interpretive strategy unfolded in this work—the "materialities" of material conditions and material others. Hospitality is not the act of a sovereign autonomous subject deciding whom to welcome; it is instead the openness to the other through which the subject is itself formed.[56] Hospitality occurs in the tensions between homelessness and homecoming, as an exposure of home to nonhome and to the welcoming of the homeless.[57] Levinas does not conceive of the ethical through concepts of community and tradition (communitarianism) or abstract equality and tolerance (liberalism) but through the radical encounter with others in their irreducible ipseity and nonsymmetrical and nonsynonymous substitution for the other.[58] The ethics of hospitality can be interpreted as an instance of or variation on such substitution. Yet what should one make of political hospitality that is mediated through the third person who demands equal and impartial consideration of all?

Derrida introduces in his discussion of Levinas how the "third" and its distinctive neutrality (illeity) cleave the ethical and the political.[59] There can be no possibility of grounding the political in the ethical; they are two distinct ways for humans to interact. Through the "introduction" of the illeity—and the impartial concern—of the third, an introduction of what was already present from the beginning, ethics is not only a question of the interpersonal asymmetry between self and other.

There is a multifaceted asymmetrical triangle involving goodness, justice, and power between three persons. For each person there are multiple fields of otherness; and, as Derrida indicates, there are two different ethical and political selves cleaved in their inseparability. It is accordingly the third that restrains the potential violence in the asymmetrical face-to-face encounter between self and other. The third is inevitably already affecting their relationship. The drama of the political and justice is at work in the face-to-face encounter such that justice and equality cannot be reduced to the love and solidarity that serve as their prophetic guides.

Derrida describes how substitution—"my absolute, singular, incalculable being-given-over to the wholly Other who comes to me from on high" in John D. Caputo's words—is broken in Levinas by the impartial justice of the third that does not concern one other but all others.[60] Tolerance, as part of justice, belongs to one facet of Levinas's triangle.

In contrast to more radical critics of tolerance as a negative, passive, and regressive concept, Levinas himself noted the broader context of the idea of tolerance and gave it an ethical orientation toward the other that brings it into kinship with hospitality, generosity, and love.[61] Levinas modifies tolerance rather than rejecting it as such, as he employed and appealed to the notion of tolerance and emphasized the Jewish tradition of tolerance.[62] In his discussion of Judaism and religion, Levinas opposed the opposition between religion and tolerance as a false dilemma, contending that tolerance can be constitutive of a religion without that religion losing its uniqueness or meaningfulness.[63]

Tolerance plays a limited role in Levinas's texts. It is substitution that indicates a more radical ethical possibility than mere tolerance conceived as a negative restraint or as a form of neutrality that does not step in for the other. Substitution is more than the equivalence of the golden rule or other forms of conventional ethics. Substitution is at times replaced with the word "love" by Levinas, who noted how the love that tolerance requires but fails to achieve is immeasurable.[64] If tolerance is not to become a neutral indifference of each self-interested ego pursuing an individual path regardless of others, or a form of intolerant condescension against those who do not belong to the tolerant community of Western cosmopolitan elites, it is in need of being radically reoriented and rethought in relation to the substitution of the self for the other.[65]

A Cosmopolitanism of the Other

As discussed in previous chapters, Honneth is committed to ethical universalism in a neo-Hegelian form that would rejuvenate its critical social potential by encompassing concrete dynamics of recognition in relationships of love, rights, and solidarity. In Habermas's abstract and formal proceduralist account, intersubjectivity becomes an anonymous and impersonal space for the exchange of reasons. It misses for Honneth the facticity and close relational bonds of ethical life and interpersonal relations visible in relations of care, esteem, friendship, respect, and solidarity. There is no separation, no adequate sense of concrete self and concrete other, in formalized intersubjectivity.[66] Honneth stresses, as a correction to the overly cognitivist and formalist tendencies of Habermas's discourse ethics, the dialectical character of processes of recognition and incorporates elements of what he considers to be the ethics of alterity, such as the asymmetrical care of parents for children.[67] Honneth has conceptualized solidarity as surpassing passive and negative understandings of tolerance. His account of a dialectic of recognition encompassing struggle and solidarity, which expresses not only tolerance but a "felt concern for what is individual and particular about the other person," offers elements of a richer and more appropriate ethics than seen in Habermas's formalistic communicative ethics.[68] Honneth, as argued above, has not gone far enough. Honneth's critical yet sympathetic correction of Habermas's discourse ethics through the logic of recognition can be pushed further by returning to the asymmetrical ethics of nonidentity indicated in the works of Adorno and Levinas.

Habermas conceives rationality as the practice of reflexive justification that is impossible to avoid in communication. Interpersonal communication provides the kernel for formal, procedural rationality and deliberative democracy.[69] Adorno emphasized doing justice to the object and reality rather than communication that must fail as a criterion of truth.[70] To recall the argumentation of part 1 of this work and think further with Adorno and Levinas, let us turn to a discussion of procedural reason and deliberative democracy. These are incomplete without the persistent reminder of their interpersonal and prophetic dimensions (part 2) as well as suffering and happiness as the contents of sensuous and material life (part 1). Democracy does not only signify the decentered society and pluralistic public sphere described by Habermas.[71] Pluralism can serve as a mask for power relations, as Adorno notes, yet a better society must be pluralistic.[72] Democracy calls further for decentered and diverse forms of rationality, argumentation, and deliberation—forms that are open to the affective and sensuous dimensions of human life—to pose the infinite prophetic and diagnostic demands of justice and the promise of happiness—articulated through the self-critique of religion (as articulated in part 2) in Levinas and the creative critical mimesis (as elucidated in part 1 above) in art, literature, and music in Adorno—to the existing social-political totality.[73]

In Levinas's thinking, there is a regard for the other that is higher than formal procedural norms of participation and mere tolerance of others, just as there is a welcoming hospitality and generosity that is more fundamental than the hospitality of cosmopolitanism.[74] In such asymmetrical and potentially tense encounters between self and other, the unique is confronted and engaged with the unique instead of being a particular occurrence subsumed within a universal law or order regulating warfare, travel, trade, and migration. Such freedom comes at a bitter cost to those who were forcibly opened up to the "free trade" and missionaries that paved the way for colonization.

Even without adopting the exaggerated accusative radicalness that Levinas's language can express, his ethical-political reflections reveal another variety of cosmopolitanism divergent from both nationalistic and cosmopolitan forms of identity that either reject or assimilate the other. A cosmopolitanism of the other person would differ from metaphysical and Enlightenment conceptions grounded in the philosophy of the autonomous subject and the "properly human" that too narrowly defines what is of worth and dignity.[75] As human rights are universal, the other is debased, the face and image disfigured, and constructed as an enemy of humanity and human rights to legitimate violence. This tendency consists of the growing facelessness of war, from mechanized war to drone warfare with its pragmatic legitimation of dehumanized and defaced targets.

Hospitality beyond Liberal Rights

If the philosophers of alterity and nonidentity discussed in this chapter—namely, Adorno, Derrida, and Levinas—and their modernistic critique of modernity are correct, centering cosmopolitanism and tolerance in the self cannot but fail due to the inherent paradox of a universalism that is contradicted by its being grounded in and overtly and tacitly committed to the prejudices of the conditional and partial perspective of the modern "universal" self-satisfied and smug and yet empty and hollow liberal subject—the banality of one-dimensional existence—characteristic of the relentlessly commodified form of life in capitalism. This conception of the self is defined through its right to persevere in existence (*conatus essendi*), which overwhelms any harm principle that would protect others, and its practices and notions of freedom and power that compel the subject to be incapable of being genuinely open to and affirmative toward material others in the ethical concretion of their singular ipseity.

Advanced capitalism continues to rearrange and redistribute its classic problems of alienation and exploitation—as analyzed by Marx from his early writings to *Capital*—without the capacity to overcome its fundamental crises. These crisis tendencies and fractures become visible each time capitalism stagnates and cannot hide its systematic inequities.[76] Given the exteriority and "other-constitution" explored throughout this work, in contrast to the idealistic tendencies in Marxism in search of a collective identity and subject, such as the free association of producers or the proletariat, the conditional, nonidentical, and infinite self or subject is disentangled and unfolded in relation to what it is not. The subject is consequently not as universal or neutral as it is ideologically construed to be in its experience and conception of its own world (*cosmos*) and political community (*polis*).

The strategies that this work has pursued through interpretations of Adorno and Levinas contest the development of Habermas's new intersubjective paradigm for critical social theory, which was intended to replace the materialism and lingering Marxist elements of its previous paradigm. Recall that Habermas's early writings (such as *The Structural Transformation of the Public Sphere*, published in German in 1962) were concerned with how capitalism endangered democracy and how the undemocratic elements of capitalist markets, ideologically obscured through ideas such as *laissez-faire*, could be democratically kept in check.[77] As his thought turned away from Marxian categories, already evident in *Legitimation Crisis*, which partially recognized yet failed to adequately address the severity of the environmental-ecological crisis tendencies that had already concerned Adorno, and became increasingly centered in ethical and political liberalism, Habermas's critical diagnosis of the distortions of democracy under capitalism weakened even if they did not entirely disappear.[78]

More recently, to consider one example, Habermas claimed, "Since 1989–90, it has become impossible to break out of the universe of capitalism; the only option is to civilize and tame the capitalist dynamics from within."[79] Habermas problematically links radical alternatives to capitalism with state-socialism: its collapse entails the disappearance of the radical critique of capitalism and the necessity of internal moderating-limits that do not confront its underlying structures. The competition of the capitalist and communist worlds had kept the excesses of capitalism in check up until the early 1990s.[80] For Habermas, an irresolvable tension between democracy and the market takes place because they are governed by different conflicting principles.[81] The alternative to a guided managerial democracy, bereft of genuine forms of participation and governed for the sake of elites, is the (political) liberal control of (economic) liberalism for Habermas, even as globalized capitalism heightens the devastation of its ecological, social, and cultural antagonisms and contradictions that are marked in the very bodies and minds of its subjects.

Conclusion

There are alternative options to the limited overly anthropocentric intersubjective strategy developed by Habermas and Honneth, as this work has repeatedly shown: by returning to earlier critical theorists of the Frankfurt school, particularly Adorno's articulation of a disintegrative dialectic suspicious of identity, the critique of capitalism—as unrestrained dominance over the means of production and communication—can be rejuvenated in conjunction with an ethics of difference that contests the logic of exchange through interruptive moments—to adopt the language of Levinas—of generosity, hospitality, and welcoming.

The alternative interpretive strategies outlined throughout this work, based on critically reinterpreting the thought of Adorno and Levinas, point to a critical materialist *ethos* of an an-archic and unrestrained solidarity—not limited to a republic of rational spirits or community of communicative and dialogical agents—between material existents.

The good occurs in ethical exposure, disrupting and potentially reorienting self and society, immanently within yet aporetically irreducible to being, its unity or multiplicity, or other ontological determinations. The promise of happiness in Adorno and the prophetically intimated good "beyond being" in Levinas, the good that is not the one, transpire in material life itself as a site imperfectly constituted in and contradicted and contested by ethical and social-political demands. Nourishing and cultivating the life of material others is demanded in fairer forms of the exchange and distribution of goods and of intersubjective and interthingly recognition.

Chapter Fourteen

Recognition, Nonidentity, and the Contradictions of Liberalism

Introduction: The Crises of Contemporary Forms of Life

Individual and collective action appears incapable of responding to the worsening ecological and social-political crisis tendencies of contemporary liberal capitalist societies. The entanglements of natural history and global life cannot be avoided, as the new nativists and nationalists contend. The globe is faced with contradictions and crisis tendencies of the environment and nonhuman and human animal life, repressive pathologies of religion that undo its prophetic aspirations, and social-political inequities and injustices that current instrumental steering and political movements have been unable to adequately answer in theory or in practice.

What would "adequate" signify in this contemporary nexus of crisis tendencies, given how incomplete and deficient human responsiveness and responsibility for animal well-being and environments has been? It would mean at the minimum contesting systematically reproduced damaged life and restricted solidarities (limited to communities of identity), but more is needed than the minimum. Liberalism, as described in the present work, is ideally concerned with defending negative liberties from the external coercion of the state or community and historically intertwined with capitalist forms of exploitation and domination. It has been historically and theoretically significant insofar as it has emphasized in theory the rights of each individual even as it has in practice undermined others' rights in the name of the hegemonic form of individuality through which actually existing individuals are forced to conform and are damaged and debased.[1] This is an insight not only expressed in Adorno, whose work critically exposes it in ways yet to be adequately appreciated. In the case of Levinas, liberalism is a necessary (as linked with human rights) yet insufficient (since it inadequately guarantees these rights) moment for political philosophy, as Annabel Herzog has shown, in response to modern economic, political, and social forms of oppression it has inadequately opposed and even legitimated.[2]

Classical liberalism, as the primacy of self-interested possessive selves (the conatus), endures in contemporary liberalism in its complexly intertwined nativist and neoliberal variations. Adorno presciently diagnosed in a 1967 lecture the persisting peril of rightwing extremism. Rightist radicalism demands its own freedoms, construed as negative liberties that cannot be restricted even by harming others, for its own actions while denying them from others. Various forms of liberalism have been fundamentally inadequate in addressing their own complicity with and perpetuation of the contemporary crisis tendencies of the environment and social-political life. Liberal forms of life are unable to address their own self-produced crisis tendencies.[3] Further, the necessity and teleology of idealist and progressive philosophies of history (whether liberal or Marxist) no longer guarantee a happy ending, as the species itself is in question and at stake. Jane Gordon and Lewis Gordon have articulated how ecological and social disasters are ubiquitous, and prophetic warnings pervasive.[4] Yet these signs and hints have not yet been adequately heard.

The Good and the Subject

How can damaged life address its own vulnerability and woundedness, given the end of nature, the loss of guaranteed hope through religion and historical progress, and the injustices of systems and theories of justice? In Adorno's strategies of dialectical negativity and Levinas's strategies of exposure to exteriority and alterity, there are intimations of nourishing life in the midst of natural history and life's damages and incompletion, as well as an infinite and unrestricted solidarity in response to ethnic, gendered, religious, and other forms of restricted identity-based fraternity and absorbed affiliation. The expression "unrestricted" is not only a norm or a value but is entangled with material and social relations.

It has been interpreted in the present work as contesting the fixed and fixating individual and collective subject, which seeks to determine its situation yet cannot, through others' ethical priority in the discourse of Levinas and the formalization, experimentation, mimetic responsiveness, and freedom toward and felt contact with the object in its priority in Adorno's lectures and writings on aesthetics, dialectics, and nonidentity.

Levinas's analysis of fraternity, despite its limitations that led to it being reimagined in the present work as unrestricted solidarity, shatters the republican confines of this concept in thematizing an excess of sociality and love that contests the ethical solitude of restricted and self-absorbed individual and collective subjects.[5] Levinas's "an-archic" or unrestricted good radically challenges not only ethnic, national, and religious identities, and the institutionalization of power in the state, but also ultimately overly restrictive visions of the collective subject—which have strategic emancipatory importance in challenging existing forms of power that can be reified into new forms of power, such as the proletariat in Marxism, the hierarchical vanguard party in Leninism, Marcuse's intersectional new forces, or Adorno's critical intellectuals. At the same time that the subject is constitutively and necessarily imperfect in relation to the good, the good itself can take on ideological forms justifying and excusing what is not good. Adorno is right to emphasize how the good is in danger of reification in the assumed taken for granted good, and that there is no good without the risk of evil.[6]

The three parts of this volume have traced the tensions and paradoxes of discourses of nature, religion, and justice. Each part has illustrated the questionable ethical character of conventional liberal accounts—based on the idea of an independent possession-driven private individual—of nature, religion, and justice. To expand on Adorno's insight, the internationalized liberal order is constructed according to the model of negotiating a "good deal" between private interests that are predictably those of stronger parties and that have detrimental consequences for individuals, communities, species, and ecosystems.

Theorists and ideologues of the contemporary order have failed to satisfactorily address in current crisis conditions (1) the use of animals and environments; (2) aesthetic, ethical, and religious experiences of the self; and (3) the justice that is indicated in the prophetic encounter with suffering and injustice. I have accordingly argued for a different strategy to reconsider the discourses of nature, religion, and justice in the context of (1) the nonidentity thinking, negative dialectics, and materialist critical social theory of Adorno, and (2) the asymmetrical ethics of alterity of Levinas.

Repeating the Question: Why Adorno? Why Levinas?

First, to return to queries posed at the outset in the introduction, why has the thinking of Adorno been stressed in this volume? Adorno's expansive materialist critique of morality and language of *minima moralia*—in contrast to the *magna moralia* of traditional ethics—is turned against conventional bourgeois moralities that reify and harm the ethical life of individuals through their material and social structural operation. Adorno's critique of ethics as ideological is not only bitter pessimism. It is ethically motivated by the aspirations and hopes of damaged life for better ways of living that have been systematically undermined and deferred in contemporary societies.[7]

The concern for the nonidentical submerged by identity orients Adorno's challenge to the liberal notion of equality that is pursued for the equality of alterity. Perpetuating injustice through justice and irrationality through rationality, equality without alterity is, Adorno notes, blind to the systematic inequalities that it helps perpetuate: "An equality in which differences perish secretly serves to promote inequality; it becomes the myth that survives amidst an only seemingly demythologized humanity."[8] In the midst of a critique of existential authenticity and nostalgic melancholy in Martin Heidegger and Karl Jaspers, Adorno describes how the liberal conception of equality legitimates violence against those who do not conform to its model and persevere in maintaining equal status: "bourgeois equality, always turned into injustice for those who could not entirely keep up."[9] Adorno justifies this critique of liberal equality for the sake of the realization of a more genuine social equality that embraces rather than subjugates and represses variance: "[O]ur critique of the inequality within equality aims at equality too, for all our skepticism of the rancor involved in the bourgeois egalitarian ideal that tolerates no qualitative difference."[10]

Second, why has this volume devoted attention to Levinas, given the many interpretive problems related to the political significance of his thought? Levinas is, as seen throughout this work, the opposite of the moralizing and ethically privileged perfectionist imagined by his detractors. Ethics does not consist in moralistic perfection, not even as a regulative ideal, but in the "saintliness," "genuine humanity," and the "greatest perfection" that transpires in the insufficiency and incompletion of everyday life in ordinary acts in which one places the other before oneself.[11] This nonperfectionist reconstruction of Levinas's intersections and tensions with Adorno has revealed how ethics is the concern of the imperfect rather than the perfect, of suffering life rather than self-satisfied life. Interrogating the ethical in the wake of the Second World War and the Holocaust, Levinas refuses to segregate the ethical from processes of exchange, commerce, violence, and war making.[12] As Levinas elucidates in the conclusion to *Existence and Existents*, the gravest sin and reification is to reduce and fixate personal existence to a time and place in the present.[13] The "I" asymmetrically encounters the thou without communion and mediation, being outside itself and receiving the other's face and name that breaks the anonymity of being, while the I and thou are materially and intersubjectively entangled with one another, the third party, and the world. Levinas accordingly neither ignores confronting ethics with such powers nor does he moralistically construct or legislate a social utopia of perpetual peace in the sense of utopia criticized by Adorno or Bloch in their thinking of critical models (Adorno) and a self-critical utopianism (Bloch) that imagines, hopes, and dreams otherwise in the midst of domination and devastation.

Levinas confronts us with how "war suspends morality" and is the ultimate ordeal from "which morality lives."[14] He imagines at times a Hobbesian situation without a Hobbesian response to it. Instead of the absolute state establishing peace, when it can only perpetuate war, ethics immanently begins in confrontation with egoism, violence, and war in Levinas, correlating with how aspirations for undamaged life commences in Adorno in a damaged life with all of its barriers, degradations, and impediments. Rather than projecting, reifying, and idealizing a telos of moral perfection, Levinas considers a saying that is "made without compromise, and without a secret betrayal" while being unable to evade betrayal and indiscretion of the saying that must become the said.[15] The responsiveness of saying is fixated in the said in a parallel way to how the ethical is solidified in society.[16] In Levinas, accordingly, as Derrida and Raffoul bring to our attention, the ethical is articulated in relation to its own impossibility—in the non- and antiethical—in violence, trauma, and war, and in conditionality, complicity, and betrayal.[17] This constant undoing of the ethical demands us—when we encounter and are confronted by someone else—to undo it as in the "unsaying" (*dédire*) of the neutral semantic content of the said (*le dit*). Yet there is no ethical saying that is not difficult and without the risks of solidification, complicity, and betrayal, and to which it is the other who reawakens the self. The self cannot be ethically self-sufficient no matter how perfect and virtuous it strives or imagines itself to be. The self is incessantly referred back to others. The paradigms of ethical perfectionism and virtue ethics are inadequate to the ethical encounter insofar as they presuppose the priority of the self instead of the ethical demand that the other places on the self. Levinas offers a model of ethical insufficiency and incompletion to interrogate the self's self-concern, self-obsession, and self-promotion in ordinary hierarchical ethical theories and forms of moral life that justify violence or neglect of the other.

The thinking of Adorno and Levinas transpires in the shadows of world wars and destruction and annihilation.[18] Their writings are not only of interest to intellectual history. They offer critical models to contest liberal modernity's complicity with economic and social power and its betrayals of its own personalist and democratic aspirations. These betrayals are not accidental but necessitated by the negative understanding of the individual as prior to and independent of ethical sociality. The reconstruction of their thought indicates a way to respond to the need for alternative ethical and political models.

Levinas shares in the personalist aspirations of liberalism while critiquing its limiting conception of the person. Levinas describes in *Totality and Infinity* how "[t]he pathos of liberalism, which we rejoin on one side, lies in the promotion of a person inasmuch as he represents nothing further, that is, is precisely a self."[19] For Levinas, a just society must be oriented and re-oriented toward living up to the demands of the other person.[20] Reading Levinas with and against him lead us to an ethics and politics of material others. Given the totalizing tendencies, limitations, and crisis tendencies of liberal capitalism with regard to nature, religion, and justice, the liberal vision of the person requires a more thoroughgoing prophetic ethics of the material other than it is capable of providing within the boundaries of its adversarial paradigm of competitive struggle: it requires a radically an-archic *res publica*, a republicanism of unrestricted civil associations, public spheres, and solidarities that contests the overreaching powers of the state, the market, and manufactured public opinion. A critical model of asymmetrical solidarities resists modern social-political pathologies such as leveling solidarity to the sameness of a collective identity, a set of interchangeable equivalents, or reciprocal exchange.[21] A solidarity without constraints contests the logic of symmetry and exchange, as—according to Adorno—the exchange principle underlies the principle of identity that does not occur as an ahistorical constant but has diverging incarnations in different configurations of the organization of the forces and relations of production.[22]

The Contradictions of Contemporary Liberalism

> One can be both liberal and reactionary at the same time in the most comfortable way.
>
> —Karl Marx, "Leading Article in No. 179 of the *Kölnische Zeitung*," July 10, 1842

Standard liberal systems presuppose and reproduce the appropriation of nonhuman and human life, as it steers and manages surface conflicts and competitions without contesting the restraints that disallow deeper interventions into materially and socially reproduced structures of domination and exploitation. Adorno and Horkheimer depicted in the *Dialectic of Enlightenment* how the liberal value of universal humanity functions as an apology for the inhumanity of the existing order with which it is more than complicit.[23] The liberal project of eliminating rage for stabilizing the peace of the free and equal exchange between private persons atavistically becomes a vengeful rage against all those who do not conform to its bourgeois ideal of humanity and business as usual.

The current market-oriented neoliberal social-cultural order that dominates the globe, and shapes even its ethnocentric critics and neonationalist opponents, is centered in the metaphysics of possessive individualism and is also involved in an ambivalent recourse to both abstract cosmopolitan internationalism and nationalist appeals to communal patriotism. Cosmopolitanism and internationalism are demanded of others while preserving patriotism and nationalism for oneself. Can the opposite be the case? Instead of rejecting cosmopolitanism for nativism or nationalism, can there be "another cosmopolitanism," a universalism capable of generating new normative models, as Seyla Benhabib and other contemporary philosophers have proposed?[24] One that is for the sake of others rather than a disguise for the exercise of power? Is such a cosmopolitanism that contests restricted borders and solidarities possible? Is it a consequence of how Levinas and Derrida think the idea of a hospitality as either infinitely demanding or nonexistent?[25]

A cosmopolitanism of the other would be not only concerned with the universal and abstract justice; it would respond to the singularity and particularity of those forgotten and suppressed by the universal as incarnated in the current social-political order. The "real is the rational" and "the state is the real" become condemnations rather than justifications in critical materialist social reflection from Marx to Adorno. Likewise, in the current situation, modern liberalism has been complicit with economic concentration (totalization) and an internationalism that privileges the particularities of the powerful while targeting the particularisms of the weak. The theoretical distinction between illiberal nationalism and enlightened patriotism does not hold in actual practice. Due to its own internally generated paradoxes and inability to countenance genuine alterity—as something other than an object of choice, exchange, and consumption—the neoliberal capitalist international system is compelled through the compulsive desire to own and consume to undermine and devalue the values of freedom, justice, and tolerance that it posits as its highest ideals and deploys to legitimate international violence.

To revise the portrait offered by Adorno and Horkheimer in the 1940s, liberal capitalism manifests its covert neocolonialism, racism, and sexism—which accord with its adversarial logic of competition and self-assertion—in the struggle to reproduce entrenched power and markets.[26] In liberal racism, which posits fair exchange as its ultimate value, the racialized other is animalized and vilified in the name of justice and universal values to excuse and legitimate marginalization, oppression, and violence. Jean-Paul Sartre noted in his analysis of the liberal legitimation of racism and colonialism how liberalism turns its opponents and enemies into "subhumans" in a state of war outside of ethics: "[O]ne of the functions of racism is to compensate the latent universalism of bourgeois liberalism: since all human beings have the same rights, the Algerian will be made a subhuman."[27] The racializing tendency of liberalism, pointed out by Adorno, Sartre, and more recent figures, such as Giorgio Agamben and Judith Butler, remains visible in contemporary Western liberal discourses about its Others whose particularity is denounced in the name of universal values to excuse oppression and war in the name of civilization.[28] The dehumanizing projection of others constructs persons as objects of "just wars" and drone strikes, of calculative manipulation and elimination, in the technocratic managerial planning characteristic of liberal warfare.[29]

Political liberalism is at its most liberal (in the sense of generous, hospitable, and tolerant) when it feels secure in its power. It cannot systematically achieve this condition of equilibrium because of the compulsive capitalist logic of competition and accumulation that—as compulsive, forced, and restrained—belies its principle of laissez-faire. Adorno's studies of the pathologies of the "authoritarian personality" in the United States of the 1940s remain pertinent in clarifying the regressive character of universalistic liberalism and its abstract conception of the private self-interested person; liberalism turns into authoritarianism and totalitarianism, and Enlightenment ideals turn into prejudice when liberal modernity's all-comprehensive and exclusive vision is threatened and endangered.[30] As illuminated in part 1, Hegel penetratingly diagnosed in the *Phenomenology of Spirit* the contradictions of an Enlightenment movement unenlightened about its own presuppositions and prejudiced about its other.[31] In *The Dialectic of Enlightenment*, which adopted Hegelian strategies from the *Phenomenology*, Horkheimer and Adorno expose the dogmas of liberal modernity in its own immanent self-critique in contrast to the nondialectical and dogmatic opposition of faith and reason, tradition and innovation, and the old and the new.[32]

Due to its ultimately competitive adversarial vision of individualism interlinked with the concentration of capital and power, which correlates with the dynamic of possession and consumption, capitalist liberalism with its fundamental right of the *conatus essendi* legitimates conflict, intervention, and war. Abstract liberal arguments against oppression that leave capitalist forms of power essentially unquestioned are complicit with systems of subjugation that exploit, marginalize, and systematically reinforce powerlessness and the vulnerability. They are compelled to sustain the machinery of globalized capitalism; its systematic control of temporality and spatiality revealed in anxiety, ennui, fatigue, and insomnia; and its destruction of environments and living beings through the "free play" of economic forces that are simultaneously social-political processes in an epoch defined by social and cultural reproduction.

Historical forms of republicanism have exaggerated the roles of fraternity, solidarity, and the collective good in overly narrow visions of collectivism that overwhelm individuals and those who do not belong to this identity. As conceived in the current reconstructions of Levinas and heterodox forms of Marxism in Benjamin, Bloch, and Rosa Luxemburg (see chapter 9), radical republicanism contests restricted affiliations and identities. The priority of the rights of others before the right of the self and the self-same community contests the modern paradigm of right based in the self, its conatus, and self-assertion in the struggle for existence.[33] The intensification and transformation of radically "an-archic" (that is, without grounding or foundations) republicanism in response to the material other, and the prophetic immanent good within damaged suffering life, in the present volume entails that the res publica be unlimited by identity and its claims. A republic of alterities (instead of a collective general will) and material others has an emancipatory potential lacking in standard liberalisms that undermine, narrow, and block solidarity through capitalist social organization and, at the theoretical level, negative accounts of individual identity, self-interested liberty, and the prioritization of the self-concerned individual person (see chapter 12).[34]

If the state of affairs interrogated in this volume is indeed the situation of the contemporary world unified and in tension through processes of globalization, then it is time to reevaluate cosmopolitanism and tolerance with respect to the self's nonidentity and asymmetry with the other, and the cosmopolitanism of multiethnic empires in relation to the cosmopolitanisms of the colonized and semicolonized who—in Sun Yat-Sen's imagery—must be more than "loose sand" exploited by those with power who end up being the particular meat and fish under the knife of the universal in order for there to be, to speak with Hannah Arendt and Levinas, another an-archic form of cosmopolitanism and internationalism of the other.[35]

The Boundaries of Universalism and the Singularity of the Material Other

Against its own emancipatory and prophetic tendencies that orient the critique of liberalism as an ideological disguise for various forms of oppression, universalism can function regressively as a false ideological pretense of possessing the universal while acting to maintain the partial and limited perspectives of those benefited by that universality. The universalizing ethics of cosmopolitanism and humanism accordingly must be persistently interrogated regarding its interconnection and complicity with power and the ideological justification of existing forms of globalized exploitation and domination (see chapter 13).

Universalism can function as a mask for the powerful in modern Western colonial empires that enslaved and eliminated entire populations. Colonial capitalism simultaneously strives for respectability and universality while exercising the systematized brutality that Marx described of the British Empire in South Asia.[36] Anticolonial nationalisms could operate as vehicles of resistance for subjugated peoples in Africa, Asia, and Latin America. Philosophical critics of colonialism such as Dussel and Fanon contested the priority of European cosmopolitan humanity.[37] Fanon, for instance, linked the weakness of national consciousness with the cosmopolitan attitude forced upon the colonized and oppressed, resulting in passivity and mediocrity.[38] Sun Yat-Sen's worries and Fanon's critical analysis of Western cosmopolitan colonialism remain trenchant: given the systematic dysfunctional characteristics of internationalism and cosmopolitanism in the developing world, there are good reasons to be suspicious of the good intentions of a universalism that legitimates an unjust international order that systematically impoverishes a majority of humanity. A reasonable and realistic unease consequently exists with this incarnation of the universal, especially when it is framed in the language of universal justice and equality insofar as they are made to serve purposes of subjugation, which not only fails to acknowledge but perpetuates systemic violence against the singular lives of others in their concrete and contingent specificities and situations.

Regimes of abstract universal justice function as a means of domination when applied without a sense of difference and asymmetry to those who do not conform to its image of the universal. The identity thinking of universalism lacks appropriate responsiveness and responsibility toward the palpable suffering and happiness of materially conditioned others who necessarily "live from" the elemental and sensuous material life. Ethics is more than a discursive exchange of reasons that risks ignoring the voiceless and inarticulate, the subaltern and other. Therefore, there is no genuine ethics that is not a material ethics addressing the sufferings and needs of sentient material life. The singularized suffering of the other should be differentiated from what Adorno criticized as the neutralization of suffering when it becomes an external object of calculation and exchange in the liberal conception of utility and the generalized happiness of primarily private interests and the negative liberties that protect them.[39]

Justice without variance to actual abjection and need and Otherness without material alterities serve to excuse oppression in the name of formal universal equality. This is not only expressed in Marx's point in the *Critique of the Gotha Program* (1875) that the "equal right" of formal equality is inadequate insofar as a genuinely social democratic society must address each individual according to their needs and material circumstances.[40] Levinas exposes how an apparently perfectly just state is oppressive insofar as it homogenizes and undoes the ethical relation: each is subordinated to administration, becoming equal as an instrumental object of technique, or excluded in being constructed as the enemy to be eliminated.[41] The state and its administration mobilize and utilize persons as resources without regard for their need and suffering, which they deem to be of secondary concern to the demands of national self-interest, social utility, and disciplinary forms of justice (to return to a quote discussed in the conclusion of chapter 6):

> But the gratuitous meaninglessness of pain already shows beneath the reasonable forms espoused by the social "uses" of suffering, which in any case do not diminish the outrage of the torture that strikes the psychically handicapped, isolating them in their pain. Behind the rational administration of pain in the penalties meted out by human courts, which immediately begin to look suspiciously like repression, the arbitrariness and strange failure of justice amidst wars, crimes, and the oppression of the weak by the strong, rejoin, in a sort of fatality, the useless suffering that springs from natural plagues, as if they were the effects of an ontological perversion.[42]

Ethics is oriented and reoriented by the material concrete other, such that all ethics is in essence an ethics of alterity, and the material life and tangible happiness and suffering of others. As stated earlier in the analysis of Adorno's ethics of suffering life and the promise of happiness in part 1, excusing and forgetting suffering is part of the destructive realization of the highest political ideas of equality, liberty, and solidarity. Truth is not a neutral positivist fact or ontological event for Adorno; it contests the reification of positivity to come closer to the object.[43] This is truth's ethical core and function. Truth is entangled with need, suffering, and injustice: "The need to let suffering speak is a condition of all truth. For suffering is objectivity that weighs upon the subject."[44]

The Other in the Dialectic of Recognition and Misrecognition

Despite the inherent cleaving of ethics and politics, described above, discourses of consensus (Habermas) and recognition (Honneth) should be referred to the horizon of material life and its suffering and happiness. Impersonal neutral justice is constitutive of legal and political fairness. At the same time, it presupposes and is in need of relentless reminder of the interpersonal ethical relationship and its prophetic concern for goodness and happiness as material orienting points to dislocate the spell of the reified forces and structures of commodified damaged and even mutilated life.[45] This is the prophetically inspired, emerging from the wounds of life itself for Adorno, prevalence of infinite an-archic justice that potentially disturbs and reorients the finite and limited justice of the state and its institutions.

The bodily material other is nonuniversalizable in its ethical singularity. Insofar as the material other is not merely one more particular subsumable under a universal category or law, including those of consensus, equality, and inclusion, justice without alterity fails to adequately respond to the other. This other in its nonadequation and nonsynchrony surpasses myself and the social totality and is excessively more than a reflection or negation of myself. In the excess of my responsibility, the other is more than the negatively defined freedom and privacy of classical Lockean liberal thought. The other who is not recognized and domesticated as another myself can be a dangerous disturbance, or perceived as such, to the self's understanding and enactment of the relation between self and other.

The occurrence of recognition and understanding are informed by the differences and asymmetries of those involved in a concrete nexus of circumstances. Processes of recognition are based in the assertion of the self and struggle for its social identity. They accordingly do not adequately encounter and distinguish the other as Other. Furthermore, control of and violence toward the other can be enacted and exercised in processes of recognition in which an equitable resolution is not guaranteed. The discourse of recognition, whether recognition is conceptualized as the agonistic struggle for being acknowledged by the other or dialogical mutual understanding, is haunted by the seemingly intractable facticity and deeply rooted systemic character of misrecognition. The self that ought to recognize the other might well be constitutively or systematically implicated in power, defined by self-interest, or conditioned by finitude, such that dialectical reversals of power and dialogical communication do not conclude with free and uncoerced reconciliation for each but a different configuration of power to incorporate and exclude.

The models of intersubjective recognition from Hegel to Honneth capture aspects of the dynamics of social life while remaining insufficient. The dialectic of misrecognition and recognition cannot be reconciled or stabilized, as the socially more powerful party demands and receives more recognition than the other party, and contemporary world spirit and liberal states have yet to adequately address real inequities in resources and recognition. Primacy is given to the one in the stronger position until the moment of its weakness, when it is overcome by another power, rather than there being an immanent transformation through the other, goodness, or justice. The dynamics of recognition threaten the perpetuation of violence toward and power over the subaltern and marginal, the dominated and exploited, by processes of not only exclusion but also inclusion, for instance, by representing and assuming their voices for them and yet—through their actual social-political location and their perceived silence—against them.

Beyond Consensus and Recognition: The An-archic Ethics of Material Others

Has unfolding the intersections between the philosophies of two pivotal twentieth-century European thinkers in this way (i.e., in interchange about nature, religion, and justice) been worthwhile?

First, Adorno and Levinas suggestively contested discourses of absorbed participation in identity (including those of consensus and recognition that need to be rethought in the context of mimesis, responsiveness, and solidarity without identification) and the philosophies of first principles, origins, and their "archic" order and measure. Their strategies challenge ideological appeals to the reenchantment of a disenchanted world or a return to the ostensibly archaic and primeval that has been constructed as "first" and "originary."

Second, despite the flourishing of discourses of alterity, difference, and nonidentity in contemporary continental philosophy, the context, significance, and consequences of these concepts require further conceptual and practical clarification.

This volume has endeavored to contribute to this task in tracing the thinking of difference and the material other with respect to the ethical and political dimensions of nature, religion, and social justice. It has sought to elucidate their ethical sources and implications by examining nonidentity thinking in Adorno's critical social theory and asymmetrical ethics in Levinas's thinking toward the other, which together—in all of their dissonances and tensions that resist reduction to a common identity and unity—has led to the explication in this work of an ethics of material others. The critical reflections and diagnoses delineated in the three parts of this volume indicate strategies for interpreting the ethical tensions operative in discourses of nature, religion, and justice with the intention of elucidating an aporetic ethics in/of "tension" and "im-possibility."[46]

Previous chapters of this volume have disclosed how Adorno and Levinas offer differing yet overlapping strategies for addressing how alterity, asymmetry, and aporia structure and destructure everyday existence and the systematically produced damages and distortions of "ethical life" (Sittlichkeit) and the lifeworld (Lebenswelt)—which require both decolonizing and intercultural revaluation—and have traced ways of reinterpreting in an ecological-environmental (in part 1) and in an an-archic materialist way (in parts 1 through 3).[47]

"An-archic" (without an ordering origin or foundation) indicates the disruptive advent of the transcendent good and prophetic call for justice inside the immanence, incompletion, and insufficiency of damaged life, and "materialism" (as constitutive, negative, and resistant in Adorno's discourse) is to be understood in an expansive, dynamic, negative dialectical sense of relational material life in confrontation with its damages. The good is aporetically interwoven with material life. Ethical an-archy signifies in this context the infinite and unrestricted solidarity of material life (intimated in the formalization of expressive and mimetic responsiveness in art, communication, and play as Adorno describes) that haunts and challenges not only capitalism but its statist and state-capitalist reification and institutionalization as well. The solidarity of nourishing life, after our reconsideration of the implications of the ethics of Adorno and Levinas, signifies an ethical demand to nourish the the ecological, economic, and social conditions of the life of material others.

Epilogue

Nourishing Life, Unrestricted Solidarity, and the Good

Against Perfection: Ethical Incompletion and the Good

This volume has not offered a prescriptive or descriptive theory of morality. Ethics, as the other's demand, does not issue commands, prescribe principles and rules, nor regulate behaviors; nor does it rest in the virtue, purity, and perfection of an individual or collective subject. Ethics is, as Levinas describes, exposure to the other and the breaking down of essence and the order of being.[1] The chapters of this book have turned to alternative ethical models and strategies: namely, those of negativity in Adorno and otherness in Levinas, as well as others from a range of thinkers from Marx, Kierkegaard, and Nietzsche through Bloch, Løgstrup, and Murdoch to Derrida, Dussel, Habermas, and Honneth.

A reevaluation of the arguments from Adorno and Levinas as critical models has indicated (1) the natural historical entanglements from which nature and history are reductively abstracted and reified as matter and spirit; (2) the fundamental "other-constitution" of the self, such that the self is persistently beholden to others and material life; (3) the other's ethical appeal and demand addressing the self and calling for a response; and (4) the disturbance of the "other-power" (as radically other than and irreducible to the individual or collective subject) or the diachrony and transcendence of the good (without the moralistic perfectionism and ideological purity derided by Adorno) in ordinary acts of generosity and kindness as well as in unordinary acts for the other in the face of annihilation, exploitation, oppression, and violence.[2]

Adorno remarked in *Minima Moralia*, "Not only is the self entwined in society; it owes society its existence in the most literal sense."[3] The social constitution of the self has been modified in the present work through the broader concept of "other-constitution." The self is other-constituted in material and communicative relations; that is, in natural history in Adorno's sense elucidated in part 1. The insufficient and incomplete self is constituted outside itself in the exteriority of its material and ethical relations. It is fundamentally yet imperfectly interpolational, relational yet asymmetrical, in regard to others and objects, as well as the natural-historically entangled material and communicative conditions and structures that form its life. In its exposedness, its conditional worldly finitude, its diachronic incompletion, and its "imperfection," this self can awaken to and respond to demands made upon it in its encounters. The temporally and worldly embodied transient self is the locus where the good transpires and is revealed in the midst of ordinary language and everyday life (see the introduction and chapter 10).

Hilary Putnam notes how Levinas audaciously asserted that ethics radically lacked any epistemological or metaphysical grounding.[4] To revise his account of Levinas as a moral perfectionist, this absence of grounding is correlated with the diachronic autonomy of the good (without reducing it to human decisions, projects, and virtues) and the asymmetrical ethical realities described in the critical model of ethical imperfectionism: the ethical demand that addresses the self-concerned self in the midst of its folly, ignorance, and immorality.[5] In contrast to the mythology of the sovereign ego and its self-formation, the other-constitution of the self and the encounter with the other's demand are prior to and make possible both the moral perfectionist's construction of the good life and how best to realize it (an attitude Putnam identifies with Levinas) as well as constructions of the right and the just society by moral legislators and lawmakers.[6] In contrast with social planning and utopian construction, existing society itself indicates its other (a just society). Levinas's discourse of transcendence intersects here from the opposite direction with Adorno's radicalization of immanent negativity.

Given the multiplicity of natural historical entanglements, ethical encounters, and moral dilemmas, the ethical demand occurs in myriad ways. Its most fundamental form is its crudest, most material one, which, according to Levinas, is hunger. Hunger is an emptiness "that cannot be compensated for with the mere hearsay of what it demands."[7] The recognition of the elemental constitutive character of hunger shares a kinship with Bloch, who—as Habermas noted—interpreted hunger not only as the most fundamental need but also as the elementary energy of hope.[8] Adorno likewise remarked concerning the ethical priority of earthly sensuous hunger against the spiritual coldness that would ignore or dismiss it: "There is tenderness only in the coarsest demand: that no-one shall go hungry any more. Every other seeks to apply to a condition that ought to be determined by human needs, a mode of human conduct adapted to production as an end in itself."[9]

The Ethical and the Political Demand

As traced throughout the present work, the prophetic demand of goodness and justice in response to each singular one, regardless of their role and status, is oriented toward the past as well as the future in addressing the present and its suffering. The prophetic demand arises within natural (part 1), religious (part 2), and political (part 3) life and awakens that life to itself and its own responsibility.

Two different expressions of the prophetic demand can be accordingly distinguished: (1) the ethical demand of the personal other (asymmetrical interpersonal ethics), which is the primary demand described by Levinas and Løgstrup, yet which is not its exclusive form; and (2) the social-political demand of an unrestricted solidarity with material others (human and non-human social ethics), which has been developed in the present work from a study of the ethical and political implications of Adorno and Levinas. These two expressions of the demand, within the context of current ecological and social-political crisis tendencies, disclose how a transformation of modern (liberal, radical republican, socialist, and anarchist) political paradigms is necessary in response to the needfulness and distress of life in its the material and social conditionality.

How is the ethical demand answered within the totalizing enclosure of material and communicative conditions? How can an undamaged life be perceived within the confines and degradations of systematically damaged life, and encountered within the systematic management and manipulation of life by economic, political, and cultural systems? The self-power of subjects appears to offer little resistance, as their desires and sacrifices conform to the imperatives of the system. If not in the spontaneity of the individual will or in the collective social will of classical republicanism and Marxism, where can resistance arise? Can that which is other than and exterior to individual and social subjects and systems (the good) replace the idea of a collective human enterprise or a revolutionary subject making its own history and destiny?

The good does not replace the activity of individuals and collectives; it addresses them and makes demands on them in their incompletion. The general will of Rousseauian republicanism and the revolutionary agency of the proletariat in Marxism is not replaced by a new agent or subject producing its history and future. They are rather contested and reoriented in relation to the priority of the object (Adorno) and the other (Levinas). An altogether different conception of the subject itself is required due to its alterity and nonidentity. The interruptive and reorienting traces of the other-power of the autonomous good are revealed through material sensibility and prophecy, such as in the suffering of and responsiveness to material others. This good is "real" in being an ethical demand encountered in nonhuman and human others rather than as a natural, ontological, or metaphysical reality. As explored in part 2, in its sovereignty, the good (as infinite, invisible, and indefinable rather than constructed) prophetically places existing systems of relations and their injustices into question, calling for dwelling with and nurturing nonhuman and human forms of life—occurring in sensuous existence amid the elemental—in response to its natural-historical damagedness, fragility, nakedness, and vulnerability.

The abject, the criminalized, the excluded, the exploited, and the impoverished do not only make a demand to be addressed by bureaucratic social-steering mechanisms; they do not only appeal to the privileged; they can and do respond to the good. In this imperfectionist critical model, ethics is not the negation of the suffering that sickens and negates life, as feared by Nietzsche (see chapter 6). It is rather a response to suffering life for the sake of nourishing the life of others that is expressed in distinctive ways in Adorno's thinking of materiality and negativity and in Levinas thinking of sensuous elemental life and alterity (as elucidated in part 1).

Critical Natural History and the Ethics of Materiality

The critical model of natural history introduced in part 1 contests the separation of nature and spirit, the environment and humanity. The critical model of imperfectionist ethics challenges moral perfectionism's stratification and exclusion of others as secondary to disciplinary ideals of the individual self and the collective community. The perfections and imperfections of the self are not the primary ethical question, as the infinity of the good is beyond the purity and impurity, the perfections and imperfections, of the virtuous and unvirtuous, who both exist in ignorance and folly (see the introduction and chapter 10). The asymmetry of material life undoes rather than excuses stratified hierarchical social-political, interpersonal, and personal schemas. The asymmetry interrupts through the priority of object (Adorno), the other (Levinas), and the infinite good over the subject, the self, and the will, thereby contesting and unfixing not only communicative, deliberative, and other hierarchies but also the perfectionist elitism and stratification typical of prevalent forms of ethical theorizing and public life.

In the opening quotation of the introduction to this work, Dussel pertinently warned of the dangers of critical social theory forgetting the materiality of existence in reflection and undermining the negativity that is indispensable to the critique of oppressive practices, institutions, and social structures.[10] Dussel also emphasized how the negative materiality at work in Adorno by itself is insufficient for the critique of contemporary lifeworlds and their systematically reproduced problems. This book has pursued Dussel's insight into materiality and the negative in order to reconsider their import in Adorno's works in relation to sensuousness and alterity in Levinas's writings. This encounter has led to a critical ethics of the material other that is indebted to, betrays, and reimagines their discourses.

In the preceding reconstruction of Adorno's conception of immanent negativity and transformation, nourishing life (the asymmetrical yet mutual nurturing of other and self) is disclosed in the insufficiency, incompletion, imperfection, and "impurity" of life itself.[11] Ethics is antimoral in problematizing the disciplinary apparatus and ideology of moralistic purity and the moralizing disregard toward others. Ethical life is an issue of natural history, and does not require presupposing or constructing an originary essence, underlying nature, or ideal of individual or collective perfection to be employed as a measure. In the reconstruction in part 3 of Levinas's ethics of alterity and his metamorphosis of radical republicanism through alterity, the demand of unrestricted solidarity confronts restricted affiliations and identities.

To briefly crystalize five strategic points, this volume has endeavored to clarify the following issues:

1. How the reproduction and repetition of quotidian life, its habits, customs, and institutionalized practices, are challenged and haunted by interruptive moments of facticity, trauma, and violence, and constituted through nonidentity and materiality, asymmetry, and the material other;

2. how these unruly disruptive moments of aporetic opening and transcendence are already constitutive conditions of and in a sense immanent to natural, religious, and social-political life;

3. how the ethical materiality advocated in this reconstruction of Adorno and Levinas does not entail but problematizes the primacy of the logic of exchange value, sacrificial exchange, and the instrumental calculative rationality characteristic of modernity and contemporary commodified culture that impedes the cultivation of a more responsive culture of nature and the solidarity of material life;

4. the ethical and social-political implications of the impossibility of conventional identity-based understandings of ethics and politics (as nonidentity contests and unfixes reified and ideological claims to pure unchanging identities unmediated by material and ethical life); and

5. the continuing promise and boundaries of the strategies unfolded in the philosophies of Adorno and Levinas in relation to earlier and later thinkers and the complexities of the contemporary interpretive situation.

Closing Words: Political Ecology and Political Economy

In closing (and conclusions are only transitions and transformations) it should be noted that in addition to the asymmetrical ethics of nonidentity, a politics and a political economy of nonidentity and the material other oriented by a critical—instead of reductive—natural history is vital. The present environmental crisis threatens the end not only of the capitalist mode of production but of the species itself. This catastrophe has yet to be adequately addressed in the critical social theory of recent generations of the Frankfurt school.

Habermas is correct in *Legitimation Crisis* that one can no longer assume that changes in objective conditions, such as the economic crisis-conditions analyzed by Marx, produce subjective and intersubjective changes in consciousness and discourse sufficient to effect radical structural changes. Contemporary crisis-tendencies concern motivation, communication, rationality, and worldview, as Habermas insightfully portrays, but more fundamentally—to return to Marx via Adorno's reinterpretation that was reconstructed in part 1—the priority of the object to which intersubjectivity must respond: the becoming and inhabiting with of natural history, material life, and the life of species.[12] Adorno sees that focusing on intersubjective and interpersonal relations without sufficient attention to relations of power and material relations, which signifies a form of intersubjective idealism when it becomes the fundamental form of constitution, is inadequate for a critique of the administered world, its ideologies, and its inscription in bodies and practices.[13] Accordingly, a new critical natural-history and materialism are needed to confront the current predicament and potentially transform it. Present ecological crisis-tendencies have compelled us to repose questions of materiality, nature, and the object—under new conditions—that twentieth-century philosophical discourses, such as that of Habermas, believed they had overcome.

The environmental crises of the Anthropocene are not only produced by discourse, ideology, and thought, which is one dimension of response. In the Capitalocene, they are primarily (albeit not exclusively or reductively as in vulgar Marxism) ones of human practices and material relations with the nature that they themselves are.[14] A serious failing of communicative and intersubjective idealism (in the senses articulated in part 1) is consequently its inadequate attention to the materiality of the other, material ecological entanglements, and the political economy of capitalism, which includes the political economy of communication and relations of recognition that were more radically interrogated in Adorno's theorizing of commodification, consumerism, and the culture industry.[15]

The first task of elucidating the potential of an ethics of material others was the motivating theme unfolded throughout this contribution, which proposed an an-archic, asymmetrical, and prophetic ethics of material others and sensuous life. Secondly, this account also engaged with a number of political questions and their implications, displaying problems of domination in contemporary political discourses and practices. A third task for a future work (to speak programmatically) would be a rethinking of political economy in the context of exteriority and nonidentity.

Contemporary regimes systematically reproduce the subordination of life to the free circulation and nourishing of capital (in neoliberal globalism) as well as its restricted concentration and stratification (in neomercantilist nationalism and ethnocentrism with its intensification of racializing society). Shifting configurations of power generate regressive and progressive forms of resistance: while identity- and exchange-based thinking justifies and intensifies the fixation and restriction of life, prophetic critical models and emancipatory social movements (structured and informed by class, gender, and racial relations) strive to contest and undo fixations and restrictions for the sake of the free circulation and nourishing of life.

Under such conditions, what could a new critique of political economy oriented toward alterity and nonidentity be like? This is beyond the scope of the present work. But, in addition to Adorno and Levinas, a significant point of departure for a new thinking of the exteriority of labor and political economy has been articulated in Dussel's reinterpretation of Marx's 1861–1863 economic manuscripts.[16] This task of a critical reconstruction of political economy might be further pursued through Dussel's account of the exteriority of labor in conjunction with a natural historical analysis of the exteriority of ecological material life that addresses the environmental and human predicaments of the modern domination of nature that has resulted in disappearing species, deteriorating ecosystems, and the wounds of damaged life.

Notes

Introduction

1. See Levinas, *OE*, 51; Levinas, *DIe*, 93. Select recent Anglophone literature on Adorno that is particularly relevant in this work includes J. M. Bernstein, *Adorno: Disenchantment and Ethics* (Cambridge: Cambridge University Press, 2001); Andrew Bowie, *Adorno and the Ends of Philosophy* (Cambridge: Polity Press, 2013); Deborah Cook, *Adorno on Nature* (Durham, NC: Acumen, 2011); Roger Foster, *Adorno: The Recovery of Experience* (Albany: State University of New York Press, 2007); Fabian Freyenhagen, *Adorno's Practical Philosophy: Living Less Wrongly* (Cambridge: Cambridge University Press, 2013); Peter E. Gordon, *Adorno and Existence* (Cambridge, MA: Harvard University Press, 2016); Espen Hammer, *Adorno and the Political* (London: Routledge, 2006); Iain Macdonald, *What Would Be Different: Figures of Possibility in Adorno* (Stanford, CA: Stanford University Press, 2019); Alastair Morgan, *Adorno's Concept of Life* (London: Continuum, 2007); Martin Shuster, *Autonomy after Auschwitz: Adorno, German Idealism, and Modernity* (Chicago, IL: University of Chicago Press, 2014). On Levinas, see Silvia Benso, *The Face of Things* (Albany: State University of New York Press, 2000); Bettina Bergo, *Levinas between Ethics and Politics: For the Beauty That Adorns the Earth* (Pittsburgh, PA: Duquesne University Press, 2003); Howard Caygill, *Levinas and the Political* (London: Routledge, 2002); Simon Critchley, *The Problem with Levinas* (Oxford: Oxford University Press, 2015); John E. Drabinski, *Levinas and the Postcolonial: Race, Nation, and Other* (Edinburgh: Edinburgh University Press, 2011); Michael Fagenblat, *A Covenant of Creatures: Levinas's Philosophy of Judaism* (Stanford, CA: Stanford University Press, 2010); Asher Horowitz, *Ethics at a Standstill: History and Subjectivity in Levinas and the Frankfurt School* (Pittsburgh, PA: Duquesne University Press, 2008); David Michael Kleinberg-Levin, *Before the Voice of Reason: Echoes of Responsibility in Merleau-Ponty's Ecology and Levinas's Ethics* (Albany: State University of New York Press, 2008); Michael L. Morgan, *Discovering Levinas* (Cambridge: Cambridge University Press, 2007); Michael L. Morgan, *Levinas's*

Ethical Politics (Bloomington: Indiana University Press, 2016); Samuel Moyn, *Origins of the Other: Emmanuel Levinas between Revelation and Ethics* (Cornell, NY: Cornell University Press, 2005); Diane Perpich, *The Ethics of Emmanuel Levinas* (Stanford, CA: Stanford University Press, 2008); Kris Sealey, *Moments of Disruption: Levinas, Sartre, and the Question of Transcendence* (Albany: State University of New York Press, 2013); Brian Schroeder, *Altared Ground: Levinas, History, and Violence* (New York: Routledge, 1996); Tom Sparrow, *Levinas Unhinged* (Winchester: Zero Books, 2013); Jill Stauffer, *Ethical Loneliness: The Injustice of Not Being Heard* (New York: Columbia University Press, 2015).

2. This is an adaptation of the conclusion of Adorno, MM, 40/66 (section/page number); Adorno, GS 4, 74.

3. On the critique of Eurocentrism, see Enrique Dussel, "Eurocentrism and Modernity (Introduction to the Frankfurt Lectures)," *Boundary 2*, 20, no. 3 (1993): 65–76; Enrique Dussel, *The Invention of the Americas: Eclipse of "the Other" and the Myth of Modernity* (New York: Continuum, 1995); and Eric S. Nelson, *Chinese and Buddhist Philosophy in Early Twentieth-Century German Thought* (London: Bloomsbury, 2017).

4. Levinas, TO, 31; Levinas, TA, 8. Note that, as the argumentation of this work will clarify, I will typically speak of (material) "others" (*les autres*). Scholars of Levinas have tried to uphold a distinction between *l'Autrui* and *l'Autre* that Levinas himself did not constantly maintain. Levinas plays on various words and senses for other that is inadequately conveyed in English by distinguishing the other (*l'autre*) and "the Other" (*l'autrui*), which in ordinary French means another person or someone else. I use capitalization to emphasize the unconditional Otherness of the Other. This work uses "Other" in line with standard translations and readings of Levinas, while—at some points and in multiple discussions—it will not be capitalized in order to loosen up the distinction and the potential essentialization and reification of the other as "Other." In particular, for reasons that will be evident throughout the text, I will speak of a multiplicity of "material others" without capitalization.

5. Levinas, GDT, 224; Levinas, DMT, 259.

6. Karl Marx and Friedrich Engels, *The Marx-Engels Reader*, 2nd ed. (New York: Norton, 1978), 66–125, 143–145.

7. On the different senses of materialism, compare Marx's "Theses on Feuerbach" (1845) in Marx, *Marx-Engels Reader*, 143–145.

8. Nourishing or nurturing life as it temporally arises is a key notion in early Daoism. See Eric S. Nelson, "Responding with Dao: Early Daoist Ethics and the Environment," *Philosophy East and West* 59, no. 3 (2009): 294–316; Eric S. Nelson, *Daoism and Environmental Philosophy: Nourishing Life* (London: Routledge, 2020). On turn taking in relation to temporal generations and the environment, compare Matthias Fritsch, *Taking Turns with the Earth: Phenom-*

enology, Deconstruction, and Intergenerational Justice (Stanford, CA: Stanford University Press, 2018).

9. Levinas, *OB*, 177; Levinas, *AE*, 223.

10. It should be noted that the expressions "liberal" and "republican" are used predominantly in the present work in their early modern senses—linked with the proper names John Locke and Jean-Jacques Rousseau—as maintaining, respectively, the priority of individual rights defined by negative liberty and the priority of the "general will" characterized by the positive liberty of equal participation. On the classical liberal and republican paradigms, see Jürgen Habermas, "Three Normative Models of Democracy," *Constellations* 1, no. 1 (1994): 1–10; Jürgen Habermas, *Philosophische Texte*, vol. 4, *Politische Theorie* (Frankfurt: Suhrkamp, 2016), 70–86.

11. On natural history as a struggle for existence, see Levinas, *EN*, xii; Levinas, *ENE*, 10. A significant analysis of the notion of forms of life and their critique is developed in Rahel Jaeggi, *Kritik von Lebensformen* (Frankfurt: Suhrkamp, 2013).

12. The entanglements between religion, politics, and secularization in Marxism and the Frankfurt school are examined in Idit Dobbs-Weinstein, *Spinoza's Critique of Religion and Its Heirs: Marx, Benjamin, Adorno* (Cambridge: Cambridge University Press, 2015). On political theology with respect to prophetic ethics in Levinas, compare Leora Faye Batnitzky, *Leo Strauss and Emmanuel Levinas: Philosophy and the Politics of Revelation* (New York: Cambridge University Press, 2006); Slavoj Žižek, Erik L. Santner, and Kenneth Reinhard, *The Neighbor: Three Inquiries in Political Theology* (Chicago, IL: University of Chicago Press, 2006).

13. Levinas, *GDT*, 142; Levinas, *DMT*, 165.

14. Levinas, *GDT*, 108–111; Levinas, *DMT*, 124–127.

15. On the concept of perfectionism at stake here, see Stanley Cavell, *Conditions Handsome and Unhandsome: The Constitution of Emersonian Perfectionism* (Chicago, IL: University of Chicago Press, 1991); on Levinas as perfectionist, see Hilary Putnam, *Jewish Philosophy as a Guide to Life: Rosenzweig, Buber, Levinas, Wittgenstein* (Bloomington: Indiana University Press, 2008), 59–60, 72–73; on Adorno as perfectionist, see Martin Shuster, "Nothing to Know: The Epistemology of Moral Perfectionism in Adorno and Cavell," *Idealistic Studies* 44, no. 1 (2014): 1–29.

16. Levinas, *GDT*, 63–65, 216–217, 222–223; also compare Levinas, *TI*, 84.

17. Levinas, *GDT*, 63–65, 216–217, 222–223.

18. Concerning Levinas's critical stance towards ordinary conceptions of naturalism, see Fiona Ellis, "Levinas on Nature and Naturalism," in *The Oxford Handbook of Levinas*, ed. Michael L. Morgan (Oxford: Oxford University Press, 2019), 689–708.

19. Levinas, *TO*, 90; Levinas, *TA*, 83.

20. Jacques Derrida, *Adieu to Emmanuel Levinas* (Stanford, CA: Stanford University Press, 1999), 49.

21. In this work, nonessentialist models of reification, ideology, fetishization, and alienation (as forms of fixation instead of loss of essence) are used. These intersect with, while differing in key ways, the analyses in Axel Honneth, *Verdinglichung* (Frankfurt: Suhrkamp, 2005); and Rahel Jaeggi, *Entfremdung: Zur Aktualität eines sozialphilosophischen Problems* (Frankfurt: Suhrkamp, 2016).

22. For an assessment of the problems of autonomy, in addition to chapter 12, see Patricia Huntington, "Toward a Dialectical Concept of Autonomy: Revisiting the Feminist Alliance with Poststructuralism," *Philosophy and Social Criticism* 21, no. 1 (1995): 37–55.

23. See, for instance, the encounter with the tree and the cat in Martin Buber, *Ich und Du* (Stuttgart: Reclam, 2002), 8, 92–93.

24. On "expansive naturalism," note the insightful account in Fiona Ellis, *God, Value, and Nature* (Oxford: Oxford University Press, 2014), 21–72. On the sovereignty of good in Levinas, and in Iris Murdoch, see chapter 10 below and Fiona Ellis, "Murdoch and Levinas on God and Good," *European Journal for Philosophy of Religion* 1, no. 2 (2009): 63–87.

25. On the concept and problem of asymmetrical reciprocity, see Patricia J. Huntington, "Asymmetrical Reciprocity and Practical Agency: Contemporary Dilemmas of Feminist Theory in Benhabib, Young, and Kristeva," in *Political Phenomenology*, ed. Hwa Yol Jung and Lester Embree (Dordrecht: Springer, 2016), 353–378.

26. Marx, *Marx-Engels Reader*, 155.

27. See de Hent de Vries, *Minimal Theologies: Critiques of Secular Reason in Adorno and Levinas* (Baltimore, MD: Johns Hopkins University Press, 2005); and Carl B. Sachs, "The Acknowledgement of Transcendence: Anti-theodicy in Adorno and Levinas," *Philosophy and Social Criticism* 37, no. 3 (2011): 273–294.

28. Levinas, OB, 165; Levinas, AE, 210.

29. On the history of mimesis, see Erich Auerbach, *Mimesis: The Representation of Reality in Western Literature* (Princeton, NJ: Princeton University Press, 1968); Stephen Halliwell, *The Aesthetics of Mimesis: Ancient Texts and Modern Problems* (Princeton, NJ: Princeton University Press, 2002).

30. Compare Adorno, HTS, 31; Levinas, GDT, 133; Levinas, DMT, 152.

31. Levinas, OB, 178; Levinas, AE, 225.

32. Levinas, OB, 36, 48; Levinas, AE, 46, 61.

Chapter 1

1. Adorno, ND, 354; Adorno, GS 6, 347.

2. Both Marx's naturalism and his mediation of history and nature in analyzing society are evident in early writings such as Marx, *Marx-Engels Reader*,

117, 170; Adorno's critical reinterpretation is made in Adorno, ND, 354–356; Adorno, GS 6, 347–349.

3. Adorno, ND, 355; Adorno, GS 6, 349.

4. On *tariki*, see Takeshi Morisato, *Faith and Reason in Continental and Japanese Philosophy: Reading Tanabe Hajime and William Desmond* (London: Bloomsbury, 2019), 155.

5. Compare Trish Morgan, "Alienated Nature, Reified Culture: Understanding the Limits to Climate Change Responses under Existing Socio-ecological Formations," *Political Economy of Communication* 5, no. 1 (2017): 3–50.

6. On the complexities concerning the concept of an ethics of nature, see Angelika Krebs, *Ethics of Nature: A Map* (Berlin: Walter de Gruyter, 1999).

7. See, for instance, his treatment of "ecological balance" in Jürgen Habermas, *Legitimation Crisis* (Boston, MA: Beacon Press, 1975), 61–63.

8. Beatrice Hanssen, *Walter Benjamin's Other History: Of Stones, Animals, Human Beings, and Angels* (Berkeley: University of California Press, 2000), 51–53.

9. Jon Elster, *Making Sense of Marx* (Cambridge: Cambridge University Press, 1985), 55. Levinas explicates the prophetic character of Marx's statements about the continuing transformation of human nature, connecting the biblical phrase "the eye hath not seen" with the "strange passages where Marx expects socialist society to bring about changes in the human condition" (Levinas, BV, 217). In contrast to Elster's analysis, Foster vigorously demonstrates in two works the significance of Marx's account of natural history in historical materialism and the contemporary ecological critique of capitalism. See John Bellamy Foster, *Marx's Ecology: Materialism and Nature* (New York: Monthly Review Press, 2000); John Bellamy Foster, *Ecology against Capitalism* (New York: Monthly Review Press, 2002); and Ariel Salleh, *Ecofeminism as Politics: Nature, Marx, and the Postmodern* (London: Zed Books, 1997).

10. Walter Benjamin, *Illuminations: Essays and Reflections* (New York: Schocken Books, 1969), 259.

11. Adorno, MM, 153/247; Adorno, GS 4, 283.

12. Adorno formulates this point about the dialectical character of progress in Adorno, AT, 284.

13. For the role of the ecological culture industry, see Trish Morgan, "Growing Ourselves to Death? Economic and Ecological Crises, the Growth of Waste, and the Role of the Media and Cultural Industries," *Human Geography* 8, no. 1 (2015): 68–81.

14. Adorno and Horkheimer, DE, 1; Adorno, GS 3, 19.

15. Adorno and Horkheimer, DE, 20, 24.

16. Generational "taking turns" is elucidated in Matthias Fritsch, *Taking Turns with the Earth: Phenomenology, Deconstruction, and Intergenerational Justice* (Stanford, CA: Stanford University Press, 2018).

17. On the Eurocentric conception of modernity that also shapes its internal critics, see Enrique Dussel, "Eurocentrism and Modernity (Introduction to

the Frankfurt Lectures)," *Boundary 2*, 20, no. 3 (1993): 65–76; Enrique Dussel, *The Invention of the Americas: Eclipse of "the Other" and the Myth of Modernity* (New York: Continuum, 1995). Also see my critique of Eurocentric philosophical modernity in favor of an intercultural model in Eric S. Nelson, *Chinese and Buddhist Philosophy in Early Twentieth-Century German Thought* (London: Bloomsbury, 2017); and Eric S. Nelson, "Zhang Junmai's Early Political Philosophy and the Paradoxes of Chinese Modernity," *Asian Studies* 8, no. 1 (2020): 183–208.

18. Compare Jürgen Habermas, *The Philosophical Discourse of Modernity: Twelve Lectures* (Cambridge, MA: MIT Press, 1987), 106–130. Concerning the problem of normativity, also see James Gordon Finlayson, "Morality and Critical Theory: On the Normative Problem of Frankfurt School Social Criticism," *Telos* 146 (2009): 7–41.

19. Habermas, *Philosophical Discourse of Modernity*, 68.

20. Habermas, *Philosophical Discourse of Modernity*, 68, 127.

21. Habermas, *Philosophical Discourse of Modernity*, 117.

22. Habermas, *Philosophical Discourse of Modernity*, 68, 129. The playful character and critical potential of human mimetic capacities are traced in Adorno, *Äs*, and Adorno, *AT*.

23. Adorno, *Äs*, 70.

24. Georg Wilhelm Friedrich Hegel, *Grundlinien der Philosophie des Rechts oder Naturrecht und Staatswissenschaft im Grundrisse* (Frankfurt: Suhrkamp: 1982), 61.

25. Adorno, *HTS*, 3–4.

26. Adorno, *HTS*, 40.

27. Adorno, *CM*, 110.

28. Adorno, *MM*, 153/247; Adorno, *GS* 4, 283.

29. Habermas identifies some of these features in Jürgen Habermas, *Philosophisch-politische Profile* (Frankfurt: Suhrkamp, 1981), 174–177.

30. Compare Habermas, *Philosophical Discourse of Modernity*, 321–322.

31. Habermas, *Philosophisch-politische Profile*, 176–178.

32. Habermas, *Philosophisch-politische Profile*, 176–177.

33. Jürgen Habermas, *The Theory of Communicative Action*, 2 vols. (Boston, MA: Beacon Press, 1984).

34. On the difficult question of making Adorno's complex and indirect strategies ethically and politically explicit, compare Nick Smith, "Making Adorno's Ethics and Politics Explicit," *Social Theory and Practice* 29, no. 3 (2003): 487–498.

35. See Adorno, *CM*, 131–132 and 134, regarding the alterity and priority of the object, the matter itself, and mimetic and material content as nonidentical moments that can interrupt, fracture, and reorient thinking.

36. Adorno's project in the early 1930s should be conceived as a hermeneutically robust and sensitive materialism, as evident in his emphasis on *Deutung*

(interpretation) as the orienting idea of philosophy, in Adorno, GS 1, 334 and 338. Unlike classical hermeneutics and phenomenology, and intersecting with Levinas's overcoming of active and passive intentionality, Adorno emphasizes the interpretation of intentionless actuality in contrast to intentional or projective meaning (Adorno, GS 1, 335–336).

37. Max Horkheimer thematized an antimetaphysical materialism in his early essay "Materialism and Metaphysics," *Critical Theory: Selected Essays* (New York: Continuum, 1982), 10–46.

38. On the priority of experience for reflection, see Adorno, PT, 348–349; Adorno, CM, 13, 17. On Adorno's "modest" or "negative" materialism, see Steven Vogel, *Against Nature: The Concept of Nature in Critical Theory* (Albany: State University of New York Press, 1996), 74. Also note Yvonne Sherratt's argument for the constructive experiential and "positive" dimension of Adorno's critical theory in Yvonne Sherratt, *Adorno's Positive Dialectic* (Cambridge: Cambridge University Press, 2002). On tabooed mimesis, see Adorno, Äs, 113–114.

39. Deborah Cook, "Adorno's Critical Materialism," *Philosophy and Social Criticism* 32, no. 6 (2006): 719–737. His early account of natural history can be read in Adorno, GS 1, 354–355. This interpretive strategy can be contextualized in relation to both Marx's historical materialism and Benjamin's formulation of the mutuality of "natural history" and "historical nature." It is justifiable given recent research in historical ecology.

Chapter 2

1. Allen Wood, *Kantian Ethics* (Cambridge: Cambridge University Press, 2007), 278. For a nuanced and insightful assessment of Adorno's relation with the concept of autonomy and its German idealist context, see Martin Shuster, *Autonomy after Auschwitz: Adorno, German Idealism, and Modernity* (Chicago, IL: University of Chicago Press, 2014).

2. This account does not signify that Adorno only negatively assessed Kant and the Enlightenment more generally. Despite the criticisms discussed here, Adorno praised Kant, including his thesis of the unity of reason, precisely in relation to its contradictory reconciling and dominating employments, in Adorno, CM, 11 and 152.

3. Adorno, BPM, 80. A shorter version of this criticism is found in Adorno HF, 209–210. Translation modified to be non-gender-exclusive. Adorno's point seems exaggerated given the importance of nature in the *Critique of the Power of Judgment*. I trace the significance of nature in Kant's sublime in the *Third Critique* in Eric S. Nelson, "Kant and China: Aesthetics, Race, and Nature," *Journal of Chinese Philosophy* 38, no. 4 (2011): 509–525.

4. Adorno, *BPM*, 80; Adorno, *HF*, 209–210. For a different reading of nature in Kant that brings him closer to ecology, see Nelson, "Kant and China," 509–525; Eric S. Nelson, "Language, Psychology, and the Feeling of Life in Kant and Dilthey," in *The Linguistic Dimension of Kant's Thought: Historical and Critical Essays*, ed. Frank Schalow and Richard Velkley (Evanston, IL: Northwestern University Press, 2014), 263–287.

5. Georg Wilhelm Friedrich Hegel, *Phänomenologie des Geistes* (Frankfurt: Suhrkamp, 1986), 398–440.

6. Compare Adorno, *PE*, 5, 7.

7. Adorno, *MM*, 92/140; Adorno, *GS 4*, 159.

8. Georg Wilhelm Friedrich Hegel, *Frühe Schriften* (Frankfurt: Suhrkamp, 1986), 234–236.

9. Adorno, *CM*, 134.

10. Adorno and Horkheimer, *DE*, xvii–xviii, 42–43.

11. Horowitz elucidates the fundamental role of natural history, and its ethical import and limits, throughout Adorno's thinking in Asher Horowitz, *Ethics at a Standstill: History and Subjectivity in Levinas and the Frankfurt School* (Pittsburgh, PA: Duquesne University Press, 2008), 43–167.

12. On Habermas's importance for democratic environmental deliberation, which I don't deny but seek to modify in a less intersubjective idealist direction, see Graham Smith, *Deliberative Democracy and the Environment* (London: Routledge, 2003).

13. Hammer construes the "ethics of nonidentity" according to a Hegelian strategy that was arguably problematized by Adorno in his critique of Hegel's dialectic and social philosophy in Espen Hammer, *Adorno's Modernism: Art, Experience, and Catastrophe* (Cambridge: Cambridge University Press, 2015), 44.

14. Habermas, *Philosophisch-politische Profile*, 176–177; Axel Honneth, *Verdinglichung* (Frankfurt: Suhrkamp, 2005), 80.

15. Honneth, *Verdinglichung*, 80.

16. Honneth, *Verdinglichung*, 66.

17. Habermas is indebted to the neo-Kantian tradition for the distinctions between validity and facticity, and value and nature. Heinrich Rickert and other neo-Kantian philosophers differentiated the intelligible realm of value and validity, which oriented practical philosophy and the cultural sciences, from the brute facticity and sensuous materiality of nature and the natural sciences. See Heinrich Rickert, *Kulturwissenschaft und Naturwissenschaft* (Stuttgart: Reclam Verlag, 1986), 38–39. Rickert defended the absolute difference between humans and animals in Rickert, *Kulturwissenschaft und Naturwissenschaft*, 43.

18. Philosophy needs to unrestrictedly experience to confront the deformation of experience (Adorno, *CM*, 17, 132, 253, and 269). Adorno distinguished the "full unregulated scope of experience" from its restriction and deformation in

doctrinal empiricism (Adorno, CM, 242). On the conception of experience at work in Adorno, see Roger Foster, *Adorno: The Recovery of Experience* (Albany: State University of New York Press, 2007).

19. Habermas, *Philosophical Discourse of Modernity*, 116.

20. Adorno, PE, 1.

21. Two of Horkheimer's classic early formulations of critical social theory are translated as "Traditional and Critical Theory" in Max Horkheimer, *Critical Theory: Selected Essays* (New York: Continuum, 1982), and "The Present Situation of Social Philosophy and the Tasks of an Institute for Social Research" in Max Horkheimer, *Between Philosophy and Social Science* (Cambridge, MA: MIT Press, 1993).

22. Angelika Krebs and Tim Hayward examine in detail the limitations of Habermas's approach to animals from the perspective of animal ethics. See Krebs, *Ethics of Nature*, 89–90; and Tim Hayward, *Political Theory and Ecological Value* (New York: St. Martin's Press, 1998), 127–131. On Habermas and the environment, see the helpful discussions in Ryan Gunderson, "Habermas in Environmental Thought," *Sociological Inquiry* 84.4 (2014): 626–653; Ryan Gunderson, "The First-generation Frankfurt School on the Animal Question: Foundations for a Normative Sociological Animal Studies," *Sociological Perspectives* 57, no. 3 (2014): 285–300.

23. Adorno, HF, 254.

24. Adorno, KCPR, 183.

25. Note chapter 12 below for a critical analysis of the ideological uses of autonomy and freedom. On diagnosing ideology, see Adorno, PS.

26. Adorno, ND, xx; Adorno, GS 6, 10.

27. Jürgen Habermas, "'Ich selber bin ja ein Stück Natur'—Adorno über die Naturverflochenheit der Vernunft," in *Dialektik der Freiheit*, ed. Axel Honneth (Frankfurt: Suhrkamp, 2005), 23–25.

28. Habermas, "Ich selber," 26, 29.

29. Habermas, "Ich selber," 31–32.

30. Contrast Jürgen Habermas, *The Future of Human Nature* (Cambridge: Polity, 2003), with the Jewish understanding of responsibility between generations in Levinas discussed by James Hatley, "Generations: Levinas in the Jewish context," *Philosophy and Rhetoric* 38, no. 2 (2005): 173–189.

31. There is not necessarily an ethical recognition of "animal otherness" in Levinas's story of a dog being "the last Kantian in Germany." The dog symbolizes a humanity absent in the behavior of his fellow humans and is construed through humanity's lack of humanity rather than the animal having a moral status of its own. For a related yet different reading, see Christina Gerhardt, "The Ethics of Animals in Adorno and Kafka," *New German Critique* 33, no. 97 (2006): 174–178. David Wood outlines Levinas's deficits concerning animals and

the environment in "Some Questions for My Levinasian Friends," in *Addressing Levinas*, ed. Eric S. Nelson, Antje Kapust, and Kent Still (Evanston, IL: Northwestern University Press, 2005), 152–169.

32. On the centrality of the body, desire, and sensuous existence in Adorno, see Lisa Yun Lee, *Dialectics of the Body: Corporeality in the Philosophy of Adorno* (London: Routledge, 2004).

33. Max Horkheimer, *Eclipse of Reason* (New York: Continuum Books, 1974), 104.

34. On the question of animals in an ecological Marxism, compare John Sanbonmatsu, "Listen, Ecological Marxist! (Yes, I Said Animals!)," *Capitalism Nature Socialism* 16, no. 2 (2005): 107–114.

35. See the analysis of the metaphysical nature of Habermas's postmetaphysical thinking in Noëlle McAfee, *Habermas, Kristeva, and Citizenship* (Ithaca, NY: Cornell University Press, 2000), 47.

36. See Habermas, *Philosophical Discourse of Modernity*, 106–130.

37. Compare Adorno, PE, 137.

38. On the nonconceptual that potentially interrupts conceptual and ideological systems, and that philosophy struggles to conceptualize, see Adorno, PT, 86–87; on the senses of mimesis in Adorno, see the introduction to Tom Huhn, *The Cambridge Companion to Adorno*, ed. Tom Huhn (Cambridge: Cambridge University Press, 2004), 9–17. On the significance of mimesis for ecological and environmental thought, see Bruce Martin, "Mimetic Moments: Adorno and Ecofeminism," in *Feminist Interpretations of Adorno*, ed. Renee Heberle (University Park: Pennsylvania State University Press, 2006), 141–172. For a critique of mimesis in Adorno, based on a critical conception of its transformative potential, see Sara Beardsworth, "From Nature in Love: The Problem of Subjectivity in Adorno and Freudian Psychoanalysis," *Continental Philosophy Review* 40, no. 4 (2007): 365–387. On Adorno's rehabilitation of mimesis as responsiveness to the object, see Nicholas Walker, "Adorno and Heidegger on the Question of Art: Countering Hegel?," in *Adorno and Heidegger: Philosophical Questions*, ed. Iain Macdonald and Krzysztof Ziarek (Stanford, CA: Stanford University Press, 2008), 96.

39. On the necessity for thought, thinking as resistance, and the interconnection between thought and happiness, see "Resignation" in Adorno CM, 293.

40. Adorno, PT, 57.

41. Adorno, MM, 152/244.

42. Adorno, CM, 12, 133.

43. Steven Vogel pursues the anthropocentric argument that nature is a social construction, rejecting Adorno's and Horkheimer's naturalism in *Against Nature*, 51–99. Andrew Biro endeavors to purify environmentalism of the metaphysical assumptions regarding nature, naturalness, and naturalism in *Denaturalizing Ecological Politics: Alienation from Nature from Rousseau to the Frankfurt*

School and Beyond (Toronto: University of Toronto Press, 2005). For an alternative understanding of the continuing relevance of experiences of nature and alienation, compare Alison Stone, "Alienation from Nature and Early German Romanticism," *Ethical Theory and Moral Practice* 17, no. 1 (2014): 41–54. For a pluralistic and nonromanticizing approach to the issue of human alienation from natures, see Simon Hailwood, "Alienations and Natures," *Environmental Politics* 21, no. 6 (2012): 882–900. On the Marxist notion of alienation and its contemporary status and import, see Rahel Jaeggi, *Entfremdung: Zur Aktualität eines sozialphilosophischen Problems* (Frankfurt: Suhrkamp, 2016); and Rahel Jaeggi, "What (If Anything) Is Wrong with Capitalism? Dysfunctionality, Exploitation and Alienation: Three Approaches to the Critique of Capitalism," supplement, *Southern Journal of Philosophy* 54, no. 1 (2016): 44–65.

44. Adorno, CM, 21. For a critique along these lines, see Stephen Eric Bronner, *Reclaiming the Enlightenment: Towards a Politics of Radical Engagement* (New York: Columbia University Press, 2004), 2–6, 112.

45. Habermas contends that the normative basis of critical social theory remained mostly implicit, and the interpretive aspect of social inquiry was ineffective and inadequate in the early Frankfurt school, in Jürgen Habermas and Peter Dews, *Autonomy and Solidarity: Interviews with Jürgen Habermas* (London: Verso, 1992), 56, 195–196. For a critical assessment of Habermas's reconstruction of ethical life and the normative basis of critical social theory, compare J. M. Bernstein, *Recovering Ethical Life: Jürgen Habermas and the Future of Critical Theory* (London: Routledge, 2014).

46. In the early essays "Traditional and Critical Theory" in Horkheimer, *Critical Theory*, 188–243, and "The Present Situation of Social Philosophy and the Tasks of an Institute for Social Research" in Horkheimer, *Between Philosophy and Social Science*, Horkheimer formulated critical theory as an "interdisciplinary materialism" integrating philosophy and the empirically oriented social sciences. Also compare the previous discussions of the early project.

47. Habermas, *Philosophical Discourse of Modernity*, 126–130.

48. Habermas, *Future of Human Nature*, 33.

49. Habermas, *Future of Human Nature*, 33.

50. Honneth, *Verdinglichung*, 37–38.

51. "In reaction to the experiences of his time, Adorno undertook a conceptual reevaluation of that dimension of social labor which he had also privileged, the upshot was a negative philosophy of history in whose framework a practical zone of prescientific critique can no longer be discerned since it is forced to see in all social action only a mere extension of the human domination of nature." Axel Honneth, *The Critique of Power: Reflective Stages in a Critical Social Theory* (Cambridge, MA: MIT Press, 1991), xvi.

52. Adorno, MM, 74/116; compare Adorno, CM, 247.

53. Adorno, MM, 74/115; translation modified to be non-gender-exclusive.

54. Honneth, *Verdinglichung*, 78.

55. "Instrumentalized subjective reason either eulogizes nature as pure vitality or disparages it as brute force, instead of treating it as a text to be interpreted by philosophy that, if rightly read, would unfold a tale of infinite suffering. Without committing the fallacy of equating nature and reason, mankind must try to reconcile the two"; in Horkheimer, *Eclipse of Reason*, 126.

56. On Bacon and modernity in Adorno and Horkheimer, see Fred Dallmayr, "Adorno and Heidegger on Modernity," in *Adorno and Heidegger: Philosophical Questions*, ed. Iain Macdonald and Krzysztof Ziarek (Stanford, CA: Stanford University Press, 2008), 167–173.

57. Horkheimer, *Eclipse of Reason*, 93.

58. Adorno, KCPR, 173; also note his remark on Kantian synthesis in Adorno, KCPR, 196.

59. Compare Habermas, *Future of Human Nature*. Also note David Chai's illuminating discussion of the critique of eugenics in Habermas and the more expansive concerns about intervening in and reconstructing nonhuman and human nature in relation to classical Daoism in David Chai, "Habermas and Zhuangzi against Liberal Eugenic," *International Journal of Chinese and Comparative Philosophy of Medicine* 14, no. 2 (2016): 97–112.

60. See Adorno, PT, 82. Philosophy is experimental in that it searches for its object rather than possesses it, tenuously striving to say what does not let itself be said.

61. Habermas, *Philosophical Discourse of Modernity*, 106–130.

62. Habermas, *Philosophical Discourse of Modernity*, 105.

63. Habermas, *Philosophical Discourse of Modernity*, pages 118 and 106, respectively.

64. Honneth, *Verdinglichung*, 80.

65. Horkheimer, *Eclipse of Reason*, chapter 3, in particular page 94.

66. Horkheimer provides a strategy for articulating the intrinsic value of nature without falling into a reified and reactionary construction of nature in Horkheimer, *Eclipse of Reason*, 101–104.

67. Adorno and Horkheimer, DE, 3; compare Adorno, CI, 92.

68. Hegel, *Phänomenologie des Geistes*, 431–440.

69. Adorno, CI, 35.

70. Horkheimer, *Between Philosophy and Social Science*, 16.

71. Adorno and Horkheimer, DE, xviii.

72. Adorno and Horkheimer, DE, 9.

73. Adorno and Horkheimer, DE, 11.

74. Adorno, ISW, 86–87.

75. Compare Adorno, ISW, 93–94, 97, 115–116.

76. Adorno, ISW, 137.

77. Adorno, KCA, 52–53, 104–105.

78. Adorno, *ISW*, 125; Adorno, *CM*, 148.
79. Adorno and Horkheimer, *DE*, 119.
80. Adorno, *ISW*, 152.
81. Jacques Derrida, *The Animal That Therefore I Am* (New York: Fordham University Press, 2008), 47–48, 52, 62.
82. Jürgen Habermas, *Knowledge and Human Interests* (Boston, MA: Beacon Press, 1971), 52–63; and Jürgen Habermas, *Theory and Practice* (Boston, MA: Beacon Press, 1973), 168–169.
83. Habermas clarifies this critique of Marxism in these terms in Habermas, *Knowledge and Human Interests*, 52–63; and Habermas, *Theory and Practice*, 168–169.
84. Adorno, *IS*, 13.
85. Adorno, *CI*, 53.
86. Compare Adorno, *LND*, 9, 19, 31; Honneth, *Verdinglichung*, 80.
87. Adorno, *Pr.*, 67.
88. Adorno, *MM*, 151/239; Adorno, *GS 4*, 273.
89. Adorno and Horkheimer, *TNM*, 20.
90. Adorno, *MM*, 149/233; Adorno, *GS 4*, 266–267. On exoticism, consumerism, and Zen, see Adorno, *ND*, 68; Adorno, *GS 6*, 76.
91. Adorno, *MM*, 59/95–96.
92. Compare Adorno, *MM*, 48, 60/77, 97; Levinas, *EE*, 10; Levinas, *DEE*, 29.

Chapter 3

1. Axel Honneth, "Communication and Reconciliation: Habermas's Critique of Adorno," *Telos* 39 (1979): 45. For a helpful analysis of the communicative turn from Adorno to Habermas, compare Martin Morris, *Rethinking the Communicative Turn: Adorno, Habermas, and the Problem of Communicative Freedom* (Albany: State University of New York Press, 2014).
2. Honneth, "Communication and Reconciliation," 45–61.
3. Habermas outlines this critique in Habermas and Dews, *Autonomy and Solidarity*, 152–154.
4. Adorno, *ND*, 356; Adorno, *GS 6*, 350.
5. Adorno, *Äs*, 41.
6. The problem with advocates of a higher role for nature in Hegel's works is that nature is "positive" and redeemed only in relationship to the activity of spirit. Nature appears as a one-sided shell when it is separated from spirit, and the truth of nature can come only through the recognition of nature when it is thoroughly, dialectically intertwined with spirit. Hegel actually does make space for a fuller sense of nature in a complicated dialectical space. Although

Hegel might give a positive account of nature to an extent, it is limited as a dialectical account in which nature finds its true meaning only in the priority and mediation of spirit, whereas in Adorno's negative dialectics, nature and spirit cannot be disentangled or one prioritized over the other without fixation. In a more minimalistic reading of the activity of spirit, Hegel is rejecting only the position that nature that has no relation to spirit. Hegel's "antinaturalistic humanism" is to this extent complicated by a dialectics that entangles that which it separates. On the complexity of Hegel's philosophy of nature, compare Alison Stone, "Hegel, Naturalism and the Philosophy of Nature," *Hegel Bulletin* 34, no. 1 (2013): 59–78. On sovereign spirit as ideology, see Adorno, PS, 142.

    7. Georg Wilhelm Friedrich Hegel, *Aesthetics: Lectures on Fine Art* (Oxford: Oxford University Press, 1998), 1:29.

    8. Hegel, *Aesthetics*, 1:2.

    9. Adorno, Äs, 36–55.

    10. Adorno, Äs, 69–70.

    11. On mimesis in literary theory and the history of philosophy, see Auerbach, *Mimesis*; Halliwell, *Aesthetics of Mimesis*.

    12. On this problematic, see Gregg Daniel Miller, *Mimesis and Reason: Habermas's Political Philosophy* (Albany: State University of New York Press, 2011).

    13. Hegel, *Aesthetics*, 1:2.

    14. This argument is unfolded in chapter 5 of Habermas, *Philosophical Discourse of Modernity*, 106–130, and in Habermas, *Theory of Communicative Action*, 1:382–390. Also see Max Pensky, *The Actuality of Adorno: Critical Essays on Adorno and the Postmodern* (Albany: State University of New York Press, 1997), 7.

    15. Compare Marie Fleming's discussion of Habermas's aesthetics in *Emancipation and Illusion: Rationality and Gender in Habermas's Theory of Modernity* (University Park: Pennsylvania State University Press, 1997), 191).

    16. Habermas and Dews, *Autonomy and Solidarity*, 152.

    17. Habermas, *Theory of Communicative Action*, 1:20.

    18. Adorno, QuF, 61–64, 315–316.

    19. Adorno, QuF, 62.

    20. Adorno, MMP, 152–154.

    21. Adorno, PMM, 64–71; Adorno, QuF, 273–275.

    22. Adorno, CM, 7; compare the similar formulation in Adorno, AT, 126; Adorno, GS 7, 191. On Heidegger and national socialism, compare Patricia J. Huntington, *Ecstatic Subjects, Utopia, and Recognition: Kristeva, Heidegger, Irigaray* (Albany: State University of New York Press, 1998), 33–75; Eric S. Nelson, "Heidegger's *Black Notebooks*: National Socialism, Antisemitism, and the History of Being," in *The Bloomsbury Companion to Heidegger*, ed. François Raffoul and Eric S. Nelson (London: Bloomsbury, 2016), 484–493.

    23. Adorno, BPM, 211.

    24. Adorno, AT, 132; Adorno, GS 7, 200.

25. Adorno, KCPR, 176.
26. Adorno, MM, 92/141.
27. Respectively Adorno, CM, 150 and 152.
28. Adorno, MM, 153/247.
29. Adorno, MM, 20/41 and 145/226.
30. Habermas takes the transcendental constructivist Kant as his point of departure. Adorno proceeds from the paradox of the integrating power of consciousness and the aporetic moment of nonidentity in Kant, in Adorno, KCPR, 176–179. One example of this radicalization to an aporia, in which the concept can neither be overcome nor justified, is Adorno's interpretation of the categorical imperative. Compare David Michael Kleinberg-Levin, "The Embodiment of the Categorical Imperative: Kafka, Foucault, Benjamin, Adorno and Levinas," *Philosophy and Social Criticism* 27, no. 4 (2001): 1–20; Itay Snir, "The 'New Categorical Imperative' and Adorno's Aporetic Moral Philosophy," *Continental Philosophy Review* 43, no. 3 (2010): 407–437.
31. On the conception of a rational society in Habermas, compare Deborah Cook, *Adorno, Habermas, and the Search for a Rational Society* (London: Routledge, 2004).
32. Jürgen Habermas, *Between Facts and Norms* (Cambridge, MA: MIT Press, 1996), xli.
33. Peter Singer, *Practical Ethics* (Cambridge: Cambridge University Press, 2011), 22.
34. Jürgen Habermas, *On the Pragmatics of Communication* (Cambridge, MA: MIT Press, 1998), 428.
35. Adorno, Pr., 67.
36. This argument is based on Adorno, Äs, 90 and Adorno, Pr., 29–31.
37. Adorno, CI, 30; on the different senses of being like a child, see 41 and 45.
38. Compare Adorno, CI, 33. For a critical account of Adorno's reservations concerning jazz and popular culture, see Theodore A. Gracyk, "Adorno, Jazz, and the Aesthetics of Popular Music," *Musical Quarterly* 76, no. 4 (1992): 526–542.
39. On the notion of a "modern archaics," developed in a discussion of poetics in republican China, see Shengqing Wu, *Modern Archaics: Continuity and Innovation in the Chinese Lyric Tradition 1900–1937* (Cambridge, MA: Harvard University Asia Center, 2013), 4–14.
40. Adorno, CI, 34, 37.
41. Adorno, CI, 88.
42. Adorno, CI, 54.
43. Adorno, Pr., 33.
44. Adorno, CM, 249–251.
45. Compare Adorno, ID, 2; Adorno, LND, 7.
46. Adorno, GS 6, 88–90.

47. Adorno, GS 6, 32.
48. On the convergence of art and philosophy, note Adorno, CM, 14.
49. Adorno and Horkheimer, DE, 7.
50. Adorno, GS 7, 192.
51. Adorno, GS 7, 52, 101.
52. In contrast to their radical separation, and consequent reification, Adorno explicitly stressed their dialectical relation and tension: "Daß Vernunft ein anderes als Natur und doch ein Moment von dieser sei . . ." (Adorno, GS 6, 283).
53. Adorno, MM, 99/154; Adorno, PT, 81.
54. Andrea Oppo, *Philosophical Aesthetics and Samuel Beckett* (Oxford: Peter Lang, 2008), 122.
55. Note the earlier description of Habermas's aesthetics of authentic self-expression.
56. Adorno, PT, 81–84.
57. Adorno, GS 7, 171–172.
58. Adorno, GS 7, 202–203.
59. On the subject in Adorno, see the analysis in David Sherman, *Sartre and Adorno: The Dialectics of Subjectivity* (Albany: State University of New York Press, 2007). On the possibility of responsiveness without a subject, in the context of Merleau-Ponty's thinking of language, see David Michael Kleinberg-Levin, "A Responsive Voice: Language without the Modern Subject," *Chiasmi International* 1 (1999): 65–102.
60. Adorno, CI, 50; Adorno, CM, 151–152.
61. Adorno, CM, 151–152.
62. Adorno, CM, 150 and 143.
63. Rodolphe Gasché, "The Theory of Natural Beauty and Its Evil Star: Kant, Hegel, Adorno," *Research in Phenomenology* 32, no. 1 (2002): 103–122.
64. Adorno, GS 7, 171–172, 181–182, 187–188.
65. Adorno, GS 7, 24, 176–178.
66. Adorno, GS 7, 168 and 25.
67. The simultaneous thinking of difference and continuity distinguishes Adorno from Derrida, who affirms difference while denying continuity as homogeneous in Derrida, *Animal*, 30. For Adorno, there can be nonhomogeneous, asymmetrical, aporetic, and irregular mediations.
68. Hegel hierarchically sublimates animality and organic life but does not fully eliminate them in spirit, insofar as spirit is life grasping itself, in Hegel, *Phänomenologie des Geistes*, 178–262, especially 262.
69. Adorno and Horkheimer, DE, 7.
70. Singer, *Practical Ethics*, 54.
71. Adorno, ISW, 146, compare Horkheimer, *Eclipse of Reason*, 104–105. On the rhetoric of animal and environmental protection in some tendencies of

national socialism, see Franz-Josef Brüggemeier, Mark Cioc, and Thomas Zeller, eds., *How Green Were the Nazis? Nature, Environment, and Nation in the Third Reich* (Athens: Ohio University Press, 2005); and chapter 5 of David Blackbourn, *The Conquest of Nature: Water, Landscape, and the Making of Modern Germany* (New York: W. W. Norton, 2006), 251–310. On the interconnections between national socialist treatment of humans and animals, see Charles Patterson, *Eternal Triblenka: Our Treatment of Animals and the Holocaust* (New York: Lantern Books, 2002).

72. For instance, see Morton Schoolman, *Reason and Horror: Critical Theory, Democracy, and Aesthetic Individuality* (London: Routledge, 2001), 30–31.

73. Adorno, PMP, 145. On Schopenhauer, Adorno, and the suffering body, see Mathijs Peters, *Schopenhauer and Adorno on Bodily Suffering: A Comparative Analysis* (New York: Palgrave Macmillan, 2014).

74. Adorno, MM, 68/105. On compulsion, reification, and identity thinking in Adorno, see Namita Goswami, "Existence Authoritarian: Compulsion, Facticity and the Philosophy of Identity," in *Rethinking Facticity*, ed. François Raffoul and Eric S. Nelson (Albany: State University of New York Press, 2008), 289–316.

75. Adorno, MMP, 9.

76. See Andrew Bowie, *Adorno and the Ends of Philosophy* (Cambridge: Polity Press, 2013), 86.

77. On the pathologies and ethics of listening in modernity, in addition to Adorno's "The Fetish-Character in Music and the Regression of Listening," also compare David Michael Kleinberg-Levin, *The Listening Self* (New York: Routledge, 1989).

78. Adorno und Horkheimer, AHB, 192.

79. Adorno associates difference with resistance in Adorno, CI, 96.

80. Compare Derrida, *Animal*, 53.

81. Adorno, GS 7, 15, 18.

82. Adorno, GS 7, 203, 335–337.

83. Adorno elucidates the nonidentity of freedom and dependence in mimesis, and identifies a moment of enlightenment and reflection in myth and enchained mimesis. Levinas perceives this mimetic moment as primarily regressive tied to mythic participation and violence, discussed further in the next two chapters, in "Reality and Its Shadow" in Levinas, UH, 88–90; LIH, 123–124. On the sharp divergence between Adorno and Levinas on art, compare Seán Hand, *Facing the Other: The Ethics of Emmanuel Lévinas* (Richmond, UK: Curzon, 1996), 76; and Nick Smith, "Adorno vs. Levinas: Evaluating Points of Contention," *Continental Philosophy Review* 40, no. 3 (2007): 275–306.

84. See Adorno, GS 7, 33; Adorno, GS 6, 58.

85. Adorno, MM, 99/154.

86. Adorno, PT, 14; Adorno, GS 6, 213.

87. See Deborah Cook, "From the Actual to the Possible: Nonidentity Thinking," *Constellations* 12, no. 1 (2005): 25.

88. Adorno, GS 7, 203.
89. Adorno, GS 7, 10, 14, 64.
90. Adorno, GS 7, 33.
91. Adorno, GS 7, 38.
92. Espen Hammer, "Metaphysics," in *Adorno: Key Concepts*, ed. Deborah Cook (Durham, NC: Acumen Publishing, 2008), 74.
93. Adorno, *HTS*, 1, 3, 8.
94. Adorno, GS 7, 148.
95. Cook, "Actual to Possible," 26–27.
96. Adorno, *MCP*, 67–68.
97. Adorno, *ND*, 144–145; Adorno, GS 7, 148.
98. Adorno, *CM*, 278.
99. Irving Wohlfarth, "Unterwegs zu Adorno," in *Adorno-Portraits*, ed. Stefan Müller-Doohm (Frankfurt: Suhrkamp, 2007), 122.
100. Compare David Michael Kleinberg-Levin, "What-Is? On Mimesis and the Logic of Identity and Difference in Heidegger and the Frankfurt School," *International Studies in Philosophy* 28, no. 4 (1996): 41–60.
101. Adorno, GS 14, 18.
102. Note how Kleinberg-Levin phenomenologically describes and confronts the pathologies and possibilities of genuine responsive listening in his *The Listening Self*.
103. Adorno, GS 7, 75.
104. Adorno, *PT*, 85.
105. Adorno, *PT*, 1–2.
106. Adorno, *PT*, 41.
107. Derrida, *Animal*, 64.
108. Adorno, GS 6, 17–18 and 36. A compelling portrayal of freedom toward the object is found in Andrea Kern, "Freiheit zum Objekt: Eine Kritik der Aporie des Erkennens," in *Dialektik der Freiheit*, ed. Axel Honneth (Frankfurt: Suhrkamp, 2005), 53–82.
109. Adorno, GS 7, 75. On the question of remembering in Adorno, see Alexander García Düttmann, *The Gift of Language: Memory and Promise in Adorno, Benjamin, Heidegger, and Rosenzweig* (Syracuse, NY: Syracuse University Press, 2000), 73–109; Mario Wenning, "Adorno, Heidegger and the Problem of Remembrance," in *Adorno and Heidegger: Philosophical Questions*, ed. Iain Macdonald and Krzysztof Ziarek (Stanford, CA: Stanford University Press, 2007), 155–166.
110. On suffering and compassion, compare William Edelglass, "Levinas on Suffering and Compassion," *Sophia* 45, no. 2 (2006): 43–59.
111. Adorno, GS 7, 176.
112. The aporetic materialist ethics of nature articulated in this work indicates an alternative to both Vogel's critique of Adorno's conception of nature and arguments for the elimination of nature in Vogel, *Against Nature*, 86–87.

113. Adorno, *GS* 7, 52, 101.
114. Adorno, *GS* 7, 101.
115. Adorno, *MM*, 121. Wohlfarth remarked, "Gegen das Leben, auch das beschädigte, hat die Dialektik, auch die negative, niemals das letzte Wort" (Wohlfarth, "Unterwegs zu Adorno," 43). On Adorno's notion of life as bioaesthetic and bioethical, compare J. M. Bernstein, *Adorno: Disenchantment and Ethics* (Cambridge: Cambridge University Press, 2001), 40. On Adorno's complex conception of life, see Alastair Morgan, *Adorno's Concept of Life* (London: Continuum, 2007).

Chapter 4

1. In regard to Levinas's interpretation of nature, naturalism, and their moral-political significance, which are further discussed in this and the following chapter, see Fiona Ellis, "Levinas on Nature and Naturalism," in *The Oxford Handbook of Levinas*, ed. Michael L. Morgan (Oxford: Oxford University Press, 2019), 689–708; Annabel Herzog, "Dogs and Fire: The Ethics and Politics of Nature in Levinas," *Political Theory* 41, no. 3 (2013): 359–379.

2. Levinas, *AIT*, 26; Levinas, *Aet*, 47; Levinas, *OB*, 122; Levinas, *AE*, 157; Levinas, *TI*, 293.

3. Levinas, *TI*, 293; Levinas, *EE*, 10; Levinas, *DEE*, 29.

4. On Levinas's relations to Husserl, see Bettina Bergo, "Levinas and Husserl," in *The Oxford Handbook of Levinas*, ed. Michael L. Morgan (Oxford: Oxford University Press, 2019), 71–102. On the philosophical complexities arising between Levinas and Heidegger, see the introduction and the essays in John Drabinski and Eric S. Nelson, eds., *Between Levinas and Heidegger* (Albany: State University of New York Press, 2014).

5. Levinas, *OE*, 51; Levinas, *DIe*, 93.

6. On the derivative character of *natura* in relation to primordial *phusis*, see Martin Heidegger, "Vom Wesen und Begriff der Phusis," in Heidegger, *Wegmarken* (Frankfurt: Klostermann, 1978), 237–299; and Martin Heidegger, *Introduction to Metaphysics*, trans. G. Fried and R. Polt (New Haven, CT: Yale University Press, 2000), 11.

7. Levinas, *EE*, 9; Levinas, *DEE*, 28.

8. Levinas, *AIT*, 169; Levinas, *Aet*, 171.

9. Edmund Husserl, "Philosophie als strenge Wissenschaft," *Logos: Internationale Zeitschrift für Philosophie der Kultur* 1 (1910/1911): 289–341. On Husserl's notion of an Occidental cultural crisis, see my discussion in chapter 6 of Nelson, *Chinese and Buddhist Philosophy*, 159–199.

10. On Levinas's intellectual formation in the 1920s, which is still insufficiently explored, see Samuel Moyn, *Origins of the Other: Emmanuel Levinas between Revelation and Ethics* (Cornell, NY: Cornell University Press, 2005),

21–56. Much has been written on Heidegger and Levinas; see in this context François Raffoul, "Being and the Other: Ethics and Ontology in Levinas and Heidegger," in *Addressing Levinas*, ed. Eric S. Nelson, Kent Still, and Antje Kapust (Evanston, IL: Northwestern University Press, 2005) 138–151; François Raffoul, "The Question of Responsibility between Levinas and Heidegger," in *Between Levinas and Heidegger*, ed. John E. Drabinski and Eric S. Nelson (Albany: State University of New York Press, 2014), 175–206; Jill Stauffer, "Heidegger and Levinas," in *The Bloomsbury Companion to Heidegger*, ed. François Raffoul and Eric S. Nelson (London: Bloomsbury, 2013), 393–398; Eric S. Nelson, "Heidegger, Levinas, and the Other of History," in *Between Levinas and Heidegger*, ed. John E. Drabinski and Eric S. Nelson (Albany: State University of New York Press, 2014), 51–72.

11. On categorical intuition, formal indication, and the hermeneutics of facticity in the development of the early thought of Heidegger, see Leslie MacAvoy, "Formal Indication and the Hermeneutics of Facticity," supplement, *Philosophy Today* 54 (2010): 84–90; Leslie MacAvoy, "The Ambiguity of Facticity in Heidegger's Early Work," *Comparative and Continental Philosophy* 5, no. 1 (2013): 99–106; Eric S. Nelson, "Questioning Practice: Heidegger, Historicity, and the Hermeneutics of Facticity," supplement, *Philosophy Today* 44 (2001): 150–159; Eric S. Nelson, "Die formale Anzeige der Faktizität als Frage der Logik," in *Heidegger und die Logik*, ed. Alfred Denker and Holger Zaborowski (Amsterdam: Rodopi, 2006), 49–64.

12. Levinas, *TI*, 34.

13. Levinas, *TIHP*.

14. Levinas, *UH*, 62; Levinas, *LIH*, 88.

15. Levinas, *UH*, 21; Levinas, *LIH*, 88.

16. Levinas, *OE*, 73; Levinas, *DIe*, 127; compare Levinas, *UH*, 18; Levinas, *LIH*, 30.

17. Levinas, *OE*, 71; Levinas, *DIe*, 124.

18. Levinas, *OE*, 51–54; Levinas, *DIe*, 93–98; Levinas, *UH*, 134; Levinas, *LIH*, 186. On Levinas, Heidegger, and the question of humanism, see Krzysztof Ziarek, "Which Other, Whose Alterity? The Human after Humanism," in *Between Levinas and Heidegger*, ed. John E. Drabinski and Eric S. Nelson (Albany: State University of New York Press, 2014), 227–244.

19. Levinas, *OS*, 136, 142; Levinas, *HS*, 193.

20. Søren Kierkegaard, *Fear and Trembling and Repetition* (Princeton, NJ: Princeton University Press, 1983), 27.

21. Contrast passages such as Adorno, *MCP*, 13; Levinas, *EN*, 116–117; Levinas, *ENE*, 126–127; Levinas, *OB*, 182; Levinas, *AE*, 230.

22. Levinas, *EN*, 116; translation modified to be gender neutral; Levinas, *ENE*, 126.

23. Levinas, *DEH*, 132.

24. Levinas, *DF*, 231–232; Levinas, *DL*, 347–349.

25. Levinas, *DF*, 233; Levinas, *DL*, 351.
26. Levinas, *DF*, 26; Levinas, *DL*, 50–51.
27. Levinas, *DF*, 233; translation modified; Levinas, *DL*, 351.
28. On Levinas's diagnosis of the struggle for existence in Heidegger, see Robert Bernasconi, "Levinas and the Struggle for Existence," in *Addressing Levinas*, ed. Eric S. Nelson, Antje Kapust, and Kent Still (Evanston, IL: Northwestern University Press, 2005), 176 and 171–173.
29. Martin Heidegger, GA 61, 134; Martin Heidegger, GA 65, 482/339.
30. Levinas, *IRB*, 136.
31. Adorno, *ND*, 179; Adorno, *GS* 6, 181.
32. Adorno, *ND*, 68; Adorno, *GS* 6, 76; Levinas, *TI*, 21–30.
33. On Heidegger's rejection of biologism, and biological racism, including in the national socialist period, see Eric S. Nelson, "Biological and Historical Life: Heidegger between Levinas and Dilthey," in *The Science, Politics, and Ontology of Life-Philosophy*, ed. Scott M. Campbell and Paul Bruno (London: Bloomsbury Press, 2013), 15–29; Nelson, "Heidegger's *Black Notebooks*, 484–493.
34. Levinas, *OE*, 53; Levinas, *DIe*, 95–96.
35. Levinas, *OE*, 54; Levinas, *DIe*, 97–98.
36. For an account of the question of history in Heidegger and Levinas, see Nelson, "Heidegger, Levinas," 51–72.
37. On moral phenomenological description in Levinas, see David Michael Kleinberg-Levin, "Tracework: Myself and Others in the Moral Phenomenology of Merleau-Ponty and Levinas," *International Journal of Philosophical Studies* 6, no. 3 (1998): 345–392.
38. In regard to the stakes and problems of a phenomenology of the inapparent, compare François Raffoul, "The Invisible and the Secret: Of a Phenomenology of the Inapparent," *Frontiers of Philosophy in China* 11, no. 3 (2016): 395–414; François Raffoul, "Phenomenology of the Inapparent," in *Unconsciousness Between Phenomenology and Psychoanalysis*, ed. Dorothée Legrand and Dylan Trigg (Dordrecht, Netherlands: Springer, 2017), 113–131.
39. Compare Tina Chanter, *Time, Death, and the Feminine: Levinas with Heidegger* (Stanford, CA: Stanford University Press, 2001), 46. Also see the illuminating analyses of the roles and problems of disruption in Levinas's works in Kris Sealey, "The Primacy of Disruption in Levinas' Account of Transcendence," *Research in Phenomenology* 40, no. 3 (2010): 363–377; and Kris Sealey, *Moments of Disruption: Levinas, Sartre, and the Question of Transcendence* (Albany: State University of New York Press, 2013).
40. On the problematic of ontology, immanence, and transcendence in Levinas, see Bettina Bergo, "Ontology, Transcendence, and Immanence in Emmanuel Levinas' Philosophy," *Research in Phenomenology* 35, no. 1 (2005): 141–180.
41. On Bergson's importance in the early thought of Levinas, note Moyn, *Origins of the Other*, 32–49.

42. Levinas repeatedly states the priority of the ethical encounter, fact, or event from which ethics and morality in the conventional sense of prescriptions and imperatives proceeds and can lose contact and consequently its ethical sense. On the ethical encounter and fact that is irreducible to norms and values, see Levinas, GCM, 147; DVI, 225.

43. Diane Perpich, *The Ethics of Emmanuel Levinas* (Stanford, CA: Stanford University Press, 2008), 159–161.

44. Levinas, BPW, 167.

45. On the issue of to what extent Levinas's ethics falls under Nietzsche's genealogical tracing of the ascetic priestly character, a topic of chapter 7, see Silvia Benso, "Levinas—Another Ascetic Priest?," *Journal of the British Society for Phenomenology* 27, no. 2 (1996): 137–156.

46. Levinas, *TIHP*, 116–119.

47. Levinas, *TIHP*, 157.

48. Martin Heidegger, SZ, 46.

49. Levinas, *TIHP*, 156–157.

50. Since Heidegger does not formally discuss the phenomenon of language until SZ, 160, it can be argued that language is implicitly crucial from the beginning through the question of meaning and the method of destructuring ordinary and metaphysical language.

51. Compare Levinas, *TIHP*, lvii. For a detailed discussion of Dilthey and Heidegger's appropriation and critique of Dilthey's hermeneutical life-philosophy, see Eric S. Nelson, "Heidegger and Dilthey: Language, History, and Hermeneutics," in *Horizons of Authenticity in Phenomenology, Existentialism, and Moral Psychology*, ed. Hans Pedersen and Megan Altman (Dordrecht, Netherlands: Springer, 2015), 109–128.

52. See my examination of this topic in Nelson, "Heidegger, Levinas," 51–72.

53. Levinas, *TIHP*, 156.

54. Levinas, UH, 13–21; Levinas, LIH, 23–33; and also note Levinas, OE.

55. Levinas, OE, 49–51; Levinas, DIe, 91–93.

56. Levinas, OB, 11; Levinas, AE, 13; Levinas, TI, 103, 105.

57. Levinas, TO, 46–47; Levinas, TA, 25–26.

58. Levinas, CPP, 52.

59. Levinas, TI, 156–158; Levinas, TO, 79; Levinas, TA, 68.

60. Levinas, TI, 23, 52, 227–228, 243–245.

61. Levinas, TI, 52; translation modified.

62. Raffoul, "Being and the Other," 138–151; François Raffoul, *The Origins of Responsibility* (Bloomington: Indiana University Press, 2010); Raffoul, "Question of Responsibility," 175–206.

63. On issues of masculinity in Heidegger's thinking and language, see the insightful analysis ("The Masculine Ethos of National Socialism or, How to Tame the Feminine") in Huntington, *Ecstatic Subjects*, 33–75. For an alternative reading and critique of the problematic of death in Heidegger, relying on Zhuangzi, note

David Chai, "On Pillowing One's Skull: Zhuangzi and Heidegger on Death," *Frontiers of Philosophy in China* 11, no. 3 (2016): 483–500.

64. Levinas, OE, 49–51; Levinas, DIe, 91–93.
65. Levinas, EN, 179; Levinas, ENE, 185.
66. Levinas, EN, 187; Levinas, ENE, 193.
67. Baruch Spinoza, *Complete Works* (Indianapolis, IN: Hackett Publishing, 2002), 283, 567.
68. Levinas, OS, 116–117; Levinas, HS, 159–160.
69. Horkheimer and Adorno, DE, 22; Adorno, GS 3, 46.
70. Arthur Schopenhauer, *The Two Fundamental Problems of Ethics* (Cambridge: Cambridge University Press, 2009), 113–258.
71. Levinas, EN, 107; Levinas, ENE, 117. Levinas continues in this passage that I am responsible for the criminal, but Schopenhauer is also concerned with the ethical status of criminals as in his argument that only deterrence against future harm against others justifies punishment.
72. Levinas, CPP, 52.
73. Levinas, EN, xii; Levinas, ENE, 10.
74. See my analysis of this problematic in Eric S. Nelson, "Heidegger's Failure to Overcome Transcendental Philosophy," in *Transcendental Inquiry: Its History, Methods and Critiques*, ed. Halla Kim and Steven Hoeltzel (Cham, Switzerland: Palgrave Macmillan, 2016), 159–179.
75. Levinas, CPP, 130.
76. Levinas, CPP, 130–131; Levinas, EE, 51–60; Levinas, DEE, 93–105.
77. Compare Levinas, OS, 119–121; Levinas, HS. 162–165.
78. Levinas, NTR, 102.
79. Adorno, CM, 102.
80. Levinas, OI, 353, 473.
81. Levinas, TI, 213.
82. Levinas, GCM, 171; Levinas, DVI, 257.
83. Levinas, BPW, 73.
84. Nick Smith opposes Adorno's materialism to Levinas's dogmatism of transcendence. His interpretation appears to underestimate the significance of the moment of nonidentity in Adorno, which allows for the critique of instrumental reason and existing society, and the materialist moment in Levinas that is the locus of the ethical. See Smith, "Adorno vs. Levinas," 299.
85. Levinas, EE, 4; Levinas, DEE, 19.

Chapter 5

1. The works of the ecohistorian William Cronon are a primary example of the cultural and social-political formation of experiences and theories of nature. On the construction of nature, and whether this insight is a threat to

or a basis for environmental thought, see his introduction to William Cronon, "Introduction: In Search of Nature," in *Uncommon Ground: Rethinking the Human Place in Nature*, ed. William Cronon (New York: Norton, 1996), 23–68. David Blackbourn's interpretation can be interpreted as a powerful example of Adorno's notion of "natural history." Blackbourn's inquiry discloses the interactions between the human transformation of the natural world and discourses concerning nature that praise as "natural" landscapes and rivers that have already repeatedly been transformed by human activities. Especially noteworthy, given Adorno and Levinas's critiques of "nature" in relation to national socialism, is the Nazi ideological and material reconstruction of nature. See Blackbourn, *Conquest of Nature*, 251–309.

2. Peter Singer, "All Animals Are Equal." *Philosophical Exchange* 1, no. 5 (1974): 103–116.

3. The outbreak of the irrational is at the service of incarnations of technical or instrumental rationality and the domination of nature, according to Adorno, HF, 15; on social Darwinism, see Adorno, HF, 211.

4. Adorno, MCP, 129–130.

5. Adorno, HF, 96; compare Marx, *Selected Writings*, 147.

6. Marx critiqued the historical school's ideological vision of nature in an early journalistic article published in 1842; see Karl Marx and Friedrich Engels, *Marx-Engels-Werke*, 43 vols. (Berlin: Dietz-Verlag, 1956–1990), 78–79. Marx has an attitude of critical appreciation toward Darwinism. Marx rejected Darwin's rediscovery of English society in nature while recognizing the theory of evolution through natural selection as promoting a materialist natural history. Compare J. B. Foster, *Marx's Ecology*, 197–199.

7. Adorno, CI, 30, 41, 45.

8. Compare Levinas, OE, 49–51; Levinas, DIe, 91–93.

9. Notably, Levinas, EN, 179; Levinas, ENE, 185.

10. Levinas, EN, 187; Levinas, ENE, 193.

11. Levinas, EE, 51; Levinas, DEE, 93.

12. Levinas, EE, 57; Levinas, DEE, 101; Levinas, CPP, 130–131.

13. Levinas, TI, 213.

14. Derrida, Animal, 12, 55.

15. John Llewelyn, "Am I Obsessed by Bobby? (Humanism of the Other Animal)," in *Re-Reading Levinas*, ed. Robert Bernasconi and Simon Critchley (Bloomington: Indiana University Press, 1991), 234–245.

16. Adorno's project of a "critical materialism" has been articulated in relation to his analysis of "natural history" in Cook, "Adorno's Critical Materialism," 719–737.

17. Adorno, ND, 321.

18. Peter Dews, *The Idea of Evil* (Malden, MA: Blackwell, 2008), 187.

19. Levinas makes his thesis concerning the immanence of things, objects, and environments clear in Levinas, AlT, 3–5; Levinas, Aet, 27–29.

20. Compare Adorno, MCP, 145.

21. Adorno, GS 1; Karl Marx, *Selected Writings*, ed. L. H. Simon (Indianapolis, IN: Hackett, 1994), 107.

22. On environmental aesthetics without nature, see Thomas Heyd, *Encountering Nature: Toward an Environmental Culture* (Aldershot, UK: Ashgate, 2007); on denaturalizing environmental movements, see Biro, *Denaturalizing Ecological Politics*; and on nature as an ideological and obsolete paradigm in the context of the "end of nature," see Vogel, *Against Nature*.

23. Levinas, DF, 22–23; Levinas, DL, 44–45.

24. Levinas, DF, 8; Levinas, DL, 22; Levinas, OO, 29, 38.

25. Benso carefully examines how Levinas prioritizes not only the human species but also the adult male human face. See Silvia Benso, *The Face of Things* (Albany: State University of New York Press, 2000), 39–43. On the possibilities of interspecies ethics in a continental philosophical context, compare Cynthia Willett, *Interspecies Ethics* (New York: Columbia University Press, 2014).

26. Levinas, EN, 17, 46–48; Levinas, ENE, 27, 57–59.

27. As noted in the previous chapter, compare Adorno, MMP, 13; Levinas, EN, 116–117; Levinas, ENE, 126–127; Levinas, OB, 182; Levinas, AE, 230.

28. Levinas, EN, 116; Levinas, ENE, 126.

29. Levinas, DF, 233; Levinas, DL, 351.

30. Levinas, DF, 231–232; Levinas, DL, 347–349.

31. Levinas, DF, 233; Levinas, DL, 351.

32. Levinas, OS, 119; Levinas, HS. 162.

33. For discussion of this issue, see Nelson, *Daoism*.

34. Levinas, DF, 26; Levinas, DL, 50–51.

35. Levinas, DF, 233; Levinas, DL, 351.

36. Levinas, DEH, 132.

37. For alternative accounts of the ethical import of Heidegger's works, see Megan Altman, "Mortality and Morality: A Heideggerian Interpretation of Kierkegaard's Either/Or," in *The Horizons of Authenticity: Essays in Honor of Charles Guignon's Work on Phenomenology, Existentialism, and Moral Psychology*, ed. Megan Altman and Hans Pedersen (Dordrecht, Netherlands: Springer, 2015), 219–237; Megan Altman, "Heidegger on the Struggle for Belongingness and Being at Home," *Frontiers of Philosophy in China* 11, no. 3 (2016): 444–462; Eric S. Nelson, "Heidegger and the Ethics of Facticity," in *Rethinking Facticity*, ed. Francois Raffoul and Eric S. Nelson (Albany: State University of New York Press, 2008), 129–147; Eric S. Nelson, "Heidegger and the Questionability of the Ethical," *Studia Phænomenologica* 8 (2008): 395–419.

38. On the difficulties of such responsiveness, in the context of aesthetics, see Malcolm Budd, *The Aesthetic Appreciation of Nature* (Oxford: Oxford University Press, 2002), 9–19, 119–121.

39. Compare Habermas, *On the Pragmatics of Communication*, 428; Habermas, *Future of Human Nature*, 33.

40. Levinas, *OB*, 11; Levinas, *AE*, 13.
41. Levinas, *DF*, 21–22; Levinas, *DL*, 43–44.
42. Levinas, *IRB*, 168.
43. Levinas, *OB*, 87, 159, 177.
44. On reason and responsibility in Levinas in the context of ecology, see David Michael Kleinberg-Levin, *Before the Voice of Reason: Echoes of Responsibility in Merleau-Ponty's Ecology and Levinas's Ethics* (Albany: State University of New York Press, 2008).
45. Levinas, *EI*, 85–86; Levinas, *Eei*, 79–80.
46. Levinas, *DF*, 153; Levinas, *DL*, 234–235. On the context of this story, also compare Herzog, "Dogs and Fire," 359–379.
47. *Pirkei Avot* 2:10, in Moïse Schuhl, S. Ulmann, and Robert Sommer, *Pirke-avot = Les Maximes des Pères: Texte Hébraïque: Traduction Francaise et Notes* (Paris: Les Editions Colbo, 1992).
48. *Pirkei Avot* 2:5, in Moïse Schuhl, S. Ulmann, and Robert Sommer, *Pirke-avot = Les Maximes des Pères: Texte Hébraïque: Traduction Francaise et Notes* (Paris: Les Editions Colbo, 1992).
49. Llewelyn, "Am I Obsessed by Bobby?," 234–245.
50. For an alternative interpretation, see Gerhardt, "Ethics of Animals," 174–178. Note Wood's assessment of Levinas's limitations regarding animals and the environment in Wood, "Some Questions," 152–169; Derrida interrogates the enchantment and idolatry of Bobby in Derrida, *Animal*, 113–117.
51. Compare Moyn, *Origins of the Other*, 190–192.
52. Levinas, *IRB*, 136, 145.
53. Levinas, *DF*, 26; Levinas, *DL*, 50–51; Levinas, *OE*, 54; Levinas, *DIe*, 96–97; Levinas, *UH*, 18; Levinas, *LIH*, 30.
54. Levinas, *UH*, 20; Levinas, *LIH*, 32.
55. Levinas, *IRB*, 128, 136.
56. Levinas, *OE*, 73; Levinas, *DIe*, 127.
57. Compare Moyn, *Origins of the Other*, 206–207.
58. By potentially conflating "nature" and fascism, it might be argued that Levinas negatively reiterates the fascist depiction of nature as a state of constant war and pseudo-Darwinian struggle for survival.
59. Levinas, *EN*, xii; Levinas, *ENE*, 10; Bernasconi illustrates how Levinas's critique of Heidegger rests on a critique of the self-assertion of the will, self-concern, and ego in the "struggle for existence" (*Kampf ums Dasein*) in Bernasconi, "Levinas and the Struggle for Existence," 171–173. Levinas's criticisms presuppose an egoistic and biologistic interpretation of Heidegger. This issue is more complicated in the case of Nietzsche, who saw himself as a critic of Darwin in interpreting life through the "will to power" rather than "survival of the fittest." Nietzsche rejected the Darwinist notion of a "struggle for life"

in favor of the self-assertion of and "struggle for power" in Friedrich Nietzsche, *Twilight of the Idols*, trans. Richard Polt (Indianapolis, IN: Hackett, 1997), 59.

60. Levinas, *TI*, 110–111.
61. Adorno, *HF*, 100.
62. Levinas, *TI*, 112.
63. Levinas, *TO*, 63; Levinas, *TA*, 45–46.
64. Wood, "Some Questions," 153–154.
65. Levinas, *TI*, 131.
66. Levinas, *TO*, 69; Levinas, *TA*, 55–56; Adorno emphasized "the sensuous actuality of the course of history as enacted by individual human beings" in his critique of Hegel in Adorno, *HF*, 42.
67. As in his discussion of Marx in Levinas, *UH*, 16–17; Levinas, *LIH*, 27–28.
68. Heidegger himself increasingly challenged the priority of pragmatic relations with things and "tool-being" in his later thought, distinguishing a responsive poetic dwelling in the midst of things from their prevailing instrumentalization.
69. Levinas, *OB*, 73–74.
70. Levinas, *OB*, 4 and 178.
71. On Levinas's purported Gnosticism, see Gillian Rose, *Mourning Becomes the Law: Philosophy and Representation* (Cambridge: Cambridge University Press, 1996), 37–38; and Slavoj Žižek, *Organs without Bodies: Deleuze and Consequences* (New York: Routledge, 2004), 106.
72. Citation from Levinas, *TO*, 42; also compare Levinas, *TO*, 43, 54, 75.
73. Levinas, *TI*, 221.
74. This is all the more apparent with the publication of his notebooks (Levinas, *O1*; *O2*; *O3*).
75. Levinas, *TI*, 115.
76. Levinas, *EN*, 13–14.
77. Levinas, *EE*, 44; Levinas, *DEE*, 67.
78. Levinas, *TO*, 43, 54.
79. Levinas, *EN*, 23, 29.
80. Levinas, *AIT*, 26–27; Levinas, *Aet*, 47–48.
81. Levinas, *OB*, 84–85.
82. Levinas, *OB*, 75; Levinas, *AE*, 95.
83. For a feminist interpretation and critique of Levinas's imaging of the feminine and the maternal, compare Chanter, *Time, Death, and the Feminine*; Luce Irigaray, "Questions to Emmanuel Levinas: On the Divinity Of Love," in *Re-Reading Levinas*, ed. Robert Bernasconi and Simon Critchley (Bloomington: Indiana University Press, 1991), 109–118; Luce Irigaray, *An Ethics of Sexual Difference* (Ithaca: Cornell University Press, 1993); Luce Irigaray, "The Fecundity of the Caress: A Reading of Levinas, Totality and Infinity, Phenomenology of

Eros," in *Feminist Interpretations of Levinas*, ed. Tina Chanter (University Park: Pennsylvania State University Press, 2001), 119–144.

84. Levinas, OB, 76; Levinas, AE, 96. Simone de Beauvoir critiqued the reification of the feminine in Levinas's images of maternity and paternity in his 1947 work *Time and the Other* in Simone de Beauvoir, *The Second Sex* (New York: Vintage, 2012), 1. On the maternal body in Levinas, which is more carefully articulated in Levinas's *Otherwise Than Being*, see the nuanced reading in Chanter, *Time, Death, and the Feminine*, 245; on the significance of natality, compare Anne O'Byrne, *Natality and Finitude* (Bloomington: Indiana University Press, 2010).

85. On natality and right, see Peg Birmingham, "The An-archic Event of Natality and the 'Right to Have Rights,'" *Social Research: An International Quarterly* 74, no. 3 (2007): 763–776; Peg Birmingham, *Hannah Arendt and Human Rights: The Predicament of Common Responsibility* (Bloomington: Indiana University Press, 2006), 4–34.

86. Levinas, OB, 81, 86.

87. Levinas, AlT, 56; Levinas, Aet, 71–72.

88. See Perpich, *Ethics of Emmanuel Levinas*, 150–176.

89. Martin Buber, *Ich und Du* (Stuttgart: Reclam, 2002), 8, 92–93.

90. Levinas, DF, 17, 22–23.

91. Levinas distinguishes natural wholes from "totalities" but does not discuss the potential ethical significance, in Levinas, AlT, 43–44; Levinas, Aet, 60–61.

92. Levinas, UH, 15–17; Levinas, LIH, 26–28.

93. On Levinas's view of Marxism, see Levinas, EN, 119–120; Levinas argued that the struggle for satisfaction and salvation are on an equal footing, such that one cannot abandon the claim for human happiness in Levinas, TO, 60–61. Levinas's relation to Marx and Marxism is more positive than argued in Moyn, *Origins of the Other*, 219–220.

94. Levinas, OB, 77, 113–114.

95. Levinas, DF, 126.

96. Levinas, CPP, 58; translation modified.

97. Levinas, IRB, 133–134.

98. Vandana Shiva examines the nexus of the environmental crisis and human injustice on the basis of class, gender, and race. On the intersection of a just and environmentally appropriate society, and of biodiversity and cultural diversity, see Vandana Shiva, *Earth Democracy: Justice, Sustainability, and Peace* (Cambridge, MA: South End Press, 2005). On the significance of postcolonial thinking for the environment, also see Namita Goswami, "Thinking Problems," *The Journal of Speculative Philosophy* 26.2 (2012): 189–199; Namita Goswami, "The (M)other of All Posts: Postcolonial Melancholia in the Age of Global Warming," *Critical Philosophy of Race* 1, no. 1 (2013): 104–120; and Namita Goswami, "Europe as an Other: Postcolonialism and Philosophers of the Future," *Hypatia* 29, no. 1 (2014): 59–74.

99. Adorno, *PMP*, 15.
100. Adorno, *HF*, 152. Also note the articulation of an expansive naturalism that addresses many concerns with naturalism in Fiona Ellis, *God, Value, and Nature* (Oxford: Oxford University Press, 2014), 21–72.
101. Adorno, *GS 1*, 325–326.
102. Adorno, *HF*, 146–147; Adorno, *ND*, 147.
103. Levinas, *EE*, 93.
104. Adorno, *ND*, 207.
105. Adorno, *ND*, 204.
106. Adorno, *ND*, 17–18.
107. Adorno, *CI*, 29.
108. Adorno, *HF*, 41, 61.
109. Adorno, *HF*, 42.
110. Adorno, *CI*, 34, 29.
111. On the relevance of the "good life" even in the midst of the "bad," damaged, or imperfect life, see "Culture Industry Reconsidered," in Adorno, *CI*, 90; and Adorno, *HF*, 262–263.
112. R. J. S. Manning, *Interpreting Otherwise Than Heidegger* (Pittsburgh, PA: Duquesne University Press, 1993), 190; Espen Hammer reaches the opposite conclusion—that without critique, theory, and the work of mourning, Levinas's ethics is infinite melancholy in *Adorno and the Political*, 120–121.
113. See "Theory and Practice," in Adorno, *CM*, 266.
114. Adorno, *PMP*, 176.
115. On the difference between mass-produced and conformist individualism, the individuals that it sacrifices, and the ones who can resist their absorption, see Adorno, *CI*, 35, 52; on the theodicy and conformist function of the category of the "individual," compare Adorno, *HF*, 60, 212, 265.
116. See Adorno, "Resignation," *CM*; and Adorno, *HF*, 97.
117. Adorno, *HF*, 78.
118. Adorno, *HF*, 23.
119. Adorno, *ND*, 192; on the priority of the object and critique of the subjective reduction, see Horowitz, *Ethics at a Standstill*, 191–194.
120. On alternative ways of conceiving and experiencing subjectivity and interpreting the subject, compare Huntington, *Ecstatic Subjects*, as well as Claudia Leeb, "Toward a Theoretical Outline of the Subject: The Centrality of Adorno and Lacan for Feminist Political Theorizing," *Political Theory* 36 no. 3 (2008): 351–376; and Claudia Leeb, *Power and Feminist Agency in Capitalism: Toward a New Theory of the Political Subject* (Oxford: Oxford University Press, 2017).
121. John E. Drabinski, *Sensibility and Singularity: The Problem of Phenomenology in Levinas* (Albany: State University of New York Press, 2001), 155; compare Levinas, *EN*, 92.
122. Levinas, *EN*, 92.
123. On negativity and nonidentity in Levinas, see Levinas, *OB*, 9 and 13.

124. On Levinas's identification of immanence with essence, note Levinas, OB, 17.

125. "The Schema of Mass Culture," in Adorno, CI, 54–55.

126. Adorno, HF, respectively 23 and 266.

127. Adorno, HF, 47, 55.

128. Adorno, KCPR, 234.

129. Adorno, HF, 11.

130. On *das Hinzutretende*, see Adorno, HF, 228, 234, 255, and 260; on the loss of empirical reality in the culture industry, see "Schema of Mass Culture," in Adorno, CI, 53.

131. On the significance of Hook, see Thomas Wheatland, *The Frankfurt School in Exile* (Minneapolis: University of Minnesota Press, 2009), 106–131.

132. Adorno, HF, 255, 266.

133. Compare Adorno, GS 1, 345, 354.

134. Adorno, GS 1, 358.

135. Marx, *Selected Writings*, 95–96, 152.

136. Adorno, HF, 116–117.

137. Levinas, CPP, 100.

138. Levinas, LR, 160–165.

139. Levinas, OO, 29, 38.

140. On the divergent ways that Adorno and Levinas endeavor to universalize the Jewish experience of what escapes conceptualization, see Oona Eisenstadt, "Levinas and Adorno: Universalizing the Jew after Auschwitz," *Journal of Jewish Thought and Philosophy* 14, no. 1–2 (2006): 131–151.

141. Levinas, OO, 38.

142. Adorno, HF, 192–193. On the question of hardening, in relation to attunement and bearing, note the discussion in Patricia J. Huntington, "Primordial Attunement, Hardening, and Bearing," in *Rethinking Facticity*, ed. François Raffoul and Eric S. Nelson (Albany: State University of New York Press, 2008), 317–344.

143. Levinas, TI, 229.

144. Horowitz, *Ethics at a Standstill*, 225.

145. Levinas, TI, 304. Compare the comprehensive and illuminating analysis of "metaphysical desire" in Drew M. Dalton, *Longing for the Other: Levinas and Metaphysical Desire* (Pittsburgh, PA: Duquesne University Press, 2009).

146. Levinas, OO, 29, 38.

147. Levinas, LR, 160–165.

148. "Reality and its Shadow," in Levinas, UH, 85–90; Levinas, LIH, 119–124; compare Jill Robbins, *Altered Readings: Levinas and Literature* (Chicago, IL: Chicago University Press, 1999), 53.

149. Adorno and Derrida converge on this question, as in Derrida, *Animal*, 54, 60, 123–124.

150. Adorno, HF, 154–155.
151. Adorno, MM, 68/105.
152. David Michael Kleinberg-Levin, *Gestures of Ethical Life: Reading Hölderlin's Question of Measure after Heidegger* (Stanford, CA: Stanford University Press, 2005), 343.
153. Adorno, MM, 68/105.
154. Levinas, EN, 33; Adorno, BPM, 80. A shorter version of this criticism is found in Adorno, HF, 209–210. Derrida discusses this passage from Adorno, an author he mostly ignores, in Derrida, *Animal*, 100–101.
155. Adorno, HF, 209.
156. Dallmayr, "Adorno and Heidegger on Modernity," 167–169.
157. Adorno questions the role of Heidegger's language of "hale life" in damaged life ("heiles Leben, als Gegensatz zu dem beschädigten") in Adorno, JA, 59.
158. Adorno, HF, 260–261.
159. Adorno, HF, 13.
160. Adorno, HF, 45.
161. Adorno, HF, 106–107.
162. Adorno, HF, 120–122.
163. Adorno, HF, 122.
164. Adorno, HF, 123–124.
165. Adorno, HF, 128.
166. Adorno, HF, 133–134.
167. Adorno, HF, 135.
168. On the conformist character of consensus, note Adorno, HF, 31–32, 64.
169. Levinas mentions the "mastery of nature" without exploring its biosocial nexus as in Levinas, AlT, 15, 47, and 131; Levinas, Aet, 37, 64, 136.
170. Adorno, HF, 174.
171. Adorno, HF, 179; Levinas, TI, 54.
172. On its social character, see Adorno, HF, 180; on its bodily character, see Adorno, HF, 213–215, 228, 234–235, 237.
173. Levinas, TI, 43; Levinas, OB, 91, 101, 107, 122.
174. On Levinas as critic of materialism, see Horowitz, *Ethics at a Standstill*, 27–31; on the materialist moment in Levinas, see the robust account in Tom Sparrow, *Levinas Unhinged* (Winchester, UK: Zero Books, 2013).
175. Levinas, TO, 57–58.
176. Levinas, OB, 108; compare Levinas, O1, 488.
177. Levinas, EE, 69–70; Levinas, DEE, 123–124; Levinas, OB, 108.
178. Levinas, OB, 101–102.
179. Levinas, TO, 89; Levinas, OB, 90; on the different senses of touching and being touched in Levinas, see Antje Kapust, *Berührung ohne Berührung: Ethik und Ontologie bei Merleau-Ponty und Lévinas* (Munich: Wilhelm Fink Verlag, 1999).

180. Adorno, *HF*, 213, 239.
181. Adorno, *PT*, 17.
182. Adorno, *HF*, 240.
183. Concerning Adorno's complicities with instrumental rationality and failures in relation to the nonidentical, see Claudia Leeb, "Desires and Fears: Women, Class and Adorno," *Theory and Event* 11, no. 1 (2008): http://doi.org/10.1353/tae.2008.0010.
184. Heyd, *Encountering Nature*, 15–36, 123–129, 181–186.
185. Levinas, *TI*, 212–214.
186. See the insightful clarification of this point in Krzysztof Ziarek, *Inflected Language: Toward a Hermeneutics of Nearness: Heidegger, Levinas, Stevens, Celan* (Albany: State University of New York Press, 1994), 93.
187. Hegel himself arguably recognized that betrayal and the beholdenness are of the same cloth in the process of sublation in the dialectic of the *Phenomenology of Spirit*. On Adorno and Hegel on dialectic, see Alison Stone, "Adorno and the Disenchantment of Nature," *Philosophy and Social Criticism* 32, no. 2 (2006): 231–253.
188. Adorno, *HF*, 150, 158.
189. On the issues of economic reductionism and the commodification of nature, see J. B. Foster, *Ecology against Capitalism*, 30–34.
190. Levinas, *TI*, 208.
191. Adorno, *HF*, 157.
192. Levinas, *AlT*, 137; Levinas, *Aet*, 141; Levinas, *TI*, preface.
193. Adorno, *MM*, 152/244.
194. Adorno, *LND*, 9, 19, 31.
195. Adorno, *LND*, 6.

Chapter 6

1. Benjamin, *Illuminations*, 254.
2. Adorno, *MM*, 153/247; Adorno, *GS* 4, 283.
3. Marx, *Selected Writings*, 28.
4. Hegel, *Phänomenologie des Geistes*, secs. 547–549.
5. Levinas, *ET*, 113; Levinas, *Eet*, 111.
6. On religion and its radical critique in critical materialism, see Idit Dobbs-Weinstein, *Spinoza's Critique of Religion and Its Heirs: Marx, Benjamin, Adorno* (Cambridge: Cambridge University Press, 2015). On Spinoza's significance for Hegel and Adorno, also compare Jeffrey Bernstein, "Spinoza, Hegel, and Adorno on Judaism and History," in *Between Hegel and Spinoza: A Volume of Critical Essays*, ed. Hasana Sharp and Jason E. Smith (London: Bloomsbury, 2012), 209–227.

7. Max Horkheimer, "Was wir 'Sinn' nennen, wird verschwinden," *Der Spiegel*, January 1970, 79–84.

8. Enrique Dussel, *Philosophy of Liberation* (Eugene, OR: Wipf and Stock, 2003), 4.

9. 2 Corinthians 4:8–9. New Testament references are to John Barton and Bruce M. Metzger, *The Holy Bible, Containing the Old and New Testaments: New Revised Standard Version* (Oxford: Oxford University Press, 2003).

10. Friedrich Nietzsche, *Genealogy of Morality* (Indianapolis, IN: Hackett, 1998), I.8.

11. Nietzsche, *Genealogy of Morality*, II.7.

12. Elaine Scarry, *The Body in Pain* (New York: Oxford University Press, 1985).

13. Scarry, *The Body in Pain*.

14. Friedrich Nietzsche, *Beyond Good and Evil* (Oxford: Oxford University Press, 1998), II.44.

15. Nietzsche, *Beyond Good and Evil*, III.46 and VII.225.

16. Friedrich Nietzsche, *Untimely Meditations* (Cambridge: Cambridge University Press, 1983), 62.

17. Friedrich Nietzsche, *Thus Spoke Zarathustra* (Oxford: Oxford University Press, 2005), II.12.

18. Friedrich Nietzsche, *Twilight of the Idols*, trans. Richard Polt (Indianapolis, IN: Hackett, 1997), IX.18/p. 60.

19. Gottfried W. Leibniz, *Theodicy: Essays on the Goodness of God, the Freedom of Man, and the Origin of Evil* (La Salle, IL: Open Court, 1988).

20. Adorno, MM, 22/43.

21. Adorno, MM, 24/46.

22. On the problematic of the logic of sacrifice and the potential to contest and overcome it, see Huntington, *Ecstatic Subjects* 119–158.

23. Adorno, MM, 61/98.

24. Nietzsche, *Twilight of the Idols*, VI.6/p. 34.

25. On the problematic nexus of karma, violence, and suffering, see Eric S. Nelson, "Questioning Karma: Buddhism and the Phenomenology of the Ethical," *Revisioning Karma: Journal of Buddhist Ethics*, ed. Charles Prebish, Damien Keown, and Dale S. Wright (2007), 353–373; Eric S. Nelson, "The Complicity of the Ethical: Causality, Karma, and Violence in Buddhism and Levinas," in *Levinas and Asian Thought*, ed. Leah Kalmanson, Frank Garrett, and Sarah Mattice (Pittsburgh, PA: Duquesne University Press, 2013), 99–114.

26. Adorno and Horkheimer, DE, 92.

27. On anti-Semitism, also see Adorno, Vo, 440–467. On suffering in Adorno and its import, see Kelly Fritsch, "On the Negative Possibility of Suffering: Adorno, Feminist Philosophy, and the Transfigured Crip to Come," *Disability Studies Quarterly* 33, no. 4 (2013); Raymond Geuss, "Suffering and Knowledge in Adorno," *Constellations* 12, no. 1 (2005): 3–20.

28. Nietzsche, *Genealogy of Morality*, III.6; Adorno, AT, 136.
29. Adorno, AT, 136.
30. Nietzsche, *Thus Spoke Zarathustra*, I.5.
31. Adorno, MM, 39/64.
32. Nietzsche, *Genealogy of Morality*, II.16.
33. Nietzsche, *Genealogy of Morality*, I.6; Nietzsche, *Thus Spoke Zarathustra*, II.4.
34. Tyrus Miller, *Late Modernism: Politics, Fiction, and the Arts between the World Wars* (Berkeley: University of California Press, 1999), 232.
35. Adorno and Horkheimer, DE, 92.
36. Marx, *Selected Writings*, 99; translation modified.
37. Marx, *Selected Writings*, 28.
38. Such as Jürgen Habermas, *Postmetaphysical Thinking II* (Cambridge: John Wiley and Sons, 2017), 3–42.
39. Nietzsche, *Genealogy of Morality*, I.6.
40. Nietzsche, *Beyond Good and Evil*, III.45.
41. On Schopenhauer's importance for Nietzsche, compare Adorno, GS 1, 98.
42. On the problematic of willing and willlessness in Nietzsche, compare Bret W. Davis, "Zen after Zarathustra: The Problem of the Will in the Confrontation between Nietzsche and Buddhism," *Journal of Nietzsche Studies*, no. 28 (2004): 89–138.
43. On Nietzsche's complex and changing relationship with Buddhism, see Jason M. Wirth, *Nietzsche and Other Buddhas: Philosophy after Comparative Philosophy* (Bloomington: Indiana University Press, 2019).
44. Compare Horkheimer, *Between Philosophy and Social Science*, 16.
45. Nietzsche, *Genealogy of Morality*, III.28.
46. On guilt in existential philosophy, compare Hye Young Kim, "Is Guilt a Feeling? An Analysis of Guilt in Existential Philosophy," *Comparative and Continental Philosophy* 9, no. 3 (2017): 1–11.
47. Nietzsche, *Genealogy of Morality*, II.24, III.11.
48. Benjamin, *Illuminations*, 254.
49. Nietzsche, *Genealogy of Morality*, I.6.
50. Nietzsche, *Genealogy of Morality*, III.15.
51. Nietzsche, *Genealogy of Morality*, I.7 and III.15; on resentment in relation to dynamics of recognition in Nietzsche, see Eric S. Nelson, "The Question of Resentment in Nietzsche and Confucian Ethics," *Taiwan Journal of East Asian Studies* 10, no. 1 (2013): 17–51.
52. Nietzsche, *Genealogy of Morality*, I.8.
53. Benjamin, *Illuminations*, 254.
54. On temporality and embodiment in Levinas's "weak messianism," compare Bettina Bergo, "Levinas's Weak Messianism in Time and Flesh, or

the Insistence of Messiah Ben David," *Journal for Cultural Research* 13, no. 3–4 (2009): 225–248.

55. Nietzsche presciently examined the skeptical and relativistic legitimization of religiosity in Nietzsche, *Genealogy of Morality*, III.6.

56. "The essential element in the black art of obscurantism is not that it wants to darken individual understanding but that it wants to blacken our picture of the world, and darken our idea of existence"; Friedrich Nietzsche, *Human, All Too Human* (Cambridge: Cambridge University Press, 1999), 27.

57. Cynthia Halpern, *Suffering, Politics, Power: A Genealogy in Modern Political Theory* (Albany: State University of New York Press, 2002), 201.

58. This occurs in Nietzsche's reaction to women when "[h]e falsely accuses woman of wielding tremendous power over him." See Katrin Froese, *Nietzsche, Heidegger, and Daoist Thought: Crossing Paths In-between* (Albany: State University of New York Press, 2006), 206. For a nuanced approach to the role of male fragility and vulnerability in the dynamics of the maintenance of male power, as articulated in the contemporary ideological discourse of "male rights," see Christa Hodapp, *Men's Rights, Gender, and Social Media* (Lanham, MD: Lexington Books, 2017).

59. On the problematic of naturalism and antinaturalism, see Ellis, *God, Value, and Nature*, 21–72; Eric S. Nelson, "Between Nature and Spirit: Naturalism and Anti-Naturalism in Dilthey," in *Anthropologie und Geschichte: Studien zu Wilhelm Dilthey aus Anlass seines 100. Todestages*, ed. G. D'Anna, H. Johach, E. S. Nelson (Würzburg: Königshausen & Neumann, 2013), 141–160; Eric S. Nelson, "Naturalism and Anti-Naturalism in Nietzsche," *Archives of the History of Philosophy and of Social Thought* 58 (2013): 213–227.

60. Adorno, GS 7, 17.

61. Adorno, MM, 152/244.

62. Adorno, MM, 85/132.

63. See the valuable accounts of antitheodicy in, for instance, Hent de Vries, *Minimal Theologies: Critiques of Secular Reason in Adorno and Levinas* (Baltimore, MD: Johns Hopkins University Press, 2005); Carl B. Sachs, "The Acknowledgement of Transcendence: Anti-Theodicy in Adorno and Levinas," *Philosophy and Social Criticism* 37, no. 3 (2011): 273–294.

64. Enrique Dussel, "'Sensibility' and 'Otherness' in Emmanuel Levinas," *Philosophy Today* 43 (1999): 129.

65. Levinas, EN, 95; Levinas, ENE, 105.

Chapter 7

1. On Levinas's reception of Kierkegaard focusing on the issue of the ethical, see especially Michael R. Paradiso-Michau, *The Ethical in Kierkegaard and*

Levinas (London: Continuum, 2012); on questions of the secular and the religious in Kierkegaard, see Eric S. Nelson, "Religious Crisis, Ethical Life, and Kierkegaard's Critique of Christendom," *Acta Kierkegaardiana* 4 (2009): 170–186. This chapter will keep in mind but not analyze Derrida's related significant account of the narrative of Abraham and Isaac in "Literature in Secret?" in Jacques Derrida, *The Gift of Death and Literature in Secret* (Chicago, IL: University of Chicago Press, 2008). On the secret, also see Raffoul, "Invisible and Secret," 395–414.

2. I examine these two versions (Confucian and Buddhist) of ethical asymmetry in further detail in relation to Levinas's ethics in, respectively, Eric S. Nelson, "Levinas and Early Confucian Ethics: Religion, Ritual, and the Sources of Morality," *Levinas Studies* 4 (2009): 177–207; and Nelson, "Complicity of the Ethical," 99–114. Also compare the intercultural discussion of the figures of the Messiah and the Bodhisattva in the context of utopianism and antiutopianism in Leah Kalmanson, "The Messiah and the Bodhisattva: Anti-Utopianism Re-Revisited," *Shofar: An Interdisciplinary Journal of Jewish Studies* 30, no. 4 (2011): 113–125.

3. Eric S. Nelson, *Daoism and Environmental Philosophy: Nourishing Life* (London: Routledge, 2020). On Daoism and Derrida's deconstruction, see Steven Burik, *The End of Comparative Philosophy and the Task of Comparative Thinking: Heidegger, Derrida, and Daoism* (Albany: State University of New York Press, 2010); Chung-Ying Cheng, "Deconstruction and Différance: Onto-Return and Emergence in a Daoist Interpretation of Derrida," supplement *Journal of Chinese Philosophy* 40 (2012): 31–50. On the early Daoist deconstructive ethics of aporia, see Dan Lusthaus, "Aporetic Ethics in the *Zhuangzi*," in *Hiding the World in the World: Uneven Discourses on the Zhuangzi*, ed. Scott Cook (Albany: State University of New York Press, 2003), 163–206; Dan Lusthaus, "Zhuangzi's Ethics of Deconstructing Moralistic Self-Imprisonment: Standards without Standards," in *Deconstruction and the Ethical in Asian Thought*, ed. Youru Wang (London: Routledge, 2007), 53–72; and Eric S. Nelson, "Questioning Dao: Skepticism, Mysticism, and Ethics in the *Zhuangzi*," *International Journal of the Asian Philosophical Association* 1, no. 1 (2008): 5–19. On the significance of intercultural philosophy, in contrast to Eurocentric and Anglocentric conceptions of philosophy, compare Eric S. Nelson, *Chinese and Buddhist Philosophy in Early Twentieth-Century German Thought* (London: Bloomsbury, 2017).

4. Genesis/Bereshit 22:1–2. Quotations from the Tanakh are based on the revised edition, *The Holy Scriptures According to the Masoretic Text* (Philadelphia, PA: Jewish Publication Society of America, 1955). On the significance of Genesis, see Avivah Gottlieb Zornberg, *The Beginning of Desire: Reflections on Genesis* (New York: Schocken Books, 1995).

5. Derrida, *Gift of Death*.

6. Jill Robbins, *Prodigal Son / Elder Brother: Interpretation and Alterity in Augustine, Petrarch, Kafka, Levinas* (Chicago, IL: University of Chicago Press, 1991), 78–79.

7. Genesis/Bereshit 4:9; Levinas, *EN*, 110.
8. Levinas, *OB*, 128; Avivah G. Zornberg, *The Murmuring Deep: Reflections on the Rabbinic Unconscious* (New York: Shocken Books, 2008), 86–89.
9. Genesis/Bereshit 3:9; compare Zornberg, *The Murmuring Deep*, 19.
10. Genesis/Bereshit 22:; *hineni* is understood as a "confession of readiness" by Mishael Caspi and John T. Greene, eds., *Unbinding the Binding of Isaac* (Lanham, MD: University Press of America, 2006), viii. Robbins emphasizes its performative and legal character in traditional Jewish readings in Robbins, *Prodigal Son / Elder Brother*, 78.
11. Levinas, *OB*, 144.
12. Levinas, *OB*, 149.
13. Levinas, *OB*, 149; Levinas, *EI*, 88; Levinas, *Eei*, 82.
14. See the Bṛhadāraṇyaka Upaniṣad 1.4.1 in Patrick Olivelle, ed. and trans., *Upaniṣads* (New York: Oxford University Press, 1996), 13. Compare Katrin Seele, *"Das bist Du!": Das "Selbst" (Ātman) und das "Andere" in der Philosophie der frühen Upaniṣaden und bei Buddha* (Würzburg: Königshausen und Neumann, 2006), 44.
15. Bṛhadāraṇyaka Upaniṣad 1.4.2–3. Much more needs to be said about loneliness and solitude with respect to Levinas than can be done at this point. On the philosophical and ethical import of loneliness and solitude, of isolation and being unheard, compare the nuanced interpretations in Patricia J. Huntington, *Loneliness and Lament: A Journey to Receptivity* (Bloomington: Indiana University Press, 2009); and Stauffer, "Heidegger and Levinas."
16. Laozi, *Daodejing: A Philosophical Translation*, trans. Roger T. Ames and David L. Hall (New York: Ballantine Books, 2004), 106.
17. On the ecological import of the feminine in early Daoism, compare Eric S. Nelson, "Responding with Dao: Early Daoist Ethics and the Environment," *Philosophy East and West* 59, no. 3 (2009): 294–316.
18. Zhuangzi, *The Essential Writings with Selections from Traditional Commentaries*, trans. Brook Ziporyn (Indianapolis, IN: Hackett, 2009), chapters 2, 11, and 18.
19. Levinas, *AT*, 4.
20. Levinas, *OB*, 149.
21. Levinas, *OB*, 114.
22. Kierkegaard, *Fear and Trembling*, 55.
23. Levinas, *OB*, 199, endnotes 11 and 17; *Isaiah*, 6:8.
24. Levinas, *OB*, 146.
25. Levinas, *OB*, 185; Levinas, *EN*, 228.
26. Levinas, *OB*, 146.
27. Confucius, *Analects*, trans. Roger Ames and Henry Rosemont Jr. (New York: Random House, 1998), 1:1 and 1:16.
28. Compare Haiming Wen, *Confucian Pragmatism as the Art of Contextualizing Personal Experience and World* (Lanham, MD: Lexington Books, 2009), 114.

29. David L. Hall and Roger T. Ames contrast Chinese experiences of immanence with the Western dualistic conception of transcendence throughout their writings; for instance, David Hall and Roger Ames, *Thinking through Confucius* (Albany: State University of New York Press, 1987), 101, 205. Ames articulates anew and defends Confucian immanence against Western transcendence in Roger T. Ames, "Getting Past Transcendence: Determinacy, Indeterminacy, and Emergence in Chinese Natural Cosmology," in *Transcendence, Immanence, and Intercultural Philosophy*, ed. Nahum Brown and William Franke (Dordrecht, Netherlands: Springer, 2016), 3–33. Also compare his account of Confucian ethics in Roger T. Ames, *Confucian Role Ethics: A Vocabulary* (Hong Kong: Chinese University Press, 2011). Lauren Pfister and others have maintained the significance of religious transcendence in early Confucian thought in "Reexamining Whole Person Cultivation: Reconsidering the Significance of Master Kong's 'Knowing the Heavenly Decree' and Yeshuah's 'Beatitudes,'" *Ching Feng* 1, no. 1 (2000): 69–96.

30. On Confucian ethics as a relational role ethics, compare Ames, *Confucian Role Ethics*. On the different modalities of alterity and asymmetry operative in early Confucian and Levinasian ethics, compare Nelson, "Levinas and Early Confucian Ethics," 177–207.

31. For a discussion of these issues, compare Nelson, "Levinas and Early Confucian Ethics," 177–207; on the problem of immanence and transcendence in Chinese philosophy, see the insightful discussion in Ames, "Getting Past Transcendence," 3–33.

32. Levinas, *AIT*, 33.

33. Compare Avivah G. Zornberg, *The Particulars of Rapture: Reflections on Exodus* (New York: Schocken Books, 2011), 309.

34. Levinas, *OB*, 126.

35. Levinas, *AIT*, 127; Levinas, *GCM*, 93–96; Levinas, *DVI*, 148–152.

36. Levinas, *EN*, 60.

37. Levinas, *OB*, 120–121.

38. On the impossibility of either differentiating or identifying God and the Other, and thus religion and ethics in Levinas, see Derrida, *Gift of Death*, 84–85.

39. I argue for this claim in Nelson, "Levinas and Early Confucian Ethics," 177–207.

40. Levinas, *OS*, 119; Levinas, *HS*, 162–163. On the character of Levinas's interpretation of Judaism, see Michael Fagenblat, *A Covenant of Creatures: Levinas's Philosophy of Judaism* (Stanford, CA: Stanford University Press, 2010); and Michael L. Morgan, "Levinas and Judaism," *Levinas Studies* 1 (2005): 1–17.

41. Isaiah, 65:24; Levinas, *OB*, 150.

42. Isaiah, 57:14–18; Levinas, *OB*, 74; Levinas, *EN*, 57.

43. Isaiah, 1:16–17.

44. Genesis/Bereshit 22:7.

45. Immanuel Kant, *Religion and Rational Theology* (Cambridge: Cambridge University Press, 2001), Akademie edition 6:87.

46. See my discussion in Eric S. Nelson, "Schleiermacher on Language, Religious Feeling, and the Ineffable," *Epoché: A Journal for the History of Philosophy* 8, no. 2 (2004): 297–312. On religion as communication, also see Eric S. Nelson, "Faith and Knowledge: Karl Jaspers on Communication and the Encompassing," *Existentia* 13, no. 3–4 (2003): 207–218.

47. Leibniz, *Theodicy*, 225–226.

48. Hermann Cohen, *Religion of Reason: Out of the Sources of Judaism*, trans. Simon Kaplan (Atlanta, GA: Scholars Press, 1995), 397. One traditional reading interprets the narrative as marking a transition from human to animal sacrifice. The transition is instigated by God as a morally transformative pedagogical exercise. However, Isaac's trauma cannot be wiped clean. Isaac becomes a tragic figure in the later tradition associated with the betrayed and the persecuted; his later blindness, which makes him fatefully unable to distinguish Jacob from Esau, is attributed to the smoke in his eyes on the sacrificial pyre on Mount Moriah.

49. Cohen, *Religion of Reason*, 397.

50. Compare Claire E. Katz, "The Responsibility of Irresponsibility: Taking (Yet) Another Look at the *Akedah*," in *Addressing Levinas*, ed. Eric S. Nelson, Antje Kapust, and Kent Still (Evanston, IL: Northwestern University Press, 2005), 28–30. Katz offers here a different account.

51. Carol Delaney interprets "this most patriarchal of stories" as an ideological construction of biological paternity and generative power that legitimates domination, exploitation, and violence; Carol Delaney, *Abraham on Trial: The Social Legacy of Biblical Myth* (Princeton, NJ: Princeton University Press, 1998), 12.

52. See Zornberg, *Murmuring Deep*, 198–199; Shalon Spiegel, *The Last Trial*, trans. Judah Goldin (Woodstock, VT: Jewish Lights Publishing, 1993), 9–12; Jerome I. Gellman, *Abraham! Abraham! Kierkegaard and the Hasidim on the Binding of Isaac* (Aldershot, UK: Ashgate, 2003), 74.

53. Philo, "On Abraham," in *The Works of Philo: Complete and Unabridged*, trans. Charles Duke (Peabody, MA: Hendrickson, 1993), 427.

54. Philo, *Works of Philo*, 32, 425.

55. Kierkegaard, *Fear and Trembling*, 53, 56, 115.

56. Spiegel, *Last Trial*, 12.

57. See Spiegel's elucidation of the diverse Jewish readings and appropriations of the *Akedah*. "Akedah" has multiple meanings, including self-sacrifice and the murder of Jews during persecutions and pogroms. See Spiegel, *Last Trial*, 92.

58. Genesis/Bereshit 22:11.

59. Michaël de Saint-Cheron, *Conversations with Emmanuel Lévinas, 1983–1994* (Pittsburgh, PA: Duquesne University Press, 2010), 15.

60. Genesis/Bereshit 22:11; Levinas, *PN*, 74.
61. Levinas, *PN*, 77.
62. Zornberg, *Murmuring Deep*, 204.
63. Levinas, *PN*, 74, 77; Levinas, *NT*, 114, 117.
64. Kierkegaard, *Fear and Trembling*, 21.
65. Levinas, *PN*, 74, 77.
66. Levinas, *NT*, 114.
67. Levinas, *NT*, 117.
68. Catherine Chalier, "Ethics and the Feminine," in *Re-Reading Levinas*, ed. Robert Bernasconi and Simon Critchley (Bloomington: Indiana University Press, 1991), 124.
69. Levinas, *NT*, 117.
70. On God and the good, compare Fiona Ellis, "Murdoch and Levinas on God and Good," *European Journal for Philosophy of Religion* 1, no. 2 (2009): 63–87.
71. Kierkegaard, *Fear and Trembling*, 7, 20.
72. Levinas, *GCM*, 75; Levinas, *DVI*, 123.
73. For a comparative study of these two forms of passivity in the context of the cultivation and practice of passivity, see Leah Kalmanson and Sarah Mattice, "The *De* of Levinas: Cultivating the Heart-Mind of Radical Passivity," *Frontiers of Philosophy in China* 10, no. 1 (2015): 113–129.
74. See Levinas, *PN*, 68–71. On the paradox of interiority in Kierkegaard, compare Stephen R. Palmquist, "The Paradox of Inwardness in Kant and Kierkegaard," *Journal of Religious Ethics* 44, no. 4 (2016): 738–751.
75. Levinas, *PM*, 171–177.
76. Levinas, *TI*, 305.
77. Levinas, *GCM*, 57; Levinas, *DVI*, 97.
78. Levinas, *GCM*, 59; Levinas, *DVI*, 99.
79. Levinas, *PN*, 74, 77.
80. Genesis/Bereshit 22:11.
81. Genesis/Bereshit 22:11; Levinas, *PN*, 13.
82. Derrida, *Gift of Death*, 68–69.
83. Kierkegaard, *Fear and Trembling*, 54.
84. Levinas, *PN*, 69.
85. Levinas, *GCM*, ix; Levinas, *DVI*, 5.
86. Levinas, *AT*, 5; Levinas, *DF*, 21–22; Levinas, *EN*, 231.
87. Levinas, *EN*, 222.
88. In contrast, Hermann Cohen proposed an arguably more classical conception of law in Judaism. See Halla Kim, "Hermann Cohen on the Concept of Law in Ethics," in *Jewish Religious and Philosophical Ethics*, ed. Curtis Hutt, Halla Kim, Berel Dov Lerner (Abingdon, UK: Routledge, 2017), 131–150.
89. Levinas, *EN*, 110.

90. On self-power and other-power, see Bret W. Davis, "Naturalness in Zen and Shin Buddhism: Before and Beyond Self- and Other-Power," *Contemporary Buddhism* 15, no. 2 (2014): 433–447.

91. G. E. Moore, *Principia Ethica* (Cambridge: Cambridge University Press, 1948). Also see chapter 10 below.

92. Moore, *Principia Ethica*, sec. 27, para. 3.

93. François Raffoul, "Derrida and the Ethics of the Im-possible," *Research in Phenomenology* 38, no. 2 (2008): 273. Raffoul notes further on the same page, "The return to the conditions of possibility of ethics would thus be an aporetic gesture, a movement leading into an aporia, into an impossibility." Also compare Raffoul, *Origins of Responsibility*.

94. Compare Raffoul, "Derrida and Ethics," 270–290; François Raffoul, *Origins of Responsibility*.

95. Karen Leslie Carr and Philip J. Ivanhoe, *The Sense of Anti-Rationalism: The Religious Thoughts of Zhuangzi and Kierkegaard* (New York: Seven Bridges Press, 1999). For a more adequate account of negativity in the *Zhuangzi*, see David Chai, *Zhuangzi and the Becoming of Nothingness* (Albany: State University of New York Press, 2019).

96. For example, see Hans-Georg Moeller, *The Moral Fool: A Case for Amorality* (New York: Columbia University Press, 2009).

97. Compare Lusthaus, "Aporetic Ethics in the *Zhuangzi*," 163–206.

98. Zhuangzi, *Zhuangzi*, 101. I examine this theme in Nelson, *Daoism and Environmental Philosophy*.

99. On Daoist conceptions of nothingness, see David Chai, "Daoism and Wu," *Philosophy Compass* 9, no. 10 (2014): 663–671; David Chai, "Nothingness and the Clearing: Heidegger, Daoism and the Quest for Primal Clarity," *Review of Metaphysics* 67, no. 3 (2014): 583–601; and Mario Wenning, "Kant and Daoism on Nothingness," *Journal of Chinese Philosophy* 38, no. 4 (2011): 556–568.

100. On the ethics of life suggested in the *Zhuangzi*, see Nelson, "Questioning Dao," 5–19; Nelson, "Responding with Dao," 294–316; Eric S. Nelson, "Kant and China: Aesthetics, Race, and Nature," *Journal of Chinese Philosophy* 38, no. 4 (2011): 509–525.

101. I discuss in fuller detail an-archic nature and ethical naturalism in early Daoism in Nelson, "Questioning Dao," 5–19; Nelson, "Responding with Dao," 294–316; Nelson, "Kant and China," 509–525; Eric S. Nelson, "The Human and the Inhuman: Ethics and Religion in the *Zhuangzi*," supplement, *Journal of Chinese Philosophy* 41 (2014): 723–739.

102. Compare Nelson, "Questioning Dao," 5–19; Nelson, "Responding with Dao," 294–316; Nelson, "Kant and China," 509–525. On Daoism's import for critical social theory, see the important discussion in Mario Wenning, "Daoism as Critical Theory," *Comparative Philosophy* 2 (2011): 50–71.

103. On the nonhuman in the *Zhuangzi*, see Nelson, "Human and Inhuman," 723–739, as well as the illuminating analysis in Mario Wenning, "Heidegger and Zhuangzi on the Nonhuman: Towards a Transcultural Critique of (Post) Humanism," in *Asian Perspectives on Animal Ethics: Rethinking the Nonhuman*, ed. Chloë Taylor and Neil Dalal (New York: Routledge, 2014), 93–111.

104. On the complex Daoist and Zhuangzian notion of "thing," see the illuminating analyses in David Chai, "Meontological Generativity: A Daoist Reading of the Thing," *Philosophy East and West* 64, no. 2 (2014): 303–318.

105. Søren Kierkegaard, *Works of Love*, trans. Howard V. Hong and Edna H. Hong (Princeton, NJ: Princeton University Press, 2013). Compare Nelson, "Religious Crisis," 170–186.

106. Martin Buber intriguingly hints at the dialogical and personalist (i.e., ethical individualist) dimensions of the *Zhuangzi* in Martin Buber, *Reden und Gleichnisse des Tschuang Tse* (Leipzig: Insel Verlag, 1910); see Jonathan R. Herman, *I and Tao: Martin Buber's Encounter with Chuang Tzu* (Albany: State University of New York Press, 1996); Nelson, *Chinese and Buddhist Philosophy*, 109–129. Eric S. Nelson, "Martin Buber's Phenomenological Interpretation of the *Daodejing*," in *Daoist Encounters with Phenomenology*, ed. David Chai (London: Bloomsbury, 2020), 105–120; Jason M. Wirth, "Martin Buber's Dao," in *Daoist Encounters with Phenomenology*, ed. David Chai (London: Bloomsbury, 2020), 121–134.

107. On aporia and impossibility, see Derrida, *Adieu to Emmanuel Levinas*, Raffoul, "Derrida and Ethics," and Lusthaus, "Aporetic Ethics in the *Zhuangzi*." Park elucidates the "ethics of tension" in the context of Buddhist and Postmodern ethics in Jin Y. Park, *Buddhism and Postmodernity: Zen, Huayan, and the Possibility of Buddhist Postmodern Ethics* (Lanham, MD: Lexington Books, 2010), 205–222; and Jin Y. Park, "Ethics of Tension: A Buddhist-Postmodern Ethical Paradigm," *Taiwan Journal of East Asian Studies* 10, no. 1 (2013): 123–142.

Chapter 8

1. Levinas, *IRB*, 89. M. L. Morgan provides an extensive discussion of Levinas's reading of Vasily Grossman's "Life and Fate" in Michael L. Morgan, *Discovering Levinas* (Cambridge: Cambridge University Press, 2007), 1–12.

2. Samuel Moyn, *Origins of the Other: Emmanuel Levinas between Revelation and Ethics* (Cornell, NY: Cornell University Press, 2005), 12f.

3. Levinas, GCM, 56; Levinas, DVI, 95f.

4. Benjamin, *Illuminations*, 254.

5. Levinas, TI, 77, 75; Levinas, TeI, 74, 73.

6. Levinas, GCM, 57; Levinas, DVI, 94. Compare Levinas, BPW, 131.

7. Levinas, AlT, 27, 166–167; Levinas Aet, 168–170; Levinas, TI, 305; Levinas, TeI, 341.

8. Levinas, *DF*, 14; Levinas, *DL*, 29f.
9. Levinas, *DF*, 7; Levinas, *DL*, 20.
10. Levinas, *OB*, 149; Levinas, *AE*, 190.
11. Levinas, *EN*, 11; Levinas, *ENE*, 19.
12. Levinas, *EE*, 89ff; Levinas, *DEE*, 150ff.
13. Kierkegaard, *Fear and Trembling*, 19; *Søren Kierkegaards Skrifter*, ed. Niels Jørgen Cappelørn, Joakim Garff, Johnny Kondrup, and Alastair McKinnon, 55 vols., Søren Kierkegaard Research Center (Copenhagen: Gads Forlag, 1997–2004), 4:115 (hereafter cited as *SKS*).
14. Dussel, "'Sensibility' and 'Otherness'," 126.
15. On the implications of Auschwitz for Levinas, compare Eisenstadt, "Levinas and Adorno," 131–151. On the question of that which can be represented and its limits, compare John Sanbonmatsu, "The Holocaust Sublime: Singularity, Representation, and the Violence of Everyday Life," *American Journal of Economics and Sociology* 68, no. 1 (2009): 101–126.
16. Levinas, *EN*, 74; Levinas, *ENE*, 110. Also note Levinas *IRB*, 77–78.
17. Levinas, *TO*, 32; Levinas, *TA*, 10.
18. Levinas, *OI*, 53.
19. Levinas, *OB*, 126; Levinas, *AE*, 200f.
20. Levinas, *GCM*, 93–96; Levinas, *DVI*, 148–153.
21. Levinas, *EN*, 60; Levinas, *ENE*, 71.
22. Levinas, *OB*, 159; Levinas, *AE*, 203.
23. See Immanuel Kant, *Anthropology, History, and Education* (Cambridge: Cambridge University Press, 2007), 296; Kant, *Religion and Rational Theology*, 297; Immanuel Kant, *The Conflict of the Faculties* (Lincoln: University of Nebraska Press, 1992), 141. Kant distinguished three kinds of predictive (*vorhersagende*) history: ordinary natural, prophetic supernatural, and a divinatory history consisting of a reflective and morally oriented prediction motivating progress and enlightenment. For a careful discussion of divination as an ethical interpretive device in Kant, see Rudolf A. Makkreel, *Imagination and Interpretation in Kant* (Chicago, IL: University of Chicago Press, 1995), 148.
24. Martin Heidegger, *Gesamtausgabe 97. Anmerkungen I–V (Schwarze Hefte 1942–1948)* (Frankfurt: Klostermann, 2015), 159.
25. Levinas, *OB*, 149; Levinas, *AE*, 190.
26. On the distinction between divination and prophecy, see Levinas, *EN*, 48; Levinas, *TI*, 22.
27. Levinas, *IRB*, 269.
28. Levinas, *PN*, 73, 76f; Levinas, *NP*, 107, 113.
29. Levinas, *PN*, 67; Levinas, *NP*, 100f.
30. Levinas, *EE*, 56; Levinas, *DEE*, 99.
31. Levinas, *DF*, 231–234; Levinas, *DL*, 299–303; Levinas, *TI*, 46f; Levinas, *TeI*, 38f.

32. Levinas, *TI*, 46f; Levinas, *TeI*, 38f; Levinas, *EN*, 17; Levinas, *ENE*, 29.

33. Kierkegaard, *Sickness unto Death*, 82f; Kierkegaard, *SKS 11*, 196f.

34. Søren Kierkegaard, *"The Moment" and Late Writings* (Princeton, NJ: Princeton University Press, 1998), 411, 574. In instances, I adopt the phrasing from Søren Kierkegaard, *Kierkegaard's Attack upon "Christendom,"* trans. Walter Lowrie (Princeton, NJ: Princeton University Press, 1968), 14, 20; Søren Kierkegaard, *Samlede Værker* (hereafter cited as SV), ed. P. P. Rohde, 20 vols. (Copenhagen: Gyldendal, 1962–1964), SV 3:19 and 25.

35. Kierkegaard, *"The Moment" and Late Writings*, 245–249; Kierkegaard, SV 3:19:234–237.

36. Levinas, *AlT*, 55; Levinas *Aet*, 71; Levinas, *TI*, 102.

37. For instance, see the introduction to Salomon Malka, *Emmanuel Levinas: His Life and Legacy* (Pittsburgh, PA: Duquesne University Press, 2006), xxi.

38. Levinas, *OI*, 419.

39. Kierkegaard, *Sickness unto Death*, 98; Kierkegaard, *SKS 4*, 188.

40. Kierkegaard, *Sickness unto Death*, 106f; Kierkegaard, *SKS 4*, 194f.

41. Søren Kierkegaard, *The Book on Adler*, trans. Howard V. Hong and Edna H. Hong (Princeton, NJ: Princeton University Press, 1990), 3–6; pap. VII 2 B 235:5–7.

42. Nietzsche, *Genealogy of Morality*, III.25.

43. Levinas contends that Kierkegaard stressed one's own abjection and its extension to the other rather than the other's violation and betrayal. James Hatley articulates how witnessing violence against others in Levinas involves two dimensions insofar as it responds to the evils of the actual suffering of the other and to the malignancy of the other's betrayal in violence. See James Hatley, "The Malignancy of Evil: Witnessing Violence beyond Justice," *Studies in Practical Philosophy* 3, no. 2 (2005): 84–106.

44. Levinas, *PN*, 69; *NP*, 102.

45. On individuation in Heidegger and Levinas's assessment of Heidegger's implicit egoism, see François Raffoul, "Otherness and Individuation in Heidegger," *Man and World* 28, no. 4 (1995): 341–358; Raffoul, "Being and the Other," 141; Raffoul, *Origins of Responsibility*, 174. On Levinas's account of Heidegger's conception of Dasein, also see Emilia Angelova, "Time's Disquiet and Unrest: The Affinity between Heidegger and Levinas," in *Between Levinas and Heidegger*, ed. John E. Drabinski and Eric S. Nelson (Albany: State University of New York Press, 2014), 90–92.

46. Levinas, *PN*, 69; Levinas, *NP*, 102.

47. Levinas, *DF*, 21f; Levinas, *DL*, 39; *EN*, 231; Levinas, *ENE*, 244.

48. Levinas, *EN*, 108; Levinas, *ENE*, 118.

49. Levinas, *GDT*, 12; Levinas, *DMT*, 21.

50. On the relation between ethics in Kant and Levinas, see Catherine Chalier, *What Ought I to Do? Morality in Kant and Levinas* (Ithaca, NY: Cornell University Press, 2002).

51. Kant, *Religion and Rational Theology*, Akademie ed., 6:87.
52. Kant, *Religion and Rational Theology*, Akademie ed., 6:87.
53. Compare Chalier, *What Ought I to Do?*; on the foundations of Kant's ethics, compare Halla Kim, *Kant and the Foundations of Morality* (Lanham, MD: Lexington Books, 2015).
54. T. P. S. Angier, *Either Kierkegaard/or Nietzsche: Moral Philosophy in a New Key* (Hampshire, UK: Ashgate, 2006), 135.
55. Kierkegaard, *Sickness unto Death*, 57; Kierkegaard, SKS 4, 151.
56. Kierkegaard, *Sickness unto Death*, 59; Kierkegaard, SKS 4, 152.
57. Kierkegaard, *Sickness unto Death*, 59; Kierkegaard, SKS 4, 152.
58. Kierkegaard, *Sickness unto Death*, 88; Kierkegaard, SKS 4, 55.
59. On ethical concretion in Kierkegaard, compare Patricia J. Huntington, "Heidegger's Reading of Kierkegaard Revisited: From Ontological Abstraction to Ethical Concretion," in *Kierkegaard in Post/Modernity*, ed. Martin Matuštík and Merold Westphal (Bloomington: Indiana University Press, 1995), 43–65.
60. Søren Kierkegaard, *Two Ages: The Age of Revolution and the Present Age: A Literary Review*, trans. Howard V. Hong and Edna H. Hong (Princeton, NJ: Princeton University Press, 1978), 61f, 64; Kierkegaard, SV 3:14:56f, 60.
61. Adorno, KDL, 414; Adorno, GS 2, 218.
62. Adorno, KDL, 415–416; Adorno, GS 2, 219–221.
63. Adorno, KDL, 423–427; Adorno, GS 2, 228–233.
64. Adorno, KDL, 429; Adorno, GS 2, 236.
65. Adorno, KDL, 427; Adorno, GS 2, 233.
66. Compare Adorno, KCA, 140–141; Adorno, KDL, 429; Adorno, GS 2, 200, 236, 258.
67. Adorno, KCA, 5, 66; Adorno, GS 2, 11–12, 97.
68. Note the different analyses in Katz, "Responsibility of Irresponsibility," 28f, and Paradiso-Michau, *Kierkegaard and Levinas*.
69. Compare Levinas, EN, 10f; Levinas, ENE, 19.
70. Levinas, EN, 70; Levinas, ENE, 80. On the reception and problematic of intentionality and its other sides in Levinas, see Leslie MacAvoy, "The Other Side of Intentionality," in *Addressing Levinas*, ed. Eric S. Nelson, Antje Kapust, and Kent Still (Evanston, IL: Northwestern University Press, 2005), 109–118.
71. Levinas, EN, 87; translation modified; Levinas, ENE, 96f.
72. Levinas, EN, 74; Levinas, ENE, 84.
73. Levinas, AlT, 107–108; Levinas Aet, 116–117.
74. Levinas, EN, 230; Levinas, ENE, 244.
75. On questions of war, violence, complicity, and betrayal in the context of Levinas, compare Margret Grebowicz, "'Between Betrayal and Betrayal': Epistemology and Ethics in Derrida's Debt to Levinas," *Addressing Levinas*, ed. in Eric S. Nelson, Antje Kapust, and Kent Still (Evanston, IL: Northwestern University Press, 2005), 75–85; Antje Kapust, *Der Krieg und der Ausfall der Sprache* (Munich: Wilhelm Fink Verlag, 2004); Antje Kapust, "Returning Violence," in

Addressing Levinas, ed. Eric S. Nelson, Antje Kapust, and Kent Still (Evanston, IL: Northwestern University Press, 2005), 236–256; Lusthaus, "Acting toward the Other with/out Violence," in *Levinas and Asian Thought*, ed. Leah Kalmanson, Frank Garrett and Sarah Mattice (Pittsburgh, PA: Duquesne University Press, 2013), 115–129; and Nelson, "Complicity of the Ethical," 99–114.

76. Levinas, *TI*, 35; Levinas, *TeI*, 23; *GDT*, 164; Levinas, *DMT*, 191.
77. Levinas, *TI*, 48; Levinas, *TeI*, 39f.
78. Levinas, *DF*, 29; Levinas, *DL*, 49.
79. Levinas, *TI*, 40; Levinas, *TeI*, 30.
80. Levinas, *TI*, 35; Levinas, *TeI*, 23.
81. Levinas, *TI*, 52f, 69; Levinas, *TeI*, 44f, 65.
82. Levinas, *TI*, 88; Levinas, *TeI*, 87.
83. Quintus Septimus Florens Tertullianus, *The Writings of Quintus Sept. Flor. Tertullianus* (Edinburgh: T. and T. Clark, 1869), 9. Compare Olli-Pekka Vainio, *Beyond Fideism: Negotiable Religious Identities* (London: Routledge, 2010), 25.
84. Tertullianus, *Writings of Tertullianus*, 9.
85. Vainio, *Beyond Fideism*, 25.
86. Levinas, *TI*, 58ff; Levinas, *TeI*, 52ff.
87. Levinas, *TI*, 77; Levinas, *TeI*, 75.
88. Levinas, *TI*, 80; Levinas, *TeI*, 79.
89. Levinas, *TI*, 78; Levinas, *TeI*, 76.
90. Levinas, *DF*, 26; Levinas, *DL*, 44.
91. Levinas, *TI*, 79; Levinas, *TeI*, 78.
92. Levinas, *TO*, 30 f.; Levinas, *TA*, 8f; on prudence in Kant's practical philosophy, and Kant's modification of the relationship between ethics and prudence in the political sphere, see Eric S. Nelson, "Moral and Political Prudence in Kant," *International Philosophical Quarterly* 44, no. 3 (2004): 305–319.
93. Levinas, *TO*, 30 f.; Levinas, *TA*, 8f.
94. Moyn, *Origins of the Other*, 12f and 256f.
95. Levinas, *GDT*, 164ff; Levinas, *DMT*, 191ff.
96. Compare Levinas, *GDT*, 137; Levinas, *HO*, 54; Levinas, *IRB*, 101.
97. On Benjamin, see Matthias Fritsch, *The Promise of Memory: History and Politics in Marx, Benjamin, and Derrida* (Albany: State University of New York Press, 2006); Idit Dobbs-Weinstein, *Spinoza's Critique*.
98. Levinas, *OB*, 128; Levinas, *AE*, 204.
99. Compare Adorno, *LND*, 9, 19, 31.
100. Levinas, *EN*, 74; Levinas, *ENE*, 84.
101. Adorno, *KDL*, 425; Adorno, *GS 2*, 230.
102. Levinas, *TA*, 92, 96, 107; Kierkegaard, *SV* 3:14:84, 87, 97.
103. Levinas, *EN*, 100f, 105; Levinas, *ENE*, 111f, 114.
104. Levinas, *EI*, 98; Levinas, *Eei*, 94–95.

Chapter 9

1. Michael Rosen, *Dignity: Its History and Meaning* (Cambridge, MA: Harvard University Press, 2012), 41.

2. Rosen also notes the retention of its hierarchical uses in Rosen, *Dignity*, 47–54.

3. On the possibility of reformulating natural theory, compare Jonathan Crowe, *Natural Law and the Nature of Law* (Cambridge: Cambridge University Press, 2019).

4. Ernst Bloch, *Naturrecht und menschliche Würde* (Frankfurt: Suhrkamp, 1985).

5. Dobbs-Weinstein, *Spinoza's Critique*. On the second dimension, also compare M. Fritsch, *Promise of Memory*.

6. Concerning the revolutionary import of utopia, see, for instance, Ernst Bloch, *Geist der Utopie*, 1918 ed. (Frankfurt: Suhrkamp, 1985). On the critical, ethical, and utopian dimensions of hope, see Ernst Bloch, *Das Prinzip Hoffnung*, 3 vols. (Frankfurt: Suhrkamp, 1976).

7. Compare Emilia Angelova, "Utopia, Metontology, and the Sociality of the Other: Levinas, Heidegger and Bloch," *Journal of Contemporary Thought* 31 (Summer 2010): 171–191.

8. See the discussion of Bloch in Adorno's essay "The Handle, the Pot, and Early Experience" in which he speaks of the "rescue of appearance" (*Rettung des Scheins*) in Bloch, and remarked, "[W]hat is specific to Bloch's philosophy is to be sought more in the gesture than in the individual ideas, not excepting his central, orienting idea of the messianic end of history, the breakthrough of transcendence [*Durchbruch der Transzendenz*]" (Adorno, NL2, 212).

9. Bloch, *Naturrecht und menschliche Würde*.

10. Bloch, *Naturrecht und menschliche Würde*, 187.

11. On critical natural law in Epicurus and Rousseau, see Ernst Bloch, *Das Materialismusproblem, seine Geschichte und Substanz* (Frankfurt: Suhrkamp, 1974), 44. On Marx's limitations as a republican political philosopher, see Ernst Bloch, *On Karl Marx* (London: Verso, 2018), 169.

12. Bloch, *Naturrecht und menschliche Würde*, 243.

13. Adorno, ND, 310; Adorno, GS 6, 305.

14. Bloch, *On Karl Marx*, 169.

15. Bloch, *Das Prinzip Hoffnung*, 1:7; 3:1613.

16. On the conservative and fascist deployment of the notion of dignity, compare Rosen, *Dignity*, 51.

17. Levinas, GDT, 96; Levinas, DMT, 111.

18. Levinas, GDT, 94; Levinas, DMT, 109.

19. Levinas, GDT, 94; Levinas, DMT, 109.

20. "Der Zielinhalt, das Zielbild im Naturrecht ist nicht das menschliche Glück (wie in den Sozialutopien; der Verfasser), sondern aufrechter Gang, menschliche Würde, Orthopädie des aufrechten Gangs, also kein gekrümmter Rücken vor Königsthronen usw., sondern Entdeckung der menschlichen Würde, die eben gleichwohl zum großen Teil nicht aus den Verhältnissen abgeleitet wird, denen man sich anpaßt, sondern . . . von dem neuen, stolzen Begriff des Menschen." "Ernst Bloch im Gespräch mit José Marchand 1974," in *Tagträume vom aufrechten Gang*, ed. Arno Münster (Frankfurt: Suhrkamp 1977), 83.

21. See Eric S. Nelson, "Zhang Junmai's Early Political Philosophy and the Paradoxes of Chinese Modernity," *Asian Studies* 8, no. 1 (2020): 183–208.

22. Ernst Bloch, "Rosa Luxemburg, Lenin und die Lehren oder Marxismus als Moral," *Gespräche mit Ernst Bloch*, ed. Rainer Traub and Harold Wieser (Frankfurt: Suhrkamp, 1975), 208–220.

23. Luxemburg, *Russian Revolution*, 71.

24. Luxemburg, *Russian Revolution*, 69.

25. Bloch, *On Karl Marx*, 169.

26. On the Stoic concept of dignity, compare Martha C. Nussbaum, *The Cosmopolitan Tradition: A Noble but Flawed Ideal* (Cambridge, MA: Belknap Press, 2019), 64–96.

27. Bloch, *Naturrecht und menschliche Würde*, 26.

28. Bloch, *Naturrecht und menschliche Würde*, 26.

29. Bloch, *Das Materialismusproblem*, 148.

30. Eric M. Nelson, *The Hebrew Republic: Jewish Sources and the Transformation of European Political Thought* (Cambridge, MA: Harvard University Press, 2011).

31. Ernst Bloch, *Atheismus im Christentum: Zur Religion des Exodus und des Reichs* (Frankfurt: Suhrkamp, 1989), 131, 459.

32. Bloch, *Das Prinzip Hoffnung*, 2:592.

33. Levinas, AlT, 83; Levinas, Aet, 96. On Eurocentrism, see Enrique Dussel, "Eurocentrism and Modernity (Introduction to the Frankfurt Lectures)," *Boundary 2*, 20, no. 3 (1993): 65–76; Dussel, "'Sensibility' and 'Otherness,'" 126–134; Enrique Dussel, "From Critical Theory to the Philosophy of Liberation: Some Themes for Dialogue," *Transmodernity: Journal of Peripheral Cultural Production of the Luso-Hispanic World* 1, no. 2 (2011): 17–43.

34. Levinas, GDT, 96–98; Levinas, DMT, 111–113.

35. Bloch, *Geist der Utopie*, 1918 ed.; Ernst Bloch, *Thomas Münzer als Theologe der Revolution* (Frankfurt: Suhrkamp, 1985).

36. For a subtler more adequate account of Levinas and Zionism, see Annabel Herzog, "Levinas's Ethics, Politics, and Zionism," in *The Oxford Handbook of Levinas*, ed. Michael L. Morgan (Oxford: Oxford University Press, 2019), 473–491.

37. The an-archic idea of a radical republicanism of unrestricted solidarity, which contests demands for identity, is further developed in part 3 below.

38. On the nexus of politics, rights, and republicanism in Hannah Arendt, see Seyla Benhabib, *The Reluctant Modernism of Hannah Arendt* (New York: Rowman and Littlefield Publishers, 2003); and the introduction to Seyla Benhabib, ed., *Politics in Dark Times: Encounters with Hannah Arendt* (Cambridge: Cambridge University Press, 2010); Birmingham, *Hannah Arendt and Human Rights*; and Margaret Canovan, *Hannah Arendt: A Reinterpretation of Her Political Thought* (Cambridge: Cambridge University Press, 1994).

39. Dussel, "'Sensibility' and 'Otherness,'," 126; Dussel, "Critical Theory," 21.

40. Levinas, *UH*, 107–112; Levinas, *LIH*, 149–151.

41. Enrique Dussel, *The Invention of the Americas: Eclipse of "the Other" and the Myth of Modernity* (New York: Continuum, 1995). Also note the discussion in Nelson, *Chinese and Buddhist Philosophy*, 213.

42. On Levinas and the question of Eurocentrism, see John E. Drabinski, *Levinas and the Postcolonial: Race, Nation, and Other* (Edinburgh: Edinburgh University Press, 2011); Oona Eisenstadt, "Eurocentrism and Colorblindness," *Levinas Studies* 7 (2012): 43–62.

43. Enrique Dussel, *Towards an Unknown Marx: A Commentary on the Manuscripts of 1861–63* (London: Routledge, 2002), 83, 191.

44. This recurrent theme is taken up in Levinas, *GDT*, 11–53; Levinas, *DMT*, 20–63.

45. Bloch, *Das Prinzip Hoffnung*, 3:1625.

46. Levinas, *GDT*, 105; Levinas, *DMT*, 121.

47. Dussel, *Towards an Unknown Marx*, 83, 191.

48. Kant claimed in the *Groundwork*, "In the kingdom of ends everything has either a price or a dignity. What has a price can be replaced by something else as its equivalent, what on the other hand is raised above all price and therefore admits of no equivalent has a dignity." Immanuel Kant, *Groundwork of the Metaphysics of Morals*, trans. and ed. Mary Gregor (Cambridge: Cambridge University Press, 1997), 42; Akademie ed., 4:434–435. See the analysis of this passage in Rosen, *Dignity*, 20–21.

49. Rosen is correct that dignity is insufficient to guarantee rights. The Kantian moral law account is itself problematic in addressing the crucial issue of the dignity of material life. Compare Rosen, *Dignity*, 55.

50. Compare Bloch, *On Karl Marx*, 23.

51. Adorno, *NL2*, 212.

52. Adorno and Horkheimer, *TNM*, 71.

53. On modality, potentiality, and possibility in Adorno, see Iain Macdonald, "Adorno's Modal Utopianism: Possibility and Actuality in Adorno

and Hegel," *Adorno Studies* 1, no. 1 (2017): 1–12; Iain Macdonald, "'What Is, Is More Than It Is': Adorno and Heidegger on the Priority of Possibility," *International Journal of Philosophical Studies* 19, no. 1 (2011): 31–57; Iain Macdonald, *What Would Be Different: Figures of Possibility in Adorno* (Stanford, CA: Stanford University Press, 2019).

54. Adorno, HF, 149.

Chapter 10

1. Knud Ejler Løgstrup, *The Ethical Demand* (Notre Dame, IN: University of Notre Dame Press, 1997), 5.
2. Levinas, TI, 53; Levinas, TeI, 23–24.
3. Levinas, EN, 100; Levinas, ENE, 111.
4. Levinas, EN, 99; Levinas, ENE, 109.
5. Løgstrup, *Ethical Demand*, 5; compare Knud Ejler Løgstrup, *Beyond the Ethical Demand* (Notre Dame: University of Notre Dame Press, 2007), 10. On the structure and import of Løgstrup's ethics, see Robert Stern, *The Radical Demand in Løgstrup's Ethics* (Oxford: Oxford University Press, 2019).
6. Knud Ejler Løgstrup, "Nazismens Filosof" (The Nazi's philosopher), published in the April 14, 1936, edition of *Dagens Nyheder*; Levinas, UH, 13–21; Levinas, LIH, 23–33.
7. Knud Ejler Løgstrup, *Kierkegaards und Heideggers Existenzanalyse und ihr Verhältnis zur Verkündigung* (Berlin: Erich Blaschker Verlag 1950); Knud Ejler Løgstrup, *Kierkegaard's and Heidegger's Existential Analysis and Its Relation to the Proclamation* (New York: Oxford University Press, 2020).
8. Løgstrup, *Ethical Demand*, 117.
9. Løgstrup, *Ethical Demand*, 18n.6.
10. See Bernasconi, "Levinas," 170–184.
11. Simon Critchley, "Leaving the Climate of Heidegger's Thinking," in *Levinas in Jerusalem: Phenomenology, Ethics, Politics, Aesthetics*, ed. Joelle Hansel (Berlin: Springer, 2009), 54.
12. Stanley Cavell, *Conditions Handsome and Unhandsome: The Constitution of Emersonian Perfectionism* (Chicago, IL: University of Chicago Press, 1991); Hilary Putnam, *Jewish Philosophy as a Guide to Life: Rosenzweig, Buber, Levinas, Wittgenstein* (Bloomington: Indiana University Press, 2008), 59–60, 72–73.
13. Levinas, OB, 138; Levinas, AE, 176; also see Levinas, OB, 11; Levinas, AE, 13.
14. Compare Levinas, OB, 123; Levinas, AE, 158.
15. Such as Joseph C. W. Chan, *Confucian Perfectionism: A Political Philosophy for Modern Times* (Princeton: Princeton University Press, 2017).
16. Murdoch, *Sovereignty of Good*, 68.

17. Adorno, MM, 119/185; Adorno, GS 4, 210–211.
18. Løgstrup, *Beyond the Ethical Demand*, 69.
19. Iris Murdoch, *Metaphysics as a Guide to Morals* (New York: Penguin Books, 2014), 428.
20. Murdoch, *Metaphysics as a Guide to Morals*, 507.
21. Murdoch, *Sovereignty of Good*, 100–101.
22. Murdoch, *Sovereignty of Good*, 101.
23. Murdoch, *Sovereignty of Good*, 41.
24. Levinas, AlT, 98; Levinas, Aet, 109. For a systematic assessment of Murdoch and Levinas, see Ellis, "Murdoch and Levinas," 63–87.
25. Murdoch, *Sovereignty of Good*, 51.
26. Murdoch, *Sovereignty of Good*, 68–70.
27. Murdoch, *Sovereignty of Good*, 73.
28. Murdoch, *Sovereignty of Good*, 76–82.
29. Iris Murdoch, *Existentialists and Mystics: Writings on Philosophy and Literature* (London: Penguin, 1999), 215.
30. Nourishing or nurturing life (*yangsheng* 養生) is a key notion in early Daoism, as discussed in Nelson, "Responding with Dao," 294–316 and Nelson, *Daoism and Environmental Philosophy*, chapter 2.
31. Levinas, GDT, 108–111; Levinas, DMT, 124–127.
32. Levinas, UH, 130; Levinas, LIH, 181.
33. Levinas, AlT, 107; Levinas, Aet, 116.
34. Compare Murdoch, *Sovereignty of Good*, 3; Levinas, OE, 49–51; Levinas, DIe, 91–93; and Levinas, TI, 21.
35. On the philosophical anthropology movement in early twentieth-century German thought, and its reception in Marjorie Grene, see Eric S. Nelson, "Exzentrische Tiere und die Selbstüberwindung des Naturalismus: Dilthey, Plessner, Grene," in *Philosophische Anthropologie zwischen Soziologie und Geschichtsphilosophie*, ed. Rainer Adolphi, Andrzej Gniazdowski, and Zdzislaw Krasnodebski (Nordhausen: Bautz-Verlag, 2018b), 369–387.
36. Levinas, GDT, 28; Levinas, DMT, 37.
37. Løgstrup, *Ethical Demand*, 68.
38. Løgstrup, *Ethical Demand*, 68.
39. Knud Ejler Løgstrup, *Metaphysics* (Milwaukee, WI: Marquette University Press, 1995), 2:355.
40. Brenda Almond, "Principles and Situations: K. E. Logstrup and British Moral Philosophy of the Twentieth Century," in *Concern for the Other: Perspectives on the Ethics of K. E. Løgstrup*, ed. Svend Andersen and Kees van Kooten Niekerk (Notre Dame, IN: University of Notre Dame Press, 2007), 92–94; Murdoch, *Sovereignty of Good*, 3–4.
41. Putnam, *Jewish Philosophy*, 94.
42. Moore, *Principia Ethica*; Murdoch, *Sovereignty of Good*.

43. For a discussion of negative ethics in relation to Adorno, see Freyenhagen, *Adorno's Practical Philosophy*.

44. There are overlapping issues in Adorno. On the problematic of ethics, the ineffable, and negative theology in Adorno, compare James Gordon Finlayson, "Adorno on the Ethical and the Ineffable," *European Journal of Philosophy* 10, no. 1 (2002): 1–25; Martin Shuster, "Adorno and Negative Theology," *Graduate Faculty Philosophy Journal* 37, no. 1 (2016): 97–130.

45. Dussel, "'Sensibility' and 'Otherness,'" 129.

46. Dussel, *Philosophy of Liberation*, 47.

47. Løgstrup, *Ethical Demand*, 15–16.

48. "Useless Suffering" in Levinas, EN, 91–101; Levinas, ENE, 100–112.

49. Levinas, EN, 95; Levinas, ENE, 105.

50. Løgstrup, *Ethical Demand*, 121.

51. Levinas, EN, 98–99; Levinas, ENE, 108–110.

Chapter 11

1. Adorno's strategy of negation is an adaptation of the double function of dialectic that is simultaneously a recognition and negation of the existing conditions. Marx described this double relation to the present in 1873 in his second afterword to *Capital* in Karl Marx and Friedrich Engels, *The Marx-Engels Reader*, 2nd ed. (New York: Norton, 1978), 302.

2. Habermas, *Philosophical Discourse of Modernity*, xvi; Habermas and Dews, *Autonomy and Solidarity*, 133.

3. Habermas, *Philosophical Discourse of Modernity*.

4. Levinas, EN, 191. On Stalin, compare Levinas, OI, 52.

5. Levinas, EN, 119.

6. Levinas, GDT, 94; Levinas, DMT, 109.

7. Compare Levinas, GCM, 48; Levinas, DVI, 84.

8. Levinas, AIT, 111–112; Levinas, Aet, 119–120.

9. Levinas, EN, 191.

10. Levinas, EN, 99.

11. On different conceptions and senses of equality in an intercultural context, see Mario Wenning, "Whose Equality?" *Confluence: Journal of World Philosophies* 2 (2015): 153–166.

12. Peter Sloterdijk, "Die Revolution der gebenden Hand," *Frankfurter Allgemeine Zeitung*, June 13, 2009; Peter Sloterdijk, "Das elfte Gebot: Die progressive Einkommenssteuer," *Frankfurter Allgemeine Zeitung*, September 27, 2009.

13. Axel Honneth, "Fataler Tiefsinn aus Karlsruhe: Zum neuesten Schrifttum des Peter Sloterdijk," *Zeit*, September 9, 2009.

14. Axel Honneth, *Das Andere der Gerechtigkeit: Aufsätze zur praktischen Philosophie* (Frankfurt: Suhrkamp, 2000), 168.

15. Honneth, *Das Andere der Gerechtigkeit*, 141. On the difference between the singular and the subsumed particular, note Levinas, *EN*, 25–26. On singularity and universality in Levinas, see Leslie MacAvoy, "Thinking through Singularity and Universality in Levinas," supplement, *Philosophy Today* 47 (2003): 147–153.

16. Adorno, *MM*, 66/102–103. Adorno examined how anti-Semitism can be seen in "works championing tolerance and humanism" in Adorno, *SDE*, 191.

17. Honneth, *Das Andere der Gerechtigkeit*, 141.

18. Claudia Moscovici, *From Sex Objects to Sexual Subjects* (New York: Routledge, 1996), 56.

19. Fleming, *Emancipation and Illusion*, 85.

20. Iris Marion Young, *Intersecting Voices: Dilemmas of Gender, Political Philosophy, and Policy* (Princeton, NJ: Princeton University Press, 1997), 39.

21. Jürgen Habermas, *The Inclusion of the Other: Studies in Political Theory* (Cambridge, MA: MIT Press, 1998).

22. Honneth, *Das Andere der Gerechtigkeit*, 167–168.

23. John William Rogerson, *Theory and Practice in Old Testament Ethics* (London: T & T Clark International, 2004), 64.

24. Habermas, "Ich selber," 33.

25. Honneth portrays his critical theory in these terms in Honneth, *Das Andere der Gerechtigkeit*, 8.

26. Critchley contends for the reconciliation of asymmetrical ethics and the ethics of recognition in Simon Critchley, *Ethics, Politics, Subjectivity: Essays on Derrida, Levinas, and Contemporary French Thought* (London: Verso, 1999), 158.

27. Gerhard Schweppenhäuser, *Die Antinomie des Universalismus: Zum moralphilosophischen Diskurs der Moderne* (Würzburg: Königshausen & Neumann, 2005), 183. Also note M. J. Monahan, "Recognition beyond Struggle: On a Liberatory Account of Hegelian Recognition," *Social Theory and Practice* 32, no. 3 (2006): 391. On Hegel's account of recognition and its implications, see Sybol Anderson, *Hegel's Theory of Recognition: From Oppression to Ethical Liberal Modernity* (London: Bloomsbury Publishing, 2009); Robert R. Williams, *Hegel's Ethics of Recognition* (Berkeley: University of California Press, 1997).

28. Honneth, *Das Andere der Gerechtigkeit*, 169–170.

29. Manuel P. Arriaga, *The Modernist-Postmodernist Quarrel on Philosophy and Justice: A Possible Levinasian Mediation* (Lanham, MD: Lexington Books, 2006), 157.

30. Arriaga, *Modernist-Postmodernist Quarrel*, 157.

31. de Vries, *Minimal Theologies*, 121; Mark Devenney, *Ethics and Politics in Contemporary Theory between Critical Theory and Post-Marxism* (London: Routledge, 2004), 135.

32. de Vries, *Minimal Theologies*, 121.

33. Honneth, *Das Andere der Gerechtigkeit*, 134–135.

34. Honneth, *Das Andere der Gerechtigkeit*, 135; Schweppenhäuser, *Die Antinomie des Universalismus*, 183; Monahan, "Recognition beyond Struggle," 391.

35. Axel Honneth, *The Struggle for Recognition: The Moral Grammar of Social Conflicts* (Cambridge, MA: MIT Press, 1995), 107–143.

36. See de Vries, *Minimal Theologies*; Devenney, *Ethics and Politics*.

37. Leora Faye Batnitzky, *Leo Strauss and Emmanuel Levinas: Philosophy and the Politics of Revelation* (New York: Cambridge University Press, 2006), 76.

38. Williams, *Hegel's Ethics of Recognition*, 410.

39. Wood, "Some Questions," 162.

40. Honneth, *Das Andere der Gerechtigkeit*, 145. Critics of the language of "obedience" in Levinas conflate ethical responsiveness, heteronomy as the other in the self that is the prerequisite of acting for-the-other, and mere sacrifice and subordination. See Moyn, *Origins of the Other*.

41. This is particularly true in the works of Slavoj Žižek; Žižek, *Organs without Bodies*, 106–107; and Slavoj Žižek, *Interrogating the Real* (London: Continuum, 2006), 343. For a more satisfying interpretation of the ethics of the impossible and its interruptive and transformative character, see Raffoul, "Derrida and Ethics," 270–290.

42. Adorno, *AT*, 215.

43. Levinas, *OB*, 115; Levinas, *AE*, 181.

44. Løgstrup, *Ethical Demand*, 53.

45. On the affinities and differences between Løgstrup and Levinas on asymmetry and the other-constitution of the self, see the helpful discussion in Robert Stern, "Others as the Ground of our Existence," in *Transcendental Inquiry: Its History, Methods, and Critiques*, ed. Halla Kim and Steven Hoeltzel (Basingstoke, UK: Palgrave Macmillan, 2016), 181–207; Stern, *Radical Demand*.

46. For an insightful consideration of questions of justice and commerce in Levinas, see John E. Drabinski, "Wealth and Justice in a U-topian Context," in *Addressing Levinas*, ed. Eric S. Nelson, Antje Kapust, and Kent Still (Evanston, IL: Northwestern University Press, 2005), 194.

47. Honneth is uncertain about this dark empirical core of Levinas's ethics and how the face can be both perceptual and morally cognitive. See Honneth, *Das Andere der Gerechtigkeit*, 145; since not only the face can function as the face, it should be interpreted as a primary exemplar of the ethical encounter for Levinas (compare Levinas, *EN*, 232). On the ethical proceeding from the Other to God, see Levinas, *EN*, 158.

48. On the discursive senses of the face, see Diane Perpich, "Figurative Language and the 'Face' in Levinas' Philosophy," *Philosophy and Rhetoric* 38, no. 2 (2005): 103–121.

49. Levinas, *EN*, 202.

50. Levinas, EN, x–xii, 103, 190, 219.

51. Levinas, EN, 170–171; I consider this issue in relation to an analogous line of thought by the early Confucian philosopher Mencius in Nelson, "Levinas and Early Confucian Ethics."

52. Levinas, EN, 91, 230.

53. Levinas, TI, 226.

54. On ethics in Heidegger, see Nelson, "Heidegger and Ethics"; Nelson, "Heidegger and Questionability"; Raffoul, "Being and the Other," 138–151; Raffoul, *Origins of Responsibility*; Raffoul, "Question of Responsibility," 175–206.

55. Levinas, TI, 150.

56. Levinas, O1, 488.

57. Levinas, EN, 228.

58. Honneth, *Das Andere der Gerechtigkeit*, 135; Levinas, EN, 196.

59. Levinas, EN, 37.

60. Levinas, EN, xii.

61. Levinas, EN, 194.

62. Levinas, TI, 53.

63. Axel Honneth, *Freedom's Right: The Social Foundations of Democratic Life* (New York: Columbia University Press, 2014), 15.

64. On the dependent and derivative character of freedom in Levinas, see Levinas, TI, 303; and Adriaan Peperzak, *To the Other: An Introduction to the Philosophy of Emmanuel Levinas* (West Lafayette, IN: Purdue University Press, 1993), 115–119. Levinas poses the question of finite liberty in his earlier notebooks, for instance in Levinas, O1, 455–456.

65. Levinas, TI, 85.

66. Levinas, OB, 124; Levinas, AE, 159.

67. Levinas, TI, 303.

68. Levinas, TI, 214.

69. Levinas, EN, 198.

70. Levinas, TI, 214.

71. Levinas, TI, 214; on the biblical background of hospitality, see Annabel Herzog, "Lecture de l'hospitalité biblique," *Revue des Etudes Juives* 171, no. 1–2 (2012): 1–25. Also note A. Z. Newton, *The Fence and the Neighbor: Levinas, Yeshayahu Leibowitz, and Israel among the nations* (Albany: State University of New York Press, 2001), 85.

72. Compare Howard Caygill, *Levinas and the Political* (London: Routledge, 2002); Simon Critchley, "Five Problems in Levinas's View of Politics and a Sketch of a Solution to Them," in *Levinas, Law, Politics*, ed. Marinos Diamantides (London: Routledge-Cavendish, 2007), 93–106.

73. Levinas, EN, 162.

74. Compare Honneth, *Freedom's Right*, 16.

75. Levinas, EN, 99.

76. On the nonconceptual in Levinas, see Jennifer McWeeny, "Origins of Otherness: Nonconceptual Ethical Encounters in Beauvoir and Levinas," *Simone de Beauvoir Studies* 26 (2009/2010): 5–17.

77. Levinas, *EN*, 157, 166.

78. Žižek, *Organs without Bodies*, 106–107; contrast Caygill, *Levinas and the Political*, 185.

79. Levinas, *EN*, 35–36.

80. Levinas, *EN*, 59–60.

81. Levinas, *EN*, 60.

82. Levinas, *EI*, 101; Levinas, *Eei*, 98; Levinas, *OB*, 146; Levinas, *AE*, 186; translation modified.

83. Levinas, *OB*, 146; Levinas, *AE*, 186.

84. Levinas, *OB*, 55, 146; Levinas, *AE*, 71, 186.

85. Levinas, *EN*, 108.

86. Levinas, *EN*, 177.

87. On the problematic of recognition and misrecognition, see Claudia Leeb, "The Politics of 'Misrecognition': A Feminist Critique," *Good Society* 18, no. 1 (2009): 70–75.

88. On the inadequacy and problematic character of the concept of "recognition," compare the analysis in Leeb, "Politics of 'Misrecognition,'" 70–75. Also note Fraser's critique of recognition in Nancy Fraser and Axel Honneth, *Redistribution or Recognition? A Political-Philosophical Exchange* (London: Verso, 2003).

89. Honneth, *Das Andere der Gerechtigkeit*, 146, 162.

Chapter 12

1. See Isaiah Berlin, *Liberty* (Oxford: Oxford University Press, 2002).

2. See Fraser and Honneth, *Redistribution or Recognition?*, for an overview of this debate about the priority of intersubjective recognition or material distribution.

3. For more extended accounts of these themes in Locke, compare Barbara Arneil, *John Locke and America: The Defence of English Colonialism* (Oxford: Clarendon Press, 1996); James Tully, *An Approach to Political Philosophy: Locke in Contexts* (Cambridge: Cambridge University Press, 1993), 137–178; Robert Bernasconi and Anika M. Mann, "The Contradictions of Racism: Locke, Slavery, and the Two Treatises," in *Race and Racism in Modern Philosophy*, ed. Andrew Valls (Ithaca, NY: Cornell University Press, 2005), 94–95.

4. See the discussion in J. E. L. Roemer et al., *Racism, Xenophobia, and Distribution: Multi-issue Politics in Advanced Democracies* (New York: Russell Sage Foundation, 2007), 77.

5. David Harvey, *Spaces of Hope* (Berkeley: University of California Press, 2000), 173.

6. On the uses of pathology and its problems in Honneth, see Fabian Freyenhagen, "Honneth on Social Pathologies: A Critique," *Critical Horizons* 16, no. 2 (2015): 131–152.

7. Brian Schroeder, *Altared Ground: Levinas, History, and Violence* (New York: Routledge, 1996), 101.

8. Frantz Fanon, *Black Skin, White Masks* (New York: Grove Press, 2008), 200.

9. Günther Anders, "Pathologie de la liberté, essai sur la non-identification," *Recherches philosophiques* 7 (1936/1937): 22–54, trans. by Katharine Wolfe as "The Pathology of Freedom: An Essay on Non-Identification," *Deleuze Studies* 3, no. 2 (2009): 278–310.

10. Compare Honneth, "Communication and Reconciliation"; Morris, *Rethinking the Communicative Turn*.

11. On normativity in Hegel, compare Iain Macdonald, "On the 'Undialectical': Normativity in Hegel," *Continental Philosophy Review* 45, no. 1 (2012): 121–141.

12. Adorno, CI, 92.

13. See Andrew Bowie, *From Romanticism to Critical Theory: The Philosophy of German Literary Theory* (London: Routledge, 1997), 289; Jennifer L. Eagan, "Unfreedom, Suffering, and the Culture Industry: What Adorno Can Contribute to a Feminist Ethics," in *Feminist Interpretations of Adorno*, ed. Renée Heberle (University Park: Pennsylvania State University Press, 2006), 292; Herbert Marcuse, *Eros and Civilization: A Philosophical Inquiry into Freud* (Boston, MA: Beacon Press, 1971), 224; and Stefano Scoglio, *Transforming Privacy: A Transpersonal Philosophy of Rights* (Westport, CT: Praeger, 1998), 17.

14. Deborah Cook, *The Culture Industry Revisited: Theodor W. Adorno on Mass Culture* (Lanham, MD: Rowman and Littlefield Publishers, 1996), 64.

15. Adorno and Horkheimer, DE, 104; Adorno, HF, 78.

16. On the controversy over popular culture, see Thomas Wheatland, *The Frankfurt School in Exile* (Minneapolis: Minnesota Press, 2009), 132–134.

17. Bronner, *Reclaiming the Enlightenment*, 5.

18. Hammer, *Adorno and the Political*, 29–31.

19. Adorno, ND, 356; Adorno, GS 6, 349.

20. Habermas and Dews, *Autonomy and Solidarity*, 28.

21. Adorno, MM, 85/131–132; Adorno, GS 4, 149–150.

22. On the dialectical image that indicates both its ideological character and its potential disruption, see Adorno, HF, 171. On the ethical beyond the ideological in Levinas, see Levinas, GCM, 3–14; Levinas, DVI, 17–33.

23. Dews, *Idea of Evil*, 130.

24. See Plato, *The Republic*, ed. and trans. G. R. F. Ferrari and T. Griffith (Cambridge: Cambridge University Press, 2001), 372e8; Hegel, *Phänomenologie des Geistes*, secs. 582–595; Alexis de Tocqueville, *Democracy in America* (New York: Library of America, 2004); compare Marcuse, *Reason and Revolution*, 96; Philip J. Harold, *Prophetic Politics: Emmanuel Levinas and the Sanctification of Suffering* (Athens: Ohio University Press, 2009), xxvi–xxviii.

25. In general, "liberty" signifies the objective social-political guarantees and maintenance of freedoms, for instance as rights, and "freedom" means the sense of liberty and the ability to act.

26. Levinas, BPW, 17.

27. Levinas, OI, 385.

28. Levinas, OI, 447, 455–456.

29. Levinas, AlT, 23; Levinas, Aet, 44.

30. Levinas, AlT, 15, 23; Levinas, Aet, 37, 44; Jeffrey Bloechl, *Liturgy of the Neighbor: Emmanuel Levinas and the Religion of Responsibility* (Pittsburgh, PA: Duquesne University Press, 2000), 33.

31. Honneth, *Freedom's Right*, 15–16.

32. Levinas, OB, 124: Levinas, AE, 159.

33. See Bernasconi, "Levinas," 170–184; and Colin Hearfield, *Adorno and the Modern Ethos of Freedom* (Aldershot, UK: Ashgate, 2004), 24.

34. Levinas, CPP, 136; compare Batnitzky, *Leo Strauss and Emmanuel Levinas*, 20; Corey Beals, *Levinas and the Wisdom of Love: The Question of Invisibility* (Waco, TX: Baylor University Press, 2007), 74.

35. Adorno's rethinking of autonomy is addressed in Iain Macdonald, "Cold, Cold, Warm: Autonomy, Intimacy and Maturity in Adorno," *Philosophy and Social Criticism* 37, no. 6 (2011): 669–689. On Adorno's reconceptualization of autonomy in Kant and German Idealism, see Martin Shuster, *Autonomy after Auschwitz: Adorno, German Idealism, and Modernity* (Chicago, IL: University of Chicago Press, 2014). On the fundamental role of autonomy in Kant, see H. Kim, *Kant and Foundations* (Lanham, MD: Lexington Books, 2015).

36. Adorno, ND, 310, 363; Adorno, GS 6, 305, 356. Note the description of this point in Habermas, *Philosophisch-politische Profile*, 165–167.

37. Chanter, *Time, Death, and the Feminine*, 270.

38. On the status and role of critique in Levinas and Derrida, in a reading that assimilates Levinas's ethics to Derrida's deconstruction, see Robert Bernasconi, "The Crisis of Critique and the Awakening of Politicisation in Levinas and Derrida," in *The Politics of Deconstruction: Jacques Derrida and the Other of Philosophy*, ed. Martin McQuillan (London: Pluto Press, 2007), 81–97.

39. Harold, *Prophetic Politics*, xvi, 191; on the problematic character of anticognitivist and antinormative interpretations of Levinas, see Perpich, *Ethics of Emmanuel Levinas*, 89–90, 126.

40. On cloture, see Simon Critchley, *The Ethics of Deconstruction: Derrida and Levinas* (West Lafayette, IN: Purdure University Press, 1999), 145.

41. Levinas, *BPW*, 90; Levinas, *PN*, 53; compare Harold, *Prophetic Politics*, 23–24.

42. Perpich, *Ethics of Emmanuel Levinas*.

43. Perpich, *Ethics of Emmanuel Levinas*.

44. Levinas, *TI*, 302. On this passage, see Chanter, *Time, Death, and the Feminine*, 270; Jeffrey Dudiak, *The Intrigue of Ethics: A Reading of the Idea of Discourse in the Thought of Emmanuel Levinas* (New York: Fordham University Press, 2001), 158.

45. Levinas, *TI*, 303; also see Ethan Kleinberg, *Generation Existential: Heidegger's Philosophy in France, 1927–1961* (Ithaca, NY: Cornell University Press, 2005), 275.

46. Rudi Visker, *The Inhuman Condition: Looking for Difference after Levinas and Heidegger* (Dordrecht: Kluwer Academic, 2004), 89; compare Jean-Luc Nancy, *The Experience of Freedom* (Stanford, CA: Stanford University Press, 1993), 189.

47. Levinas, *DF*, 225; Levinas, *DL*, 290.

48. Levinas, *GCM*, 70; Levinas, *DVI*, 116; Levinas, *NT*, 65.

49. Levinas, *GDT*, 178; Levinas, *DMT*, 208.

50. C. Fred Alford, *Levinas, the Frankfurt School, and Psychoanalysis* (Middletown, CT: Wesleyan University Press, 2002), 121.

51. Levinas distinguishes passivity from receptiveness in Levinas, *GCM*, 89; Levinas, *DVI*, 142; he contrasts Heidegger's openness and letting be, as an inadequate responsiveness lacking responsibility, with invocation and summoning in "Is Ontology Fundamental?" in Levinas, *BPW*, 5–6; on responsibility for the other's freedom, and heteronomy as the condition of autonomy, see Levinas, *NT*, 58; Levinas, *BV*, 104.

52. Levinas, *GCM*, 70; Levinas, *DVI*, 116.

53. On the problem of asymmetrical freedom, see Susan Wolf, "Asymmetrical Freedom," *Journal of Philosophy* 7, no. 7 (1980): 151–166.

54. Ewa P. Ziarek, "The Ethical Passions of Levinas," in *Feminist Interpretations of Levinas*, ed. Tina Chanter (University Park: Pennsylvania State University Press, 2001), 89.

55. Levinas, *HO*, 55.

56. Levinas, *TI*, 271.

57. Bettina Bergo, *Levinas between Ethics and Politics: For the Beauty That Adorns the Earth* (Pittsburgh, PA: Duquesne University Press, 2003), 120.

58. Hent de Vries, *Philosophy and the Turn to Religion* (Baltimore, MD: Johns Hopkins University Press, 1999), 60.

59. Levinas, *BV*, 107; compare Levinas, *NT*, 58.

60. Levinas, *GDT*, 176; translation modified; Levinas, *DMT*, 206.

61. Milan Zafirovski, *Democracy, Economy, and Conservatism: Political and Economic Freedoms and Their Antithesis in the Third Millennium* (Lanham, MD: Lexington Books, 2009), 321.

62. Slavoj Žižek, Erik L. Santner, and Kenneth Reinhard, *The Neighbor: Three Inquiries in Political Theology* (Chicago, IL: University of Chicago Press, 2006), 155.

63. James Kalb, *The Tyranny of Liberalism* (Wilmington, DE: ISI Books, 2008).

64. See Harold, *Prophetic Politics*; and Batnitzky, *Leo Strauss and Emmanuel Levinas*.

65. On Levinas's republicanism, see Caygill, *Levinas and the Political*, 7–9, 151–158.

66. Critchley, "Five Problems," 94.

67. Adorno, *IS*, 54.

68. Harvey, *Spaces of Hope*, 173.

69. Richard Stivers, *The Illusion of Freedom and Equality* (Albany: State University of New York Press, 2008), 29.

70. Nancy, *Experience of Freedom*, 46.

71. On the problems of autonomy, see Patricia Huntington, "Toward a Dialectical Concept of Autonomy: Revisiting the Feminist Alliance with Poststructuralism," *Philosophy and Social Criticism* 21, no. 1 (1995): 37–55; Timothy J. Reiss, *Against Autonomy: Global Dialectics of Cultural Exchange* (Stanford, CA: Stanford University Press, 2002); Molly Anne Rothenberg, *The Excessive Subject: A New Theory of Social Change* (Cambridge: Polity, 2009), 201.

72. Beyond the literature on Adorno and Levinas, a number of important works have addressed the question of the contemporary subject. See Namita Goswami, *Subjects That Matter: Philosophy, Feminism, and Postcolonial Theory* (Albany: State University of New York Press, 2019); Huntington, *Ecstatic Subjects*; Leeb, *Power and Feminist Agency in Capitalism*; John Sanbonmatsu, *The Postmodern Prince: Critical Theory, Left Strategy, and the Making of a New Political Subject* (New York: New York University Press, 2004); John Sanbonmatsu, "The Subject of Freedom at the End of History: Socialism beyond Humanism," *American Journal of Economics and Sociology* 66, no. 1 (2007): 217–235.

73. Levinas, *EN*, 191.

74. Levinas, *OI*, 114.

75. Levinas, *OI*, 115–121.

76. For example, Levinas, *OI*, 114–115.

77. Levinas, *PN*, 54.

78. Levinas, *IRB*, 192.

79. Levinas, *OB*, 138: Levinas, *AE*, 176.

80. Friedrich Nietzsche, *Sämtliche Werke: Kritische Studienausgabe*, ed. Giorgio Colli and Mazzino Montinari (Berlin: De Gruyter, 1980), 4:61–64.

81. Adorno, CI, 105.
82. Anders, "Pathology of Freedom," 307–308.
83. Adorno, MM, 97/149–150; Adorno, GS 4, 169–171.
84. Adorno, HF, 266.
85. Adorno, HF, 57, 60.
86. Levinas, TI, 85–87.
87. Benda Hofmeyr, *Radical Passivity: Rethinking Ethical Agency in Levinas* (Dordrecht: Springer, 2009), 19.
88. Adorno, CI, 35.
89. Adorno, HF, 212. On de Tocqueville, Adorno, and America, see Claus Offe, *Reflections on America: Tocqueville, Weber, and Adorno in the United States* (Cambridge: Polity, 2005).
90. Adorno, HF, 197; compare Rose, *Mourning Becomes the Law*, 60.
91. Compare Adorno, ND, 146; Adorno, GS 6, 149.
92. Adorno, HF, 198.
93. Levinas, EN, 60; also note Chalier, *What Ought I to Do?*, 75–77.
94. Levinas, TI, 241; compare the discussion of this passage in Oona Eisenstadt, *Driven Back to the Text: The Premodern Sources of Levinas' Postmodernism* (Pittsburgh, PA: Duquesne University Press, 2001), 51.
95. Alford, *Levinas*, 124.
96. Levinas, TI, 302; Levinas, IRB, 192–193.
97. Compare Macdonald, "Cold, Cold, Warm," 669–689.
98. See again Caygill, *Levinas and the Political*, 7–9, 151–158.
99. Levinas, OS, 125; Levinas, HS, 170; compare Levinas, BV, 104.
100. Levinas, AlT, 148–149; Levinas, Aet, 152–153.
101. Levinas, NTR, 37.
102. Levinas, DF, 284–285; Levinas, DL, 396–397; compare Adriaan Peperzak, *Ethics as First Philosophy* (New York: Routledge, 1995), 190.
103. Jean-Jacques Rousseau, *The Government of Poland*, trans. W. Kendall (Indianapolis, IN: Hackett Publishing, 1985), 29.
104. Adorno and Horkheimer, DE, 91.

Chapter 13

1. April Carter, *The Political Theory of Global Citizenship* (New York: Routledge, 2001), 17.
2. Martha C. Nussbaum has recently described the aspirations and deficits of cosmopolitanism in Martha C. Nussbaum, *Cosmopolitan Tradition*. This chapter will focus on her earlier account.
3. Rainer Forst, *Toleranz im Konflikt: Geschichte, Gehalt, und Gegenwart eines umstrittenen Begriffs* (Frankfurt: Suhrkamp, 2003); also see Wendy Brown

and Rainer Forst, *The Power of Tolerance: A Debate* (New York: Columbia University Press, 2014).

4. Martin Buber, *Meetings: Autobiographical Fragments* (London: Routledge, 2002), 28.

5. Sun Yat-Sen 孫中山, *Sanmin zhuyi* 三民主義 [The three principles of the people], 18th ed. (Taipei: Sanmin Press, 1996).

6. Since the patriotism of the oppressed can be a needed response to cosmopolitan empires, as Sun Yat-Sen argued, Martha Nussbaum's argumentation goes too far in problematizing the anticolonial nationalist responses to colonialism—by way of an analysis of Rabindranath Tagore's novel *The Home and the World* (1916)—in Martha C. Nussbaum, "Patriotism and Cosmopolitanism," in *For Love of Country?*, ed. Joshua Cohen (Boston, MA: Beacon Press, 1996), 3–17. She has further modified her position in subsequent writings. See Martha C. Nussbaum, *Cosmopolitan Tradition*.

7. Herbert Marcuse, "Repressive Tolerance," in *A Critique of Pure Tolerance*, ed. Robert Paul Wolff, Herbert Marcuse, and Barrington Moore (Boston, MA: Beacon Press, 1969), 81.

8. Wendy Brown, *Regulating Aversion: Tolerance in the Age of Identity and Empire* (Princeton, NJ: Princeton University Press, 2006).

9. Levinas, *TI*, 27.

10. Stephen Eric Bronner, *Ideas in Action: Political Tradition in the Twentieth Century* (Lanham, MD: Rowman and Littlefield Publishers, 1999), 331.

11. For a discussion of Kant and Hegel that problematizes and formulates an alternative to this standard account, see Andrew Buchwalter, *Hegel and Global Justice* (Dordrecht: Springer, 2012), 23.

12. Hegel remarked, "[O]nce the substantial form of the spirit has inwardly reconstituted itself, all attempts to preserve the forms of an earlier culture are utterly in vain; like withered leaves they are pushed off by the new buds already growing at their roots." Georg Wilhelm Friedrich Hegel, *Science of Logic* (London: George Allen and Unwin, 1969), sec. 5.

13. Georg Wilhelm Friedrich Hegel, *Elements of the Philosophy of Right* (Cambridge: Cambridge University Press, 1991), sec. 270.

14. Georg Wilhelm Friedrich Hegel, *Lectures on the Philosophy of World History* (Cambridge: Cambridge University Press, 1981), 66.

15. Hegel, *Elements of the Philosophy of Right*, sec. 209.

16. Adorno, *HF*, 110.

17. Adorno's critical stance toward the student movement is noticeable in Adorno, *CM*.

18. Adorno, *SDE*, 191.

19. Adorno, *MM*, 66/102–103. For an analysis of Adorno's apparently ambiguous attitude toward tolerance in this passage, compare Hammer, *Adorno and the Political*, 160–161.

20. Adorno, MM, 4/25. This passage suggests that tolerating the other involves denying the other's alterity in Andrew G. Fiala, *Tolerance and the Ethical Life* (London: Continuum, 2005), 106–107. Such a tolerance is read as a variety of tact, calculative prudence, and artifice according to Kleinberg-Levin, *Gestures of Ethical Life*, 112.

21. Brown, *Regulating Aversion*.

22. On the context and implications of the difference between Derrida and Habermas on tolerance and hospitality, see Lasse Thomassen, "The Inclusion of the Other? Habermas and the Paradox of Tolerance," *Political Theory* 34, no. 4 (2006): 439–462; Mengwei Yan, "Tolerance or Hospitality?" *Frontiers of Philosophy in China* 7, no. 1 (2012): 154–163.

23. Jacques Derrida and Maurizio Ferraris, *A Taste for the Secret* (Malden, MA: Polity, 2001), 62–63. Compare Jacques Derrida and Gil Anidjar, *Acts of Religion* (New York: Routledge, 2002), 59.

24. John D. Caputo, *Deconstruction in a Nutshell: A Conversation with Jacques Derrida* (New York: Fordham University Press, 1997), 45.

25. Marcuse, *One-Dimensional Man*, 7.

26. On Levinas's problematic relationship with colonialism and Eurocentrism, see Caygill, *Levinas and the Political*; Drabinski, *Levinas and the Postcolonial*; as well as Nelson, *Chinese and Buddhist Philosophy*, 60, 180, 213.

27. Jacques Derrida, *On Cosmopolitanism and Forgiveness* (London: Routledge, 2001), ix.

28. Jacques Derrida, *Paper Machine* (Stanford, CA: Stanford University Press, 2005), 123.

29. See Jacques Derrida and Elisabeth Roudinesco, *For What Tomorrow: A Dialogue*, 123 (Stanford, CA: Stanford University Press, 2004).

30. Derrida, *On Cosmopolitanism and Forgiveness*, 20–21. Note the related discussion in Jacques Derrida, *Aporias: Dying-Awaiting (One Another at) the "Limits of Truth"* (Stanford, CA: Stanford University Press, 1995), 84.

31. Jacques Derrida, *Monolingualism of the Other, or, the Prosthesis of Origin* (Stanford, CA: Stanford University Press, 1998), 25.

32. Derrida, *Monolingualism of the Other*, 25.

33. Compare David Gauthier, "Levinas and the Politics of Hospitality," *History of Political Thought* 28, no. 1 (2007): 158–180. Levinas's ambiguous and at times troubling relationship with Eurocentrism, colonialism, and racism should be addressed in this context.

34. Jacques Derrida, *Adieu to Emmanuel Levinas* (Stanford: Stanford University Press, 1999), 87–88.

35. On the problematic of republicanism in Levinas, in addition to the previous discussions, see Caygill, *Levinas and the Political*, 58; Critchley, *Ethics of Deconstruction*, 304; Simon Critchley, *Very Little . . . Almost Nothing: Death, Philosophy, Literature*, 2nd ed. (London: Routledge, 2004), 173.

36. On the advantages and disadvantages of republican democracy, see Jürgen Habermas, "Three Normative Models of Democracy," *Constellations* 1, no. 1 (1994): 1–10; Jürgen Habermas, *Philosophische Texte* (Philosophical texts), vol. 4, *Politische Theorie* (Political theory) (Frankfurt: Suhrkamp, 2009), 70–86. Levinas does not consider at length a number of elements of the republican tradition, such as civil society and the public sphere, articulated in Arendt's works on totalitarianism and Habermas's on the public.

37. Hannah Arendt, *The Origins of Totalitarianism* (New York: Houghton Mifflin Harcourt, 1973).

38. Arendt, *Origins of Totalitarianism*, 296.

39. See Levinas, OI, 398. Prophecy is an inspiration rather than an established institution by definition.

40. Marx, *Selected Writings*, 176. This statement from the *Communist Manifesto* has analogous expressions in the *German Ideology* (Marx, *Selected* Writings, 147) and *Capital* (Marx, *Selected Writings*, 239).

41. Habermas, "Three Normative Models of Democracy," 1–10; Habermas, *Philosophische Texte*, 4:70–86.

42. Derrida, *Adieu to Emmanuel Levinas*, 72.

43. On universal charity as justice in Leibniz, see Patrick Riley, *Leibniz' Universal Jurisprudence: Justice as the Charity of the Wise* (Cambridge, MA: Harvard University Press, 1996), 143.

44. The difference between "universal" cosmopolitan justice and the "infinite" and open-ended responsibility articulated by Levinas is discussed in Eduard Jordaan, "Cosmopolitanism, Freedom, and Indifference: A Levinasian View," *Alternatives: Global, Local, Political* 34, no. 1 (2009): 83–106.

45. On asymmetrical reciprocity, compare Patricia J. Huntington, "Asymmetrical Reciprocity and Practical Agency: Contemporary Dilemmas of Feminist Theory in Benhabib, Young, and Kristeva," in *Political Phenomenology*, ed. Hwa Yol Jung and Lester Embree (Dordrecht: Springer, 2016), 353–378.

46. Compare Immanuel Kant, *Practical Philosophy* (Cambridge: Cambridge University Press, 1996), Ak. 6:332; "An Eye for an Eye," in Levinas, DF, 147.

47. See Levinas, EN, 98, 121; Levinas, IRB, 194; compare M. Morgan, *Discovering Levinas*, 451.

48. Compare Derrida, *Adieu to Emmanuel Levinas*, 4, 39.

49. Levinas, UH, 130; Levinas, LIH, 181.

50. Dussel, *Towards an Unknown Marx*.

51. Derrida, *Adieu to Emmanuel Levinas*, 72.

52. On the complex and problematic relationship between ethical Judaism and Zionism, see Judith Butler, *Parting Ways: Jewishness and the Critique of Zionism* (New York: Columbia University Press, 2012); Herzog, "Levinas's Ethics, Politics, and Zionism," 473–491. On Levinas's question-worthy relationship with Zionism and the political status of Palestinians, see Jason Caro, "Levinas and the Palestinians," *Philosophy and Social Criticism* 35, no. 6 (2009): 671–684.

53. Levinas, *DF*, 51.
54. Derrida and Anidjar, *Acts of Religion*, 88.
55. Compare the discussion of French soil in Derrida, *Monolingualism of the Other*, 91.
56. See the discussion in Raffoul, *Origins of Responsibility*, 179.
57. Compare Cecil Eubanks, "The Politics of the Homeless Spirit: Heidegger and Levinas on Dwelling and Hospitality," *History of Political Thought* 32, no. 1 (2011): 125–146.
58. See C. Fred Alford, "Levinas and the Limits of Political Theory," in *Levinas, Law, Politics*, ed. Marinos Diamantides (London: Routledge-Cavendish, 2007), 119.
59. Concerning the contested issue of the relation between ethics and politics in Levinas and Derrida, see Diane Perpich, "A Singular Justice: Ethics and Politics between Levinas and Derrida," supplement, *Philosophy Today* 42 (1998): 59–70.
60. Caputo, *Prayers and Tears*, 205. On the problem of the third party in Levinas, see Robert Bernasconi, "The Third Party: Levinas on the Intersection of the Ethical and the Political," *Journal of the British Society for Phenomenology* 30, no. 1 (1999): 76–87; and William Simmons, "The Third: Levinas' Theoretical Move from An-archical Ethics to the Realm of Justice and Politics," *Philosophy and Social Criticism* 25, no. 6 (1999): 83–104.
61. Ze'ev Levy, "Emmanuel Levinas on Secularization in Modern Society," *Levinas Studies* 1 (2005): 31–32.
62. On tolerance as a noncontingent constitutive characteristic of Judaism, see Levinas, *DF*, 173; Levy, "Emmanuel Levinas," 31–32; Malka, *Emmanuel Levinas*, 13.
63. Levinas, *DF*, 173–174.
64. Levinas, *NTR*, 27.
65. Concerning the issue of the intolerant and condescending "tolerance" of the privileged and the elite, see Levinas, *BV*, 95. On the face-to-face situation and substitution, see Bettina Bergo, "The Face in Levinas: Toward a Phenomenology of Substitution," *Angelaki* 16, no. 1 (2011): 17–39.
66. Compare Levinas, *OI*, 476.
67. In particular, chapter 5 of Axel Honneth, *Das Andere der Gerechtigkeit: Aufsätze zur praktischen Philosophie* (Frankfurt: Suhrkamp, 2000), 133–170; Axel Honneth, *Disrespect: The Normative Foundations of Critical Theory* (Cambridge: Polity Press, 2007), 99–128.
68. See Honneth, *Struggle for Recognition*, 129.
69. Habermas's basic formulation of deliberative democracy in these terms appears in Habermas, "Three Normative Models of Democracy," 1–10; Habermas, *Philosophische Texte*, 4:70–86.
70. Adorno, *ND*, 41; Adorno, *GS* 6, 51.
71. Habermas, "Three Normative Models of Democracy," 1–10; Habermas, *Philosophische Texte*, 4:70–86.

72. Adorno, *PE*, 127–128.

73. Compare the argument of part 1 above. On the promise of happiness and redemption in literature, see David Michael Kleinberg-Levin, *Redeeming Words and the Promise of Happiness: A Critical Theory Approach to Wallace Stevens and Vladamir Nabokov* (Lanham, MD: Rowman and Littlefield, 2012); David Michael Kleinberg-Levin, *Redeeming Words: Language and the Promise of Happiness in the Stories of Döblin and Sebald* (Albany: State University of New York Press, 2013).

74. Compare Rosalyn Diprose, *Corporeal Generosity: On Giving with Nietzsche, Merleau-Ponty, and Levinas* (Albany: State University of New York Press, 2002), 167.

75. On the complex question of cosmopolitanism, humanism, and the properly human in Derrida's thought, see Jin Y. Park, ed., *Comparative Political Theory and Cross-Cultural Philosophy: Essays in Honor of Hwa Yol Jung* (Lanham, MD: Lexington Books, 2009), 5–6.

76. Compare Adorno, *IS*, 40.

77. Jürgen Habermas, *The Structural Transformation of the Public Sphere: An Inquiry into a Category of Bourgeois Society* (Cambridge, MA: MIT Press, 1991).

78. Jürgen Habermas, *Legitimation Crisis* (Boston, MA: Beacon Press, 1975).

79. Jürgen Habermas, *Europe: The Faltering Project* (Cambridge: Polity, 2009), 187.

80. Habermas, *Europe*, 209.

81. Habermas, *Europe*, 190.

Chapter 14

1. On the classical idea of liberalism, note Berlin, *Liberty*; Habermas, "Three Normative Models of Democracy," 1–10; Habermas, *Philosophische Texte*, 4:70–86.

2. On liberalism and oppression in Levinas, see Annabel Herzog, "Is Liberalism 'All We Need'? Levinas's Politics of Surplus," *Political Theory* 30, no. 2 (2002): 204–227; Annabel Herzog, "Levinas, Benjamin, and the Oppressed," *Journal of Jewish Thought and Philosophy* 12, no. 2 (2003): 123–138.

3. On forms of life, see Rahel Jaeggi, *Kritik von Lebensformen* (Frankfurt: Suhrkamp, 2013).

4. Jane Anna Gordon and Lewis R. Gordon, *Of Divine Warning: Disaster in a Modern Age* (London: Routledge, 2015).

5. Compare Levinas, *AlT*, 137; Levinas, *Aet*, 142.

6. Adorno, *PE*, 115.

7. Adorno, *ND*, 147, 309; Adorno, *GS 6*, 143, 304; regarding Adorno's ethically motivated critique of conventional morality, see J. M. Bernstein, *Adorno*, 143.

8. Adorno, *ND*, 309; Adorno, *GS 6*, 304.

9. Adorno, JA, 47; Adorno, GS 6, 445.
10. Adorno, ND, 147; Adorno, GS 6, 150.
11. Levinas, UH, 128–129; Levinas, LIH, 178–179.
12. Compare Edith Wyschogrod, *Emmanuel Levinas: The Problem of Ethical Metaphysics* (New York: Fordham University Press, 2000), 114; however, it is a question in the present work whether these should be considered exclusively negative for Levinas.
13. Levinas, EE, 101; Levinas, DEE, 168.
14. Levinas, TI, 21.
15. Respectively Levinas, IRB, 257; Levinas, BPW, 7, 113.
16. Levinas, EI, 88; Levinas, Eei, 82.
17. On the impossibility of ethics and the ethics of the impossible, see Raffoul, "Derrida and Ethics," 270–290.
18. See Eisenstadt, "Levinas and Adorno," 131–151.
19. Levinas, TI, 120.
20. Levinas, EN, 174–175; Levinas, ENE, 181–182.
21. This point extends the one made in Levinas, EE, 98–99; Levinas, DEE, 163–164.
22. Adorno, ND, 147; Adorno, GS 6, 150. Habermas rightly warns of overgeneralizing Adorno's critique of identity and exchange such that they become ahistorical constants without a specific configuration in capitalist societies in Habermas, *Philosophisch-politische Profile*, 178–179.
23. Adorno and Horkheimer, DE, 138.
24. Seyla Benhabib, *Another Cosmopolitanism* (Oxford: Oxford University Press, 2006).
25. Derrida, *Adieu to Emmanuel Levinas*, 48.
26. Adorno and Horkheimer, DE, 138.
27. Jean-Paul Sartre, *Colonialism and Neocolonialism*, trans. Azzedine Haddour, Steve Brewer, and Terry McWilliams (London: Routledge, 2001), 18. Agamben articulates a related point about "otherization" in his conception of the *homo sacer* in Giorgio Agamben, *Homo Sacer: Sovereign Power and Bare Life* (Stanford, CA: Stanford University Press, 1998).
28. Compare Agamben, *Homo Sacer*, and Judith Butler, *Frames of War: When Is Life Grievable?* (London: Verso, 2009), 93, 128.
29. Consider, for two examples among many, the accounts of the racialization of Muslim veils in Alia Al-Saji, "The Racialization of Muslim Veils: A Philosophical Analysis," *Philosophy and Social Criticism* 36, no. 8 (2010): 875–902; and the ideological discourse of the American-Iraq war in Bassam Romaya, *The Iraq War: A Philosophical Analysis* (Basingstoke, UK: Palgrave Macmillan, 2012).
30. Compare Adorno, SDE, 121.
31. Hegel, *Phänomenologie des Geistes*, secs. 549–550.
32. Horkheimer and Adorno, DE; Adorno, GS 3.

33. In addition to the modified Levinasian argument of the present book, also see Seyla Benhabib, *The Rights of Others: Aliens, Residents, and Citizens* (Cambridge: Cambridge University Press, 2004).

34. This point and the argument developed in this section is in accord with the description of the limitations of classical models of liberalism and republicanism developed in Habermas, "Three Normative Models of Democracy," 1–10; Habermas, *Philosophische Texte*, 4:70–86. Instead of embracing Habermas's formulation of an alternative procedural, discursive, and deliberative democracy, I have argued for a pluralistic an-archic democracy of a community of nonidentity.

35. Herzog, "Political Itineraries," 20–41.

36. Marx, *Marx-Engels Reader*, 663–664.

37. Dussel, *Invention of the Americas*; Frantz Fanon, *The Wretched of the Earth* (New York: Grove Press, 2004). For a systematic account of Fanon's challenge and its implications, see Lewis R. Gordon, *Fanon and the Crisis of European Man: An Essay on Philosophy and the Human Sciences* (London: Routledge, 1995).

38. Fanon, *Wretched of the Earth*, 98.

39. Adorno, HF, 155.

40. Marx, *Marx-Engels Reader*, 531; Karl Marx, "Kritik des Gothaer Programms," in *Karl Marx / Friedrich Engels Gesamtausgabe* (MEGA), part I, vol. 25, May 1875–May 1883 (Berlin: Dietz Verlag, 1981), 15.

41. Levinas, OS, 120; Levinas, HS, 164.

42. Levinas, EN, 95; Levinas, ENE, 105.

43. Adorno, PE, 12; Adorno and Horkheimer, TNM, 5.

44. Adorno, ND, 17–18; Adorno, GS 6, 28–29.

45. Adorno, PE, 124.

46. On the significance of an "ethics of tension," see Park, *Buddhism and Postmodernity*, 205–222; Park, "Ethics of Tension," 123–142; on the ethics of impossibility, see Raffoul, "Derrida and Ethics," 270–290; Raffoul, *Origins of Responsibility*.

47. On the intercultural pluralization of lifeworlds, in the context of an analysis and intercultural critique of the lifeworld conceptions of Husserl and Habermas, see Nelson, *Chinese and Buddhist Philosophy*, 178–187 and 255–258; and also the conclusion regarding intercultural lifeworlds and modernity in Nelson, "Zhang Junmai's Early Political Philosophy," 183–208.

Epilogue

1. Levinas, OB, 14–15; Levinas, AE, 17–18.

2. Although Adorno mocks perfectionist moralizing and posturing, and, in contrast to my imperfectionist interpretation, there are other senses of perfectionism that could be at work in his thought, see Martin Shuster, "Nothing

to Know: The Epistemology of Moral Perfectionism in Adorno and Cavell," *Idealistic Studies* 44, no. 1 (2014): 1–29.

3. Adorno, MM, 99/154; Adorno, GS 4, 176.

4. Putnam, *Jewish Philosophy*, 72.

5. The good's diachronic autonomy is thematized in Levinas, OB, 122; Levinas, AE, 157.

6. Putnam, *Jewish Philosophy*, 72.

7. Levinas, OB, 96; Levinas, AE, 122.

8. See Bloch, *Das Prinzip Hoffnung*, 1:74, 357; Habermas, *Philosophisch-politische Profile*, 141.

9. Adorno, MM, 100/156; Adorno, GS 4, 178.

10. Dussel, "Critical Theory," 22.

11. For further discussion of "nourishing life," see my discussions of its ethical role in Daoist discourses in Nelson, *Daoism and Environmental Philosophy*, chapter 2.

12. Jürgen Habermas, *Legitimation Crisis* (Boston, MA: Beacon Press, 1975).

13. Compare Adorno, PE, 131. On the persistent problems with and transformative positionality of the notion of ideology (the bewitchment and fixation of social mediations as natural) and its critique (oriented toward emancipation), see Adorno, PS, 135–277; Adorno, PE, 70–76, 130–139; and Adorno, IS, 84–86.

14. In light of Levinas, "becoming-with" can be read as an "inhabiting with." On reimagining multi-species "becoming-with" in the Capitalocene (the capitalistically determined Anthropocene), see Donna J. Haraway, *Staying with the Trouble: Making Kin in the Chthulucene* (Durham, NC: Duke University Press, 2016).

15. See Adorno, CI, 61–106; Adorno, Vo, 156–176. Compare Cook, *Culture Industry Revisited*; Trish Morgan, "Adorno and the Political Economy of Communication," *Political Economy of Communication* 1, no. 2 (2014): 44–64.

16. Dussel, *Towards an Unknown Marx*.

Bibliography

Works of Theodor W. Adorno

AHB. Theodor W. Adorno and Max Horkheimer. *Briefwechsel 1945–1949*. Edited by Christoph Godde and Henri Lonitz. Frankfurt: Suhrkamp, 2005.

Äs. *Ästhetik (1958/1959)*. Frankfurt: Suhrkamp, 2009.

AT. *Aesthetic Theory*. Edited by Gretel Adorno and Rolf Tiedemann. Translated by Robert Hullot-Kentor. Minneapolis: University of Minnesota Press, 1997.

BPM. *Beethoven: The Philosophy of Music*. Translated by Edmund Jephcott. Stanford, CA: Stanford University Press, 1998.

CI. *The Culture Industry*. Edited by J. M. Bernstein. London: Routledge, 1991.

CM. *Critical Models: Interventions and Catchwords*. Translated by H. W. Pickford. New York: Columbia University Press, 2005.

DE. Coauthored with Max Horkheimer. *Dialectic of Enlightenment*. Translated by Edmund Jephcott. Stanford, CA: Stanford University Press, 2002.

GS 1–20. *Gesammelte Schriften*. Edited by Rolf Tiedemann, with Gretel Adorno. Frankfurt: Suhrkamp, 1970–1986.

HF. *History and Freedom*. Translated by Rodney Livingstone. Stanford, CA: Stanford University Press, 2007.

HTS. *Hegel: Three Studies*. Translated by Shierry Weber Nicholsen. Cambridge, MA: MIT Press, 1994.

ID. *An Introduction to Dialectics*. Cambridge: John Wiley and Sons, 2017.

IS. *Introduction to Sociology*. Translated by Edmund Jephcott. Stanford, CA: Stanford University Press, 2002.

ISW. *In Search of Wagner*. Translated by Rodney Livingstone. London: Verso, 1981.

JA. *The Jargon of Authenticity*. Translated by K. Tarnowski and F. Will. London: Routledge and Kegan Paul, 1973.

KCA. *Kierkegaard: Construction of the Aesthetic*. Translated by R. Hullot-Kentor. Minneapolis: Minnesota University Press, 1989.

KDL. "On Kierkegaard's Doctrine of Love." *Zeitschrift fur Sozialforschung / Studies in Philosophy and Social Science*, 8, no. 3 (1939): 413–429.

KCPR. *Kant's Critique of Pure Reason*. Translated by Rodney Livingstone. Stanford, CA: Stanford University Press, 2001.
LND. *Lectures on Negative Dialectics: Fragments of a Lecture Course 1965/1966*. Cambridge: John Wiley and Sons, 2014.
MCP. *Metaphysics: Concept and Problems*. Translated by Edmund Jephcott. Stanford, CA: Stanford University Press, 2001.
MM. *Minima Moralia: Reflections on a Damaged Life*. Translated by E. F. N. Jephcott. London: Verso, 1974. (Cited by section number / page number).
MMP. *Mahler: A Musical Physiognomy*. Translated by Edmund Jephcott. Chicago, IL: University of Chicago Press, 1992.
ND. *Negative Dialectics*. Translated by E. B. Ashton. New York: Continuum Books, 1973.
NL1 and NL2. *Notes to Literature*. 2 vols. Translated by Shierry Weber Nicholsen. New York: Columbia University Press, 1992.
PE. *Philosophical Elements of a Theory of Society*. Cambridge: Polity Press, 2019.
PMM. *Philosophy of Modern Music*. London: Bloomsbury, 2007.
PMP. *Problems of Moral Philosophy*. Edited by Thomas Schröder. Translated by Rodney Livingstone. Stanford, CA: Stanford University Press, 2001.
Pr. *Prisms*. Translated by Samuel Weber and Shierry Weber. Cambridge, MA: MIT Press, 1981.
PS. *Philosophie und Soziologie*. Frankfurt: Suhrkamp, 2011.
PT. *Philosophische Terminologie*. Frankfurt: Suhrkamp, 2016.
QuF. *Quasi una Fantasia: Essays on Modern Music*. London: Verso, 1998.
SDE. *The Stars Down to Earth and Other Essays on the Irrational in Culture*. Edited by Stephen Crook. London: Routledge, 1994.
TNM. Coauthored with Max Horkheimer. *Towards a New Manifesto*. Translated by Rodney Livingstone. London: Verso, 2011.
Vo. *Vorträge 1949–1968*. Frankfurt: Suhrkamp, 2019.

Works of Emmanuel Levinas

AlT. *Alterity and Transcendence*. Translated by Michael B. Smith. New York: Columbia University Press, 1999. / Aet. *Altérité et transcendance*. Paris: Fata Morgana, 1995.
BPW. *Basic Philosophical Writings*. Edited by Adriaan T. Peperzak, Simon Critchley, and Robert Bernasconi. Bloomington: Indiana University Press, 1996.
BV. *Beyond the Verse: Talmudic Readings and Lectures*. Translated by Gary D. Mole. Bloomington: Indiana University Press, 1994.
CPP. *Collected Philosophical Papers*. Translated by Alphonso Lingis. Pittsburgh, PA: Duquesne University Press, 1979.

DEH. *Discovering Existence with Husserl.* Translated by Richard A. Cohen and Michael B. Smith. Evanston, IL: Northwestern University Press, 1998.

DF. *Difficult Freedom: Essays on Judaism.* Translated by Seán Hand. Baltimore, MD: Johns Hopkins University Press, 1990. / DL. *Difficile liberté: Essais sur le Judaïsme.* Paris: Editions Albin Michel, 1963.

EE. *Existence and Existents.* Translated by Alphonso Lingis. The Hague: Nijhoff, 1978. / DEE. *De l'existence à l'existant.* Paris: Fontaine, 1947.

EI. *Ethics and Infinity.* Translated by Richard A. Cohen. Pittsburgh, PA: Duquesne University Press, 1985. / *Eei. Éthique et infini.* Paris: Fayard, 1982.

EN. *Entre nous: On Thinking-of-the-Other.* Translated by Michael B. Smith and Barbara Harshav. New York: Columbia University Press, 1998. / *ENE. Entre nous: Essais sur le penser-à-l'autre.* Paris: Bernard Grasset, 1998.

GCM. *Of God Who Comes to Mind.* Translated by Bettina Bergo. Stanford, CA: Stanford University Press, 1998. / DVI. *De Dieu qui vient à l'idée.* Paris: J. Vrin, 1982.

GDT. *God, Death and Time.* Translated by Bettina Bergo. Stanford, CA: Stanford University Press, 2000. / DMT. *Dieu, la mort et le temps.* Paris: Grasset, 1993.

HO. *Humanism of the Other.* Translated by Nidra Poller. Urbana: University of Illinois Press, 2003.

IRB. *Is It Righteous to Be?* Edited by Jill Robbins. Stanford, CA: Stanford University Press, 2001.

LR. *The Levinas Reader.* Edited by Sean Hand. Oxford: Basil Blackwell, 1989.

NT. *New Talmudic Readings.* Translated by Richard A. Cohen. Pittsburgh, PA: Duquesne University Press, 1999.

NTR. *Nine Talmudic Readings.* Translated by Annette Aronowicz. Bloomington: Indiana University Press, 1990.

O1. *Œuvres 1: Carnets de captivité suivi de Écrits sur la captivité et Notes philosophiques diverses.* Paris: Grasset-IMEC, 2009.

O2. *Œuvres 2: Parole et silence et autres conférences inédites au Collège philosophique.* Paris: Grasset-IMEC, 2011.

O3. *Œuvres 3: Eros, littérature et philosophie.* Paris: Grasset-IMEC, 2013.

OB. *Otherwise Than Being or Beyond Essence.* Translated by Alphonso Lingis. The Hague: Nijhoff, 1981. / AE. *Autrement qu'être, ou, Au-delà de l'essence.* The Hague: Nijhoff, 1974.

OE. *On Escape.* Translated by Bettina Bergo. Stanford, CA: Stanford University Press, 2003. / Dle. *De l'évasion.* Montpellier: Fata Morgana, 1982.

OO. *On Obliteration: An Interview with Françoise Armengaud Concerning the Work of Sacha Sosno.* Zürich: Diaphanes, 2019.

OS. *Outside the Subject.* Translated by Michael B. Smith. Stanford, CA: Stanford University Press, 1994. / HS. *Hors sujet.* Montpellier: Fata Morgana, 1987.

PM. "The Paradox of Morality: An Interview with Emmanuel Levinas." In *The Provocation of Levinas: Rethinking the Other*, edited by R. Bernasconi and D. Wood, 168–188. London: Routledge, 2002.
PN. *Proper Names*. Translated by Michael B. Smith. Stanford, CA: Stanford University Press, 1996. / *NP. Noms propres*. Montpellier: Fata Morgana, 1976.
TI. *Totality and Infinity: An Essay on Exteriority*. Translated by Alphonso Lingis. Pittsburgh, PA: Duquesne University Press, 1979. / *TeI. Totalité et infini: Essai sur l'exteriorité*. The Hague: M. Nijhoff, 1961.
TIHP. *The Theory of Intuition in Husserl's Phenomenology*. 2nd ed. Translated by Andre Orianne. Evanston, IL: Northwestern University Press, 1995.
TO. *Time and the Other*. Translated by Richard A. Cohen. Pittsburgh, PA: Duquesne University Press, 1987. / *TA. Le temps et l'autre*. Paris: PUF, 1983.
UH. *Unforeseen History*. Translated by Nidra Poller. Urbana: University of Illinois Press, 2004. / *LIH. Les imprévus de l'histoire*. Montpellier: Fata Morgana, 1994.

Other Works

Agamben, Giorgio. *Homo Sacer: Sovereign Power and Bare Life*. Stanford, CA: Stanford University Press, 1998.
Alford, C. Fred. "Levinas and the Limits of Political Theory." In *Levinas, Law, Politics*, edited by Marinos Diamantides, 107–126. London: Routledge-Cavendish, 2007.
Alford, C. Fred. *Levinas, the Frankfurt School, and Psychoanalysis*. Middletown, CT: Wesleyan University Press, 2002.
Almond, Brenda. "Principles and Situations: K. E. Logstrup and British Moral Philosophy of the Twentieth Century." In *Concern for the Other: Perspectives on the Ethics of K. E. Løgstrup*, edited by Svend Andersen and Kees van Kooten Niekerk, 85–112. Notre Dame, IN: University of Notre Dame Press, 2007.
Al-Saji, Alia. "The Racialization of Muslim Veils: A Philosophical Analysis." *Philosophy and Social Criticism* 36, no. 8 (2010): 875–902.
Altman, Megan. "Heidegger on the Struggle for Belongingness and Being at Home." *Frontiers of Philosophy in China* 11, no. 3 (2016): 444–462.
Altman, Megan. "Mortality and Morality: A Heideggerian Interpretation of Kierkegaard's Either/Or." In *The Horizons of Authenticity: Essays in Honor of Charles Guignon's Work on Phenomenology, Existentialism, and Moral Psychology*, edited by Megan Altman and Hans Pedersen, 219–237. Dordrecht: Springer, 2015.
Ames, Roger T. *Confucian Role Ethics: A Vocabulary*. Hong Kong: Chinese University Press, 2011.

Ames, Roger T. "Getting Past Transcendence: Determinacy, Indeterminacy, and Emergence in Chinese Natural Cosmology." In *Transcendence, Immanence, and Intercultural Philosophy*, edited by Nahum Brown and William Franke, 3–33. Dordrecht: Springer, 2016.

Anders, Günther. "Pathologie de la liberté, essai sur la non-identification." *Recherches philosophiques* 7 (1936/1937): 22–54. Translated by Katharine Wolfe as "The Pathology of Freedom: An Essay on Non-Identification," *Deleuze Studies* 3, no. 2 (2009): 278–310.

Anderson, Sybol. *Hegel's Theory of Recognition: From Oppression to Ethical Liberal Modernity*. London: Bloomsbury Publishing, 2009.

Angelova, Emilia. "Utopia, Metontology, and the Sociality of the Other: Levinas, Heidegger and Bloch." *Journal of Contemporary Thought* 31 (Summer 2010): 171–191.

Angelova, Emilia. "Time's Disquiet and Unrest: The Affinity between Heidegger and Levinas." In *Between Levinas and Heidegger*, edited by John E. Drabinski and Eric S. Nelson, 85–108. Albany: State University of New York Press, 2014.

Angier, T. P. S. *Either Kierkegaard/or Nietzsche: Moral Philosophy in a New Key*. Hampshire, UK: Ashgate, 2006.

Arendt, Hannah. *The Origins of Totalitarianism*. New York: Houghton Mifflin Harcourt, 1973.

Arneil, Barbara. *John Locke and America: The Defence of English Colonialism*. Oxford: Clarendon Press, 1996.

Arriaga, Manuel P. *The Modernist-Postmodernist Quarrel on Philosophy and Justice: A Possible Levinasian Mediation*. Lanham, MD: Lexington Books, 2006.

Auerbach, Erich. *Mimesis: The Representation of Reality in Western Literature*. Princeton, NJ: Princeton University Press, 1968.

Barton, John, and Bruce M. Metzger. *The Holy Bible, Containing the Old and New Testaments: New Revised Standard Version*. Oxford: Oxford University Press, 2003.

Batnitzky, Leora Faye. *Leo Strauss and Emmanuel Levinas: Philosophy and the Politics of Revelation*. New York: Cambridge University Press, 2006.

Beals, Corey. *Levinas and the Wisdom of Love: The Question of Invisibility*. Waco, TX: Baylor University Press, 2007.

Beardsworth, Sara. "From Nature in Love: The Problem of Subjectivity in Adorno and Freudian Psychoanalysis." *Continental Philosophy Review* 40, no. 4 (2007): 365–387.

Benhabib, Seyla. *Another Cosmopolitanism*. Oxford: Oxford University Press, 2006.

Benhabib, Seyla. *The Reluctant Modernism of Hannah Arendt*. New York: Rowman and Littlefield, 2003.

Benhabib Seyla, ed. *Politics in Dark Times: Encounters with Hannah Arendt*. Cambridge: Cambridge University Press, 2010.

Benhabib, Seyla. *The Rights of Others: Aliens, Residents, and Citizens*. Cambridge: Cambridge University Press, 2004.

Benjamin, Walter. *Illuminations: Essays and Reflections*. New York: Schocken Books, 1969.

Benso, Silvia. *The Face of Things*. Albany: State University of New York Press, 2000.

Benso, Silvia. "Levinas—Another Ascetic Priest?" *Journal of the British Society for Phenomenology* 27, no. 2 (1996): 137–156.

Bergo, Bettina. "The Face in Levinas: Toward a Phenomenology of Substitution." *Angelaki* 16, no. 1 (2011): 17–39.

Bergo, Bettina. "Levinas and Husserl." In *The Oxford Handbook of Levinas*, edited by Michael L. Morgan, 71–102. Oxford: Oxford University Press, 2019.

Bergo, Bettina. *Levinas between Ethics and Politics: For the Beauty That Adorns the Earth*. Pittsburgh, PA: Duquesne University Press, 2003.

Bergo, Bettina. "Levinas's Weak Messianism in Time and Flesh, or the Insistence of Messiah Ben David." *Journal for Cultural Research* 13, no. 3–4 (2009): 225–248.

Bergo, Bettina. "Ontology, Transcendence, and Immanence in Emmanuel Levinas' Philosophy." *Research in Phenomenology* 35, no. 1 (2005): 141–180.

Berlin, Isaiah. *Liberty*. Oxford: Oxford University Press, 2002.

Bernasconi, Robert. "The Crisis of Critique and the Awakening of Politicisation in Levinas and Derrida." In *The Politics of Deconstruction: Jacques Derrida and the Other of Philosophy*, edited by Martin McQuillan, 81–97. London: Pluto Press, 2007.

Bernasconi, Robert. "Levinas and the Struggle for Existence." In *Addressing Levinas*, edited by Eric S. Nelson, Kent Still, and Antje Kapust, 170–184. Evanston, IL: Northwestern University Press, 2005.

Bernasconi, Robert. "The Third Party: Levinas on the Intersection of the Ethical and the Political." *Journal of the British Society for Phenomenology* 30, no. 1 (1999): 76–87.

Bernasconi, Robert, and Anika M. Mann. "The Contradictions of Racism: Locke, Slavery, and the Two Treatises." In *Race and Racism in Modern Philosophy*, edited by Andrew Valls, 89–107. Ithaca, NY: Cornell University Press, 2005.

Bernstein, J. M. *Adorno: Disenchantment and Ethics*. Cambridge: Cambridge University Press, 2001.

Bernstein, J. M. *Recovering Ethical Life: Jürgen Habermas and the Future of Critical Theory*. London: Routledge, 2014.

Bernstein, Jeffrey. "Spinoza, Hegel, and Adorno on Judaism and History." In *Between Hegel and Spinoza: A Volume of Critical Essays*, edited by Hasana Sharp and Jason E. Smith, 209–227. London: Bloomsbury, 2012.

Birmingham, Peg. "The An-archic Event of Natality and the 'Right to have Rights.'" *Social Research: An International Quarterly* 74, no. 3 (2007): 763–776.

Birmingham, Peg. *Hannah Arendt and Human Rights: The Predicament of Common Responsibility*. Bloomington: Indiana University Press, 2006.

Biro, Andrew. *Denaturalizing Ecological Politics: Alienation from Nature from Rousseau to the Frankfurt School and Beyond*. Toronto: University of Toronto Press, 2005.

Blackbourn, David. *The Conquest of Nature: Water, Landscape, and the Making of Modern Germany*. New York: W. W. Norton, 2006.

Bloch, Ernst. *Atheismus im Christentum: Zur Religion des Exodus und des Reichs*. Frankfurt: Suhrkamp, 1989. Translated by J. T. Swann as *Atheism in Christianity: The Religion of the Exodus and the Kingdom* (London: Verso, 2009).

Bloch, Ernst. *Das Materialismusproblem, seine Geschichte und Substanz*. Frankfurt: Suhrkamp, 1974.

Bloch, Ernst. *Das Prinzip Hoffnung*. 3 vols. Frankfurt: Suhrkamp, 1985.

Bloch, Ernst. "Ernst Bloch im Gespräch mit José Marchand 1974." In *Tagträume vom aufrechten Gang*, edited by Arno Münster, 20–100. Frankfurt: Suhrkamp, 1977.

Bloch, Ernst. *Experimentum Mundi: Frage, Kategorien des Herausbringens*. Frankfurt: Suhrkamp, 1974.

Bloch, Ernst. *Geist der Utopie*. 1918 ed. Frankfurt: Suhrkamp, 1985.

Bloch, Ernst. *Naturrecht und menschliche Würde*. Frankfurt: Suhrkamp, 1985. Translated by Dennis Schmidt as *Natural Law and Human Dignity* (Cambridge, MA: MIT Press, 1986).

Bloch, Ernst. *On Karl Marx*. London: Verso, 2018.

Bloch, Ernst. "Rosa Luxemburg, Lenin und die Lehren oder Marxismus als Moral." In *Gespräche mit Ernst Bloch*, edited by Rainer Traub and Harold Wieser, 208–220. Frankfurt: Suhrkamp, 1975.

Bloch, Ernst. *Thomas Münzer als Theologe der Revolution*. Frankfurt: Suhrkamp, 1985.

Bloechl, Jeffrey. *Liturgy of the Neighbor: Emmanuel Levinas and the Religion of Responsibility*. Pittsburgh, PA: Duquesne University Press, 2000.

Bowie, Andrew. *Adorno and the Ends of Philosophy*. Cambridge: Polity Press, 2013.

Bowie, Andrew. *From Romanticism to Critical Theory: The Philosophy of German Literary Theory*. London: Routledge, 1997.

Bronner, Stephen Eric. *Ideas in Action: Political Tradition in the Twentieth Century*. Lanham, MD: Rowman and Littlefield, 1999.

Bronner, Stephen Eric. *Reclaiming the Enlightenment: Towards a Politics of Radical Engagement*. New York: Columbia University Press, 2004.

Brown, Wendy. *Regulating Aversion: Tolerance in the Age of Identity and Empire*. Princeton, NJ: Princeton University Press, 2006.

Brown, Wendy, and Rainer Forst. *The Power of Tolerance: A Debate*. New York: Columbia University Press, 2014.

Brüggemeier, Franz-Josef, Mark Cioc, and Thomas Zeller, eds. *How Green Were the Nazis? Nature, Environment, and Nation in the Third Reich*. Athens: Ohio University Press, 2005.

Buber, Martin. *Ich und Du*. Stuttgart: Reclam, 2002.
Buber, Martin. *Meetings: Autobiographical Fragments*. London: Routledge, 2002.
Buber, Martin. *Reden und Gleichnisse des Tschuang Tse*. Leipzig: Insel Verlag, 1910.
Buchwalter, Andrew. *Hegel and Global Justice*. Dordrecht: Springer, 2012.
Budd, Malcolm. *The Aesthetic Appreciation of Nature*. Oxford: Oxford University Press, 2002.
Burik, Steven. *The End of Comparative Philosophy and the Task of Comparative Thinking: Heidegger, Derrida, and Daoism*. Albany: State University of New York Press, 2010.
Butler, Judith. *Frames of War: When Is Life Grievable?* London: Verso, 2009.
Butler, Judith. *Parting Ways: Jewishness and the Critique of Zionism*. New York: Columbia University Press, 2012.
Canovan, Margaret. *Hannah Arendt: A Reinterpretation of Her Political Thought*. Cambridge: Cambridge University Press, 1994.
Caputo, John D. *Deconstruction in a Nutshell: A Conversation with Jacques Derrida*. New York: Fordham University Press, 1997.
Caputo, John D. *The Prayers and Tears of Jacques Derrida: Religion without Religion*. Bloomington: Indiana University Press, 1997.
Caro, Jason. "Levinas and the Palestinians." *Philosophy and Social Criticism* 35, no. 6 (2009): 671–684.
Carr, Karen Leslie, and Philip J. Ivanhoe. *The Sense of Anti-Rationalism: The Religious Thoughts of Zhuangzi and Kierkegaard*. New York: Seven Bridges Press, 1999.
Carter, April. *The Political Theory of Global Citizenship*. New York: Routledge, 2001.
Caspi, Mishael, and John T. Greene, eds. *Unbinding the Binding of Isaac*. Lanham, MD: University Press of America, 2006.
Cavell, Stanley. *Conditions Handsome and Unhandsome: The Constitution of Emersonian Perfectionism*. Chicago, IL: University of Chicago Press, 1991.
Caygill, Howard. *Levinas and the Political*. London: Routledge, 2002.
Chai, David. "Daoism and *Wu*." *Philosophy Compass* 9, no. 10 (2014): 663–671.
Chai, David. "Habermas and Zhuangzi against Liberal Eugenic." *International Journal of Chinese and Comparative Philosophy of Medicine* 14, no. 2 (2016): 97–112.
Chai, David. "Meontological Generativity: A Daoist Reading of the Thing." *Philosophy East and West* 64, no. 2 (2014): 303–318.
Chai, David. "Nothingness and the Clearing: Heidegger, Daoism and the Quest for Primal Clarity." *Review of Metaphysics* 67, no. 3 (2014): 583–601.
Chai, David. "On Pillowing One's Skull: Zhuangzi and Heidegger on Death." *Frontiers of Philosophy in China* 11, no. 3 (2016): 483–500.
Chai, David. *Zhuangzi and the Becoming of Nothingness*. Albany: State University of New York Press, 2019.
Chalier, Catherine. "Ethics and the Feminine." In *Re-Reading Levinas*, edited by Robert Bernasconi and Simon Critchley, 119–129. Bloomington: Indiana University Press, 1991.

Chalier, Catherine. *What Ought I to Do? Morality in Kant and Levinas*. Translated by Jane Marie Todd. Ithaca, NY: Cornell University Press, 2002.
Chan, Joseph C. W. *Confucian Perfectionism: A Political Philosophy for Modern Times*. Princeton, NJ: Princeton University Press, 2017.
Chanter, Tina. *Time, Death, and the Feminine: Levinas with Heidegger*. Stanford, CA: Stanford University Press, 2001.
Cheng, Chung-Ying. "Deconstruction and Différance: Onto-Return and Emergence in a Daoist Interpretation of Derrida." Supplement, *Journal of Chinese Philosophy* 40 (2012): 31–50.
Cohen, Hermann. *Religion of Reason: Out of the Sources of Judaism*. Translated by Simon Kaplan. Atlanta, GA: Scholars Press, 1995.
Confucius. *Analects*. Translated by Roger Ames and Henry Rosemont Jr. New York: Random House, 1998.
Cook, Deborah. *Adorno, Habermas, and the Search for a Rational Society*. London: Routledge, 2004.
Cook, Deborah. *Adorno on Nature*. Durham, NC: Acumen, 2011.
Cook, Deborah. "Adorno's Critical Materialism." *Philosophy and Social Criticism* 32, no. 6 (2006): 719–737.
Cook, Deborah. *The Culture Industry Revisited: Theodor W. Adorno on Mass Culture*. Lanham, MD: Rowman and Littlefield, 1996.
Cook, Deborah. "From the Actual to the Possible: Nonidentity Thinking." *Constellations* 12, no. 1 (2005): 21–35.
Critchley, Simon. *The Ethics of Deconstruction: Derrida and Levinas*. West Lafayette, IN: Purdue University Press, 1999.
Critchley, Simon. *Ethics, Politics, Subjectivity: Essays on Derrida, Levinas, and Contemporary French Thought*. London: Verso, 1999.
Critchley, Simon. "Five Problems in Levinas's View of Politics and a Sketch of a Solution to Them." In *Levinas, Law, Politics*, edited by Marinos Diamantides, 93–106. London: Routledge-Cavendish, 2007.
Critchley, Simon. "Leaving the Climate of Heidegger's Thinking." In *Levinas in Jerusalem: Phenomenology, Ethics, Politics, Aesthetics*, edited by Joelle Hansel, 45–55. Berlin: Springer, 2009.
Critchley, Simon. *The Problem with Levinas*. Oxford: Oxford University Press, 2015.
Critchley, Simon. *Very Little . . . Almost Nothing: Death, Philosophy, Literature*. 2nd ed. London: Routledge, 2004.
Cronon, William, ed. *Uncommon Ground: Rethinking the Human Place in Nature*. New York: Norton, 1996.
Crowe, Jonathan. *Natural Law and the Nature of Law*. Cambridge: Cambridge University Press, 2019.
Dallmayr, Fred. "Adorno and Heidegger on Modernity." In *Adorno and Heidegger: Philosophical Questions*, edited by Iain Macdonald and Krzysztof Ziarek, 167–182. Stanford, CA: Stanford University Press, 2008.

Dalton, Drew M. *Longing for the Other: Levinas and Metaphysical Desire*. Pittsburgh, PA: Duquesne University Press, 2009.
Davis, Bret W. "Naturalness in Zen and Shin Buddhism: Before and Beyond Self- and Other-Power." *Contemporary Buddhism* 15, no. 2 (2014): 433–447.
Davis, Bret W. "Zen after Zarathustra: The Problem of the Will in the Confrontation between Nietzsche and Buddhism." *Journal of Nietzsche Studies*, no. 28 (2004): 89–138.
De Beauvoir, Simone. *The Second Sex*. New York: Vintage, 2012.
Delaney, Carol. *Abraham on Trial: The Social Legacy of Biblical Myth*. Princeton, NJ: Princeton University Press, 1998.
Derrida, Jacques. *Adieu to Emmanuel Levinas*. Stanford, CA: Stanford University Press, 1999.
Derrida, Jacques. *The Animal That Therefore I Am*. New York: Fordham University Press, 2008.
Derrida, Jacques. *Aporias: Dying-Awaiting (One Another at) the "Limits of Truth."* Stanford, CA: Stanford University Press, 1995.
Derrida, Jacques. *The Gift of Death and Literature in Secret*. Chicago, IL: University of Chicago Press, 2008.
Derrida, Jacques. *Monolingualism of the Other, or, the Prosthesis of Origin*. Stanford, CA: Stanford University Press, 1998.
Derrida, Jacques. *On Cosmopolitanism and Forgiveness*. London: Routledge, 2001.
Derrida, Jacques. *Paper Machine*. Stanford, CA: Stanford University Press, 2005.
Derrida, Jacques, and Elisabeth Roudinesco. *For What Tomorrow: A Dialogue*. Stanford, CA: Stanford University Press, 2004.
Derrida, Jacques, and Gil Anidjar. *Acts of Religion*. New York: Routledge, 2002.
Derrida, Jacques, and Maurizio Ferraris. *A Taste for the Secret*. Malden, MA: Polity, 2001.
de Saint-Cheron, Michaël. *Conversations with Emmanuel Lévinas, 1983–1994*. Pittsburgh, PA: Duquesne University Press, 2010.
de Tocqueville, Alexis. *Democracy in America*. New York: Library of America, 2004.
Devenney, Mark. *Ethics and Politics in Contemporary Theory between Critical Theory and Post-Marxism*. London: Routledge, 2004.
de Vries, Hent. *Minimal Theologies: Critiques of Secular Reason in Adorno and Levinas*. Baltimore, MD: Johns Hopkins University Press, 2005.
de Vries, Hent. *Philosophy and the Turn to Religion*. Baltimore, MD: Johns Hopkins University Press, 1999.
Dews, Peter. *The Idea of Evil*. Malden, MA: Blackwell, 2008.
Diprose, Rosalyn. *Corporeal Generosity: On Giving with Nietzsche, Merleau-Ponty, and Levinas*. Albany: State University of New York Press, 2002.
Dobbs-Weinstein, Idit. *Spinoza's Critique of Religion and Its Heirs: Marx, Benjamin, Adorno*. Cambridge: Cambridge University Press, 2015.

Drabinski, John E. *Levinas and the Postcolonial: Race, Nation, and Other.* Edinburgh: Edinburgh University Press, 2011.
Drabinski, John E. *Sensibility and Singularity: The Problem of Phenomenology in Levinas.* Albany: State University of New York Press, 2001.
Drabinski, John E. "Wealth and Justice in a U-topian Context." In *Addressing Levinas,* edited by Eric S. Nelson, Antje Kapust, and Kent Still, 185–198. Evanston, IL: Northwestern University Press, 2005.
Drabinski, John E., and Eric S. Nelson, eds. *Between Levinas and Heidegger.* Albany: State University of New York Press, 2014.
Dudiak, Jeffrey. *The Intrigue of Ethics: A Reading of the Idea of Discourse in the Thought of Emmanuel Levinas.* New York: Fordham University Press, 2001.
Dussel, Enrique. "Eurocentrism and Modernity (Introduction to the Frankfurt Lectures)." *Boundary 2,* 20, no. 3 (1993): 65–76.
Dussel, Enrique. "From Critical Theory to the Philosophy of Liberation: Some Themes for Dialogue." *Transmodernity: Journal of Peripheral Cultural Production of the Luso-Hispanic World* 1, no. 2 (2011): 17–43.
Dussel, Enrique. *The Invention of the Americas: Eclipse of "the Other" and the Myth of Modernity.* New York: Continuum, 1995.
Dussel, Enrique. *Philosophy of Liberation.* Eugene, OR: Wipf and Stock, 2003.
Dussel, Enrique. "'Sensibility' and 'Otherness' in Emmanuel Levinas." *Philosophy Today* 43 (1999): 126–134.
Dussel, Enrique. *Towards an Unknown Marx: A Commentary on the Manuscripts of 1861–63.* London: Routledge, 2002.
Düttmann, Alexander García. *The Gift of Language: Memory and Promise in Adorno, Benjamin, Heidegger, and Rosenzweig.* Syracuse, NY: Syracuse University Press, 2000.
Eagan, Jennifer L. "Unfreedom, Suffering, and the Culture Industry: What Adorno Can Contribute to a Feminist Ethics." In *Feminist Interpretations of Theodor Adorno,* edited by Renée Heberle, 277–300. University Park: Pennsylvania State University Press, 2006.
Edelglass, William. "Levinas on Suffering and Compassion." *Sophia* 45, no. 2 (2006): 43–59.
Eisenstadt, Oona. *Driven Back to the Text: The Premodern Sources of Levinas' Postmodernism.* Pittsburgh, PA: Duquesne University Press, 2001.
Eisenstadt, Oona. "Eurocentrism and Colorblindness." *Levinas Studies* 7 (2012): 43–62.
Eisenstadt, Oona. "Levinas and Adorno: Universalizing the Jew after Auschwitz." *Journal of Jewish Thought and Philosophy* 14, no. 1–2 (2006): 131–151.
Ellis, Fiona. *God, Value, and Nature.* Oxford: Oxford University Press, 2014.
Ellis, Fiona. "Levinas on Nature and Naturalism." In *The Oxford Handbook of Levinas,* edited by Michael L. Morgan, 689–708. Oxford: Oxford University Press, 2019.

Ellis, Fiona. "Murdoch and Levinas on God and Good." *European Journal for Philosophy of Religion* 1, no. 2 (2009): 63–87.
Elster, Jon. *Making Sense of Marx.* Cambridge: Cambridge University Press, 1985.
Eubanks, Cecil. "The Politics of the Homeless Spirit: Heidegger and Levinas on Dwelling and Hospitality." *History of Political Thought* 32, no. 1 (2011): 125–146.
Fagenblat, Michael. *A Covenant of Creatures: Levinas's Philosophy of Judaism.* Stanford, CA: Stanford University Press, 2010.
Fanon, Frantz. *Black Skin, White Masks.* New York: Grove Press, 2008.
Fanon, Frantz. *The Wretched of the Earth.* New York: Grove Press, 2004.
Fiala, Andrew G. *Tolerance and the Ethical Life.* London: Continuum, 2005.
Finlayson, James Gordon. "Adorno on the Ethical and the Ineffable." *European Journal of Philosophy* 10, no. 1 (2002): 1–25.
Finlayson, James Gordon. "Morality and Critical Theory: On the Normative Problem of Frankfurt School Social Criticism." *Telos* 146 (2009): 7–41.
Fleming, Marie. *Emancipation and Illusion: Rationality and Gender in Habermas's Theory of Modernity.* University Park: Pennsylvania State University Press, 1997.
Forst, Rainer. *Toleranz im Konflikt: Geschichte, Gehalt, und Gegenwart eines umstrittenen Begriffs.* Frankfurt: Suhrkamp, 2003.
Foster, John Bellamy. *Ecology against Capitalism.* New York: Monthly Review Press, 2002.
Foster, John Bellamy. *Marx's Ecology: Materialism and Nature.* New York: Monthly Review Press, 2000.
Foster, Roger. *Adorno: The Recovery of Experience.* Albany: State University of New York Press, 2007.
Fraser, Nancy, and Axel Honneth. *Redistribution or Recognition? A Political-Philosophical Exchange.* London: Verso, 2003.
Fraser, Nancy, and Rachel Jaeggi. *Capitalism: A Conversation in Critical Theory.* Cambridge: Polity Press, 2018.
Freyenhagen, Fabian. *Adorno's Practical Philosophy: Living Less Wrongly.* Cambridge: Cambridge University Press, 2013.
Freyenhagen, Fabian. "Honneth on Social Pathologies: A Critique." *Critical Horizons* 16, no. 2 (2015): 131–152.
Fritsch, Kelly. "On the Negative Possibility of Suffering: Adorno, Feminist Philosophy, and the Transfigured Crip to Come." *Disability Studies Quarterly* 33, no. 4 (2013): https://dsq-sds.org/article/view/3869.
Fritsch, Matthias. *The Promise of Memory: History and Politics in Marx, Benjamin, and Derrida.* Albany: State University of New York Press, 2006.
Fritsch, Matthias. *Taking Turns with the Earth: Phenomenology, Deconstruction, and Intergenerational Justice.* Stanford, CA: Stanford University Press, 2018.

Froese, Katrin. *Nietzsche, Heidegger, and Daoist Thought: Crossing Paths In-between.* Albany: State University of New York Press, 2006.

Gasché, Rodolphe. "The Theory of Natural Beauty and Its Evil Star: Kant, Hegel, Adorno." *Research in Phenomenology* 32, no. 1 (2002): 103–122.

Gauthier, David. "Levinas and the Politics of Hospitality." *History of Political Thought* 28, no. 1 (2007): 158–180.

Gellman, Jerome I. *Abraham! Abraham! Kierkegaard and the Hasidim on the Binding of Isaac.* Aldershot, UK: Ashgate, 2003.

Gerhardt, Christina. "The Ethics of Animals in Adorno and Kafka." *New German Critique* 33, no. 97 (2006): 159–178.

Geuss, Raymond. "Suffering and Knowledge in Adorno." *Constellations* 12, no. 1 (2005): 3–20.

Gordon, Jane Anna, and Lewis R. Gordon. *Of Divine Warning: Disaster in a Modern Age.* London: Routledge, 2015.

Gordon, Lewis R. *Fanon and the Crisis of European Man: An Essay on Philosophy and the Human Sciences.* London: Routledge, 1995.

Gordon, Peter E. *Adorno and Existence.* Cambridge, MA: Harvard University Press, 2016.

Goswami, Namita. "Europe as an Other: Postcolonialism and Philosophers of the Future." *Hypatia* 29, no. 1 (2014): 59–74.

Goswami, Namita. "Existence Authoritarian: Compulsion, Facticity and the Philosophy of Identity." In *Rethinking Facticity*, edited by François Raffoul and Eric S. Nelson, 289–316. Albany: State University of New York Press, 2008.

Goswami, Namita. "The (M)other of All Posts: Postcolonial Melancholia in the Age of Global Warming." *Critical Philosophy of Race* 1, no. 1 (2013): 104–120.

Goswami, Namita. *Subjects That Matter: Philosophy, Feminism, and Postcolonial Theory.* Albany: State University of New York Press, 2019.

Goswami, Namita. "Thinking Problems." *Journal of Speculative Philosophy* 26, no. 2 (2012): 189–199.

Gracyk, Theodore A. "Adorno, Jazz, and the Aesthetics of Popular Music." *Musical Quarterly* 76, no. 4 (1992): 526–542.

Grebowicz, Margret. " 'Between Betrayal and Betrayal': Epistemology and Ethics in Derrida's Debt to Levinas." In *Addressing Levinas*, edited by Eric S. Nelson, Antje Kapust, and Kent Still, 75–85. Evanston, IL: Northwestern University Press, 2005.

Gunderson, Ryan. "The First-generation Frankfurt School on the Animal Question: Foundations for a Normative Sociological Animal Studies." *Sociological Perspectives* 57, no. 3 (2014): 285–300.

Gunderson, Ryan. "Habermas in Environmental Thought." *Sociological Inquiry* 84, no. 4 (2014): 626–653.

Habermas, Jürgen. *Between Facts and Norms*. Cambridge, MA: MIT Press, 1996.
Habermas, Jürgen. *Europe: The Faltering Project*. Cambridge: Polity, 2009.
Habermas, Jürgen. *The Future of Human Nature*. Cambridge: Polity, 2003.
Habermas, Jürgen. "'Ich selber bin ja ein Stück Natur'—Adorno über die Naturverflochenheit der Vernunft." In *Dialektik der Freiheit*, edited by Axel Honneth, 13–40. Frankfurt: Suhrkamp, 2005.
Habermas, Jürgen. *The Inclusion of the Other: Studies in Political Theory*. Cambridge, MA: MIT Press, 1998.
Habermas, Jürgen. *Knowledge and Human Interests*. Boston, MA: Beacon Press, 1971.
Habermas, Jürgen. *Legitimation Crisis*. Boston, MA: Beacon Press, 1975.
Habermas, Jürgen. *On the Pragmatics of Communication*. Cambridge, MA: MIT Press, 1998.
Habermas, Jürgen. *The Philosophical Discourse of Modernity: Twelve Lectures*. Translated by Frederick Lawrence. Cambridge, MA: MIT Press, 1987.
Habermas, Jürgen. *Philosophisch-politische Profile*. Frankfurt: Suhrkamp, 1981.
Habermas, Jürgen. *Philosophische Texte*. Vol. 4, *Politische Theorie*. Frankfurt: Suhrkamp, 2009.
Habermas, Jürgen. *Postmetaphysical Thinking II*. Cambridge: John Wiley and Sons, 2017.
Habermas, Jürgen. *The Structural Transformation of the Public Sphere: An Inquiry into a Category of Bourgeois Society*. Cambridge, MA: MIT Press, 1991.
Habermas, Jürgen. *Theory and Practice*. Boston, MA: Beacon Press, 1973.
Habermas, Jürgen. *The Theory of Communicative Action*. 2 vols. Boston, MA: Beacon Press, 1984.
Habermas, Jürgen. "Three Normative Models of Democracy." *Constellations* 1, no. 1 (1994): 1–10.
Habermas, Jürgen, and Peter Dews. *Autonomy and Solidarity: Interviews with Jürgen Habermas*. London: Verso, 1992.
Hailwood, Simon. "Alienations and Natures." *Environmental Politics* 21, no. 6 (2012): 882–900.
Hall, David, and Roger Ames. *Thinking through Confucius*. Albany: State University of New York Press, 1987.
Halliwell, Stephen. *The Aesthetics of Mimesis: Ancient Texts and Modern Problems*. Princeton, NJ: Princeton University Press, 2002.
Halpern, Cynthia. *Suffering, Politics, Power: A Genealogy in Modern Political Theory*. Albany: State University of New York Press, 2002.
Hammer, Espen. *Adorno and the Political*. London: Routledge, 2006.
Hammer, Espen. *Adorno's Modernism: Art, Experience, and Catastrophe*. Cambridge: Cambridge University Press, 2015.
Hammer, Espen. "Metaphysics." In *Theodor Adorno: Key Concepts*, edited by Deborah Cook, 63–76. Durham, NC: Acumen, 2008.

Hand, Seán. *Facing the Other: The Ethics of Emmanuel Lévinas*. Richmond, UK: Curzon, 1996.
Hanssen, Beatrice. *Walter Benjamin's Other History: Of Stones, Animals, Human Beings, and Angels*. Berkeley: University of California Press, 2000.
Haraway, Donna J. *Staying with the Trouble: Making Kin in the Chthulucene*. Durham, NC: Duke University Press, 2016.
Harold, Philip J. *Prophetic Politics: Emmanuel Levinas and the Sanctification of Suffering*. Athens: Ohio University Press, 2009.
Harvey, David. *Spaces of Hope*. Berkeley: University of California Press, 2000.
Hatley, James. "Generations: Levinas in the Jewish Context." *Philosophy and Rhetoric* 38, no. 2 (2005): 173–189.
Hatley, James. "The Malignancy of Evil: Witnessing Violence beyond Justice." *Studies in Practical Philosophy* 3, no. 2 (2003): 84–106.
Hayward, Tim. *Political Theory and Ecological Value*. New York: St. Martin's Press, 1998.
Hearfield, Colin. *Adorno and the Modern Ethos of Freedom*. Aldershot, UK: Ashgate, 2004.
Hegel, Georg Wilhelm Friedrich. *Aesthetics: Lectures on Fine Art*. 2 vols. Oxford: Oxford University Press, 1998.
Hegel, Georg Wilhelm Friedrich. *Elements of the Philosophy of Right*. Cambridge: Cambridge University Press, 1991.
Hegel, Georg Wilhelm Friedrich. *Frühe Schriften*. Frankfurt: Suhrkamp, 1986.
Hegel, Georg Wilhelm Friedrich. *Lectures on the Philosophy of World History*. Cambridge: Cambridge University Press, 1981.
Hegel, Georg Wilhelm Friedrich. *Grundlinien der Philosophie des Rechts oder Naturrecht und Staatswissenschaft im Grundrisse*. Frankfurt: Suhrkamp, 1982.
Hegel, Georg Wilhelm Friedrich. *Phänomenologie des Geistes*. Frankfurt: Suhrkamp, 1986.
Hegel, Georg Wilhelm Friedrich. *Science of Logic*. London: George Allen and Unwin, 1969.
Heidegger, Martin. *Gesamtausgabe* [GA]. Frankfurt am Main: Vittorio Klostermann, 1975–ongoing.
Heidegger, Martin. *Gesamtausgabe* 61 [GA61]. *Phänomenologische Interpretationen zu Aristoteles*. 2nd ed. Frankfurt: Klostermann, 1994.
Heidegger, Martin. *Gesamtausgabe* 65 [GA65]. *Beiträge zur Philosophie: (Vom Ereignis)*. Frankfurt: Klostermann, 1989. Translated by P. Emad and K. Maly as *Contributions to Philosophy: From Enowning* (Bloomington: Indiana University Press, 1999).
Heidegger, Martin. *Gesamtausgabe* 90 [GA90]. *Zu Ernst Jünger*. Frankfurt: Klostermann, 2004.
Heidegger, Martin. *Gesamtausgabe* 97 [GA97]. *Anmerkungen I–V (Schwarze Hefte 1942–1948)*. Frankfurt: Klostermann, 2015.

Heidegger, Martin. *Introduction to Metaphysics*. Translated by G. Fried and R. Polt. New Haven, CT: Yale University Press, 2000.
Heidegger, Martin. SZ. *Sein und Zeit*. Tübingen: Niemeyer Verlag. 16th ed. 1985. Translated by J. Macquarrie and E. Robinson as *Being and Time* (New York: Harper and Row, 1962). Translated by Joan Stambaugh as *Being and Time* (Albany: State University of New York Press, 1996).
Heidegger, Martin. "Vom Wesen und Begriff der Phusis." In Heidegger, *Wegmarken*, 237–299. Frankfurt: Klostermann, 1978.
Herman, Jonathan R. *I and Tao: Martin Buber's Encounter with Chuang Tzu*. Albany: State University of New York Press, 1996.
Herzog, Annabel. "Dogs and Fire: The Ethics and Politics of Nature in Levinas." *Political Theory* 41, no. 3 (2013): 359–379.
Herzog, Annabel. "Is Liberalism 'All We Need'? Levinas's Politics of Surplus." *Political Theory* 30, no. 2 (2002): 204–227.
Herzog, Annabel. "Lecture de l'hospitalité biblique." *Revue des Etudes Juives* 171, no. 1–2 (2012): 1–25.
Herzog, Annabel. "Levinas, Benjamin, and the Oppressed." *Journal of Jewish Thought and Philosophy* 12, no. 2 (2003): 123–138.
Herzog, Annabel. "Levinas's Ethics, Politics, and Zionism." In *The Oxford Handbook of Levinas*, edited by Michael L. Morgan, 473–491. Oxford: Oxford University Press, 2019.
Herzog, Annabel. "Political Itineraries and Anarchic Cosmopolitanism in the Thought of Hannah Arendt." *Inquiry* 47, no. 1 (2004): 20–41.
Heyd, Thomas. *Encountering Nature: Toward an Environmental Culture*. Aldershot, UK: Ashgate, 2007.
Hodapp, Christa. *Men's Rights, Gender, and Social Media*. Lanham, MD: Lexington Books, 2017.
Hofmeyr, Benda. *Radical Passivity: Rethinking Ethical Agency in Levinas*. Dordrecht: Springer, 2009.
Honneth, Axel. "Communication and Reconciliation: Habermas' Critique of Adorno." *Telos* 39 (1979): 45–61.
Honneth, Axel. *The Critique of Power: Reflective Stages in a Critical Social Theory*. Cambridge, MA: MIT Press, 1991.
Honneth, Axel. *Das Andere der Gerechtigkeit: Aufsätze zur praktischen Philosophie*. Frankfurt: Suhrkamp, 2000. Translated as *Disrespect: The Normative Foundations of Critical Theory* (Cambridge: Polity Press, 2007).
Honneth, Axel. "Fataler Tiefsinn aus Karlsruhe: Zum neuesten Schrifttum des Peter Sloterdijk." *Zeit*, September 9, 2009.
Honneth, Axel. *Freedom's Right: The Social Foundations of Democratic Life*. New York: Columbia University Press, 2014.
Honneth, Axel. *The Struggle for Recognition: The Moral Grammar of Social Conflicts*. Cambridge, MA: MIT Press, 1995.

Honneth, Axel. *Verdinglichung*. Frankfurt: Suhrkamp, 2005.
Horkheimer, Max. *Between Philosophy and Social Science*. Cambridge, MA: MIT Press, 1993.
Horkheimer, Max. *Critical Theory: Selected Essays*. New York: Continuum, 1982.
Horkheimer, Max. *Eclipse of Reason*. New York: Continuum Books, 1974.
Horkheimer, Max. "Materialism and Metaphysics." *Critical Theory: Selected Essays*. New York: Continuum, 1982.
Horkheimer, Max. "Was wir 'Sinn' nennen, wird verschwinden." *Der Spiegel*, January 1970, 79–84.
Horowitz, Asher. *Ethics at a Standstill: History and Subjectivity in Levinas and the Frankfurt School*. Pittsburgh, PA: Duquesne University Press, 2008.
Huhn, Tom. "Introduction." In *The Cambridge Companion to Adorno*, edited by Tom Huhn, 1–18. Cambridge: Cambridge University Press, 2004.
Huntington, Patricia J. "Asymmetrical Reciprocity and Practical Agency: Contemporary Dilemmas of Feminist Theory in Benhabib, Young, and Kristeva." In *Political Phenomenology*, edited by Hwa Yol Jung and Lester Embree, 353–378. Dordrecht: Springer, 2016.
Huntington, Patricia J. *Ecstatic Subjects, Utopia, and Recognition: Kristeva, Heidegger, Irigaray*. Albany: State University of New York Press, 1998.
Huntington, Patricia J. "Heidegger's Reading of Kierkegaard Revisited: From Ontological Abstraction to Ethical Concretion." In *Kierkegaard in Post/Modernity*, edited by Martin J. Matuštík and Merold Westphal, 43–65. Bloomington: Indiana University Press, 1995.
Huntington, Patricia J. *Loneliness and Lament: A Journey to Receptivity*. Bloomington: Indiana University Press, 2009.
Huntington, Patricia J. "Primordial Attunement, Hardening, and Bearing." In *Rethinking Facticity*, edited by François Raffoul and Eric S. Nelson, 317–344. Albany: State University of New York Press, 2008.
Huntington, Patricia J. "Toward a Dialectical Concept of Autonomy: Revisiting the Feminist Alliance with Poststructuralism." *Philosophy and Social Criticism* 21, no. 1 (1995): 37–55.
Husserl, Edmund. "Philosophie als strenge Wissenschaft." *Logos: Internationale Zeitschrift für Philosophie der Kultur* 1 (1910/1911): 289–341.
Irigaray, Luce. *An Ethics of Sexual Difference*. Ithaca, NY: Cornell University Press, 1993.
Irigaray, Luce. "The Fecundity of the Caress: A Reading of Levinas, *Totality and Infinity*, Phenomenology of Eros." In *Feminist Interpretations of Emmanuel Levinas*, edited by Tina Chanter, 119–144. University Park: Pennsylvania State University Press, 2001.
Irigaray, Luce. "Questions to Emmanuel Levinas: On the Divinity of Love." In *Re-Reading Levinas*, edited by Robert Bernasconi and Simon Critchley, 109–118. Bloomington: Indiana University Press, 1991.

Jaeggi, Rahel. *Entfremdung: Zur Aktualität eines sozialphilosophischen Problems*. Frankfurt: Suhrkamp, 2016.

Jaeggi, Rahel. *Kritik von Lebensformen*. Frankfurt: Suhrkamp, 2013.

Jaeggi, Rahel. "What (If Anything) Is Wrong with Capitalism? Dysfunctionality, Exploitation and Alienation: Three Approaches to the Critique of Capitalism." Supplement, *Southern Journal of Philosophy* 54 (2016): 44–65.

Jewish Publication Society of America. *The Holy Scriptures According to the Masoretic Text*. Philadelphia, PA: Jewish Publication Society of America, 1955.

Jordaan, Eduard. "Cosmopolitanism, Freedom, and Indifference: A Levinasian View." *Alternatives: Global, Local, Political* 34, no. 1 (2009): 83–106.

Kalb, James. *The Tyranny of Liberalism*. Wilmington, DE: ISI Books, 2008.

Kalmanson, Leah. "The Messiah and the Bodhisattva: Anti-Utopianism Re-Revisited." *Shofar: An Interdisciplinary Journal of Jewish Studies* 30, no. 4 (2011): 113–125.

Kalmanson, Leah, and Sarah Mattice. "The De of Levinas: Cultivating the Heart-Mind of Radical Passivity." *Frontiers of Philosophy in China* 10, no. 1 (2015): 113–129.

Kant, Immanuel. *Anthropology, History, and Education*. Cambridge: Cambridge University Press, 2007.

Kant, Immanuel. *The Conflict of the Faculties*. Lincoln: University of Nebraska Press, 1992.

Kant, Immanuel. *Groundwork of the Metaphysics of Morals*. Translated and edited by Mary Gregor. Cambridge: Cambridge University Press, 1997.

Kant, Immanuel. *Practical Philosophy*. Cambridge: Cambridge University Press, 1996.

Kant, Immanuel. *Religion and Rational Theology*. Cambridge: Cambridge University Press, 2001.

Kapust. Antje. *Berührung ohne Berührung: Ethik und Ontologie bei Merleau-Ponty und Lévinas*. Munich: Wilhelm Fink Verlag, 1999.

Kapust, Antje. *Der Krieg und der Ausfall der Sprache*. Munich: Wilhelm Fink Verlag, 2004.

Kapust, Antje. "Returning Violence." In *Addressing Levinas*, edited by Eric S. Nelson, Antje Kapust, and Kent Still, 236–256. Evanston, IL: Northwestern University Press, 2005.

Katz, Claire E. "The Responsibility of Irresponsibility: Taking (Yet) Another Look at the *Akedah*." In *Addressing Levinas*, edited by Eric S. Nelson, Antje Kapust, and Kent Still, 17–33. Evanston, IL: Northwestern University Press, 2005.

Kern, Andrea. "Freiheit zum Objekt: Eine Kritik der Aporie des Erkennens." In *Dialektik der Freiheit*, edited by Axel Honneth, 53–82. Frankfurt: Suhrkamp, 2005.

Kierkegaard, Søren. *The Book on Adler*. Translated by Howard V. Hong and Edna H. Hong. Princeton, NJ: Princeton University Press, 1990.

Kierkegaard, Søren. *Fear and Trembling and Repetition*. Translated by Howard V. Hong and Edna H. Hong. Princeton, NJ: Princeton University Press, 1983.

Kierkegaard, Søren. *Kierkegaard's Attack upon "Christendom."* Translated by Walter Lowrie. Princeton, NJ: Princeton University Press, 1968.

Kierkegaard, Søren. *"The Moment" and Late Writings*. Translated by Howard V. Hong and Edna H. Hong. Princeton, NJ: Princeton University Press, 1998.

Kierkegaard, Søren. *The Sickness unto Death*. Translated by Howard V. Hong and Edna H. Hong. Princeton, NJ: Princeton University Press, 1980.

Kierkegaard, Søren. *Søren Kierkegaards Skrifter* [SKS]. Edited by Niels Jørgen Cappelørn, Joakim Garff, Johnny Kondrup, and Alastair McKinnon. 55 vols. Søren Kierkegaard Research Center. Copenhagen: Gads Forlag, 1997–2004.

Kierkegaard, Søren. *Samlede Værker* [SV]. Edited by P. P. Rohde. 20 vols. Copenhagen: Gyldendal, 1962–1964.

Kierkegaard, Søren. *Two Ages: The Age of Revolution and the Present Age: A Literary Review*. Translated by Howard V. Hong and Edna H. Hong. Princeton, NJ: Princeton University Press, 1978.

Kierkegaard, Søren. *Works of Love*. Translated by Howard V. Hong and Edna H. Hong. Princeton, NJ: Princeton University Press, 2013.

Kim, Halla. "Hermann Cohen on the Concept of Law in Ethics." In *Jewish Religious and Philosophical Ethics*, edited by Curtis Hutt, Halla Kim, and Berel Dov Lerner, 131–150. Abingdon, UK: Routledge, 2017.

Kim, Halla. *Kant and the Foundations of Morality*. Lanham, MD: Lexington Books, 2015.

Kim, Hye Young. "Is Guilt a Feeling? An Analysis of Guilt in Existential Philosophy." *Comparative and Continental Philosophy* 9, no. 3 (2017): 1–11.

Kleinberg, Ethan. *Generation Existential: Heidegger's Philosophy in France, 1927–1961*. Ithaca, NY: Cornell University Press, 2005.

Kleinberg-Levin, David Michael. *Before the Voice of Reason: Echoes of Responsibility in Merleau-Ponty's Ecology and Levinas's Ethics*. Albany: State University of New York Press, 2008.

Kleinberg-Levin, David Michael. "The Embodiment of the Categorical Imperative: Kafka, Foucault, Benjamin, Adorno and Levinas." *Philosophy and Social Criticism* 27, no. 4 (2001): 1–20.

Kleinberg-Levin, David Michael. *Gestures of Ethical Life: Reading Hölderlin's Question of Measure after Heidegger*. Stanford, CA: Stanford University Press, 2005.

Kleinberg-Levin, David Michael. *The Listening Self*. New York: Routledge, 1989.

Kleinberg-Levin, David Michael. *Redeeming Words and the Promise of Happiness*: A Critical Theory Approach to Wallace Stevens and Vladimir Nabokov. Lanham, MD: Rowman and Littlefield, 2012.

Kleinberg-Levin, David Michael. *Redeeming Words: Language and the Promise of Happiness in the Stories of Döblin and Sebald*. Albany: State University of New York Press, 2013.

Kleinberg-Levin, David Michael. "A Responsive Voice: Language without the Modern Subject." *Chiasmi International* 1 (1999): 65–102.

Kleinberg-Levin, David Michael. "Tracework: Myself and Others in the Moral Phenomenology of Merleau-Ponty and Levinas." *International Journal of Philosophical Studies* 6, no. 3 (1998): 345–392.

Kleinberg-Levin, David Michael. "What-Is? On Mimesis and the Logic of Identity and Difference in Heidegger and the Frankfurt school." *International Studies in Philosophy* 28, no. 4 (1996): 41–60.

Krebs, Angelika. *Ethics of Nature: A Map*. Berlin: Walter de Gruyter, 1999.

Laozi. *Daodejing: A Philosophical Translation*. Translated by Roger T. Ames and David L. Hall. New York: Ballantine Books, 2004.

Lee, Lisa Yun. *Dialectics of the Body: Corporeality in the Philosophy of Theodor Adorno*. London: Routledge, 2004.

Leeb, Claudia. "Desires and Fears: Women, Class and Adorno." *Theory and Event* 11, no. 1 (2008): doi:10.1353/tae.2008.0010.

Leeb, Claudia. "Toward a Theoretical Outline of the Subject: The Centrality of Adorno and Lacan for Feminist Political Theorizing." *Political Theory* 36, no. 3 (2008): 351–376.

Leeb, Claudia. "The Politics of 'Misrecognition': A Feminist Critique." *Good Society* 18, no. 1 (2009): 70–75.

Leeb, Claudia. *Power and Feminist Agency in Capitalism: Toward a New Theory of the Political Subject*. Oxford: Oxford University Press, 2017.

Leibniz, Gottfried W. *Theodicy: Essays on the Goodness of God, the Freedom of Man, and the Origin of Evil*. La Salle, IL: Open Court, 1988.

Levy, Ze'ev. "Emmanuel Levinas on Secularization in Modern Society." *Levinas Studies* 1 (2005): 19–35.

Llewelyn, John. "Am I Obsessed by Bobby? (Humanism of the Other Animal)." In *Re-Reading Levinas*, edited by Robert Bernasconi and Simon Critchley, 234–245. Bloomington: Indiana University Press, 1991.

Løgstrup, Knud Ejler. *Beyond the Ethical Demand*. Notre Dame, IN: University of Notre Dame Press, 2007.

Løgstrup, Knud Ejler. *The Ethical Demand*. Notre Dame, IN: University of Notre Dame Press, 1997.

Løgstrup, Knud Ejler. *Kierkegaard's and Heidegger's Existential Analysis and Its Relation to the Proclamation*. New York: Oxford University Press, 2020.

Løgstrup, Knud Ejler. *Kierkegaards und Heideggers Existenzanalyse und ihr Verhältnis zur Verkündigung*. Berlin: Erich Blaschker Verlag, 1950.

Løgstrup, Knud Ejler. *Metaphysics*. 3 vols. Milwaukee, WI: Marquette University Press, 1995.
Løgstrup, Knud Ejler. "Nazismens Filosof" [The Nazi's Philosopher]. *Dagens Nyheder*, April 14, 1936.
Löwenthal, Leo. *Critical Theory and Frankfurt Theorists: Lectures, Correspondence, Conversations*. New Brunswick, NJ: Transaction Books, 1989.
Löwenthal, Leo. *Schriften*. 5 vols. Frankfurt: Suhrkamp, 1984.
Lusthaus, Dan. "Acting toward the Other with/out Violence." In *Levinas and Asian Thought*, edited by Leah Kalmanson, Frank Garrett and Sarah Mattice, 99–114. Pittsburgh, PA: Duquesne University Press, 2013.
Lusthaus, Dan. "Aporetic Ethics in the *Zhuangzi*." In *Hiding the World in the World: Uneven Discourses on the Zhuangzi*, edited by Scott Cook, 163–206. Albany: State University of New York Press, 2003.
Lusthaus, Dan. "Zhuangzi's Ethics of Deconstructing Moralistic Self-Imprisonment: Standards without Standards." In *Deconstruction and the Ethical in Asian Thought*, edited by Youru Wang, 53–72. London: Routledge, 2007.
Luxemburg, Rosa. *The Russian Revolution, and Leninism or Marxism?* Ann Arbor: University of Michigan Press, 1961.
MacAvoy, Leslie. "The Ambiguity of Facticity in Heidegger's Early Work." *Comparative and Continental Philosophy* 5, no. 1 (2013): 99–106.
MacAvoy, Leslie. "Formal Indication and the Hermeneutics of Facticity." Supplement, *Philosophy Today* 54 (2010): 84–90.
MacAvoy, Leslie. "The Other Side of Intentionality." In *Addressing Levinas*, edited by Eric S. Nelson, Antje Kapust, and Kent Still, 109–118. Evanston, IL: Northwestern University Press, 2005.
MacAvoy, Leslie. "Thinking through Singularity and Universality in Levinas." Supplement, *Philosophy Today* 47 (2003): 147–153.
Macdonald, Iain. "Adorno's Modal Utopianism: Possibility and Actuality in Adorno and Hegel." *Adorno Studies* 1, no. 1 (2017): 1–12.
Macdonald, Iain. "Cold, Cold, Warm: Autonomy, Intimacy and Maturity in Adorno." *Philosophy and Social Criticism* 37, no. 6 (2011): 669–689.
Macdonald, Iain. "On the 'Undialectical': Normativity in Hegel." *Continental Philosophy Review* 45, no. 1 (2012): 121–141.
Macdonald, Iain. "'What Is, Is More Than It Is': Adorno and Heidegger on the Priority of Possibility." *International Journal of Philosophical Studies* 19, no. 1 (2011): 31–57.
Macdonald, Iain. *What Would Be Different: Figures of Possibility in Adorno*. Stanford, CA: Stanford University Press, 2019.
Makkreel, Rudolf A. *Imagination and Interpretation in Kant*. Chicago, IL: University of Chicago Press, 1995.
Malka, Salomon. *Emmanuel Levinas: His Life and Legacy*. Pittsburgh, PA: Duquesne University Press, 2006.

Manning, R. J. S. *Interpreting Otherwise Than Heidegger*. Pittsburgh, PA: Duquesne University Press, 1993.
Marcuse, Herbert. *Eros and Civilization: A Philosophical Inquiry into Freud*. Boston, MA: Beacon Press, 1971.
Marcuse, Herbert. *One-Dimensional Man: Studies in the Ideology of Advanced Industrial Society*. Boston, MA: Beacon, 1964.
Marcuse, Herbert. *Reason and Revolution: Hegel and the Rise of Social Theory*. Boston, MA: Beacon Press, 1970.
Marcuse, Herbert. "Repressive Tolerance." In *A Critique of Pure Tolerance*, edited by Robert Paul Wolff, Herbert Marcuse, and Barrington Moore, 81–118. Boston, MA: Beacon Press, 1969.
Martin, Bruce. "Mimetic Moments: Adorno and Ecofeminism." In *Feminist Interpretations of Theodor Adorno*, edited by Renée Heberle, 141–172. University Park: Pennsylvania State University Press, 2006.
Marx, Karl. "Kritik des Gothaer Programms." In *Karl Marx / Friedrich Engels Gesamtausgabe* (MEGA), part I, vol. 25, May 1875–May 1883. Berlin: Dietz Verlag, 1981.
Marx, Karl. *Selected Writings*. Edited by L. H. Simon. Indianapolis, IN: Hackett, 1994.
Marx, Karl. *Writings of the Young Marx on Philosophy and Society*. Indianapolis, IN: Hackett, 1997.
Marx, Karl, and Friedrich Engels. *Karl Marx / Friedrich Engels Gesamtausgabe* (MEGA). Berlin: Dietz Verlag, 1975–.
Marx, Karl, and Friedrich Engels. *Marx-Engels-Werke*. 43 vols. Berlin: Dietz-Verlag, 1956–1990.
Marx, Karl, and Friedrich Engels. *The Marx-Engels Reader*. 2nd ed. New York: Norton, 1978.
McAfee, Noëlle. *Habermas, Kristeva, and Citizenship*. Ithaca, NY: Cornell University Press, 2000.
McWeeny, Jennifer. "Origins of Otherness: Nonconceptual Ethical Encounters in Beauvoir and Levinas." *Simone de Beauvoir Studies* 26 (2009–2010): 5–17.
Miller, Gregg Daniel. *Mimesis and Reason: Habermas's Political Philosophy*. Albany: State University of New York Press, 2011.
Miller, Tyrus. *Late Modernism: Politics, Fiction, and the Arts between the World Wars*. Berkeley: University of California Press, 1999.
Moeller, Hans-Georg. *The Moral Fool: A Case for Amorality*. New York: Columbia University Press, 2009.
Monahan, M. J. "Recognition beyond Struggle: On a Liberatory Account of Hegelian Recognition." *Social Theory and Practice* 32, no. 3 (2006): 389–414.
Moore, G. E. *Principia Ethica*. Cambridge: Cambridge University Press, 1948.
Morgan, Alastair. *Adorno's Concept of Life*. London: Continuum, 2007.

Morgan, Michael L. *Discovering Levinas*. Cambridge: Cambridge University Press, 2007.
Morgan, Michael L. "Levinas and Judaism." *Levinas Studies* 1 (2005): 1–17.
Morgan, Michael L. *Levinas's Ethical Politics*. Bloomington: Indiana University Press, 2016.
Morgan, Trish. "Adorno and the Political Economy of Communication." *Political Economy of Communication* 1, no. 2 (2014): 44–64.
Morgan, Trish. "Alienated Nature, Reified Culture: Understanding the Limits to Climate Change Responses under Existing Socio-ecological Formations." *Political Economy of Communication* 5, no. 1 (2017): 3–50.
Morgan, Trish. "Growing Ourselves to Death? Economic and Ecological Crises, the Growth of Waste, and the Role of the Media and Cultural Industries." *Human Geography* 8, no. 1 (2015): 68–81.
Morisato, Takeshi. *Faith and Reason in Continental and Japanese Philosophy: Reading Tanabe Hajime and William Desmond*. London: Bloomsbury, 2019.
Morris, Martin. *Rethinking the Communicative Turn: Adorno, Habermas, and the Problem of Communicative Freedom*. Albany: State University of New York Press, 2014.
Moscovici, Claudia. *From Sex Objects to Sexual Subjects*. New York: Routledge, 1996.
Moyn, Samuel. *Origins of the Other: Emmanuel Levinas between Revelation and Ethics*. Cornell, NY: Cornell University Press, 2005.
Müller-Doohm, Stefan, ed. *Adorno-Portraits*. Frankfurt: Suhrkamp, 2007.
Münster, Arno, ed. *Tagträume vom aufrechten Gang*. Frankfurt: Suhrkamp, 1977.
Murdoch, Iris. *Existentialists and Mystics: Writings on Philosophy and Literature*. London: Penguin, 1999.
Murdoch, Iris. *Metaphysics as a Guide to Morals*. New York: Penguin Books, 2014.
Murdoch, Iris. *The Sovereignty of Good*. Abingdon, UK: Routledge, 2001.
Nancy, Jean-Luc. *The Experience of Freedom*. Stanford, CA: Stanford University Press, 1993.
Nelson, Eric M. *The Hebrew Republic: Jewish Sources and the Transformation of European Political Thought*. Cambridge, MA: Harvard University Press, 2011.
Nelson, Eric S. "Between Nature and Spirit: Naturalism and Anti-Naturalism in Dilthey." In *Anthropologie und Geschichte: Studien zu Wilhelm Dilthey aus Anlass seines 100. Todestages*, edited by G. D'Anna, H. Johach, and E. S. Nelson, 141–160. Würzburg: Königshausen & Neumann, 2013.
Nelson, Eric S. "Biological and Historical Life: Heidegger between Levinas and Dilthey." In *The Science, Politics, and Ontology of Life-Philosophy*, edited by Scott M. Campbell and Paul Bruno, 15–29. London: Bloomsbury Press, 2013.
Nelson, Eric S. *Chinese and Buddhist Philosophy in Early Twentieth-Century German Thought*. London: Bloomsbury, 2017.

Nelson, Eric S. "The Complicity of the Ethical: Causality, Karma, and Violence in Buddhism and Levinas." In *Levinas and Asian Thought*, edited by Leah Kalmanson, Frank Garrett, and Sarah Mattice, 99–114. Pittsburgh, PA: Duquesne University Press, 2013.

Nelson, Eric S. "Confucian Relational Hermeneutics, the Emotions, and Ethical Life." In *Relational Hermeneutics: Essays in Comparative Philosophy*, edited by Paul Fairfield and Saulius Geniusas, 193–204. London: Bloomsbury, 2018.

Nelson, Eric S. *Daoism and Environmental Philosophy: Nourishing Life*. London: Routledge, 2020.

Nelson, Eric S. "Die formale Anzeige der Faktizität als Frage der Logik." In *Heidegger und die Logik*, edited by Alfred Denker and Holger Zaborowski, 49–64. Amsterdam: Rodopi, 2006.

Nelson, Eric S. "Exzentrische Tiere und die Selbstüberwindung des Naturalismus: Dilthey, Plessner, Grene." In *Philosophische Anthropologie zwischen Soziologie und Geschichtsphilosophie*, edited by Rainer Adolphi, Andrzej Gniazdowski, and Zdzislaw Krasnodebski, 369–387. Nordhausen: Bautz-Verlag, 2018.

Nelson, Eric S. "Faith and Knowledge: Karl Jaspers on Communication and the Encompassing." *Existentia* 13, no. 3–4 (2003): 207–218.

Nelson, Eric S. "Heidegger and the Ethics of Facticity." In *Rethinking Facticity*, edited by François Raffoul and Eric S. Nelson, 129–147. Albany: State University of New York Press, 2008.

Nelson, Eric S. "Heidegger and Dilthey: Language, History, and Hermeneutics." In *Horizons of Authenticity in Phenomenology, Existentialism, and Moral Psychology*, edited by Hans Pedersen and Megan Altman, 109–128. Dordrecht: Springer, 2015.

Nelson, Eric S. "Heidegger and the Questionability of the Ethical." *Studia Phænomenologica* 8 (2008): 395–419.

Nelson, Eric S. "Heidegger, Levinas, and the Other of History." In *Between Levinas and Heidegger*, edited by John E. Drabinski and Eric S. Nelson, 51–72. Albany: State University of New York Press, 2014.

Nelson, Eric S. "Heidegger's *Black Notebooks*: National Socialism, Antisemitism, and the History of Being." In *The Bloomsbury Companion to Heidegger*, edited by François Raffoul and Eric S. Nelson, 484–493. London: Bloomsbury, 2016.

Nelson, Eric S. "Heidegger's Daoist Turn." *Research in Phenomenology* 49, no. 3 (2019): 362–384.

Nelson, Eric S. "Heidegger's Failure to Overcome Transcendental Philosophy." In *Transcendental Inquiry: Its History, Methods and Critiques*, edited by Halla Kim and Steven Hoeltzel, 159–179. Cham, Switzerland: Palgrave Macmillan, 2016.

Nelson, Eric S. "The Human and the Inhuman: Ethics and Religion in the *Zhuangzi*." Supplement, *Journal of Chinese Philosophy* 41 (2014): 723–739.

Nelson, Eric S. "Introduction: Wilhelm Dilthey in Context." In *Interpreting Dilthey: Critical Essays*, edited by Eric S. Nelson, 10–36. Cambridge: Cambridge University Press, 2019.

Nelson, Eric S. "Kant and China: Aesthetics, Race, and Nature." *Journal of Chinese Philosophy* 38, no. 4 (2011): 509–525.

Nelson, Eric S. "Language, Psychology, and the Feeling of Life in Kant and Dilthey." In *The Linguistic Dimension of Kant's Thought: Historical and Critical Essays*, edited by Frank Schalow and Richard Velkley, 263–287. Evanston, IL: Northwestern University Press, 2014.

Nelson, Eric S. "Levinas and Early Confucian Ethics: Religion, Rituality, and the Sources of Morality." *Levinas Studies* 4 (2009): 177–207.

Nelson, Eric S. "Martin Buber's Phenomenological Interpretation of the *Daodejing*." In *Daoist Encounters with Phenomenology*, edited by David Chai, 105–120. London: Bloomsbury, 2020.

Nelson, Eric S. "Moral and Political Prudence in Kant." *International Philosophical Quarterly* 44, no. 3 (2004): 305–319.

Nelson, Eric S. "Naturalism and Anti-Naturalism in Nietzsche." *Archives of the History of Philosophy and of Social Thought* 58 (2013): 213–227.

Nelson, Eric S. "Questioning Dao: Skepticism, Mysticism, and Ethics in the Zhuangzi." *International Journal of the Asian Philosophical Association* 1, no. 1 (2008): 5–19.

Nelson, Eric S. "Questioning Karma: Buddhism and the Phenomenology of the Ethical." Edited by Charles Prebish, Damien Keown, and Dale S. Wright. *Revisioning Karma: Journal of Buddhist Ethics* (2007): 353–373.

Nelson, Eric S. "Questioning Practice: Heidegger, Historicity, and the Hermeneutics of Facticity." Supplement, *Philosophy Today* 44 (2001): 150–159.

Nelson, Eric S. "The Question of Resentment in Nietzsche and Confucian Ethics." *Taiwan Journal of East Asian Studies* 10, no. 1 (2013): 17–51.

Nelson, Eric S. "Religious Crisis, Ethical Life, and Kierkegaard's Critique of Christendom." *Acta Kierkegaardiana* 4 (2009): 170–186.

Nelson, Eric S. "Responding with Dao: Early Daoist Ethics and the Environment." *Philosophy East and West* 59, no. 3 (2009): 294–316.

Nelson, Eric S. "Revisiting the Dialectic of Environment: Nature as Ideology and Ethics in Adorno and the Frankfurt School." *Telos*, no. 155 (2011): 105–126.

Nelson, Eric S. "Schleiermacher on Language, Religious Feeling, and the Ineffable." *Epoché: A Journal for the History of Philosophy* 8, no. 2 (2004): 297–312.

Nelson, Eric S. "Zhang Junmai's Early Political Philosophy and the Paradoxes of Chinese Modernity." *Asian Studies* 8, no. 1 (2020): 183–208.

Newton, Adam Z. *The Fence and the Neighbor: Emmanuel Levinas, Yeshayahu Leibowitz, and Israel among the Nations*. Albany: State University of New York Press, 2001.

Nietzsche, Friedrich. *Beyond Good and Evil.* Oxford: Oxford University Press, 1998.
Nietzsche, Friedrich. *Genealogy of Morality.* Indianapolis, IN: Hackett, 1998.
Nietzsche, Friedrich. *Human, All Too Human.* Cambridge: Cambridge University Press, 1999.
Nietzsche, Friedrich. *Sämtliche Werke: Kritische Studienausgabe,* Edited by Giorgio Colli and Mazzino Montinari. 15 vols. Berlin: De Gruyter, 1980.
Nietzsche, Friedrich. *Thus Spoke Zarathustra.* Oxford: Oxford University Press, 2005.
Nietzsche, Friedrich. *Twilight of the Idols.* Translated by Richard Polt. Indianapolis, IN: Hackett, 1997.
Nietzsche, Friedrich. *Untimely Meditations.* Cambridge: Cambridge University Press, 1983.
Nussbaum, Martha C. *The Cosmopolitan Tradition: A Noble but Flawed Ideal.* Cambridge, MA: Belknap Press, 2019.
Nussbaum, Martha C. "Patriotism and Cosmopolitanism." In *For Love of Country?,* edited by Joshua Cohen, 2–17. Boston, MA: Beacon Press, 1996.
O'Byrne, Anne. *Natality and Finitude.* Bloomington: Indiana University Press, 2010.
Offe, Claus. *Reflections on America: Tocqueville, Weber, and Adorno in the United States.* Cambridge: Polity, 2005.
Olivelle, Patrick, ed. and trans. *Upaniṣads.* New York: Oxford University Press, 1996.
Oppo, Andrea. *Philosophical Aesthetics and Samuel Beckett.* Oxford: Peter Lang, 2008.
Palmquist, Stephen R. "The Paradox of Inwardness in Kant and Kierkegaard." *Journal of Religious Ethics* 44, no. 4 (2016): 738–751.
Paradiso-Michau, Michael R. *The Ethical in Kierkegaard and Levinas.* London: Continuum, 2012.
Park, Jin Y. *Buddhism and Postmodernity: Zen, Huayan, and the Possibility of Buddhist Postmodern Ethics.* Lanham, MD: Lexington Books, 2010.
Park, Jin Y., ed. *Comparative Political Theory and Cross-Cultural Philosophy: Essays in Honor of Hwa Yol Jung.* Lanham, MD: Lexington Books: Lexington Books, 2009.
Park, Jin Y. "Ethics of Tension: A Buddhist-Postmodern Ethical Paradigm." *Taiwan Journal of East Asian Studies* 10, no. 1 (2013): 123–142.
Patterson, Charles. *Eternal Triblenka: Our Treatment of Animals and the Holocaust.* New York: Lantern Books, 2002.
Pensky, Max. *The Actuality of Adorno: Critical Essays on Adorno and the Postmodern.* Albany: State University of New York Press, 1997.
Peperzak, Adriaan T. *Ethics as First Philosophy.* New York: Routledge, 1995.
Peperzak, Adriaan T. *To the Other: An Introduction to the Philosophy of Emmanuel Levinas.* West Lafayette, IN: Purdue University Press, 1993.
Perpich, Diane. "A Singular Justice: Ethics and Politics between Levinas and Derrida." Supplement, *Philosophy Today* 42 (1998): 59–70.

Perpich, Diane. *The Ethics of Emmanuel Levinas*. Stanford, CA: Stanford University Press, 2008.
Perpich, Diane. "Figurative Language and the 'Face' in Levinas' Philosophy." *Philosophy and Rhetoric* 38, no. 2 (2005): 103–121.
Peters, Mathijs. *Schopenhauer and Adorno on Bodily Suffering: A Comparative Analysis*. New York: Palgrave Macmillan, 2014.
Pfister, Lauren. "Re-examining Whole Person Cultivation: Reconsidering the Significance of Master Kong's 'Knowing the Heavenly Decree' and Yeshuah's 'Beatitudes.'" *Ching Feng* 1, no. 1 (2000): 69–96.
Philo. *The Works of Philo: Complete and Unabridged*. Translated by Charles Duke Yonge. Peabody, MA: Hendrickson, 1993.
Plato. *The Republic*. Edited and translated by G. R. F. Ferrari and T. Griffith. Cambridge: Cambridge University Press, 2001.
Putnam, Hilary. *Jewish Philosophy as a Guide to Life: Rosenzweig, Buber, Levinas, Wittgenstein*. Bloomington: Indiana University Press, 2008.
Raffoul, François. "Being and the Other: Ethics and Ontology in Levinas and Heidegger." In *Addressing Levinas*, edited by Eric S. Nelson, Kent Still, and Antje Kapust, 138–151. Evanston, IL: Northwestern University Press, 2005.
Raffoul, François. "Derrida and the Ethics of the Im-possible." *Research in Phenomenology* 38, no. 2 (2008): 270–290.
Raffoul, François. "The Invisible and the Secret: Of a Phenomenology of the Inapparent." *Frontiers of Philosophy in China* 11, no. 3 (2016): 395–414.
Raffoul, François. *The Origins of Responsibility*. Bloomington: Indiana University Press, 2010.
Raffoul, François. "Phenomenology of the Inapparent." In *Unconsciousness between Phenomenology and Psychoanalysis*, edited by Dorothée Legrand and Dylan Trigg, 113–131. Dordrecht: Springer, 2017.
Raffoul, François. "Otherness and Individuation in Heidegger." *Man and World* 28, no. 4 (1995): 341–358.
Raffoul, François. "The Question of Responsibility between Levinas and Heidegger." In *Between Levinas and Heidegger*, edited by John E. Drabinski and Eric S. Nelson, 175–206. Albany: State University of New York Press, 2014.
Reiss, Timothy J. *Against Autonomy: Global Dialectics of Cultural Exchange*. Stanford, CA: Stanford University Press, 2002.
Rickert, Heinrich. *Kulturwissenschaft und Naturwissenschaft*. Stuttgart: Reclam Verlag, 1986.
Riley, Patrick. *Leibniz' Universal Jurisprudence: Justice as the Charity of the Wise*. Cambridge, MA: Harvard University Press, 1996.
Robbins, Jill. *Altered Readings: Levinas and Literature*. Chicago, IL: Chicago University Press, 1999.
Robbins, Jill. *Prodigal Son / Elder Brother: Interpretation and Alterity in Augustine, Petrarch, Kafka, Levinas*. Chicago, IL: University of Chicago Press, 1991.

Roemer, J. E. L., et al. *Racism, Xenophobia, and Distribution: Multi-issue Politics in Advanced Democracies*. New York: Russell Sage Foundation, 2007.

Rogerson, John W. *Theory and Practice in Old Testament Ethics*. London: T & T Clark International, 2004.

Romaya, Bassam. *The Iraq War: A Philosophical Analysis*. Basingstoke, UK: Palgrave Macmillan, 2012.

Rose, Gillian. *Mourning Becomes the Law: Philosophy and Representation*. Cambridge: Cambridge University Press, 1996.

Rosen, Michael. *Dignity: Its History and Meaning*. Cambridge, MA: Harvard University Press, 2012.

Rothenberg, Molly Anne. *The Excessive Subject: A New Theory of Social Change*. Cambridge: Polity, 2009.

Rousseau, Jean-Jacques. *Collected Writings*. Edited by Roger Masters and Christopher Kelly. 13 vols. Lebanon, NH: University Press of New England, 1990–2010.

Rousseau, Jean-Jacques. *The Government of Poland*. Translated by W. Kendall. Indianapolis, IN: Hackett, 1985.

Sachs, Carl B. "The Acknowledgement of Transcendence: Anti-theodicy in Adorno and Levinas." *Philosophy and Social Criticism* 37, no. 3 (2011): 273–294.

Salleh, Ariel. *Ecofeminism as Politics: Nature, Marx, and the Postmodern*. London: Zed Books, 1997.

Sanbonmatsu, John. "The Holocaust Sublime: Singularity, Representation, and the Violence of Everyday Life." *American Journal of Economics and Sociology* 68, no. 1 (2009): 101–126.

Sanbonmatsu, John. "Listen, Ecological Marxist! (Yes, I Said Animals!)." *Capitalism Nature Socialism* 16, no. 2 (2005): 107–114.

Sanbonmatsu, John. *The Postmodern Prince: Critical Theory, Left Strategy, and the Making of a New Political Subject*. New York: New York University Press, 2004.

Sanbonmatsu, John. "The Subject of Freedom at the End of History: Socialism beyond Humanism." *American Journal of Economics and Sociology* 66, no. 1 (2007): 217–235.

Sartre, Jean-Paul. *Colonialism and Neocolonialism*. Translated by Azzedine Haddour, Steve Brewer, and Terry McWilliams. London: Routledge, 2001.

Scarry, Elaine. *The Body in Pain*. New York: Oxford University Press, 1985.

Schoolman, Morton. *Reason and Horror: Critical Theory, Democracy, and Aesthetic Individuality*. London: Routledge, 2001.

Schopenhauer, Arthur. *The Two Fundamental Problems of Ethics*. Edited by Christopher Janaway. Cambridge: Cambridge University Press, 2009.

Schroeder, Brian. *Altared Ground: Levinas, History, and Violence*. New York: Routledge, 1996.

Schuhl, Moïse, S. Ulmann, and Robert Sommer. *Pirḳe-avot* = *Les Maximes des Pères: Texte Hébraïque: Traduction Francaise et Notes*. Paris: Les Editions Colbo, 1992.

Schweppenhäuser, Gerhard. *Die Antinomie des Universalismus: Zum moralphilosophischen Diskurs der Moderne*. Würzburg: Königshausen & Neumann, 2005.

Scoglio, Stefano. *Transforming Privacy: A Transpersonal Philosophy of Rights*. Westport, CT: Praeger, 1998.

Sealey, Kris. *Moments of Disruption: Levinas, Sartre, and the Question of Transcendence*. Albany: State University of New York Press, 2013.

Sealey, Kris. "The Primacy of Disruption in Levinas' Account of Transcendence." *Research in Phenomenology* 40, no. 3 (2010): 363–377.

Seele, Katrin. *"Das bist Du!": Das "Selbst" (Ātman) und das "Andere" in der Philosophie der frühen Upaniṣaden und bei Buddha*. Würzburg: Königshausen & Neumann, 2006.

Sherman, David. *Sartre and Adorno: The Dialectics of Subjectivity*. Albany: State University of New York Press, 2007.

Sherratt, Yvonne. *Adorno's Positive Dialectic*. Cambridge: Cambridge University Press, 2002.

Shiva, Vandana. *Earth Democracy: Justice, Sustainability, and Peace*. Cambridge, MA: South End Press, 2005.

Shuster, Martin. "Adorno and Negative Theology." *Graduate Faculty Philosophy Journal* 37, no. 1 (2016): 97–130.

Shuster, Martin. *Autonomy after Auschwitz: Adorno, German Idealism, and Modernity*. Chicago, IL: University of Chicago Press, 2014.

Shuster, Martin. "Nothing to Know: The Epistemology of Moral Perfectionism in Adorno and Cavell." *Idealistic Studies* 44, no. 1 (2014): 1–29.

Simmons, William. "The Third: Levinas' Theoretical Move from An-archical Ethics to the Realm of Justice and Politics." *Philosophy and Social Criticism* 25, no. 6 (1999): 83–104.

Singer, Peter. "All Animals Are Equal." *Philosophical Exchange* 1, no. 5 (1974): 103–116.

Singer, Peter. *Practical Ethics*. Cambridge: Cambridge University Press, 2011.

Slabodsky, Santiago. *Decolonial Judaism: Triumphal Failures of Barbaric Thinking*. New York: Palgrave Macmillan, 2014.

Sloterdijk, Peter. "Das elfte Gebot: Die progressive Einkommenssteuer." *Frankfurter Allgemeine Zeitung*, September 27, 2009.

Sloterdijk, Peter. "Die Revolution der gebenden Hand." *Frankfurter Allgemeine Zeitung*, June 13, 2009.

Snir, Itay. "The 'New Categorical Imperative' and Adorno's Aporetic Moral Philosophy." *Continental Philosophy Review* 43, no. 3 (2010): 407–437.

Smith, Graham. *Deliberative Democracy and the Environment*. London: Routledge, 2003.

Smith, Nick. "Adorno vs. Levinas: Evaluating Points of Contention." *Continental Philosophy Review* 40, no. 3 (2007): 275–306.

Smith, Nick. "Making Adorno's Ethics and Politics Explicit." *Social Theory and Practice* 29, no. 3 (2003): 487–498.

Sparrow, Tom. *Levinas Unhinged*. Winchester, UK: Zero Books, 2013.

Spiegel, Shalom. *The Last Trial*. Translated by Judah Goldin. Woodstock, VT: Jewish Lights, 1993.

Spinoza, Baruch. *Complete Works*. Translated by Samuel Shirley. Indianapolis, IN: Hackett Publishing, 2002.

Stauffer, Jill. *Ethical Loneliness: The Injustice of Not Being Heard*. New York: Columbia University Press, 2015.

Stauffer, Jill. "Heidegger and Levinas." In *The Bloomsbury Companion to Heidegger*, edited by François Raffoul and Eric S. Nelson, 393–398. London: Bloomsbury, 2013.

Stern, Robert. "Others as the Ground of our Existence." In *Transcendental Inquiry: Its History, Methods, and Critiques*, edited by Halla Kim and Steven Hoeltzel, 181–207. Basingstoke, UK: Palgrave Macmillan, 2016.

Stern, Robert. *The Radical Demand in Løgstrup's Ethics*. Oxford: Oxford University Press, 2019.

Stivers, Richard. *The Illusion of Freedom and Equality*. Albany: State University of New York Press, 2008.

Stone, Alison. "Adorno and the Disenchantment of Nature." *Philosophy and Social Criticism* 32, no. 2 (2006): 231–253.

Stone, Alison. "Alienation from Nature and Early German Romanticism." *Ethical Theory and Moral Practice* 17, no. 1 (2014): 41–54.

Stone, Alison. "Hegel, Naturalism and the Philosophy of Nature." *Hegel Bulletin* 34, no. 1 (2013): 59–78.

Sun Yat-Sen 孫中山. *Sanmin zhuyi* 三民主義 [The Three Principles of the People]. 18th ed. Taipei: Sanmin Press, 1996.

Tahmasebi-Birgani, Victoria. *Emmanuel Levinas and the Politics of Non-violence*. Toronto: University of Toronto Press, 2014.

Tertullianus, Quintus Septimius Florens. *The Writings of Quintus Sept. Flor. Tertullianus*. Edinburgh: T. and T. Clark, 1869.

Thomassen, Lasse. "The Inclusion of the Other? Habermas and the Paradox of Tolerance." *Political Theory* 34, no. 4 (2006): 439–462.

Tully, James. *An Approach to Political Philosophy: Locke in Contexts*. Cambridge: Cambridge University Press, 1993.

Vainio, Olli-Pekka. *Beyond Fideism: Negotiable Religious Identities*. London: Routledge, 2010.

Visker, Rudi. *The Inhuman Condition: Looking for Difference after Levinas and Heidegger*. Dordrecht: Kluwer Academic, 2004.

Vogel, Steven. *Against Nature: The Concept of Nature in Critical Theory*. Albany: State University of New York Press, 1996.

Walker, Nicholas. "Adorno and Heidegger on the Question of Art: Countering Hegel?" In *Adorno and Heidegger: Philosophical Questions*, edited by Iain Macdonald and Krzysztof Ziarek, 87–104. Stanford, CA: Stanford University Press, 2008.

Wen, Haiming. *Confucian Pragmatism as the Art of Contextualizing Personal Experience and World*. Lanham, MD: Lexington Books, 2009.

Wenning, Mario. "Adorno, Heidegger and the Problem of Remembrance." In *Adorno and Heidegger: Philosophical Questions*, edited by Iain Macdonald and Krzysztof Ziarek, 155–166. Stanford, CA: Stanford University Press, 2007.

Wenning, Mario. "Daoism as Critical Theory." *Comparative Philosophy* 2 (2011): 50–71.

Wenning, Mario. "Heidegger and Zhuangzi on the Nonhuman: Towards a Transcultural Critique of (Post)Humanism." In *Asian Perspectives on Animal Ethics: Rethinking the Nonhuman*, edited by Chloë Taylor and Neil Dalal, 93–111. New York: Routledge, 2014.

Wenning, Mario. "Kant and Daoism on Nothingness." *Journal of Chinese Philosophy* 38, no. 4 (2011): 556–568.

Wenning, Mario. "Whose Equality?" *Confluence: Journal of World Philosophies* 2 (2015): 153–166.

Wheatland, Thomas. *The Frankfurt School in Exile*. Minneapolis: University of Minnesota Press, 2009.

Willett, Cynthia. *Interspecies Ethics*. New York: Columbia University Press, 2014.

Williams, Robert R. *Hegel's Ethics of Recognition*. Berkeley: University of California Press, 1997.

Wirth, Jason M. "Martin Buber's Dao." In *Daoist Encounters with Phenomenology*, edited by David Chai, 121–134. London: Bloomsbury, 2020.

Wirth, Jason M. *Nietzsche and Other Buddhas: Philosophy after Comparative Philosophy*. Bloomington: Indiana University Press, 2019.

Wohlfarth, Irving. "Unterwegs zu Adorno, unterwegs zu sich." In *Adorno-Portraits*, edited by Stefan Müller-Doohm. Frankfurt: Suhrkamp, 2007, 40–94.

Wolf, Susan. "Asymmetrical Freedom." *Journal of Philosophy* 7, no. 7 (1980): 151–166.

Wood, Allen. *Kantian Ethics*. Cambridge: Cambridge University Press, 2007.

Wood, David. "Some Questions for My Levinasian Friends." In *Addressing Levinas*, edited by Eric S. Nelson, Kent Still, and Antje Kapust, 152–169. Evanston, IL: Northwestern University Press, 2005.

Wu, Shengqing. *Modern Archaics: Continuity and Innovation in the Chinese Lyric Tradition 1900–1937*. Cambridge, MA: Harvard University Asia Center, 2013.

Wyschogrod, Edith. *Emmanuel Levinas: The Problem of Ethical Metaphysics*. New York: Fordham University Press, 2000.

Yan, Mengwei. "Tolerance or Hospitality?" *Frontiers of Philosophy in China* 7, no. 1 (2012): 154–163.

Young, Iris Marion. *Intersecting Voices: Dilemmas of Gender, Political Philosophy, and Policy*. Princeton, NJ: Princeton University Press, 1997.

Zafirovski, Milan. *Democracy, Economy, and Conservatism: Political and Economic Freedoms and Their Antithesis in the Third Millennium*. Lanham, MD: Lexington Books, 2009.

Zhuangzi. *Zhuangzi: The Essential Writings with Selection from Traditional Commentaries*. Translated by Brook Ziporyn. Indianapolis, IN: Hackett, 2009.

Ziarek, Ewa P. "The Ethical Passions of Levinas." In *Feminist Interpretations of Emmanuel Levinas*, edited by Tina Chanter, 78–95. University Park: Pennsylvania State University Press, 2001.

Ziarek, Krzysztof. *Inflected Language: Toward a Hermeneutics of Nearness: Heidegger, Levinas, Stevens, Celan*. Albany: State University of New York Press, 1994.

Ziarek, Krzysztof. "Which Other, Whose Alterity? The Human after Humanism." In *Between Levinas and Heidegger*, edited by John E. Drabinski and Eric S. Nelson, 227–244. Albany: State University of New York Press, 2014.

Žižek, Slavoj. *Interrogating the Real*. London: Continuum, 2006.

Žižek, Slavoj. *Organs without Bodies: Deleuze and Consequences*. New York: Routledge, 2004.

Žižek, Slavoj, Erik L. Santner, and Kenneth Reinhard. *The Neighbor: Three Inquiries in Political Theology*. Chicago, IL: University of Chicago Press, 2006.

Zornberg, Avivah Gottlieb. *The Beginning of Desire: Reflections on Genesis*. New York: Schocken Books, 1995.

Zornberg, Avivah Gottlieb. *The Murmuring Deep: Reflections on the Rabbinic Unconscious*. New York: Schocken Books, 2008.

Zornberg, Avivah Gottlieb. *The Particulars of Rapture: Reflections on Exodus*. New York: Schocken Books, 2011.

Index

Abel, 173, 181, 187, 301
Abraham, 97–98, 119, 169, 171–174, 178–187, 199, 201, 206–210, 306
Adam, 49, 173–174, 187
Adorno, Theodor W., *passim*; and bourgeois society 77, 241; and constitutive subject, 6, 28, 35, 47, 69, 95, 108, 279; and critical model (defined), 30; and culture industry, 18, 32, 43, 52, 84, 158, 221, 290–291, 294, 302, 304, 355; and damaged life (*beschädigten Leben*), 2, 10–11, 13, 31–33, 83, 88–89, 138, 149–150, 154, 158–159, 238, 251, 337, 351; and experimentation, 10, 18, 35–36, 40, 50, 56, 67–68, 75, 84–87, 335; and *das Hinzutretende*, 87, 135; and Kierkegaard, 59, 208–209; and mimesis, 2, 31, 35–36, 50, 67–69, 75, 77–79, 82–86, 136–137, 166; and natural history, 26, 29–30, 34, 39–40, 43, 47–48, 56, 63, 74–75, 82, 117, 136, 140, 145, 350, 352, 355; and negative dialectics, 3, 5–6, 26, 35, 66, 144, 217, 336; and negative ethics, 19, 239, 256–257, 273; and nonidentity, 2–9, 12–17, 21–22, 30, 38–39, 41, 44, 48, 50, 54, 59, 68–69, 73–75, 79, 85, 89, 117, 131, 133–137, 250, 272, 322, 354. Works: *Aesthetic Theory*, 18, 79, 87–88, 140; with Horkheimer, *Dialectic of Enlightenment*, 32–34, 36–38, 41–43, 47–48, 51–52, 54–58, 61–62, 72–73, 77, 79–80, 99, 107, 138–139, 157–158, 163, 290, 293, 307, 339–341; *The Jargon of Authenticity*, 70, 96, 99; *Kierkegaard: Construction of the Aesthetic*, 59, 209; *Minima Moralia*, 2, 10, 12, 18, 30, 35, 62, 81, 138; 143, 150, 156, 158–159, 239, 241, 251, 268, 305, 316, 336, 350; *Negative Dialectics*, 26, 66, 70, 99; with Horkheimer, *Towards a New Manifesto*, 38, 62, 88, 144, 161, 289
the aesthetic, 18, 35, 65–70, 83–85, 89, 136, 209, 335
aesthetic modernism, 35, 50, 66, 68, 75
Agamben, Giorgio, 340
Akedah (*aqedah* עֲקֵדָה), 171, 173, 177–187, 194, 208
alienation, 83, 159
an-archy/an-archic, 4, 191–193, 266, 273, 321, 346–347; of the good, 9–10, 15, 189, 191–192, 245, 275, 281, 302, 335; of the republic, 307–309, 321–322, 338, 342

anarchism, 245, 321
Anders, Günther, 288, 302, 304
animals, 9, 14, 16, 25, 27–28, 30–31, 37, 41–42, 44–46, 48–49, 53–56, 60–63, 69–71, 73–75, 79–83, 87–88, 91, 113–118, 120–123, 126–130, 136, 138–139, 142–145, 220, 269, 333; and ethics, 74, 80, 87, 127–128, 130; and rights, 27, 80–81; and suffering, 31, 42, 48, 79–82
Anthropocene, 25, 29, 34, 355; and Capitalocene, 25, 355
anti-Semitism, 42, 80, 154, 157, 164, 316–318, 320–321
Apel, Karl-Otto, 268–269
archaism, 29, 36, 54, 58, 75, 92, 115, 124, 137, 346
Arendt, Hannah, 127, 234, 309, 321–322, 342
Aristotle, 46, 79, 137, 214, 246; and *phronesis*, 214, 247, 295
artwork, 77, 83–85, 118
asceticism, 95, 103, 126, 143, 150, 153, 157, 160–162, 165, 169, 200, 205, 216, 245, 326
Auschwitz, 15, 138, 149, 157, 294. See also Holocaust; Shoah
authenticity, 246–247, 295, 302, 336; aesthetic as expressions of, 67–69, 83
autonomy, 141, 253, 276, 279, 290–292, 298, 300, 306

Bacon, Francis, 55, 139
Badiou, Alain, 234
Benhabib, Seyla, 234, 339
Benjamin, Walter, 5, 18, 26, 28–29, 34, 36, 67, 117, 149–151, 163, 165, 198, 205, 216, 229–230, 232–233
Bentham, Jeremy, 37, 46

Bergson, Henri, 102–103
Berlin, Isaiah, 286
Biro, Andrew, 51
Bloch, Ernst, 1, 5, 36, 38, 149, 165, 219–239, 265–266, 337, 341, 349, 351; and the experimental, 225–226; and the not-yet (*noch nicht*), 223–224, 232; and tendency-latency, 221, 231. Works: *Natural Law and Human Dignity*, 220–221, 224–227, 234–235; *The Principle of Hope*, 220; *The Spirit of Utopia*, 232, 238
Bréhier, Émile, 95
Bṛhadāraṇyaka Upaniṣad, 174
Brown, Wendy, 313, 317
Buber, Martin, 14, 110, 128, 218, 312
Buddhism, 5–6, 26, 74, 162, 172, 176, 188, 250
Butler, Judith, 340

Cain, 173, 181, 187, 190, 301
capitalism, 14–17, 31–32, 34–35, 286–291, 200, 312–313, 315–317, 330–333, 340–343, 347; and neoliberalism, 32, 260, 286–289, 315, 340, 355; and neomercantilism, 260, 355
Cassirer, Ernst, 101
Cavell, Stanley, 88, 245–246
Caygill, Howard, 234
Christianity, 74, 114, 156–157, 164–165, 180–184, 202–205, 209, 212–213, 229–230, 320
civil society, 278, 314–315
commodity: commodification, 59, 61–62, 84, 133, 143, 247, 291, 307, 316; commodity fetishism, 31, 133, 143, 291–292
Cohen, Hermann, 180
colonialism, 287, 312–313, 316–319, 321, 340, 343

communism, 117, 150, 219–222, 225–227, 230, 234–235, 265–266, 301, 321, 323, 331
Comte, Auguste, 210
conatus essendi (persevering in or striving for existence), 17, 98–99, 106–108, 124, 184, 199, 277, 279, 293, 330, 334, 341–342. *See also* struggle for existence
Confucianism (*rujia* 儒家), 83, 119, 176, 178, 225, 246, 312, 316–317
Confucius (Kongzi 孔子), 172, 176–177
consequentialism, 189, 222, 225, 247, 305. *See also* utilitarianism
consumerism/consumption, 3, 32, 34, 59, 62, 76–77, 86, 132, 143, 158, 290–291, 294, 307, 340–341, 355
Cook, Deborah, 85
cosmopolitanism, 227–228, 235, 275, 279, 309, 311–321, 324, 326, 328–330, 339–340, 342–343
creation and createdness, 99, 174, 244, 252, 254
crisis tendencies, 26, 60, 333–334, 355; as ecological/environmental, 26, 29–31, 33, 37–38, 54, 56, 62, 331, 355
critique; as immanent, 76, 133, 140
Critchley, Simon, 234, 245, 253, 299, 321, 326

Daodejing 道德經, 172, 174, 184, 191–194
Daoism (*daojia* 道家), 119, 172, 174, 184, 191–194
Darwin, Charles, 99, 123
Darwinism: and evolution, 74; social Darwinism, 26, 39, 98–100, 106–107, 115
Delhomme, Jeanne, 295
democracy, 63, 72, 158, 225–226, 290–292, 321–322, 329, 331

deontological ethics, 43, 47, 120, 179, 189, 191, 207–209, 237, 247, 269, 278, 322
de Sade, Marquis, 158, 163
Derrida, Jacques, 4, 10, 50, 173, 229–230, 232–234, 260, 264, 272, 284; and animals, 60, 87, 116, 122, 139; and aporia, 52, 189–191, 337; and cosmopolitanism, 313–314, 317–320, 330; and hospitality, 12, 325–327, 340; and tolerance, 313–314, 317–318, 322, 330
Descartes, René, 10, 203
de Tocqueville, Alexis, 292, 302–303
de Vries, Hent, 15, 168, 271, 298
Dewey, John, 135, 290
dialectic: negative dialectic, 3, 5–6, 26, 35, 66, 144, 217, 270, 336; positive dialectic, 217, 270
dignity, 41–42, 55, 66, 69, 79, 104, 108, 114, 116, 121–122, 219–231, 233, 235–238, 330
Dilthey, Wilhelm, 102–103
Dobbs-Weinstein, Idit, 221
Dostoevsky, Fyodor: and Grand Inquisitor, 153, 161; and infinite responsibility, 282
Dussel, Enrique, 1, 4–5, 9–10, 34, 152, 166, 229–230, 232–233, 235–237, 256–257, 260, 325, 343, 349, 353, 356

earth, 21, 33, 97–98, 119–120, 124, 128, 130, 156–157, 167
ecology: deep ecology, 130; social ecology, 34, 44, 97
Elster, Jon, 29
Emerson, Ralph Waldo, 245–246, 287
emptiness: as *śūnyatā*, 5; and hunger, 350; of hands, 97–98, 119
Engels, Friedrich, 117, 219

Enlightenment, 32–34, 41–43, 72–74, 77, 129, 179, 205, 290–291, 314–316; Enlightenment project, 34, 57, 73, 315–316
environment, crisis of, 26, 29–33, 37–38, 54–56, 62, 331, 354–355
environmental ethics/ethics of nature, 26, 54–55, 67, 74, 106, 113–116, 118, 123, 128, 130, 142; and anthropocentrism, 9, 63, 71, 116, 120, 145, 311; and biocentrism, 51, 118, 130, 145; and turn taking, 33
Epicurus, 222
equality, 8–9, 12, 74, 83, 120, 157, 200, 209, 218–219, 230, 236, 242, 258–260, 263–271, 275–279, 281–284, 286–287, 291, 299–301, 309, 325, 327, 336, 344
ethics: and aporia, 7, 181, 186, 190–195, 347; and asymmetry, 4, 7, 22, 73, 78–80, 83–84, 120, 122, 142, 173, 176–177, 186, 200–201, 206, 218, 242–243, 245, 258–259, 263–274, 276–284, 298–301, 309, 312–314, 323–325, 327, 329, 338, 347, 350, 353–355; and the demand, 241–247, 252–255, 273, 278, 350–351; and eudaemonia, 222; and imperfection, 1–2, 10–11, 88–89, 152, 162, 165, 168, 239, 245, 249–251, 259, 271–272, 276, 350–353; and impossibility, 4, 7, 12–13, 20, 111, 125, 172, 182, 185, 190–192, 195, 199, 211, 216, 233, 259, 266, 271–272, 280–281, 284, 337; and material others, 2, 7, 9, 14, 37, 95, 97, 237, 343, 256, 259, 263, 338, 347, 352–353, 355; and nature, 26, 54–55, 67, 74, 106, 113–116, 118, 123, 128, 130, 142; and nonidentity, 7, 12–14, 314, 329, 354; and the prophetic, 19, 152, 160, 177, 221, 229, 232–234, 237–238, 260, 338, 355
Eurocentrism, 3, 34, 230, 235, 279, 318, 320
existentialism, 101–104, 163, 193, 207, 232, 246–247, 295, 336
Exodus, 109, 177, 181

facticity, 27–28, 34, 43, 45, 57, 61, 67, 92, 95, 100–101, 104, 106, 115, 123–124, 128, 132–133, 142, 155, 211, 214, 237–238, 265, 273, 281, 283, 292, 294, 317, 328, 345, 354
Fanon, Frantz, 288, 343
fascism, 22, 42, 45, 59, 71, 80–81, 95, 97, 104, 115, 123–124, 131, 266, 321
feminism, 44, 174, 269
Feuerbach, Ludwig; and Marx's critique, 159–160; and natural history, 117
fideism, 177, 181, 185, 194, 204, 212–213
Fink, Eugen, 295
freedom: freedom toward the object (*Freiheit zum Objekt*), 10, 35, 44, 50, 84, 87, 335; free will, 285, 289, 297. *See also* liberty
French Revolution: and republicanism, 18, 72, 278, 292, 299, 306, 317–318, 321
Freud, Sigmund, 153–154, 166
Froese, Katrin, 166

Gasché, Rodolphe, 78
gender, 180, 269, 276, 278, 286
Genesis, 97, 172
Gerhardt, Christina, 122
God: divine command of, 101, 154, 172, 176, 183, 185, 198, 208; existence of, 184, 203; transcendence of, 92, 180, 213, 215–216

the good: as good beyond being (*epekeina tês ousias*), 10–11, 17, 188–189, 199, 203, 255–256
Gordon, Jane, 334
Gordon, Lewis, 334
Grossmann, Vasily, 211

Habermas, Jürgen, *passim*; and communicative action, 37, 53, 67–69, 78, 89, 252, 269; and discourse ethics, 38, 44, 215, 269–270, 328–329; and labor/interaction, 37, 61; and lifeworld (*Lebenswelt*), 36–37, 44, 61, 74, 82, 86, 160, 252, 347; and postmetaphysical, 28, 49, 74, 277; and public sphere, 28, 269, 291, 322, 329, 331, 338. Works: *The Future of Human Nature*, 48, 53, 55; *Legitimation Crisis*, 28, 331, 355; *The Philosophical Discourse of Modernity*, 34–35, 52, 56, 264; *The Theory of Communicative Action*, 37, 53, 69
Haraway, Donna J., 22
Hegel, Georg Wilhelm Friedrich, 4, 10, 16, 19–20, 35, 42–43, 57, 66–68, 71, 79, 84–85, 105, 117, 132, 136, 142, 144, 151, 190, 203, 217, 247, 263, 270, 290, 292, 299, 304, 314–315, 341; and dialectic, 16, 19, 35, 142, 144, 217, 270, 274, 292; and world spirit, 16, 66, 346. Works: *Phenomenology of Spirit*, 42, 57, 79, 151, 341
Heidegger, Martin, 15, 17, 19–20, 22, 31, 70, 76, 92–105, 107–108, 110–111, 118–120, 123–125, 129, 131, 135, 139, 154–155, 190, 199, 201–203, 206, 224, 236–237, 243–244, 246–247, 253, 271, 274, 295, 297, 326, 336; and letting/releasing (*Gelassenheit*), 20, 97, 101, 297; and national socialism 95–101, 104–105, 243. Works: *Being and Time*, 19–20, 103, 105, 206, 253
Heraclitus, 124, 244
Hering, Jean, 92, 243
Heyd, Thomas, 142
Hobbes, Thomas, 115, 124, 211, 337
Holocaust, 13, 97, 122, 157, 199, 266, 321, 337. See also Auschwitz; Shoah
Hōnen 法然, 250
Honneth, Axel, 9–10, 54–57, 62, 65, 207, 259, 264–268, 270–272, 274–277, 279; and autonomy, 276–277, 285, 288, 293; and equality, 44, 264–267, 270, 284; and recognition, 37, 44–46, 51, 54, 57, 190, 270–271, 274, 283–285, 328–329, 345–346; and reification, 44–46, 54–55
Horkheimer, Max, 34, 36, 39, 45, 55, 83, 135, 151, 162, 233; with Adorno, *Dialectic of Enlightenment*, 32–34, 36–38, 41–43, 47–48, 51–52, 54–58, 61–62, 72–73, 77, 79–80, 99, 107, 138–139, 157–158, 163, 290, 293, 307, 339–341; with Adorno, *Towards a New Manifesto*, 38, 62, 88, 144, 161, 289
Horowitz, Asher, 137
humanism, 38, 48, 57, 63, 116–117, 122, 127–130, 178, 183, 191, 224, 266, 279, 316, 342
human dignity, 41–43, 69, 108, 116, 219–229, 233–237
human rights, 119, 131, 220, 226, 229, 233, 279, 299, 321, 330, 334; and "rights of man" (*droits de l'homme*), 299, 321
hunger, 11, 16, 19, 97, 103, 118–120, 125–128, 350–351

Hurcanus, Eliezer ben, 122
Husserl, Edmund, 17, 19–20, 22, 76, 91–95, 101, 103–105, 109–111, 246–247, 252, 253, 297

idealism, 31, 41–44, 47–48, 61–63, 66–67, 85, 89, 99, 108–110, 114, 131, 139, 160, 275, 330, 355; constitutive idealism, 25, 30–31, 38, 41, 47, 69, 79, 89, 268; German idealism, 35, 38, 42–43, 74, 115
identity: identity formation, 4, 144, 245, 284; identity thinking, 5–6, 16, 25, 32, 74, 131, 137, 143, 217, 265, 280, 302, 308–309, 343; and nonidentity, 2–9, 12–17, 21–22, 30, 38–39, 41, 44, 48, 50, 54, 59, 68–69, 73–75, 79, 85, 89, 117, 131, 133–137, 250, 272, 322, 354
ideology critique, 50–52, 57, 72, 169, 314
images: ban on image (*Bilderverbot*), 43, 137, 141, 216; dialectical image, 115; and idolatry, 43, 50, 84, 136–137, 216
imperfection: and ethics, 1–2, 10–11, 88–89, 152, 162, 165, 168, 239, 245, 249–251, 259, 271–272, 276, 350–353. *See also* perfectionism
impossibility: and ethics, 4, 7, 12–13, 20, 111, 125, 172, 182, 185, 190–192, 195, 199, 211, 216, 233, 259, 266, 271–272, 280–281, 284, 337; and faith, 199, 213
individualism, 58, 158, 289–292, 302–303, 308, 339, 341
individuation, 78, 84, 98, 104, 163, 175, 206, 213, 282, 286, 290–291, 302
Isaac, 169, 171–173, 178–179, 181–182, 185–187, 202, 206, 210

Isaiah, 173, 175, 178, 229–230, 278

Jaeggi, Rahel, 10
Jaspers, Karl, 347
Job, 154
Jonah, 173, 175
Judaism, 18, 108, 178, 180, 183, 197, 230, 325, 327

Kafka, Franz, 82
Kant, Immanuel, 4, 10–11, 41–42, 45–48, 55–56, 66–69, 73–74, 85, 89, 95, 107, 139, 141, 166, 179, 181–182, 199, 201, 207–208, 215, 278, 290, 294, 306, 314–315, 319–320, 323; and categorical imperative, 56, 207; and duty, 278, 322–323. Works: *Critique of Judgment*, 68–69, 73, 85
Kierkegaard, Søren, 10, 164, 168–169, 171, 175–176, 178, 180–188, 191, 193–194, 198–210, 213, 217–218; and the absurd, 199, 213; and Adorno, 59, 208–209; and Johannes de Silentio, 96, 180–183, 201, 207; and Judge William, 209; and Løgstrup, 243–244, 247–248. Works: *Either/Or*, 209–210; *Fear and Trembling*, 171, 181, 184, 193–194, 199, 201, 207–208, 211, 217; *The Moment*, 202, 214; *Works of Love*, 184, 194, 207–209
kindness (*chesed* חסד), 198, 216, 274, 322
Kyōto school, 26, 250

labor, 29, 49–50, 53, 77, 131–132, 236–237, 292; and dignity, 224, 227; and exteriority, 236–237, 325, 356; and interaction, 37, 61
Lacan, Jacques, 283

language games, 31–32
Laozi 老子, 174, 193
Leibniz, Gottfried Wilhelm, 48, 89, 156, 179, 183, 186, 246, 322
Lenin, Vladimir, 226
Levinas, Emmanuel, *passim*; and the an-archic, 4, 9–10, 15, 189–193, 266, 273–275, 307–309, 321–322, 346–347; and animals, 120–122, 251; and chosenness, 172, 175, 187, 206; and diachrony, 10, 21, 39, 123, 189, 232, 251, 255, 274, 349–350; and disruption, 15, 101–102, 106, 125, 187, 190, 242, 252, 272, 275, 347; and earthly needs, 103, 109, 116, 127, 131; and the elemental, 102, 116, 124–125, 129, 193, 250, 343, 350, 352; and the face, 102, 109, 120–121, 127–128, 180, 186, 191–192, 194, 200, 212, 216, 242, 266, 273, 275, 281, 322, 327, 330, 337; and fatigue and insomnia, 20, 131, 301, 324, 341; and "Here I am" (*me voici*), 129, 172–179, 182–184; and incompletion, 2, 10–11, 250–251, 337–338, 350–353; and inhabiting, 98, 120, 193; and prophecy, 9, 151–153, 167, 175, 178, 185, 188, 199–201, 230, 233–234, 238, 264, 338; and republicanism, 2, 8–9, 234–235, 278, 299, 307, 309, 342, 351–353; and substitution, 175–177, 200, 281, 294, 326–328; and the "there is" (*il y a*), 108, 116, 124, 232, 324; and the third, 109, 116, 294, 299, 305, 320, 327, 337. Works: *Existence and Existents*, 92, 126, 129, 232, 337; *God, Death and Time*, 10, 220, 236, 265; *On Escape*, 17, 95, 124; *Otherwise Than Being*, 17, 20–21, 125, 177, 254, 293; *The Philosophy of Hitlerism*, 104, 123, 243; *The Theory of Intuition in Husserl's Phenomenology*, 101–104; *Time and the Other*, 12, 126; *Totality and Infinity*, 12, 17, 19, 99, 124, 129, 137, 168, 211, 251, 254–255, 258, 321, 338
liberalism, 227, 271, 286–287, 289, 294, 299–300, 313–314, 324–327, 331, 333–334, 338, 340–342; and neoliberalism, 72, 286, 316–317, 320
liberty: as natural 290, 308; as negative 141, 286, 289, 303, 306, 333–334, 343; as positive, 292, 315; in French republicanism, 2, 8–9, 222, 235, 266, 278–279, 299, 344; in libertarianism, 267, 286–291, 301–303. *See also* freedom
life: bare life, 63, 92, 124; biological life, 60, 91–92, 167; bodily life, 17, 103, 111, 273, 283; damaged life (*beschädigten Leben*), 2, 10–11, 13, 31–33, 83, 88–89, 138, 149–150, 154, 158–159, 238, 251, 337, 351; the good life, 33, 89, 132, 153, 161–164, 167–168, 245–246, 294, 309, 311, 350; nourishing life, 22, 142, 145, 194, 264, 332, 334, 347, 353; nurturing life (*yangsheng* 養生), 191, 194
life-philosophy (*Lebensphilosophie*), 89, 92, 100–104, 243–244
lifeworld (*Lebenswelt*), 3, 36–37, 44, 61, 74, 82, 86, 160, 252, 347, 353
Lipps, Hans, 252
Llewelyn, John, 116, 122, 127
Locke, John, 287, 289, 308, 345
Løgstrup, Knud Ejler, 188, 241–244, 246–258, 273, 349, 351
love, 9, 18, 36, 78, 109, 141, 150, 152, 154, 164, 180, 184, 187, 194, 208–209, 224, 230, 237,

love (continued)
241, 249–250, 255, 258–259, 304, 307, 316–317, 322–324, 327–328, 335; as eros, 11, 18, 20, 36, 78, 125–126, 137, 209, 250

Lukács, György, 49, 56–57, 63, 309

Luxemburg, Rosa, 224–226, 341

Mahler, Gustav, 70, 80, 82, 84; and *Song of the Earth*, 70

Marcuse, Herbert, 36, 61, 235, 266, 309, 335; and repressive tolerance, 313–314, 316–317

Marx, Karl, 6, 9–10, 14–15, 25–26, 28–30, 34, 39, 44–46, 49, 56–57, 61, 74, 108, 115, 117, 125, 136, 150–151, 153–154, 159–160, 166, 175, 219, 222–227, 229–230, 235–238, 259, 263, 265, 290–292, 321, 325, 330, 339–340, 343–344, 355–356

Marxism, 9, 15, 22, 26, 28–30, 36–37, 44–46, 49, 57, 61, 129, 151, 221–227, 229–230, 235–236, 265–266, 300

material others: and ethics, 2, 7, 9, 14, 37, 95, 97, 237, 343, 256, 259, 263, 338, 347, 352–353, 355; and politics, 264, 338

Mencius (Mengzi 孟子), 190, 316

Mill, James, 289

Mill, John Stuart, 46, 289–290, 318

Mīmāṃsā, 173

mimesis: as imitative, 18, 31, 36, 50, 67–69, 75, 77–78, 84, 166; as responsive, 35–40, 75–79, 82–86, 89, 136–138, 172, 335, 347; as unrestricted, 18, 36, 166, 172

Misch, Georg, 252

monotheism, 97, 114, 119, 176, 180, 183, 197, 199, 202–204, 210, 213–216, 244

Moore, G. E.: and the good, 188–190, 255–256

More, Sir Thomas, 223

Moscovici, Claudia, 269

Mount Moriah, 172–173, 181

Mozi 墨子, 178; and Mohism (*mojia* 墨家), 316

Murdoch, Iris: and the good, 188–189, 241–242, 246, 248–252, 255–258, 349

music: and atonality, 35, 70; and dialectic of nature, 70, 75, 82, 84; and dissonance, 21; and jazz, 75–76; and regression in listening, 82, 86

Nāgārjuna, 5

national socialism, 17, 21, 32, 70, 80–81, 121, 123, 149, 202, 288; and Heidegger, 95–101, 104–105, 243

nationalism, 32, 123, 235, 260, 278, 306, 309, 312, 316, 321, 325, 329, 333, 339–340, 343, 355

natural history (*Naturgeschichte*), 26, 28–30, 34, 37, 39–40, 43–44, 47–48, 51, 53–54, 56, 59–63, 66, 74–75, 82, 86–87, 89, 108, 111, 117, 133, 135–136, 140, 145, 167, 231, 233, 238–239, 256, 259, 265, 324, 333–334, 349–350, 352–356

natural law (political), 26, 106–107, 219–229, 231, 233–235, 237, 254

nature: as *phusis*, 92–93, 100; domination of, 8, 22, 29–30, 33–36, 41–45, 48–50, 53–56, 62–63, 66–67, 70–73, 83–84, 99, 130, 133, 138–140, 149, 290, 356; freedom of, 51, 59, 70; instrumentalization of, 41, 46–47, 53, 55, 94, 114, 125, 140, 167;

sublimity of, 42, 66, 69–70, 86, 100
Nelson, Eric M., 229
Nemo, Philippe, 121
neo-Aristotelianism, 214
neo-Kantianism, 28, 54, 67, 91, 93, 95, 243
Nietzsche, Friedrich, 10, 50, 56, 68, 95, 98, 107–108, 123–124, 150, 153–167, 190, 205, 207, 213, 231, 259, 264, 299, 302, 306, 352; and genealogy, 153–155, 158–162, 164–166, 205; and the passion (of Christ), 154, 164; and *ressentiment*, 163–164
Nussbaum, Martha, 311, 313

other-constitution, 2, 6, 8, 26, 31, 47, 109, 206, 234, 274, 277, 330, 349–350. See also self-constitution
other-power (*tariki* 他力), 2, 5, 11, 26, 74, 188, 199, 245, 249–251, 257, 349, 352. See also self-power

Pascal, Blaise, 161
perfectionism, 2, 5, 10–11, 18, 153, 189, 238–239, 245–246, 249–250, 253, 324, 336–338, 349–350, 352–353. See also imperfection
Perpich, Diane, 128, 295
phenomenology, 13–17, 19–20, 22, 76, 91–97, 101–104, 109–111, 113–114, 119, 121, 216, 221, 243, 246, 252–253, 271, 273, 322
Philo of Alexandria (Philo Judaeus), 180–181
Plato: and aporia, 7; and city in fever, 292; and eros, 249–250; and the good 10–11, 17, 188–190, 203, 255–257; and mimesis, 77–78, 84, 136
Plessner, Helmuth, 252

political economy, 3, 16, 27, 30–31, 59–60, 145, 163, 265, 354–356
positivism, 26, 39, 75, 114, 135, 344; legal positivism, 179, 183
prophecy/the prophetic, 2, 9, 18–19, 149–153, 160, 165–169, 177–178, 188, 198–201, 221, 229–234, 237–238, 260, 301, 321, 331, 338, 342, 345, 352, 355; and divination, 200–201; and justice, 151, 165, 216; and temporality, 221, 229–234
Putnam, Hilary, 245, 256, 350

racism, 70, 81, 95, 99, 123–124, 138–139, 235, 287, 316–317, 320–321, 325, 340
Raffoul, François, 105, 337
rationalism, 25, 79, 136, 193
rationality: communicative rationality, 36–37, 53–57, 269, 283, 350; Enlightenment rationality, 43, 57; instrumental rationality, 27, 34, 36, 41, 47, 50, 53, 60, 81, 84, 125, 143, 201, 308; rationalization, 33–34, 43, 50, 53, 72, 143, 167, 289
Rawls, John, 200, 311
republicanism: and revolutionary thought, 8–9, 18, 72, 222, 235, 266, 278–279, 292, 299, 306, 317–318, 321, 344
Ricœur, Paul, 153
romanticism: of nature, 57, 70, 75, 118, 139
Rosen, Michael, 219
Rosenzweig, Franz, 110
Rousseau, Jean-Jacques, 9, 84, 115, 222, 234, 246, 269, 278, 299, 307, 352
Ruge, Arnold, 223

Śāntideva, 172

Sartre, Jean-Paul, 295, 340
Scarry, Elaine, 155
Scheler, Max, 252
Schleiermacher, Friedrich, 179
Schönberg, Arnold, 70
Schopenhauer, Arthur, 37, 81, 107–108, 111, 154–155, 161–163
self: self-constitution, 2, 8, 28, 35, 47, 69, 95, 108–109, 279; self-power (*jiriki* 自力), 26, 188, 245, 351. *See also* other-constitution and other-power
Shoah, 15, 21, 157, 199. *See also* Auschwitz; Holocaust
Singer, Peter, 74, 80, 113
Sloterdijk, Peter, 267
Smith, Adam, 287, 289, 304
socialism, 22, 44–45, 119, 129, 222–226, 229, 231, 234, 259–260, 265–266, 281, 284, 300–301, 307, 309, 331, 344, 351
solidarity: as republican fraternity, 18, 235, 278, 299, 306, 322, 334–335, 341; as unrestricted, 2, 7, 150, 169, 234–237, 250, 264, 309, 334–335, 351–353
Spinoza, Baruch, 98, 106–107, 123, 151, 203, 221
Stalinism, 45, 52, 265, 301, 321
Stendhal (Marie-Henri Beyle): and promise of happiness (*promesse du bonheur*), 131, 156–157
Stoicism: and dignity, 228; and cosmopolitanism, 317, 320
struggle: struggle as polemos, 100; struggle for dignity, 222; struggle for existence (*Kampf um Existenz*), 8, 12, 20–21, 63, 92, 98–100, 106–107, 116, 123–124, 133, 140, 167, 244, 254, 278, 293, 342; struggle for recognition (*Kampf um Anerkennung*), 190, 199, 271, 274, 283, 345
Sun Yat-Sen 孫中山, 312, 342–343

telos, 73, 88, 208, 214, 250, 337
temporality, 104, 141, 165, 188, 201, 217, 221, 229–233, 236, 274
Ten Commandments, 181
Tertullianus, Quintus Septimus Florens, 212–213
theodicy, 15, 71, 105–106, 132, 156–157, 167–168, 179, 199, 214, 229, 231, 257–258, 287, 303
thereness, 96, 111, 123, 232
Thoreau, Henry David, 287
tikkun olam תיקון עולם, 322
tolerance, 268, 309, 311–320, 322–324, 326–329, 340–342; and repressive tolerance, 313, 316–317
truth content (*Wahrheitsgehalt*), 26, 43, 71, 85

universalism, 206–208, 279, 299, 312–313, 318–321, 342–343
utilitarianism, 74, 222, 322. *See also* consequentialism
utility, 46, 343–344
utopianism, 38, 131, 220–224, 230–232, 337

validity (*Geltung*), 28, 67, 84, 104, 237; validity claims, 61, 67–68, 84, 89, 294
value: anthropocentric value, 46–47, 128; exchange value, 14, 43, 59, 76–77, 286, 354; intrinsic value, 57
Vico, Giambattista: and *verum factum*, 71
violence, 9, 13, 79, 97–100, 108, 119, 124, 150, 152–154, 156–157,

163–165, 169, 180–182, 186, 199, 211–213, 326, 337, 340
virtue ethics, 11, 153, 161, 214, 249, 338
Voltaire (François-Marie Arouet), 318
Vogel, Steven, 51

Wagner, Richard, 58–59, 70, 82, 84, 139, 154
war, 12, 20, 124, 151, 168, 211, 213, 275; facelessness of 330; justice of 315; technization of 340–341
will: free will, 285, 297; self-assertion of will, 92, 98, 107, 124, 162, 250

will (political): general will (*volonté générale*), 63, 309, 342, 352; will formation, 234, 321–322
Wittgenstein, Ludwig, 31
witnessing, 150, 175, 206, 212, 229–230
wuwei 無爲, 184, 192

Xunzi 荀子, 119

Zhang Junmai 张君劢, 225
Zhuangzi 莊子, 119, 172, 174, 184, 191–193
Zionism: and Palestinians, 234, 325
Žižek, Slavoj, 234, 272, 281, 299

www.ingramcontent.com/pod-product-compliance
Lightning Source LLC
Chambersburg PA
CBHW020118240426
43673CB00038B/518